What Is Cost Containment?
How Does it Work?
What Does it Do?

EMPLOYEE BENEFITS

Third Edition

Burton T. Beam, Jr.
John J. McFadden

Dearborn
Financial Publishing, Inc.

While a great deal of care has been taken to provide accurate and current information, the ideas, suggestions, general principles and conclusions presented in this text are subject to local, state and federal laws and regulations, court cases and any revisions of same. The reader is thus urged to consult legal counsel regarding any points of law—this publication should not be used as a substitute for competent legal advice.

Publisher: Carol Luitjens
Editorial Assistant: Betsy Ireland
Cover Design: Lucy Jenkins

Published by Dearborn Financial Publishing, Inc.

Printed in the United States of America

92 93 94 10 9 8 7 6 5 4 3 2 1

Library of Congress Cataloging-in-Publication Data

Beam, Burton T.
    Employee benefits / Burton T. Beam, Jr., John J. McFadden.
        p.   cm.
    Includes bibliographic references and index.
    ISBN 0-7931-0338-X : $48.00
    1. Employee fringe benefits—United States. 2. Compensation management—United States. I. McFadden, John J. II. Title.
HD4928.N62U623 1992
658.3′25—dc20

        91-29732
        CIP

To
Betsy, Greg, Grant, and Lindsay
B. T. B.

To
Diana, Rhoda, and Susanna
J. J. McF.

Contents

13. Group Dental Coverage and Other Group Insurance Benefits   246

14. Alternative Funding Methods   270

15. Group Insurance Rate Making   284

Part Four   Other Nonretirement Benefits and Cafeteria Plans

16. Other Nonretirement Benefits   313

17. Cafeteria Plans   332

Selection. Cost. Issues in Plan Design: *The Type and Amount of Benefits to Include. Level of Employer Contributions. Including an FSA Option. Change of Benefits.* Study Questions.

Part Five Retirement Plans

Preface

Over the last two decades, few fields have changed as dramatically as employee benefits. Employers are spending an ever-increasing portion of total compensation dollars on benefit plans. Some of this increased spending is a result of new or expanded benefits being offered. However, a significant portion of the increase arises because the cost of certain benefits, such as medical expense coverage, has risen at a faster rate than wages. This spiraling cost has made employers increasingly concerned with containing benefit costs.

Legislation has also had a significant effect on employee benefit plans, causing employers to continually monitor and often to revise their plans. The impact of the Employee Retirement Income Security Act of 1974 (ERISA) and subsequent legislation such as the Tax Reform Act of 1986 drastically altered the area of pensions. The Age Discrimination in Employment Act resulted in benefits being provided to persons who previously had coverages terminated at a certain age, such as 65. Coverage under health maintenance organizations (HMOs) must now be offered to many employees, and the Consolidated Omnibus Budget Reconciliation Act of 1985 (COBRA) requires that medical expense coverage be made available to certain employees and dependents after such coverage would otherwise cease. In addition, the states are increasingly mandating the types of benefits that employees must be provided.

The federal tax treatment of employee benefit plans also has had a particularly significant impact on employee benefit plans. Certain types of plans, such as medical expense plans and qualified retirement plans, owe their popularity in large part to federal tax advantages. Cafeteria plans and Section 401(k) cash-or-deferred plans have become more widespread largely because of legislative clarification of their tax treatment. Since the tax benefits for employee benefit plans result in a substantial annual loss of federal tax revenues, Congress has imposed an elaborate and ever-changing scheme of regulation on these plans; in the last 15 years, there have been eight major tax law changes. The information in this text reflects current law through late 1991.

This changing environment and the resultant need for up-to-date materials was one reason for the first edition of this book and has remained a major consideration in the two revisions. New and revised material has been added where needed. Some of the major changes include the following:

- Objectives at the beginning of each chapter.
- Study questions at the end of each chapter.
- Recent changes in social insurance programs.
- New developments in the Age Discrimination in Employment Act.
- New material on the Americans with Disabilities Act.
- Significant updating of the chapters on medical expense coverage to reflect the changing role of alternative providers of medical expense coverage and increased emphasis on cost containment, particularly managed care.
- New coverage on open-ended HMOs and the latest changes in the HMO Act of 1973.
- Updated material on coordination of benefits, Medicare secondary rules and COBRA.
- New coverage on the FASB rules for postretirement medical benefits.
- New material on group long-term care benefits.
- Significant updating to reflect the massive new pension regulations following the Tax Reform Act of 1986.
- New emphasis on management objectives in retirement plan design.

In addition, we have continued to use four other major guidelines in preparing this book. First, the book covers the broad spectrum of employee benefits, from social insurance programs to executive benefits. Second, the book is applicable to all sizes of employer groups, from the small employer using a multiple-employer trust to the large employer relying on alternative funding methods, including self-insurance. Third, the book explains the decisions involved in designing an employee plan; it doesn't just describe the products available. Finally, we have tried to write a book that can be used not only in courses given by college and professional organizations but also as a reference resource for practitioners.

We have also tried to write a book that can be flexible for classroom use. If students have had other insurance courses, perhaps the material on social insurance could be eliminated. Depending on the length of the course and student backgrounds, the detailed material on group insurance taxation and rate making might be skipped or covered superficially. In the retirement plan part, Chapters 25, 26 and possibly 27 could also be omitted.

A difficult decision involved where we should place the chapter on employee benefit planning and management. On one hand, readers should be aware of the importance of planning and management issues before they pursue the material further. On the other hand, they will probably better understand the issues after they are familiar with the benefit environment and the products and services that exist in this environment. We recommend that the principles of the chapter not be ignored after an initial reading. This is an important chapter that should be reviewed again after the remainder of the book is read.

The changing nature of employee benefits makes it essential to remain up-to-date. For this reason, we have included a list of additional readings. We particularly urge readers to become familiar with the loose-leaf services and periodicals mentioned.

LEGAL REFERENCES IN THIS TEXT

In this text, legal authorities will be cited occasionally to help in finding further information about the subject, if the reader wishes. The term *the Code* will be used in referring to the Internal Revenue Code, and the Treasury Regulations will be cited as *the regulations,* with other citations given more fully. ERISA *Section 000* will be used to refer to the indicated section of the Employee Retirement Income Security Act of 1974.

No attempt is made to provide a complete citation of authorities for all of the propositions set forth. However, the general discussion in this text should be adequate to enable the interested reader to obtain citations of the necessary legal authorities from one of the loose-leaf qualified plan or tax services, or one of the handbooks in the field of qualified plans. If accurate legal references are to be obtained, it is important to have thorough and up-to-date materials, because the legal authorities are voluminous and subject to very frequent change.

ACKNOWLEDGMENTS

As with any undertaking of this scope, we owe gratitude to the many persons who have been helpful in making this book a reality, from those persons who were immensely helpful in preparing the first edition to those who have offered valuable suggestions for its two revisions.

We would like to thank the following reviewers of the third edition: Mark Dorfman, University of Arkansas–Little Rock, R.B. Drennan, Temple University, Rebecca A. Luzadis, Miami University, and Nancy Sutton-Bell, Florida State University.

We owe a particular gratitude to Nancy Cornman and Evelyn Rice for their hard work in helping us finish this edition.

Finally, we wish to acknowledge The American College, Bryn Mawr, Pennsylvania, for giving us permission to use the copyrighted material previously written by Burton T. Beam, Jr., and contained in *Group Benefits: Basic Concepts and Alternatives,* 4th edition (1991) and "Social Security and Other Social Insurance Programs" from the CLU/ChFC course *HS 323 Life Insurance.*

Burton T. Beam, Jr.
John J. McFadden

PART ONE

Introduction

1

Introduction to Employee Benefits

Objectives

- Explain the meaning of the term *employee benefits*.
- Explain the significance of employee benefits in terms of both employer cost and benefits provided to employees.
- Identify the factors that have influenced the growth of group insurance and explain the significance of each factor.

In the early part of the century, very few employees received any compensation from their employers other than direct wages for time actually worked. Employees or their families were responsible for meeting the needs of old age, poor health and death. Vacations, if allowed at all, were usually without pay.

The 1940s and 50s witnessed the increasing use and acceptance of employee benefits as a form of compensation in addition to direct wages. During the last two decades, this growth has accelerated as new types of benefits have been added and existing benefits have expanded. Further, while employee benefits were once fairly standardized and free of government regulation, employers must now make more complex decisions regarding the benefits to be provided and the methods with which these benefits are funded.

DEFINITION OF EMPLOYEE BENEFITS

Before continuing, it is best to define exactly what is meant by *employee benefits*. The narrowest definition of the term includes only employer-provided benefits for death, accident, sickness, retirement or unemployment. Even with this approach, there is disagreement as to whether the definition should include those benefits that

3

are financed by employer contributions but provided under social insurance programs, such as workers' compensation insurance, unemployment insurance and social security.[1] On the other hand, the broadest definition of employee benefits includes all benefits and services, other than wages for time worked, that are provided to employees in whole or in part by their employers.

This text will use a broad definition and define employee benefits as including benefit plans for employees that arise from the following five categories of employer payments or costs:[2]

1. Legally required social insurance payments. These include employer contributions to such programs as:
   social security
   unemployment compensation insurance
   workers' compensation insurance
   nonoccupational disability insurance

2. Payments for private insurance and retirement plans. These include the cost of establishing such plans, as well as contributions in the form of insurance premiums or payments through alternative funding arrangements. Benefits are provided under these plans for personal loss exposures such as:

   old age   dental expenses
   death   legal expenses
   disability income   property damage
   medical expenses   liability judgments

3. Payments for time not worked. These include:
   vacations and holidays   maternity leave
   sick leave   sabbatical leaves
   jury duty

4. Extra cash payments to employees. These are cash payments other than wages and bonuses based on performance. Benefits in this category include:
   educational expense allowances   savings plans
   moving expenses   Christmas bonuses
   current profit-sharing payments suggestion awards

5. Cost of services to employees. These include such items as:
   subsidized cafeterias   van pools
   recreation programs   wellness programs
   clothing allowances   day care centers
   financial counseling   free parking
   retirement counseling

Part Two of this book is devoted to the programs that comprise legally required social insurance payments. Group insurance benefits are discussed in Part Three

---

[1]The Social Security Administration uses a narrow definition in its studies of employee benefit plans. This definition includes only those benefits not underwritten or paid directly by the federal, state or local governments.

[2]These categories are based on those listed in Robert M. McCaffery, *Managing the Employee Benefits Program* (New York: American Management Association, 1972). They also are similar to those used by the Chamber of Commerce of the United States in its broad definition of employee benefits.

and retirement plans are covered in Part Five. The remaining categories of benefits are described in Part Four.

SIGNIFICANCE OF EMPLOYEE BENEFITS

In a recent study of nearly 1,000 companies, the Chamber of Commerce of the United States found that the average payment for employee benefits was equal to 37.6 percent of payroll.[3] Of this figure, 8.7 percent of payroll went for the employer's share of legally required social insurance payments, 5.1 percent for payments to private pension plans and 9.8 percent for payments to insurance plans. The remaining 14.0 percent was for all other types of benefits, with paid vacations being the single most costly item. The study showed substantial variations among business firms, with overall percentages ranging from less than 20 percent to more than 60 percent. Large variations were also shown by industry, with the highest percentages belonging to fabricated metals and rubber, leather and plastics products; the lowest percentages were found in the textile and apparel industries. Furthermore, benefit payments generally increased for firms within specific industries as the number of employees increased; benefit payments tended to be higher in the Southeast and Midwest than in the Northeast and West.

The Chamber of Commerce study also estimated that employee benefits for all employees within the United States amounted to $911 billion in 1989, and that this figure was equal to 37.5 percent of payroll. The reason for the discrepancy between this estimated percentage and that found in the survey mentioned above (37.6) is that the survey was weighted in favor of larger firms. The Chamber of Commerce estimated that the 37.5 percent figure had grown from 3.0 percent in 1929, 21.5 percent in 1965 and 30.0 percent in 1975. As a percentage of payroll, the cost of employee benefits has remained relatively stable during the last ten years. However, there have been some interesting trends. Payments to social insurance programs have continued to grow on a percentage basis. Once the largest single employee benefit item, these payments have now been surpassed by the payments made for medical expense coverage, which has risen to over $200 billion and almost 9 percent of payroll. Payments to private pension plans have decreased on a percentage basis. This has resulted from favorable pension investment returns, tighter funding restrictions and an increased reliance on contributory plans.

While aggregate statistics clearly show the significance of employee benefits as a portion of the total compensation of employees, specific statistics regarding certain categories of benefits can also be given.

Social Insurance Plans[4]

- Almost all workers are now covered under the social security program.

---

[3]Chamber of Commerce of the United States, *Employee Benefits 1990*. This study is updated annually.

[4]Social Security Administration, *Social Security Bulletin, Annual Statistic Supplement*, 1990, and Chamber of Commerce of the United States, *Employee Benefits 1990*.

- Almost 40 million persons are now receiving some type of cash benefit under social security. Thirty million are receiving Medicare benefits.
- Cash benefits under social security were nearly $248 billion in 1989; Medicare benefits were almost $100 billion.
- The present value of survivors' benefits under the social security program is over $5.0 trillion. This compares to $8.7 trillion for the amount of private life insurance in force.
- Employers' contributions to the social security program are approximately 7 percent of payroll.
- Unemployment insurance programs cover approximately 99 percent of all wage and salary workers and about 90 percent of all workers.
- Unemployment insurance taxes on employers are equal to between 1 and 2 percent of total payroll.
- Almost 95 percent of the working population is covered by workers' compensation programs.
- Workers' compensation costs to employers are equal to about 1½ percent of payroll and have been increasing faster than the general inflation rate.

Group Life Insurance[5]

- Coverage amounting to $3.5 trillion is in force under approximately 700,000 master contracts and 140 million certificates of insurance. This is double the amount of insurance in force in 1980.
- Over 99 percent of the coverage in force is term insurance.
- Employer-employee groups account for approximately 90 percent of coverage in force.
- Group insurance amounts to 40 percent of total life insurance coverage, up from 20 percent in 1950.
- The amount of coverage under the average-size group life insurance certificate covering employees is $24,510. This compares to $34,410 for the average-size ordinary life insurance policy in force.

Group Disability Income Insurance[6]

- About 60 percent of the work force has some type of short-term protection provided through group arrangements. Slightly more than half of these persons have some or all of their coverage under group insurance contracts, while the remainder have coverage solely under completely self-funded plans.
- The number of persons with short-term group protection remained relatively stable during the previous ten-year period, but an increasing portion of the coverage is provided by self-funded plans.
- Approximately one-fourth of the work force has some form of long-term protection through employer-provided plans.

[5]American Council of Life Insurance, *Life Insurance Fact Book,* 1990.
[6]Health Insurance Association of America, *Source Book of Health Insurance Data,* 1990.

- Group coverage accounts for approximately 80 percent of disability income protection. During the previous ten-year period, the number of persons covered under group arrangements grew at a faster rate than the number of persons covered under individual insurance contracts.

Group Medical Expense Insurance[7]

- Since 1970, premiums for medical expense coverage have risen from approximately $20 billion to almost $200 billion. In 1970, this represented less than 3 percent of disposable personal income; in 1989, it represented almost 6 percent. Almost 90 percent of these premiums represent the cost of coverage under group insurance arrangements, as opposed to individual insurance.
- In recent years, the percentage of persons with medical expense protection under group arrangements with insurance companies, Blue Cross and Blue Shield, and independent plans (including health maintenance organizations [HMOs] and preferred provider organizations [PPOs]) has increased, while the percentage of persons having individual coverage has decreased. During the last ten years, the number of persons with coverage from group contracts of insurance companies has remained stable at about 100 million. The number covered by Blue Cross and Blue Shield has decreased somewhat to about 75 million while the number covered by HMOs, PPOs and self-funded plans has more than doubled to 70 million. Note that some persons have coverage from more than one type of provider, and the total number of persons represented by these statistics is about 180 million.
- During the last ten years, the percentage of the civilian population under age 65 having some form of hospital and surgical benefits from nongovernmental sources remained relatively stable at about 80 percent. However, the percentage of those with major medical benefits rose from less than 60 percent to over 70 percent, while the percentage of persons with dental coverage grew from less than 20 percent to over 60 percent.

Retirement Plans[8]

- Over 70 million persons are covered under pension plans or other retirement programs of private employers, and another 22 million are covered under plans of federal, state or local governments.
- The assets of pension plans amount to about $1.8 trillion.
- About 15 million persons receive pension income from sources other than social security.

---

[7]Health Insurance Association of America, *Source Book of Health Insurance Data*, 1990.

[8]American Council of Life Insurance, *Pension Facts*, 1988, and Employee Benefit Research Institute, *EBRI Databook on Employee Benefits*, 1990.

FACTORS INFLUENCING THE GROWTH
OF EMPLOYEE BENEFITS

No one factor can be singled out as the reason for the substantial growth in employee benefits. Rather, this growth has resulted from a combination of factors, including industrialization, the influence of organized labor, wage controls, cost advantages, tax advantages, inflation and legislation.

Industrialization

During the 19th century, the United States made the transition from an agrarian economy to one characterized by increasing industrialization and urbanization. The economic consequences of death, sickness, accidents and old age became more significant as individuals began to depend more on monetary wages than on self-reliance and family ties to meet their basic needs. As a result, some employers began to provide retirement, death and medical benefits to their employees. While benevolence may have influenced the decision to provide such benefits, the principal reason was probably the realization by employers that it was in their own best interest to do so. Not only did such benefits improve morale and productivity, they also reduced employee turnover and the expenses associated with it.

While some of the earlier benefits were paid directly by employers, the development of group insurance enabled these benefits to be funded by systematic payments to an insurance company. As group insurance became more common, employers were faced with adopting new or better plans to remain competitive in attracting and keeping employees. This competitiveness in employee benefits continues to exist.

Influence of Organized Labor

Since a Supreme Court ruling in 1949, there has been no question about the right of labor unions to negotiate legally for retirement and insurance plans. Although union pressures prior to that time had frequently resulted in the establishment or broadening of employee benefit plans, this ruling strengthened the influence of labor unions.

Labor unions have also influenced benefits for nonunion employees. Some employers provide generous benefit plans in an effort to discourage their employees from unionizing. In addition, employers with both union and nonunion employees often provide the same benefits for the nonunion employees as are stipulated in the union contracts.

Wage Controls

Employee benefit plans grew substantially during World War II and the Korean War when wage freezes were in effect. Although wages were frozen, no restrictions were imposed on employee benefits. Therefore, employee benefits became an important factor in attracting and retaining employees in labor markets characterized by little unemployment. When wage controls were instituted in the early 1970s, however, no unusual growth took place in employee benefit plans because the duration of the controls was relatively short and the unemployment rate was higher than in previous years.

Cost Advantages

Because of the economics associated with group underwriting and administration, benefits can usually be obtained at a lower cost through group arrangements than through separate contracts purchased by individual employees.

Tax Advantages

The Internal Revenue Code also provides favorable tax treatment to employer contributions for certain types of employee benefits. The employer may deduct the contributions as usual business expenses, and, within limits, employees will often have no taxable income as a result of employer contributions on their behalf. In addition, payments received from some types of employee benefit plans may be received tax free by employees, even if provided by employer contributions. Benefits from other types of plans may not result in taxable income until payments are actually received. The extent of the favorable tax treatment applicable to specific benefits will be discussed in detail in later chapters. Nevertheless, it should be noted here that the types of employee benefits with the most favorable tax treatment also tend to be the most prevalent.

Inflation

The high inflation rate in recent years has also affected employee benefits. When benefit levels are related to employees' wages, the level and cost of these benefits will increase as wages increase; when benefit levels are stated as fixed amounts, inflation results in employee pressure for increases. For most employers, the total cost of benefit programs has been increasing at a rate faster than wages, primarily because of the skyrocketing increase in the cost of providing medical expense benefits.

Legislation

Most states have traditionally limited the types of groups that are eligible for group insurance benefits. In addition, the types, and possibly the amounts, of coverage that could be written were also subject to restrictions. In recent years, the majority of these states have liberalized their laws and have allowed more group insurance coverage to be available to an increasing variety of groups.

The federal government and many states have also passed legislation mandating that certain benefits be included in group insurance contracts or that existing benefits be broadened. Examples include legislation requiring benefits for maternity, alcoholism and drug abuse. These increased benefits have also increased the cost of providing group insurance coverage.

STUDY QUESTIONS

1. Explain the different ways in which the term *employee benefits* may be defined.
2. The Chamber of Commerce of the United States estimates that the cost of employee benefit programs averages about 35 percent of payroll.
   a. How has this percentage changed over time?
   b. What factors may account for a particular firm having a percentage-of-payroll figure that deviates from the average?
   c. What categories of employee benefits have had the most rapid cost increase in recent years?
3. How has organized labor influenced the growth of employee benefit plans?
4. How does inflation affect the cost of employee benefit plans?
5. Briefly explain how favorable tax laws have contributed to the growth of many types of employee benefits.

2

Employee Benefit Planning and Management

Objectives

- Explain the rationale for having employee-benefit-plan objectives and identify the forms such objectives might take.
- Identify the methods by which the benefit needs of employees may be determined.
- Analyze the provisions contained in employee benefit plans for controlling costs.
- Identify the objectives of an effective employee benefit communications program and describe the methods by which it might be implemented.

The significant growth in employee benefits requires increasingly complex decisions. Whether these decisions are made by employers providing benefits, unions negotiating for benefits or employees selecting benefit options, the need for proper benefit planning is crucial. Employee benefit planning is a dynamic process that must continually be reviewed and modified if an overall benefit plan is to meet the changing needs of a changing environment.

If either a single type of employee benefit plan or an overall benefit plan is to be properly designed and managed, many questions must be asked. For example, should the plan reflect the wants of employees or the needs of employees as perceived by the employer? Should it have a probationary period for eligibility? Under what circumstances should the plan be self-insured? These questions are only subparts of five much broader issues:

1. What are the employer's objectives?
2. What types of benefits should be provided in the plan?

3. How should the plan be funded?
4. What provisions for controlling costs should be contained in the plan?
5. How should the plan be communicated to employees?

Unfortunately for those who like precise answers, plan design and management is an art rather than a science. However, decisions must be made. In some cases, the advantages and disadvantages of the various alternative answers to these five questions must be weighed; in other cases, compromises must be made when the answers to two or more questions conflict.

Too often, the proper design of an employee benefit plan is viewed as a one-time decision rather than as an evolving process. As times and organizations change, employers' answers to the questions raised in this chapter may also have to change. For this reason, these issues must be frequently restudied to determine whether a group benefit plan is continuing to meet its desired purpose.

Because the question of funding is addressed in detail in Chapter 14, only the remaining four questions will be discussed in this chapter.

One difficulty in writing a textbook of this nature is determining where to discuss the many issues and decisions that must be faced if proper planning is to take place. While some issues and decisions can easily be handled at the beginning of a textbook, many others are best discussed along with specific types of benefit plans. Still others are most meaningfully treated only after the basic coverages, provisions and funding methods have been described. However, a treatment of the benefit-planning process seems appropriate in an introductory chapter to make readers aware that benefit planning is much more than a description of the many types of coverages and provisions that are the subject of most of this book. While this chapter is devoted entirely to planning and is the first and only place where certain issues are discussed, other planning issues are handled where appropriate throughout the book. Readers may wish to return to this chapter after they have completed the remainder of the book.

WHAT ARE THE EMPLOYER'S OBJECTIVES?

No benefit plan is properly designed unless it meets the employer's objectives. Unfortunately, these objectives may be unclear or nonexistent, particularly in small firms. However, most large corporations have—and all firms should have—specific written objectives that have been approved by the board of directors or by the owners of the firm. These objectives will vary for each individual organization, depending upon such factors as size, location, industry, the results of collective bargaining and the philosophy of the employer. Without such objectives, it is difficult for the agent, broker, benefit consultant or third-party administrator to make recommendations, or for the benefit specialist within a firm to make decisions.

Objectives for benefit plans can be general and part of a firm's overall compensation objective, that is, cash and employee benefits in the aggregate. This may be done to achieve a compensation package that is competitive within the firm's geographic area or industry. Such an average objective usually means that the firm wants both its wages and salaries and its employee benefits to be similar to what the competition is offering its employees. There is usually some, but not much, room for creativity in the design of a group benefit plan, unless the plans of the competition are quite diverse.

Some firms have separate objectives for cash compensation and employee benefits. For example, a growing firm may want its cash compensation to be competitive, but it may want its overall employee benefit plan to be above average in order to attract new employees. A difficulty with this type of objective for the plan designer is determining whether the firm wants all aspects of the employee benefit plan to be better than average, or whether it would be willing to accept, for example, an average program of group insurance benefits, but a better-than-average pension plan and more vacation time for its employees. Note that most objectives, even when they are very detailed, tend to apply to all employee benefits rather than to specific types.

It has become increasingly common for firms, particularly large firms, to maintain a lengthy and often detailed list of objectives for their employee benefit programs. The following are the objectives of one such firm:

- To establish and maintain an employee benefit program that is based primarily on the employees' needs for leisure time and on protection against the risks of old age, loss of health and loss of life.
- To establish and maintain an employee benefit program that complements the efforts of employees on their own behalf.
- To evaluate the employee benefit plan annually for its effect on employee morale and productivity, giving consideration to turnover, unfilled positions, attendance, employees' complaints and employees' opinions.
- To compare the employee benefit plan annually with that of other leading companies in the same field and to maintain a benefit plan with an overall level of benefits based on cost per employee that falls within the second quintile of these companies.
- To maintain a level of benefits for nonunion employees that represents the same level of expenditures per employee as for union employees.
- To determine annually the cost of new, changed and existing programs as a percentage of salaries and wages and to maintain this percentage as much as possible.
- To self-fund benefits to the extent that a long-run cost savings can be expected for the firm and catastrophic losses can be avoided.
- To coordinate all benefits with social insurance programs to which the company makes payments.
- To provide benefits on a noncontributory basis, except benefits for dependent coverage for which employees should pay a portion of the cost.
- To maintain continual communications with all employees concerning benefit programs.

Most lists of objectives contain few, if any, specific details regarding what provisions or what types of benefits should be contained in an employee benefit plan.

Rather, they establish guidelines—instead of specific performance goals—within which management must operate. For example, the objectives listed above indicate this firm wants a plan that is understood and appreciated by employees and that is designed with employee opinion in mind. No mention, however, is made of how this is to be done. As will be seen later in this chapter, there may be alternative ways for this firm to achieve its objectives. Similarly, the objectives establish guidelines for the cost of providing benefits. Although the firm wants to have a better-than-average plan, it does not want to be a leader. There is a very specific objective about what the relationship between the cost of benefits for union and nonunion employees should be. However, nothing is mentioned to indicate that the benefits for the two groups must also be identical. If the two groups have different needs, different types and levels of benefits may be desired.

One additional point about employer objectives should be made. Often the primary, and possibly the only, objective of a firm is to establish an overall employee benefit plan that channels as large a portion of the benefits as possible to the owner or owners. Although this is a poor objective for an overall plan, it is a reality that must be recognized, most commonly in small firms or in firms that have a small number of owners. Large, publicly held corporations sometimes wish to provide better benefits for their executives than for other employees. However, these extra benefits are likely to be provided under separate executive compensation plans, rather than under the benefit plan that applies to all employees.

WHAT TYPES OF BENEFITS SHOULD BE PROVIDED IN THE PLAN?

A major decision for any employer is what types and levels of benefits to include in an overall employee benefit plan. For those few firms that do not have an employee benefit program, this decision involves choosing which benefits to offer initially. However, in most cases, the decision is ongoing and involves either the offering of new or improved benefits or the redesigning of all or a major portion of the benefit plan. An objective of most employee benefit plans is to meet the needs of employees. But what are these needs? If they vary for different groups of employees, should different benefit plans be established? Or should a single plan be designed in which employees are allowed to choose from alternative benefits?

Determining Needs

Every employer wants its employees to appreciate the benefits that are provided. However, employers are becoming increasingly aware that employee benefit programs are failing to achieve this desired level of appreciation. To some extent, this is due to the fact that as employee benefit plans have grown more comprehensive, employees have begun to take the benefits for granted. In addition, the growing consensus seems to be that the traditional methods of determining the types and levels of benefits to offer have lost much of their effectiveness. These include basing benefits on the following factors:

- *The employer's perception of the employees' needs.* This perception is largely based on the opinions of a firm's top management employees whose compensation is much higher than that of the average employee. Therefore, it is not surprising that many recent studies have shown that management's perception of employees' needs often differs from what the employees themselves feel they need.
- *What competitors are doing.* Too often, the emphasis is placed on having an employee benefit package that is virtually identical to that of the competition, even though the makeup of the work force may be different and the employees may have different needs.
- *Collectively bargained benefits.* Many employers pattern their benefit plans for salaried employees after their negotiated plans for union employees. Again, the needs of salaried employees may be substantially different and may call for a totally different plan.
- *Tax laws and regulations.* Benefit plans are often designed to include those benefits that are best suited to the high tax brackets of top executives. The average employee who is in a modest tax bracket may actually have a preference for certain benefits even though they will result in currently taxable income.

In the last few years, employers have increasingly taken a marketing research approach to employee benefit planning. The employees' preferences for benefits are determined in a way similar to that in which consumers' demands for products are determined. For the most part, this approach has been used only for nonunion employees, since benefits for union employees are decided by collective bargaining. However, some employers and some unions use this procedure as a guide in their negotiations with union employees.

A marketing research approach can be used for different purposes. Most often it is selected as a way to determine

1. How funds should be allocated to new types of benefits.
2. How funds should be used to improve current benefits.

This can be for a one-time change in a firm's benefit plan or for changes that are implemented over time. In addition, a marketing research approach can also help an employer to determine what alternative provisions employees would prefer regarding a specific type of benefit. For example, a firm that allocates additional funds to a long-term disability plan could determine whether employees would prefer a shorter waiting period or an increase in the size of the monthly benefit.

Marketing research techniques must be used with caution. They can have a negative effect on employee morale unless the employer is committed to using their results in benefit decision making. Therefore, this approach should not be undertaken unless the employer intends to base expenditures for benefits on satisfying what employees perceive as their needs. In addition, employees must be made aware that changes in an overall benefit program will be subject to financial constraints and, possibly, trade-offs among benefits.

Although a variety of marketing research techniques can be used in benefit planning, those most commonly chosen fall into three major categories:

1. Personal interviews.
2. Simplified questionnaires.
3. Sophisticated research methods.

Personal Interviews

Personal interviews with employees either alone or in small groups probably constitute the most effective marketing research technique for a small firm or for a benefit program that is limited to a small number of employees. On this scale, it is also the least expensive technique. An advantage of personal interviewing is that it can be used to collect the same type of information as both simplified questionnaires and sophisticated research techniques. It is important in personal interviewing that the employees feel they can speak candidly. For this reason, it may be desirable to have the interviews conducted by someone outside the firm and to hold group interviews without the supervisor's presence.

Simplified Questionnaires

A simplified questionnaire often has two major parts: one determines benefit preferences, the other determines demographic data, such as age, sex, marital status, years of service and salary range. The questionnaire is called simplified because employees are basically asked only to indicate and/or rank their preferences. However, the actual analysis of the data that are gathered may be a complex task, and unless a firm is small, it will probably require the use of a computer. It is important to use a clear, brief questionnaire that is not annoying to employees. Consequently, it is best that the questionnaire be initially given to only a few employees in order to test their reactions.

Figure 2-1 contains a sample of a portion of a simplified questionnaire on benefit preferences. Note that the questionnaire is essentially a structured one and is not open-ended. Employees are requested only to rank their preferences, and they are not given the opportunity to state whether each benefit is important or whether it should be improved. They are also required to make their preferences known regarding possible trade-offs between benefits and pay. Even though the questionnaire is structured, employees are still given the opportunity to make general comments. Such a feature should be incorporated into any questionnaire as a way of letting employees know that their opinions will be heard. It also may result in useful, and sometimes surprising, information for the employer.

Sophisticated Research Methods

One difficulty with simplified questionnaires, and to some extent personal interviews, is that they fail to measure the intensity of employees' preferences. Consequently, some firms have used more sophisticated marketing research techniques in an attempt to measure the degree of importance that employees place on various benefit alternatives. These more sophisticated research techniques are typically used only when specific alternatives have been formulated by the employer. Therefore, they are often used as a follow-up to personal interviews and simplified questionnaires; they frequently also involve additional interviews and/or questionnaires.

FIGURE 2-1

EMPLOYEE BENEFIT QUESTIONNAIRE

1. In the right column below, rank the benefits from 1 to 7 in their importance to you and your family. Use 1 for the most important, 2 for the next important, etc.

Benefit	*Importance*
Holidays	_____
Life Insurance	_____
Long-Term Disability Income	_____
Medical Expense Insurance	_____
Pension Plan	_____
Sick Pay	_____
Vacations	_____

2. To the list of benefits below, add the two benefits you would most like to see added by this company. In the right column, rank the benefits listed according to their need for improvement or adoption. Use 1 for the benefit you feel should have the highest priority for improvement or adoption, 2 for the next highest, etc.

Benefit	*Need for Improvement or Adoption*
Holidays	_____
Life Insurance	_____
Long-Term Disability Income	_____
Medical Expense Insurance	_____
Pension Plan	_____
Sick Pay	_____
Vacations	_____
_____	_____
_____	_____

3. How would you prefer that additional funds for benefits be used? (check one)
   _____ Improve or add benefit programs
   _____ Reduce currently required employee contributions

4. Which of the following statements reflects your opinion? (check one)
   _____ More emphasis should be placed on improving wages and salaries and less on improving benefits.
   _____ More emphasis should be placed on improving benefits and less on improving wages and salaries.
   _____ The same emphasis as in the past should be placed on improving both benefits and wages and salaries.

5. Please use the back of this form to make any additional comments you feel will be of use to the company in its desire to improve the employee benefit programs.

Figure 2-2 illustrates one example of how preferences might be measured in a questionnaire.

Once the information is gathered, the firm must decide which benefits to adopt, based on employees' preferences and other cost and administrative considerations. For example, assume that the firm using the questionnaire is willing to

FIGURE 2-2

EMPLOYEE BENEFIT QUESTIONNAIRE

The following benefit changes are being considered for adoption by this company in the next fiscal year. Although the company is committed to making improvements in its benefit package, financial considerations dictate that only some of these proposed changes can be adopted at that time. The first item on the list has been given a value of 100. Please rank the other items in their relative importance to you. For example, if item 2 is three times as important, it should be given a value of 300. If it is only half as important, it should be given a value of 50.

Proposed Change	*Value*
1. Increase lifetime major medical maximum from $250,000 to $500,000.	100
2. Eliminate employee contributions to long-term disability coverage.	_____
3. Increase life insurance coverage from 1½ to 2 times base earnings.	_____
4. Add Columbus Day to the list of holidays.	_____
5. Provide reimbursement up to $250 for annual physical.	_____

---

spend up to $200 annually per employee to improve its benefit package. Also assume that the following figures represent the average importance of each proposed benefit to employees, as well as the expected annual cost per employee of providing each benefit:

Change	Average Value	Annual Cost per Employee
1	100	$ 50
2	310	100
3	140	50
4	240	100
5	190	150

It is clear that the employees feel the second proposed change, which has an annual cost of $100 per employee, is most important by a substantial margin. Therefore, it will most likely be adopted. However, it is difficult to determine what other benefit or benefits will be offered. The last proposed change will definitely not be made because only $100 per employee remains for additional benefit changes. The firm is therefore faced with two alternatives—either add Columbus Day as a holiday or increase both the life insurance coverage and the major medical lifetime maximum. Because the average importance of each alternative to employees is 240, and only one can be made within the cost constraint, the deciding factor will hinge on other considerations. The firm may look at the administrative aspects of each change or the effect of inflation on long-range costs. The firm may also analyze the data in terms of the demographic characteristics of employees. For example, long-time employees may have a slight preference for the insurance benefits, while younger employees would like the extra holiday. If the firm wishes to favor the older employees, it will change the insurance benefits; if morale is low among younger employees, it might decide to add the holiday instead.

It should be pointed out that these other considerations may also be the deciding factor for employers even when employee preferences are clear. However, if employees are led to believe that their preferences will be the primary consideration, other considerations should be weighed only when there are modest differences in employee preferences.

Different Plans

From an administrative standpoint, it is easiest for a firm to have a single employee benefit plan that applies to all employees. Nevertheless, some firms have different plans for different groups of employees. This most commonly occurs when the benefits for union employees are determined by collective bargaining. If the benefits for the union employees are provided through a negotiated trusteeship, a separate plan must be designed for the nonunion employees. The employer must then decide whether to play "follow the leader" and provide identical benefits to the nonunion employees or whether to design a plan that reflects their different needs. When benefits are provided through a negotiated trusteeship, the employer is more likely to develop a different plan for nonunion employees than when the employer is required to provide benefits to union employees through group insurance or pension contracts that are purchased or self-funded by the employer. Under these circumstances, employers often find it simpler administratively to purchase a single contract that covers all employees.

Even when unions are not involved, an employer may still decide to have different plans for different groups of employees. Usually one plan will be limited to hourly employees; another to salaried employees. In addition, a plan that offers supplemental benefits to top management may also be provided, but it will often only be publicized to those employees who are eligible for these benefits. Some firms that have employees located in different parts of the country have also found it desirable to provide somewhat different benefits at some or all locations in order to remain competitive locally.

Having different plans for different groups of employees is not without its disadvantages. Administrative costs are usually increased, communications with employees become more difficult and resentment can occur if one group of employees feels its benefit plan is inferior to that of another group. To minimize this latter possibility, some firms have designed their plans so that an overall comparison is difficult. Each plan will have its own positive and negative features when a comparison is made with the plans for other groups of employees.

A trend in recent years has been the growth of cafeteria plans. Because of their popularity, a separate chapter (Chapter 17) is devoted to them.

WHAT PROVISIONS FOR CONTROLLING COSTS SHOULD BE CONTAINED IN THE PLAN?

Employers have always been concerned about the costs of providing employee benefits. Traditionally, this concern has led to plan provisions that transfer these costs to employees rather than reduce them. These include probationary periods, benefit limitations and contributory financing. More recent attempts to control costs have been primarily directed toward the rapidly increasing costs of medical care, and, for the most part, cost-containment provisions have been designed to reduce administrative and claim costs without transferring them to employees. Methods for controlling the costs of medical expenses are discussed throughout Chapters 9 through 14. The focus here will be on provisions and activities that can be used with other types of benefit plans.

Probationary Periods

Probationary periods reduce costs to employers, because any claims that are incurred by employees during this time must be borne by the employees. In addition, probationary periods reduce the adverse selection that would most likely exist without their use. Administrative costs are also minimized for those employees who terminate employment shortly after being hired. However, probationary periods do impose hardships on newer employees who incur claims but find themselves without benefits. Primarily for competitive reasons in attracting employees, the use and length of probationary periods, particularly in medical expense plans, have been decreasing except in high turnover situations.

Benefit Limitations

Benefit limitations in the form of deductibles, coinsurance, maximum benefits and exclusions for certain types of expenses are common in medical expense insurance. However, some of these techniques can also be used in other types of insurance. The following are some examples:

- The limiting of benefits to a maximum percentage of income in disability income plans. In addition to reducing the amount of benefits paid by the employer, a maximum percentage also minimizes the possibility of feigned and unnecessarily prolonged disabilities.
- The setting of maximum benefits under dental plans for expenses such as orthodontics. There is little doubt that the availability of benefits will encourage treatment of orthodontic conditions, particularly when the treatment is primarily sought for cosmetic reasons. There is also the feeling that dentists will encourage the treatment of relatively minor orthodontic conditions if a patient has coverage for orthodontics.

Contributory Financing

Many benefit plans require each employee to pay a portion of the costs for his or her own coverage. This may lower the employer's costs and/or may enable the employer to use these saved dollars to provide additional or improved benefits. There are several arguments both for and against contributory financing, but in many instances it is a moot point, since the decision is determined by collective bargaining or competition.

When contributory financing is used for benefits other than pension plans, employees are generally able to voluntarily elect or decline coverage. To the extent that some employees decline coverage, the costs to the employer will be further lowered. However, this savings may be offset by the adverse selection that can result because of those who did elect coverage. Furthermore, having the option to decline coverage could mean that employees or their dependents will be without coverage should a loss occur. Finally, there tend to be more administrative costs associated with a contributory plan than with a noncontributory plan.

Advocates of a contributory plan feel that sharing in the cost will increase the employees' awareness and appreciation of both the plan and the contribution the employer is making. However, this can be countered by the argument that payroll deductions for benefits are a source of employee dissatisfaction, since they may view the employer as "cheap" for not paying the entire cost of the plan.

Although there are no empirical studies to support the contention, it has been argued that employees are less likely to misuse medical and dental benefits under a contributory plan, because they realize that such misuse will probably lead to an increase in their future contributions.

Cost Containment

Recent attempts to control benefit costs have concentrated on either reducing the size of claims or minimizing the administrative costs associated with benefit plans. Rather than transfer the costs to employees, these techniques try to lower costs, or to at least lower the rate at which costs are increasing. Although employers are concerned primarily with their own costs, some of the advantages of this cost containment will impact on the employees in the form of increased benefits or a lower rate of increase for out-of-pocket expenses.

Other than provisions or practices associated solely with medical expense plans, the following are some of the more common cost-containment techniques that are currently being used by employers:

- Alternative funding methods that lower administrative costs and improve cash flow. (Discussed in Chapter 14.)
- Competitive bidding among insurance companies and third-party administrators that lowers administrative costs.
- Wellness programs and employee-assistance plans that reduce future medical claims as well as minimize absences from work. (Discussed in Chapter 16.)

HOW SHOULD THE PLAN BE COMMUNICATED TO EMPLOYEES?

Traditionally, employers placed a low priority on the communication of their benefit plans to employees. They took the attitude that employees appreciated any benefits that were given to them. The little information that was made available tended only to be the literature that had been prepared by the insurance companies providing the coverage. Over the last few years, this situation has changed dramatically. Employers are required by federal law to disclose a substantial amount of information to employees about their benefit plans. In addition, employers have come to realize that many employees take their benefit plans for granted, that they fail to realize the value of these benefits to themselves and their families and that they are unaware of the employer's dollar outlay. Not only will effective communication solve this problem, it may also minimize the dissatisfaction that arises from misunderstandings about the benefit program, and it may reduce turnover to the extent that employees realize the true value of their benefits. Employers have also learned that effective communication is necessary to obtain employee support if cost-containment efforts are to be successful.

Most benefit consultants feel an effective communication program should have three primary objectives. These are:

1. To create an awareness of and an appreciation for the way current benefits improve the financial security of employees.
2. To provide a high level of understanding about available benefits.
3. To encourage the wise use of benefits.

The communication of benefit plans to employees is now regarded as a highly sophisticated task. No single method of communication is likely to accomplish all the desired objectives, so several methods should be combined. To meet these objectives, many employers hire communications experts who generally report to the person who is responsible for employee benefits. Other employers use the services of benefit-consulting firms, many of which have developed specialized units for advising their clients in this particular area. Benefit plans can be communicated to employees in audiovisual presentations, in face-to-face meetings, through printed materials and, more recently, with computers.

Audiovisual Presentations

Audiovisual presentations are a very effective way to communicate benefit plans to new employees, or to explain significant changes in existing benefit plans to current employees. It is much easier to require employees to view audiovisual presentations than to read printed materials. In addition, if properly done, audiovisual presentations can convey the employer's concern for the well-being of its employees, and they can explain proper benefit use more effectively than printed materials. In the past, many audiovisual presentations have been dull and sometimes uninformative. Recently, however, many employers have adopted more sophisticated communications methods, and they view these presentations, if not their entire communication program, as a way of advertising their employee benefit plans. In fact, some employers have actually hired advertising firms to design not only their audiovisual programs but other aspects of their communication program as well.

Meetings with Employees

Face-to-face meetings with employees can also be an effective way to explain employee benefit plans and to answer employees' questions. For small employers, this technique is generally used to present benefit plans to new employees or to explain the changes in existing plans. Large employers often combine meetings with audiovisual presentations. It is obvious that whoever conducts these meetings—be it the employer, agent, broker, consultant or provider representative—must be truly knowledgeable about the plan. In addition, it is just as important that they be able to effectively communicate this knowledge to the employees.

The number of employees that attend a meeting may impact on its effectiveness. A large meeting may be satisfactory if its purpose is primarily to present information. However, a series of small meetings may be more manageable and appropriate if employees' opinions or questions are being solicited. These small meetings can be used in lieu of a large meeting or as follow-up meetings to a large group presentation. When employees must make decisions regarding their benefit plans, meetings with individual employees may also be necessary.

Group meetings can be used for purposes other than explaining new or changed benefit plans. They can be held periodically to reexplain benefits, to answer employees' questions, or to listen to employees' concerns and suggestions. However, every employer should also have a procedure by which employees can have ready access to a knowledgeable person when they have any problems to discuss or questions to ask. Although this can often be accomplished by telephone, face-to-face meetings should be used when necessary.

The employer's attitude toward a group meeting can influence its effectiveness. Employers should not regard these meetings as necessary formalities, but rather they should view them as a way to communicate their concern about the security of their employees and the benefits with which they are provided. The success of face-to-face meetings may also be affected by when and where they are held. To achieve maximum employee interest and attention, the facilities should be comfortable and not overcrowded. In addition, meetings should be held during normal working hours, but not at the end of the working day, when many employees may be concerned with whether the meeting will end on time.

Printed Materials

Virtually every employer provides employees with some printed materials about its employee benefit plans. At a minimum, this material consists of group insurance certificates and the information that is required to be distributed under the disclosure provisions of The Employee Retirement Income Security Act (ERISA). The next most commonly provided source of information is the benefit handbook. If there is a typical benefit handbook, it can best be described as a reference book that summarizes the benefit plans that are available to all employees. In addition to describing group insurance benefits, it will include information about an organization's retirement plan, vacation policy and possibly other benefits, such as educational assistance. Each plan will be described in terms of eligibility, benefits and what employee contributions are required.

Traditionally, these benefit handbooks merely described each benefit plan separately; they did not discuss the relationship between the various benefit plans or what social insurance benefits might be available. Newer benefit handbooks are more likely to focus on the potential causes of lost income to an employee or his or her family. For example, rather than discuss short-term and long-term disability income plans separately, they will include a single section on disability income that describes how a short-term disability plan will initially pay benefits, and at what point it will be replaced by the long-term disability plan and social security.

Because of the general nature of benefit handbooks, many employers also give each employee a personalized benefit statement, usually on an annual basis. The most common form of personalized benefit statement specifies the plans for which the employee is eligible and what benefits are available to that particular employee (or his or her family) under each of these plans. (Note that such a statement will comply with the personal benefit statement that is required for qualified retirement plans.) Figure 2-3 shows a portion of one such statement. In addition, some employers feel that employees will better appreciate the value of their benefits if they are aware of the magnitude of the cost to the employer. Figure 2-4 is an example of one form that is used for reporting this information.

FIGURE 2-3

PERSONAL STATEMENT OF BENEFITS

This Personal Statement of Benefits lists the benefits that both protect you and your family now and provide security for your future. We know you will find this statement informative, and we hope it will be useful in your personal planning.

HEALTH-CARE BENEFITS

You have elected coverage for
☐ yourself   ☐ your family   ☐ You have not elected coverage.

The highlights of your Comprehensive Medical Plan are summarized in the following table. See your employee handbook for further details.

In-Hospital Benefits	Out-of-Hospital Benefits	Special Benefits
$100 deductible per person each calendar year (3-deductible maximum per family)		100% of outpatient emergency treatment of accidental injury (no deductible).
100% of covered expenses, including maternity care, after the deductible is met.	80% of first $3,000 of covered expenses, then 100% of remaining covered expenses. 50% of psychiatric treatment up to $1,000 a year ($20-a-visit maximum benefit).	80% of diagnostic X-ray and laboratory tests (deductible applies).
OVERALL PLAN MAXIMUM: $1 million per person		

FIGURE 2-3 *(concluded)*

DISABILITY INCOME BENEFITS

Salary Continuation Plan
- Your full salary continues for _____ weeks, then ¾ of your salary continues for _____ weeks.

Long-Term Disability Income Plan
- If disabled over 26 weeks, you will receive _____ a month. This is 60% of your base pay and includes benefits under the corporation's plan and any social security benefits, other than family benefits, for which you are eligible.
- If you have eligible dependents, you can receive additional family benefits under social security up to _____ a month.
- If total long-term disability income from the above sources exceeds 80% of your base pay, disability benefits under the corporation's plan will be reduced to bring the total to the 70% level.

SURVIVOR'S BENEFITS

Group Life Insurance
- If you die from any cause, your survivors will receive _____ from the corporation's group life insurance plan.

Supplemental Life Insurance
- If you participate in the corporation's supplemental life insurance plan, your survivors will receive an additional _____ upon your death from any cause.

Travel Accident Insurance
- An additional benefit of _____ will be paid to your survivors if your death results from an accident while traveling on corporate business.

Social Security
- Social security will provide a monthly income of up to _____ a month if you have an eligible spouse with 2 or more children.

Medical Coverage
- Dependent's coverage can continue on a contributory basis.

RETIREMENT BENEFITS

Normal Retirement
- At age 65, you will receive an estimated _____ a month from the corporation's retirement plan and social security. Additional social security benefits are payable for an eligible spouse age 62 or older.
- Your spouse will receive an estimated _____ a month from the corporation's retirement plan and social security if your spouse is age 65 or older at your death.
- If you leave the corporation before retirement, you will be eligible to receive a pension amounting to the vested portion of your accrued benefit. The pension is payable at age 65, but reduced benefits are available as early as age 55. Your current accrued benefit is approximately _____ a month. Your vested benefit is _____ a month.

Early Retirement
- You may retire as early as age 55 with five years' service and receive a reduced benefit. For example, at age 62, your retirement income from the corporation's plan and social security would be approximately _____ .

Other Retirement Benefits
- Medical coverage continues after retirement and is coordinated with Medicare.
- Group life insurance coverage continues in the amount of $5,000.

FIGURE 2-4

BENEFIT STATEMENT REVIEW

FOR

_____

Many of us forget that there is more to our paycheck than the amount we take home. The following are the "extras" that were provided in 19 _____ and their value as determined by the cost to your employer.

	Annual Value	*Value per Hour*
(1) Social Security (employer's contribution)	$_____	$_____
(2) Worker's Compensation Insurance Premium	_____	_____
(3) State Unemployment Insurance Premium	_____	_____
(4) Paid Holidays	_____	_____
(5) Vacation Days	_____	_____
(6) Pension	_____	_____
(7) Salary Continuation	_____	_____
(8) Long-Term Disability Income Insurance	_____	_____
(9) Life Insurance	_____	_____
(10) Medical Expense Insurance (employer's contribution)	_____	_____
(11) Others	_____	_____
_____	_____	_____
_____	_____	_____

The $ _____ value of these sometimes forgotten benefits is equal to _____ % of the $ _____ you received as salary or wages in 19 _____ . These benefits are provided to protect you and your family from certain financial risks and to help provide for your future retirement.

Other types of printed information, such as company newsletters, personal letters to employees at home, or notices in pay envelopes, may also be of value. This may be the simplest and least expensive way of announcing benefit changes that need little explanation, such as an increase in daily hospital room-and-board benefits. In addition, they are an effective way to advertise or remind employees about the wellness programs that are available, or what cost-containment provisions are included in their medical expense coverage. Experience has shown that without occasional reminders, the use of these programs and provisions by the employees will decrease.

Computers

An increasing number of employers are turning to computers to help communicate various provisions of their benefits plan to employees. A few employers actually provide diskettes to those employees who have access to personal computers, but the most common approach is to have computer kiosks located in central locations. The monitors at these kiosks can be accessed through the use of a keyboard. By pressing the appropriate key, an employee can get a general description of the company's various plans. By inputting appropriate data (including an identification number), an employee may also be able to obtain information about his or her own particular situation. For example, an employee could determine his or her potential disability income or retirement benefit. An employee may also be able to obtain the answers to "what if" questions. For example, if I contribute $100 per month to a 401(k) plan that is expected to earn 9 percent annually, how much will I have at age 65? Or if I elect these options under a cafeteria plan, will any additional employer dollars remain for other benefits, or will I have to make an additional contribution through a payroll deduction?

As the last question indicates, the use of computers can facilitate the administration of a cafeteria plan. In fact, some employers are actually using the computer as the process by which benefit selections are made. To have some verification in writing, a form is either printed on the spot for an employee to sign and return or generated in the personnel office, reviewed and sent to the employee for signing.

There seems to be little doubt that as the role of the computer expands in the business world, its uses for communicating with employees will also increase.

STUDY QUESTIONS

1. Why is it important for an organization to have specific written objectives for its benefit plans?
2. Explain how the benefit objectives of an organization may vary in both length and specific details for realizing the objectives.
3. Describe the traditional approaches for determining the benefit needs of employees and explain the drawbacks of each approach.
4. What is the potential negative impact of using a marketing-research approach to determine the needs of employees?
5. a. What are the advantages of using personal interviews to determine employee needs?
   b. Why should these interviews be conducted without the presence of the employee's supervisor?
6. What advantages does a structured questionnaire for determining employee needs have over an open-ended questionnaire?
7. Some firms have different plans for different groups of employees.
   a. Under what circumstances are different benefits often used?
   b. What are the disadvantages of having different plans?
8. Identify the potential advantages of requiring employees to pay a portion of the premiums for their own coverage.

9. What should be the objectives of an effective program for communicating benefit plans to employees?
10. Explain why some personalized benefit statements may be more effective techniques than benefit handbooks for communicating with employees.
11. What are some of the ways in which computers can be used to communicate employee benefit plans?

PART TWO

Social Insurance

3

Social Security Benefits

Objectives

- Identify the reasons why social insurance exists and describe the basic features of social insurance programs.
- Identify the types of benefits available under OASDI and Medicare.
- Explain the requirements necessary for benefit eligibility under OASDI and Medicare.
- Describe the financing of social security benefits including (1) the purpose and significance of the social security trust funds and (2) the financial soundness of the program.

Social insurance programs in the United States fall into four categories:

1. Social security.
2. Workers' compensation insurance.
3. Temporary disability insurance.
4. Unemployment insurance.

Social security, a totally federal program, is described in this chapter; the remaining three programs, either state or joint federal and state programs, are covered in Chapter 4.

These programs are significant for several reasons. First, the most significant insurance expense for most individuals is their contribution to social insurance programs—primarily social security. For many persons, this contribution will exceed the combined cost of all other types of insurance purchased directly by the individual.

Second, in the United States nearly one-fourth of the dollars employers spend on benefits for their employees is used to make legally required payments to social insurance programs. For employers with meager benefit plans, this proportion will be much higher and may even account for the majority of the benefit package.

Third, these programs form the foundation on which many individual insurance plans and employee benefit programs are built. For example, it is impossible to do a proper job of life insurance programming without taking potential social security benefits into consideration. In addition, the medical expense, disability income and retirement plans of employers are often designed in light of the benefits already available to employees under social insurance programs. Some benefit plans apply only to those employees not adequately covered under comparable social insurance programs; other benefit plans may cover all employees but may provide reduced benefits in those areas where similar social insurance benefits are available.

Many books have been devoted entirely to social insurance programs. Because of space limitations, the treatment in this book is rather brief and is devoted primarily to a description of eligibility requirements, financing and benefits. However, a few words should also be said about the reasons why social insurance programs exist and the general characteristics of such programs.

REASONS FOR SOCIAL INSURANCE

The existence and scope of social insurance programs are the result of several factors, probably the most significant of which is the need to solve major social problems that affect a large portion of society. The industrialization of American society and the decreasing self-sufficiency of families have resulted in a greater dependence on monetary income to provide economic security. The widespread lack of such income during the Depression led to the passage of the Social Security Act of 1935 as an attempt to provide economic security by attacking the sources of economic insecurity, including old age and unemployment.

A second reason for social insurance programs results from the difficulty of privately insuring certain types of losses. For example, the inability to predict future unemployment rates and the potential for catastrophic losses make the peril of unemployment virtually uninsurable in the private sector. In addition, broad medical expense coverage for the elderly can be marketed commercially only at a price beyond the financial means of many retirees.

Finally, many Americans have come to expect the government to provide at least a degree of economic security against the consequences of premature death, old age, disability and unemployment. As a result, social insurance programs enjoy widespread acceptance by the public.

CHARACTERISTICS OF SOCIAL INSURANCE

Even though there are variations between social insurance programs and exceptions to the rule always exist, social insurance programs tend to have certain distinguishing characteristics. These include the following:

- Compulsory employment-related coverage.
- Benefits prescribed by law.
- Benefits as a matter of right.
- Emphasis on social adequacy.
- Partial or total employer financing.

Compulsory Employment-Related Coverage

Most social insurance programs are compulsory and require that the persons covered be attached—either presently or by past service— to the labor force. If a social insurance program is to meet a social need through the redistribution of income, it is necessary to have widespread participation.

Benefits Prescribed by Law

Benefit amounts and the eligibility requirements for social insurance benefits are prescribed by law. This does not mean that benefits are uniform for everyone. They may vary by such factors as wage level, length of covered employment or family status. However, these factors are incorporated into benefit formulas specified by law, and covered persons are unable to either increase or decrease their prescribed level of benefits.

Benefits As a Matter of Right

Social insurance benefits are paid as a matter of right under the presumption that a need for the benefits exists. This feature distinguishes social insurance programs from public assistance or welfare programs under which applicants, in order to qualify for benefits, must meet a needs test by demonstrating that their income or assets are below some specified level.

Emphasis on Social Adequacy

Benefits under social insurance programs are based more on social adequacy than on individual equity. Under the principle of social adequacy, benefits are designed to provide a minimum floor of income to all beneficiaries under the program regardless of their economic status. Above this floor of benefits, persons are expected to provide additional resources from their own savings, employment or private insurance programs. This emphasis on social adequacy also results in disproportionately large benefits in relation to contributions for some groups of beneficiaries. For some programs, high-income persons, single persons or small families and the young are subsidizing low-income persons, large families and the retired.

If social insurance programs were based solely on individual equity, benefits would be actuarially related to contributions just as they are under private insurance programs. While this degree of individual equity does not exist, there is some relationship between benefits and income levels (and thus contributions). Within certain maximum and minimum amounts, benefits are a function of a person's covered earnings under social insurance programs. However, the major emphasis is on social adequacy.

Partial or Total Employer Financing

While significant variations exist between social insurance programs, most require that the cost of the program be borne fully or at least partially by the employers of the covered persons. This is the basis for including these programs under the broad definition of employee benefits. The remaining cost of most social insurance programs is paid primarily by the persons covered under the programs. With the exception of Medicare and certain unemployment benefits, the general revenues of the federal government and state governments finance only a small portion of social insurance benefits.

SOCIAL SECURITY (OASDHI)

When most people use the term *social security,* they are actually referring to Old Age, Survivors, Disability and Health Insurance (OASDHI)—a program of the federal government. This is the meaning that is used here. However, OASDHI is only one of several programs resulting from the Social Security Act of 1935 and its frequent amendments over the years. The Act established four programs aimed at providing economic security for the American society:

1. Old-age insurance.
2. Unemployment insurance.
3. Federal grants for assistance to certain needy groups: the aged, the blind and children.
4. Federal grants for maternal and child welfare, public health work and vocational rehabilitation.

The old-age insurance program and the benefits that have been added to that program over the years to make it what we now call social security will be discussed here. These additional benefits include survivors' insurance (1939), disability insurance (1956), hospital insurance (1965) and supplementary medical insurance (1965). The latter two parts of social security comprise Medicare and are often referred to as part A and part B, respectively.

The following discussion of social security begins with a description of the extent of coverage under the program and the way the program is financed. It then focuses on the eligibility requirements and benefits under the various parts of the program. Because of the many differences between Medicare and the rest of the program, the discussion treats each part separately beginning with old age, survivors and disability insurance, or OASDI. Finally, a description of the tax implications of social security benefits and contributions is found at the end of this chapter.

Extent of Coverage

Over 90 percent of the workers in the United States are in covered employment under the social security program. This means that these workers have wages (if they are employees) or self-employment income (if they are self-employed) on which social security taxes must be paid. The following are the major categories of workers who are not covered under the program or who are covered only if they meet specific conditions:

- Civilian employees of the federal government who were employed by the government prior to 1984 and who are covered under the Civil Service Retirement System or certain other federal retirement programs. These workers are covered by government plans that provide benefits similar to those available under social security. Coverage for new civilian federal employees under the entire program was one of the most significant changes resulting from the 1983 amendments to the Social Security Act. It should be noted, however, that *all* federal employees have been covered under social security for purpose of Medicare since 1983.
- Railroad workers. Under the Railroad Retirement Act, employees of railroads have their own benefit system that is similar to OASDI. However, they are covered under social security for purposes of Medicare. In addition, there are certain circumstances under which railroad workers receive benefits from the social security program even though their contributions were paid to the railroad program.
- Employees of state and local governments unless the state has entered into a voluntary agreement with the Social Security Administration. Under such an agreement, the state may either require that employees of local governments also be covered or allow the local governments to decide whether to include their employees. In addition, the state may elect to include all or only certain groups of its employees. Beginning in mid-1991, this exemption for state and local government employees applies only to those employees who are covered under their employer's retirement plan. A state or local government can no longer be exempt and not provide retirement benefits to employees. Prior to 1984, states and local government units were allowed to withdraw their employees from social security coverage. However, this withdrawal privilege is no longer available.
- American citizens working abroad for foreign affiliates of U.S. employers, unless the employer owns at least a 10 percent interest in the foreign affiliate and has made arrangements with the secretary of the treasury for the payment of social security taxes. However, Americans working abroad are covered under social security if they are working for U.S. employers rather than their foreign subsidiaries.
- Ministers who elect out of coverage because of conscience or religious principles.
- Workers in certain jobs, such as student nurses, newspaper carriers under age 18 and students working for the school at which they are regularly enrolled or doing domestic work for a local college club, fraternity or sorority.
- Certain family employment. This includes the employment of a child under age 18 by a parent. This exclusion, however, does not apply if the employment is for a corporation owned by a family member.

- Certain workers who must satisfy special earnings requirements. For example, self-employed persons are not covered unless they have net annual earnings of $400 or more. In addition, certain agricultural workers must have annual cash wages of $150 or more, and domestic workers must earn more than $50 in cash wages in a calendar quarter.

Financing

Medicare part B is financed by a combination of monthly premiums paid by persons eligible for benefits and contributions from the federal government. Medicare part A and all the benefits of the OASDI program are financed through a system of payroll and self-employment taxes paid by all persons covered under the program. In addition, employers of covered persons are also taxed.

In 1991, an employee and his or her employer pay a tax of 7.65 percent each on the first $53,400 of the employee's wages. (6.2 percent of the tax rate is for OASDI; 1.45 percent is for Medicare.) For persons who have annual wages in excess of $53,400, the Medicare tax of 1.45 percent is also levied on wages between $53,400 and $125,000. The tax rates are scheduled to remain the same after 1991. However, the wage bases are adjusted annually for changes in the national level of wages. Therefore, if wage levels increase by 10 percent in a particular year, the wage base for the following year will also increase by 10 percent. The tax rate for the self-employed is 15.3 percent on the first $53,400 of self-employment income and 2.9 percent on the balance of any income up to $125,000. This is equal to the combined employee and employer rates.

Over the years, both the tax rate and wage base have been dramatically increased to finance increased benefit levels under social security as well as the new benefits that have been added to the program. Table 3-1 shows the magnitude of these increases for selected years.

The social security program is essentially based on a system of pay-as-you-go financing with limited trust funds. This means that current payroll taxes and other contributions received by the program are used to pay the current benefits of persons who are no longer paying social security taxes because of death, old age or disability. This is in direct contrast to private insurance or retirement plans, which are based on advance funding, whereby assets are accumulated from current contributions to pay the future benefits of those making the contributions.

All payroll taxes and other sources of funds for social security are deposited into four trust funds: an old-age and survivors' fund, a disability fund and two Medicare funds. Benefits and administrative expenses are paid out of the appropriate trust fund from contributions to that fund and any interest earnings on excess contributions. The social security program does have limited reserves to serve as emergency funds in periods when benefits exceed contributions, such as in times of high unemployment. However, these reserves are currently relatively small and could pay benefits for only a limited time if contributions to a fund ceased.

In the early 1980s, considerable concern arose over the potential inability of payroll taxes to pay promised benefits in the future. Through a series of changes, the most significant being the 1983 amendments to the Social Security Act, these

TABLE 3-1
Changes in Wage Base and Tax Rate under Social Security

Year	Wage Base	Tax Rate	Maximum Employee Tax
1950	$3,000	1.50%	$45.00
1955	4,200	2.00	84.00
1960	4,800	3.00	144.00
1965	4,800	3.65	174.00
1970	7,800	4.80	374.40
1975	14,100	5.85	824.85
1980	25,900	6.13	1,587.67
1981	29,700	6.65	1,975.05
1982	32,400	6.70	2,170.80
1983	35,700	6.70	2,391.90
1984	37,800	7.00	2,532.60
1985	39,600	7.05	2,791.80
1986	42,000	7.15	3,003.00
1987	43,800	7.15	3,131.70
1988	45,000	7.51	3,379.50
1989	48,000	7.51	3,604.80
1990	51,300	7.65	3,924.45
1991	first 53,400	7.65	
	next 71,600	1.45	5,123.30
1992 and after	*	**	

*Subject to automatic adjustment
**Same as 1991

problems seem to have been solved for the OASDI portion of the program—at least in the short run. The changes approached the problem from two directions. On the one hand, payroll tax rates were increased; on the other hand, some benefits were eliminated and future increases in other benefits were scaled back.

The trust fund for old-age and survivors' benefits will continue to grow and will be very large by the time the current baby boomers retire. At that time, the fund will begin to decrease as the percentage of retirees grows rapidly. If current projections are realized, the size of the fund will stabilize at the desired level as the baby boomers die and the percentage of elderly returns to a more normal level. This increase in the size of the trust fund has caused some concerns. Since social security revenues and expenses are part of the federal budget, the excess contributions to the fund actually make the budget deficit look less severe than it really is. There is a fear that this may lull Congress into a false sense of security about the deficit, which will prevent budget reform of the magnitude that should be undertaken. In addition, the large trust fund surplus will lead to pressure for benefit increases, even though the surplus will be needed in later years. There is also the fear that Congress may decide to spend some of the surplus, thus leading to future financial problems for the OASDI program. To counter both of these issues, some experts advocate a short-run decrease in the tax rate. Rather than have a stable rate of 7.65 percent, they would lower the rate by at least one percentage point and then gradually raise the rate in the future. This strategy would result in a tax rate approaching 9 percent during the retirement years of the baby boomers.

There is still concern about the Medicare portion of the program. In the minds of many experts, some combination of increasing contributions or decreasing bene-fits will be needed to keep the program viable into the next century, when the percentage of elderly persons in the population will increase dramatically. Some changes of this nature were part of the 1990 deficit reduction bill, but there is still a feeling that these changes are only short-term measures. Much more will have to be done. However, tinkering with Medicare has significant political implications.

OASDI: Eligibility

To be eligible for benefits under OASDI, an individual must have credit for a mini-mum amount of work under social security. This credit is based on quarters of coverage. For 1991, a worker receives credit for one quarter of coverage for each $540 in annual earnings on which social security taxes are paid. However, credit for no more than four quarters of coverage may be earned in any one calendar year. Consequently, a worker paying social security taxes on as little as $2,160 (i.e., $540 × 4) during the year will receive credit for the maximum of four quarters. As in the case of the wage base, the amount of earnings necessary for a quarter of coverage is adjusted annually for changes in the national level of wages. Prior to 1978, a worker could receive credit for only one quarter of coverage in any given calendar quarter. Therefore, it was necessary to be earning wages throughout the year in order to receive the maximum number of credits. Now a worker with the appropriate level of wages can receive credit for the maximum number of quarters even if all wages are earned within one calendar quarter.

Quarters of coverage are the basis for establishing an insured status under OASDI. The three types of insured status are fully insured, currently insured and disability insured.

Fully Insured

A person is fully insured under OASDI if either of two tests is met. The first test requires credit for 40 quarters of coverage. Once a person acquires such credit, he or she is fully insured for life even if covered employment under social security ceases.

Under the second test, a person who has credit for a minimum of six quarters of coverage is fully insured if he or she has credit for at least as many quarters of coverage as there are years elapsing after 1950 (or after the year in which age 21 is reached, if later) and before the year in which he or she dies, becomes disabled or reaches age 62, whichever occurs first. Therefore, a worker who turned 62 in 1988 would need credit for only 38 quarters of coverage in order to be fully insured and eligible for full retirement benefits in 1991 at age 65. Similarly, a worker who reached age 21 in 1979 and who dies in 1991 would need credit for 11 quarters of coverage for his or her family to be eligible for survivors' benefits.

Currently Insured

If a worker is fully insured under OASDI, there is no additional significance to being currently insured. However, if a worker is not fully insured, certain survivors' benefits are still available if a currently insured status exists. To be currently insured, it is only necessary that a worker have credit for at least six quarters of coverage out of the 13-quarter period ending with the quarter in which death occurs.

Disability Insured

In order to receive disability benefits under OASDI, it is necessary to be disability insured. At a minimum, a disability insured status requires that a worker (1) be fully insured and (2) have a minimum amount of work under social security within a recent time period. In connection with the latter requirement, workers age 31 or older must have credit for at least 20 of the last 40 quarters ending with the quarter in which disability occurs; workers between the ages of 24 and 30, inclusively, must have credit for at least half the quarters of coverage from the time they turned 21 and the quarter in which disability begins; and workers under age 24 must have credit for six out of the last 12 quarters, ending with the quarter in which disability begins.

A special rule for the blind states that they are exempt from the recent-work rules and are considered disability insured as long as they are fully insured.

OASDI: Types of Benefits

As its name implies, the OASDI portion of social security provides three principal types of benefits:

1. Retirement (old-age) benefits.
2. Survivors' benefits.
3. Disability benefits.

Retirement Benefits

A worker who is fully insured under OASDI is eligible to receive monthly retirement benefits as early as age 62. However, the election to receive benefits prior to age 65 results in a permanently reduced benefit. (Note: Beginning in 2003, the retirement age for nonreduced benefits will gradually increase until it reaches 67 in 2027.) In addition, the following dependents of persons receiving retirement benefits are also eligible for monthly benefits:

- A spouse age 62 or older. However, benefits are permanently reduced if this benefit is elected prior to the spouse's reaching age 65. This benefit is also available to a divorced spouse under certain circumstances if the marriage lasted at least ten years.
- A spouse of any age if the spouse is caring for at least one child of the retired worker who is (1) under age 16 or (2) disabled or entitled to a child's benefit as described below. This benefit is commonly referred to as a mother's or father's benefit.

- Dependent, unmarried children under 18. This child's benefit will continue until age 19 as long as the child is a full-time student in elementary or secondary school. In addition, disabled children of any age are eligible for benefits as long as they were disabled before reaching age 22.

It is important to note that retirement benefits, as well as all other benefits under social security, are not automatically paid upon eligibility but must be applied for.

Survivors' Benefits

All categories of survivors' benefits are payable if a worker is fully insured at the time of death. However, three types of benefits are also payable if a worker is only currently insured. The first is a lump-sum death benefit of $255, payable to a surviving spouse living with the worker at the time of the worker's death or, if there is no such spouse, to children eligible for monthly benefits. If neither category exists, the benefit is not paid.

There are two categories of persons who are eligible for income benefits as survivors if a deceased worker was either fully or currently insured at the time of death:

1. Dependent, unmarried children under the same conditions as previously described for retirement benefits.
2. A spouse (including a divorced spouse) caring for a child or children under the same conditions as previously described for retirement benefits.

The following categories of persons are also eligible for benefits, but only if the deceased worker was fully insured:

- A widow or widower at age 60. However, benefits are reduced if taken prior to age 65. This benefit is also payable to a divorced spouse if the marriage lasted at least ten years. In addition, the widow's or widower's benefit is payable to a disabled spouse at age 50 as long as the disability commenced no more than seven years after (1) the worker's death or (2) the end of the year in which entitlement to a mother's or father's benefit ceased.
- A parent age 62 or over who was dependent on the deceased worker at the time of death.

Disability Benefits

A disabled worker under age 65 is eligible to receive benefits under OASDI as long as he or she is disability insured and meets the definition of disability under the law. The definition of disability is very rigid and requires a mental or physical impairment that prevents the worker from engaging in any substantial gainful employment. The disability must also have lasted (or be expected to last) at least 12 months or be expected to result in death. A more liberal definition of disability applies to blind workers who are age 55 or older. They are considered disabled if they are unable to perform work that requires skills or abilities comparable to those required by the work they regularly performed before reaching age 55 or before becoming blind, if later.

Disability benefits are subject to a waiting period and are payable beginning with the sixth full calendar month of disability. In addition to the benefit paid to a disabled worker, the other categories of benefits available are the same as those described under retirement benefits.

As previously mentioned, certain family members not otherwise eligible for OASDI benefits may be eligible if they are disabled. Disabled children are subject to the same definition of disability as workers. However, disabled widows or widowers must be unable to engage in any gainful (rather than substantial gainful) employment.

Eligibility for Dual Benefits

In many cases, a person is eligible for more than one type of OASDI benefit. Probably the most common situation occurs when a person is eligible for both a spouse's benefit and a worker's retirement benefit based on his or her own social security record. In this case, and in any other case when a person is eligible for dual benefits, only an amount equal to the highest benefit is paid.

Termination of Benefits

Monthly benefits to any social security recipient cease upon death. When a retired or disabled worker dies, the family members' benefits that are based on the worker's retirement or disability benefits also cease, but the family members are then eligible for survivors' benefits.

Disability benefits for a worker technically terminate at age 65 but are then replaced by comparable retirement benefits. In addition, any benefits payable because of disability cease if the definition of disability is no longer satisfied. However, the disability benefits continue during a readjustment period that consists of the month of recovery and two additional months.

As long as children are not disabled, benefits will usually terminate at age 18, but may continue until age 19 if the child is a full-time student in elementary or secondary school.

The benefit of a surviving spouse terminates upon remarriage unless remarriage takes place at age 60 or later.

OASDI: Benefit Amounts

With the exception of the $255 lump-sum death benefit, the amount of all OASDI benefits is based on a worker's primary insurance amount (PIA). The PIA, in turn, is a function of the worker's average indexed monthly earnings (AIME) on which social security taxes have been paid.

Calculation of AIME

Even though they may initially seem rather complex, the steps in calculating a worker's AIME are relatively simple. They are outlined below and will be best

TABLE 3-2
Calculation of AIME

Year	Covered Earnings	×	Indexing Factor	=	Indexed Earnings	Earnings for Years to Be Included in Calculation
1983	$15,000	×	1.31893	=	$19.783.95	excluded
1984	16,000	×	1.24571	=	19,931.36	$19,931.36
1985	17,500	×	1.19480	=	20,909.00	20,909.00
1986	19,000	×	1.16036	=	22,046.84	22,046.84
1987	21,000	×	1.09080	=	22,906.80	22,906.80
1988	22,500	×	1.03960	=	23,391.00	23,391.00
1989	24,000	×	1.00000	=	24,000.00	24,000.00
1990	26,500	×	1.00000	=	26,500.00	26,500.00

$$\text{AIME} = \frac{\$159,685.00}{84} = \$1,901 \text{ (rounded to the next lower dollar)}$$

understood by referring to Table 3-2, which shows the computation of the AIME for a worker who attained age 30 in 1991 and became disabled.

- First, list the earnings on which social security taxes were paid for each year beginning with 1951 (or the year when age 22 was attained, if later) up to and including the year of death or the year prior to disability or retirement. The example in Table 3-2 begins with 1983 because that was the year the worker attained age 22.
- Second, index these earnings by multiplying them by an indexing factor that reflects changing wage levels. The only years that are indexed are those prior to the indexing year, which is the year a worker turned 60 for retirement purposes or two years preceding the year of death or disability for purposes of survivors' or disability benefits. Therefore, the indexing factor for the indexing year (1989 in the example) and subsequent years is one. For years prior to the indexing year, the indexing factor for each year is equal to the *average annual covered wages* in the indexing year divided by the average annual covered wages in the year in which earnings are to be indexed. Average annual covered wages are the average wages on which social security taxes were paid. This figure is made available annually by the government for the previous year. In the example, the indexing factor for 1983 is 1.31893 because average annual covered wages were $20,099.55 in 1989 and $15,239.24 in 1983.
- Third, determine the number of years to be included in the calculation. For retirement and survivors' benefits, the number of years is five less than the minimum number of quarters necessary to be fully insured. For disability benefits, a subtraction may also be made from the minimum number of quarters necessary for fully insured status. This subtraction is five for workers age 47 or over, four for workers age 42 through 46, three for workers age

37 through 41, two for workers age 32 through 36, one for workers age 27 through 31, and none for workers under age 27. However, for survivors' or disability benefits, at least two years must remain for purposes of calculating benefits. In the example, the worker needs a minimum of eight quarters to be fully insured, since eight is the number of years after the worker reached age 21 and prior to the year of disability. Because the worker is age 30, one year can be subtracted, which leaves seven years to be included in the calculation. (Note: Up to three additional years may be dropped from the calculation if the worker had no income during the year and had a child under the age of three living in his or her household during the entire year.)

- Fourth, determine the years to be excluded from the calculation. These will be the years with the lowest indexed earnings. Of course, the number of years determined in the previous step must remain. In the example, only one year (1983) can be excluded.
- Fifth, add the indexed earnings for the years to be included in the AIME calculation and divide the result by the number of months in these years. In the example, the divisor is 84 months, which represents the seven years of earnings included in the calculation.

As mentioned earlier, the calculation of the AIME for retirement or disability benefits excludes the year in which retirement or disability takes place. However, the indexed earnings for that year can be substituted for the lowest year in the calculation if the result will be a larger AIME.

Determination of PIA and Monthly Benefits

Once a worker's AIME has been calculated, his or her PIA is determined by applying a formula to the AIME. The 1991 formula is as follows:

> 90% of the first $370 of AIME
> + 32% of the AIME in excess of $370 through $2,230
> + 15% of the AIME in excess of $2,230

The dollar figures in this formula are adjusted annually for changes in the national level of wages. The formula used to determine a worker's retirement benefit is the formula for the year in which the worker turned age 62. Therefore, a worker retiring at age 65 in 1991 would use the 1988 formula rather than the 1991 formula. The formula used to determine survivors' and disability benefits is the formula in existence for the year in which death or disability occurs, even if application for benefits is made in a later year.

Using the formula for 1991, a disabled worker with an AIME of $2,300 would have a PIA of $938.70, calculated as follows:

> 90% of $370 = $333.00
> +32% of $1,860 = 595.20
> +15% of $70 = 10.50
> $938.70

The PIA is the amount a worker will receive if he or she retires at age 65 or becomes disabled, and it is the amount on which benefits for family members are based. In 1991, a worker who had average earnings during his or her lifetime can expect a PIA of about $600. A worker who continually earned the maximum income subject to social security taxes can expect a PIA of nearly $1,000 for retirement purposes and a PIA of between $950 and $1,150 for purposes of disability and survivors' benefits. The higher PIA occurs for workers who are disabled or die at younger ages.

If a worker is retired or disabled, the following benefits are paid to family members:

Category	Percentage of Worker's PIA
Spouse age 65	50%
Spouse caring for disabled child or child under 16	50%
Child under 18 or disabled child	50% each

If the worker dies, survivors' benefits are as follows:

Category	Percentage of Worker's PIA
Spouse age 65	100%
Spouse caring for disabled child or child under 16	75%
Child under 18 or disabled child	75% each
Dependent parent	82.5% for one, 75% each for two

However, the full benefits described above may not be payable because of a limitation imposed on the total benefits that may be paid to a family. This family maximum will usually be reached if three or more family members (including a retired or disabled worker) are eligible for benefits. The family maximum for purposes of retirement and survivors' benefits can be determined for 1991 from the following formula, which, like the PIA formula, is adjusted annually based on changing wage levels:

150% of the first $473 of PIA
+272% of the PIA in excess of $473 through $682
+134% of the PIA in excess of $682 through $890
+175% of the PIA in excess of $890

The family maximum for purposes of disability benefits is limited to 85 percent of the worker's AIME or 150 percent of the worker's PIA, whichever is lower. However, in no case can the maximum be reduced below the worker's PIA.

If the total amount of benefits payable to family members exceeds the family maximum, the worker's benefit (in the case of retirement and disability) is not affected, but the benefits of other family members are reduced proportionately. For example, assume a worker dies leaving a spouse under age 65 and three children who are each eligible for 75 percent of his or her PIA of $800. Ignoring the family maximum, the benefits would total $2,400 ($600 for each family member). However, the family maximum using the above formula is $1,436.10. Therefore, each family member would have his or her benefit reduced to $359 (family benefits are rounded to the next lowest dollar). When the first child loses benefits at age 18, the other family members will each have benefits increased to $478 (ignoring any automatic increases in benefit amounts, including the family maximum). When a second family member loses eligibility, the remaining two family members will each receive the full benefit of $600 because the total benefits received by the family will now be less than $1,436.10.

Special Minimum PIA. There is a minimum PIA for workers who have been covered under OASDI for at least ten years but at very low wages. The PIA is used only if it is higher than a worker's PIA based on actual wages, which is usually not the case. The benefit is first determined by multiplying $11.50 times the number of years of coverage less ten, subject to a maximum of 20. This figure is then adjusted for the cumulative change in the consumer price index (CPI) since 1979. In 1991, a worker with 30 or more years of coverage under OASDI will have a minimum PIA at age 65 of $461.20.

Benefits Taken Early. If a worker elects to receive retirement benefits prior to age 65, benefits are permanently reduced by $5/9$ of 1 percent for every month that the early retirement precedes age 65. For example, for a worker who retires at age 62, the monthly benefit will only be 80 percent of that worker's PIA. A spouse who elects retirement benefits prior to age 65 will have benefits reduced by $25/36$ of 1 percent per month, and a widow or widower will have benefits reduced by $19/40$ of 1 percent per month. In the latter case, benefits at age 60 will be 71½ percent of the worker's PIA. If the widow or widower elects benefits at an earlier age because of disability, there is no further reduction.

Delayed Retirement. Workers who delay applying for retirement benefits until after age 65 are eligible for an increased benefit. For persons born from 1917 to 1924, the increase is 3 percent for each year of delay up to age 70. For persons born in 1925 or 1926 the increase is 3.5 percent per year. To encourage delayed retirement, the percentage will gradually increase to 8 percent by 2009.

Earnings Test. Benefits are reduced for social security beneficiaries under the age of 70 if they have wages from work that exceed a specified level. The rationale behind having such a reduction tied to wages, referred to as an earnings test, is that social security benefits are intended to replace lost wages but not other income such as dividends or interest. In 1991, social security beneficiaries age 65 through 69 are allowed annual wages of $9,720 without any reduction in their benefits. Beneficiaries under age 65 are allowed earnings of $7,080. These figures are also adjusted annually on the basis of national wage levels. If a beneficiary earns in excess of the allowable amount, his or her social security benefit is reduced. For persons age 65 through 69, the reduction is $1 for every $3 of excess earnings; for persons under age 65, the reduction is $1 for every $2 of excess earnings. Social security beneficiaries age 70 or older can earn any amount of wages without a reduction in benefits.

The reduction in a retired worker's benefits from excess earnings is charged against the entire benefits that are paid to a family as a result of the worker's social security record. If large enough, this reduction may totally eliminate all benefits otherwise payable to the worker and family members. In contrast, excess earnings of family members are charged against their individual benefits only. For example, a widowed mother who holds a job outside the home may lose her mother's benefit, but any benefits received by her children will be unaffected.

Cost-of-Living Adjustments. OASDI benefits are increased automatically each January as long as there has been an increase in the Consumer Price Index (CPI) for the one-year period ending in the third quarter of the prior year. The increase is the same as the increase in the CPI since the last cost-of-living adjustment, rounded to the nearest 0.1 percent.

There is one exception to this adjustment. In any year that the combined reserves of the OASDI trust funds drop below 20 percent of expected benefits, the cost-of-living adjustment will be limited to the lesser of the increase in the CPI or the increase in national wages used to adjust the wage base for social security taxes. When benefit increases have been based on wage levels, future cost-of-living increases can be larger than changes in the CPI to make up for the lower benefit increases in those years when the CPI was not used. However, this extra cost-of-living increase can be made only in years when the reserve is equal to at least 32 percent of expected benefits.

Offset for Other Benefits. Disabled workers under age 65 who are also receiving workers' compensation benefits or disability benefits from certain other federal, state or local disability programs will have their OASDI benefits reduced to the extent that the total benefits received (including family benefits) exceed 80 percent of their average current earnings at the time of disability. In addition, the monthly benefit of a spouse or surviving spouse is reduced by two-thirds of any federal, state or local government pension that is based on earnings not covered under OASDI.

Medicare: Eligibility

Part A, the hospital portion of Medicare, is available to any person age 65 or older as long as the person is entitled to monthly retirement benefits under social security or the railroad retirement program. In addition, civilian employees of the federal government age 65 or older are also eligible. It is not necessary for the workers to actually receive retirement benefits, but they must be fully insured for purposes of retirement benefits. The following persons are also eligible for Medicare at no monthly cost:

- Dependents age 65 or older of fully insured workers age 62 or older.
- Survivors age 65 or older who are eligible for OASDI survivors' benefits.
- Disabled persons at any age who have been eligible to receive OASDI benefits for two years because of their disability. This includes workers under age 65, disabled widows and widowers age 50 or over and children 18 or older who were disabled prior to age 22.
- Workers who are either fully or currently insured and their spouses and dependent children with end-stage renal (kidney) disease who require renal dialysis or kidney transplants. Coverage begins either the first day of the third month after dialysis begins or earlier for admission to a hospital for kidney transplant surgery.

Most persons age 65 or over who do not meet the previously discussed eligibility requirements may voluntarily enroll in Medicare. However, they must pay a monthly part A premium and must also enroll in part B. The part A premium, $177 in 1991, is adjusted annually to reflect the full cost of the benefits provided.

Any person eligible for Medicare part A is also eligible for part B. However, a monthly premium must be paid for part B. This premium—$29.90 in 1991, is adjusted annually and represents only about 25 percent of the cost of the benefits provided. The remaining cost of the program is financed from the general revenues of the federal government.

Persons receiving social security or railroad retirement benefits are automatically enrolled in Medicare if they are eligible. If they do not want part B, they must reject it in writing. Other persons eligible for Medicare must apply for benefits. Anyone who rejects part B or who does not enroll when initially eligible may later apply for benefits during a general enrollment period that occurs between January 1 and March 31 of each year. However, the monthly premium will be increased by 10 percent for each 12-month period during which the person was eligible but failed to enroll.

Medicare: Part A Benefits

Medicare part A provides benefits for expenses incurred in hospitals, skilled nursing facilities and hospices. In addition, home health care benefits are covered. In order for benefits to be paid, it is necessary that the facility or agency providing benefits participate in the Medicare program. Virtually all hospitals are participants, as are most other facilities or agencies that meet the requirements of Medicare.

Hospital Benefits

Part A pays for inpatient hospital services for up to 90 days in each benefit period (also referred to as a spell of illness). A benefit period begins the first time a Medicare recipient is hospitalized and ends only after the recipient has been out of a hospital or skilled nursing facility for 60 consecutive days. A subsequent hospitalization then begins a new benefit period.

In each benefit period, covered hospital expenses are paid in full for 60 days, subject to an initial deductible of $628 in 1991. This deductible is adjusted annually to reflect increasing health care costs. Benefits for an additional 30 days of hospitalization are also provided in each benefit period, but the patient must pay a daily coinsurance charge ($157 in 1991) equal to 25 percent of the initial deductible amount. Each recipient also has a lifetime reserve of 60 additional days that may be used if the regular 90 days of benefits have been exhausted. However, once a reserve day is used, it cannot be restored for use in future benefit periods. When using reserve days, patients must pay a daily coinsurance charge ($314 in 1991) equal to 50 percent of the initial deductible amount.

There is no limit to the number of benefit periods a person may have during his or her lifetime. However, there is a lifetime limit of 190 days of benefits for treatment in psychiatric hospitals.

Covered inpatient expenses include the following:

- Room and board in semiprivate accommodations. Private rooms are covered only if required for medical reasons.
- Nursing services (except private-duty nurses).
- Use of regular hospital equipment, such as oxygen tents or wheelchairs.
- Drugs and biologicals ordinarily furnished by the hospital.
- Diagnostic or therapeutic items or services.
- Operating room costs.
- Blood transfusions after the first three pints of blood. Patients must pay for the first three pints of blood unless they get donors to replace the blood.

There is no coverage under part A for the services of physicians or surgeons.

Skilled Nursing Facility Benefits

In many cases, a patient may no longer require continuous hospital care but may not be well enough to go home. Consequently, part A provides benefits for care in a skilled nursing facility if a physician certifies that skilled nursing care or rehabilitative services are needed for a condition that was treated in a hospital within the last 30 days. In addition, the prior hospitalization must have lasted at least three days. Benefits are paid in full for 20 days in each benefit period and for an additional 80 days with a daily coinsurance charge ($78.50 in 1991) that is equal to 12.5 percent of the initial hospital deductible. Covered expenses are the same as those described for hospital benefits.

A skilled nursing facility may be a separate facility for providing such care or a separate section of a hospital or nursing home. The facility must have at least one full-time registered nurse and nursing services must be provided at all times. Every patient must be under the supervision of a physician. A physician must always be available for emergency care.

One very important point should be made about skilled nursing facility benefits. Custodial care is not provided under any part of the Medicare program unless skilled nursing or rehabilitative services are also needed.

Home Health Care Benefits

If a patient can be treated at home for a medical condition, part A will pay the full cost for an unlimited number of home visits by a home health agency. Such agencies specialize in providing nursing services and other therapeutic services. To receive these benefits a person must be confined at home and be treated under a home health plan set up by a physician. No prior hospitalization is required. The care needed must include skilled nursing services, physical therapy or speech therapy. In addition to these services, Medicare will also pay for the cost of part-time home health aides, medical social services, occupational therapy and medical supplies and equipment provided by the home health agency. There is no charge for these benefits other than a required 20 percent copayment for the cost of durable medical equipment, such as iron lungs, oxygen tanks and hospital beds. Medicare does not cover home services furnished primarily to assist people in activities such as housecleaning, preparing meals, shopping, dressing or bathing.

Hospice Benefits

Hospice benefits are available under Medicare part A for terminally ill persons who have a life expectancy of six months or less. While a hospice is thought of as a facility for treating the terminally ill, Medicare benefits are available primarily for hospice-type benefits provided to patients in their own homes. However, up to 20 percent of the days of hospice treatment may be as an inpatient in a facility of the organization providing home treatment or in a hospital or other facility with which it cooperates. In addition to including the types of benefits described for home health care, hospice benefits also include drugs, bereavement counseling and respite care when family members need a break from caring for the ill person.

In order to qualify for hospice benefits, a Medicare recipient must elect such coverage in lieu of other Medicare benefits, except for the services of the attending physician or services and benefits that do not pertain to the terminal condition. There are modest copayments for some services.

Exclusions

There are some circumstances under which Medicare part A will not pay benefits. In addition, there are times when Medicare will act as the secondary payer of benefits. Exclusions under part A include the following:

- Services outside the United States and its territories or possessions. However, there are a few exceptions to this rule for qualified Mexican and Canadian hospitals. Benefits will be paid if an emergency occurs in the United States and the closest hospital is in one of these countries. However, persons living closer to a hospital in one of these countries than to a hospital in the United States may use the foreign hospital even if an emergency does not exist. Finally, there is coverage for Canadian hospitals if a person needs hospitalization while traveling the most direct route between Alaska and another state in the United States. However, this latter provision does not apply to persons vacationing in Canada.

- Elective luxury services, such as private rooms or televisions.
- Hospitalization for services not necessary for the treatment of an illness or injury, such as custodial care or elective cosmetic surgery.
- Services performed in a federal facility, such as a veterans' hospital.
- Services covered under workers' compensation.

Under the following circumstances, Medicare is the secondary payer of benefits:

- When primary coverage under an employer-provided medical expense plan is elected by (1) an employee or spouse age 65 or older or (2) a disabled beneficiary. (This is discussed in more detail in Chapters 5 and 12.)
- When medical care can be paid under any liability policy, including policies providing automobile no-fault benefits.
- In the first 18 months for end-stage renal disease when an employer-provided medical expense plan provides coverage. By law, employer plans cannot specifically exclude this coverage during this 18-month period.

Medicare only pays if complete coverage is not available from these sources and then only to the extent that benefits are less than would otherwise be payable under Medicare.

Medicare: Part B Benefits

Medicare part B provides benefits for the following medical expenses not covered under part A:

- Physicians' and surgeons' fees. These fees may result from house calls, office visits or services provided in a hospital or other institution. Under certain circumstances, benefits are also provided for the services of chiropractors, podiatrists and optometrists.
- Diagnostic tests in a hospital or in a physician's office.
- Physical therapy in a physician's office, or as an outpatient of a hospital, skilled nursing facility or other approved clinic, rehabilitative agency or public-health agency.
- Drugs and biologicals that cannot be self-administered.
- Radiation therapy.
- Medical supplies, such as surgical dressings, splints and casts.
- Rental of medical equipment, such as oxygen tents, hospital beds and wheelchairs.
- Prosthetic devices, such as artificial heart valves or lenses after a cataract operation.
- Ambulance service if a patient's condition does not permit the use of other methods of transportation.
- Mammograms.
- Pneumococcal vaccine and its administration.
- Home health services as described for part A when a person does not have part A coverage.

Exclusions

Although the preceding list may appear to be comprehensive, there are numerous medical products and services not covered by part B, some of which represent significant expenses for the elderly. They include the following:

- Drugs and biologicals that can be self-administered except drugs for osteoporosis.
- Routine physical, eye and hearing examinations except mammograms.
- Routine foot care.
- Immunizations, except pneumococcal vaccinations or immunization required because of an injury or immediate risk of infection.
- Cosmetic surgery unless it is needed because of an accidental injury or to improve the function of a malformed part of the body.
- Dental care unless it involves jaw or facial bone surgery or the setting of fractures.
- Custodial care.
- Eyeglasses, hearing aids or orthopedic shoes.

In addition, benefits are not provided to persons eligible for workers' compensation or to those treated in government hospitals. Benefits are provided only for services received in the United States, except for physicians' services and ambulance services rendered for a hospitalization that is covered in Mexico or Canada under part A. Part B is also a secondary payer of benefits under the same circumstances described for part A.

Amount of Benefits

With some exceptions, part B pays 80 percent of the approved charges for covered medical expenses after the satisfaction of a $100 annual deductible. Annual maximums apply to outpatient psychiatric benefits ($450) and physical therapy in a therapist's office or at the patient's home ($400). A few charges are paid in full without any cost sharing. These include:

- Home health services.
- Pneumococcal vaccine and its administration.
- Certain surgical procedures that are performed on an outpatient basis in lieu of hospitalization.
- Diagnostic preadmission tests performed on an outpatient basis within seven days prior to hospitalization.

The approved charge for doctors' services covered by Medicare is based on a complex formula, but it is less than what many doctors normally charge. A patient will be reimbursed for only 80 percent of the approved charges above the deductible—regardless of the doctor's actual charge. Since late 1990, doctors have been required to submit all bills directly to Medicare whether they accept assignments of Medicare benefits or not. Previously, doctors could bill patients directly, which required the patients to file the Medicare claims. Beginning in 1991, limits were placed on the size of the fees in excess of approved charges that doctors can charge Medicare patients.

TAXATION OF SOCIAL SECURITY BENEFITS AND CONTRIBUTIONS

Employers may deduct the amount of any social security taxes paid for their employees as an ordinary business expense in calculating their federal income taxes. Employees and self-employed persons, however, receive no such deduction. Their portion of social security taxes must be paid with after-tax dollars. Individual taxpayers who itemize their federal income tax deductions, however, are allowed a deduction for medical expenses that exceed a specified limit. For purposes of this deduction (discussed fully in Chapter 12), Medicare part B premiums are considered.

Until 1984, all social security benefits were received tax free. Social security income benefits (and railroad retirement benefits) are now subject to taxation, but only for beneficiaries with moderately high incomes. The amount of the annual benefit that is subject to taxation is equal to the lesser of (1) one-half the social security benefit received or (2) one-half of the "excess" specified in the Internal Revenue Code. The "excess" is the amount by which one-half of the annual social security benefit raises a recipient's "modified adjusted gross income" above a specified base amount which is $25,000 for a single individual or $32,000 for a married person filing jointly. For purposes of the tax code, modified adjusted gross income is defined to include a taxpayer's adjusted gross income plus otherwise tax-free interest, such as interest on municipal bonds. For example, assume a single person had a modified adjusted gross income of $22,000 and received $8,000 in social security benefits. Adding one-half of the social security benefit to the modified adjusted gross income yields a total amount of $26,000, or an excess of $1,000 over the base amount. One-half of this excess is $500. Because it is less than one-half of the annual social security benefit, the $500 is the amount subject to taxation.

STUDY QUESTIONS

1. Why are social insurance programs necessary?
2. Describe the characteristics of social insurance programs.
3. a. How is the social security program financed?
   b. What is the purpose of the social security trust funds?
4. As of this year, Nancy Westman, age 37, had 28 quarters of coverage under social security. Twenty-four of these quarters were earned prior to the birth of her first child 11 years ago. Four quarters have been earned since she re-entered the labor force one year ago.
   a. Is Nancy fully insured? Explain.
   b. Is Nancy currently insured? Explain.
   c. Is Nancy disability insured? Explain.

5. Describe the retirement benefits available under social security.
6. What categories of persons are eligible for social security survivors' benefits?
7. a. What is the definition of disability under social security?
   b. What categories of persons may be eligible for disability benefits?
8. Explain how earnings are indexed under social security.
9. a. Explain the relationship between a worker's PIA and the benefits available for dependents and survivors.
   b. What happens if the total benefits for a family exceed the maximum family benefit?
10. Explain how a worker's retirement benefits under OASDI will be affected if that person elects early or delayed retirement.
11. Describe the earnings test applicable to the OASDI program.
12. Describe the automatic cost-of-living adjustment provision under OASDI as it relates to benefit amounts.
13. With respect to the hospital insurance portion of Medicare,
    a. Describe the types of benefits that are available.
    b. Explain the extent to which deductibles and copayments are required.
    c. Identify the major exclusions.
14. With respect to the supplementary medical insurance portion of Medicare,
    a. Describe the types of benefits that are available.
    b. Explain the extent to which copayments are required.
    c. Identify the major exclusions.

4

Other Social Insurance Programs

Objectives

- Describe unemployment insurance programs with respect to objectives, eligibility requirements, benefits and financing.
- Describe the typical workers' compensation program with respect to type of law, eligibility requirements, benefits and financing.
- Describe the nature of temporary disability insurance.
- Explain the extent to which social security benefits are subject to income taxation.

This chapter focuses on the three major social insurance programs other than social security—unemployment insurance, workers' compensation insurance and temporary disability laws. Unemployment insurance is a joint federal and state program, and workers' compensation insurance and temporary disability laws are solely under state control. Because the programs of each state are unique, the discussion in this chapter is general in nature. Readers should familiarize themselves with the programs in their own states and not assume that these programs will always conform to the generalizations that follow.

UNEMPLOYMENT INSURANCE

Prior to the passage of the Social Security Act in 1935, relatively few employees had any type of protection for income lost during periods of unemployment. The Act provided for a payroll tax to be levied on covered employers for the purpose of financing unemployment insurance programs that were to be established by the states under guidelines issued by the federal government. Essentially, the federal law levied a federal tax on certain employers in all states. If a state established an acceptable program of unemployment insurance, the taxes used to finance its program could offset up to 90 percent of the federal tax. If a state failed to establish a program, the federal tax would still be levied, but no monies collected from employers in the state would be returned to provide benefits to the unemployed in that state. Needless to say, all states quickly established unemployment insurance programs. These programs (along with a federal program for railroad workers) now cover over 95 percent of all working persons, with the major gaps in coverage occurring for domestic workers, agricultural workers and the self-employed.

There are several objectives to the current unemployment insurance program. The primary objective is to provide periodic cash income to workers during periods of involuntary unemployment. Benefits generally are paid as a matter of right with no demonstration of need required. While legislation of the federal government has extended benefits during times of high unemployment, the unemployment insurance program is basically designed for workers whose periods of unemployment are short-term; the long-term and hard-core unemployed must rely on other measures, such as public assistance and job retraining programs, when unemployment insurance benefits are exhausted.

A second major objective of unemployment insurance is to help the unemployed find jobs. Workers must register at local unemployment offices, and unemployment benefits are received through these offices. Another important objective is to encourage employers to stabilize employment. As described later, this is accomplished through the use of experience rating in determining an employer's tax rate. Finally, unemployment insurance contributes to a stable labor supply by providing benefits so that skilled and experienced workers are not forced to seek other jobs during short-term layoffs, thereby remaining available to return to work when called back.

Financing of Benefits

Unemployment insurance programs are financed primarily by unemployment taxes levied by both the federal and state governments. The federal tax is equal to 6.2 percent of the first $7,000 of wages for each worker, but this tax is reduced by up to 5.4 percentage points for taxes paid to state programs. The practical effect of this offset is that the federal tax is actually equal to 0.8 percent of covered payroll. A few states levy an unemployment payroll tax equal only to the maximum offset (5.4 percent on the first $7,000) of wages, but many states have a higher tax rate and/or levy their tax on a higher amount of earnings.

No state levies the same tax on all employers. Rather they use a method of experience rating whereby all employers, except those in business for a short time or those with a small number of employees, pay a tax rate that, within limits, reflects their actual experience. Thus, an employer who has laid off a large percentage of employees will have a higher tax rate than an employer whose employment record has been stable.

An employer with good experience will often pay a state tax of less than 1 percent of payroll, and possibly as little as 0.1 percent. Other employers may pay a state tax as high as 9 or 10 percent. Regardless of the actual state tax paid, the employer will still pay the 0.8 federal tax.

The major argument for experience rating is that it will provide a financial incentive for employers to stabilize employment. However, those opposed to its use contend that many employers have little control over economic trends that affect employment. In addition, they argue that tax rates will tend to rise in bad economic times and may thus actually thwart economic recovery.

The entire unemployment insurance tax is collected by the individual states and deposited in the Federal Unemployment Insurance Trust Fund, which is administered by the Secretary of the Treasury. Each state has a separate account that is credited with its taxes and its share of investment earnings on assets in the fund. Unemployment benefits in the state are paid from this account. The federal share of the taxes received by the fund is used for administering the federal portion of the program and for giving grants to the states to administer their individual programs. In addition, the federal funds are available for loans to states whose accounts have been depleted during times of high unemployment.

Eligibility for Benefits

In order to receive unemployment benefits, a worker must meet the following eligibility requirements:

- Have a prior attachment to the labor force.
- Be able to work and be available for work.
- Be actively seeking work.
- Satisfy any prescribed waiting period.
- Be free of disqualification.

Attachment to the Labor Force

The right to benefits is subject to an attachment to the labor force within a prior *base period*. In most states, this base period is either the 52 weeks or four quarters prior to the time of unemployment. During this base period, the worker must have earned a minimum amount of wages or worked a minimum period of time, or both.

Able to Work and Available for Work

The right to benefits is contingent upon an unemployed worker being both physically and mentally capable of working. The worker must also be available for work. Benefits may be denied if suitable work is refused or if substantial restrictions are placed upon the type of work that will be accepted.

Actively Seeking Work

In addition to registering with a local unemployment office, most states require a worker to make a reasonable effort to seek work.

Waiting Period

Most unemployment programs have a one-week waiting period before benefits commence, and benefits are not paid retroactively for that time of unemployment.

Free of Disqualification

All states have provisions in their laws under which a worker may be disqualified from receiving benefits. This disqualification may take the form of (1) a total cancellation of benefit rights, (2) the postponement of benefits or (3) a reduction in benefits. Common reasons for disqualification include:

- Voluntarily leaving a job without good cause.
- Discharge for misconduct.
- Refusal to accept suitable work.
- Involvement in a labor dispute.
- Receipt of disqualifying income. This includes dismissal wages, workers' compensation benefits, benefits from an employer's pension plan or primary insurance benefits under OASDI.

Benefits

The majority of states pay regular unemployment insurance benefits for a maximum of 26 weeks; the remaining states pay benefits for slightly longer periods. In most states, the amount of the weekly benefit is equal to a specified fraction of a worker's average wages during the highest calendar quarter of the base period. The typical fraction is $\frac{1}{26}$ which yields a benefit equal to 50 percent of earnings. Other states determine benefits as a percentage of average weekly wages or annual wages during the base period. Some states also modify their benefit formulas to provide relatively higher benefits (as a percentage of past earnings) to lower paid workers. Benefits in all states are subject to minimum and maximum amounts. Minimum benefits typically fall within the range from $5 to $50, maximum benefits from $100 to $300, and the average benefit from $90 to $175. In addition, 13 states currently provide additional benefits if there are dependents receiving regular support from the worker.

Most states also provide reduced benefits for partial unemployment. Such a condition occurs if a worker is employed less than full time and has a weekly income less than his or her weekly benefit amount for total unemployment.

In 1970, a permanent federal-state program of "extended" unemployment benefits was established to provide benefits for an additional period of time when a worker's regular benefits are exhausted during periods of high unemployment. These benefits are financed equally by the federal government and the states involved and can be paid for up to 13 weeks, as long as the total of regular and extended benefits does not exceed 39 weeks. The program is operable only when the *insured unemployment rate* in a state exceeds a specified level. The insured unemployment rate is the percentage of workers covered by unemployment insurance who are receiving regular benefits.

WORKERS' COMPENSATION LAWS

Prior to the passage of workers' compensation laws, it was difficult for employees to receive compensation for their work-related injuries or diseases. Group benefits were meager and the social security program had not been enacted. The only recourse for employees was to sue their employers for damages. In addition to the time and expense of such actions (as well as the possibility of being fired), the probability of a suit being successful was small because of the three common-law defenses available to the employer:

1. Under the contributory negligence doctrine, a worker could not collect if his or her negligence had contributed in any way to the injury.
2. Under the fellow-servant doctrine, the worker could not collect if the injury had resulted from the negligence of a fellow worker.
3. Under the assumption-of-risk doctrine, a worker could not collect if he or she had knowingly assumed the risks inherent in the trade.

To help solve the problem of uncompensated injuries, workers' compensation laws were enacted to require employers to provide benefits to employees for losses resulting from work-related accidents or diseases. These laws are based on the principle of liability without fault. An employer is absolutely liable for providing the benefits prescribed by the workers' compensation law regardless of whether the employer would be considered legally liable in the absence of the workers' compensation law. However, benefits, with the possible exception of medical expense benefits, are subject to statutory maximums.

All states have workers' compensation laws. In addition, several similar laws have been enacted by the federal government. The Federal Workers' Compensation Act provides benefits for the employees of the federal government and the District of Columbia. Railroad employees and seamen aboard ships are covered under the Federal Employer's Liability Act and stevedores, longshore workers and workers who repair ships are covered under the United States Longshoremen's and Harbor Workers' Act.

Type of Law

Most workers' compensation laws are compulsory for all employers covered under the law. A few states have elective laws, but the majority of employers do elect coverage. If they do not, their employees are not entitled to workers' compensation benefits and must sue for damages resulting from occupational accidents or diseases. However, the employer loses the right to the three common-law defenses previously described.

Financing of Benefits

Most states allow employers to comply with the workers' compensation law by purchasing coverage from insurance companies. Several of these states also have competitive state funds from which coverage may be obtained, but these funds usually provide coverage for fewer employers than insurance companies. Six states have monopolistic state funds that are the only source for obtaining coverage under the law.

Almost all states, including some with monopolistic state funds, allow employers to self-insure their workers' compensation exposure. These employers must generally post a bond or other security and receive the approval of the agency administering the law. While the number of firms using self-insurance for workers' compensation is small, these firms account for approximately one-half of the employees covered under such laws.

In virtually all cases, the full cost of providing workers' compensation benefits must be borne by the employer. Obviously, if an employer self-insures benefits, the ultimate cost will be the benefits paid plus any administrative expenses.

Employers who purchase coverage pay a premium that is calculated as a percentage of their payroll and that is based upon the occupations of their workers. For example, premiums for office workers may be less than 1 percent of payroll, and premiums for a few extremely hazardous occupations may be close to 100 percent of payroll. Most states also require that employers with total workers' compensation premiums above a specified amount be subject to experience rating. That is, the employer's premium is a function of benefits paid for past injuries to the employer's workers. To the extent that safety costs are offset or eliminated by savings in workers' compensation premiums, experience-rating laws encourage employers to take an active role in correcting conditions that may cause injuries.

Covered Occupations

Although it is estimated that about 90 percent of the workers in the United States are covered by workers' compensation laws, the percentage varies among the states from less than 70 percent to more than 95 percent. Many laws exclude certain agricultural, domestic and casual employees. Some laws also exclude employers with a small number of employees. Coverage for employees of state and local governments is also often less than universal.

Eligibility

Before an employee can be eligible for benefits under a workers' compensation law, he or she must work in an occupation covered by the law and be disabled or killed by a covered injury or illness. The typical workers' compensation law provides coverage for *accidental occupational injuries (including death) arising out of and in the course of employment.* In all states, this includes injuries arising out of accidents, which generally are defined as sudden and unexpected events that are definite in time and place. Most workers' compensation laws exclude self-inflicted injuries and accidents resulting from an employee's intoxication or willful disregard of safety rules.

Every state has some coverage for illnesses resulting from occupational diseases. While the trend is toward full coverage for occupational diseases, some states cover only those diseases that are specifically listed in the law.

Benefits

Workers' compensation laws typically provide four types of benefits:

1. Medical care.
2. Disability income.
3. Death benefits.
4. Rehabilitative services.

Medical Care

Benefits for medical expenses are usually provided without any limitations as to time or amount. In addition, they are not subject to a waiting period.

Disability Income

For an employee to collect disability income benefits under workers' compensation laws, his or her injuries must result in one of the following four categories of disability:

1. *Temporary total.* The employee cannot perform any of the duties of his or her regular job. However, full recovery is expected. Most workers' compensation claims involve this type of disability.
2. *Permanent total.* The employee will never be able to perform any of the duties of his or her regular job or any other job. Several states also list in their laws certain disabilities (such as loss of both eyes or both arms) that result in an employee's automatically being considered permanently and totally disabled even though future employment might be possible.
3. *Temporary partial.* The employee can perform some of the duties of his or her regular job but is neither totally nor permanently disabled. For example, an employee with a sprained back might be able to work part time.
4. *Permanent partial.* The employee has a permanent injury, such as the loss of an eye, but may be able to perform his or her regular job or may be retrained for another job.

Most workers' compensation laws have a waiting period for disability income benefits that varies from two to seven days. However, benefits are frequently paid retroactively to the date of the injury if an employee is disabled for a specified period of time or is confined to a hospital.

Disability income benefits under workers' compensation laws are based on an employee's average weekly wage over some period of time, commonly the 13 weeks immediately preceding the disability. For total disabilities, benefits are a percentage (usually 66⅔ percent) of an employee's average weekly wage, subject to maximum and minimum amounts that vary substantially by state. Benefits for temporary total disabilities continue until an employee returns to work; benefits for permanent total disabilities usually continue for life but have a limited duration, such as ten years, in a few states.

Benefits for partial disabilities are calculated as a percentage of the difference between an employee's wages before and after the disability. In most states, the duration of these benefits is subject to a statutory maximum. Several states also provide lump-sum payments to employees whose permanent partial disabilities involve the loss (or loss of use) of an eye, an arm or other body member. These benefits, which are determined by a schedule in the law, may be in lieu of, or in addition to, periodic disability income benefits.

Death Benefits

Most workers' compensation laws provide two types of death benefits: burial allowances and cash income payments to survivors.

Burial allowances are a flat amount in each state and vary from $300 to $5,000, with benefits of $1,000 and $1,500 being common.

Cash income payments to survivors, like disability income benefits, are a function of the worker's average wage prior to the injury resulting in death. Benefits usually are paid only to a surviving spouse and children under 18. In some states, benefits are paid until the spouse dies or remarries and all children have reached 18. In other states, benefits are paid for a maximum duration of time, such as ten years, or until a maximum dollar amount has been paid, such as $50,000.

Rehabilitation Benefits

All states have provisions in their workers' compensation laws for rehabilitative services for disabled workers. Benefits are included for medical rehabilitation as well as for vocational rehabilitation, including training, counseling and job placement.

A difficulty faced in providing vocational rehabilitation is that employers are reluctant to hire workers with a permanent physical impairment because a subsequent work-related injury may result in their total disability, and thus an increased workers' compensation premium. For example, a worker who lost an arm in a previous work-related accident would probably be totally and permanently disabled if the other arm were lost in a later accident. Consequently, most states have established second-injury funds. If a worker is disabled by a second injury, the employer is only responsible for providing benefits equal to those that would have been provided to a worker who had not suffered the first injury. Any remaining benefits are provided by the second-injury fund.

TEMPORARY DISABILITY LAWS

In the beginning, state unemployment insurance programs were usually designed to cover only unemployed persons who were both willing and able to work. Benefits were denied to anyone unable to work for any reason, including disability. Some states amended their unemployment insurance laws to provide coverage to the unemployed who subsequently became disabled. However, five states—California, Hawaii, New Jersey, New York and Rhode Island—and Puerto Rico went one step further by enacting temporary disability laws, under which employees can collect disability income benefits regardless of whether their disability begins while they are employed or unemployed. These laws are often referred to as nonoccupational disability laws since benefits are not provided for disabilities covered under workers' compensation laws. While variations exist among the states, these laws are generally patterned after the state unemployment insurance law and provide similar benefits.

In the six jurisdictions with temporary disability laws, most employers are required to provide coverage to their employees. In all jurisdictions except Rhode Island, which has a monopolistic state fund, coverage may be obtained from either a competitive state fund or private insurance companies. Private coverage must provide at least the benefits prescribed under the law, but it may be more comprehensive. As with workers' compensation insurance, self-insurance is generally permitted. Under all six of these programs, employees must pay all or a portion of the cost, which in all cases is based upon a percentage of wages up to some statutory weekly or annual maximum.

Eligibility

Before an employee is eligible for benefits under a temporary disability law, the employee must satisfy an earnings or employment requirement, the definition of disability and a waiting period.

Earnings or Employment Requirement

Every jurisdiction requires that an employee must have worked for a specified period of time and/or have received a minimum amount of wages within some specific period prior to disability in order to qualify for benefits.

Definition of Disability

Most laws define disability as the inability of the worker to perform his or her regular or customary work because of a nonoccupational injury or illness. New Jersey has the most stringent definition of disability, which requires that an employee be unable to perform any work for remuneration. As with workers' compensation laws, certain types of disabilities are not covered. In most jurisdictions, these include disabilities caused by self-inflicted injuries or by illegal acts.

Waiting Period

The usual waiting period for benefits is seven days. However, in some jurisdictions, the waiting period is waived if the employee is hospitalized.

Benefits

Benefits are a percentage, ranging from 50 percent to 66⅔ percent, of the employee's average weekly wage for some period prior to disability, subject to maximum and minimum amounts. Benefits are generally paid for up to 26 weeks if the employee remains disabled that long.

TAXATION OF OTHER SOCIAL INSURANCE BENEFITS

Employer contributions to the social insurance programs described in this chapter are tax deductible for federal income tax purposes. Any employee contributions must be paid with after-tax dollars.

Unemployment insurance benefits are included in a recipient's gross income. However, workers' compensation benefits are free of income taxation.

Benefits received by persons under temporary disability laws are treated the same for income tax purposes as any other insured disability income benefits. This tax treatment is discussed in Chapter 8. In those jurisdictions where benefits can also be received by unemployed persons, any benefits paid to unemployed persons are considered unemployment insurance benefits and taxed accordingly.

STUDY QUESTIONS

1. What are the objectives of unemployment insurance?
2. Explain how unemployment insurance benefits are financed.
3. What requirements must be satisfied before a worker is eligible for unemployment insurance benefits?
4. For the extended benefits program of unemployment compensation, explain
   a. The circumstances under which benefits are made available.
   b. The method by which benefits are financed.
5. How did the passage of workers' compensation laws alter the traditional system of common law with respect to employee injuries?
6. What are the usual eligibility requirements for receiving workers' compensation benefits?
7. Briefly describe the types and amounts of benefits available under workers' compensation laws.
8. Explain the nature of temporary disability laws.

PART THREE

Group Insurance

5

The Group Insurance Environment

Objectives

- Identify the characteristics that distinguish group insurance from individual insurance.
- Identify the factors that are of concern to group underwriters and explain the significance of each factor.
- Describe the major aspects of state regulation applying to group insurance.
- Identify the types of groups eligible for coverage under the laws of most states and explain the significant characteristics and regulations pertaining to each.
- Explain the provisions of the Age Discrimination in Employment Act.
- Explain how employee benefit plans are affected by the provision of the Civil Rights Act that pertains to pregnancy.
- Explain how the passage of the Americans with Disabilities Act affects employee benefit plans.

The term *group insurance*, like the term *employee benefits*, can have different meanings to different persons. Most employees view group insurance in a very broad sense as any arrangement under which an employer makes benefits available to employees for life insurance, disability income, medical and dental expenses, legal expenses and property and liability insurance. To employees, it usually makes little difference whether a benefit plan is funded with a traditional insurance contract or through some type of alternative arrangement; it still is group insurance.

Even though the broad meaning of group insurance is used in this book, it is important to make a distinction between group insurance plans that are funded with traditional insurance contracts and those that use alternative funding methods. Although alternative funding methods, including total self-funding, are becoming more common, the majority of group insurance is still fully insured through insurance contracts. This chapter begins with a discussion of these traditional arrangements. Alternative funding methods are described in detail in Chapter 14. It should also be emphasized at this point that although much of the discussion in following chapters centers on the provisions found in insurance contracts, similar provisions must also be contained in group insurance plans that are funded in other ways.

The character of group insurance has been greatly influenced by the numerous laws and regulations that have been imposed by state governments and the federal government. These laws and regulations are discussed in the remainder of the chapter. The major impact of state regulation has been felt through the insurance laws governing insurance companies and the products they sell. Traditionally, these laws have affected only those benefit plans funded with insurance contracts. However, as a growing number of employers are turning toward self-funding of benefits, there has been an increasing interest on the part of state regulatory officials to extend these laws to plans using alternative funding methods. The federal laws affecting group insurance, on the other hand, have generally been directed toward any benefit plans that are established by employers for their employees, regardless of the funding method used.

CHARACTERISTICS OF TRADITIONAL GROUP INSURANCE

Traditionally, group insurance has been characterized by a group contract, experience rating of larger groups and group underwriting. Perhaps the best way to define group insurance is to compare its characteristics with those of individual insurance, which is underwritten on an individual basis.

Group Contract

In contrast to most individual insurance contracts, the group insurance contract provides coverage to a number of persons under a single contract issued to someone other than the persons insured. The contract, referred to as a *master contract,* provides benefits to a group of individuals who have a specific relationship to the policyholder. Most commonly, group contracts cover individuals who are full-time employees, and the policyholder is either their employer or a trust established to provide benefits for the employees. Although the employees are not actual parties to the master contract, they can legally enforce their rights. Consequently, employees are often referred to as third-party beneficiaries of the insurance contract.

Employees covered under the contract receive *certificates of insurance* as evidence of their coverage. A certificate is merely a description of the coverage provided and is not part of the master contract. In general, a certificate of insurance is not even considered to be a contract and usually contains a disclaimer to that effect. However, some courts have held the contrary to be true when the provisions of the certificate, or even the explanatory booklet of a group insurance plan, vary materially from the master contract.

In individual insurance, the coverage of the insured normally begins with the inception of the insurance contract and ceases with its termination. However, in group insurance, individual members of the group may become eligible for coverage long after the inception of the group contract, or they may lose their eligibility status long before the contract terminates.

Experience Rating

A second distinguishing characteristic of traditional group insurance is the use of experience rating. If a group is sufficiently large, the actual experience of that particular group will be a factor in determining the premium the policyholder will be charged. The experience of an insurance company will also be reflected in the dividends and future premiums associated with individual insurance. However, such experience will be determined on a class basis and will apply to all insureds in that class. This is also true for group insurance contracts when the group's membership is small. The use of experience rating will be discussed in Chapter 15.

Group Underwriting

The applicant for individual insurance must generally show evidence of insurability. For group insurance, on the other hand, individual members of the group are usually not required to show any evidence of insurability when initially eligible for coverage. This is not to say that there is no underwriting, but rather that underwriting is focused on the characteristics of the group instead of on the insurability of individual members of the group. As with individual insurance, the underwriter must appraise the risk, decide on the conditions of the group's acceptability and establish a rating basis.

The purpose of group insurance underwriting is twofold:

1. To minimize the problem of *adverse selection* (those who are most likely to have claims are also those who are most likely to seek insurance).
2. To minimize the administrative costs associated with group insurance.

Because of group underwriting, coverage can be provided through group insurance at a lower cost than through individual insurance.

Underwriting considerations peculiar to specific types of group insurance will be discussed in appropriate sections of later chapters. However, there are certain general underwriting considerations applicable to all or most types of group insurance that affect the contractual provisions contained in group insurance contracts as well as insurance company practices pertaining to group insurance. These general underwriting considerations include:

- The reason for the existence of the group.
- The stability of the group.
- The persistency of the group.
- The method of determining benefits.
- The provisions for determining eligibility.

- The source and method of premium payments.
- The administrative aspects of the group insurance plan.
- The prior experience of the plan.
- The size of the group.
- The composition of the group.
- The industry represented by the group.
- The geographic location of the group.

Reason for Existence

Probably the most fundamental group underwriting principle is that a group must have been formed for some purpose other than to obtain insurance for its members. Such a rule protects the group insurance company against the adverse selection that would likely exist if poor risks were to form a group just to obtain insurance. Groups based on an employer-employee relationship present little difficulty with respect to this rule.

Stability

Ideally, an underwriter would like to see a reasonable but steady flow of persons through a group. A higher than average turnover rate will result in increased administrative costs for the insurance company as well as for the employer. If turnover exists among recently hired employees, these costs can be minimized by requiring employees to wait a period of time before becoming eligible for coverage. However, such a *probationary period* does leave newly hired employees without protection if their previous group insurance coverage has terminated.

A lower than average turnover rate often results in an increasing average age for the members of a group. To the extent that a plan's premium is a function of the mortality (death rates) and the morbidity (sickness and disability rates) of the group, such an increase in average age will result in an increasing premium rate for that group insurance plan. This may cause the better risks to drop out of a plan, if they are required to contribute to its cost, and may ultimately force the employer to terminate the plan because of its increasing cost.

Persistency

An underwriter is concerned with the length of time a group insurance contract will remain on the insurance company's books. Initial acquisition expenses, often including higher first-year commissions, frequently cause an insurance company to lose money during the first year the group insurance contract is in force. Only through the renewal of the contract for a period of time, often three or four years, can these acquisition expenses be recovered. For this reason, firms with a history of frequently changing insurance companies or those with financial difficulty are often avoided.

Determination of Benefits

In most types of group insurance, the underwriter will require that benefit levels for individual members of the group be determined in some manner that precludes individual selection by either the employees or the employer. If employees could choose their own benefit levels, there would be a tendency for the poorer risks to select greater amounts of coverage than the better risks would select. Similarly, adverse selection could also exist if the employer were able to choose a separate benefit level for each individual member of the group. As a result, this underwriting rule has led to benefit levels that are either identical for all employees or determined by a benefit formula that bases benefit levels on some specific criterion, such as position or salary.

Benefits based on salary or position may still lead to adverse selection since disproportionately larger benefits will be provided to the owner or top executives who may have been involved in determining the benefit formula. Consequently, most insurance companies have rules for determining the maximum benefit that may be provided for any individual employee without evidence of insurability. Additional coverage either will not be provided or will be subject to individual evidence of insurability.

The general level of benefits for all employees is also of interest to the underwriter. For example, benefit levels that are too high may encourage overutilization and malingering while benefit levels that are unusually low may lead to low participation if a plan is voluntary.

Determination of Eligibility

The underwriter is also concerned with the eligibility provisions that will be contained in the group insurance plan. Many group insurance plans contain probationary periods that must be satisfied before an employee is eligible for coverage. In addition to minimizing administrative costs, a probationary period will also discourage persons with known medical conditions from seeking employment primarily because of a firm's group insurance benefits. This latter problem is also addressed by the requirement that an employee be actively at work before coverage commences or, particularly with major medical coverage, by limiting coverage for preexisting conditions.

Most group insurance plans normally limit eligibility to full-time employees since, from an underwriting standpoint, the coverage of part-time employees may not be desirable. In addition to having a high turnover rate, some part-time employees may be seeking employment primarily to obtain group insurance benefits. Similar problems exist with seasonal and temporary employees and, consequently, eligibility is often restricted to permanent employees.

Premium Payments

Group insurance plans may be *contributory* or *noncontributory*. Members of *contributory plans* pay a portion, or possibly all, of the cost of their own coverage. When the entire portion is paid by employees, these plans are often referred to as fully contributory or employee-pay-all plans. Under *noncontributory plans*, the policyholder pays the entire cost. Since all eligible employees are usually covered, noncontributory plans are desirable from an underwriting standpoint because adverse selection is minimized. In fact, most insurance companies and the laws of many states require 100 percent participation of eligible employees under noncontributory plans. In addition, the absence of employee solicitation, payroll deductions and underwriting of late entrants into the plan results in administrative savings to both the policyholder and the insurance company, thus favoring the noncontributory approach to the financing of group insurance benefits.

Most state laws prohibit an employer from requiring an employee to participate in a contributory plan. The insurance company is then faced with the possibility of adverse selection since those who elect coverage will tend to be the poorer risks. From a practical standpoint, 100 percent participation in a contributory plan would be unrealistic because, for many reasons, some employees neither desire nor even need the coverage provided under the plan. However, insurance companies will require that a minimum percentage of the eligible members elect to participate before the contract will be issued. The common requirement is 75 percent, although a lower percentage is often acceptable for large groups and a higher percentage may be required for small groups. A 75 percent minimum requirement is also often a statutory requirement for group life insurance and sometimes for group health insurance.

A key issue in contributory plans is how to treat employees who did not elect to participate when first eligible but who later desire coverage, or who dropped coverage and want it reinstated. Unfortunately, this desire for coverage may arise when these employees or their dependents have medical conditions that will lead to claims once coverage is provided. To control this adverse selection, insurance companies commonly require individual evidence of insurability by these employees or their dependents before coverage will be made available. However, there is one exception: Some plans have periodic open enrollment periods during which the evidence-of-insurability requirement is lessened or waived for a short period of time.

Insurance companies frequently require that the employer pay a portion of the premium under a group insurance plan. This is also a statutory requirement for group life insurance in most states and occasionally for group health insurance. Many group insurance plans set an average contribution rate for all employees, which in turn leads to the subsidizing of some employees by other employees, particularly in those types of insurance where the frequency of claims increases with age. Without a requirement for employer contributions, younger employees might actually find coverage at a lower cost in the individual market, thereby leaving the group with only the older risks. Even when group insurance already has a cost advantage over individual insurance, its attractiveness to employees is enhanced by employer contributions. With constantly increasing health-care costs, employer contributions help cushion rate increases to employees and thus minimize participation problems as contributions are raised. In addition, underwriters feel that the lack of employer contributions may lead to a lack of employer interest in the plan and, consequently, poor cooperation with the insurance company and poor plan administration.

Administration

To minimize the expenses associated with group insurance, the underwriter will often require that certain administrative functions be carried out by the employer. These commonly include communicating the plan to the employees, handling enrollment procedures, collecting employee contributions on a payroll-deduction basis and keeping certain types of records. In addition, employers are often involved in the claims process. Underwriters are concerned not only with the employer's ability to carry out these functions but also with the employer's willingness to cooperate with the insurance company.

Prior Experience

For most insurance companies, a large portion of newly written group insurance consists of business that was previously written by other insurance companies. Therefore, it is important for the underwriter to ascertain the reason for the transfer. If the transferred business is a result of dissatisfaction with the service provided by the prior insurance company, the underwriter must determine whether the insurance company can provide the type and level of service desired. Because an employer is most likely to shop for new coverage when faced with a rate increase, the underwriter must evaluate whether the rate increase was due to excessive claims experience. Often, particularly with larger groups, poor claims experience in the past is an indication of poor experience in the future. Occasionally, however, the prior experience may be due to circumstances that will not continue in the future, such as a catastrophe or large medical bills for an employee who has died, totally recovered, or terminated employment.

Excessive past claims experience may not result in coverage denial for a new applicant, but it will probably result in a higher rate. As an alternative, changes in the benefit or eligibility provisions of the plan might eliminate a previous source of adverse claims experience.

The underwriter must determine the new insurance company's responsibility for existing claims. Some states prohibit a new insurance company from denying (by using a pre-existing-conditions clause) the continuing claims of persons that were covered under a prior group insurance plan if these claims would otherwise be covered under the new contract. The rationale for this "no-loss no-gain" legislation is that claims should be paid neither more liberally nor less liberally than if no transfer had taken place. Even in states that have no such regulation, an employer may still wish to provide employees with continuing protection. In either case, the underwriter must evaluate these continuing claims as well as any liability of the previous insurance company for their payment.

Finally, the underwriter must be reasonably certain that the employer will not present a persistency problem by changing insurance companies again in the near future.

Size

The size of a group is a significant factor in the underwriting process. With large groups, prior group insurance experience can usually be used as a factor in determining the premium, and considerable flexibility also exists with both rating and plan design. In addition, adjustments for adverse claims experience can be made at future renewal dates under the experience-rating process.

The situation is different for small groups. In many cases, coverage is being written for the first time. Administrative expenses tend to be high in relation to the premium. There is also an increased possibility that the owner or major stockholder might be interested in coverage primarily because he or she, or a family member, has a medical problem that will result in large immediate claims. As a result, contractual provisions and the benefits available tend to be standardized to control administrative costs. Also, because past experience for small groups is not necessarily a realistic indicator of future experience, most insurance companies use pooled rates under which a uniform rate is applied to all groups that have a specific coverage. Since poor claims experience for a particular group is not charged to that group at renewal, more restrictive underwriting practices relating to adverse selection are used. These include less liberal contractual provisions and, in some cases, individual underwriting of group members.

Composition

The age, sex and income of employees in a group will affect the experience of the group. As employees age, the mortality rate increases. Excluding maternity claims, both the frequency and duration of medical and disability claims also increase with age.

At all ages, the death rate is lower for females than for males. However, the opposite is true for medical expenses and disability claims. Even if maternity claims are disregarded, women as a group tend to be hospitalized and disabled more frequently and require medical and surgical treatment more often than men.

Employees with high income levels tend to incur higher than average medical and dental expenses. This is partly because practitioners sometimes base charges on a patient's ability to pay. In addition, persons with higher incomes are more likely to seek specialized care or care in more affluent areas, where the charges of practitioners are generally higher. On the other hand, low-income employees can also pose difficulties. Turnover rates tend to be higher, and there is often difficulty in getting and retaining proper levels of participation in contributory plans.

Adjustments can be made for all of these factors when determining the proper rate to charge the policyholder. The major problem arises in contributory plans. To the extent that higher costs for a group with a less-than-average mix of employees are passed on to these employees, a lower participation rate may result.

Industry

The nature of the industry represented by a group is also a significant factor in the underwriting process. In addition to different occupational hazards among industries, employees in some industries have higher-than-average health insurance claims that cannot be directly attributed to their jobs. Therefore, insurance companies commonly make adjustments in their life and health insurance rates based on the occupations of the employees covered as well as on the industries in which they work.

In addition to occupational hazards, the underwriter must weigh other factors as well. Certain industries are characterized by a lack of stability and persistency and thus may be considered undesirable risks. The underwriter must also be concerned with what impact changes in the economy will have on a particular industry.

Geographic Location

The size of medical claims varies considerably among geographic regions and must be considered in determining a group insurance rate. For example, medical expenses tend to be higher in the Northeast than in the South, and higher in large urban areas than in rural areas.

A group with geographically scattered employees will also pose more administrative problems and probably result in greater administrative expense than a group in a single location. In addition, the underwriter must determine whether the insurance company has the proper facilities to service policyholders at their various locations.

STATE REGULATION

Even though the United States Supreme Court has declared insurance to be commerce and thus subject to federal regulation when conducted on an interstate basis, Congress gave the states substantial regulatory authority by the passage of the McCarran-Ferguson Act (Public Law 15) in 1945. This act exempts insurance from certain federal regulations to the extent that individual states actually regulate insurance. In addition, it provides that most other federal laws are not applicable to insurance unless they are specifically directed at the business of insurance.

As a result of the McCarran-Ferguson Act, a substantial body of laws and regulations has been enacted in every state. While no two states have identical laws and regulations, there have been attempts to encourage uniformity among the states. The most significant influence in this regard has been the National Association of Insurance Commissioners (NAIC), which is composed of state regulatory officials. Because the NAIC has as one of its goals the promotion of uniformity in legislation and administrative rules affecting insurance, it has developed numerous model laws. Although states are not bound to adopt these model laws, many have been enacted by many states.

Some of the more significant state laws and regulations affecting group insurance include those pertaining to the types of groups eligible for coverage, contractual provisions, benefit limitations and taxation. Moreover, since many employers have employees in several states, the extent of the regulatory jurisdiction of each state is a question of some concern.

Eligible Groups

Most states do not allow group insurance contracts to be written unless a minimum number of persons are insured under the contract. This requirement, which may vary by type of coverage and type of group, is most common in group life insurance, where the minimum number required for plans established by individual employers is generally ten persons. A few states have either a lower minimum or no such requirement. A higher minimum, often 100 persons, may be imposed on other plans, such as those established by trusts, labor unions or creditors. Only about half the states impose any minimum number requirement on group health insurance contracts. Where one exists, it usually is either five or ten persons.

Most states also have insurance laws concerning the types of groups for which insurance companies may write group insurance. Most of these laws specify that a group insurance contract cannot be delivered to a policyholder in the state unless the group meets certain statutory eligibility requirements for its type of group. In some states these eligibility requirements even vary by type of coverage. While the categories of eligible groups may vary, at least four types of groups involving employees are acceptable in virtually all states:

1. Individual employer groups.
2. Negotiated trusteeships.
3. Trade associations.
4. Labor union groups.

Other types of groups, including multiple-employer trusts, are also acceptable in some states. Some states have no insurance laws regarding the types or sizes of groups for which insurance companies may write group insurance. Rather, eligibility is determined on a contract-by-contract basis by the underwriting standards of the insurance company.

Individual Employer Groups

The most common type of eligible group is the individual employer group—a corporation, partnership, or sole proprietorship. Many state laws are very specific about what constitutes an employee for group insurance purposes. In addition to those usually considered to be employees of a firm, coverage can generally be written for retired employees and employees of subsidiary and affiliated firms as well. Furthermore, individual proprietors or partners usually are eligible for coverage as long as they are actively engaged in and devote a substantial part of their time to the conduct of the organization. Similarly, directors of a corporation may be eligible for coverage if they are also employees of the corporation.

Negotiated Trusteeships (Taft-Hartley Trusts)

Negotiated trusteeships are formed as a result of collective bargaining over benefits between a union and the employers of the union members. Generally, the union employees are in the same industry or a related one. For the most part, these industries, such as trucking or construction, are characterized by frequent movement of union members among employers. The Taft-Hartley Act prohibits employers from paying funds directly to a labor union for the purpose of providing group insurance coverage to members, but payments may be made to a trust fund established for the purpose of purchasing insurance. The group insurance contract is then issued to the trustees of the fund, who must be made up of equal numbers of representatives from the employers and the union. Since eligible employees include only members of the collective bargaining unit, benefits for other employees must be provided in some other manner.

Negotiated trusteeships differ from other types of groups in how benefits are financed and how eligibility for benefits is determined. Contributions are often made by employers based on the number of hours worked by the employees covered under the collective bargaining agreement, regardless of whether these employees are eligible for benefits. Eligibility for benefits during a given time period usually is based only on some minimum number of hours worked during a previous time period. For example, a union member might receive coverage during a calendar quarter (even while unemployed) if he or she worked at least 300 hours in the previous calendar quarter. This situation, where the employees for whom contributions are made may differ from those eligible for benefits, presents a unique problem for the underwriter. Rates must be adequate to build up the contingency reserves necessary to pay benefits in periods of heavy layoffs, during which a large portion of contributions would cease, but eligibility for benefits would continue.

While negotiated trusteeships normally provide benefits for the employees of several employers, they can also be established for the employees of a single employer. However, situations involving collective bargaining with a single employer will usually result in the employer being required to purchase a group insurance contract and provide benefits. Although benefits and eligibility are specified in the bargaining agreement, the employer is the policyholder and the group is an individual employer group rather than a negotiated trusteeship. This approach also enables the employer to provide benefits for employees not represented by the bargaining unit under the same contract.

Trade Associations

A trade association, for eligibility purposes, is an association of employers that has been formed for reasons other than obtaining insurance. In most cases, these employers are in the same industry or type of business. Many such associations contain a large number of employers who do not have the minimum number of employees necessary to qualify for an individual employer group insurance contract. While in some states the master contract is issued directly to the trade association, in most states it is necessary that a trust be established. Through payment of premiums to the association or the trust, individual employers may provide coverage for their employees.

Both adverse selection and administrative costs tend to be greater in trade association groups than in many other types of groups. Therefore, most underwriters and state laws require that a minimum percentage of the employers belonging to the association, such as 50 percent, participate in the plan and that a minimum number of employees, possibly as high as 500, be covered. In addition, individual underwriting or strict provisions regarding pre-existing conditions may be used, and employer contributions are usually required. To ensure adequate enrollment, the underwriter must determine whether the association has the resources as well as the desire to promote the plan enthusiastically and to administer it properly.

Labor Union Groups

Labor unions may establish group insurance plans to provide benefits for their members, with the master contract issued to the union. In addition to the prohibition by the Taft-Hartley Act of employer payments to labor unions for insurance premiums, state laws generally prohibit plans in which union members pay the entire cost from their own pockets. Consequently, the premiums come solely from union funds or partially from union funds and partially from members' contributions. Labor union groups account for a relatively small amount of group insurance, most of which is life insurance.

Multiple-Employer Trusts

The final type of eligible group designed to provide benefits for employees is the multiple-employer trust (MET). These are also often referred to as MEWAs or multiple-employer welfare arrangements. In the last few years, METs have become a popular, and often controversial, method of marketing group benefits to employers who have a small number of employees. METs are legal entities in the form of trusts (1) sponsored by an insurance company, an independent administrator or some other person or organization and (2) organized for the purpose of providing group benefits to participants. Each trust must have an administrator and a trustee. The administrator may be either an insurance company or a professional administrator. The trustee may be an individual, but is usually a corporate trustee, such as a commercial bank.

METs generally are established to provide group benefits to employers within a specific industry, such as construction, agriculture or banking. METs may provide either a single type of insurance, such as life insurance, or a wide range of coverages—for example, life, medical expense and disability income insurance. In some cases, alternative forms of the same coverage are available, such as comprehensive health insurance or basic health insurance.

An employer desiring to obtain insurance coverage for its employees from a MET must subscribe by becoming a member of the trust. The employer is issued a joinder agreement, which spells out the relationship between the trust and the employer and specifies the coverages to which the employer has subscribed. It is not necessary for an employer to subscribe to all the coverages offered by a MET.

A MET may either provide benefits on a self-funded basis or fund benefits with a contract purchased from an insurance company. In the latter case, the trust—rather than the subscribing employers—is the master contract holder. In either case, the employees of subscribing employers are provided with benefit descriptions (certificates of insurance in insured METs) in a manner similar to the usual group insurance arrangement.

In addition to alternative methods of funding benefits, METs can also be categorized according to how they are administered—by an insurance company or by a third-party administrator. It is generally agreed that there are three types of METs. Unfortunately, the terminology used to describe the three types is often misleading and not uniform. In this text, the following terminology and definitions will be used:

1. *Fully insured MET.* Benefits are insured and the MET is administered by an insurance company.
2. *Insured third-party-administered MET.* Benefits are insured and the MET is administered by a third party.
3. *Self-insured MET.* Benefits are self-funded and the MET is administered by a third party.

Fully Insured METs. Fully insured METs are established and administered by insurance companies, with a commercial bank usually acting as trustee. Coverage under such METs is normally marketed by the sales force of the insurer involved and may be made available to other licensed producers. Note that the trust purchases coverage from the insurance company, and what is being marketed to employers is the availability of insurance through participation in the trust, not an insurance contract from the insurance company.

Fully insured METs were developed to provide group insurance to small employer groups. A single insurance company may have one MET or several, with each designed for a different industry (such as construction or manufacturing). Through the use of METs, insurance companies have attempted to provide group insurance at a cost lower than the cost of a direct sale to the employer or to individual employees. Regulatory restrictions regarding minimum group size are overcome because the employees of many small employers are insured under a single group contract issued to the trust. Costs are also minimized because each type of coverage offered by the trust tends to be standardized for all employers using the trust.

In addition, underwriting standards have been developed to minimize the problems of adverse selection and the higher administrative costs associated with providing coverage to small groups of employees. While these standards vary among companies, some common examples include:

- More stringent participation requirements, such as 100 percent, for employers with fewer than five employees.
- A requirement that life insurance coverage be purchased. This tends to be a profitable and stable form of coverage for insurance companies. In some cases the more life insurance coverage purchased, the more comprehensive are the medical expense benefits made available.
- Limitations on the period of time for which rates are guaranteed, rarely more than six months.
- Probationary periods for new employees, often two or three months.
- Restrictive provisions for pre-existing conditions.
- Limitations on the amounts of life insurance coverage available on a simplified or guaranteed-issue basis; for example, $10,000 for four or fewer

employees; $20,000 for five or more. Additional coverage may be available, but individual evidence of insurability will be required.

- Limitations on the amount of long-term disability insurance coverage that will be issued, such as 50 percent or 60 percent of income, subject to a $1,000 monthly maximum.
- Ineligible groups. Most METs have a lengthy list of ineligible groups, including those characterized by poor loss experience or high turnover rates.

Since it generally has been accepted under insurance regulatory law that an insurance contract is subject to regulation by the state in which the contract was delivered, many insurers have established METs where they consider the regulatory climate to be favorable. This has allowed an insurance company, in effect, to offer a nationally standardized contract to small employers who subscribe to the trust rather than different contracts to comply with the regulatory requirements in each subscriber's state. In the past few years, however, some state insurance departments have begun to regulate METs marketed in their states. In some states, this had led to the requirement that METs make their coverage conform with applicable state law when an employer from that state becomes a subscriber. Furthermore, with recent rulings by some courts and the Department of Labor that certain METs are not exempted from state regulation by ERISA (Employee Retirement Income Security Act), it appears that the extent of state regulation may increase further.

Insured Third-Party-Administered METs. Insured third-party-administered METs are similar to fully insured METs in that benefits are provided through an insurance contract issued to the trust. However, these METs are administered by some person or organization other than an insurance company.

The impetus for the establishment of an insured third-party-administered MET may come from either the insurance company or the administrator. An insurance company desiring to enter the MET field may feel it lacks the expertise or resources to administer METs properly at a competitive cost. Consequently, a number of insurance companies have sought out third-party administrators to provide many of the necessary administrative functions. The third-party administrators under such arrangements normally are organizations either specializing in the administration of various types of insurance programs or specializing solely in the management of METs. In addition to general administrative duties and subject to the insurance company's rules, the third-party administrator may be involved in any or all of the following functions associated with METs: underwriting, claims administration, benefit design or marketing.

Third-party administrators desiring to enter the MET field, or hoping to increase their share of MET business, might seek out insurance companies to provide the insurance coverages for the METs they wish to establish. Some of these administrators specialize in the administration of insurance programs; others are insurance agents or brokers who desire a product over which they can have marketing control.

Unfortunately, the experience of insured third-party-administered METs was not always satisfactory. There were several instances of mismanagement that caused some of these METs to cease operations. In some instances, eagerness to enter the field resulted in inadequate rates or lax underwriting; in other instances, administrators were more interested in management fees and sales commissions than in making a profit for the insurance company. While these types of situations tarnished the image of insured third-party-administered METs in the past, it should be noted that many operated successfully and were managed by capable administrators. Two factors have minimized these difficulties in recent years. First, insurance companies, aware of past experiences, are cautious as they enter the field, giving particular regard to the selection of their administrators. Second, some states have passed legislation aimed at regulating administrators of METs and other insurance arrangements.

Self-Funded METs. Self-funded METs normally are established and marketed by the persons or organizations who will administer them. The trust does not purchase an insurance contract; benefits are self-funded with premiums paid by subscribing employers. While some self-funded METs have operated successfully and have been well administered, others have gone bankrupt and left participants with unpaid claims, particularly medical bills. (Under an insured MET, the insurer would be responsible for paying claims even if the MET failed.) Again, administrators often did not charge enough to establish proper reserves for future benefits; or they were more concerned with generating management fees and sales commissions than in properly managing the trust.

In 1982, Congress enacted legislation that provides for state regulation of self-funded METs. For several years, state insurance departments had tried to obtain the power to shut down mismanaged METs, but the administrators of these plans argued that they were exempted from state regulation by ERISA. Under federal legislation, a self-funded MET can apply for ERISA certification, but even if it is granted, the trust will still be subject to state rules governing reserves and contributions. In addition, while ERISA certification is pending, a MET will have to meet all state insurance regulations, or the state can force it to cease operations. State regulation also applies if a MET either fails to apply for certification or is denied certification. The overall effect of federal legislation has been to significantly reduce the number of self-funded METs.

Contractual Provisions in Group Insurance

Through its insurance laws, every state provides for the regulation of contractual provisions. In many instances, certain contractual provisions must be included in group insurance policies. These mandatory provisions may be altered only if they result in more favorable treatment of the policyholder. Such provisions tend to be most uniform from state to state in the area of group life insurance, primarily because of the widespread adoption of the NAIC model bill pertaining to group life insurance standard provisions. As a result of state regulation, coupled with industry practices, the provisions of most group life and health insurance policies are relatively uniform from company to company. In most instances, an insurance company's policy forms can be used in all states. However, riders may be necessary to bring certain provisions into compliance with the regulations of some states.

Traditionally, the regulation of contractual provisions has focused on provisions pertaining to such factors as the grace period, conversion, and incontestability rather than on factors pertaining to the types or levels of benefits. These latter provisions have been a matter between the policyholder and the insurance company. However, in recent years this has changed in many states. In some states, certain benefits—such as well-baby care and treatment for alcoholism or drug abuse—must be included in any group insurance contract; in other states, they must be offered to group policyholders as optional benefits. Still other state laws and regulations specify minimum levels for certain benefits if those benefits are included.

It is interesting to note that, with few exceptions, the regulation of contractual provisions affects only those employee benefit plans funded with insurance contracts. This is because provisions of ERISA seem to exempt employee benefit plans from most types of state regulation. However, there are exceptions to this exemption; these include insurance regulation and therefore the provisions in insurance contracts. As a result of this ERISA exemption, states have few laws and regulations applying to the provisions of uninsured benefit plans. However, ERISA does not exempt uninsured plans from state regulation in such areas as age and sex discrimination, and laws pertaining to these areas commonly apply to all benefit plans. A few states are also trying to mandate other types of benefits for uninsured plans, and ultimately the issue will probably have to be settled by Congress or the Supreme Court.

Benefit Limitations

Statutory limitations may be imposed on the level of benefits that can be provided under group insurance contracts issued to certain types of eligible groups. With the exception of group life insurance, these limitations rarely apply in situations involving an employer-employee relationship. In the past, most states limited the amount of group life insurance that could be provided by an employer to an employee, but only Texas still has such a restriction. However, several states limit the amount of coverage that can be provided under contracts issued to groups other than individual employer groups. In addition, some states limit the amount of life insurance coverage that may be provided for dependents.

Taxation

Every state levies a premium tax on out-of-state insurance companies licensed to do business in their state, and most states tax the premiums of insurance companies domiciled in their state. These taxes, which are applicable to premiums written within a state, average about 2 percent.

The imposition of the premium tax has placed insurance companies at a competitive disadvantage with alternative methods of providing benefits. Premiums paid to health maintenance organizations (HMOs) are not subject to the tax, nor are premiums paid to Blue Cross and Blue Shield Plans in many states. In addition, the elimination of this tax is one cost saving under self-funded plans. Because the trend toward self-funding of benefits by large corporations has resulted in the loss of substantial premium tax revenue to the states, there have been suggestions that all premiums paid to any type of organization or fund for the purpose of providing insurance benefits to employees be subject to the premium tax.

Where state income taxation exists, the tax implications of group insurance premiums and benefits to both employers and employees are generally similar to those of the federal government. Employers may deduct any premiums paid as business expenses, and employees have certain exemptions from taxation with respect to both premiums paid on their behalf and benefits attributable to employer-paid premiums.

Regulatory Jurisdiction

A group insurance contract will often insure individuals living in more than one state—a situation that raises the question of which state or states have regulatory jurisdiction over the contract. The issue is a crucial one because factors such as minimum enrollment percentages, maximum amounts of life insurance and required contract provisions vary among the states.

Few problems usually arise if the insured group qualifies as an eligible group in all the states where insured individuals reside. Individual employer groups, negotiated trusteeships and labor union groups fall into this category. Under the *doctrine of comity,* by which states recognize within their own territory the laws of other states, it is generally accepted that the state in which the group insurance contract is delivered to the policyholder has governing jurisdiction. Therefore, the contract must conform only to the laws and regulations of this one state, even though certificates of insurance may be delivered in other states. However, a few states have statutes that prohibit insurance issued in other states from covering residents of their state unless the contract conforms to their laws and regulations. While these statutes are effective with respect to insurance companies licensed within the state (that is, admitted companies), their effectiveness with respect to nonadmitted companies is questionable, because states lack regulatory jurisdiction over these companies.

This does not mean that the policyholder may arbitrarily seek out a situs (place of delivery) that is most desirable from a regulatory standpoint. Unless the place of delivery has a significant relationship to the insurance transaction, other states may seek to exercise their regulatory authority. Therefore, it has become common practice that an acceptable situs must be at least one of the following:

1. The state where the policyholder is incorporated (or the trust is created if the policyholder is a trust).
2. The state where the policyholder's principal office is located.
3. The state where the greatest number of insured individuals are employed.
4. Any state where an employer or labor union that is a party to a trust is located.

While a policyholder may have a choice of situs if these locations differ, most insurers are reluctant to issue a group contract in any state unless a corporate officer or trustee who can execute acceptance of the contract is located in that state and unless the principal functions related to the administration of the group contract will be performed there.

The issue of regulatory jurisdiction is more complex for those types of groups that are not considered to be eligible groups in all states. METs are a typical example. If the state has no regulation to the contrary and if the insured group would be eligible for group insurance in other states, the situation is the same as previously described. In addition, most other states will accept the doctrine of comity and not interfere with the regulatory jurisdiction of the state where the contract is delivered. However, some states either prohibit coverage from being issued or require that it conform with the state's laws and regulations other than those pertaining to eligible groups.

FEDERAL REGULATION

Many aspects of federal regulation have affected the establishment and character of group insurance. Those most significant include:

- The Age Discrimination in Employment Act.
- The Civil Rights Act.
- ERISA (Employee Retirement Income Security Act).
- The Americans with Disabilities Act.
- The Social Security Act.
- The Health Maintenance Organization Act.
- The Internal Revenue Code.

This chapter will focus on the first four acts listed, since these have had a similar influence on most types of group insurance. Nondiscrimination rules will also be discussed. The Social Security Act was discussed in Chapter 3. The Health Maintenance Organization Act will be described in Chapter 9 along with a general discussion of HMOs. The income tax implications of the Internal Revenue Code, which may vary for different types of group insurance coverage, will be described in those chapters pertaining to each type of coverage.

The Age Discrimination in Employment Act

In 1986, the Age Discrimination in Employment Act was amended to drop the upper age limitation from the prohibition against age discrimination for most working persons. The law, first passed in 1967, applied only to employers with 20 or more employees and originally affected employees between the ages of 40 and 65. A 1978 amendment increased the maximum age to 70, and the latest change (1986) completely eliminates the cap. With some exceptions, such as individuals in executive or high policy-making positions, compulsory retirement is no longer allowed. Employee benefits, which traditionally ceased or were severely limited at age 65, have also been affected by the act. In 1979, the Department of Labor, which was responsible for the enforcement of the Act, issued an interpretative bulletin requiring benefits to be continued for older workers. However, some reductions in benefits were allowed. The responsibility for enforcement was later transferred to the Equal Employment Opportunity Commission, which continued to use the interpretative bulletin of the Department of Labor. It should be noted that an interpretative bulletin is not a law or regulation, but rather an indication of what the enforcing agency believes to be correct. It should also be noted that while the federal act does not prohibit age discrimination in benefits for employees under age 40 or for all employees of firms that employ fewer than 20 persons, some states may prohibit such discrimination under their own laws or regulations.

The status of the provisions of the interpretative bulletin became unclear following a 1989 Supreme Court decision stating that the bulletin went beyond the provisions of the Age Discrimination in Employment Act. The Court said that employee benefits were beyond the scope of the act unless they are used to achieve a prohibited, *nonbenefit* discrimination in employment. As a result, Congress in 1990 explicitly brought employee benefits under the provisions of the Age Discrimination in Employment Act by codifying the provisions contained in the interpretative bulletin.

The Act currently permits a reduction in the level of some benefits for older workers as long as the cost of providing older workers with benefits is no greater than the cost of providing benefits for younger workers. The most expensive benefit, however—medical expense coverage—cannot be reduced. The following discussion is limited to reductions after age 65—probably the most common age for reducing benefits—even though reductions could start at an earlier age if they are justified on a cost basis. It should be emphasized that these restrictions apply only to benefits for active employees. There are no requirements under the act that any benefits be continued for retired workers.

When participation in an employee benefit plan is voluntary, an employer can generally require larger employee contributions instead of reducing benefits for older employees, as long as the proportion of the premiums paid by older employees does not increase with age. Thus, if an employer pays 50 percent of the cost of benefits for younger employees, it must pay at least 50 percent of the cost for older employees. If employees pay the entire cost of a benefit, older employees may be required to pay the full cost of their coverage to the extent that this is a condition of participation in the plan. However, this provision does not apply to medical expense benefits. Employees over age 65 cannot be required to pay any more for their coverage than is paid by employees under age 65.

In cases where benefits are reduced, two approaches are permitted: a benefit-by-benefit approach or a benefit-package approach. Under the *benefit-by-benefit approach*, each employee benefit may be reduced to a lesser amount as long as each reduction can be justified on a cost basis. Under a *benefit-package approach*, the overall benefit package may be altered. Some benefits may be eliminated or reduced to a lesser amount than can be justified on a cost basis, as long as other existing benefits are not reduced or the benefit package is increased by adding new benefits for older workers. The only cost restriction is that the cost of the revised benefit package may be no less than if a benefit-by-benefit reduction had been used. The Act also places two other restrictions on the benefit-package approach by prohibiting any reduction in medical expense benefits or retirement benefits.

In reducing a benefit, an employer must use data that approximately reflect the actual cost of the benefit to the employer over a reasonable period of years. Unfortunately, such data either have not been kept by employers or are not statistically valid. Consequently, the reductions that have taken place have been based on estimates provided by insurance companies and consulting actuaries. This approach appears to have been satisfactory to the Equal Employment Opportunity Commission. The Act allows reductions to take place on a yearly basis or to be based on age brackets of up to five years. Any cost comparisons must be made with the preceding age bracket. For example, if five-year age brackets are used, the cost of providing benefits to employees between the ages of 65 and 69 must be compared with the cost of providing the same benefits to employees between the ages of 60 and 64.

While reductions in group insurance benefits for older employees are permissible, they are not required. Some employers make no reductions for older employees, but most employers reduce life insurance benefits at age 65 and long-term disability benefits at age 60 or 65.

Group Term Life Insurance Benefits

Based on mortality statistics, most insurance companies feel that group term life insurance benefits can be reduced to the following percentages of the amount of coverage provided immediately prior to age 65.

Age	Percentage
65–69	65
70–74	45
75–79	30
Over 79	20

Therefore, if employees are normally provided with $20,000 of group term life insurance, those employees between the ages of 65 and 69 can be provided with only $13,500; employees between the ages of 70 and 74 can be provided with $9,000, and so forth. Similarly, if employees normally receive coverage equal to 200 percent of salary, this may be reduced by 35 to 130 percent of salary at age 65, with additional reductions at later ages.

Reductions may also be made on an annual basis. If an annual reduction is used, it appears that a reduction of up to 11 percent of the previous year's coverage can be actuarially justified, starting at age 65 and continuing through age 69. Starting at age 70, the reduction should be 9 percent.

In a plan with employee contributions, the employer may either reduce benefits as described above and charge the employee the same premium as those employees in the previous age bracket, or continue full coverage and require the employee to pay an actuarially increased contribution.

Group Disability Income Benefits

The Act allows reductions in insured short-term disability income plans. However, no reductions are allowed in uninsured salary continuation plans. While disability statistics for those age 65 and older are limited, some insurance companies feel a benefit reduction of approximately 20 percent is appropriate for employees between the ages of 65 and 69, with additional decreases of 20 percent of the previous benefit for each consecutive five-year period. However, the laws of the few states that require short-term disability income benefits to be provided allow neither a reduction in benefits nor an increase in any contribution rate for older employees.

Under the Act, two methods are allowed for reducing long-term disability income benefits for those employees who become disabled at older ages. Either the level of benefits may be reduced without altering benefit eligibility or duration, or the benefit duration may be reduced without altering the level of benefits. These reductions again must be justified on a cost basis. Unfortunately, no rough guidelines can be given since any possible reductions will vary considerably, depending upon the eligibility requirements and the duration of benefits under a long-term disability plan. For example, one insurance company suggests that if a plan previously provided full benefits until age 70, then the duration of the benefits could be reduced to 12 months for disabilities occurring between the ages of 70 and 74 and six months for disabilities occurring after age 74.

Group Medical Expense Benefits

Prior to 1983, most employers were taking the availability of Medicare into consideration in designing their medical expense plans. In many cases, this required an employer to provide additional benefits so that employees between the ages of 65 and 69 had medical expense benefits equivalent to those provided for employees under age 65. However, the Age Discrimination in Employment Act requires employers to now offer *all* employees over age 65 (and any employees' spouses who are also over age 65) the same medical coverage they provide for younger employees (and their spouses). The employer's plan is the primary payer of benefits, with Medicare assuming the secondary payer role. However, employees may reject the employer's plan and have Medicare be the primary payer of benefits, but regulations prevent an employer from offering a health plan or option designed to induce such a rejection. This effectively prohibits an employer from offering any type of supplemental plan to employees who have elected Medicare as their primary medical coverage. (However, supplemental and carve-out plans can be used for retirees.) Therefore, most employees will elect to remain with the employer's plan unless it requires large employee contributions. When Medicare is secondary, the employer may pay the part B premium for those employees who are also eligible for Medicare, but there is no legal responsibility to do so.

The Civil Rights Act

Traditionally, pregnancy has been treated differently from other medical conditions under both individual and group insurance policies. However, the 1978 amendment to the Civil Rights Act requires that women affected by pregnancy, childbirth or related medical conditions be treated the same for employment-related purposes (including receipt of benefits under an employee benefit plan) as other persons who are not so affected but who are similar in their ability to work. The amendment (also referred to as the Pregnancy Discrimination Act) applies only to the benefit plans (both insured and self-funded) of those employers who have 15 or more employees. While employers with fewer employees are not subject to the provisions of the amendment, they may be subject to comparable state laws. Similarly, since the amendment applies only to employee benefit plans, pregnancy may be treated differently from other medical conditions under insurance policies that are not part of an employee benefit plan.

While the amendment itself is brief, enforcement falls under the jurisdiction of the Equal Employment Opportunity Commission, which has issued detailed guidelines for interpreting the amendment. The highlights of these guidelines are as follows:

- If an employer provides any type of disability income or sick-leave plan for employees, the employer must provide coverage for pregnancy and its related medical conditions on the same basis as for other disabilities. For example, maternity cannot be treated as a named exclusion in a disability income plan. Similarly, an employer cannot limit disability income benefits for pregnancies to a shorter period than that applicable to other disabilities.
- If an employer provides medical expense benefits for employees, the employer must provide coverage for the pregnancy-related conditions of employees (regardless of marital status) on the same basis as for all other medical conditions. For example, an employer cannot limit hospitalization coverage to $1,500 for pregnancy-related conditions while paying up to 80 percent of expenses for other medical conditions; nor can the employer have a pre-existing condition clause applying to pregnancy unless the clause also applies to other pre-existing conditions in the same manner.
- If an employer provides medical expense benefits for dependents, the employer must provide equal coverage for the medical expenses (including those arising from pregnancy-related conditions) of spouses of both male and female employees. The guidelines do allow a lower level of benefits for the pregnancy-related conditions of spouses of male employees than for female employees, but only if all benefits for spouses are lower than those for employees. The guidelines also allow an employer to exclude pregnancy-related benefits for female dependents other than spouses as long as such an exclusion applies equally to the nonspouse dependents of both male and female employees.
- Extended medical expense benefits after termination of employment must apply equally to pregnancy-related medical conditions and other medical conditions. Thus, if pregnancy commencing during employment is covered until delivery, even if the employee is not disabled, a similar nondisability extension of benefits must apply to all other medical conditions. No extension is required under the guidelines as long as all medical conditions are treated in the same manner.

- Medical expense benefits relating to abortions may be excluded from coverage except when the life of the woman is endangered. However, complications from an abortion must be covered. In addition, abortions must be treated like any other medical condition with respect to sick leave and other fringe benefit plans.

ERISA (Employee Retirement Income Security Act)

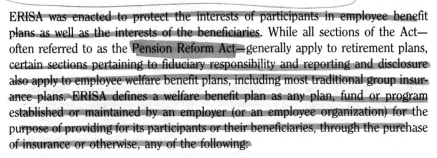

ERISA was enacted to protect the interests of participants in employee benefit plans as well as the interests of the beneficiaries. While all sections of the Act—often referred to as the Pension Reform Act—generally apply to retirement plans, certain sections pertaining to fiduciary responsibility and reporting and disclosure also apply to employee welfare benefit plans, including most traditional group insurance plans. ERISA defines a welfare benefit plan as any plan, fund or program established or maintained by an employer (or an employee organization) for the purpose of providing for its participants or their beneficiaries, through the purchase of insurance or otherwise, any of the following:

- Medical, surgical or hospital care or benefits.
- Benefits in the event of sickness, accident, disability, death or unemployment.
- Vacation benefits.
- Apprenticeship or other training programs.
- Day-care centers.
- Scholarship funds.
- Prepaid legal services.
- Any benefit described in Section 302(c) of the Labor Management Relations Act of 1947, such as holiday pay and severance pay.

Certain types of employee welfare benefit plans are specifically exempt from regulation under ERISA. Among these are:

- Governmental plans.
- Church plans (unless they elect to be covered).
- Plans maintained solely to comply with workers' compensation, unemployment compensation or disability insurance laws.

In addition, through regulations issued by the Department of Labor, certain types of plans have been declared not to be employee benefit welfare plans and are thus exempt from the regulations of ERISA. Among these are:

- Compensation for work performed under other than normal circumstances (including overtime pay and shift, holiday or weekend premiums).
- Compensation for absences from work due to sickness, vacation, holidays, military duty, jury duty or sabbatical leave and training programs to the extent such compensation is paid out of the general assets of the employer.
- Group insurance programs under which (1) no contributions are made by the employer; (2) participation is completely voluntary for employees; (3) the sole function served by the employer, without endorsing the program, is to

collect premiums through payroll deduction and remit the amount collected to the insurer; and (4) no consideration is paid to the employer in excess of reasonable compensation for administrative services actually performed. (Most of the mass-marketed plans described in Chapter 13 fall into this category.)

Because of its greater impact on retirement plans, the complete discussion of ERISA is contained in Part Five. The provisions of most relevance to employee welfare benefit plans—fiduciary responsibilities and reporting and disclosure requirements—are found in Chapter 26.

Americans with Disabilities Act of 1990

In late 1990, Congress passed the Americans with Disabilities Act. The Act will have a major impact on employment practices, but employee benefits are largely exempt from its provisions. As with any act of this type, it is impossible to determine its full impact until regulations are issued. However, the act specifically allows insurers, HMOs, third-party administrators, other similar organizations and employers the same opportunities they would have without the legislation to design and administer benefit plans in a manner consistent with basic insurance risk classification principles.

Under the Act, a benefit plan will not be considered discriminatory merely because it does not address the special needs of every disabled person. For example, employers are not required to give disabled persons extra medical coverage or additional sick leave.

The Act, however, does impose some restrictions on employers with respect to employee benefits. For example, a person with a disability that does not pose increased risks cannot be denied coverage or be subject to different terms based on the disability alone. Similarly, a blind person cannot be denied coverage based on blindness independent of actuarial risk classifications. An employer also cannot deny a qualified applicant a job merely because the employer's plan does not cover the applicant's disability or because increased insurance costs might result. However, it appears that employers can deny coverage or require higher employee contributions based on medical underwriting.

Nondiscrimination Rules

For many years, nondiscrimination rules have applied to employee benefit plans that provide retirement benefits. The purpose of these rules is to deny favorable tax treatment to plans that do not provide equitable benefits to a large cross section of employees. In effect, the owners and executives of a business cannot receive tax-favored benefits if a plan is designed primarily for them. Nondiscrimination rules in recent years have slowly been applied to various other types of employee benefit plans, but these rules, each of which is complex, have not been uniform.

Congress attempted to eliminate this lack of uniformity by adding Section 89 to the Internal Revenue Code as part of the Tax Reform Act of 1986. This code section was extremely far-reaching and complex, and it would have been very costly both for the government to implement and for employers to comply with. As a result, Section 89 was repealed in 1989, and all the old nondiscrimination rules it replaced were reinstated. These rules are discussed where appropriate throughout this book.

STUDY QUESTIONS

1. What general characteristics distinguish group insurance from individual insurance?
2. a. What factors do underwriters take into consideration when evaluating group benefit proposals?
   b. What is the significance of each factor?
3. a. How do negotiated trusteeships (Taft-Hartley trusts) differ from other types of groups with respect to financing of benefits and determination of eligibility?
   b. How do labor union groups differ from negotiated trusteeships?
4. Providing group insurance coverage to small groups of employees through trade association plans or METS presents unique problems with respect to adverse selection and high administrative costs. Explain how insurance company underwriting standards have been modified to confront these problems.
5. Describe the alternative ways in which METS may be funded and administered.
6. Explain the extent to which states regulate the provisions found in group insurance contracts.
7. How do state premium taxes put insurance companies at a competitive disadvantage with alternative methods of providing benefits?
8. The Felton Corporation is incorporated in the state of Pennsylvania where it was established. However, its principal office is now located in Wilmington, Delaware, where all administrative functions are performed. While it has some employees in these two states, the majority of its work force of 500 are employed in New Jersey. The corporation has been told by its benefit consultant that most insurance companies will deliver the group insurance contracts for its employees in any of these three states.
   a. Is the agent correct? Explain.
   b. From a practical standpoint, why might the corporation prefer a situs other than the state where its administrative functions are performed?
9. Describe the general approaches that are acceptable for reducing benefits under the Age Discrimination in Employment Act.
10. Explain the extent to which reductions in group term life insurance and group disability income insurance appear justified (using a benefit-by-benefit approach) under the Age Discrimination in Employment Act.
11. The medical expense plan of the Mallory Corporation provides benefits for pregnancy-related conditions to married female employees but excludes such coverage for unmarried female employees and unmarried female dependents of employees. Abortions are excluded unless the life of the mother is in danger. In

addition, the corporation limits benefits under its short-term disability insurance plan to a maximum of six weeks for pregnancy-related conditions. Assuming the Mallory Corporation is subject to the pregnancy provisions of the Civil Rights Act, do these plans conform to the requirements of the act? Explain.

12. What effect has the passage of the Americans with Disabilities Act had on employee benefits?

6

Group Life Insurance: Term Coverage

Objectives

- Explain how the benefit schedules under group term life insurance plans might be determined.
- Describe the eligibility requirements usually found in group term life insurance plans.
- Describe the provisions contained in group term insurance contracts.
- Describe the following coverages often written in conjunction with group term insurance for employees:
  1. Supplemental life insurance.
  2. Accidental death and dismemberment insurance.
  3. Survivor income benefit insurance.
  4. Dependent life insurance.
- Explain the tax implications of group term insurance to both employers and employees.

Traditionally, most group life insurance plans were designed to provide coverage during an employee's working years, with coverage usually ceasing upon termination of employment for any reason. Today, the majority of employees are provided with coverage that will continue, often at a reduced amount, when termination is due to retirement. Term insurance, which provides preretirement coverage, is described in this chapter. The methods and contracts used to provide coverage that continues after retirement will be discussed in Chapter 7.

The oldest and most common form of group life insurance is group term insurance. Coverage virtually always consists of yearly renewable term insurance that provides death benefits only, with no build-up of cash values. The widespread use of yearly renewable term in the group insurance marketplace contrasts with the individual marketplace, where until recently such coverage has accounted for only a small percentage of life insurance in force. This is primarily due to the increasing annual premiums which become prohibitive for many insureds at older ages. In group life insurance plans, the overall premium, in addition to other factors, is determined by the age distribution of the group's members. While the premium for any individual employee will increase with age, the flow of younger workers into the plan and the retirement of older workers tend to result in a relatively stable age distribution. Thus, the average group insurance rate remains constant or rises only slightly.

The following discussion of group term insurance focuses primarily on common contract provisions, other coverages that are often added to the basic contract and relevant federal tax laws.

CONTRACT PROVISIONS

The provisions contained in group term insurance contracts are more uniform than those found in other types of group insurance. Much of this uniformity is a result of the adoption by most states of the NAIC Group Life Insurance Standard Provisions Model Bill. This, coupled with the insurance industry's attempts at uniformity, has resulted in provisions that are virtually identical among insurance companies. While the following contract provisions represent the norm and are consistent with the practices of most insurance companies, some states may require slightly different provisions, and some companies may vary their contract provisions somewhat. In addition, negotiations between a policyholder and an insurance company may result in the modification of contract provisions.

Benefit Schedules

The purpose of the benefit schedule is twofold: It classifies the employees who are eligible for coverage and specifies the amount of life insurance that will be provided to the members of each class. This has the effect of minimizing adverse selection because the amount of the coverage for individual employees is predetermined. A benefit schedule can be as simple as providing a single amount of life insurance for all employees or as complex as providing different amounts of insurance for different classes of employees. For individual employer groups, the most common benefit schedules are those in which the amount of life insurance is based on either earnings or position.

Earnings Schedules

Under an earnings schedule, the amount of life insurance is determined as a multiple, or percentage, of each employee's earnings. For example, the amount of life insurance for each employee may be twice the employee's annual earnings. The amount of insurance is often rounded to the next higher $1,000, and for underwriting purposes may be subject to a maximum benefit, such as $100,000. For purposes of the benefit schedule, an employee's earnings usually consist of base salary only and do not include additional compensation like overtime pay or bonuses.

An alternative to using a flat percentage of earnings is to use a schedule of earnings such as the following:

Annual Earnings	Amount of Life Insurance
Less than $10,000	$ 10,000
$10,000–$19,999	20,000
$20,000–$29,999	40,000
$30,000–$39,999	75,000
$40,000–$49,999	100,000
$50,000 and over	150,000

This type of schedule may be designed so that all employees receive an amount of coverage which is approximately equal to the same multiple of annual earnings or, as in this example, larger multiples with higher earnings. Benefit schedules usually provide for a change in the amount of an employee's coverage when the employee moves into a different classification, even if this does not occur on the policy anniversary date. For example, the preceding schedule indicates that the amount of coverage for an employee earning $28,000 would increase from $40,000 to $75,000 if the employee received a $4,000 raise. Some schedules, however, specify that adjustments in amounts of coverage will only be made annually or on monthly premium due dates.

Position Schedules

Position schedules are similar to earning schedules except that, as the example below shows, the amount of life insurance is based upon an employee's position within the firm rather than on the employee's annual earnings.

Position	Amount of Life Insurance
President	$200,000
Vice President	100,000
Managers	60,000
Salesmen	40,000
Other employees	20,000

Because individuals in higher positions are often involved in designing the benefit schedule, underwriters are concerned that the benefits for these individuals be reasonable in relation to the overall plan benefits. Position schedules may also pose problems with respect to meeting nondiscrimination rules if excessively large amounts of coverage are provided to persons in high positions.

Even though position schedules are often used when annual earnings can be easily determined, they are particularly useful when it is difficult to determine an employee's annual income. This is the situation when income is materially affected by such factors as commissions earned, number of hours worked or bonuses that are based on either the employee's performance or the profits of the firm.

Flat-Benefit Schedules

Under flat-benefit schedules, the same amount of life insurance is provided for all employees regardless of salary or position. This type of benefit schedule is commonly used in group insurance plans covering hourly paid employees, particularly when benefits are negotiated with a union. In most cases, the amount of life insurance under a flat-benefit schedule is relatively small, such as $5,000 or $10,000. When an employer desires to provide only a minimum amount of life insurance for all employees, a flat-benefit schedule is often used.

Length-of-Service Schedules

In the early days of group life insurance, length-of-service schedules were relatively common and viewed as a method for rewarding longtime employees. However, because of the current view that the primary purpose of group life insurance is to replace income, such schedules are not extensively used. These schedules may also be considered discriminatory if a disproportionate number of the persons with longer service records are also the most highly paid employees. Here is a typical length-of-service schedule:

Length of Service	Amount of Life Insurance
Less than 2 years	$ 4,000
2 years but less than 5 years	8,000
5 years but less than 10 years	12,000
10 years but less than 15 years	16,000
15 years but less than 20 years	20,000
20 years or more	24,000

Pension Schedules

Under pension schedules, the amount of life insurance is based on an employee's projected pension at retirement. For example, under the employer's pension plan, the amount of life insurance for each employee might be 100 times the monthly pension that will be payable to the employee at normal retirement age. However, the amount of life insurance may be subject to a maximum benefit.

Combination Benefit Schedules

It is not unusual for employers to have benefit schedules that incorporate elements from several of the various types previously discussed. While there are numerous possible combinations, a common benefit schedule of this type provides salaried employees with an amount of insurance that is determined by a multiple of their annual earnings, and provides hourly employees with a flat amount of life insurance.

Reduction in Benefits

It is common for a group life insurance plan to provide for a reduction in benefits for active employees who reach a certain age, commonly 65 or 70. Such a reduction, which is due to the high cost of providing benefits for older employees, will be specified in the benefit schedule of a plan. Any reduction in the amount of life insurance for active employees is subject to the provisions of the Age Discrimination in Employment Act discussed in Chapter 5.

Benefit reductions fall into three categories:

1. A reduction to a flat amount of insurance.
2. A percentage reduction, such as 50 percent of the amount of insurance that was previously provided.
3. A gradual reduction over a period of years (for example, a 10 percent reduction in coverage each year until a minimum benefit amount is reached).

Eligibility Requirements

Group insurance contracts are very precise in their definition of what constitutes an eligible person for coverage purposes. In general, an employee must be in a covered classification, must work full time and must be actively at work. In addition, any requirements concerning probationary periods, insurability or premium contributions must be satisfied.

Covered Classifications

All group insurance contracts specify that an employee must fall into one of the classifications contained in the benefit schedule. While these classifications may be broad enough to include all employees of the organization, they may also be so limited as to exclude many employees from coverage. In some cases, these excluded employees may have coverage through a negotiated trusteeship or under other group insurance contracts provided by the employer; in other cases, they may have no coverage because the employer wishes to limit benefits to certain groups of employees. No employee may be in more than one classification, and the responsibility for determining the appropriate classification for each employee falls on the policyholder.

Full Time

Most group insurance contracts limit eligibility to full-time employees. A full-time employee is generally defined as one who works no fewer than the number of hours in the normal work week (at least 30 hours) established by the employer. Subject to insurance company underwriting practices, an employer can provide coverage for part-time employees. When this is done, part time is generally defined as less than full time but more than some minimum number of hours per week. In addition, part-time employees may be subject to more stringent eligibility requirements. For example, full-time hourly paid employees may be provided with $20,000 of life insurance immediately upon employment, while part-time employees may be provided with only $10,000 of life insurance and may be subject to a probationary period.

Actively at Work

Most group insurance contracts contain an actively-at-work provision, whereby an employee is not eligible for coverage if absent from work because of sickness, injury or other reasons on the otherwise effective date of his or her coverage under the contract. Coverage will commence when the employee returns to work. The actively-at-work provision is often waived for employers with a large number of employees in situations when coverage is transferred from one insurance company to another and the employees involved have been insured under the previous insurance company's contract.

Probationary Periods

Group insurance contracts may contain probationary periods that must be satisfied before an employee is eligible for coverage. When a probationary period exists, it rarely exceeds six months. An employee will be eligible for coverage on either the first day after the probationary period or on the first day of the month following the end of the probationary period.

Insurability

While most group insurance contracts are issued without individual evidence of insurability, some underwriting practices will require evidence of insurability. This commonly occurs when an employee fails to elect coverage under a contributory plan and later wants coverage or when an employee is eligible for a large amount of coverage. In these cases, an employee will not be eligible for coverage until the employee has submitted proper evidence of insurability and the insurance company has determined that the evidence is satisfactory.

Premium Contribution

If a group insurance plan is contributory, an employee will not be eligible for coverage until the policyholder has been provided with the proper payroll deduction authorization. If this is done before the employee otherwise becomes eligible, coverage will commence on the eligibility date. During the next 31 days, coverage will commence when the policyholder receives the employee's authorization. If the authorization is not received within 31 days, the employee must furnish evidence of insurability at his or her own expense to obtain coverage. Evidence of insurability will also be required if an employee drops coverage under a contributory plan and at a future date wishes to regain coverage.

Beneficiary Designation

With few exceptions, an insured person has the right to name the beneficiary under his or her group life insurance coverage. These exceptions include credit life insurance (the creditor is the beneficiary) and dependent life insurance (the employee is the beneficiary). In addition, the laws and regulations of some states prohibit the employer from being named as beneficiary. Unless a beneficiary designation has been made irrevocable, an employee has the right to change the designated beneficiary at any time. While all insurance contracts require that the insurance company be notified of any beneficiary change in writing, the effective date of the change may vary depending on contract provisions. Some contracts specify that a change will be effective on the date it is received by the insurance company; others make it effective on the date the change was requested by the employee.

Under individual life insurance policies, death benefits are paid to an insured person's estate if no beneficiary has been named or if all beneficiaries have died before the insured. Some group term insurance contracts contain an identical provision; others provide that the death benefits will be paid through a *successive beneficiary provision*. Under the latter provision, the proceeds will be paid, at the option of the insurance company, to any one or more of the following survivors of the insured person: spouse, children, parents, brothers and sisters or the executor of the employee's estate. In most cases, insurance companies will pay the proceeds to the person or persons in the first of these categories with eligible survivors.

Two other provisions, each of which is often called a *facility-of-payment provision*, are sometimes found in group term insurance contracts. The first of these provisions provides that a specified amount, generally $500 or less, may be paid to any person who appears to be entitled to such a sum by reason of having incurred funeral or other expenses relating to the last illness or death of the person insured. The other provision applies to any beneficiary who is a minor or who is physically, mentally or otherwise incapable of giving a valid release for any payment received. Under this provision, the insurance company has the option, until a claim is made by the guardian for the beneficiary, of paying the proceeds to any person or institution that appears to have assumed responsibility for the care, custody or support of the beneficiary. These payments will be made in installments in the amount specified under any optional method of settlement previously selected by the person insured, or, in the absence of such a selection, in installments not to exceed some specified amount, such as $100 per month.

Settlement Options

With the exception of the survivor income benefit insurance plans discussed later in this chapter, group term insurance contracts covering employees provide that death benefits will be payable in a lump sum unless an optional mode of settlement has been selected. Each employee insured under the contract has the right to select and change any available mode of settlement during his or her lifetime. If no optional mode of settlement is in force at the death of the employee, the beneficiary generally has the right to elect any of the available options. The most common provision in group term insurance contracts is that the available modes of settlement are those customarily offered by the insurance company at the time the selection is made. The available options are not generally specified in the contract, but information about them is usually provided to the group policyholder. In addition, many insurance companies have brochures available for employees that describe either all or the most common options available. Any guarantees associated with these options will be those that are in effect when the option is selected.

In addition to a lump sum option, most insurance companies offer all of the following options and possibly other options as well:

- *An interest option.* The proceeds are left on deposit with the insurance company and the interest on the proceeds is paid to the beneficiary. The beneficiary usually can withdraw the proceeds at any time. The amount of any periodic installment depends on the interest rate paid by the insurance company.
- *An installment option for a fixed period.* The proceeds are paid in equal installments for a specified period of time. The amount of any periodic installment is determined by the time period and the amount of the death proceeds.
- *An installment option for a fixed amount.* The proceeds are paid in equal installments of a specified amount until the proceeds plus any interest earnings are exhausted.
- *A life income option.* The proceeds are payable in installments during the lifetime of the beneficiary. A choice of guarantee periods is usually available during which a secondary beneficiary or the beneficiary's estate will continue to receive benefits even if the beneficiary should die. The amount of any periodic installment depends on the age and sex of the beneficiary, the period for which payments are guaranteed and the amount of the death proceeds.

Premiums

Group insurance contracts stipulate that it is the responsibility of the policyholder to pay all premiums to the insurance company, even if the group insurance plan is contributory. Any required contributions from employees will be incorporated into the employer's group insurance plan, but they are not part of the insurance contract, and therefore, do not constitute an obligation to the insurance company by the employees. Rather, these contributions represent an obligation to the employer by the employees and are commonly paid by payroll deduction. Subject to certain limitations, any employee contributions are determined by the employer or as a result of labor negotiations. Most states require the employer to pay at least a portion of the premium for group term insurance (but not for other group insurance coverages), and a few states impose limitations on the amounts that may be paid by any employee. The most common restriction limits the contribution of any employee to the greater of 60 cents per month per $1,000 of coverage or 75 percent of the premium rate for that employee. This limitation is adhered to by companies licensed to do business in the state of New York and is often incorporated into their contracts. However, for some hazardous industries a higher contribution than 60 cents per month is permitted.

Premiums are payable in advance to the insurance company or any authorized agent for the time period specified in the contract. In most cases, premiums are payable monthly but may be paid less frequently. The rates used to determine the premium for any policyholder are guaranteed for a period of time, usually one year. The periodic premium is determined by applying these rates to the amount of life insurance in force. Consequently, the premium actually payable will change each month as the total amount of life insurance in force under the group insurance plan varies. Premium computations are discussed in Chapter 15.

Group insurance contracts state that any dividends or experience refunds are payable to the policyholder in cash or, at the policyholder's option, may be used to reduce any premium due. To the extent these exceed the policyholder's share of the premium, they must be used for the benefit of the employees. This is usually accomplished by reducing employee contributions or by providing increased benefits.

Claims

The provision concerning death claims under group life insurance policies is very simple. It states that the amount of insurance under the contract is payable when the insurance company receives written proof of death. No time period is specified in which a claim must be filed. However, most companies require the completion of a brief form by the policyholder and the beneficiary before the claim is processed.

Assignment

For many years, the owners of individual life insurance policies have been able to transfer any or all of their rights under the insurance contract to another party. Such assignments have been commonly used to avoid federal estate tax by removing the proceeds of an insurance contract from the insured's estate at death. Historically, assignments have not been permitted under group life insurance contracts, often because of state laws and regulations prohibiting them. In recent years, most states have eliminated such prohibitions; many insurance companies have modified their contracts to permit assignments, or waive the prohibition upon request. Essentially, an assignment will be valid as long as it is permitted by and conforms with state law and the group insurance contract. It should be noted that insurance companies generally require any assignment to be in writing and to be filed with the company.

Grace Period

Group life insurance contracts provide for a grace period (usually 31 days) during which a policyholder may pay any overdue premium without interest. If the premium is not paid, the contract will lapse at the end of the grace period unless the policyholder has notified the insurance company that an earlier termination should take place. Even if the policy is allowed to lapse or is terminated during the grace period, the policyholder is legally liable for the payment of any premium due during the portion of the grace period when the contract was still in force.

Entire Contract

The entire-contract clause states that the insurance policy, the policyholder's application that is attached to the policy, and any individual applications of any insured persons (which would not be attached) constitute the entire insurance contract. All statements made in these applications are considered to be representations rather than warranties, and no other statements made by the policyholder or by any insureds can be used by the insurance company as the basis for contesting coverage. When compared with the application for individual life insurance, the policyholder's application that is attached to a group insurance contract may be relatively short. Most of the information needed by the insurance company often is contained in a preliminary application that is not part of the insurance contract. On the delivery of many group insurance contracts, the policyholder signs an acceptance application, which states that the coverage as applied for has been delivered. Consequently, a greater burden is placed on the insurance company to verify the statements made by the policyholder in the preliminary application.

The entire-contract clause also stipulates that no agent has any authority to waive or amend any provisions of the insurance contract and that a waiver or amendment to the contract will be valid only if it is signed by certain specified corporate officers of the insurance company.

Incontestability

Like individual life insurance contracts, group insurance contracts contain an incontestability provision. Except for the nonpayment of premiums, the validity of the contract cannot be contested after it has been in force for a specified time period, generally one or two years. During this time, the insurance company can contest the contract based on statements made by the policyholder in the application attached to the contract that are considered to be material misrepresentations. Statements by any insured person can be used as the basis for denying claims during this period only if such statements relate to the insurability of the individual. In addition, the statements must have been made in a written application signed by the individual, and a copy of the application must have been furnished to either the individual or his or her beneficiary. It should be pointed out that the incontestability clause will not be of concern to most covered persons, because evidence of insurability is not usually required and thus no statements concerning individual insurability will be made.

Misstatement of Age

If the age of any person covered under a group term insurance policy is misstated, the benefit payable will be the amount that is specified under the benefit schedule. However, the premium will be adjusted to reflect the true age of the individual. This is in contrast to individual life insurance contracts where benefits are adjusted to the amount that the premium paid would have purchased at the true age of the individual. Under a group insurance contract, the responsibility for paying any additional premium or the right to receive a refund belongs to the policyholder and not to the individual employee whose age is misstated, even if the plan is contributory. If the misstated age would have affected the employee's contribution, this is a matter to be resolved between the employer and the employee.

Termination

All group insurance contracts stipulate the conditions under which the contract may be terminated by either the insurance company or the policyholder. The circumstances under which the coverage for a particular insured person will terminate are also specified.

A group term insurance contract can be terminated for nonpayment of premium at the end of the grace period. Insurance companies may also terminate coverage for an individual employer group on any premium due date if certain conditions exist and notice of termination has been given to the policyholder at least 31 days in advance. These conditions include the failure to maintain a stated minimum number of participants in the plan and, in contributory plans, the failure to maintain a stated minimum percentage participation. The policyholder may also terminate the contract at any time by giving the insurance company 31 days' advance written notice. Moreover, the policyholder has the right to request the amendment of the contract at any time by notifying the insurance company.

The coverage on any insured person will terminate automatically (subject to any provisions providing for a continuation or conversion of coverage) when any of the following conditions exist:

- The employee terminates employment.
- The employee ceases to be eligible; for example, if the employee no longer satisfies the full-time work requirement or no longer is in a covered classification.
- The master contract is terminated by the policyholder or the insurance company.
- Any required contribution by the employee has not been made—generally because the employee has notified the policyholder to cease the required payroll deduction.

Temporary Interruption of Employment

Most group term insurance contracts provide that the employer may elect to continue coverage on employees during temporary interruptions of active full-time employment. These may arise from leaves of absence, layoffs or the inability to work due to illness or injury. The employer must continue paying the premium and the coverage may be continued only for a relatively short period of time, such as three months, unless the time period is extended by mutual agreement between the employer and the insurance company. Also, in electing to continue coverage, the policyholder must act in such a way as to preclude individual selection.

Continuation of Coverage for Disabled Employees

Most group term insurance contracts make some provision for the continuation of coverage on employees whose active employment has terminated due to disability. By far the most common provision in use today is the *waiver-of-premium provision.* Under this provision, life insurance coverage is continued without the payment of premiums as long as the employee is totally disabled, even if the master contract is terminated. However, certain requirements must be met:

- The disability must commence while the employee is insured under the master contract.
- The disability must commence prior to a specified age, commonly age 60.
- The employee must be totally disabled. Total disability normally is defined as the complete inability of the employee to engage in any gainful occupation for which he or she is or becomes qualified by reason of education, training, or experience.
- The employee must file a claim within a prescribed time period (normally 12 months) and must submit annual evidence of continuing disability.

If an employee no longer meets the definition of disability and returns to work, the employee may again be insured under the group insurance contract on a premium-paying basis as long as the employee meets the eligibility requirements of the contract. If for any reason the employee is not eligible for insurance under the group insurance contract, the conversion privilege can be exercised.

A few insurance companies refer to their waiver-of-premium provision as an *extended-death benefit.* This terminology is somewhat confusing since, historically, an extended-death-benefit provision has only allowed coverage to continue on a disabled employee for a maximum of one year. After that time, coverage ceases. This type of provision, once quite common, is still used occasionally. However, it has generally been replaced by a waiver-of-premium provision.

Another provision relating to disabled employees is a maturity-value benefit. Under this type of provision, the face amount of a totally disabled employee's group life insurance will be paid to the employee in a lump sum or in monthly installments. Like the extended-death-benefit provision, a maturity-value-benefit provision was once widely used; it is no longer common today.

A small but growing trend is for disabled employees to be continued as eligible employees under a group insurance contract, with the employer paying the periodic cost of their coverage just as if they were active employees. At the termination of the contract, the insurance company has no responsibility to continue coverage unless a disabled employee is eligible and elects to convert coverage and pays any required premiums. However, depending on the provisions of the group insurance plan, the employer may have a legal responsibility to continue coverage on disabled employees in some manner.

Conversion

All group term insurance contracts covering employees contain a conversion privilege that gives any employee whose coverage ceases the right to convert to an individual insurance policy. The terms of the conversion privilege vary, depending on the reason for termination of coverage under the group contract. The most generous conversion rights are available to those employees who have either terminated employment or who no longer fall into one of the eligible classifications still covered by the master contract. These employees have the right to purchase from the insurance company, without evidence of insurability, an individual life insurance policy—usually one without disability or other supplementary benefits. However, this right is subject to the following conditions:

- The employee must apply for conversion within 31 days after the termination of employment or membership in an eligible classification. During this 31-day period, the employee is provided with a death benefit equal to the amount of life insurance that is available under the conversion privilege, even if the employee does not apply for conversion. Disability and supplementary benefits are not extended during this period unless they are also subject to conversion. The premium for the individual policy must accompany the conversion application and coverage will be effective at the end of the conversion period.
- The individual policy selected by the employee generally may be any form, except term insurance, customarily issued by the insurance company at the age and amount applied for. Some insurance companies also make term insurance coverage available, and a few states require that employees be allowed to purchase term insurance coverage for a limited time, such as one year, after which an employee must convert to a cash-value form of coverage.
- The face amount of the individual policy may not exceed the amount of life insurance that terminated under the group insurance contract.
- The premium for the individual policy will be determined using the insurance company's current rate applicable to the type and amount of the individual policy for the attained age of the employee on the date of conversion and for the class of risk to which the employee belongs. While no extra premium may be charged for reasons of health, an extra premium may be charged for any other hazards considered in an insurance company's rate structure, such as occupation or avocation.

It is estimated that only 1 or 2 percent of employees eligible actually take advantage of the conversion privilege. Several reasons account for this: Many employees will obtain coverage with new employers; others are discouraged by the high cost of the permanent insurance to which they must convert. Still others, if they are insurable at standard rates, may find coverage at a lower cost with other insurers and be able to purchase supplementary coverages, such as disability benefits, that are not available under conversion policies. In addition, insurance companies have not actively encouraged group conversions since those who convert tend to be the poorer risks. Finally, because some employers are faced with conversion charges due to experience rating (see Chapter 15), they are also unlikely to encourage conversion.

A more restrictive conversion privilege exists if an employee's coverage is terminated because the master contract is terminated for all employees or is amended to eliminate eligible classifications. Under these circumstances, the employee is given a conversion right only if he or she was insured under the contract for a period of time—generally five years—immediately preceding the date on which coverage was terminated. In addition, the amount of insurance that can be converted is limited to the lesser of $2,000 or the amount of the employee's life insurance under the contract at the date of termination reduced by any amount of life insurance for which the employee becomes eligible under any group life insurance policy issued or reinstated by the same or another insurance company within 31 days after such termination.

ADDED COVERAGES

Group term insurance contracts often provide additional insurance benefits through the use of riders. These benefits are also forms of group term insurance and consist of the following:

1. Supplemental life insurance.
2. Accidental death and dismemberment insurance.
3. Survivor income benefit insurance.
4. Dependent life insurance.

These added benefits may be provided for all employees insured under the basic group term contract or may be limited to certain classes of employees. With the exception of dependent life insurance, these coverages may also be written as separate contracts.

Supplemental Life Insurance

Some group life insurance plans enable all or certain classes of employees to purchase additional life insurance. Generally, the employer will provide a basic amount of life insurance to all eligible employees on a noncontributory basis. This is commonly a flat amount of coverage or multiple of annual earnings. The supplemental coverage is contributory and may be either incorporated into the basic group life insurance contract or contained in a separate contract. The latter method tends to be more common when the supplemental coverage is available to only a select group of employees. Although the employee may pay the entire cost of the supplemental coverage, either state laws that require employer contributions or insurance company underwriting practices will often result in the employer paying a portion of the cost.

The amount of supplemental coverage available will be specified in a benefit schedule. Under some plans, an employee must purchase the full amount of coverage; under other plans, an employee may purchase a portion of the coverage. The following are two examples of benefit schedules for a basic plus supplemental life insurance plan:

Type of Coverage	Amount of Life Insurance
Basic insurance	$10,000
Supplemental insurance	20,000

Type of Coverage	Amount of Life Insurance
Basic insurance	1 times salary
Supplemental insurance	½, 1, 1½ or 2 times salary, subject to a maximum (including basic insurance) of $100,000

Giving employees the right to choose their benefit amounts leads to adverse selection. As a result, more stringent underwriting requirements are usually associated with supplemental coverage. These often include requiring individual evidence of insurability, except possibly when the additional coverage is modest. In addition, higher rates may be charged for supplemental insurance than for basic coverage.

Accidental Death and Dismemberment Insurance

Many group life insurance contracts contain an accidental death and dismemberment provision that gives additional benefits if an employee dies accidentally or suffers certain types of injuries. Traditionally, this group coverage was available only as a rider to a group life insurance contract. Now, however, it is common to find these benefits provided through separate group insurance contracts in which coverage usually is contributory on the part of employees. Such contracts are referred to as voluntary accidental death and dismemberment insurance.

Traditional Coverage

Under the traditional form of accidental death and dismemberment insurance, an employee eligible for group life insurance coverage, and electing the life insurance coverage if it is contributory, will automatically have the accidental death and dismemberment coverage if it has been added by the employer. Under the typical accidental death and dismemberment rider, the insurance company will pay an additional amount of insurance that is equal to the amount of coverage under the basic group life insurance contract—referred to as the principal sum—if an employee dies as a result of accidental bodily injuries while he or she is covered under the policy. It is specified that death must occur within 90 days following the date that injuries are sustained; however, some courts have ruled this time period to be invalid and have required insurance companies to pay claims when longer periods have been involved. In addition to an accidental death benefit, the following benefit schedule is provided for certain specific injuries:

Type of Injury	Benefit Amount
Loss of (including loss of use of):	
Both hands or both feet	The principal sum
The sight of both eyes	The principal sum
One hand and sight of one eye	The principal sum
One foot and sight of one eye	The principal sum
One foot and one hand	The principal sum
One hand	One half the principal sum
One foot	One half the principal sum
The sight of one eye	One half the principal sum

In some cases, the accidental death and dismemberment rider provides the same benefits for any accident covered under the contract. However, it is not unusual to have a higher level of benefits for accidents that occur while the employee is traveling on business for the employer. They may also be limited to accidents occurring while the employee is occupying (or entering, alighting from, or struck by) a public conveyance or by a company-owned or personally owned vehicle. The following benefit schedule reflects some of these variations:

Type of Loss	Benefit Amount
Death while traveling on business when occupying, boarding, alighting from or struck by any motor vehicle, airplane or other conveyance including company-owned or personally owned vehicles	3 times the principal sum
Death at all other times	2 times the principal sum
Dismemberment	Up to the principal sum (as shown in the previous schedule)

Death benefits are paid in accordance with the beneficiary provision of the group life insurance contract, and dismemberment benefits are paid to the employee. Coverage is usually written to cover both occupational and nonoccupational accidents. However, when employees are in hazardous occupations, coverage may apply only to nonoccupational accidents, in which case employees would still have workers' compensation coverage for any occupational accidents.

Coverage generally is not subject to a conversion privilege. When life insurance coverage continues after retirement, accidental death and dismemberment benefits normally cease. Like life insurance coverage, however, it may be continued during temporary periods of unemployment. In contrast to the group term insurance policy to which it is attached, group accidental death and dismemberment insurance contains some exclusions. These include losses resulting from:

- Suicide at any time. It is interesting to note that, except for a few METs, group term life insurance does not contain a suicide provision.
- Disease or bodily or mental infirmity, or medical or surgical treatment thereof.
- Ptomaines or any infection other than one occurring simultaneously with and through an accidental cut or wound.
- War.
- Travel or flight in any type of aircraft as a pilot, student pilot, officer or member of the crew. (There is a trend toward eliminating this exclusion, particularly when coverage is written on large groups.)

Voluntary Coverage

The provisions of voluntary group accidental death and dismemberment insurance are almost identical to those contained in a group life insurance contract with an accidental death and dismemberment insurance rider. However, there are a few differences: Voluntary plans usually require the employee to pay the entire cost of coverage, and they virtually always provide both occupational and nonoccupational coverage. Subject to limitations, the employee may select the amount of coverage desired, with the maximum amount of coverage available tending to be larger than when coverage is provided through a rider. Another difference is the frequent use in voluntary plans of a common accident provision, whereby the amount payable by the insurance company is limited to a stipulated maximum for all employees killed or injured in any single accident. If this exceeds the sum of the benefits otherwise payable for each employee, benefits are prorated.

Survivor Income Benefit Insurance

Survivor income benefit insurance represents an attempt to more closely relate life insurance benefits to the actual needs of each employee's survivors. Instead of paying death benefits in a lump sum to a named beneficiary, benefits are paid in the form of periodic income to specified dependents who survive the employee. No death benefits are paid unless an employee has qualified survivors, and benefit payments will cease when survivors no longer are eligible. Like regular group term insurance, a survivor income benefit insurance plan may be contributory or noncontributory.

Survivor income benefit insurance plans, which have been available since the 1960s, never gained widespread acceptance. Employees without qualified survivors often view such plans as discriminatory since these employees have no life insurance coverage. Consequently, survivor income benefit insurance is normally written in conjunction with a group term insurance plan that will provide a basic amount of life insurance to all eligible employees. This basic amount of life insurance will serve as a means of providing for the burial and other last expenses associated with the death of any employee. In addition, there is a feeling among employers that employees are not as appreciative of a benefit expressed as a certain amount of dollars per month as they would be of one expressed as a larger lump-sum amount. Also, the final decision as to what type of group life insurance coverage to buy frequently is made by an older executive. Such a person may not view survivor income benefit plans with enthusiasm since they generally provide potentially greater benefits to younger workers who tend to have younger survivors.

Under survivor income benefit insurance coverage, eligible survivors generally include only the spouse and any dependent children of the employee. The spouse typically is defined as a person who has been lawfully married to the employee for at least 90 days and who is not legally separated from the employee. A spouse's eligibility to receive benefits usually ceases if the spouse remarries or reaches a certain age, such as 65. At this age, it is assumed that the spouse will be eligible for benefits under social security. Some plans make benefit payments of one or two years to spouses who remarry. The purpose of this "dowry payment" is to encourage the spouse to report the remarriage.

Dependent children are defined as unmarried dependent children of the employee, including stepchildren and children who have been legally adopted by the employee. Benefits to dependent children will cease upon marriage or the attainment of a certain age, such as 19. Benefits may be paid longer for unmarried children who are in school.

Under some survivor income benefit insurance plans, the benefit amount is determined by the number of eligible survivors even though the entire benefit will be paid to the surviving spouse. Only if there is no surviving spouse, or if the spouse later dies, will the benefits be paid directly to the children. Under other plans, separate benefits are made available to the surviving spouse and the dependent children. These benefits may be based on specified dollar amounts or be determined by the salary of the deceased employee.

Some survivor income benefit insurance plans provide a monthly benefit—either a flat amount or a percentage of salary—regardless of the number and types of survivors. In some instances, a larger benefit is paid for a certain period of time following the employee's death. This transitional benefit will give survivors a better opportunity to adjust their standard of living to a level consistent with the regular survivor income benefits. Survivor income benefits generally are substantially less than the employee's former income and are viewed as a supplement to any social security benefits for which the survivors will be eligible. In those few instances where benefits are more generous, they are likely to be reduced by any social security benefits that will be received. Here are two examples of benefit schedules under group life insurance plans that have been supplemented with survivor income benefit insurance:

Benefit	Amount of Benefit
Basic life insurance for each employee	$25,000
Surviving spouse benefit*	10% of the employee's average monthly salary during the year prior to death
Surviving child benefit*	5% of the employee's average monthly salary during the year prior to death for each child

*Subject to a maximum family benefit of $400 per month.

Benefit	Amount of Benefit
Basic life insurance for each employee	$10,000
Transition survivor benefit for 24 months	$1,000 per month
Survivor benefit after the transition period	$500 per month

For regulatory purposes, most states treat survivor income benefit insurance the same as group term insurance, including the requirement for a conversion provision. The amount eligible for conversion by an employee is the commuted value of the benefit payments that would be received by eligible survivors if the employee died at the time of conversion. This amount is determined by calculating the present value of potential benefits by using the mortality table and interest rates employed by the insurance company. The present value of these benefits, which is determined by the number and ages of eligible survivors, can be substantial for an employee with young survivors.

Because of the adverse selection accompanying conversion, insurance companies have been concerned about the size of the conversion benefit. Some states allow the conversion amount to be expressed as a multiple of the potential monthly benefit. On the average, this results in a lower conversion amount than if the commuted value is used. A few states also allow insurance companies to market their survivor income benefit product as an annuity with contingencies. One advantage to having the product considered an annuity is that no conversion provision is required.

Dependent Life Insurance

Some group life insurance contracts provide insurance coverage on the lives of employees' dependents. Dependent life insurance has been viewed as a method of providing the employee with resources to meet the funeral and burial expenses associated with the death of a dependent. Consequently, the employee is automatically the beneficiary. The employee also elects and pays for this coverage if it is contributory. Coverage for dependents is almost always limited to employees who are themselves covered under the group contract. Thus, if an employee's coverage is contributory, the employee must elect coverage for himself or herself to be eligible for dependent coverage.

For purposes of dependent life insurance coverage, dependents are usually defined as including an employee's spouse who is not legally separated from the employee, and an employee's unmarried dependent children (including stepchildren and adopted children) who are over 14 days of age but under some specified age, commonly 19 or 21. To prevent adverse selection, an employee cannot select coverage on individual dependents. Rather, if dependent coverage is selected, all dependents fitting the definition are insured. When dependent coverage is in effect for an employee, any new eligible dependents are automatically insured.

The amount of coverage for each dependent usually is quite modest. Some states limit the maximum amount of life insurance that can be written and a few states actually prohibit writing any coverage on dependents. In addition, employer contributions used to purchase more than $2,000 of coverage on each dependent will result in income to the employee for the purpose of federal taxation. However, amounts in excess of $2,000 may be purchased with employee contributions without adverse tax consequences. In some cases, the same amount of coverage will be provided for all dependents; in other cases, a larger amount will be provided for the spouse than for the children. It is also not unusual for the amount of coverage on children to be less until the children attain some specified age, such as six months. Here are examples of benefit schedules under dependent coverage:

Class	Amount of Insurance
Each dependent	$2,000

Class	Amount of Insurance
Spouse	50% of the employee's insured amount, subject to a maximum of $5,000
Dependent children:	
At least 14 days but less than 6 months of age	$ 500
6 months of age or older	$1,000

A single premium applies to the dependent coverage for each employee and is independent of the number of dependents. In some cases, the premium may vary, depending on the age of the employee (not the dependents), but, more commonly, it is the same amount for all employees regardless of age. Dependent coverage usually contains a conversion privilege applicable only to spousal coverage. However, some states require that the conversion privilege apply to the coverage on all dependents. Assignment is almost never permitted, and no waiver of premium is available if a dependent becomes disabled. However, if the basic life insurance contract contains a waiver-of-premium provision applicable to the employee, the disability of the employee will sometimes result in a waiver of premium for the dependent coverage. A provision similar to the actively-at-work provision pertaining to employees is often included for dependents. It specifies that dependents will not be covered when otherwise eligible if they are confined in a hospital, except for newborn children who are covered after 14 days. Coverage will commence when the dependent is discharged from the hospital.

TAXATION

A discussion of group term insurance is incomplete without an explanation of the tax laws affecting its use. While discussions of these laws are often limited to federal income and estate taxation, federal gift taxation and taxation by the states should also be considered.

Federal Taxation

The growth of group term insurance has been greatly influenced by the favorable tax treatment afforded it under federal tax laws. This section will discuss the effects of these tax laws on basic group term insurance and on coverages that may be added to a basic group term insurance contract. A complete explanation of the federal tax laws pertaining to group term insurance and their interpretation by the Internal Revenue Service (IRS) would be lengthy and is beyond the scope of this book. Consequently, this discussion and subsequent discussions of federal tax laws will only highlight these laws.

Deductibility of Premiums

In general, employer contributions for an employee's group term insurance coverage are fully deductible to the employer under Section 162 of the Internal Revenue Code as an ordinary and necessary business expense as long as the overall compensation of the employee is reasonable. The reasonableness of compensation, which includes wages, salary and other fringe benefits, is usually only a potential issue for the owners of small businesses or the stockholder-employees of closely held corporations. Any compensation that is determined by the IRS to be unreasonable may not be deducted by a firm for income tax purposes. In addition, the Internal Revenue Code does not allow a firm to take an income tax deduction for contributions (1) that are made on behalf of sole proprietors or partners under any circumstances or (2) that are made on behalf of stockholders, unless they are providing substantive services to the corporation. Finally, no deduction is allowed under Code Section 264 if the employer is named as beneficiary.

Contributions by any individual employee are considered payments for personal life insurance and are not deductible for income tax purposes by that employee. Thus, the amount of any payroll deductions authorized by an employee for group term insurance purposes will be included in the employee's taxable income.

Income Tax Liability of Employees

In the absence of tax laws to the contrary, the amount of any compensation for which an employer receives an income tax deduction (including the payment of group insurance premiums) represents taxable income to the employee. However, Code Section 79 provides favorable tax treatment to employer contributions for life insurance that qualifies as group term insurance.

Section 79 Requirements. In order to qualify as group term insurance under Section 79, life insurance must meet the following conditions:

- It must provide a death benefit excludable from federal income tax.
- It must be provided to a group of employees. A group of employees is defined to include all employees of an employer. If all employees are not covered, membership must be determined on the basis of age, marital status or factors relating to employment.

- It must be provided under a policy carried directly or indirectly by the employer. This includes (1) any policy for which the employer pays any part of the cost or (2) any noncontributory policy arranged by the employer if at least one employee is charged less than his or her cost (under Uniform Premium Table 1) and at least one other employee is charged more than his or her cost. If no employee is charged more than the Uniform Premium Table 1 cost, a policy is not group term insurance for purposes of Section 79.

  A policy is defined to include a master contract or a group of individual policies. The term *carried indirectly* refers to those situations where the employer is not the policyholder, but rather provides coverage to employees through master contracts issued to organizations such as negotiated trusteeships or METs.

- The plan must be arranged in such a manner as to preclude individual selection of coverage amounts. However, it is acceptable to have alternative benefit schedules based upon the amount an employee elects to contribute. Supplemental plans where an employee is given a choice, such as either 1, 1½ or 2 times salary, are considered to fall within this category.

All life insurance that qualifies under Section 79 as group term insurance is considered to be a single plan of insurance, regardless of the number of insurance contracts used. For example, an employer might provide coverage for union employees under a negotiated trusteeship, for other employees under an individual employer group insurance contract, and additional coverage for top executives under a group of individual life insurance policies. Under Section 79, these would all constitute a single plan. This plan must be provided for at least ten full-time employees at some time during the calendar year. For purposes of meeting the ten-full-time requirement, employees who have not satisfied any required waiting periods may be counted as participants. In addition, employees who have elected not to participate are also counted as participants—but only if they would not have been required to contribute to the cost of other benefits besides group term insurance if they had participated. As will be described later, a plan with fewer than ten full-time employees may still qualify for favorable tax treatment under Section 79 if more restrictive requirements are met.

Exceptions to Section 79. Even when all the previous requirements are met, there are some situations in which Section 79 does not apply. In some cases, different sections of the Internal Revenue Code provide alternative tax treatment. For example, when group term insurance is issued to the trustees of a qualified pension plan and is used to provide a death benefit under the plan, the full amount of any life insurance paid for by employer contributions will result in taxable income to the employee, as discussed in Chapter 21.

There are three situations for which employer contributions for group term insurance will not result in taxable income to an employee, regardless of the amount of insurance:

1. If an employee has terminated employment because of disability.
2. If a qualified charity (as determined by the Internal Revenue Code) has

been named as beneficiary for the entire year.
3. If the employer has been named as beneficiary for the entire year.

Prior to the Tax Reform Act of 1984, employer contributions did not result in taxable income to retired employees. Coverage on retired employees is now subject to Section 79, and these persons are treated in the same manner as active employees. Thus, they will have taxable income in any year in which the amount of coverage received exceeds $50,000. However, a grandfather clause to this new rule stipulates that it does not apply to group term life insurance plans (or to comparable successor plans or to plans of successor employers) in existence for covered employees who (1) retired before 1984 or (2) were at least 55 years of age before 1984 and were employed by the employer any time during 1983. There is one exception to this grandfather clause: It does not apply to persons (either key or nonkey employees) retiring after 1986 if a plan is discriminatory. The factors that make a plan discriminatory are discussed later.

General Tax Rules. Under Section 79, the cost of the first $50,000 of coverage is not taxed to the employee. Since all group term insurance provided by an employer that qualifies under Section 79 is considered to be one plan, this exclusion applies only once to each employee. For example, an employee who has $10,000 of coverage that is provided to all employees under one policy, and $75,000 of coverage provided to executives under a separate insurance policy, would have a single $50,000 exclusion. The cost of coverage in excess of $50,000, less any employee contributions for the entire amount of coverage, represents taxable income to the employee. For purposes of Section 79, the cost of this excess coverage is determined by a government table called the Uniform Premium Table 1, but often referred to only as Table 1. This table will often result in a lower cost than would be calculated using the actual premium paid by the employer for the coverage.

Uniform Premium Table 1

Age	Cost per Month per $1,000 of Coverage
29 and under	$ .08
30–34	.09
35–39	.11
40–44	.17
45–49	.29
50–54	.48
55–59	.75
60–64	1.17
65–69	2.10
70 and over	3.76

To calculate the cost of an employee's coverage for one month of protection under a group term insurance plan, the Uniform Premium Table 1 cost shown for the employee's age bracket—based on the employee's attained age at the end of the tax year—is multiplied by the number of thousands in excess of 50 of group term insurance on the employee. For example, if an employee age 57 was provided with $150,000 of group term insurance, assuming no employee contributions, the employee's monthly cost could be calculated as follows:

Coverage provided	$150,000
Less Section 79 exclusion	50,000
Amount subject to taxation	$100,000
Uniform Premium Table 1 monthly cost per $1,000 of coverage at age 57	$0.75
Monthly cost ($0.75 × 100)	$75

The monthly costs are then totaled to obtain an annual cost. Assuming no change in the amount of coverage during the year, the annual cost would be $900. Any employee contributions for the entire amount of coverage are subtracted from the annual cost to determine the taxable income that must be reported by an employee. If the employee contributed $.30 per month ($3.60 per year) per $1,000 of coverage, the employee's total annual contribution for $150,000 of coverage would be $540. This reduces the amount reportable as taxable income from $900 to $360.

One final point is worthy of attention. Group term insurance coverage can often be purchased at a lower cost than Uniform Premium Table 1 rates. There are some who argue that in these instances the actual cost of coverage can be used in place of the Table 1 cost for determining an employee's taxable income. From the standpoint of logic and consistency with tax laws, this view makes sense. However, the regulations for Section 79 are very specific: Only Uniform Premium Table 1 costs are to be used.

Nondiscrimination Rules. Any plan that qualified as group term insurance under Section 79 is subject to nondiscrimination rules, and the $50,000 exclusion will not be available to key employees if a plan is discriminatory. Such a plan favors key employees in either eligibility or benefits. In addition, the value of the full amount of coverage for key employees, less their own contributions, will be considered taxable income, based on the greater of actual or Uniform Premium Table 1 costs. A key employee of a firm is defined as any employee who at any time during the current year or the preceding four plan years is any of the following:

- An officer of the firm who earns from the firm more than 50 percent of the Internal Revenue Code limit on the amount of benefits payable by a defined benefit plan. This amount (50 percent of $108,963, or $54,481.50, for 1991) is indexed annually. For purposes of this rule, the number of employees treated as officers is the greater of three people or 10 percent of the firm's employees, subject to a maximum of 50 people. In applying the rule, the following employees can be excluded: part-time persons, persons who are under 21, and persons with less than six months of service with the firm.

- One of the ten employees owning the largest interests in the firm and having an annual compensation from the firm of more than $30,000.
- A more-than-5-percent owner of the firm.
- A more-than-1-percent owner of the firm who earns over $150,000 per year.
- A retired employee who was a key employee when he or she retired or terminated service.

Note that the definition of key employee includes not only active employees but also retired employees who were key employees at the time of retirement or separation from service.

Eligibility requirements are not discriminatory if (1) at least 70 percent of all employees are eligible, (2) at least 85 percent of all employees who are participants are not key employees, or (3) participants comprise a classification that the IRS determines is nondiscriminatory. For purposes of the 70-percent test, employees with less than three years service, part-time employees and seasonal employees may be excluded. Employees covered by collective bargaining agreements may also be excluded if plan benefits were the subject of good-faith bargaining.

Benefits are not discriminatory if neither the type nor amount of benefits discriminate in favor of key employees. The act specifies that it is permissible to base benefits on a uniform percentage of salary.

One issue that arose after the passage of the nondiscrimination rules in 1984 was whether they applied separately to active and to retired employees. A technical correction in the Tax Reform Act of 1986 clarifies the issue by stating that the rules do apply separately to the extent provided in IRS regulations. However, such regulations have yet to be issued.

Groups with Fewer Than Ten Full-Time Employees. A group insurance plan that covers fewer than ten employees must satisfy an additional set of requirements before it is eligible for favorable tax treatment under Section 79. These rules predated the general nondiscrimination rules previously described, and it was assumed that the under-ten rules would be abolished when the new rules were adopted. However, that was not done, so smaller groups are subject to two separate and somewhat overlapping sets of rules. It should also be noted that this section applies to an employer's overall plan of group insurance, not separate group insurance contracts. For example, an employer providing group insurance coverage for its 50 hourly employees under one group insurance contract and for its six executives under a separate contract is considered to have a single plan covering 56 employees, and thus is exempt from the under-ten requirements. While the stated purpose of the under-ten requirements is to preclude individual selection, their effect is to prevent the group insurance plan from discriminating in favor of the owners or stockholder-employees of small businesses.

With some exceptions, plans covering fewer than ten employees must provide coverage for all full-time employees. For purposes of this requirement, employees who are not customarily employed for more than 20 hours in any one week or five months in any calendar year are considered part-time employees. It is permissible to exclude full-time employees from coverage under the following circumstances:

- The employee has reached 65.
- The employee has not satisfied the waiting period under the plan. However, the waiting period may not exceed six months.
- The employee has elected not to participate in the plan, but only if the employee would not have been required to contribute to the cost of other benefits besides group term life insurance if he or she had participated.
- The employee has not satisfied the evidence of insurability required under the plan. This evidence of insurability must be determined solely on the basis of a medical questionnaire completed by the employee and not by a medical examination.

The amount of coverage must be a flat amount, a uniform percentage of salary or an amount based on different employee classifications. These employee classifications, which are referred to as coverage brackets in Section 79, may be determined in the manner described earlier in this chapter in the section on benefit schedules. The amount of coverage provided each employee in any classification may be no greater than 2½ times the amount of coverage provided each employee in the next lower classification. In addition, each employee in the lowest classification must be provided with an amount of coverage that is equal to at least 10 percent of the amount provided each employee in the highest classification. There must also be a reasonable expectation that there will be at least one employee in each classification. The following benefit schedule would be unacceptable for two reasons: First, the amount of coverage provided for the hourly employees is only 5 percent of the amount of coverage provided for the president. Second, the amount of coverage on the supervisor is more than 2½ times the amount of coverage provided for the hourly employees.

Classification	Amount of Coverage
President	$50,000
Supervisor	20,000
Hourly employees	2,500

The following benefit schedule, however, would be acceptable:

Classification	Amount of Coverage
President	$50,000
Supervisor	20,000
Hourly employees	10,000

If a group insurance plan covering fewer than ten employees does not qualify for favorable tax treatment under Section 79, any premiums paid by the employer for such coverage will represent taxable income to the employees. The employer, however, will still receive an income tax deduction for any premiums paid on behalf of the employees as long as overall compensation is reasonable.

Taxation of Proceeds

In most instances, Code Section 101 provides that life insurance proceeds under a group term insurance contract do not result in any taxable income to the beneficiary if paid in a lump sum. If the proceeds are payable in installments over more than one taxable year of the beneficiary, only the interest earnings attributable to the proceeds will be included in the beneficiary's income for tax purposes.

Under certain circumstances, the exemption of the proceeds from income taxation does not apply if the coverage was transferred (either in whole or in part) for a valuable consideration. Such a situation will arise when the stockholder-employees of a corporation name each other as beneficiaries under their group term insurance coverage as a method of funding a buy-sell agreement. The mutual agreement to name each other as beneficiaries is the valuable consideration. Under these circumstances, any proceeds paid to a beneficiary constitute ordinary income to the extent that the proceeds exceed the beneficiary's tax basis, as determined by the Internal Revenue Code.

In many cases, benefits paid by an employer to employees or their beneficiaries from the firm's assets receive the same tax treatment as benefits provided under an insurance contract. This is not true for death benefits. If they are provided other than through an insurance contract, the amount of the proceeds in excess of $5,000 will represent taxable income to the beneficiary. For this reason, employers are less likely to use alternative funding arrangements for death benefits than for disability and medical expense benefits.

Under Code Section 2042, the proceeds of a group term insurance contract, even if paid to a named beneficiary, are included in an employee's gross estate for federal estate tax purposes as long as the employee possessed incidents of ownership in the coverage at the time of death. However, no estate tax is levied on any amounts, including life insurance proceeds, left to a surviving spouse. In addition, taxable estates of $600,000 or less are generally free of estate taxation regardless of the beneficiary.

When an estate would otherwise be subject to estate taxation, an employee may remove the proceeds of group term insurance from his or her taxable estate by absolutely assigning all incidents of ownership to another person, usually the beneficiary of the coverage. Incidents of ownership include the rights to change the beneficiary, to terminate coverage, to assign coverage or to exercise the conversion privilege. For this favorable treatment, however, the Internal Revenue Code requires that such an assignment be permissible under both the group term insurance master contract and the laws of the state having jurisdiction. The absolute assignment is usually in the form of a gift, which is not without its own tax implications. The amount of insurance is considered a gift made each year by the employee to the person to whom the absolute assignment was granted. Consequently, if the value of the gift is of sufficient size, federal gift taxes will be payable. As the Internal Revenue Code and the IRS Regulations are silent on the specific gift tax consequences of assigned group term insurance, there is disagreement as to whether the gift should be valued at Uniform Premium Table 1 cost or at the actual premium for the coverage.

The assignment of group term life insurance also results in the inclusion of some values in the employee's estate. If the employee dies within three years of making the assignment, the full amount of the proceeds will be included in the employee's estate. If death occurs more than three years after the assignment is made, only the premiums paid within the three years prior to death will be included in the employee's taxable estate. In the past, a problem arose if the employer changed group insurance carriers. In effect, this would require the employee to make a new assignment which would again be subject to the three-year time limit. However, the IRS now considers this type of situation to be a continuation of the original assignment as long as the amount and provisions of the new coverage are essentially the same as those of the old coverage.

Treatment of Added Coverage

For purposes of Section 79, supplemental life insurance can be written as either a separate contract or as part of the contract providing basic group term life insurance coverage. If it is a separate contract and if the supplemental group life insurance meets the conditions of qualifying as group term insurance under Section 79, the amount of coverage provided is added to all other group term insurance for purposes of calculating the Uniform Premium Table 1 cost. Any premiums paid by the employee for the supplemental coverage are included in the deduction used to determine the final taxable income. In all other ways supplemental life insurance is treated the same as group term insurance. When supplemental life insurance coverage is written in conjunction with a basic group life insurance plan, employers have the option of treating the supplemental coverage as a separate policy of insurance as long as the premiums are properly allocated among the two portions of coverage. There is no advantage in treating the supplemental coverage as a separate policy if it, by itself, would still qualify as group term insurance under Section 79. However, this election will minimize taxable income to employees if the cost of the supplemental coverage is paid totally by the employees, and all employees are charged rates at or below Uniform Premium Table 1 rates.

Premiums paid for accidental death and dismemberment insurance are considered to be health insurance premiums rather than group term insurance premiums. However, these are also deductible to the employer as an ordinary and necessary business expense the same as for group term insurance. Benefits paid to an employee under the dismemberment portion of the coverage are treated as benefits received under a health insurance contract and are received tax free. Death benefits received under the coverage are treated like death benefits received under group term life insurance.

For federal tax purposes, survivor income benefit insurance is considered to be a group term insurance coverage. Under Section 79, the amount of the benefit is considered to be the commuted value of benefit payments that would have been received by eligible survivors if the employee had died during the year. This amount normally is provided annually by the insurance company. A commuted value is also used for estate tax purposes. In all other respects, survivor income benefit insurance is treated the same as group term insurance.

Employer contributions for dependent life insurance coverage are fully deductible by the employer as an ordinary and necessary business expense if overall compensation of the employee is reasonable. Employer contributions do not result in taxable income to an employee as long as the value of the benefits is *de minimis*. This means that the value is so small that it is administratively impractical for the employer to account for the cost on a per-person basis. Dependent coverage of $2,000 or less on any person falls into this category. The IRS considers amounts of coverage in excess of $2,000 on any dependent to be more than *de minimis*. If more than $2,000 of coverage is provided for any dependent from employer contributions, the cost of the entire amount of coverage for that dependent (as determined by Uniform Premium Table 1 rates) will be considered taxable income to the employee. (Note: Dependent life insurance provided through a cafeteria plan is treated as cash and is fully taxable, regardless of the amount of coverage.) Death benefits will be free of income taxation and will not be included in the taxable estate of the dependent for estate tax purposes.

State Taxation

In most instances, state tax laws affecting group term insurance are similar to the federal laws. However, two major differences do exist: In most states, the payment of group term insurance premiums by the employer will not result in any taxable income to the employee, even if the amount of coverage exceeds $50,000. In addition, death proceeds receive favorable tax treatment under the estate and inheritance tax laws of most states. Generally, the death proceeds are partially, if not totally, exempt from such taxation.

STUDY QUESTIONS

1. Describe the following types of benefit schedules:
   a. Earnings schedules.
   b. Position schedules.
   c. Flat-benefit schedules.
   d. Length-of-service schedules.
2. What are the criteria that generally must be satisfied before an employee is eligible for group term insurance coverage?
3. a. Under what circumstances will the assignment of group life insurance coverage be valid?
   b. What requirements do insurance companies impose on assignments of group life insurance coverage?
4. The owner of the Midtown Garage decided to amend his group insurance contract to provide coverage for part-time employees. His agent said such a change presented no problem and wrote the owner a letter stating that the change had been made. Two weeks later, the agent called and informed the owner that the insurance company had refused to amend the contract. Can the insurance company overrule its agent? Explain.

5. Describe the methods for continuing coverage on retired or disabled employees.

6. Because of severe business difficulties, the Newtown Manufacturing Company permanently laid off 20 percent of its employees last March. All had been employed by the company for less than three years. In June, salaries and fringe benefits were reduced for the remaining employees. This included amending the company's group term insurance contract to eliminate all eligible classifications except those pertaining to four executives. Explain the extent, if any, to which the following groups of employees would have had the right to convert any coverage that was terminated under the plan:
   a. Employees who were laid off in March.
   b. Employees whose coverage was terminated in June.

7. How have insurance companies handled the problem of adverse selection associated with supplemental life insurance?

8. How may the amount of an accidental death benefit vary depending on when and how an employee dies?

9. How does dependent life insurance differ from group term insurance on employees with respect to
   a. Conversion privilege?
   b. Ability to assign benefits?
   c. Availability of a waiver-of-premium provision?

10. What requirements must be met in order for life insurance to qualify as group term insurance under Code Section 79?

11. a. Last year, Sarah Robbins, age 32, was provided with $75,000 of group term insurance by her employer for the entire year. Sarah is not a key employee, and the employer paid the entire premium. Assuming Sarah lives in a state with no limit on the amount of life insurance that can be provided to employees, calculate the amount of taxable income Sarah had because of this coverage.
    b. What if Sarah had contributed $3 per month for her coverage?

12. a. To what extent are group life insurance proceeds included in an employee's gross estate for federal estate tax purposes?
    b. What are the potential tax implications to an employee if an absolute assignment is used to remove life insurance proceeds from his or her estate?

7

Group Life Insurance: Lifetime Coverage

Objectives

- Describe the methods available to fund the continuation of group term insurance after retirement.
- Describe the characteristics of group paid-up and group ordinary insurance.
- Describe the characteristics of group univeral life insurance.
- Describe the tax treatment of group life insurance that provides coverage after retirement.

Group term insurance plans were traditionally designed to provide employees with preretirement life insurance coverage. At retirement, an employee was faced with the decision of whether to let coverage terminate or whether to convert to an individual policy at an extremely high premium rate. In recent years, however, an increasing number of group life insurance plans have been designed to provide postretirement, as well as preretirement, life insurance coverage. In some cases, this has been accomplished by continuing group term insurance coverage, often at a reduced amount, after retirement. In other cases, it has been done through life insurance that provides permanent (or cash value) benefits that have been funded during the working years of employees.

CONTINUATION OF GROUP TERM INSURANCE

The continuation of group term insurance on employees after retirement requires the employer to make two important decisions:

1. How much coverage should be continued?
2. What method should be used for paying the cost of the continued coverage?

Although the full amount of coverage prior to retirement may be continued, the high cost of group term insurance coverage for employees at older ages frequently results in a reduction in the amount of coverage. In some cases, employees are provided with a flat amount of coverage, such as $2,000 or $5,000; in other cases, employees are provided with a percentage, such as 50 percent, of the amount of coverage they had on the date of retirement.

Current Revenue Funding

Particularly among larger employers, the cost of providing postretirement life insurance is paid from current revenue, with each periodic premium paid to the insurance company based on the lives of all employees covered, both active and retired. Because retired employees have no salary or wages from which payroll deductions can be made, most postretirement life insurance coverage is noncontributory. The tax implications of providing postretirement group term insurance on a current-revenue basis are the same as those discussed in Chapter 6.

Retired Lives Reserves

In the late 1970s and early 1980s, increasing interest was shown in prefunding the cost of postretirement group term insurance coverage through retired lives reserve arrangements. Much of this interest stemmed from IRS regulations regarding Section 79 that made group paid-up and group ordinary products less attractive. The concept was not new; retired lives reserves, while not extensively used prior to that time, had been in existence for many years, primarily for very large employers. The trend in the 1970s was to establish them for smaller employers as well, since the tax laws allowed the plans to be designed so that they often provided significant benefits to the firm's owners or key employees. Because the Tax Reform Act of 1984 imposed more stringent requirements on retired lives reserves, there is no longer a great interest in establishing new plans. However, many plans are still in existence, and under certain circumstances, they remain a viable option for prefunding postretirement life insurance benefits.

A retired life reserve is best defined as a fund established during the working years of employees for the purpose of paying all or a part of the cost of group term insurance for employees after retirement. In some cases, the term has been used to describe a fund that is designed to pay the cost of coverage for active as well as retired employees. However, the term retired lives reserve, properly used, refers only to that portion of the fund applying to postretirement benefits. The fund may be established and maintained through a trust—either a tax-exempt Section 501(c)(9) trust or a nonexempt trust—or with an insurance company. If properly designed, a retired lives reserve (1) will enable an employer to make currently tax deductible contributions to the fund during the working years of employees and (2) will not result in any taxable income to employees before retirement.

Tax Deductibility of Employer Contributions

The contributions of an employer to a retired lives reserve are deductible for federal income tax purposes under Code Section 162 as long as certain conditions are met:

- The contributions must be an ordinary and necessary business expense.
- The balance in the reserve must be held solely for the purpose of providing life insurance coverage for currently retired employees or for active employees when they retire.
- The amount added annually to the reserve must be no greater than an amount that would be required to allocate, on an actuarially level basis, the unfunded cost of the postretirement life insurance coverage over the remaining working lives of the employees involved. There is no requirement that the entire permissible annual contribution be made. Any missed contributions may be made at a later date on an actuarially level basis only, and not in a lump sum.
- The employer must not have a right to recapture any portion of the assets in the reserve as long as any employees covered under the plan, whether active or retired, are still alive. The effect of this condition is of considerable significance and is often the reason that a retired lives reserve is not established. Even if a retired lives reserve plan is discontinued, assets must be used to provide the promised postretirement benefits to active and retired employees previously covered under the plan as long as such employees are living and the reserve has any assets.

Current deductions may be taken only for prefunding coverage that will be received tax free by retired employees under Section 79. This amount is generally $50,000, but may be higher for certain employees, subject to a grandfather clause. In addition, contributions on behalf of key employees cannot be deducted if the plan is discriminatory under Section 79.

Taxation to Employees

As long as an employee has no rights in a retired lives reserve except to receive postretirement group term insurance coverage until his or her death, Code Sections 83 and 162 provide that the employee will incur no income taxation as a result of either employer contributions to the reserve or investment earnings on the reserve.

Prior to the Tax Reform Act of 1984, the continuance of group term life insurance after retirement did not result in any income taxation to employees. As mentioned in Chapter 6, this is no longer the case. Except for certain persons subject to a grandfather clause, the Act now results in identical Section 79 treatment for both active and retired employees. Thus, retired employees will be taxed on the amount of coverage that exceeds $50,000 in each year for which postretirement coverage is provided.

In those instances where death benefits are paid directly from trust assets, the tax consequences to the employee are the same as if death benefits were provided through group term insurance contracts, except that death proceeds in excess of $5,000 will represent taxable income to the beneficiary.

Methods for Funding

A retired lives reserve may be established and maintained through either a tax-exempt Section 501(c)(9) trust, a nonexempt trust, or an insurance company reserve account.

Tax-Exempt Trust. A retired lives reserve that provides postretirement group term insurance may be funded through a tax-exempt Section 501(c)(9) trust described further in Chapter 14. This trust may either pay the premiums for group term insurance on retired employees or pay death benefits directly from trust assets. Because of its tax-exempt nature, investment earnings of the trust are not subject to federal income taxation.

In order for a trust to qualify for tax-exempt status under Code Section 501(c)(9), certain requirements must be met:

- Benefits must be offered to all members of one or more classes of employees on a basis that does not limit membership to shareholders or highly compensated employees.
- Coverage must be voluntary.
- The trust must be operated only for the purpose of providing for the payment of life, health or other benefits to employees or their dependents.
- No portion of the earnings of the trust may inure, other than by payment of benefits, to the benefit of any shareholder or other individual. Disproportionate benefits to highly compensated personnel and the return of contributions to an employer upon termination of the plan constitute inurement and will prevent a plan from qualifying.

It is generally felt that because of these restrictions—particularly the first and the fourth restrictions—a Section 501(c)(9) trust is better suited for larger corporations than for smaller, closely held corporations. In addition, an employee has no guarantee that the assets of the trust will be sufficient to either provide the annual premiums for group term insurance or pay death benefits.

The assets of the trust can also be used to provide paid-up insurance policies for each employee at retirement rather than to continue the group term coverage or to pay death benefits directly from the trust. However, the cost of such policies will not qualify for the income tax exemption of Section 79.

Nonexempt Trust. A nonexempt trust or taxable trust allows more flexibility than a Section 501(c)(9) trust as to which employees may be covered and the amount of insurance that may be provided for each employee. Consequently, it allows a small, closely held corporation to provide disproportionate benefits as well as to offer benefits to a more select group of employees. However, the plan of group insurance must satisfy Section 79 requirements if employees are to receive favorable income tax treatment for the benefits provided.

One disadvantage of a nonexempt trust is that investment earnings are taxable to the trust. Taxation can be avoided, however, if the assets of the trust are invested in tax-exempt securities. Moreover, taxation can be deferred until the date of surrender or until benefit payments begin if the assets are invested in cash value life insurance or annuity contracts. As with a Section 501(c)(9) trust, employees have no guarantee that the assets of the trust will be adequate to meet all future obligations.

Insurance Company Reserve Account. If a retired lives reserve is maintained with an insurance company, IRS regulations provide that any investment income credited to the reserve will not result in income taxation to the reserve, the employer, the employees or the insurance company.

A retired lives reserve maintained with an insurance company is usually established in conjunction with a preretirement group term insurance plan. It is then used to pay the cost of continued coverage, possibly at a different level, for employees after retirement. In the past, the typical approach has been to use a group term insurance contract with a deposit administration fund rider.[1] The deposit administration fund is the retired lives reserve. However, some newer retired lives reserve products use individual term insurance contracts with a separate retired lives reserve fund. Under either approach, the retired lives reserve is not allocated to any particular employee. Thus, if an employee terminates employment prior to retirement, any contributions made in anticipation of continuing his or her coverage remain in the fund and can be used to provide benefits to other employees who do remain until retirement. After an employee retires, funds are withdrawn from the reserve as needed to pay the cost of postretirement benefits provided by the term insurance contract. Neither the future group term insurance rates nor the sufficiency of the retired lives reserve to pay the cost of promised benefits have traditionally been guaranteed by insurance companies. This lack of guarantee has been particularly unattractive to smaller businesses. Consequently, many insurance companies have modified their retired lives reserve products to provide guaranteed rates in future years for the group term coverage.

Many retired lives reserve products are now designed so that an employee's future benefits can be guaranteed at retirement. Essentially, the retired lives reserve is divided into two accounts: an accumulation account and a retired life account. The accumulation account is not allocated to individual employees. However, at retirement, a lump-sum amount—as determined by insurance company rates—can be transferred to the retired life account. Once this transfer takes place, the funds are allocated to that particular employee and, with accruing interest, are used to pay the premium for the employee's coverage as needed. If the employee dies before the funds are depleted, any excess funds belong to the insurance company; if the funds are insufficient, the insurance company guarantees continued coverage without any additional premium payments.

The following illustration is typical of the retired lives reserve products offered by many insurance companies. As mentioned earlier, most of these products provide both preretirement and postretirement coverage.

---

[1]For further discussion of this concept, see the discussion of deposit administration contracts in Chapter 22.

Assumptions	
Amount of preretirement insurance:	$100,000
Amount of postretirement insurance:	$ 50,000
Current age of employee:	45
Retirement age of employee:	65
Sex of employee:	Male
Current assumed interest rate for retired lives reserve deposits:	9%
Minimum guaranteed interest rate for retired lives reserve deposits:	4%

Age	Annual Cost of $100,000 Term Insurance	Annual Retired Lives Reserve Deposit	Annual Total Employer Cost (before tax)	Accumulated Retired Lives Reserve Fund (end of year)
45	$ 468	$ 560	$ 1,028	$ 25
46	582	560	1,142	390
47	628	560	1,188	795
—	—	—	—	—
—	—	—	—	—
62	2,264	560	2,824	17,284
63	2,506	560	3,066	19,632
64	2,778	560	3,338	22,250
Total at age 65	$26,606	$11,200	$37,806	

This illustration is based on a target figure of $22,250 as the amount needed in the retired lives reserve to guarantee the postretirement insurance to an employee at age 65. Many insurance companies will guarantee that, upon the retirement of an employee, the amount that must be transferred from the accumulation account to the retired life account will not exceed the target figure. In fact, it may actually be lower at that time because of insurance company actuarial assumptions. In this example, the annual deposit of $560 to the retired lives reserve is based on a current assumed interest rate of 9 percent. Most insurers will only guarantee such rates for one year. Consequently, if interest rates drop in the future, increased retired lives reserve deposits will be necessary to reach the targeted accumulation. And conversely, rising interest rates will lower the annual deposit. The current interest rate, however, is subject to a minimum guarantee (only 4 percent in this case) below which the interest rate cannot fall.

Two other points are worthy of mention: First, even though the illustration is for a single employee, amounts in the accumulation account are not allocated to individual employees. If the employee in the illustration terminates employment, any amounts deposited in anticipation of his retirement will remain in the reserve and can be used to reduce the contributions otherwise necessary for employees who do remain until retirement. Second, the first-year accumulation of $25 in the retired lives reserve fund indicates a heavy front-end load in early years which, in turn, reflects administrative and acquisition charges, including the agent's commission.

In some cases, retired lives reserve products are sold to supplement existing group term insurance plans. While such products are occasionally sold to provide only postretirement coverage, additional preretirement coverage is usually also included. These products are often referred to as either superimposed (or supplemental) plans or wraparound plans. Under a superimposed plan (Figure 7-1A), the retired lives reserve only continues the preretirement coverage added by the retired lives reserve product. Under a wraparound plan (Figure 7-1B), an amount equal to both the existing and the added preretirement coverage is continued. However, the full amount of this continued coverage is provided under the retired lives reserve product.

FIGURE 7-1

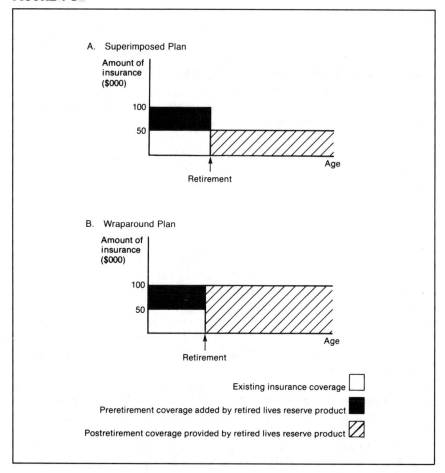

A group insurance plan may use a retired lives reserve to continue coverage after retirement for all employees or for only selected employees. However, the nondiscrimination rules and the provisions governing coverage of fewer than ten lives in Section 79 are applicable.

GROUP INSURANCE WITH PERMANENT BENEFITS

Group insurance offering permanent insurance coverage that will continue after retirement is available. While terminology may differ, the products used to provide this permanent protection after retirement generally have been placed in two categories:

1. Group paid-up insurance.
2. Group ordinary insurance.

(These coverages should be distinguished from group permanent insurance, the term normally used to describe cash value life insurance used to fund pension plans.) If properly designed, group insurance products that provide permanent life insurance coverage may qualify for favorable tax treatment under Section 79. Consequently, such products, particularly those providing group ordinary insurance, are frequently referred to as Section 79 products.

A new product that can be used to provide postretirement life insurance coverage—group universal life insurance—has recently come on the scene. This product is covered in the last section of the chapter.

Group Paid-Up

Although once a popular type of group insurance coverage, relatively few group paid-up insurance plans have been written in recent years. However, a number of such plans, generally those of large employers, still exist. (The trend is toward providing noncontributory coverage on a current revenue basis.) Under the typical group paid-up insurance plan, the total amount of insurance coverage is determined the same way as it is for group term insurance plans; for example, a schedule related to earnings or a flat amount. The amount of insurance consists of accumulating units of single-premium whole life insurance and decreasing amounts of group term insurance, with the total amount of coverage remaining constant.

The typical plan is contributory, with employee contributions used to purchase the increments of single-premium whole life insurance. The employer pays the cost of the group term insurance and the amount of the term coverage decreases as employee contributions are used to purchase additional units of whole life insurance. The amount of employee contributions normally is uniform for all employees, with a monthly contribution rate commonly ranging between $1 and $1.50 per $1,000 of insurance. These contributions are accumulated during each policy year and are used to purchase paid-up insurance on the anniversary date of the group insurance contract. Consequently, an employee is provided only with term insurance from the date of initial participation until the next anniversary date of the contract.

The following illustration is based on a monthly contribution of $1 per month for an employee entering a group paid-up plan at age 29.

Age	Annual Paid-Up Insurance Purchased by $1 Monthly Contribution	Accumulated Paid-Up Insurance Purchased by Employee's Contribution	Decreasing Amount of Term Insurance Paid by Employer	Total Amount of Life Insurance
29	$-0-	$-0-	$1,000.00	$1,000
30	44.10	44.10	955.90	1,000
31	43.20	87.30	912.70	1,000
32	41.88	129.18	870.82	1,000
—	—	—	—	—
—	—	—	—	—
63	18.96	948.48	51.52	1,000
64	18.60	967.08	32.92	1,000

If this employee retires on his or her 65th birthday, $967.08 of paid-up insurance can be continued in force with no further contributions required. Since the amount of paid-up insurance purchased by any employee is determined by the employee's attained age at the time a contribution is made, younger employees will accumulate more paid-up insurance for a given contribution than older employees. As a result, some plans provide for increased employee contributions for employees entering the plan at older ages.

While cash values accumulate under the policy, they are not available to employees during employment. At termination of employment, an employee may surrender the policy for its cash value or maintain the paid-up portion in force without further premiums. In addition, a terminating employee has the right to convert the term insurance coverage to an individual policy in the same manner as for regular group term insurance. However, this conversion privilege may be available only if the employee continues the paid-up coverage.

Group Ordinary

Because of the many variations, it is impossible to describe a typical group ordinary insurance product. However, it can be viewed essentially as dividing a whole life insurance policy into two segments: a term portion and a permanent or cash value portion. The total amount of coverage available to an employee is determined the same way it is in group term insurance. The cost of the term portion of the coverage is paid by the employer and the permanent portion, which the employee may be able to decline, generally is paid by the employee.

There is no typical group ordinary product. Rather, the terminology is used to describe any product (except group paid-up insurance) that provides cash value life insurance to a group of employees and that will qualify for favorable income tax treatment under Section 79.

Some group ordinary products are not actually group insurance contracts, but consist of single individual insurance policies for each employee, with premiums and coverage allocated between the term and permanent portions. Other group ordinary products consist of separate individual policies for each portion. Some group ordinary products actually are group term insurance policies with the permanent element added as a rider to the basic term coverage. Other group ordinary products use individual contracts for the permanent portion of coverage but use a single group contract for the term portion. Under these various forms, the product may be structured in one of several ways with respect to the allocation of premiums and coverage. These include:

- Decreasing term insurance with an increasing premium (to be paid by the employer) and increasing permanent insurance with a decreasing premium (probably to be paid by the employee). This will result in a level death benefit and a level total premium.
- Decreasing term insurance with a level premium and increasing permanent insurance with a level total premium. This will also result in a level death benefit and a level premium.
- Level term insurance with an increasing premium and increasing permanent insurance with a decreasing premium. This will result in a level total premium but in an increasing death benefit.

Upon termination of employment, an employee may surrender the policy for its cash value or continue coverage. If individual policies are used, the employee may continue paying the premium—whether or not this is already being done—to keep coverage in force. If group contracts are used, then the employee may convert coverage to an individual contract just like with group term insurance or group paid-up insurance.

Taxation

With the exception of the income tax liability of employees, group paid-up insurance and group ordinary insurance are treated in essentially the same manner as group term insurance, described in Chapter 6. Favorable tax treatment for the term portion of group insurance contracts that have permanent benefits (that is, cash value life insurance) has been available for many years to employees under Section 79, if certain requirements are satisfied. However, changes to Section 79 in 1979 reduced this favorable tax treatment and diminished the prior popularity of group insurance contracts providing permanent benefits. No favorable tax treatment is given to the premium for the permanent portion of coverage. If paid by an employer, the premiums for permanent coverage will be fully taxable to the employee as additional compensation.

The Section 79 regulations pertaining to group insurance with permanent benefits can be divided into three segments:

1. The general requirements that a policy having permanent benefits must satisfy in order to have a portion of the policy considered as group term life insurance for purposes of Section 79.

2. A mandatory actuarial procedure for determining the cost of the permanent benefits.
3. The provisions for the tax treatment of dividends.

General Requirements

The regulations define a *policy* as including two or more obligations of an insurer (or its affiliates) that are offered to a group of employees as a result of their employment relationship. The definition is broad enough to include a group of individual policies provided to a group of employees. In addition, term insurance benefits and permanent benefits provided under separate contracts can be considered a policy, even if one of the benefits is provided to employees who decline the other. The regulations also specify that a *permanent benefit* is an economic value extending beyond one policy year. This includes, for example, paid-up insurance or cash surrender values.

Before any part of a policy may be treated as group term life insurance, two requirements must be met:[2]

1. The policy or the employer must designate in writing the portion of each employee's death benefit that is considered group term insurance.
2. The portion of each employee's death benefit that is designated as group term insurance for any policy year must not be less than the difference between the total death benefit provided under the policy and the employee's *deemed death benefit* at the end of the policy year.[3]

If these requirements are met, the portion of the policy representing group term insurance will receive favorable income tax treatment under Section 79. When added to any other coverage that qualifies for Section 79 treatment, only the cost of the total term protection that exceeds $50,000 will represent taxable income to an employee. This cost is calculated by using Uniform Premium Table 1 rates (See page 115) and is reduced by the aggregate of any employee contributions for the entire term coverage but not for the permanent coverage.

The Cost of Permanent Benefits

The regulations also establish a mandatory allocation procedure for determining the cost of permanent benefits for an employee in a given policy year.[4] This cost

---

[2]In addition, plans covering fewer than ten lives and providing permanent protection must also satisfy the same requirement described in Chapter 6 for group term insurance plans covering fewer than ten lives.

[3]The deemed death benefit for a given policy year is defined as R/Y, where R = the net level premium reserve at the end of that policy year for all benefits provided to the employee by the policy or, if greater, the cash value of the policy at the end of that policy year; and Y = the net single premium for insurance (the premium for $1 of paid-up whole life insurance) at the employee's age at the end of that policy year. R and Y are based on the 1958 CSO Mortality Table and a 4 percent interest rate.

[4]The cost of permanent benefits for any employee is $X(DDB^2 - DDB^1)$, where DDB^2 = the employee's deemed death benefit at the end of the policy year; DDB^1 = the employee's deemed death benefit at the end of the preceding policy year; and X = the net single premium for insurance (the premium for $1 of paid-up whole life insurance) at the employee's attained age at the beginning of the policy year. X is based on the 1958 CSO Mortality Table and a 4 percent interest rate.

represents taxable income to the employee to the extent it is paid by the employer. The cost as determined by this formula is independent of the annual premium for permanent benefits actually specified in the policy. For example, if an employee were required to pay the cost of permanent benefits and this cost is specified in the policy as $300, the employee will have taxable income to the extent the mandatory allocation procedure yields a cost in excess of $300.

The effect of the mandatory allocation procedure often has been to increase the amount of premium attributable to permanent benefits. This has resulted in employees either having to pay a larger contribution for permanent benefits or having a larger portion of employer contributions treated as taxable income. In either case, the attractiveness of group products with permanent benefits has been diminished.

Treatment of Dividends

If the employer pays the entire cost of the permanent benefits, any dividends that are actually or constructively received by the employee must be included in the employee's income for federal income tax purposes. In all other cases, the amount of dividends included in an employee's taxable income is determined by a formula specified in the regulations.[5] The effect of this formula is that any dividend will result in currently taxable income unless the employee has paid more than the aggregate costs from the inception of coverage for the permanent protection, as determined by the mandatory allocation formula.

GROUP UNIVERSAL LIFE INSURANCE[6]

Beginning in the mid-1980s, many large writers of group insurance started to sell group universal life insurance, a trend that has been warmly greeted by insurers, employers and even employees. This enthusiasm seems to stem primarily from the following five factors:

1. The phenomenal success of universal life in the individual marketplace. Introduced in the 1970s, universal life insurance now accounts for about 25 percent of newly written individual life insurance premiums.
2. Tax legislation that made employer-provided term life insurance in excess of $50,000 taxable after retirement.

---

[5]The amount included in an employee's income is $(D + C) - (PI + DI + AP)$, where D = the total amount of dividends actually or constructively received under the policy by the employee in the current and all preceding tax years of the employee; C = the total cost of the permanent benefits for the current and all preceding tax years of the employee (determined under the formula in footnote 4); PI = the total amount of premium included in the employee's income under the formulas for the current and all preceding tax years of the employee; DI = the total amount of dividends included in the employee's income under this dividend formula in all preceding tax years of the employee; and AP = the total amount paid for permanent benefits by the employee in the current and all preceding taxable years of the employee.

[6]This material is based on "Group Universal Life Insurance as an Employee Benefit" by Burton T. Beam, Jr. and Edward E. Graves, which appeared in *Benefits Quarterly 11*, No. 3 (Third Quarter 1986).

3. The clarification of the tax treatment of universal life insurance. For the first few years after the introduction of universal life insurance, there was concern that the IRS would not grant it the same favorable tax treatment that was granted to traditional cash-value life insurance policies. There was speculation that the interest paid on the cash value might become subject to taxation and also that the death benefit would be considered taxable income to the beneficiary. For the most part, these fears have been laid to rest by tax legislation as long as a universal life insurance policy meets certain prescribed guidelines. Therefore, the cash value of a universal life insurance policy accumulates tax free, and death benefits are free of income taxation.

4. The interest of employers in containing employee benefit costs. Little needs to be said about the attempts of employers to minimize the costs of their employee benefit plans. Group universal life insurance plans can make life insurance available to employees with little cost to the employer.

5. Less favorable tax treatment for two popular products for prefunding postretirement life insurance—Section 79 plans and retired lives reserves.

Group universal life insurance products are being marketed primarily as supplemental life insurance plans—either to replace existing supplemental group term life insurance plans or as additional supplemental plans. Some insurers are selling them as a way of providing the basic life insurance plan of the employee as well. Marketing efforts are touting group universal life insurance as having the following advantages to the employer:

- No direct costs other than those associated with payroll deductions and possibly enrollment since the entire premium cost is borne by the employee. In this sense group universal life insurance plans are much like mass-marketed insurance plans (described in Chapter 13).
- No ERISA filing and reporting requirements as long as the master contract is issued to a trust and as long as there are no employer contributions for the cost of coverage. The current products are marketed through multiple-employer trusts with the trust being the policyholder.
- The ability of employees to continue coverage into retirement, alleviating pressure for the employer to provide postretirement life insurance benefits.

The following advantages are being claimed for employees:

- The availability of a popular life insurance product at group rates.
- The opportunity to continue insurance coverage after retirement, possibly without any postretirement contributions.
- Flexibility in designing coverage to best meet the needs of the individual employee.

The current plans being marketed are still evolving, and differences do exist among the plans being offered by competing insurance companies. Because of the flexibility given to policyholders, the administrative aspects of a group universal plan are formidable, and most insurers originally designed their plans only for employers with a large number of employees, usually at least 1,000. However, most insurers that write the product now make it available for as few as 100 employees. There seems to be cautious optimism among insurance companies that group universal life insurance will become a popular and successful product even though early growth has been modest and several insurers have achieved sales below their expectations.

Skeptics, including employees of some insurance companies offering group universal life, wonder if the administrative aspects can be accomplished in such a manner that it can be offered at a cost that is significantly lower than coverage in the individual marketplace. In raising this question, they point out the administrative problems and costs that have arisen when universal life insurance has been included in mass-marketed individual insurance plans, as well as the highly competitive market for individual universal life insurance that has resulted in rates with extremely low margins for contributions to surplus. These drawbacks, coupled with the lack of employer contributions, make the potential for savings to employees through the group insurance approach less than for many other types of insurance. Other critics point out that the popularity of universal life insurance in general has decreased as interest rates have dropped over the last few years, and they wonder how successful universal life will be if interest rates drop further. However, the initial plans that have been installed have been well received by employees, and participation has generally met or exceeded expectations.

General Nature

Group universal life insurance is a flexible premium policy that, unlike traditional cash value life insurance, divides the pure insurance protection and the cash value accumulation into separate and distinct components. The employee is required to pay a specified initial premium. A charge is subtracted from this premium for one month's mortality. This mortality charge is used to purchase the required amount of pure or term insurance (often referred to as the amount at risk) at a cost that is a function of the insured's current age. Under some policies, an additional deduction is made for expenses. The balance of the initial premium becomes the initial cash value of the policy. This initial cash value, when credited with interest, becomes the cash value at the end of the period. The process continues in succeeding periods. New premiums are added to the cash value, charges are made for expenses and mortality and interest is credited to the remaining cash value. Employees receive periodic disclosure statements showing all charges made for the period as well as any interest earnings.

Group universal life insurance offers an employee considerable flexibility to meet several life-cycle financial needs with a single type of insurance coverage. The death benefit can be increased because of marriage, the birth of a child or an increase in income. The death benefit can be reduced later when the need for life insurance decreases. Cash withdrawals can be made for the down payment on a home or to pay college tuition. Premium payments can be reduced during those periods when a young family has pressing financial needs. As financial circumstances improve, premiums can be increased so that an adequate retirement fund can be accumulated. The usual settlement options found in traditional cash-value life insurance are available, so an employee can elect to periodically liquidate the cash accumulation as a source of retirement income.

Types of Group Universal Products

Two approaches have been used in designing group universal life insurance products. Under the first approach, there is a single group universal life insurance plan. An employee who wants only term insurance can pay a premium equal to the mortality and expense charges so that there is no accumulation of cash values. Naturally, an employee who wants to accumulate cash values must pay a larger premium.

Under the second approach, there are actually two group insurance plans—a term insurance plan and a universal life insurance plan. An employee who wants only term insurance contributes to the term insurance plan, and an employee who wants only universal life insurance contributes to the universal life insurance plan. With this approach, an employee purchasing universal life insurance must make premium payments that are sufficient to generate a cash value accumulation. Initially, the employee may be required to make minimum premium payments, such as two or three times the cost of the pure insurance. If an employee who has only the term insurance coverage later wants to switch to universal life insurance coverage, the group term insurance certificate is cancelled, and the employee is issued a new certificate under the universal life insurance plan. An employee can also withdraw his or her cash accumulation under the universal life insurance plan and switch to the term insurance plan. It is also possible for an employee to have coverage under both plans. Typically, an employee is eligible to purchase a maximum aggregate amount of coverage under the two plans. For example, if the maximum is three times the employee's annual salary, the employee could purchase term insurance equal to two times salary and universal life insurance that has a pure insurance amount equal to one times salary.

Underwriting

Insurance companies that write group universal life insurance have underwriting standards concerning group size, the amounts of coverage available and insurability.

Currently, most group universal life insurance products are being limited primarily to employers who have at least 100 or 200 employees. However, a few insurers write coverage for even smaller groups. Some insurance companies also have an employee percentage participation requirement, such as 20 or 25 percent, that must be satisfied before a group can be installed. Other insurance companies feel their marketing approach is designed so that adequate participation will result and, therefore, they have no participation requirements.

Employees can generally elect amounts of pure insurance equal to varying multiples of their salaries. These multiples typically start at one-half or one and range as high as three or five. There may be a minimum amount of coverage that must be purchased, such as $10,000. The maximum multiple an insurance company will offer is influenced by factors such as the size of the group, the amount of insurance provided under the employer's basic employer-pay-all group term insurance plan and the percentage of participation in the plan. In general, the rules regarding amounts of coverage are the same as those that have been traditionally applied to supplemental group term life insurance plans. The initial premium, which is a function of the employee's age and death benefit, is frequently designed to accumulate a cash value at age 65 equal to approximately 20 percent of the total death benefit.

Other approaches for determining the death benefit may be used, depending on insurance company practices and employer desires. Under some plans, employees may elect specific amounts of insurance, such as $25,000, $50,000 or $100,000. Again, an employee's age and the death benefit selected determine the premium. Some plans allow an employee to select the premium he or she wants to pay. The amount of the premium and the employee's age then automatically determine the amount of the death benefit.

The extent to which evidence of insurability is required of individual employees is also similar to that found under most supplemental group term life insurance plans. When an employee is initially eligible, coverage is usually issued on a guaranteed basis up to specified limits, which again are influenced by the size of the group, the amount of coverage provided under the employer's basic group term insurance plan, and the degree of participation in the plan. If an employee chooses a larger death benefit, simplified underwriting is used up to a second amount, after which regular underwriting is used. Guaranteed issue is often unavailable for small groups; hence, underwriting on the basis of a simplified questionnaire is used up to a specific amount of death benefit, after which regular underwriting is used.

With some exceptions, future increases in the amount of pure insurance are subject to evidence of insurability. These exceptions include additional amounts resulting from salary increases as long as the total amount of coverage remains within the guaranteed issue limit. Some insurance companies also allow additional purchases without evidence of insurability when certain events occur, such as marriage or the birth of a child.

The Death Benefit

The policyholder under an individual group universal life insurance policy typically has a choice of two death benefit options. Option A provides a level death benefit in the early policy years. As the cash value increases, the amount of pure insurance decreases so that the total amount paid to a beneficiary upon the insured's death remains constant. Without any provision to the contrary, the cash value would eventually approach the amount of the total death benefit. To prevent this from occurring, and also to keep the policy from failing to qualify as a life insurance policy under existing tax regulations, it is provided that the amount of pure insurance will not decrease further once the cash value reaches a predetermined level. Thereafter, the total death benefit will increase unless the cash value decreases. Figure 7-2 graphically demonstrates option A.

FIGURE 7-2

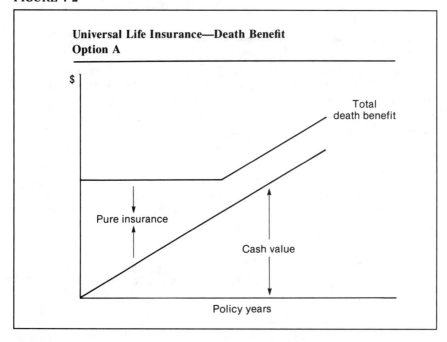

Universal Life Insurance—Death Benefit Option A

FIGURE 7-3

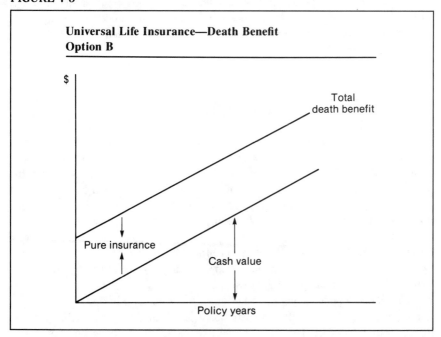

Universal Life Insurance—Death Benefit Option B

Under option B, the amount of pure insurance is constant, and the death benefit increases each period by the change in the policy cash value. This is shown graphically in Figure 7-3.

Under group universal life insurance products, an employee usually has only one death benefit option available, and whether it is option A or option B depends on which one has been selected by the employer. In general, there seems to be a feeling that the availability of both options makes a plan more difficult to explain to employees and more costly to administer. Most employers have selected option B because it is generally felt that it can be marketed more easily to employees since the increasing total death benefit is a visible sign of any increase in their cash value or "investment." As a result, several insurers now make only option B available with their group products.

Universal life insurance products give the insured the right to increase or decrease the death benefit from the level originally selected as circumstances change. For example, the policyholder might have initially selected a pure death benefit of $100,000 under option B. Because of the birth of a child, this might be increased to $150,000. Increases, but not decreases, generally require that the insured provide evidence of insurability.

Mortality Charges

Most products have a guaranteed mortality charge for three years. After that time, the mortality charge will be based on the experience of each particular group. As with experience rating in general, the credibility given to a group's actual experience will be greater for larger groups. Most insurance companies guarantee that any future increases in the mortality charge will not exceed a stated maximum.

The products designed for small groups typically use pooled rates that apply to all groups insured through a particular trust. Therefore, the mortality charge for any employer will vary not with the employer's overall experience, but rather with the overall experience of the trust.

Expense Charges

Probably, the most variations that exist among group universal life insurance products occur in the expense charges that are levied. Typically, a percentage of each premium, such as 2 percent, is deducted for expenses. In addition, there is a flat monthly charge, normally ranging from $1 to $3, to maintain the accumulation account. Some insurance companies levy this charge against all certificate holders, even those who are contributing only enough to have the pure insurance coverage. Other insurance companies levy the charge only against those accounts that have a positive cash-value accumulation. A few insurance companies also load their mortality charges for expenses. Finally, many companies levy a transaction charge, such as $25, that often applies to withdrawals in early policy years. A transaction charge may also apply to policy loans and additional lump-sum contributions. In evaluating the expense charges of different insurers, it is important to remember that an insurer with a lower than average charge may be subtly compensating for this by having a higher mortality charge or crediting a lower interest rate to cash-value accumulations than otherwise would be paid.

Interest Rates

Most insurance companies guarantee that the initial interest rate credited to cash-value accumulations will be in effect for one year. After that time, the rate is typically adjusted quarterly or semiannually, but cannot go below some contractual minimum such as 4 or 4.5 percent. The interest rate credited is usually determined on a discretionary basis but is influenced by the insurance company's investment income and competitive factors. However, some insurers provide that it will be linked to some money market instrument, such as three-month Treasury bills. In general, the same interest is credited to all groups that an insurance company has underwritten.

Several insurance companies are exploring the possibility of establishing separate accounts for group universal life insurance accumulations and allowing individual employees to direct the types of assets in which their accumulations are invested. Such a change will give employees much of the investment flexibility that is currently available under many 401(k) plans.

Premium Adjustments

Employees are allowed considerable flexibility in the amount and timing of premium payments. Premiums can be raised or lowered and even suspended. In the latter case the contract will terminate if an employee's cash-value accumulation is inadequate to pay current mortality and expense charges. Of course, premium payments could be reinstated to prevent this from happening. Additional lump-sum contributions may also be made to the accumulation account.

Two restrictions are placed on premium adjustments. First, the premium payment cannot be such that the size of the cash-value accumulation becomes so large in relationship to the pure protection that an employee's coverage fails to qualify as a policy of insurance under IRS regulations. Second, changes in premium payments through payroll deductions are costly for employers to administer. Therefore, many employers limit the frequency with which adjustments are allowed.

Loans and Withdrawals

Employees are allowed to make loans and withdrawals from their accumulated cash values, but the frequency of loans and withdrawals may be limited for administrative reasons. There are also minimum loan and withdrawal amounts, such as $250 or $500. In addition, an employee is usually required to leave a minimum balance in the cash-value account sufficient to pay mortality and expenses charges for some time period, possibly as long as one year. If an option A death benefit is in effect, the amount of the pure insurance is increased by the amount of the loan or withdrawal so that the total death benefit remains the same. With an option B death benefit, the amount of the total death benefit is decreased.

The interest rate charged on policy loans is usually pegged to some index, such as Moody's composite bond yield. In addition, the interest rate credited to an amount of the cash value equal to the policy loan is reduced. This reduced interest rate may be the guaranteed policy minimum or may also be based on some index, such as 2 percent less than Moody's composite bond yield.

An employee can withdraw his or her entire cash value accumulation and terminate coverage. Total withdrawals are subject to a surrender charge during early policy years. The charge decreases with policy duration and usually is in addition to any transaction charge that might also be levied.

Dependent Coverage

Most products allow an employee to purchase a rider that provides term insurance coverage on his or her spouse and children. For example, one insurance company allows an employee to elect spousal coverage of $10,000 to $50,000 in $10,000 increments and coverage on children in the amount of either $5,000 or $10,000. Other insurers make varying amounts available.

Some insurance companies allow separate universal life insurance coverage to be elected, but usually only for the spouse. In such cases, the coverage is provided under a separate group insurance certificate rather than a rider.

Accidental Death and Waiver of Premium

A group universal life insurance plan may provide accidental death benefits and a disability waiver of premium. These benefits are not optional for each employee; rather, they are part of the coverage only if the employer has elected to include them in the plan. When a waiver of premium is included, all that is waived in case of disability is the portion of the premium necessary to pay the cost of the pure insurance protection for the employee and any dependents.

Employee Options at Retirement and Termination

Several situations may arise in which an employee is no longer actively working. In addition, a group universal plan might be terminated by the employer.

Several options are available to the retiring employee. First, the employee can continue the group insurance coverage in the same manner as an active employee. However, if premium payments are continued, the employee will be billed by the insurance company, probably on a quarterly basis. Because of the direct billing, the employee may also be subject to a higher monthly expense charge. Second, the employee can terminate the coverage and completely withdraw his or her accumulated cash value. Third, the employee can elect one of the settlement options under the policy for the liquidation of the cash value in the form of annuity income. Finally, some insurers allow the retiring employee to decrease the amount of pure insurance enough so that the cash value will be adequate to keep the policy in force without any more premium payments. In effect, the employee then has a paid-up policy.

The same options are generally available to an employee who terminates employment prior to retirement. In contrast to most other types of group insurance arrangements, the continuation of coverage does not involve a conversion and the accompanying conversion charge. Rather, the employee usually remains in the same group. This ability to continue group coverage after termination of employment is commonly referred to as *portability*. If former employees who continue coverage have higher mortality rates, this will be reflected in the mortality charge for the entire group. However, at least one insurer places terminated employees into a separate group consisting of terminated employees from all plans. These persons will be subject to a mortality charge based solely on the experience of this group. Thus, any higher mortality due to adverse selection will not be shared by the actively working employees.

If the employer terminates the group insurance arrangement, some insurance companies keep the group in force on a direct bill basis, even if the coverage has been replaced with another insurer. Other insurance companies only continue the group coverage if the employer has not replaced the plan. If replacement occurs, the insurance company terminates the pure insurance amount and either gives the cash value to participants or transfers it to the trustee of the new plan.

Enrollment and Administration

Variations exist in the method by which employees are enrolled in group universal life insurance plans. Some early plans used agents who were compensated in the form of commissions or fees, but several insurance companies have dropped this practice. The actual enrollment typically is done by the employer with materials provided by the insurance company. However, salaried or commissioned representatives of the insurer usually meet with the employees in group meetings to explain the plan.

The main administrative function of the employer is to process the payroll deductions associated with a plan. As previously mentioned, employee flexibility may be somewhat limited to minimize the costs of numerous changes in payroll deductions.

Other administrative functions are performed by the insurance company or a third-party administrator. These functions include providing employees with annual statements about their transactions and cash-value accumulation under the plan. Toll-free telephone lines are often maintained to provide information and advice to employees.

Taxation

Group universal life insurance products are not designed to be policies of insurance under Section 79. In addition, each employee pays the full cost of his or her coverage. Therefore, the tax treatment is the same to employees as if they had purchased a universal life policy in the individual insurance marketplace.

STUDY QUESTIONS

1. Why is postretirement life insurance coverage usually noncontributory?
2. Identify the methods by which a retired lives reserve may be funded and explain any advantages and disadvantages of each method of funding.
3. Compare group paid-up life insurance and group ordinary life insurance with respect to
   a. The provisions for continuing coverage after retirement.
   b. Employee contributions.
4. a. In certain cases, Section 79 provides favorable tax treatment to a policy having permanent benefits. Explain what is meant by (1) a policy and (2) permanent benefits.
   b. Explain the requirements that must be satisfied before a policy providing permanent benefits will qualify for favorable tax treatment under Section 79.
5. What circumstances have sparked the current interest in group universal life insurance?
6. What are the advantages of group universal life insurance for (a) the employer and (b) employees?
7. What underwriting requirements are often found in group universal life insurance products with respect to
   a. Group size?
   b. Amounts of coverage available?
   c. Insurability?
8. Briefly describe the typical group universal life insurance product with respect to
   a. Guarantees of mortality charges.
   b. Types of expense charges.
   c. Interest rates credited.
   d. Premium flexibility.
   e. Loans and withdrawals.
   f. Dependent coverage.
   g. Waiver of premiums for accidental death.
9. What options are available under group universal life insurance plans to employees who retire or terminate employment?
10. Why is group universal life insurance not treated as group term life insurance for tax purposes?

8

Group Disability Income Coverage

Objectives

- Describe the characteristics of salary continuation plans.
- Describe the characteristics of short-term group disability income insurance.
- Describe the characteristics of long-term group disability income insurance.
- Explain the tax implications of group disability income premiums and benefits for both the employer and the employees.

The purpose of disability income coverage is to partially, and sometimes totally, replace the income of employees who are unable to work because of sickness or accident. While missing a few days of work may occur from time to time, there is often a tendency to underestimate both the frequency and severity of disabilities that last for longer periods of time. At all working ages, the probability of being disabled for at least 90 consecutive days is much greater than the chance of dying. One out of every three employees will have a disability that lasts at least 90 days during his or her working years, and one out of every ten employees can expect to be permanently disabled prior to age 65.

In terms of its financial impact on the family, permanent disability is more severe than death. In both cases, income ceases. In the case of permanent disability, however, family expenses—instead of decreasing because of one less family member—may actually increase because of the cost of providing care for the disabled person.

Employers are less likely to provide employees with disability income benefits than either life insurance or medical expense benefits. It is difficult to estimate the exact extent of disability income coverage because benefits often are not insured and workers are sometimes covered under overlapping plans. A reasonable consensus would be that no more than two-thirds of all employees have some form of short-term employer-provided protection, and only about one-third have protection for long-term disabilities. This does not mean that almost all employees have some sort of disability income coverage, because many employees have both short-term and long-term protection and thus are included in both estimates. In addition, these estimates are also somewhat misleading because most employees have long-term disability coverage under social security as well as coverage for certain types of disabilities under other governmental programs.

Group disability income protection consists of two distinct types of coverage:

1. Short-term coverage provides benefits for a limited period of time, usually six months or less. Benefits may be provided under uninsured salary continuation plans or under insured plans, often referred to as accident and sickness insurance or weekly indemnity benefits.
2. Long-term coverage provides extended benefits (possibly for life) after an employee has been disabled for a period of time, usually six months. This is typically provided on an insured basis.

Two important tasks in designing and underwriting insured group disability income plans are to coordinate them with each other where both a short-term and a long-term plan are provided for employees, and to coordinate them with other benefits to which employees might be entitled under social insurance programs or uninsured salary continuation plans. A lack of coordination can lead to such a generous level of benefits for employees that absences from work because of disability might be either falsified or unnecessarily prolonged.

SALARY CONTINUATION (SICK LEAVE) PLANS

Salary continuation plans, often called sick-leave plans, are uninsured and generally fully replace lost income for a limited time starting on the first day of disability. In contrast, short-term disability income insurance plans, which are covered in the next section of this chapter, usually provide benefits that replace only a portion of an employee's lost income and often contain a waiting period before benefits start, particularly for sickness.

Traditionally, many salary continuation plans were informal with the availability, amount and duration of benefits for an employee being discretionary on the part of the employer. Some plans used by small firms or for a limited number of executives still operate in this manner. However, the vast majority of salary continuation plans are now formalized and have written rules concerning eligibility and benefits.

Eligibility

Almost all salary continuation plans are limited to permanent full-time employees, but benefits may also be provided for permanent part-time employees. Most plans also require an employee to satisfy a short probationary period—one to three months being common—before being eligible for benefits. Salary continuation plans may also be limited to certain classes of employees, such as top management or nonunion employees. The latter is common when union employees are covered under a collectively bargained, but insured, plan.

Benefits

Most salary continuation plans are designed to provide benefits equal to 100 percent of an employee's regular pay. Some plans, however, provide a reduced level of benefits after an initial period of full pay.

Several approaches are used in determining the duration of benefits. The most traditional approach credits eligible employees with a certain amount of sick leave each year, such as ten days. The majority of plans using this approach allow employees to accumulate sick leave up to some maximum amount, which rarely exceeds six months, sometimes specified as 130 days or 26 weeks. A variation of this approach is to credit employees with an amount of sick leave, such as one day, for each month of service. Here is an example of a benefit schedule using this variation:

Length of Service	Amount of Sick Leave*
Less than 3 months of service	None
3 or more months of service	1 day at full pay for each month of service (retroactive to date of employment)

*Maximum unused sick leave: 130 days

Another approach, as shown below, bases the duration of benefits on an employee's length of service:

Length of Service	Maximum Days of Sick Leave per Year
Less than 3 months	0
3 months to 1 year	5
2 years	10
3 years	15
5 years	20
7 years	25
10 years	30

An alternative to this approach provides benefits for a uniform duration of time to all employees, except possibly those with short periods of service. However, benefits are reduced to a level less than full pay after some period of time that is related to an employee's length of service. Here is an illustration of this increasingly common approach.

Length of Service	Weeks of Sick Leave per Disability		
	100% of Pay	50% of Pay	Total Weeks
Less than 6 months	0	0	0
6 months to 1 year	2	0	2
1 year	4	22	26
2 years	8	18	26
3 years	12	14	26
4 years	16	10	26
5 years	20	6	26
6 years or more	26	0	26

In some instances, an employee is not eligible for salary continuation benefits if he or she is eligible for benefits under social insurance plans, such as workers' compensation. However, most salary continuation plans are coordinated with social insurance programs. For example, if an employee is entitled to 100 percent of pay and receives 60 percent of pay as a workers' compensation benefit, the salary continuation plan will pay the remaining 40 percent.

A problem for the employer is how to verify an employee's disability. In general, the employee's word is accepted for disabilities that last a week or less. Under most salary continuation plans, there is a provision that benefits for longer periods will be paid only if the employee is under the care of a physician, and the physician certifies that the employee is unable to work.

INSURED DISABILITY INCOME PLANS

As mentioned, insured disability income plans consist of two distinct products: short-term coverage and long-term coverage. Approximately twice as many employees have group short-term coverage than have group long-term coverage. However, over the last few years, the number of employees with insured benefits for short-term disability has remained almost constant, while the number of employees with insured benefits for group long-term disability has more than doubled.

In many respects, the contractual provisions of both short-term and long-term disability income contracts are the same or very similar. In other respects—notably, the eligibility requirements, the definition of disability and the amount and duration of benefits—there are significant differences.

Eligibility

The eligibility requirements contained in group disability income insurance contracts are similar to those found in group term insurance contracts. In addition to being in a covered classification, an employee must usually work full time and be actively at work before coverage will commence. Any requirements concerning probationary periods, insurability and premium contributions must also be satisfied.

Short-term and long-term disability income insurance plans frequently differ in both the classes of employees eligible for coverage and the length of the probationary period. Employers are more likely to provide short-term benefits to a wider range of employees, and it is not unusual for short-term plans to cover all full-time employees. However, these plans may be the result of collective bargaining and apply only to union employees. In this situation, other employees frequently have short-term disability benefits under uninsured salary continuation plans.

Long-term disability plans often limit benefits to salaried employees. Claims experience has traditionally been less favorable for hourly paid employees for several reasons: Claims of hourly paid employees tend to be more frequent, particularly in recessionary times, when the possibility of temporary layoffs or terminations increases. Such claims also tend to be of longer duration, possibly because these employees may hold repetitive and nonchallenging jobs. Some long-term plans also exclude employees below a certain salary level since this category of employees, like hourly paid employees, is considered to have a reasonable level of benefits under social security.

Long-term disability income plans tend to have longer probationary periods than short-term disability income plans. While the majority of short-term disability plans (as well as group term insurance plans and medical expense plans) either have no probationary period or have a probationary period of three months or less, it is common for long-term disability plans to have probationary periods ranging from three months to one year. While short-term plans only require that an employee be actively at work on the date he or she is otherwise eligible for coverage, long-term plans sometimes require that the employee be on the job for an extended period, such as 30 days, without illness or injury before coverage will become effective.

Definition of Disability

Benefits are paid under disability income insurance contracts only if the employee meets the definition of disability as specified in the contract. Virtually all short-term disability income insurance contracts define disability as *the total and continuous inability of the employee to perform any and every duty of his or her regular occupation.* A small minority of contracts use a more restrictive definition, requiring that an employee be unable to engage in any occupation for compensation. Partial disabilities are not covered. In addition, the majority of short-term contracts limit coverage to nonoccupational disabilities, because employees have workers' compensation benefits for occupational disabilities. This limitation tends to be most common when benefits under the short-term contract are comparable to or lesser in amount than those under the workers' compensation law. In those cases where workers' compensation benefits are relatively low and the employer desires to provide additional benefits, coverage may be written under the short-term contract for both occupational and nonoccupational disabilities, with an offset for any workers' compensation benefits payable.

A few long-term disability income contracts use the same liberal definition of disability commonly used in short-term contracts. However, the term *each and every duty* is often replaced by *material duties.* A few other contracts define disability as *the total and continuous inability of the employee to engage in any and every gainful occupation for which he or she is qualified or shall reasonably become qualified by reason of training, education or experience.* However, the majority of long-term disability contracts use a dual definition that combines these definitions. Under a dual definition, benefits will be paid for some period of time, usually 24 or 36 months, as long as an employee is unable to perform his or her regular occupation. After that time, benefits will only be paid if the employee is unable to engage in any occupation for which he or she is qualified by reason of training, education or experience. The purpose of this combined definition is to require and encourage a disabled employee, if that employee becomes able after a period of time, to readjust his or her lifestyle and earn a livelihood in another occupation.

A more recent definition of disability found in some long-term contracts contains an occupation test and an earnings test. Under the occupation test, a person is totally disabled if he or she meets the definition of disability as described in the previous paragraph. However, if the occupation test is not satisfied, a person will still be considered totally disabled as long as an earnings test is satisfied. This means that the person's income has dropped by a stated percentage, such as 50 percent, because of injury or sickness. This newer definition makes a group insurance contract similar to an individual disability income policy that provides residual benefits.

The definition of disability in long-term contracts may differ from that found in short-term contracts in two other respects. Long-term contracts occasionally provide benefits for partial disabilities in a manner similar to workers' compensation insurance. However, both the amount and duration of such benefits may be limited when compared with those for total disabilities, and the receipt of benefits is usually contingent upon a prior period of total disability. In addition, most long-term contracts provide coverage for both occupational and nonoccupational disabilities.

Exclusions

Under certain circumstances, disability income benefits will not be paid even when an employee satisfies the definition of disability. Common exclusions under both short-term and long-term disability income contracts specify that no benefits will be paid:

- For any period during which the employee is not under the care of a physician.
- For any disability caused by an intentionally self-inflicted injury.
- Unless the period of disability commenced while the employee was covered under the contract. For example, an employee who previously elected not to participate under a contributory plan cannot obtain coverage for an existing disability by deciding to pay the required premium.
- If the employee is engaged in any occupation for remuneration. This exclusion applies in those situations when an employee is totally disabled with respect to his or her regular job but is engaged in other employment that can be performed despite the employee's condition.

Until the 1978 amendment to the Civil Rights Act, it was common for disabilities as a result of pregnancy to be excluded. Such an exclusion is now illegal under federal law if an employer has 15 or more employees. Employers with fewer than

15 employees may still exclude pregnancy disabilities unless they are subject to state laws to the contrary.

Additional exclusions are often found in long-term contracts. These commonly deny benefits for disabilities resulting from:

- War, whether declared or undeclared.
- Participation in an assault or felony.
- Mental disease, alcoholism or drug addiction. However, some contracts provide benefits if an employee is confined in a hospital or institution specializing in the care and treatment of such disorders; other contracts provide benefits but limit their duration, such as for 24 months.
- Pre-existing conditions.

The exclusion for pre-existing conditions is designed to counter adverse selection and potentially large claims that could occur if an employer established a group disability income plan or if an employee elected to participate in the plan because of some known condition that is likely to result in disability. Although variations exist, a common provision for pre-existing conditions excludes coverage for any disability that commences during the first 12 months an employee is covered under the contract if the employee received treatment or medical advice for the disabling condition both (1) prior to the date the employee became eligible for coverage and (2) within 90 consecutive days prior to the commencement of the disability.

When coverage is transferred from one insurance company to another, it is not unusual, particularly in the case of large employers, for the new insurance company to waive the limitation for pre-existing conditions for those employees who were insured under the previous contract. In some instances, the provision is modified so that benefits are limited to those that would have been provided under the previous contract, possibly for a specified duration, such as one year.

Benefits

A discussion of the benefits under disability income contracts is more complex than a discussion of the benefits under group life insurance contracts. A similarity exists in that there are benefit schedules that classify employees and specify the amount of disability income that will be provided. However, the relationship between an employee's earnings and the employee's potential benefits is more important in disability income insurance than group life insurance. In addition, disability benefits are subject to several provisions not found in group life insurance contracts. These pertain to the length of time benefits will be paid and the coordination of benefits with other types of disability income.

Benefit Schedules

As in group life insurance, there are a variety of benefit schedules found in group disability income contracts. Benefits may be available to all employees or limited to specific groups of employees. In addition, benefits may be expressed as either flat-dollar amounts, varying dollar amounts by classification or a percentage of earnings.

A major difficulty in disability insurance is determining the appropriate level of benefits to provide. Absenteeism is encouraged and the incentive to return to work is diminished if a disabled employee is given a level of income that is comparable to his or her regular earnings. In general, disability income plans are designed to provide a level of benefits that replaces between 50 and 70 percent of an employee's gross income. While this may appear to represent a substantial reduction from regular earnings, it should be remembered that a disabled employee does not have the usual expenses associated with working, such as transportation costs. In addition, disability income benefits are not subject to social security taxation after a period of time and, depending on the source and amount, may be free of income taxation. Despite the logic in providing a reduced level of income, some short-term disability income plans provide employees with 100 percent of their predisability earnings. In most cases, this level of benefits is either a result of collective bargaining or an effort by employers to provide nonunion employees with a level of benefits comparable to that of union employees.

Many short-term disability income plans and most long-term plans base benefits on a single percentage of regular earnings, excluding bonuses and overtime. This percentage varies widely for short-term plans, and benefits as low as 50 percent or as high as 100 percent are not unusual. However, many insurers are reluctant to underwrite plans providing benefits higher than 70 percent of earnings. In some instances, short-term plans, like salary continuation plans, may use different percentages, such as 100 percent of earnings for four weeks and 70 percent of earnings for the remaining benefit period. The length of time that the higher level of benefits will be provided may also be a function of the length of an employee's service.

Long-term plans provide benefits that range from 50 to 70 percent of earnings, with 60 and 66⅔ being the most prevalent percentages. Some plans also use a sliding scale, such as 66⅔ percent of the first $4,000 of monthly earnings and 40 percent of earnings in excess of $4,000.

It is common for plans that determine benefits as a percentage of earnings to also place a maximum dollar amount on the benefit that will be provided, regardless of earnings. For example, a short-term plan covering hourly employees may have a benefit equal to 70 percent of earnings that might be subject to a maximum of $250 per week. Similarly, a long-term plan may provide benefits equal to 66⅔ percent of earnings, but might be subject to a monthly maximum that varies from $1,000 for some small groups to $4,000 or $5,000 (and sometimes higher) for larger groups. The purpose of such a maximum is to prevent the absolute benefit from being so high that an employee, by adjusting his or her lifestyle, could live comfortably on the disability income benefit and thus have no financial incentive to return to work.

Other types of benefit schedules are found in short-term disability income plans, particularly when these plans are designed for hourly paid employees. If the weekly earnings of most employees fall within a narrow range, the benefit might be expressed as a flat-dollar amount. For example, if all employees earned between $300 and $400 per week, a benefit of $225 per week might be used. If earnings varied widely, a benefit schedule such as the following might be used:

Weekly Earnings	Weekly Benefit
$221–$260	$170
$261–$300	200
$301–$340	220
$341–$380	250
Over $381	280

A similar approach is occasionally used in long-term disability income plans, as shown by the following benefit schedule for salaried employees earning in excess of $18,000 per year:

Monthly Earnings	Monthly Benefit
$1,500–$2,500	$1,200
$2,501–$3,500	1,500
$3,501–$4,500	2,400
Over $4,501	3,000

Period of Benefits

To determine the period for which disability income benefits will be paid, it is necessary to determine when benefits will begin and how long they will be paid. In both respects, differences exist between short-term and long-term plans.

Short-Term Plans. Short-term disability income contracts commonly contain a waiting period, referred to as an elimination period in disability income contracts. The waiting period is the length of time that an employee covered under the contract must be disabled before benefits begin. In the typical short-term contract, there is no waiting period for disabilities resulting from accidents, but a waiting period ranging from one to seven days is used for disabilities resulting from sicknesses. However, in some plans a single waiting period applies to disabilities from either accidents or sicknesses; in a few plans there are no waiting periods for either cause. Waiting periods longer than seven days are occasionally used, particularly when there is a salary continuation plan to provide benefits during the initial portion of a disability. In addition to lowering the cost of a disability income plan, the waiting period discourages unwarranted absences from work because of sickness. In a few cases, benefits are paid retroactively to the date of disability if the disability lasts for a predetermined time. However, it is generally felt that retroactive benefits cause employees to prolong their return to work in order to receive benefits for the full period of their disability.

Once an employee begins to receive benefit payments under a short-term disability contract, the benefits continue until the end of the benefit period specified in the contract, assuming the employee remains disabled for that length of time. Although short-term contracts may provide benefits up to two years (with long-term contracts providing benefits for periods in excess of two years), it is unusual for benefits to continue for more than one year. In fact, the majority of short-term contracts stipulate that benefits will be paid for either 13 or 26 weeks, with the latter period being most prevalent. It is also common for short-term plans to be described in terms of their elimination period and their duration of benefits. For example, a "1-8-26" plan pays benefits for a maximum of 26 weeks beginning with the first day of disability in the case of an accident and with the eighth day of disability in the case of a sickness.

In a few cases, the maximum period of benefits applies to a specified time, such as any consecutive 12 months, regardless of the number of separate disabilities. However, in most plans, both the maximum benefit period and the elimination period apply to each separate disability. Moreover, successive periods of disability caused by the same accident or the same or related sickness generally are considered to be a single disability unless they are separated by a period—normally two weeks—of continuous resumption of active employment. This provision prevents an employee from briefly returning to work to obtain a second maximum period of benefits for the same disability.

Even though a reduction in short-term disability income benefits for older employees can probably be justified on a cost basis, few plans have incorporated such a reduction.

Long-Term Plans. While waiting periods in long-term disability income plans may be as short as 30 days or as long as one year or more, the vast majority of plans contain elimination periods ranging from three to six months, with six months being most common. In many cases, the length of the waiting period will correspond to the length of time benefits will be paid under a firm's short-term disability income plan or salary continuation plan. In contrast to short-term plans, there is no difference between the waiting periods for sicknesses and accidents.

Long-term disability income benefits may be paid for as short a period as two years or as long as the lifetime of the disabled employee. The length of the benefit period may differ, however, depending upon whether the disability was a result of an accident or a sickness. Prior to the amending of the Age Discrimination in Employment Act, it was common for long-term disability income benefits to cease at age 65. Since that time, several different approaches have been used with respect to older employees. In a few cases, benefits are paid until age 70 for any disability that occurred before that age. For disabilities occurring at age 70 or later, benefits are paid for a reduced duration. A more common approach is to provide benefits to age 65 for employees who are disabled prior to a specified age. Employees disabled after the specified age are given benefits for a limited time. For example, a plan may provide the following:

Age at Commencement of Disability	Benefit Duration
59 and younger	to age 65
60–64	5 years
65–69	to age 70
70–74	1 year
75 and older	6 months

A similar approach uses a sliding level of benefit durations after a certain age. For example, a plan may provide that employees disabled prior to age 60 will receive benefits until age 65. The following schedule might then be used for employees disabled at age 60 or older:

Age at Commencement of Disability	Benefit Duration (in years)
60	5
61	4
62	3½
63	3
64	2½
65	2
66	2
67	1
68	1
69	1

As in short-term disability income plans, provisions are made in long-term plans for successive disabilities. The majority of contracts stipulate that successive periods of disability which are separated by less than some period (usually varying from three to six months) of continuous, active full-time employment will be considered a single disability, unless the subsequent disability (1) arises from an unrelated cause and (2) begins after the employee has returned to work.

Coordination with Other Benefits

To minimize the possibility that an employee will receive total benefits higher than his or her predisability earnings, disability income plans commonly stipulate that benefits will be integrated with other sources of disability income. The effect of this integration is to reduce (either totally or partially) the benefits payable under the disability income contract to the extent that certain other benefits are available. In general, the insurance laws or regulations of most states allow such reductions to be made as a result of benefits from social insurance programs and group insurance or retirement plans provided by the employer, but not as a result of benefits from individual disability income contracts unless they were purchased by the employer. Employers and employees often resent the fact that disability income benefits they have paid for may be reduced. However, such reductions are considered in determining the rates charged for disability income insurance. In effect, the employer is purchasing a contract that is only a supplement to these other available sources of disability income.

For various reasons, including the limited duration of benefits and the desire for simplified operating procedures, integration with other benefits is less likely to exist in short-term plans than in long-term plans. If a short-term plan covers only nonoccupational disabilities, there is no need for integration with workers' compensation benefits; and unless benefits are provided for disabilities lasting longer than five months, there is no need to integrate benefits with social security. In general, benefits under short-term plans are integrated with (1) workers' compensation benefits, if the plan covers occupational disabilities; (2) temporary disability laws, if they are applicable; and (3) social security benefits, if the maximum benefit period is longer than five months.

Some insurance companies will sell group long-term disability income coverage without any provision for coordination with other disability income benefits. However, the availability and potential magnitude of other benefits will be an underwriting factor in determining the maximum amount of coverage written. Long-term disability income benefits are usually integrated with benefits provided under the following:

- Social security.
- Workers' compensation laws.
- Temporary disability laws.
- Other insurance plans for which the employer makes a contribution or payroll deduction.
- Pension plans for which the employer has made a contribution or deduction to the extent the employee elects to receive retirement benefits because of disability.
- Salary continuation plans.
- Earnings from other employment, either with the employer or from other sources.

The integration with social security may be based solely on the benefit a disabled worker receives for himself or herself, referred to as the employee's primary insurance amount. It may also be based on the employee's total family benefit when the employee has eligible dependents.

Two basic approaches to integration are used: a full-integration approach and a dual-percentage approach. Under the *full-integration approach,* long-term disability income benefits are reduced to the extent that any benefits subject to integration are received. For example, assume that an employee earning $2,500 per month is entitled to a disability income benefit of 60 percent, or $1,500 per month. In addition, suppose the employee is entitled to a disability benefit under social security of $800, as well as additional family benefits of $400 (a total of $1,200). If the long-term disability income benefit plan provides for integration with total family benefits, the employee would receive $1,500 ($1,200 from social security and the remaining $300 from the long-term plan). However, if full integration were provided only with respect to the primary insurance amount (in other words, the $400 of family benefits are not considered), the employee would receive $1,900 ($1,200 from social security and $700 from the long-term disability plan).

Under the *dual-percentage approach,* two percentages are used: one that is applicable to benefits which will be provided under the long-term plan when there are no other benefits subject to integration, and another higher percentage that is applicable to total benefits payable from the long-term plan and other sources subject to integration. For example, an insured plan might provide benefits equal to

60 percent of earnings in the absence of other benefits subject to integration. If there are benefits subject to integration, benefits under the insured plan will be reduced to the extent that the sum of the benefits under the long-term disability plan and the benefits subject to integration exceed another percentage, such as 70 percent. Using these percentages and the previous example, 70 percent of earnings would be $1,750. Since the long-term disability benefit and all the social security benefits total $2,700, the long-term disability benefit would be reduced by $950 if the plan provided for integration with total family benefits. Therefore, the employee would receive a total benefit of $1,750 ($1,200 from social security and $550 from the long-term plan).

It is possible for the integration with other benefits to eliminate totally a long-term disability benefit. To prevent this situation from happening, many plans provide and some states require that a minimum benefit, such as $25 or $50 per month, be paid. Most plans also contain a provision freezing the amount of any social security reduction at the initial level established when the claim began. For example, assume an employee is entitled to receive $1,000 per month in disability income benefits under a long-term plan that contains a provision for full integration with social security. If the employee initially receives $600 from the long-term plan and $400 from social security, the $600 will continue to be paid under a provision that freezes the offset even if social security benefits are increased. If a 10 percent increase is later granted in social security benefits, the employee will receive a total benefit of $1,040. Without such a provision, the intended effect of increases in social security benefits would be erased by equivalent reductions in other disability income benefits provided to the employee. This is seen by some regulators as being contrary to public policy and thus a reason for requiring insured plans to contain a freeze in the amount of the social security offset.

Other Contract Provisions

Many provisions contained in group disability income contracts are similar to those contained in group term insurance contracts and will not be discussed further in this chapter. These include provisions pertaining to incontestability, a grace period, the entire contract and the payment of premiums. The provisions that will be discussed either are unique to group disability income benefit contracts or differ in certain respects from similar provisions found in group term insurance contracts.

Claims

The provisions concerning claims under both short-term and long-term disability income contracts are essentially the same. The insurance company must be notified within a relatively short time period, 20 or 30 days or as soon as is reasonably possible, after the disability for which benefits are being claimed begins. A formal proof of loss must then be filed with the insurance company, usually within 90 days after the commencement of the disability or after the end of the week, month, or other time period for which benefits are payable. The proof of loss normally consists of a statement by the employee concerning the disability, a statement by the attending physician, and a statement by the employer indicating the date and reason that active employment ceased. Provisions are also included that require periodic reports from the attending physician or that permit the insurance company to request such reports at reasonable intervals. The insurance company also has the right to have the employee examined by a physician of its own choice (and at its own expense) at reasonable time periods during the duration of the claim.

Payment of Benefits

The insurance company is not obligated to make benefit payments until a proof of loss has been filed. In general, benefits are payable to the employee. However, a facility-of-payment provision is included to allow payments to a guardian if the employee is physically, mentally or otherwise incapable of giving a valid release for any payment received. Benefits may be assigned to another party if such an assignment is permissible under state law and the insurance contract.

Rehabilitation

As an incentive to encourage disabled employees to return to active employment as soon as possible, but possibly at a lower-paying job, most insurance companies include a rehabilitation provision in their long-term disability income contracts. This provision permits the employee to enter a trial work period of one or two years in rehabilitative employment. During this time disability benefits will continue but will be reduced by some percentage (varying from 50 to 80 percent) of the earnings from rehabilitative employment. For example, with a 50 percent reduction, an employee who is otherwise entitled to a disability benefit of $1,500 per month would have this benefit reduced by only $600 if he or she could earn $1,200 in the new job. If the trial work period indicates that the employee is unable to perform the rehabilitative employment, the original long-term benefits will be continued and the employee will not be required to satisfy a new waiting period.

While there are no other provisions in long-term disability income contracts that require the insurance company to aid in the rehabilitation of disabled employees, it is not unusual for insurance companies to provide benefits for rehabilitation when it is felt that the cost of these benefits will be offset by shortening an employee's disability period. These benefits may be in the form of physical therapy, job training, adaptive aids to enable a disabled person to perform job functions or even the financing of a business venture.

Termination

For the most part, the provisions in disability income contracts concerning either the termination of the master contract or an employee's coverage are the same as those found in group life insurance. However, there is one notable exception—a conversion privilege is rarely included. The rationale for not including such a provision is based on the theory that the termination of employment will also terminate an employee's income and thus the need for disability income protection.

One other situation should be mentioned. When an employee meets the definition of total disability under a disability income contract, the employee is considered to have terminated employment by reason of ceasing to be an active, full-time employee. Without some provision to the contrary, an employee who resumes work would then be required to resatisfy any eligibility requirements, including a new probationary period. Most group disability income contracts allow the employer to consider disabled employees as not having terminated employment for insurance purposes. The employer may continue coverage as long as it is done on a nondiscriminatory basis and as long as the required premiums are paid. In short-term contracts, coverage is generally continued by the payment of premiums on the same basis as for active employees. However, it is common for long-term contracts to contain a waiver-of-premium provision.

The only practical effect of continuing coverage on a disabled employee is to guarantee that the employee will again be eligible for disability income benefits after he or she has returned to active employment. The continuation or termination of coverage has no effect on the future disability income benefits to an employee who is currently disabled and, therefore, entitled to receive benefits.

Supplemental Benefits

Three types of supplemental benefits are occasionally found under group long-term disability income contracts: a cost-of-living adjustment, a pension supplement and a survivors' benefit. Some disability income plans have cost-of-living adjustments (COLAs) so that the purchasing power of disability income benefits being received is not eroded by inflation. Under the typical COLA formula, benefits increase annually with changes in the consumer price index.

Many firms make provisions in their pension plans for treating disabled employees as if they were still working and accruing pension benefits. Such a provision requires that contributions on behalf of disabled employees be made to the pension plan. In most cases, these are paid from the current revenues of the employer. However, some disability income plans stipulate that the contributions necessary to fund a disabled employee's accruing pension benefits be paid from the disability income contract.

Some pension plans provide disability income benefits by allowing disabled employees to begin receiving retirement benefits when they are totally and permanently disabled. It is common, however, to limit these early benefits to employees who have satisfied some minimum period of service or who have reached some minimum age. In recent years, the feeling among employee benefit consultants seems to be that it is preferable to have separate retirement and disability income plans.

Some long-term contracts provide a benefit to survivors in the form of continued payments after the death of a disabled employee. In effect, the disability income payments will be continued, possibly at a reduced amount, for periods ranging up to 24 months. Payments generally are made only to eligible survivors, who commonly include the spouse and unmarried children under age 21.

FEDERAL TAXATION

As with group life insurance, employer contributions to disability income insurance are fully deductible as an ordinary and necessary business expense under Code

Section 162 if the overall compensation of the employee is reasonable. Salary continuation payments are similarly tax deductible. Contributions by an individual employee are considered payments for personal disability income insurance and are not tax deductible.

Income Tax Liability of Employees

In contrast to group life insurance, for which employer contributions may result in some taxable income to an employee, Code Section 106 provides that employer contributions for disability income insurance do not result in taxable income to an employee. However, the payment of benefits under an insured plan or salary continuation plan may or may not result in the receipt of taxable income. In making this determination, it is necessary to look at whether the plan is fully contributory, noncontributory or partially contributory.

Fully Contributory Plans

Under a fully contributory plan, the entire cost is paid by employee contributions and benefits are received free of income taxation.

Noncontributory Plans

Under a noncontributory plan, the entire cost is paid by the employer and benefits are included in an employee's gross income. However, Code Section 22 provides a tax credit to persons who are permanently and totally disabled. This credit is subtracted from an individual's federal income tax liability rather than deducted from gross income as was the $100 per week sick-pay exclusion that existed prior to 1984. For purposes of this tax credit, the IRS uses the social security definition of disability (an employee must be unable to engage in any kind of gainful work because of a medically determinable physical condition that has lasted or is expected to last at least 12 months or to result in death).

The maximum credit is $750 for a single person, $1,125 for a married person filing jointly, and $562.50 for a married person filing separately. The credit cannot exceed the taxable disability benefit actually received. The maximum credit is reduced if a single individual has an adjusted gross income (including the disability benefit) over $7,500, if a married person filing jointly has an adjusted gross income over $10,000, or if a married person filing separately has an adjusted gross income over $5,000. The reduction is equal to 7.5 percent of any income over the limit. In addition, the credit is reduced by 15 percent of any tax-free income received as a pension, annuity or disability benefit from certain government programs, including benefits from social security. Since disability income plans are usually integrated with social security, this will substantially reduce or eliminate the tax credit available to most persons receiving disability benefits from employer plans.

Partially Contributory Plans

Under a partially contributory plan, benefits attributable to employee contributions are received free of income taxation; benefits attributable to employer contributions are includable in gross income, but employees are eligible for the tax credit described previously.

The portion of the benefits attributable to employer contributions (and thus subject to income taxation) are based on the ratio of the employer's contributions to the total contributions for the employee under the plan for some period of time. For example, if the employer paid 75 percent of the cost of the plan, 75 percent of the benefits would be considered attributable to employer contributions and 25 percent to employee contributions. The time period used to calculate this percentage varies, depending upon the type of disability income plan and the length of time that the plan has been in existence. Under group insurance policies, the time period used is the three policy years ending prior to the beginning of the calendar year in which the employee is disabled. If coverage has been in effect for a shorter time, the regulations of the IRS specify the appropriate time period to use. Similar provisions pertain to contributory salary continuation plans, the major exception being that the time period is based on calendar years rather than policy years. If benefits are provided under individual disability income insurance policies, the proportion is determined on the basis of the premiums paid for the current policy year.

Tax Withholding and Social Security Taxes

Benefits paid directly to an employee by an employer under a salary continuation plan are treated like any other wages for the purpose of tax withholding. Disability income benefits paid by a third party, such as an insurance company or a trust, are subject to the withholding tax rules and regulations only if the employee requests that taxes be withheld. In both cases, benefits that are attributable to employer contributions are subject to social security taxes. However, social security taxes are payable only during the last calendar month in which the employee worked and the six calendar months that follow.

STATE TAXATION

For income tax purposes, some states consider an individual's taxable income to be the figure shown on the individual's federal income tax return, and those states treat disability income and salary continuation benefits in the same manner as does the federal government. While considerable variations exist in other states, disability income and salary continuation benefits are generally treated more favorably than under the federal tax laws and are often totally exempt from state income taxation.

STUDY QUESTIONS

1. Why is it important to coordinate insured group disability income plans with other sources of disability income benefits?
2. Describe the approaches used to determine the duration of benefits under salary continuation plans.

3. Why are long-term disability income plans less likely to cover all employees than are short-term disability income plans?
4. What is the rationale for providing disability benefits that are less than an employee's earnings prior to disability?
5. Compare insured short-term and long-term disability income contracts with respect to
   a. Definition of disability.
   b. Coverage for partial disabilities.
   c. Coverage for nonoccupational disabilities.
6. Compare insured short-term and long-term disability income contracts with respect to
   a. Exclusions.
   b. Waiting (elimination) period.
   c. Duration of benefits.
   d. Extent to which benefits are usually reduced for older employees.
   e. Extent to which benefits are usually coordinated with other disability income benefits.
7. Lindsay Grant, who earns $1,600 per month, is covered under a group long-term disability income plan that provides benefits equal to 60 percent of predisability earnings. If disabled, she will also receive social security disability benefits of $780—$520 as her primary insurance amount and an additional $260 as a family benefit. If the group plan contains an integration provision that reduces benefits to the extent that the long-term disability income benefit and the primary insurance amount exceed 75 percent of earnings, how much will Lindsay receive from each source if she is disabled?
8. Describe the rehabilitation provision often found in long-term disability income contracts.
9. Explain how long-term disability income contracts are sometimes modified to provide
   a. A pension supplement.
   b. Survivor benefits.
10. Under the federal income tax laws, to what extent are employer contributions for disability income insurance
    a. Deductible to the employer?
    b. Taxable as income to an employee?

9

Providers of Group Medical Expense Coverage

Objectives

- Describe the characteristics of Blue Cross and Blue Shield Plans and compare them with the characteristics of medical expense plans offered by insurance companies.
- Describe the characteristics of health maintenance organizations (HMOs).
- Explain the effect on employers of the Health Maintenance Organization Act of 1973.
- Describe the characteristics of preferred-provider organizations (PPOs).

Medical expense insurance is the most significant type of group insurance in terms of both the number of persons covered and the dollar outlay. With the exception of employers with very few employees, virtually all employers offer some type of medical expense plan. In almost all cases, coverage identical to that offered for employees is also available for eligible dependents. In the absence of employee contributions, the cost of providing medical coverage for employees will be several times greater for most employers than the combined cost of providing life insurance and disability income insurance.

Group medical expense contracts are not as standardized as group life insurance or group disability income insurance. Coverage may be provided through Blue Cross and Blue Shield Plans and HMO and PPO's as well as insurance companies. In addition, a large and increasing percentage of benefits is provided under plans that are partially or totally self-funded. An overall medical expense plan may be limited to specific types of medical expenses, or may be broad enough

to cover almost all medical expenses. Even when broad coverage is available, benefits may be provided either under a single contract or under a combination of
contracts. Furthermore, in contrast to other types of group insurance already discussed, benefits may be in the form of services rather than in the form of cash
payments. Finally, the skyrocketing cost of providing medical expense benefits in
recent years has led to many changes in coverage and plan design aimed at controlling these costs. Many of these changes have resulted in more similarities among
the providers of medical expense coverage than existed in the past.

Chapter 9 discusses the providers of medical expense coverage. The *basic*
coverages available for specific types of medical expenses are described in Chapter
10, and *major medical* coverages that provide more comprehensive benefits are
discussed in Chapter 11. Chapter 12 is devoted to the contractual provisions of
medical expense contracts and the relevant tax laws. Alternative methods of funding
medical expense benefits are discussed in Chapter 14, but other attempts at cost
containment are discussed throughout Chapters 9, 10, 11 and 12.

ALTERNATE PROVIDERS OF MEDICAL EXPENSE COVERAGE

When providing death benefits and disability income benefits to their employees,
employers have a limited number of choices. Coverage can be purchased from an
insurance company, provided on a self-funded basis or funded by a combination of
these two approaches. However, when providing medical expense benefits, an employer has more options. Many employers purchase coverage from Blue Cross and
Blue Shield (which compete vigorously with insurance companies), while some employers also provide benefits through HMOs or PPOs. In most cases, coverage
under an HMO or a PPO is not offered to employees as the only plan available, but
as an alternative to a more traditional insurance company plan or Blue Cross and
Blue Shield Plan.

Precise statistics concerning the relative significance of these alternate providers of medical expense coverage are difficult to obtain, particularly for group
insurance. For example, many Blue Cross and Blue Shield Plans and HMOs report
only the total number of persons covered and make no distinction between individual coverage and group coverage. Many persons receive portions of their coverage
from different types of providers, such as hospital coverage from a Blue Cross Plan,
and other medical expense coverages from an insurance company under a supplemental major medical contract. In addition, self-funded plans may purchase stop-
loss coverage and/or utilize PPOs.

Even though precise statistics cannot be obtained, there is no doubt that a
significant change has taken place over the last decade. In 1980, approximately
90 percent of all insured workers were covered under "traditional" medical expense
plans and 5 percent were covered under HMOs. *Traditional* means that if a worker
or family member was sick, he or she had complete freedom in choosing a doctor or
a hospital. Medical bills were paid by the plan, and no attempts were made to
control costs or the utilization of services. It is estimated that between 10 and
15 percent of the employees under these traditional plans were in

plans that were totally self-funded by the employer; the remainder of the employees were split fairly evenly between plans written by insurance companies and Blue Cross and Blue Shield.

By 1990, the figures had changed dramatically, with the majority of employees now covered under plans that control costs and the access to medical care. (Managed care is discussed more fully in Chapter 12.) In 1990, it was estimated that fewer than 30 percent of all employees were covered under traditional plans.[1] Another 35 to 40 percent were still covered under plans that were self-funded or written by insurance companies or Blue Cross and Blue Shield. However, these plans incorporated varying degrees of managed care. The remaining 30 to 35 percent of employees received their medical expense benefits from HMOs and PPOs. The latter have grown rapidly since 1985 and provide benefits to almost the same number of persons as do HMOs.

One important change is hidden in this statistic—the trend toward self-funding of medical expense benefits by employers. It is estimated that as many as 50 percent of all workers are covered under plans that are totally or substantially self-funded. Self-funding is more prevalent as the number of employees increases. Between 80 and 90 percent of persons who work for employers with more than 20,000 employees are covered under self-funded plans; the percentage is about 20 percent for persons in companies with fewer than 500 employees.

INSURANCE COMPANIES

Prior to the Great Depression, health insurance contracts provided by insurance companies were primarily designed to give income benefits to individuals who were disabled by accidents and, to a limited degree, illnesses. However, it was generally accepted that individuals should pay their own medical expenses from their savings. During the Depression, the savings of many individuals disappeared, unemployment was severe and most insurance companies even ceased writing disability income contracts. It was not until the 1940s that insurance companies again offered health insurance coverage to any great extent. By that time attitudes had changed, disability insurance was again being written and coverage for medical expenses was no longer considered an undesirable line of business. While there are approximately 700 insurance companies writing group life and health insurance, virtually all medical expense coverage is written by fewer than 100 companies, and over half the coverage is written by approximately 30 companies. Most writers of group medical expense coverage are life insurance companies, but coverage may also be obtained from property and liability insurers. Few companies specialize in writing group health insurance only.

---

[1]These statistics are a composite of several surveys of which the author of this book is aware. These surveys have been conducted by trade associations, insurance companies and benefit consulting firms. Precise statistics are difficult to estimate. Many employers fund benefits in a combination of ways. For example, benefits up to a certain limit may be self-funded, while benefits above the limit may be insured. In addition, employees are often able to choose between different types of plans such as Blue Cross and Blue Shield, an HMO and a PPO.

BLUE CROSS AND BLUE SHIELD

Faced with financial difficulties arising from the inability of many patients to pay their bills during the Great Depression, many hospitals established plans for the prepayment of hospital expenses. By paying a monthly fee to the hospital, a subscriber—the term used to describe persons covered by such plans—was entitled to a limited number of days of hospitalization per year. The early plans were limited to a single hospital, but by the mid-1930s, many plans had become community-wide or statewide operations, offering subscribers the choice of using any participating hospital. Much of this expansion resulted from actions by the American Hospital Association to promote and control this type of plan. In the late 1930s, the American Hospital Association adopted the Blue Cross name and emblem and permitted them to be used only by plans that met standards established by the association. As a general rule, only one plan within a geographic area was allowed to use the Blue Cross name. Eventually, the activities of the American Hospital Association were transferred to a separate national organization, the Blue Cross Association.

The success of the early Blue Cross Plans and the inability of physicians to collect bills for their services during the Depression resulted in the development of Blue Shield Plans. These were established by local medical associations for the purpose of prepaying physicians' charges. The evolution of Blue Shield Plans has paralleled that of Blue Cross Plans, with the American Medical Association acting similarly to the American Hospital Association. Eventually, the role of the American Medical Association was transferred to the National Association of Blue Shield Plans, which then became the national coordinating body.

To a large extent, the persons covered by Blue Shield Plans for physicians' charges have been the same persons covered by Blue Cross Plans for hospital expenses, and, in many geographic regions, this led to a close working relationship between the two plans. For many years in some areas of the country, one plan administered the other. However, this administration typically was on a fee-for-administration basis, with the two plans being separate legal entities. In recent years, there has been a consolidation of more than half of the Blue Cross and Blue Shield Plans. In most cases, this consolidation has taken the form of a complete merger; in other cases, the consolidation has only been partial. These partial consolidations have resulted in Blue Cross and Blue Shield Plans that have a single staff but separate governing boards.

There has been consolidation at the national level also. In 1978, the staffs of the two national organizations were merged, and a new association—the Blue Cross and Blue Shield Associations—was formed to act on matters of mutual interest to both Blue Cross Plans and Blue Shield Plans. It was governed by members of the boards from both the Blue Cross Association and the National Association of Blue Shield Plans. In 1982, a complete merger took place with the resulting organization called the Blue Cross and Blue Shield Association.

As of mid-1990, there were 53 plans in existence that jointly wrote Blue Cross and Blue Shield coverage. In addition, there were 8 separate Blue Cross Plans and 13 separate Blue Shield Plans. Most states are served by a single joint plan or only one Blue Cross Plan and one Blue Shield Plan. However, in a few states there is more than one plan, each operating within a specific geographic region. In a few sparsely populated states, plans may cover more than one state. Only in rare instances is there any overlapping of the geographic areas served by individual plans.

Each local Blue Cross, Blue Shield or Blue Cross and Blue Shield Plan is a legally separate entity operated by a governing board that establishes specific practices for the plan in accordance with the broad standards of the national Blue Cross and Blue Shield Association. Consequently, individual plans may differ substantially from one another. The boards of these plans used to be dominated by the providers of coverage, but now the boards of most plans are dominated by "nonproviders," including representatives of consumer organizations, foundations, labor unions, businesses and the general public.

COMPARING INSURANCE COMPANIES AND BLUE CROSS AND BLUE SHIELD PLANS

Perhaps the best way to describe the two major providers of medical expense coverage is to compare the characteristics of Blue Cross and Blue Shield Plans with the characteristics of insurance companies. Traditionally, the similarities between Blue Cross and Blue Shield Plans and insurance companies were overshadowed by their differences. Over time, however, intense competition has often caused one type of provider to adopt the more popular practices of the other. As a result, insurance companies and Blue Cross and Blue Shield Plans are becoming increasingly similar, in spite of their many distinctly different characteristics.

Regulation and Taxation

In a few states, Blue Cross and Blue Shield Plans are regulated under the same laws that apply to insurance companies. However, in most states, Blue Cross and Blue Shield Plans are considered nonprofit organizations and are regulated under special legislation. Typically, this regulation is carried out by the same body that regulates insurance companies. In some respects, Blue Cross and Blue Shield Plans receive preferential treatment over insurance companies. Probably the most significant example of this treatment is their exemption from premium taxation and income taxation by the majority of states. Since premium taxes (usually about 2 percent of premiums) are passed on to consumers, this gives Blue Cross and Blue Shield Plans a cost advantage. In many other respects, however, Blue Cross and Blue Shield Plans are subject to more stringent regulation than insurance companies. For example, in most states, their rates are subject to regulatory approval. With recent trends toward consumerism, this approval has become more burdensome and expensive.

In addition, Blue Cross and Blue Shield Plans are also accorded favorable tax treatment under the federal income tax laws. Prior to the Tax Reform Act of 1986, Blue Cross and Blue Shield Plans (except for the few plans that were incorporated as insurance companies) were exempt from federal income taxation. The tax act eliminated this complete exemption. Because of various deductions that can be taken, however, the average effective tax rate for Blue Cross and Blue Shield Plans is below the average tax rate for insurance companies.

Form of Benefits

Traditionally, Blue Cross and Blue Shield Plans have offered benefits in the form of services, while insurance companies have offered benefits on an indemnity or reimbursement basis. Under the service benefit concept, benefits are expressed in terms of the services that will be provided by the hospitals or physicians participating in the plan rather than in terms of dollar maximums. For example, a Blue Cross Plan might provide up to 90 days of hospitalization per year in semiprivate accommodations. In contrast, an insurance company might provide reimbursement for hospital charges subject to both dollar and duration limits, such as $400 per day for 90 days. In both cases, however, any charges in excess of the benefits must be borne by the covered person.

Blue Cross and Blue Shield Plans involve two separate types of contractual relationships:

1. A plan promises to provide specified services to a subscriber for whom a premium has been paid.
2. It has contracts with providers of services, whereby the providers are reimbursed for the cost of services rendered to subscribers.

In general, subscribers are not billed for the cost of covered services or required to file claim forms. Rather, this is negotiated between the plan and the providers. This type of arrangement generally requires that subscribers receive their services from providers participating in the plan; however, most hospitals and physicians are participants. If nonparticipating providers can be used (such as for emergencies), benefits usually are paid on an indemnity basis as is done by insurance companies.

In contrast, an insurance company agrees only to reimburse a covered person for medical expenses up to the limits specified in the insurance contract. There is no contractual relationship between the providers of medical services and the insurance company. Thus, covered persons must file the appropriate claim forms. While covered persons have a legal obligation to pay their medical bills, the insurance company's obligation (unless benefits are assigned) is only to reimburse the covered person, not to actually pay the providers. However, many providers, particularly hospitals, require that any potential insurance benefits be assigned to them by a patient before they will render services. In effect, this requires the insurance company to pay benefits directly to the provider on behalf of the covered person.

In the past, insurance companies incorporated maximum daily room-and-board limits into their contracts and did not cover medical expenses in full. However, to compete with Blue Cross and Blue Shield Plans, many insurance companies now frequently write contracts that provide full reimbursement for certain medical expenses. Even though a covered person may see little difference in the benefits received from either type of provider, the traditional distinction still exists: Blue Cross and Blue Shield Plans are providing services while insurance companies provide reimbursement for the cost of services.

Types of Benefits

Over the years, Blue Cross and Blue Shield Plans have specialized in providing basic medical benefits, with Blue Cross providing coverage for hospital expenses and Blue Shield providing coverage for surgical expenses and physicians' visits. Major medical benefits were rarely available. However, competition from insurance companies and increased cooperation between Blue Cross and Blue Shield have resulted in these Plans now offering virtually the same coverages as insurance companies. It is interesting to note that Blue Cross and Blue Shield Plans have expanded the scope of benefits offered by often including deductible and coinsurance provisions similar to those used by insurance companies. When there is a deductible, a covered person is required to pay expenses up to some limit (such as $100 per year or per illness) out of his or her own pocket before benefits will be paid. When coinsurance is used, a covered person is required to pay a percentage (such as 20 percent) of some or all expenses, the remaining portion being covered under the medical expense plan.

The advantage many insurance companies have had over Blue Cross and Blue Shield Plans has been the insurance company's ability to offer a wide variety of group benefits, including life insurance coverage and disability income coverage. Until a few years ago, most states had laws and regulations that prevented Blue Cross and Blue Shield Plans from offering any coverages other than medical expense benefits. However, because of changes in these laws and regulations, Blue Cross and Blue Shield Plans can now offer a wider range of group benefits to their subscribers. While competition between Blue Cross and Blue Shield Plans and insurance companies over writing these other benefits is increasing, Blue Cross and Blue Shield currently write relatively little coverage other than medical expense benefits.

Reimbursement of Providers

The method by which Blue Cross and Blue Shield Plans reimburse the providers often results in their having a competitive advantage over insurance companies. Most Blue Cross Plans pay participating hospitals on a per diem basis for each day a subscriber is hospitalized. Periodic negotiations with Blue Cross determine the amount of this payment, which includes room-and-board charges as well as other covered charges, for each hospital. For example, if the per diem amount is $600, the hospital will receive $600 for each day a subscriber is hospitalized, regardless of what the actual charges might be. While this per diem amount will on the average be adequate, the hospital will "lose money" on some patients and "make money" on others.

In addition to the administrative simplicity of this method of reimbursement, the per diem amount is often less than the average daily hospital charges. Frequently, it is determined by excluding such hospital costs as bad debts, charity care and nursing school costs. These costs, however, are used in determining charges for patients who are not Blue Cross subscribers. Therefore, Blue Cross subscribers, in effect, receive a discount on the charges made to other patients, including those whose benefits are provided by insurance companies. This discount, except to the extent it results from administrative savings, has not been allowed in some states and has come under increasing criticism where it is the normal practice. In general, the discount size has been reduced in recent years, often due to legislation or regulation. It is interesting to note that there have been some experimental attempts by insurance companies to lower their cost of claims handling by using a similar reimbursement procedure with hospitals.

Under some Blue Shield Plans, physicians may also be reimbursed at less than their actual charges, as will be discussed in Chapter 10.

National Coverage

While Blue Cross and Blue Shield Plans operate in precise geographic regions, many insurance companies operate on a national basis. Therefore, Blue Cross and Blue Shield Plans have had a more difficult time competing with insurance companies for the group insurance business of employers whose employees are located in areas served by various Blue Cross and Blue Shield Plans. Even though Blue Cross and Blue Shield have developed procedures for providing coverage to these national accounts, most benefit specialists seem to feel that insurance companies have the competitive advantage in this regard.

Flexibility

There also seems to be a feeling among benefit consultants that insurance companies have a greater degree of flexibility in modifying their group contracts to meet the needs and desires of employers. Blue Cross and Blue Shield contracts have traditionally been quite standardized, with few, if any, variations allowed. One major reason for this rigidity is that changes in the benefits promised to subscribers also have an effect on the contracts between Blue Cross and Blue Shield and the providers. However, with employers increasingly wanting new approaches to medical expense benefits, often for cost-containment reasons, many Blue Cross and Blue Shield Plans have taken a more flexible approach. Considerable variations exist among plans, and some have been very innovative in meeting the demands of the marketplace, even going so far as to administer benefit plans that are self-funded by employers.

Rating

In their early years, Blue Cross and Blue Shield Plans used only a *community-rating* approach in determining what premium rates to charge. Under this approach, each plan uses the same rate structure for all subscribers, regardless of their past or potential loss experience and regardless of whether coverage is written on an individual or group basis. Usually, the only variations in the rate structure result from variations in coverage—whether it is for an individual, a couple without children or a family. The philosophy behind the community-rating approach is that coverage should be made available to the widest range of persons possible at an affordable cost. Charging lower premium rates to segments of the community with better-than-average loss experience is thought to result in higher, and possibly unaffordable, premium rates for other segments of the community.

The use of community rating placed Blue Cross and Blue Shield at a competitive disadvantage when insurance companies began to aggressively market group medical expense insurance and use experience rating. With experience rating, insurance companies frequently were able to charge certain employer groups considerably lower premiums than those charged by Blue Cross and Blue Shield. As a result, by the mid-1950s, insurance companies surpassed Blue Cross and Blue Shield in the number of persons covered. Blue Cross and Blue Shield Plans were faced with the increasing dilemma that rate increases necessary to compensate for the loss of better-than-average business tended to drive even more business to the insurance companies. Therefore, Blue Cross and Blue Shield initiated the use of experience rating for groups. Today, there is little difference in this regard between these two major providers with respect to group business. However, Blue Cross and Blue Shield still use community rating in pricing products for smaller employers and for the individual marketplace.

Marketing

Blue Cross and Blue Shield Plans tend to have lower acquisition expenses than insurance companies, and most coverage is marketed by salaried employees. However, more than half of the plans also market coverage through agents and/or brokers in addition to their own sales forces. In general, the commissions paid to agents or brokers are below the commissions paid by insurance companies.

HEALTH MAINTENANCE ORGANIZATIONS

Since the early 1970s, the concept of health maintenance organizations (HMOs) has received considerable attention. Because the nature of these organizations varies, a precise definition is difficult. However, HMOs generally are regarded as organized systems of health care that provide a comprehensive array of medical services on a prepaid basis to voluntarily enrolled persons living within a specified geographic region. HMOs act like insurance companies and Blue Cross and Blue Shield Plans in that they finance health care. However, unlike insurance companies and Blue Cross and Blue Shield Plans, they also deliver medical services.

Even though the term *health maintenance organization* is relatively new, its concept is not. For many years, prepaid practice plans, as they were called, have operated successfully in many parts of the country.[2] However, growth was relatively slow until the passage of the Health Maintenance Organization Act of 1973. This Act resulted from a belief on the part of the federal government that HMOs were a viable alternative method of financing and delivering health care and thus should be encouraged. In fact, the Act has also resulted in many employers being required to offer their employees the option of coverage by an HMO instead of by a more traditional medical expense plan. As of 1991, there were approximately 600 HMOs in existence.

---

[2]The better-known of these early HMOs include the Ross-Loos Medical Group in Los Angeles; the Kaiser Foundation Health Plan, which operates six plans in several western states and Ohio; the Group Health Association in Washington, D.C.; and the Health Insurance Plan of Greater New York.

Characteristics of HMOs

HMOs have several characteristics that distinguish them from insurance companies and Blue Cross and Blue Shield.

Comprehensive Care

HMOs offer their subscribers a comprehensive package of health-care services, generally including benefits for outpatient services as well as for hospitalization. These services are usually provided to subscribers at no cost except the periodically required premium, referred to as a capitation payment. However, in some cases, a modest copayment, such as $2 per physician's visit or $3 per drug prescription, may be imposed. HMOs emphasize preventive care and provide such services as routine physicals and immunizations. The cost of such preventive care usually is not covered under the contracts of insurance companies or Blue Cross and Blue Shield, even when major medical coverage is provided. (A comparison of an HMO plan with a major medical plan of an insurance company is presented in Chapter 11.)

Delivery of Medical Services

HMOs provide for the delivery of medical services, which in many cases are performed by salaried physicians and other personnel employed by the HMO. This is in contrast to the usual fee-for-service delivery system of medical care. However, some HMOs do contract with providers on a fee-for-service basis.

Subscribers are required to obtain their care from the providers of medical services who are affiliated with the HMO. Since HMOs rarely operate in a geographic region any larger than a single metropolitan area, this may result in limited coverage for subscribers if treatment is received elsewhere. Most HMOs do have out-of-area coverage, but only in the case of medical emergencies.

Cost Control

A major emphasis of HMOs is the control of medical expenses. By providing and encouraging preventive care, HMOs attempt to detect and treat medical conditions at an early stage, thereby avoiding costly medical treatment in the future. There has also been an attempt by HMOs to provide treatment on an outpatient basis whenever possible. Because insurance companies and Blue Cross and Blue Shield Plans have in the past provided more comprehensive coverage for a hospitalized person, less costly outpatient treatments were often not performed. This emphasis on outpatient treatment and preventive medicine has resulted in a much lower hospitalization rate for HMO subscribers than the population as a whole. However, it appears that some of this decreased hospitalization rate is a result of younger and healthier employees being more likely to elect HMO coverage.

The use of salaried employees by many HMOs also may result in lower costs since the physician or other provider of care has no financial incentive to prescribe additional, and possibly unnecessary, treatment. In fact, the physicians and other medical professionals in some HMOs may receive bonuses if the HMO operates efficiently and has a surplus from the capitation fees received.

Sponsorship of HMOs

Traditionally, most HMOs were operated as nonprofit organizations, and these organizations currently have the majority of subscribers. However, the majority of new HMOs are profit making. While many subscribers are covered by HMOs that have been sponsored by consumer groups, a sizable and increasing portion are covered by plans sponsored by insurance companies or Blue Cross and Blue Shield. Sponsorship may also come from physicians, hospitals or labor unions.

The issue of whether insurance companies should be involved with HMOs has been a source of disagreement within the industry. Some insurance companies view HMOs as competitors with the potential of putting them out of the health insurance business. Other insurance companies view them as a viable alternative method of financing and delivering health care that can be offered to employers as one of the products in their portfolio. In addition to actually sponsoring and owning HMOs, some insurance companies are actively involved with HMOs in a variety of ways. These include:

- Consulting on such matters as plan design and administration.
- Administrative services, such as actuarial advice, claims monitoring, accounting and computer services.
- Marketing assistance, such as designing sales literature. In a few cases, the agents of insurance companies have been used to market HMOs. This has been done in conjunction with the marketing of the insurance company's hospitalization plan when the HMO does not provide hospitalization coverage to its subscribers.
- Providing hospitalization coverage. HMOs that do not control their own hospital facilities may provide this benefit by purchasing coverage for their subscribers.
- Providing emergency out-of-area coverage. An insurance company operating on a national basis may be better equipped to administer these claims than an HMO.
- Providing financial support in a variety of ways, including reinsurance if an HMO experiences greater than expected demand for services and agreements to bail out financially troubled HMOs.

Types of HMOs

There are three basic types of HMOs—group-practice plans, individual practice association plans and open-ended plans.

The earliest type of HMO is the group-practice plan. While this type of plan accounts for only about 15 percent of the total number of HMOs, slightly more than half of HMO subscribers are covered under group-practice plans. Under this arrangement, physicians (and other medical personnel) are either (1) employees of the HMO, which pays their salary, or (2) employees of another legal entity that has a contractual relationship with the HMO to provide medical services for its subscribers. The first approach is often referred to as a staff model and the second approach as a group model when the contractual arrangement is with one group of providers and a network model when the contractual relationship is with two or more provider groups. These physicians normally consist of general practitioners and medical specialists who practice as a group, sharing facilities and support personnel. The plan may have a single facility for physicians, frequently one that is located in or near a hospital owned by the HMO or with which the HMO has an agreement to provide the necessary care for subscribers. Some of the larger group practice plans may also have other facilities, often staffed only by general practitioners, that are located throughout the geographic area served by the plan. If a plan or the legal entity contracting with the plan is not large enough to justify the hiring of certain types of specialists on a salaried basis, contractual relationships are frequently entered into with such specialists to provide their services to subscribers as needed. These specialists tend to be paid on a fee-for-service basis.

Group practice plans are often referred to as *closed-panel plans* since subscribers must use physicians employed by the plan or the organization with which it contracts. With most plans having several general practitioners, subscribers may usually select their physicians from among those accepting new patients and make medical appointments just as if the physician were in private practice. However, there frequently is little choice among specialists since a plan may employ or have a contract with only one physician in a given field of specialty.

In *individual practice association plans,* participating physicians practice individually or in small groups at their own offices. In most cases, these physicians accept non–HMO patients, on a traditional fee-for-service basis, as well as HMO subscribers. Individual practice association plans are often referred to as *open-panel plans* since subscribers choose from a list of participating physicians. The number of physicians participating in this type of HMO frequently is larger than the number participating in group practice plans and may include several physicians within a given specialty. In some geographic areas, most physicians may participate; in other geographic areas only a relatively small percentage of the physicians may participate. Most of the newer HMOs are individual practice associations and, therefore, the percentage of HMO subscribers served by these plans is growing.

Several methods may be used to compensate physicians participating in an individual practice association. The most common is a fee schedule based on the services provided to subscribers. To encourage physicians to be cost effective, it is common for plans to have a provision reducing payments to physicians if the experience of the plan is worse than expected. In addition, the physicians may receive a bonus if the experience of the plan is better than expected. Particularly with respect to general practitioners, some individual practice association plans pay each physician a flat annual amount for each subscriber who has elected to use that physician. For this annual payment, the physician must see these subscribers as often as is necessary during the year.

It is unusual for individual practice association plans to own their own hospitals. Rather, they enter into contracts with local hospitals to provide the necessary services for their subscribers.

The newest type of HMO is the open-ended plan. Under this approach, employees are allowed to receive treatment from non–HMO providers at reduced benefit levels. For example, one HMO of this type has no deductibles or copayments if an

HMO physician is used. However, there is a $300 annual deductible for outside office visits, and only 70 percent of the costs above the deductible are reimbursed. An open-ended HMO is an example of a point-of-service plan. At the time an employee needs medical care, he or she can decide what type of plan to use—the HMO or an alternative indemnity plan.

Employers that use open-ended plans hope that these plans will encourage a greater number of older and illness-prone employees to leave more expensive traditional benefit plans and join HMOs, which are viewed as being better able to control escalating medical costs. The early experience has shown this to be the case. One interesting result is that while new HMO subscribers still have the security of occasionally seeing an outside specialist, most subscribers have confined their visits solely to HMO physicians.

Extent of HMO Use

It is estimated that between 15 and 20 percent of employees are covered under HMOs. However, this percentage varies considerably by geographic region and by employers. Except in rare instances, employees covered by HMO plans have elected this form of coverage as an alternative to their employer's insurance company plan or Blue Cross and Blue Shield Plan. Although many employers are required by state and/or federal law to offer an HMO option, other employers voluntarily make the option available. The administrative details of such an option may be burdensome and expensive for small employers, but they seem to pose few problems for large employers with specialized employee benefit staffs. In many cases, the financial consequences to the employer of such an option are insignificant since the employer will make the same contribution on an employee's behalf regardless of which plan is selected.

Until recently, the general attitude of employers toward HMOs seems to have been somewhat ambivalent: some employers have been in favor of HMOs, others against, and the majority indifferent. However, several recent studies have shown that most employers feel that HMOs have been a very effective technique for controlling benefit costs. On the other hand, some employers feel that HMOs may actually increase an employer's cost of providing medical care. HMOs have tended to attract younger, healthier employees. And, in fact, many HMOs have designed their plans to appeal most to this group by providing benefits popular to the group, such as well-baby care. When these younger, healthier persons leave the insurance company plan or Blue Cross and Blue Shield Plan, its average cost per remaining employee will increase if the plan is experience rated. Unless the employer's cost for the HMO coverage drops correspondingly, the employer's aggregate medical expense premiums will increase.

Most employees do not elect an HMO option. However, studies have revealed that employees who have elected HMOs are for the most part satisfied with their choice and are unlikely to switch back to an insurance company plan or Blue Cross and Blue Shield Plan as long as the HMO option remains available. The success of an HMO in attracting subscribers seems to be related primarily to the following factors:

- The reputation of the HMO. To some extent, this is a function of the experience of the HMO. In those areas where HMOs have been established for many years, a larger percentage of employees participate.
- The extent to which employees have established relationships with physicians. Employees are reluctant to elect an HMO option if it requires them to give up a physician with whom they are satisfied. However, in some cases, this physician may also participate in the HMO. In general, new employees are more likely to elect an HMO option if they are new residents of the area or just entering the labor force.
- The attitude of the employer. Employees are more likely to elect HMO coverage if the HMO option is effectively and enthusiastically communicated by their employer.
- Cost. HMOs obviously are attractive to employees when they offer a less expensive alternative to coverage under insurance company plans. However, in some cases, an HMO option will be more expensive to an employee, but this may be more than offset by broader coverage and the lack of deductibles and coinsurance. The more that employees view an HMO alternative as being less expensive in the long run, the greater the employee participation will be.

THE HEALTH MAINTENANCE ORGANIZATION ACT OF 1973

The Health Maintenance Organization Act of 1973 has had a significant influence on the interest in and the growth of HMOs. The Act introduced the concept of the *federally qualified* HMO. Most HMOs formed since the passage of the Act have been organized to take advantage of this federal qualification, which entitles them to federal grants for feasibility studies and development—including grants to solicit subscribers—and federal loans or loan guarantees to assist them in covering initial operating deficits. In addition, employers may be required to offer the HMO as a dual option to employees. Most of the older HMOs have also become federally qualified, primarily because of this dual-choice provision of the Act.

Federal Qualification

To become federally qualified, an HMO must meet certain requirements set forth in the Act to the satisfaction of the Secretary of Health and Human Services. In return for a periodic prepaid fee, an HMO must provide the following basic benefits to its subscribers at no cost or with nominal copayments:

- Physicians' services, including consultant and referral services, up to 10 percent of which may be provided by physicians who are not affiliated with the HMO.
- Inpatient and outpatient hospital services.
- Medically necessary emergency health services.
- Short-term (up to 20 visits) outpatient mental health services.

- Medical treatment and referral services for alcohol or drug abuse or addiction.
- Diagnostic laboratory services and diagnostic and therapeutic radiologic services.
- Home health services.
- Preventive health services, such as immunizations, well-baby care, periodic physical examinations and family planning services.
- Medical social services, including education in methods of personal health maintenance and in the use of health services.

The HMO may also provide the following supplemental benefits either as part of its standard benefit package or as optional benefits for which an additional fee may be charged:

- Services of intermediate and long-term facilities.
- Vision care.
- Dental care.
- Additional mental health services.
- Rehabilitative services.
- Prescription drugs.

In addition to the benefits that either are required or may be included, an HMO must meet other requirements with respect to its operations. These include:

- A fiscally sound operation including provisions against the risk of insolvency.
- Annual open enrollment periods.
- An ongoing quality assurance program.

Prior to 1988, the HMO Act required HMOs to determine their rates on the basis of community rating for all employer groups. This provision of the Act decreased the attractiveness of HMOs to employers whose employees had lower-than-average benefit claims. Since a 1988 amendment to the Act, HMOs can establish advance rates based on an employer's past and projected claims experience if a group has 100 or more employees. Experience rating can also be used for groups of fewer than 100 employees, but the advance rate cannot be more than 10 percent higher than the HMO's community rates. In contrast to the usual practice of experience rating (see Chapter 15), HMOs are *not* allowed to make retrospective rate adjustments if claims turn out to be higher or lower than expected.

Dual-Choice Provision

Under the Act, an employer must offer one, or possibly more, federally qualified HMOs to its employees as an option to its insurance company, Blue Cross and Blue Shield or self-funded health care plan if all the following circumstances exist:

- The employer is required to pay its employees the minimum wage specified by the Fair Labor Standards Act.
- The employer has 25 or more employees, including both full-time and part-time employees.

- The employer covers eligible employees with a health-care plan for which the employer makes a monetary contribution.
- The employer has received a request to make coverage available to its employees from one or more federally qualified HMOs operating in a defined geographic area where at least 25 employees reside.

The request by an HMO must be in writing and contain specific information, such as a current financial report, the geographic area to be served, the facilities to be used and rates to be charged. In addition, the request must be received by an employer at least 180 days prior to the expiration or renewal date of any existing health benefit plans. If employees are represented by a collective bargaining unit, the HMO option must first be offered to the bargaining unit for its acceptance or rejection. If the bargaining unit rejects the option, the employer is under no further obligation with respect to employees represented by the unit. However, if the bargaining unit accepts the option or if some employees are not subject to collective bargaining, the employer must make the HMO option available to employees who reside in the service area of the HMO.

The dual-choice option applies separately to group practice plans and to individual practice association plans. Thus, an employer may be required to offer one of each type. Furthermore, an employer must also offer the option of coverage in other qualified HMOs to its employees, provided the other HMOs request inclusion and have service areas that include the residence of at least 25 employees who either (1) do not reside in the service area of a qualified HMO that is already offered as an option or (2) cannot obtain coverage because the current HMO is no longer accepting new subscribers. Again, the employer is not required to offer more than one of each type of HMO covering the same geographic area.

When an employer is initially contacted by a federally qualified HMO serving an area in which eligible employees reside, the employer may deal with any qualified HMO of the same type serving that area, and is not limited to the one making the initial contact. The decision of which HMO to include as an option is up to the employer.

This dual-choice provision as previously described is subject to a sunset provision on October 1, 1995. After that date, no employer will be required to offer an HMO to its employees.

Once an HMO option is made available, an employer must provide for a group enrollment period of at least ten working days each year in which eligible employees may transfer between any available health insurance plans without the application of waiting periods, exclusions or limitations based on health status. During this open enrollment period and at least 30 days prior to it, an employer must allow any participating HMOs to have fair and reasonable access to eligible employees for purposes of presenting and explaining their programs.

Prior to a 1988 amendment to the HMO Act, an employer was required to contribute as much toward the cost of an employee's coverage under an HMO as would have been paid for medical expense benefits if the employee had elected the employer's insurance company plan or a Blue Cross and Blue Shield Plan. Employers are now required only to make nondiscriminatory contributions to HMOs. This change allows an employer to make the same percentage contribution toward an HMO's premium as is made toward premiums of other medical expense plans.

Some states also have laws requiring employers to offer HMO coverage under certain circumstances. In general, these laws apply to any HMO within the state, whether it is federally qualified or not. In at least one state, coverage must be offered and administered on a payroll-deduction basis even if the employer does not have an existing medical expense plan.

A problem may arise if an HMO ceases operations because of financial difficulties. Unfortunately, this has occurred in several cases, even among those HMOs that have met the standards of federal qualification. Unless the cessation of HMO coverage coincides with an open enrollment period, these employees may not be able to join or rejoin their employer's insurance company plan or Blue Cross and Blue Shield Plans without showing evidence of insurability. However, many insurance companies and Blue Cross and Blue Shield Plans will include provisions in their contracts to provide coverage without evidence of insurability for employees under these circumstances.

PREFERRED-PROVIDER ORGANIZATIONS

A concept that continues to receive considerable attention from employers and insurance companies is the preferred-provider organization (PPO). A few PPOs have existed on a small scale for many years, but since the early 1980s, PPOs have grown in number and are now viewed as a new weapon to control increased medical care costs. In 1990, an estimated 700 PPOs were in existence, and an estimated 40 million employees had the option of using them for receiving medical care.

While many variations exist, PPOs can basically be described as groups of health-care providers that contract with employers, insurance companies, union trust funds, third-party administrators or others to provide medical care services at a reduced fee. PPOs may be organized by the providers themselves or by other organizations such as insurance companies, Blue Cross and Blue Shield or groups of employers. Like HMOs, they may take the form of group practices or separate individual practices. They may provide a broad array of medical services, including physicians' services, hospital care, laboratory costs and home health care, or they may be limited only to hospitalization or physicians' services. Some PPOs are very specialized and provide specific services such as dental care, mental health benefits, substance abuse services, maternity care or prescription drugs.

PPOs typically differ from HMOs in two major respects. First, they do not provide benefits on a prepaid basis. The participants in the PPO are paid on a fee-for-service basis as their services are used. However, fees are usually subject to a schedule that is the same for all participants in the PPO, and participants may have an incentive to control utilization through bonus arrangements. Second, employees are not required to use the practitioners or facilities of PPOs that contract with their group insurance company, Blue Cross and Blue Shield Plan or employer; rather, a choice can be made each time medical care is needed. However, employees are offered incentives to use the PPO, including lower or reduced deductibles and copayments as well as increased benefits such as preventive health care.

Employers were disappointed with some of the early PPOs. While discounts were received, they seemed to have little effect on benefit costs because discounts were from higher-than-average fees or providers were more likely to perform diagnostic tests or prolong hospital stays to generate additional fees to compensate for the discounts. Needless to say, these PPOs seldom lasted long.

The successful PPOs today emphasize quality care and utilization review. In selecting physicians and hospitals, PPOs look at both the type of care provided and the cost-effectiveness of the provider. In this era of fierce competition among medical care providers, these physicians and hospitals are often willing to accept discounts in hopes of increasing patient volume. It is also important for a PPO to monitor and control utilization on an ongoing basis. In some cases, bonuses are provided if the quantity of care is below specified utilization targets. However, there is always the risk that a low quantity of care may also be associated with a low quality of care.

Although a few years ago there was little doubt that HMOs were more effective than PPOs in controlling medical expense costs, recent surveys seem to indicate that the two types of organizations are now fairly comparable in this regard. However, it must be pointed out that there are wide variations among HMOs as well as among PPOs. Therefore, a careful analysis of quality of care, cost and financial stability is necessary before a particular HMO or PPO is selected.

MULTIPLE-OPTION PLANS

Until recently, an employer who wanted to make an HMO option available to employees had to enter into a separate contractual arrangement with the HMO. Unless a PPO was sponsored by the insurance company or Blue Cross and Blue Shield Plan of an employer, a similar contractual agreement was also required. Several insurance companies and Blue Cross and Blue Shield Plans are now providing all of these options under a single medical expense contract. For example, one insurer is marketing a so-called triple option plan that gives employees the choice among a traditional fee-for-service indemnity plan, an indemnity plan using a PPO or an HMO. In most cases, the HMOs and PPOs used in such arrangements have been formed or purchased by the insurance company or Blue Cross and Blue Shield Plan; however, in other cases, a contractual relationship has been established with an existing HMO or PPO.

These plans offer certain advantages to the employer. First, administration is easier since all elements of the plan are purchased from a single provider. Second, costs may be lower since the entire plan, including the HMO, is normally subject to experience rating. Because federally qualified HMOs cannot fully use experience rating, only nonfederally qualified HMOs are typically used in multiple-option plans.

Self-Funded Plans

It should be obvious from the first few pages of this chapter that self-funding of medical expense plans is becoming increasingly common. Self-funding, which is discussed in detail in Chapter 14, may result in cost savings and improvement of the employer's cash flow.

The discussion of medical benefits in the following chapters focuses primarily on insured plans. However, it is important to remember that a self-funded plan must be properly designed. Most self-funded plans have "borrowed" liberally from insured plans and contain similar if not identical provisions.

STUDY QUESTIONS

1. Describe the origins and purposes of Blue Cross and Blue Shield Plans.
2. Compare Blue Cross and Blue Shield Plans with private insurance companies with respect to
   a. Regulation and taxation.
   b. Form of benefits provided.
   c. Types of benefits provided.
   d. Reimbursement of providers.
   e. Rating.
   f. Marketing.
3. Describe the characteristics of HMOs that distinguish them from insurance companies.
4. Compare open-panel, closed-panel and open-ended HMOs with respect to
   a. Choice of physicians.
   b. Reimbursement of physicians.
5. What factors are likely to affect the success of an HMO in attracting subscribers?
6. What requirements must be satisfied by an HMO to obtain federal qualification?
7. The Radnor Corporation has been contacted by an HMO and was requested to offer the HMO plan as an option to its employees. Under what circumstances must the corporation comply with this request?
8. Explain how PPOs differ from HMOs.
9. What advantages do multiple-option medical expense plans have for employers?

10

Basic Group Medical Expense Coverage

Objectives

- Describe the benefits and exclusions contained in each of the following basic medical expense coverages:

    1. Hospital expense benefits.
    2. Surgical expense benefits.
    3. Physicians' visits expense benefits.
    4. Extended-care facility benefits.
    5. Home health-care benefits.
    6. Hospice benefits.
    7. Ambulatory-care expense benefits.
    8. Birthing centers.
    9. Diagnostic X-ray and laboratory expense benefits.
    10. Radiation therapy expense benefits.
    11. Prescription drug expense benefits.
    12. Vision-care expense benefits.
    13. Supplemental accident benefits.

Traditionally, medical expense coverage has consisted of separate benefits for hospital expenses, surgical expenses and physicians' charges. Coverage was limited and many types of medical expenses were not covered. In this environment, two developments took place:

    1. Basic coverages for other types of medical expenses were developed.
    2. A vast majority of employers began to provide more extensive benefits to

employees than had previously been available through the commonly written basic coverages.

While this broader coverage is increasingly being provided through a single comprehensive contract, the majority of employees are still covered under medical expense plans that consist of selected basic coverages supplemented by a major medical contract. This is particularly true for large employers. Small employers are much more likely to use a single major medical contract. This chapter will describe these basic coverages, consisting of three traditional coverages for

1. Hospital expense benefits.
2. Surgical expense benefits.
3. Physicians' visits expense benefits.

As well as the following newer coverages for

- Extended-care facilities.
- Home health care.
- Hospice care.
- Ambulatory care.
- Birthing centers.
- Diagnostic X-ray and laboratory services.
- Radiation therapy.
- Prescription drugs.
- Vision care.
- Supplemental accident benefits.

While many of these coverages can be written separately, it is not unusual for them to be incorporated into a single contract. In addition, many of the medical expenses for which basic benefit coverage is either limited or excluded will be covered under a supplemental major medical contract.

HOSPITAL EXPENSE BENEFITS

Hospital expense coverage provides benefits for charges incurred in a hospital by a covered person—that is, the employee or his or her dependents—who is an inpatient or, in some circumstances, an outpatient. Every medical expense contract defines what is meant by a hospital. While the actual wording may vary among insurance companies and in some states, the following definition is typical:

> The term *hospital* means (1) an institution which is accredited as a hospital under the hospital accreditation program of the Joint Commission on Accreditation of Hospitals, or (2) any other institution which is legally operated under the supervision of a staff of physicians and which has 24-hour-a-day nursing service. In no event should the term *hospital* include a convalescent nursing home or include any institution or part thereof which (1) is used principally as a convalescent facility, rest facility, nursing facility or facility for the aged; or (2) furnishes primarily domiciliary or custodial care, including training in the routines of daily living; or (3) is operated primarily as a school.

Inpatient Benefits

Hospital inpatient benefits fall into two categories: coverage for room-and-board charges and coverage for other charges.

Room and Board

Coverage for room-and-board charges includes the cost of the hospital room, meals and the services normally provided to all inpatients, including routine nursing care. Separate charges for such items as telephones and televisions usually are not covered. Benefits are commonly provided for a specific number of days for each separate hospital confinement, and this may vary from 31 days to 365 days. Some contracts provide coverage for an unlimited number of days. For purposes of this time period as well as for other benefits, most contracts stipulate that successive periods of hospital confinement will be treated as a single hospital confinement unless they (1) arise from entirely unrelated causes, or (2) are separated by the employee's return to continuous full-time active employment for some period of time, such as two weeks. For dependents, this latter requirement is replaced by one specifying that they must completely recover or remain out of the hospital for some period of time, such as three months.

The amount of the daily room-and-board benefit may be expressed in one of two ways: either a flat-dollar maximum or the cost of semiprivate accommodations. Under the first approach, benefits are provided for actual room-and-board charges up to a maximum daily amount; for example, $400. Employers using this approach may have different maximum benefits for employees in different locations to reflect geographic variations in hospital costs.

The majority of hospital expense contracts cover actual room-and-board charges up to the cost of semiprivate accommodations in the hospital in which the covered person is confined. This is the traditional approach used by Blue Cross Plans and is increasingly used by insurance companies. The cost of a private room may be covered in full if such accommodations are medically necessary. If a private room is not medically necessary, covered persons electing such accommodations must usually pay any charges above the normal semiprivate room rate. However, a few insurance plans provide additional coverage, usually a fixed daily dollar amount, for elective private room occupancy.

Most hospital expense contracts include additional room-and-board benefits for confinement in an intensive care unit. In some cases, particularly when normal room-and-board benefits are subject to a dollar maximum, intensive care benefits are expressed as some multiple, commonly two, of the normal room-and-board benefit. In those cases where benefits are provided for the cost of semiprivate accommodations, intensive care charges frequently are covered in full. However, in both cases, intensive care benefits may be subject to either a time limit or an overall dollar maximum.

Other Charges

Coverage for other charges, often referred to as miscellaneous charges, ancillary charges or hospital extras, provides benefits for certain services and supplies ordered by a physician during a covered person's hospital confinement, such as drugs, operating room charges, laboratory services and X-rays. However, with a few exceptions, only the hospital portion of these charges is covered; any associated charges for professional services, such as physicians' fees, are not covered. The exceptions often include charges for anesthesia and ambulance services. Traditionally, anesthesia and its administration were provided and billed by the hospital and considered a covered expense. As anesthesia came to be administered and separately billed by physicians not employed by the hospital, many hospital expense benefit contracts were altered to cover anesthesia if it was administered in a hospital, whether the patient was billed by the hospital or by a physician. Recently, however, the trend has been toward covering anesthesia as a surgical expense benefit instead of a hospital expense benefit.

The amount of the benefit for other charges is usually expressed in one of the following three ways:

1. Full coverage up to a dollar maximum. This approach is most commonly found in contracts when the daily room-and-board benefit is also subject to a dollar limit. In most cases, this maximum is some multiple, often 20, of the daily room-and-board benefit. For example, a contract with a daily room-and-board benefit of $400 might have an $8,000 maximum for other charges.
2. Full coverage up to a dollar maximum, again often expressed as a multiple of the room-and-board benefit, and partial coverage for a limited amount of additional expenses. For example, a contract might cover the first $1,500 of charges in full and 75 percent of the next $3,000 in charges.
3. Full payment subject only to the duration for which room-and-board benefits are payable. While this approach is normally associated with contracts that provide room-and-board benefits equal to the cost of semiprivate accommodations, it may also be used when room-and-board benefits are subject to a daily maximum.

When coverage for ambulance services is provided, it is common to limit the benefit to a dollar maximum, such as $50 per hospital confinement.

Preadmission Certification

As a method of controlling costs, medical expense plans are increasingly adopting utilization review programs. One aspect of these programs, which are discussed in more detail in Chapter 12, is preadmission certification. Such a program requires that a covered person or his or her physician obtain prior authorization for any nonemergency hospitalization. Authorization usually must also be obtained within 24 to 48 hours of admission for emergencies.

The initial reviewer, typically a registered nurse, determines whether hospitalization or some type of alternative care is most appropriate and what the appropriate length of stay for the medical condition should be. If the preapproved length of stay is insufficient, the patient's physician must obtain prior approval for any extension.

Most plans reduce benefits if the preadmission certification procedure is not followed. Probably the most common reduction is to pay only 50 percent of the benefit that would otherwise be paid. If a patient enters the hospital after a preadmission certification has been denied, many plans will not pay for any hospital expenses. Other plans will provide a reduced level of benefits.

Outpatient Benefits

Traditionally, hospital expense contracts did not cover outpatient expenses. However, it is not unusual today to find coverage for hospital outpatient expenses arising from the following:

- *Surgery.* When broader coverage exists for surgery performed on inpatients than on outpatients, there is no question that unnecessary hospitalization is encouraged. The purpose of this benefit is to provide comparable coverage, thus lowering hospital utilization when surgical procedures can be performed on an outpatient basis. This benefit covers only hospital charges, such as the use of operating facilities, not the surgeon's fee.
- *Preadmission testing.* The first day or two of hospital confinements, particularly for surgical procedures, are often devoted to necessary diagnostic tests and X-rays. This benefit encourages the performing of these procedures on an outpatient basis prior to hospitalization by covering the costs as if the person were an inpatient. For benefits to be paid, these procedures generally must be (1) performed after a hospital confinement for surgery has been scheduled, (2) ordered by the same physician who ordered the hospital confinement, (3) performed in the hospital where the confinement will take place and (4) accepted by the hospital in lieu of the same tests that normally would be performed during confinement. Benefits are paid even if the preadmission testing leads to a cancellation of the scheduled confinement. Even when benefits for preadmission testing are available, they are often not used since physicians and patients find it easier to have such testing performed on an inpatient basis.
- *Emergency room treatment.* Hospital expense contracts commonly provide coverage for emergency room treatment of accidental injuries within a specified time period, varying from 24 to 72 hours, after an accident. In a few cases, similar benefits are also provided for sudden and serious illnesses. It should be noted that any emergency room charges incurred immediately prior to hospitalization are considered inpatient expenses.

In most cases, these outpatient expenses are treated like other charges, but in some hospital expense plans, separate benefits may apply to outpatient surgery and emergency room treatment.

Exclusions

Although variations exist among the providers of hospital coverage—some of which result from state legislation—most hospital expense contracts usually do not cover expenses resulting from:

- Occupational injury or disease to the extent benefits are provided by workers' compensation laws or similar legislation. Many contracts exclude coverage for benefits available through workers' compensation laws. Thus, work-related hospital expenses are excluded even if the employer has not purchased workers' compensation coverage.
- Cosmetic surgery unless such surgery is to correct a condition resulting from an accidental injury incurred while the covered person is insured under the contract.
- Physical examinations, including diagnostic tests and X-rays, unless such examinations are necessary for the treatment of an injury or illness.
- Convalescent, custodial or rest care.
- Private-duty nursing.
- Services furnished by or on behalf of government agencies unless there is a requirement for either the patient or the patient's medical expense plan to pay for the services. Prior to the passage of the Consolidated Omnibus Budget Reconciliation Act of 1985 (COBRA), it was common for employee benefit plans to exclude payment for medical services received in a Veterans Administration or military hospital since the patient had no legal obligation to pay. Under provisions of the Act, medical expense plans must generally pay benefits to the government on the same basis as they would have paid if care had been received elsewhere. However, if a plan does not pay charges in full because of deductibles, coinsurance or plan limitations, the patient is not responsible for the balance. With respect to VA hospitals, the provisions of the Act apply only to non-service-connected disabilities. The rules for military hospitals apply to retired (but not active) members of the armed services and most spouses and dependent children of active or retired military persons.

Hospital expense contracts may also exclude, or only provide limited coverage for, expenses arising from mental illness, alcoholism and drug addiction unless these exclusions are prohibited by law. Until the amendment of the Civil Rights Act in 1978, it was not unusual to exclude maternity-related expenses from hospital expense contracts. However, the Act now requires that benefit plans of employers with 15 or more employees treat pregnancy, childbirth and related conditions in the same manner as any other illness. (See Chapter 5.)

In the absence of state laws to the contrary, pregnancy may be, and often is, excluded under group insurance contracts written for employers with fewer than 15 employees. If these employers wish to provide such coverage, it can usually be added as an optional benefit. In some cases, pregnancy is treated like any other illness covered under the contract. In other cases, benefits are determined in accordance with a schedule that most commonly provides an all-inclusive benefit for hospital, surgical and certain other expenses associated with delivery. Regular physician visits and diagnostic tests may or may not be covered. Here is a typical maternity schedule:

Type of Pregnancy	Benefit
Normal delivery	$1,500
Cesarian	3,000
Miscarriage	750

A variation of this schedule that is often used by Blue Cross and Blue Shield Plans provides a scheduled surgery benefit (possibly including visits prior to delivery) and covers hospital expenses on a semiprivate room basis.

An expense associated with maternity is the nursery charge for a newborn infant. In most cases, this will be equal to at least 50 percent of a hospital's normal room-and-board charge. This expense is not covered as part of a maternity benefit and is not covered under many hospital expense contracts if the infant is healthy since the contract only covers expenses associated with accidents and illnesses. However, some contracts do cover nursery charges, and a number of states require that they be covered.

Deductibles and Coinsurance

It is common for deductibles and coinsurance to apply to major medical expense coverages. In contrast, hospital expenses under basic hospital expense coverage, as well as benefits under other basic medical expense coverages, usually are not subject to deductibles or coinsurance. Rather, any limitations that exist are most likely to be in the form of maximum amounts that will be paid.

SURGICAL EXPENSE BENEFITS

Surgical expense coverage provides benefits for physicians' charges associated with surgical procedures. While one tends to think of a surgical procedure as involving cutting, insurance contracts typically define the term broadly to include such procedures as suturing, electrocauterization, removal of a stone or foreign body by endoscopic means and the treatment of fractures or dislocations.

Even though surgical expense coverage is frequently sold in connection with hospital expense coverage, surgical expense coverage normally provides benefits for surgery performed not only in the hospital either as an inpatient or an outpatient, but also as an outpatient in a free-standing (separate from a hospital), ambulatory surgical center and in a physician's office. To discourage unnecessary hospitalization, some surgical expense benefit contracts actually provide larger benefits if a surgical procedure is performed as outpatient surgery.

Outpatient surgery also results in charges for medical supplies, nurses and the use of facilities. As mentioned, these charges are often covered if surgery is performed on an outpatient basis in a hospital. However, neither hospital expense coverage nor surgical expense coverage usually provides such benefits if the surgery is performed in a physician's office or in an ambulatory surgical center. Even though not specifically covered, costs of alternate facilities are paid by some insurance companies, and required by some states, when their use clearly has prevented hospital expenses from being incurred. As will be discussed later in this chapter, benefits for ambulatory care centers are sometimes included as an additional basic coverage.

Benefits

Surgical expense coverage traditionally provided benefits only for the fee of the primary surgeon. However, newer contracts often provide separate benefits for assistant surgeons and anesthesiologists as well. Since both hospital expense coverage and surgical expense coverage often cover anesthesia, it is important that an overall medical expense plan be properly designed to make sure this benefit is neither omitted nor overlapping. The major difficulty in this regard occurs when different providers are used for the hospital and surgical benefits.

Benefit amounts may be expressed in several ways, ranging from a schedule of fees to the full payment of actual charges.

Fee Schedule

In providing basic surgical expense benefits, many insurance companies and some Blue Shield Plans use either a fee schedule or a relative value schedule in which charges are paid up to the maximum amounts specified in the schedule of surgical procedures contained in the master contract. The following is an excerpt from one such schedule:

Surgical Procedure	Maximum Benefit
Cardiovascular system:	
Aortic valve replacement	$2,000
Pericardiectomy	1,200
Digestive system:	
Adenoidectomy	100
Appendectomy	400
Tonsillectomy, under age 18 years	150
Tonsillectomy, over age 18 years	200

It is common to refer to a fee schedule by the maximum amount that will be paid for the most expensive procedure. For example, the previous excerpt is from a $2,000 schedule. For the vast majority of procedures, however, the maximum benefits that will be paid are less, reflecting the relatively lower cost for such procedures.

The benefit specified in the schedule of surgical procedures is the maximum amount that will be paid to the primary surgeon for all charges, including follow-up visits. To the extent the charges of the primary surgeon are below this amount, the balance generally can be applied to charges of assistant surgeons and, possibly, anesthesiologists. If separate benefits are provided for an assistant surgeon, they are usually a percentage, commonly 20 percent, of this amount. If benefits are provided for an anesthesiologist, a separate dollar maximum also varying by procedure will usually be specified. The typical fee schedule contains only between 100 and 200 of the more common surgical procedures. When other surgical procedures are performed, payment is based on an amount determined by the insurance company, but consistent with the fee schedule. For example, if the charge for an unlisted procedure typically is the same as for an appendectomy, the benefit maximum for that procedure would most likely be used. If more than one surgical procedure is performed at the same time, the total benefit normally is limited to the maximum benefit payable for the most costly procedure plus 50 percent of the maximum benefit payable for any other procedures. However, no additional amounts will usually be paid for the second procedure if it is considered incidental and performed through the same incision.

Relative Value Schedule

A variation of the fee schedule is the relative value schedule in which the value of each surgical procedure is expressed in unit values that are relative to each other. For example, a surgical procedure with the unit value of 50 is considered to be twice as expensive as one with a unit value of 25. These relative values are based on statistics from insurance companies or state medical associations and may vary depending on the source of the statistics. This is an excerpt from a relative value schedule:

Surgical Procedure	Relative Value Units
Skin:	
Biopsy	3
Excision of pilonidal cyst	30
Stomach:	
Excision of ulcer or tumor	60
Total gastrectomy	100

To determine the actual maximum benefit that will be paid, the relative value is multiplied by a dollar conversion factor selected by the policyholder and specified in the master contract. For example, with a $20 conversion factor $60 would be paid for a skin biopsy and $1,200 for the removal of a stomach ulcer. Providers using relative value schedules usually have the same schedule in all contracts, but vary the levels of benefits for different policyholders by using different dollar conversion factors. Employers can also take geographic variations in surgical costs into consideration by using different dollar conversion factors for employees in different locations.

Reasonable-and-Customary Charges

The majority of surgical expense plans follow the approach used in major medical contracts and provide benefits to the extent surgical charges are reasonable and customary. Unfortunately, insurance contracts are vague as to the precise meaning of these terms, and each company determines what it considers reasonable and customary. In general, reasonable-and-customary charges—sometimes referred to as usual, customary and reasonable or prevailing charges—are considered to be those that fall within the range of fees normally charged for a given procedure by physicians of similar training and experience within a geographic region.

The usual practice of insurance companies is to pay charges in full as long as the charges do not exceed some percentile, usually ranging from the 85th to the 95th, of the range of charges for a specific surgical procedure within a certain geographic region. For example, if an insurance company uses the 90th percentile and if for a certain procedure 90 percent of the charges are $300 or less, this is the maximum amount that will be paid. The covered person will be required to absorb any additional charges if he or she uses a more expensive physician. Through the use of computers, insurance companies now have statistics that categorize expenses by geographic regions as small as by the zip codes of medical care providers. Thus, while $300 may be the maximum reasonable-and-customary amount in one part of a metropolitan area, $350 may be considered reasonable and customary in another part of the same metropolitan area.

Blue Shield Plans often use a somewhat modified approach in determining the maximum amount that will be paid. Each year, physicians file their charges for the coming year with the Blue Shield Plan. During that year, the association will pay charges in full up to some percentile of these filed charges. Under some plans, the physicians agree not to charge Blue Shield patients amounts in excess of their filed fees. In addition, participating physicians in other Blue Shield Plans agree to accept any Blue Shield payment as payment in full, particularly for employees with an income level below a certain amount, such as $10,000 for an individual and $15,000 for a family.

Second Surgical Opinions

In an attempt to control medical costs by eliminating unnecessary surgery, many medical expense plans, both basic and major medical, now provide benefits for second surgical opinions. There is no question that as a result of such opinions some patients will decide against surgery. However, it is still unclear whether the cost savings of second surgical opinions might be illusionary. For example, surgery may still be required at a later date, or long-term costs may be incurred for alternative treatment.

A voluntary approach for obtaining second surgical opinions is often used. If a physician or surgeon recommends surgery, a covered person can seek a second opinion and the cost will be borne by the medical expense plan. In some instances, the benefit is limited to a specific maximum, but in most cases, the costs of the second opinion, including X-rays and diagnostic tests, are paid in full. Some plans will also pay for a third opinion if the first two opinions disagree. When there are divergent opinions, the final choice is up to the patient, and the regular benefits of the plan will usually be paid for any resulting surgery. As an incentive to encourage second opinions, some plans actually provide larger benefits for a covered person who has obtained a second opinion, even if it does not agree with the first opinion.

In the last few years, it has become increasingly common for medical expense plans to require mandatory second opinions. These provisions may apply to any elective and nonemergency surgery, but frequently apply only to a specified list of procedures. In most cases, the second opinion must be performed by a surgeon selected by the insurance company or other provider of benefits. If conflicting opinions arise, a third opinion may be obtained. The costs of the second and third opinions are paid in full. In contrast to voluntary provisions, mandatory provisions generally specify that benefits will be paid at a reduced level if surgery is performed either without a second opinion or contrary to the final opinion.

The trend toward mandatory second opinions has had an interesting result. Since many employers felt money was being saved under their voluntary programs, wouldn't it be logical to save more money by making the program mandatory? Unfortunately, the opposite situation has often been the case: People who voluntarily seek a second opinion are frequently looking for an alternative to surgery, while those who obtain a second opinion only because it is required are more likely to accept surgery as the best alternative. Employers have also found that a second opinion by a surgeon is still likely to call for surgery. As a result, there seems to be a growing feeling that the cost of mandatory second opinions may exceed any decrease in surgical benefits paid. Consequently, some employers have returned to voluntary programs or stopped providing coverage for second opinions altogether.

Exclusions

As with hospital coverage and virtually all other types of medical expense coverage, exclusions exist under basic surgical expense contracts for occupational injuries or disease, certain services provided by governmental agencies and cosmetic surgery. All surgical expense contracts have an exclusion for certain types of dental surgery. However, the extent of the exclusion varies and care must be taken in properly integrating any dental coverage with other basic coverages. At one extreme, some contracts exclude virtually all procedures associated with the teeth or disease of their surrounding tissue or bone structure. At the other extreme, a more common exclusion eliminates coverage for most dental procedures but provides surgical benefits if a covered person is hospitalized for the removal of impacted teeth or for surgery of the gums or bone structure surrounding the teeth. Note that although benefits for oral surgery may not be paid even if a covered person is hospitalized, the hospital expenses are often covered under hospital expense contracts.

PHYSICIANS' VISITS EXPENSE BENEFITS

Often referred to as medical expense coverage or regular medical expense coverage, physicians' visits expense coverage provides benefits for fees of attending physicians other than surgeons; the charges of the latter are paid under surgical expense benefits coverage. Benefits are usually provided only for physicians' visits while a covered person is hospitalized. However, coverage may also include office and home visits.

In-Hospital Coverage

In-hospital coverage is designed to provide benefits for physicians' charges when a covered person is hospitalized as an inpatient. Three general approaches are used to determine the amount and duration of benefits:

1. Physicians' fees are paid on a reasonable-and-customary basis, up to a specific number of visits per hospitalization. In most cases, this will correspond to the period of time for which hospital expense benefits are provided.
2. Benefits are limited to a daily maximum, again, up to a specified period of time. The daily maximum may be expressed as a dollar amount (such as $30) or in terms of a relative value (such as 1.5) that is generally multiplied by the same dollar conversion factor applicable to surgical expense benefits. However, a separate conversion factor might be used. A difficulty here is that physicians often charge more for initial hospital visits. Consequently, the daily maximum in some contracts is increased for the first day (or two to three days) of hospitalization.
3. The total benefit is expressed as a lump-sum amount equal to the daily benefit times the number of days hospitalized. For example, if the daily benefit is $25 and the covered person is hospitalized for ten days, physicians' charges would be paid in full up to $250, regardless of the charges incurred on any specific day or the number of visits made by the physician.

Three additional types of benefits are sometimes included when in-hospital coverage is provided:

1. Coverage for physicians' visits when a covered person is in an intensive care unit. If benefits are paid on a reasonable-and-customary basis, these charges will be covered in the same manner. Under plans with a daily maximum, the maximum may be increased to reflect the more expensive charges normally associated with intensive care.
2. Coverage for consultation services. Most plans only cover the charges of attending physicians. However, some plans provide benefits for the consultation services of other physicians. This benefit may be subject to a dollar maximum or paid on a reasonable-and-customary basis.
3. Coverage for physicians' visits in other types of medical care facilities, such as extended care centers. This benefit is most commonly provided when room-and-board charges for these alternative facilities are also covered.

In-Hospital and Out-of-Hospital Coverage

In addition to the benefits previously described, coverage for physicians' visits may also include physicians' charges incurred in a physician's office or in a covered person's home. This broader coverage is usually not written as a separate and distinct benefit, but rather as a single overall coverage for all types of physicians' visits. Benefits may be paid on a reasonable-and-customary basis or be subject to a dollar maximum per visit. In the latter case, it is not unusual to have two different dollar maximums: one for hospital visits and home visits and a lesser one for office visits. Benefits will be subject to some overall maximum limit, which may be expressed as either a dollar amount (such as $1,000) or a specified number of visits (such as 60). This limit may be applied on an annual basis or for any single illness or injury. Most plans contain a waiting period, commonly ranging from one to five visits, before benefits for home and office visits will be paid. However, this waiting period is often waived in the case of an accident.

Some plans also provide coverage for well-baby care. This includes benefits for inoculations and physicians' examinations—both in and out of the hospital—of healthy infants for a limited period of time, such as three months after birth. Some states require that medical expense contracts cover these benefits for newborns only until the infant is discharged from the hospital.

Exclusions

Most of the exclusions mentioned previously in connection with surgical expense coverage also apply to physicians' visits expense coverage. In addition to these exclusions, there usually are no benefits for physical examinations, eye examinations or dentistry. Fees charged when a physician did not actually see a patient, such as for a telephone consultation, are also often excluded. Finally, charges made by a physician who is a salaried staff member of a hospital are frequently not covered.

OTHER BENEFITS

When medical expense plans consist of basic coverages supplemented by major medical insurance, it is not unusual for the basic benefits to cover only hospital expenses, surgical expenses and sometimes physicians' visits. Other types of basic benefits might also be provided, which generally cover expenses that either are included, or may be included, in a supplemental major medical contract. However, providing such coverage in the form of separate basic benefits may result in a greater reimbursement to an employee since deductibles and coinsurance often do not apply.

Extended-Care Facility Benefits

Many hospital patients recover to a point where they no longer require the full level of medical care provided by a hospital, but they cannot be discharged because they still require a period of convalescence under supervised medical care. Extended-care facilities, often called convalescent nursing homes or skilled nursing facilities, have been established in many areas to provide this type of care. To the extent patients can be treated in these facilities which are often adjacent to hospitals, daily room-and-board charges can be reduced—often substantially. Obviously, this type of care is discouraged if it is not covered on a comparable basis with confinement in a hospital. Even when comparable coverage is provided, however, there seems to be a reluctance on the part of both patients and physicians to use such facilities. It becomes an additional facility for physicians to visit, and concerns are often expressed about the quality of care provided.

Extended-care facility coverage provides benefits to the person who is an inpatient in an extended-care facility, which is typically defined as an institution that furnishes room and board and 24-hour-a-day skilled nursing care under the supervision of a physician or a registered professional nurse. It does not include facilities that are designed as places for rest or domiciliary care for the aged. In addition, facilities for the treatment of drug abuse and alcoholism are often excluded. To receive benefits, the following conditions must usually be satisfied:

- The confinement must be recommended by a physician.
- 24-hour-a-day nursing care must be needed.
- The confinement must commence within (1) 14 days after termination of a specified period of hospital confinement, generally 3 days, for which room-and-board benefits were payable, or (2) 14 days of a previous confinement in an extended care facility for which benefits were payable. A few but increasing number of contracts include benefits for situations where extended-care facilities are used in lieu of hospitalization.
- The confinement must be for the same or a related condition for which the covered person was hospitalized.

Benefits are provided in much the same manner as under hospital expense coverage. If hospital expense benefits are on a semiprivate accommodation basis, extended-care facility benefits generally are paid on the same basis. If hospital expense benefits are subject to a daily dollar maximum, extended-care facility benefits are usually likewise subject to a daily dollar maximum, most typically equal to 50 percent of the daily hospital benefit. The maximum length of time for which extended-care benefits will be paid may be independent of the time a person is hospitalized. A maximum of 60 days' coverage is fairly common. Alternatively, the benefit period may be related to the number of unused hospital days. The most common approach in this instance is to allow two days in an extended-care facility for each unused hospital day. For example, if a hospital expense plan provides benefits for a maximum of 90 days and if a covered person is hospitalized for 50 days, the 40 unused hospital days can be exchanged for 80 days of benefits in an extended-care facility. Other charges incurred in an extended-care facility may be treated in one of several ways. They may be covered in full, subject to a separate dollar limit, or be treated as part of the maximum benefit payable for other charges under hospital expense coverage.

Home Health-Care Benefits

Home health-care coverage is similar to extended-care facility benefits; however, it is designed for those situations when the necessary part-time nursing care ordered by a physician following hospitalization can be provided in the patient's home. Coverage is for (1) nursing care (usually limited to a maximum of two hours per day) under the supervision of a registered professional nurse; (2) physical, occupational and speech therapy; and (3) medical supplies and equipment, such as wheelchairs and hospital beds.

In most cases, the benefits payable are equal to a percentage, frequently 80 percent, of reasonable-and-customary charges. Benefit payments are limited to either a maximum number of visits (such as 60 per calendar year) or to a period of time (such as 90 days after benefits commence). In the latter case, the time period may be based on the unused hospital days, such as three days of home visits for each unused hospital day.

Hospice Benefits

A newer development in the area of medical care is hospice care for the treatment of terminally ill persons. Hospice care does not attempt to cure medical conditions, but rather is devoted to easing the physical and psychological pain associated with death. In addition to providing services for the dying patient, counseling may also be provided to surviving family members. While a hospice is thought of as a separate facility, this type of care can also be provided on an outpatient basis in the dying person's home. Where hospice care is available, the cost of treating patients is usually much less than the cost of traditional hospitalizations. Currently, few benefit plans provide hospice coverage, but considerable interest has been generated among employers as a means of controlling medical costs.

Ambulatory-Care Expense Benefits

Recent years have also seen the development of medical facilities called ambulatory-care centers, or surgicenters. These centers, designed for the purpose of outpatient surgery, are separate from hospitals. Since these facilities fail to meet the definition of a hospital, benefits for their use are not included under hospital expense coverage. Consequently, some basic medical expense plans provide benefits for ambulatory-care expenses. Ambulatory-care centers are generally defined as permanent facilities that (1) are operated primarily for the purpose of performing surgical procedures, (2) have continuous physician services and professional nursing services and (3) do not provide services or other accommodations for patients to stay overnight. In most cases, benefits are paid as if the covered person were an inpatient in a hospital. However, to encourage the use of such facilities as a less expensive alternative to hospitals, benefits may be paid at a higher level or even in full. Benefits cover any charges for use of the facility as well as other charges, such as medical supplies, X-rays, and diagnostic tests.

Birthing Centers

Another recent development in medical care is birthing centers, which are designed to provide a homelike facility for the delivery of babies. Like ambulatory-care centers, they are separate from hospitals.

The cost of using birthing centers is considerably less than using hospitals. Deliveries are performed by nurse-midwives, and mothers and babies are released shortly after birth. Benefits may be paid as if the mother used a hospital and obstetrician, but are frequently paid in full as an incentive to use these lower-cost facilities.

Diagnostic X-Ray and Laboratory Expense Benefits

In recent years, the number of diagnostic X-rays and laboratory services performed has increased substantially, often because of defensive medicine practiced by physicians. Under the previous coverages mentioned, benefits include the cost of these services if a covered person is an inpatient. However, outpatient benefits only cover costs connected with surgery at a hospital or ambulatory-care center or preadmission testing. Diagnostic X-ray and laboratory coverage provides benefits for the cost of these services (including physicians' charges) when performed on an outpatient basis and when not otherwise covered under other portions of a basic medical expense plan. While benefits are usually provided for both illnesses and injuries, they may be provided only for illnesses if a medical expense plan contains a separate supplemental accident expense benefit, which will be described later in this chapter.

Several approaches are used to provide diagnostic X-ray and laboratory coverage.

1. A schedule of procedures, similar to a surgical schedule, with maximum benefits specified for each procedure. Plans taking this approach usually contain a single overall maximum benefit, or possibly separate overall maximum benefits for X-rays and laboratory services. This maximum benefit may apply on a per-illness or per-injury basis or on an annual basis.
2. All charges are covered in full up to a specified maximum amount per procedure.
3. Benefits are paid as if the X-rays and laboratory examinations had been performed while the covered person was an inpatient in a hospital. In this situation, the maximum benefit specified for other charges under hospital expense coverage applies to the aggregate of these outpatient charges and any other miscellaneous charges that are incurred while the covered person is hospitalized if they are associated with the same illness or injury.

Because diagnostic X-ray and laboratory expense coverage is designed to complement other basic coverages, benefits that might be provided under these other coverages are generally excluded from diagnostic X-ray and laboratory expense coverage. In addition, exclusions generally exist for routine physical examinations and dentistry.

Radiation Therapy Expense Benefits

The widespread use of radiation therapy is a relatively new but common form of treatment for some illnesses, particularly cancer. Under the traditional basic coverages, benefits are provided under hospital expense coverage only as long as a covered person is hospitalized. Therefore, the primary purpose of radiation therapy expense benefits is to cover the cost of these treatments when performed on an outpatient basis. However, coverage may also be written to supplement any such benefits under hospital expense coverage. There is no coverage for the use of radiation for diagnostic purposes because such benefits are provided by diagnostic X-ray and laboratory expense benefits. Coverage is often provided for the treatment of both malignant and benign conditions, but is sometimes limited to cancerous conditions only.

Benefits are generally provided for the administration of the therapy, the use of facilities, and any materials and their preparation. Some insurance companies treat radiation therapy as a single category of benefits, while others divide it into two categories:

1. Treatments involving the use of X-ray machines.
2. Treatments involving the use of radioactive isotopes, radioactive iodine or other radioactive substances that are applied to the body or taken internally.

Benefits may be paid on a reasonable-and-customary basis or paid in accordance with a fee or relative value schedule. An overall maximum limit, or limits if two categories of benefits are used, may also apply. This limit may be based on some time period, such as 12 months, or it may apply to the entire course of treatment for a condition, regardless of duration.

Prescription Drug Expense Benefits

With the exception of drugs administered in a hospital or in an extended-care facility, the cost of prescription drugs is covered as a basic benefit only if prescription drug expense coverage is purchased. The cost of prescription drugs has typically been covered under major medical insurance. Separate prescription drug plans, however, are often a result of collective bargaining even when there is a major medical plan. This benefit is highly visible to employees who will periodically have prescriptions that must be filled either for themselves or for members of their family. Some benefit consultants also feel that a separate prescription drug plan may result in cost savings since the large number of relatively small claims lends itself to more economical methods of administration and processing of claims.

The typical basic prescription drug plan covers the cost of drugs that are required by either state or federal law to be dispensed by prescription, except those dispensed in a hospital or in an extended-care facility. Drugs for which prescriptions are not required by law are usually not covered even though they are ordered by the physician on a prescription form. One frequent exception to this general rule is injectable insulin, which generally is covered despite the fact that in many states it is a nonprescription drug. No coverage is provided for charges to administer drugs or the cost of therapeutic devices or appliances, such as bandages or hypodermic needles. It is common to exclude benefits for a quantity of drugs in excess of a specified amount. In some plans, this quantity is expressed as the amount normally prescribed by physicians; in other plans, it is expressed as a supply for a certain time period, often 30 days. Refills, however, are considered new prescriptions.

Some plans cover maintenance drugs, such as medicine for the treatment of high blood pressure; other plans exclude them. Excluding these drugs, however, may be false economy. Although the current cost of a prescription drug plan will be lowered, medical conditions may remain untreated and preventable surgical and hospital expenses may result. Contraceptive drugs may also be covered or excluded. Some prescription drug plans take a middle approach by covering these drugs only when they are prescribed for treating a medical condition rather than for preventing conception.

Most prescription drug plans have a deductible—often referred to as a copayment—that must be paid by a covered person for any prescription filled. In most cases, this is a flat amount varying from $1 to $3 per prescription.

Two basic methods are used to provide prescription drug coverage: a reimbursement approach and a service approach. Under plans using a reimbursement approach, a covered individual personally pays the cost of prescription drugs, using any pharmacy he or she chooses. A claim for reimbursement is then filed with the provider of benefits. Subject to any copayments, reimbursement is made to the covered person on the basis of either billed charges or reasonable-and-customary charges.

While coverage for prescription drugs under major medical plans is often on a reimbursement basis, the majority of basic medical plans use a service approach. Under this approach, drugs are provided to covered persons by participating pharmacies upon receipt of a prescription, proper identification which is usually a card issued by the plan, and any required copayments. The pharmacy then bills the provider of coverage for the remaining cost of any prescription filled. This provider may be a Blue Cross and Blue Shield Plan, an insurance company or a third-party administrator acting on behalf of either an insurance company or an employer with a self-insured plan. Because of the specialization that can be used in handling many small claims and the need to establish a system of participating pharmacies, most insurance companies, except for a few large ones, use third-party administrators for their prescription drug plans.

Under virtually all service plans, the provider of coverage or the third-party administrator negotiates a contract with participating pharmacies to provide the drugs at a reduced cost. This cost is usually equal to the wholesale cost of the drug plus a flat dispensing fee, such as $3 for each prescription. Prescriptions filled at nonparticipating pharmacies generally are covered but handled on a reimbursement basis. In addition, reimbursement in these cases is typically less than the cost of the prescription. The usual provision under Blue Cross and Blue Shield Plans is to pay 75 percent of the cost of a prescription drug purchased at a nonparticipating pharmacy, less any copayment, while insurance companies usually pay up to the amount that would have been paid to a participating pharmacy.

Vision-Care Expense Benefits

The previous coverages discussed do not provide benefits for the cost of eyeglasses and only rarely cover the cost of routine eye examinations. Vision-care expense coverage is designed to provide benefits for these expenses. Coverage may be provided by insurance companies, Blue Cross and Blue Shield Plans, plans of state optometric associations patterned after Blue Shield, closed-panel HMO-type plans established by local providers of vision services, vision-care PPOs or third-party administrators.

Benefits are occasionally provided on a reasonable-and-customary basis or are subject to a flat benefit per year that may be applied to any covered expenses. Normally, however, a benefit schedule will be used that specifies the types and amounts of benefits and the frequency with which they will be provided. Here is one such schedule:

Type of Benefit	Maximum Amount
Any 12-month period:	
Eye examination	$ 45
Lenses, pair:	
Single vision	45
Bifocal	75
Trifocal	125
Lenticular	200
Contact (when medically necessary)	300
Contact (when not medically necessary)	125
Any 24-month period:	
Frames	60

Under some plans, most benefits are provided on a service basis rather than being subject to a maximum benefit. However, these plans usually cover only the cost of basic frames, which the covered person can upgrade at an additional expense.

Exclusions commonly exist for any extra charge for plastic lenses, or the cost of safety lenses or prescription sunglasses. Benefits are generally provided for eye examinations by either an optometrist or an ophthalmologist. Larger benefits are sometimes provided if the latter is used. Vision-care plans do not pay benefits for eye surgery or treatment of eye diseases since these are covered under other basic coverages or major medical coverage.

Supplemental Accident Expense Benefits

Many basic medical expense plans, as well as major medical plans, include a supplemental accident expense benefit. The purpose of this benefit is to cover expenses associated with accidents to the extent that they are not provided under other medical expense coverages. There would probably be little need for this type of coverage if a basic medical expense plan included all the coverages previously described in this chapter. Most basic medical expense plans consist only of hospital, surgical and physicians' visits coverage; little coverage exists for the treatment of accidental injuries on an outpatient basis.

Benefits usually apply to expenses incurred within 90 days after an accident and pay for such items as professional fees, diagnostic X-rays, laboratory examinations and physical therapy. In addition, benefits are subject to a maximum limit, with $300 and $500 limits most commonly used.

Supplemental accident coverage has been the subject of controversy inasmuch as there seems to be no logical reason for providing different benefits for accidental injuries than for illnesses. However, the benefit is popular among employees and its cost is relatively small.

STUDY QUESTIONS

1. Describe the coverage that may be contained in a hospital expense contract for
   a. Room and board.
   b. Other inpatient charges.
   c. Outpatient expenses.
2. a. What is the purpose of hospital preadmission certification?
   b. What are the possible penalties if the preadmission process is not followed?
3. How are benefit limitations under medical expense contracts usually expressed?
4. How does a surgical fee schedule differ from a relative value schedule?
5. How do most insurance companies determine whether a surgical fee is reasonable and customary?
6. Explain how surgical benefits may be affected by (a) voluntary provisions and (b) mandatory provisions for second surgical opinions.
7. Describe the approaches used to determine the amount and duration of benefits for physicians' visits when each of the following is provided:
   a. In-hospital coverage only.
   b. Both in-hospital and out-of-hospital coverage.
8. Why has hospice care become topic of interest among employers?
9. How is the amount of benefits usually determined when coverage is provided for surgery in ambulatory-care centers?
10. Why are radiation therapy expense benefits often limited to outpatient expenses?
11. Why are benefits for prescription drugs often provided under a separate prescription drug plan rather than under a major medical contract?
12. Why are benefits for eye surgery and the treatment of eye diseases excluded from vision-care coverage?

11

Group Major Medical Expense Coverage

Objectives

- Describe the approaches used to provide major medical coverage.
- Explain why supplemental major medical coverage continues to be used.
- Describe the characteristics of major medical coverage with respect to covered expenses and benefit limitations.
- Explain the purpose of deductibles and coinsurance and describe the differences found in deductible and coinsurance provisions.

Most employees have some type of major medical expense coverage that provides substantial protection against catastrophic medical expenses, with relatively few exclusions or limitations. However, the employee frequently must pay a portion of the cost of these medical expenses in the form of a deductible and/or coinsurance.

TYPES OF MAJOR MEDICAL COVERAGE

Two general types of plans for providing major medical coverage are supplemental (or superimposed) plans and comprehensive plans. In supplemental plans, major medical coverage is coordinated with various basic medical expense coverages. One example of this kind of coordinated medical expense plan is shown in Figure 11-1.

Subject to its own limitations and exclusions, a supplemental major medical plan covers expenses that are not included under basic coverages. These include:

- Expenses not within the scope of the basic coverages. For example, office

FIGURE 11-1

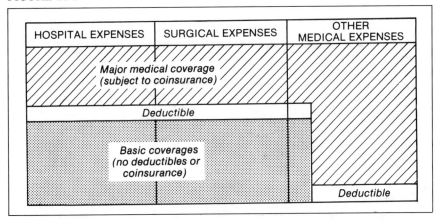

visits to a physician may be excluded if the basic coverages only include in-hospital physicians' visits.

- Expenses no longer covered under the basic coverages because those benefits have been exhausted. For example, if the basic coverages provide room-and-board benefits in full, but only for a maximum of 60 days, the cost of room and board would be covered by the major medical plan beginning on the 61st day.
- Expenses specifically excluded under the basic coverages. For example, if the basic coverages exclude hospital charges for the treatment of alcoholism, the major medical coverage may provide benefits. However, expenses that are excluded under the basic coverages are often excluded under the major medical plan.

In the comprehensive type of major medical coverage, a single contract covers all medical expenses. This is illustrated in Figure 11-2. In this example, once the deductible is satisfied, most medical expenses are covered subject to a coinsurance provision. Although this illustration shows a comprehensive major medical plan in its purest form, most comprehensive medical expense contracts contain modifications that either eliminate or reduce the deductible or coinsurance provision for certain expenses. These variations will be discussed later in this chapter.

SUPPLEMENTAL VERSUS COMPREHENSIVE

At first glance, it might appear that the simplicity of a comprehensive major medical plan makes it preferable to a supplemental plan. Yet, supplemental plans continue to cover the majority of employees, even though most newly written plans are

FIGURE 11-2

HOSPITAL EXPENSES	SURGICAL EXPENSES	OTHER MEDICAL EXPENSES
	Major medical coverage (subject to coinsurance)	
	Deductible	

comprehensive. In a few instances, the continued use of supplemental plans has been based on tradition. When some firms with basic medical plans found it necessary to expand that coverage, they added a supplemental plan instead of redesigning the entire medical expense plan itself. In most cases, however, there have been a number of more valid reasons for choosing separate coverages. These include the employer's desire

1. To use more than one provider of coverage.
2. To offer first-dollar coverage.
3. To use different employer contribution rates for the basic and supplemental coverages. But there are also disadvantages, including more difficult administration and communication.

More than One Provider of Coverage

Frequently, the provider of a supplemental major medical plan is different from the provider of the underlying basic coverages. Usually Blue Cross or Blue Cross and Blue Shield Plans provide the basic coverages and an insurance company provides the supplemental coverage. In the past, only a few Blue Cross and Blue Shield Plans offered major medical coverage because

1. Some of them felt such coverage was not within the scope of their traditional benefit structure.
2. Some states legally prohibited it.
3. Some experienced administrative difficulties over the effective and efficient coordination of these broader benefits.

Although most Blue Cross and Blue Shield Plans now offer major medical coverage (often referred to as extended benefits), insurance companies are still by far the largest providers of major medical benefits.

The most common type of supplemental plan is the one shown in Figure 11-1, but occasionally a major medical plan is designed to supplement only a basic Blue Cross plan, as shown in Figure 11-3. This type of plan is most common in those geographic areas where Blue Cross and Blue Shield Plans do not operate jointly and thus cannot offer a single coordinated basic plan.

First-Dollar Coverage

Under the traditional comprehensive major medical plan, a deductible and coinsurance apply to all covered expenses. However, because of competition or labor negotiations, employers frequently offer their employees *first-dollar coverage* for certain medical expenses. With first-dollar coverage, there is no deductible and usually no coinsurance, and the basic medical expense plan will consist only of those benefits provided on a first-dollar basis. Because first-dollar coverage has been characteristic of Blue Cross and Blue Shield, they are frequently used as the providers of basic coverages. Therefore, in order to compete with them, most insurance companies now offer comprehensive major medical plans that are modified to provide similar first-dollar coverage.

All other things being equal, first-dollar coverage will increase the cost of a medical expense plan. In recent years, employers have become increasingly concerned with the cost of providing medical expense coverage and are less likely than in the past to provide first-dollar coverage.

Different Contribution Rates

Some employers still maintain separate basic medical and major medical expense plans because different employer contributions are made for each plan. The most

FIGURE 11-3

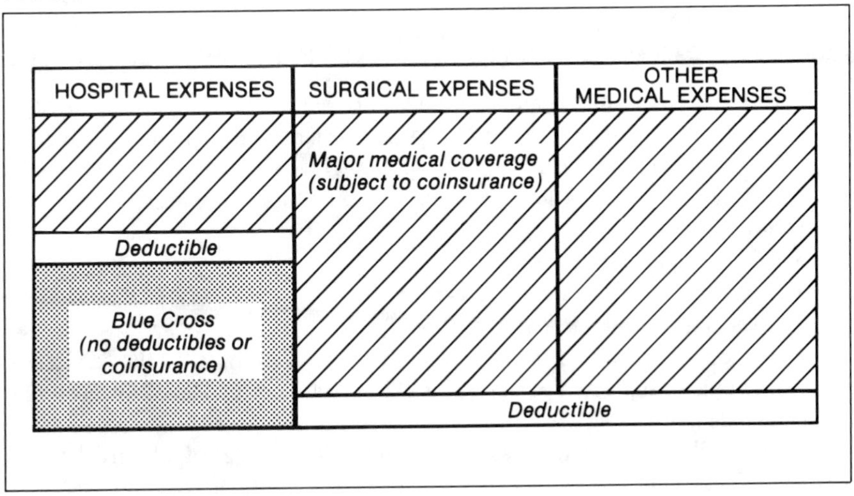

common arrangement under these circumstances has the employer paying the entire cost of the basic coverages for the employee and possibly his or her dependents, and the employee paying a portion, if not all, of the costs of the major medical coverage. The current trend, however, is to have a single plan even when the contribution rates for the basic and major medical coverages differ.

Administration and Communication

A goal of most employers is to have benefit plans that minimize administrative problems and that can be easily communicated to employees. In both regards, comprehensive plans have the advantage. When a supplemental plan is used, the employer must often deal with two providers of coverage. The two plans must be properly coordinated so that no undesired gaps in coverage exist. The processing of claims also becomes more burdensome for both the employer and the employees. In addition, the complexity of medical expense plans makes them difficult to communicate to employees, and the task becomes even more complex when two plans are used.

Even when a single provider is used for a basic medical expense plan and a supplemental major medical plan, the same problems may also exist. The employer must often negotiate the plans with separate divisions of the provider's organization, and separate claims forms and claims departments are frequently used.

CHARACTERISTICS OF MAJOR MEDICAL COVERAGE

The distinguishing features of major medical expense plans, either supplemental or comprehensive, include a broad range of covered expenses, deductibles, coinsurance and high overall maximum benefits.

Covered Expenses

Major medical plans give broad coverage for necessary expenses incurred for medical services and supplies that have been ordered or prescribed by a physician. These services and supplies, which are specified in the contract, generally include:

- Hospital room and board. Coverage has not traditionally been provided either for confinements in extended-care facilities or for home health care. However, major medical plans now often include such coverage. Some plans also provide benefits for room and board in alternative facilities, such as birthing centers.
- Other hospital charges.
- Charges of outpatient surgical centers.
- Anesthetics and their administration.
- Services of doctors of medicine or osteopathy. Coverage for the services of other medical practitioners, such as chiropractors or podiatrists, may also be included.
- Private-duty nursing by a registered nurse. The services of a licensed practical nurse may also be included.

- Prescription drugs.
- Physical and speech therapy.
- Diagnostic X-ray and laboratory services.
- Radiation therapy.
- Blood and blood plasma.
- Artificial limbs and organs.
- Pacemakers.
- Casts, splints, trusses, braces and crutches.
- Rental of wheelchairs, hospital beds or iron lungs.
- Ambulance services.

The expenses of dental care may also be included as a major medical benefit. However, dental benefits (described in Chapter 13) are usually provided for under a separate dental expense plan.

Even though coverage is broad, major medical contracts contain exclusions and limitations for certain types of medical expenses.

Exclusions

Common exclusions found in major medical contracts include charges arising from the following:

- Occupational injuries or diseases to the extent that benefits are provided by workers' compensation laws or similar legislation.
- Services furnished by or on behalf of government agencies, unless there is a requirement that the patient or the patient's medical expense plan pay.
- Cosmetic surgery, unless such surgery is to correct a condition resulting from either an accidental injury or a birth defect if the parent has dependent coverage when the child is born.
- Physical examinations, unless such examinations are necessary for the treatment of an injury or illness. While most major medical plans contain this exclusion, it should be noted that some employers provide coverage for physical examinations. In most cases, however, benefits will be provided under a separate, and often self-funded, plan and not as part of the major medical coverage.
- Convalescent, custodial or rest care.
- Dental care except for (1) treatment required because of injury to natural teeth and (2) hospital and surgical charges associated with hospital confinement for dental surgery. This exclusion will not be included if dental coverage is provided under the major medical contract.
- Eye refraction, or the purchase or fitting of eyeglasses or hearing aids. Like the dental care exclusion, this exclusion will not be included if the major medical coverage provides benefits for vision and hearing care. These benefits, however, normally are provided under a separate plan.
- Expenses either paid or eligible for payment under Medicare or other federal, state or local medical expense programs.
- Benefits provided by any other benefit program to which the employer

makes a contribution. This includes any benefits provided under basic medical expense plans if a supplementary major medical plan is used.

To minimize the problem of adverse selection, most major medical plans also contain an exclusion for pre-existing conditions. However, this exclusion applies only for a limited time, after which the condition will no longer be considered preexisting and will be covered in full, subject to any other contract limitations or exclusions. It is interesting to note that a pre-existing-conditions clause is common in major medical contracts; it is rarely found in basic medical expense contracts.

A *pre-existing condition* is usually defined as any illness or injury for which a covered person received medical care during the three-month period prior to becoming eligible for coverage. Usually, the condition is no longer considered preexisting after the earlier of (1) a period of three consecutive months during which no medical care is received for the condition or (2) 12 months of coverage under the contract by the individual.

Some insurance companies provide limited coverage rather than exclude coverage for pre-existing conditions. During the time a condition is considered preexisting, benefits may be paid subject to limitations, such as a 50 percent coinsurance provision or a calendar-year maximum of $1,000. It is also not unusual, particularly with large employers, for the pre-existing-conditions clause to be waived for persons who are eligible for coverage on the date a master contract becomes effective. However, future employees will be subject to the provision.

Limitations

Major medical plans also contain "internal limits" for certain types of medical expenses. Although the expense is covered, the amount that will be paid under the contract is limited. With rare exceptions, benefits are not paid for charges that exceed what is reasonable and customary. In addition, limitations are often placed on the following expenses:

- Hospital room and board. Benefits generally are limited to the charge for semiprivate accommodations unless other accommodations are medically necessary. However, in some cases, a flat-dollar maximum is placed on the daily semiprivate accommodation rate.
- Extended-care facilities, home health-care benefits, and hospice benefits (if provided). Benefits for extended-care facilities are often subject to a dollar limit per day for room-and-board charges as well as a time limit on the number of days that coverage will be provided. Similarly, home health-care benefits are often subject to a maximum daily benefit and limited to a certain number of visits within a specific time period. Hospice benefits are usually limited to a specific maximum amount, such as $5,000.
- Treatment for mental and nervous disorders, alcoholism and drug addiction. Unless state laws require that such conditions be treated like any other medical condition, inpatient coverage is often limited to a specific number of days each year, commonly 30 or 60. Outpatient benefits are even more limited. Benefits usually are subject to 50 percent coinsurance and to a

specific dollar limit per visit. An annual maximum benefit, such as $1,000, may also be imposed. In addition, it is not unusual to have an overall maximum lifetime benefit; for example, $25,000.
- Surgery. Although most major medical contracts pay surgical expenses on a reasonable-and-customary basis, some use a surgical schedule as was described in Chapter 10.

When major medical contracts provide coverage for dental care, vision and hearing care and physical examinations, benefits are frequently subject to schedules and annual limitations.

Deductibles

A deductible is the initial amount of covered medical expenses an individual must pay before he or she will receive benefits under a major medical plan. For example, if a plan has an annual deductible of $200, the covered person is responsible for the first $200 of medical expenses incurred each year. Covered expenses in excess of $200 are then paid by the major medical plan, subject to any limitations or coinsurance. In addition to the different types of deductibles, there are variations in (1) the amounts of the deductible, (2) the frequency with which it must be satisfied and (3) the expenses to which it applies.

Types of Deductibles

Probably the simplest form of deductible is the *initial deductible* commonly used in comprehensive medical expense plans (see Figure 11-2). Essentially, a covered person must satisfy this deductible before any insurance benefits will be paid by the plan.

Most supplemental medical expense plans use a *corridor deductible* (see Figure 11-1) under which no benefits are paid by the major medical plan until an individual has incurred a specific amount of covered expenses above those paid under his or her basic coverages. For example, assume an individual incurs $4,000 of covered medical expenses, $2,500 of which are paid by the basic coverages. If the supplemental major medical plan has a $200 corridor deductible, the plan will pay $1,300 of the expenses, subject to any limitations or coinsurance. This is determined as follows:

Covered expenses	$4,000
Less expenses covered under basic protection	2,500
	$1,500
Less deductible	200
	$1,300

In those situations when no benefits are paid under the basic coverages, the corridor deductible operates as if it were an initial deductible.

Some supplemental major medical expense plans contain an *integrated deductible*, which tends to be large—at least $500—but any amounts paid under the basic coverages can be used to satisfy it. For example, assume the specified deductible is $1,000 per year. If an individual incurs $1,000 or more of covered expenses under the basic coverages, the annual deductible is satisfied. As another example, assume a person incurs $1,500 of medical expenses, $800 of which is for hospital charges that are covered in full under the individual's basic coverages and $700 of which consists of noncovered outpatient expenses. The $800 for hospital charges can be used toward satisfying the deductible. However, the individual must pay the next $200 of medical expenses out of his or her own pocket in order to satisfy the remaining deductible amount. Therefore, only $500 of the $700 of outpatient charges would be paid, subject to any other limitations and coinsurance, under the major medical coverage.

Although the integrated deductible was once quite common, its complexity has never made it as popular as the corridor deductible. Currently, it is found in only a few supplemental major medical expense plans.

Deductible Amounts

With the exception of the integrated deductible, deductible amounts for any covered person tend to be relatively small. Most deductibles are fixed-dollar amounts that apply separately to each person and range between $100 and $250. A few major medical expense plans contain deductibles that are based on a percentage of an employee's salary (such as 1 or 2 percent), possibly subject to a maximum annual limit (such as $250).

In most major medical expense plans, the deductible must be satisfied only once during any given period, usually a calendar year, regardless of the number of causes from which medical expenses arise. This type of deductible is often referred to as an *all-causes deductible*. However, a few plans have *per-cause deductibles*, also referred to as per-disability deductibles, under which the deductible amount must be satisfied for each separate accident or illness before major medical benefits will be paid.

Deductibles apply to each covered individual, including the dependents of an employee. However, to minimize the family's burden of satisfying several deductibles, most major medical expense plans also contain a *family deductible*. Once the family deductible is satisfied, future covered medical expenses of all family members will be paid just as if every member of the family had satisfied his or her individual deductible.

Two basic types of family deductibles are found in major medical expense plans. The most common type waives any deductible requirements for other family members once a certain number of family members (generally two or three) have satisfied their individual deductibles. However, two important points should be noted: First, major medical benefits will be paid for each individual family member once his or her individual deductible is satisfied, even though the family deductible has not been met. Second, when the family deductible has been satisfied, the waiver of any deductible requirements does not apply to medical expenses incurred prior to the date the deductible is satisfied. For example, assume a family deductible is satisfied when three family members incur $200 each in covered medical expenses.

If a fourth family member has had $60 in medical expenses up to that point, future medical expenses for that person will be paid under the major medical coverage. The $60, however, will not be covered. In effect, the satisfaction of the family deductible freezes the deductible for each family member at the lesser of the individual deductible or the amount of medical expenses incurred up to that time.

Another approach used in some major medical plans is to have a fixed-dollar amount for the family deductible, such as $500. In addition, each family member has to meet an individual deductible, such as $200. Major medical benefits will be paid for any given family member once his or her deductible is satisfied, and future deductible requirements for all family members will be waived once the family maximum has been reached. Although the same expenses can satisfy both the family deductible and an individual deductible, any amount that is applied toward the family deductible cannot exceed the individual deductible. For example, if a family has deductibles of $200 for an individual and $500 for the family and if one family member incurs $1,000 in covered medical expenses, the $800 exceeding the individual deductible will be paid under the major medical plan, subject to any limitations and coinsurance. The $200 used to satisfy the individual deductible, but no more, can also be applied to the family deductible. However, the family deductible will not be completely satisfied until other family members incur another $300 in covered expenses, but no more than $200 from any one family member.

Most major medical expense contracts contain a *common accident provision*, whereby if two or more members of the same family are injured in the same accident, the covered medical expenses for all family members will at most be subject to a single deductible, usually equal to the individual deductible amount. In effect, this deductible establishes the maximum amount of medical expenses that must be borne by an employee for his or her family before major medical benefits will be paid. In some cases, the employee may actually bear a smaller portion of the medical expenses if the amount satisfies the family or individual deductibles. For example, if three family members incur medical expenses of $300 each in an accident under a plan that contains a $200 deductible, at least $700 of these expenses will be covered under the major medical coverage. However, if because of previous medical expenses only $40 is needed to satisfy the family deductible, then $860 of these expenses will be covered under the major medical plan.

Deductible Frequency

An all-causes deductible usually applies to medical expenses incurred within a 12-month period, which is usually a calendar year, January 1 to December 31. Under such a *calendar-year deductible*, expenses incurred from January 1 apply toward the deductible and once the deductible has been satisfied, the balance of any covered expenses incurred during the year will then be paid by the major medical plan, subject to any limitations and coinsurance.

Most plans with a calendar-year deductible also have a carryover provision that allows any expenses (1) applied to the deductible, and (2) incurred during the last three months of the year, to also be applied to the deductible for the following year. For example, assume an individual only satisfies $150 of a $200 deductible prior to

October 1. If less than $50 of covered expenses are incurred in the last three months of the year, the deductible will not be totally satisfied for the year, but this amount can be applied to the deductible for the following year. If $50 or more of covered expenses are incurred in this three-month period, not only will the deductible be satisfied for the year, but $50 can also be applied to the deductible for the following year. No carryover is allowed if the deductible for the year is satisfied prior to the last three months of the year.

A rarely used variation of the calendar-year deductible allows expenses incurred during any 12-month period to satisfy the deductible. Once an individual incurs covered medical expenses in any consecutive 12-month period that are equal to the deductible, major medical benefits will be paid for the remainder of the period.

With a per-cause deductible, a different approach is normally taken. Medical expenses used to satisfy the deductible for each illness or accident must be incurred within a specified *accumulation period*. Although the accumulation period can be a calendar year or some other 12-month period, most accumulation periods consist of any consecutive two-, three-, or six-month period. Once the deductible for an accumulation period has been met, benefits will be paid for a *benefit period*, which usually begins when the deductible is satisfied, but sometimes begins on the date the first expense toward the deductible is incurred. In the latter case, expenses used to satisfy the deductible are not paid by the major medical plan. The benefit period typically lasts until the earlier of (1) two years or (2) the end of some time period (usually 60 or 90 days) in which covered medical expenses from that cause are less than a small but specified dollar amount (such as $25 or $50). Once the benefit period ends, an individual must again satisfy the deductible before a new benefit period will begin.

Expenses to Which the Deductible Applies

Most major medical plans have a single deductible that applies to all medical expenses. However, some plans have two or more deductibles that apply separately to different categories of medical expenses. While many variations exist, the most common plan of this type has a small deductible, such as $50, that applies to those expenses over which individuals have the least control; for example, hospital charges, surgical charges and charges resulting from accidents. A larger deductible, such as $100, applies to all other medical expenses.

In some major medical plans, the deductible does not apply to certain expenses. In effect, this gives the covered person first-dollar coverage for these charges. Insurance companies sometimes write major comprehensive medical expense plans without any deductible for hospital and/or surgical expenses as their way of competing with the first-dollar coverage offered by Blue Cross and Blue Shield. In addition, these expenses are often not subject to a coinsurance provision. Rather, a dollar maximum may be placed on the amount of benefits that will be paid in full. Above this maximum, coinsurance will apply.

Coinsurance

Major medical expense plans contain a coinsurance provision, whereby the plan will only pay a specified percentage, often 80 percent, of the covered expenses that exceed the deductible.[1] For example, if a $200 calendar-year deductible and an 80 percent coinsurance provision apply to all expenses, the individual who incurs $1,200 of covered medical expenses during the year will receive an $800 reimbursement under a comprehensive major medical expense plan, as shown below:

Covered expenses	$1,200
Less deductible	200
	$1,000
Times coinsurance percentage	.80
	$ 800

The individual will have to pay the remaining $400 from his or her own pocket; that is, the deductible plus 20 percent of those expenses exceeding the deductible. It has been argued that having such provisions is a financial incentive for employees to control their use of medical care, since they must bear a portion of the cost of any expenses incurred.

Just as deductibles vary, so do coinsurance provisions. Sometimes different coinsurance percentages apply to different categories of medical expenses. For example, outpatient psychiatric charges may be subject to 50 percent coinsurance, while other covered medical expenses are subject to 80 percent coinsurance. In addition, certain medical expenses may be subject to 100 percent coinsurance and usually no deductible, which means that the expenses are paid in full, subject to any limitations. Such full coverage is most likely to exist (1) for those expenses over which an individual has little control; (2) when there is a desire to provide first-dollar coverage for certain expenses; or (3) when there is a desire to encourage the use of the most cost-effective treatment, such as outpatient surgery, preadmission testing or birthing centers.

Figures 11-4 through 11-7 show how the deductible and coinsurance provisions might be modified in a comprehensive major medical expense plan.

Figure 11-4 illustrates a medical expense plan that has both the deductible and coinsurance provisions waived for hospital expenses, surgical expenses and certain other expenses up to specified limits. This type of modification results in a plan similar to a Blue Cross and Blue Shield Plan that has supplemental major medical coverage but no corridor deductible. Figure 11-5 shows a comprehensive major medical expense plan that is designed to provide first-dollar coverage for hospital

---

[1]The term *coinsurance* as used in this book refers to the percentage of covered expenses paid by a medical expense plan. A plan with 80 percent coinsurance, sometimes referred to as an 80/20 plan, will pay 80 percent of covered expenses while a person who receives benefits under the plan must pay the remaining 20 percent. In some plans, the term *coinsurance* is not used, but rather a percentage participation, such as 20 percent, is specified. As commonly used, a percentage participation (sometimes also referred to as a copayment) refers to the percentage of covered medical expenses that will not be paid by a medical expense plan and that must be paid by a person receiving benefits.

FIGURE 11-4

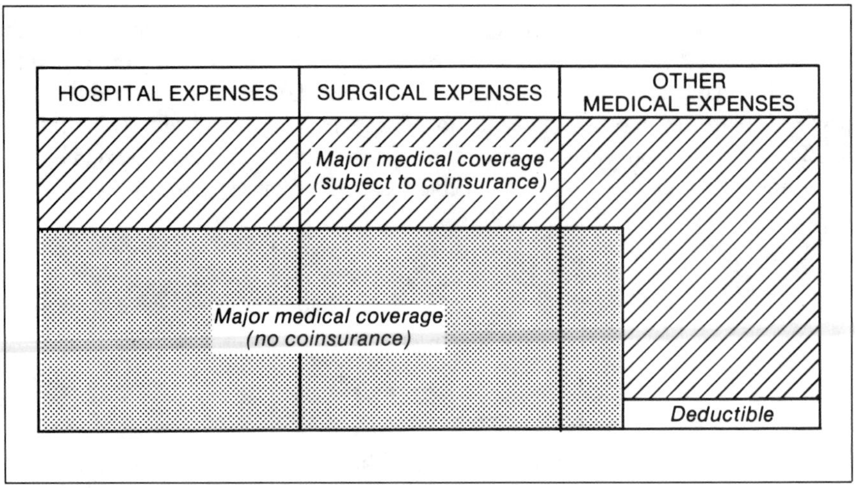

HOSPITAL EXPENSES | SURGICAL EXPENSES | OTHER MEDICAL EXPENSES

Major medical coverage (subject to coinsurance)

Major medical coverage (no coinsurance)

Deductible

FIGURE 11-5

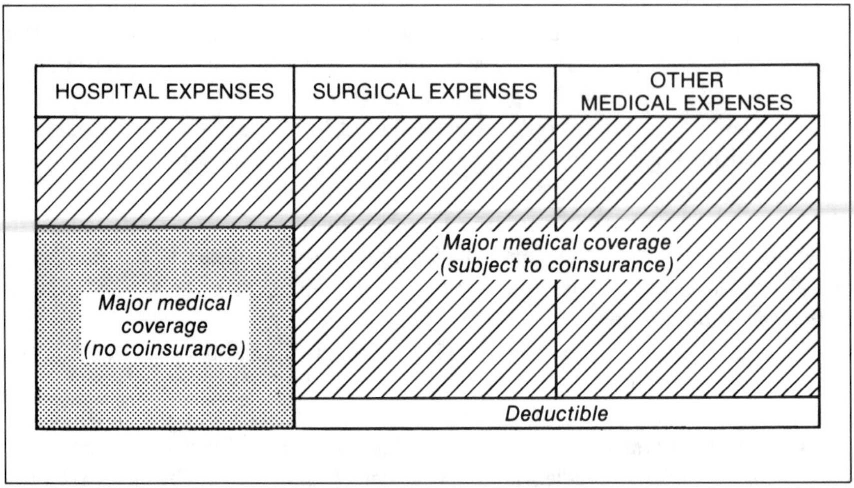

HOSPITAL EXPENSES | SURGICAL EXPENSES | OTHER MEDICAL EXPENSES

Major medical coverage (subject to coinsurance)

Major medical coverage (no coinsurance)

Deductible

expenses only. Notice the similarity between this plan and a Blue Cross Plan that has supplemental major medical coverage (Figure 11-3). Figures 11-6 and 11-7 illustrate two other possible variations. In Figure 11-6 the deductible and coinsurance provisions are completely waived for certain medical expenses. In Figure 11-7 only the coinsurance—and not the deductible—is waived.

In the case of catastrophic medical expenses, the coinsurance provision could result in an individual being required to assume a large dollar amount of his or her

FIGURE 11-6

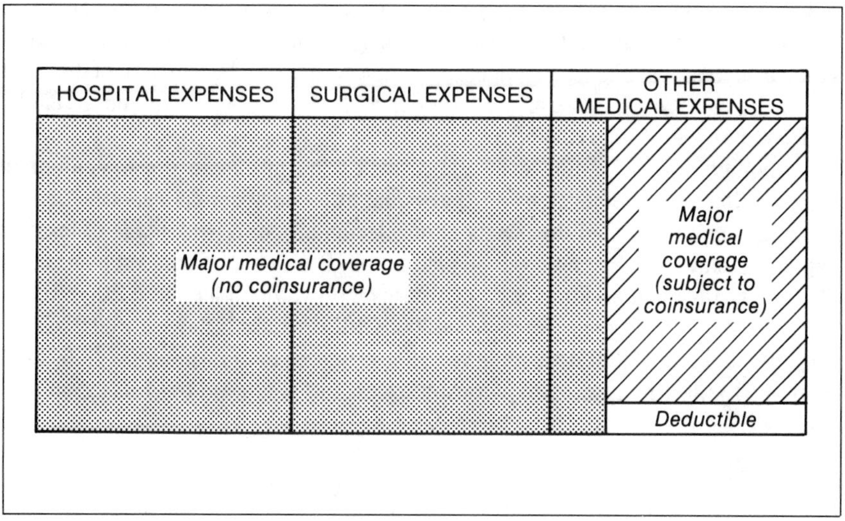

FIGURE 11-7

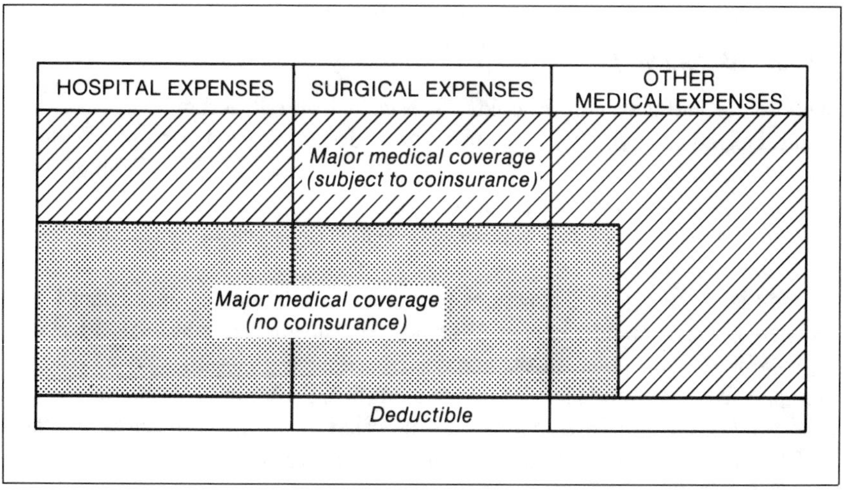

own medical expenses. Consequently, many major medical expense plans place a limit, often referred to as a stop-loss or coinsurance limit or cap, on the amount of out-of-pocket expenses that must be borne by a covered person during any time period. It is sometimes specified that the coinsurance provision only applies to a limited amount of expenses and that expenses in excess of this limit will be paid in full. For example, the plan may have a $200 deductible, an 80 percent coinsurance provision that applies to the next $3,000 of covered expenses, and full coverage for any remaining covered expenses. Therefore, the most an individual will have to pay out of his or her own pocket in any year is the $200 deductible and 20 percent of $3,000 (for a total of $800). Occasionally, this type of plan is modified to allow a gradual increase in the coinsurance percentage, such as 80 percent of the first $2,000 of covered expenses above the deductible, 90 percent of the next $2,000, and 100 percent of the remainder.

Another way of limiting coinsurance states the maximum dollar amount of expenses that must be borne by any individual or a family during a specific period. Once this limit is reached, by paying either deductibles or a percentage of medical expenses, additional expenses will be paid in full. For example, under a plan with a $200 deductible and an 80 percent coinsurance provision, a limit of $1,000 will be met if total medical expenses reach $4,200. Of this amount, the individual will be responsible for the $200 deductible and 20 percent of the remaining $4,000, for a total of $1,000. Any medical expenses in excess of $4,200 will be paid in full.

Maximum Benefits

The maximum benefits that will be paid for any covered person under a major medical contract may be determined in one of two ways. Although the use of a *lifetime maximum* is most common, a few contracts contain a *per-cause maximum*. In both instances, the benefit maximum applies separately to each employee and each dependent covered under the contract.

Lifetime Maximum

When a lifetime maximum is used, the specified overall maximum applies to all medical expenses paid, after the application of deductibles and coinsurance, during the entire period an individual is covered under the contract. It is no longer common to find benefit maximums of less than $100,000, and most benefit maximums fall within the range of $250,000 to $1 million. In some instances, the benefit amount is unlimited.

In the absence of any provisions to the contrary, the lifetime maximum will be reduced by the amount of any benefits paid. For example, an individual with a $200 calendar-year deductible, an 80 percent coinsurance provision, and a $100,000 lifetime maximum, who incurs $4,000 of medical expenses in his or her first year of coverage (assuming it corresponds with the calendar year), will receive benefits of $3,040 (that is, 80 percent of $3,800). This will reduce the remaining lifetime benefit to $96,960.

Major medical contracts commonly contain provisions for either partially or totally restoring the lifetime maximum to its original level. Most contracts stipulate that on some date each year, often January 1, the entire deficit in the lifetime maximum will be automatically restored, subject to a maximum annual restoration that may vary from $1,000 to $5,000. However, the overall maximum cannot be increased above its original limit. If the plan in the previous example has a $1,000 automatic annual restoration, the amount of the remaining benefit will be initially increased to $97,960. Ignoring any future reductions for benefits paid, this limit will continue to increase by $1,000 each year until the original $100,000 maximum is restored.

Most contracts also state that after a covered person has used up a specified amount, often $1,000 or $2,000, he or she may have the maximum benefit restored to its original level upon supplying satisfactory evidence of insurability to the insurance company. Although insurance contracts are silent on what constitutes evidence of insurability, most insurance companies use the same standards and procedures that apply to applicants for individual medical expense insurance.

In addition to the overall lifetime maximum, *internal maximums* are sometimes found in major medical contracts. For example, a plan may have a $1 million overall lifetime maximum, but a $10,000 lifetime maximum for mental and nervous disorders. In other words, only $10,000 of the $1 million will be paid for expenses relating to these conditions. This is probably the most common type of an internal maximum, but a few plans contain calendar-year or per-disability maximums. The provisions for restoring benefits do not apply to the calendar-year or per-disability maximums, and may or may not apply to the mental and nervous disorder maximum.

Per-Cause Maximum

A few plans contain maximum limits for each cause of medical expenses, but this type of maximum limit is generally only used when the deductible is also applied on a per-cause basis. Most plans of this type do not have an automatic restoration-of-benefits provision, but do allow benefits to be reinstated upon satisfactory evidence of insurability. If this evidence is not—or cannot be—provided, coverage will terminate for any cause for which the maximum benefits have been paid. However, coverage will remain in force for expenses arising from other causes.

HMO COVERAGE AS AN ALTERNATIVE TO MAJOR MEDICAL

Most HMOs also provide broad protection for medical expenses. In fact, federally qualified HMOs often give more comprehensive protection than most major medical plans, because, in addition to covering such items as routine examinations and immunizations, they tend to require fewer out-of-pocket expenses by the members. HMOs that meet the requirements for federal qualification are allowed to use copayments for services (1) if the copayment for any single service does not exceed 50 percent of the cost for that service, and (2) if the total of all copayments does not exceed more than 20 percent of the cost of supplying all basic health services. In practice, if copayments are used at all, they are usually substantially below these permissible limits. In addition, no subscriber is required to copay more than 50 percent of the annual subscriber fee that would have been charged if coverage had been written without any copayments.

The following chart compares the major medical plan and two HMOs that are offered to the employees of one organization. All three plans are reasonably representative of their respective plan types.

A COMPARISON: INSURED PLAN VERSUS HMOs

	Insurance Company Comprehensive Major Medical Expense Plan	Group Practice HMO	Individual Practice Association HMO
Choice of physician	Member may select any licensed physician or surgeon.	Member selects a personal physician from the medical group who coordinates and directs all health care needs including referrals to specialists.	Members select a personal primary care physician from among the health plan physicians.
Where primary and specialty care is available	Care is provided in physician's office or outpatient facility.	Care is provided at four multispecialty centers.	Care is provided in participating private physicians' offices.
Choice of hospitals	Member may select any accredited hospital—choice depends on where physician has admitting privileges.	Selection is from participating hospitals.	Selection is from participating hospitals.
Deductible and coinsurance	There is a $200 annual deductible. The plan has no coinsurance for hospitalization, but it does have 80% coinsurance for other covered services. There is no coinsurance on covered services after $3,000 in benefits is paid.	There is no deductible and no coinsurance, except small copayments for home visits and outpatient mental health.	There is no deductible and no coinsurance, except small copayments for home visits, outpatient mental health, and a deductible for prescription drugs.
Maximum benefit	$1 million lifetime maximum	No overall maximum limit	No overall maximum limit
Preventive care:			
Routine physicals	Not covered	Covered in full	Covered in full
Well-baby care	Not covered	Covered in full	Covered in full
Pap smears	Routine exams not covered	Covered in full	Covered in full
Immunizations	Not covered	Covered in full	Covered in full

Eye exam	Not covered	Covered in full, including written prescriptions for lenses	Paid in full for children up to age 18
Hearing exam	Not covered	Covered in full	Covered in full
Health education	Available through some physicians' offices	Periodic classes held on diet, prenatal care and physical fitness	Covered in full through participating hospital programs
Physician care:			
Surgery	Covered at 80% after satisfying deductible	Covered in full	Covered in full
Inpatient visits	Covered at 80% after satisfying deductible	Covered in full	Covered in full
Office and home	Covered at 80% after satisfying deductible	Office visits covered in full, home visits covered in full, $3 per allied health professional home visit	Office visits covered in full, charge of $5 per doctor's home visit
X-rays and lab	Covered at 80% after satisfying deductible	Covered in full	Covered in full
Hospital services:			
Room and board	Covered in full for unlimited days after satisfying deductible in semiprivate room	Covered in full for unlimited days in semiprivate room	Covered in full for unlimited days in semiprivate room
Supplies, tests, medication, etc.	Covered in full for covered benefit days	Covered in full	Covered in full
Private-duty nurse	Covered in full while hospitalized. (Outpatient licensed practical nurse services covered at 50% up to $250 per year.)	Covered in full	Covered in full

A COMPARISON: INSURED PLAN VERSUS HMOs *(continued)*

	Insurance Company Comprehensive Major Medical Expense Plan	Group Practice HMO	Individual Practice Association HMO
Emergency care	Covered in full for care received in hospital outpatient department within 24 hours of an accident	Covered in full for around-the-clock emergency care by plan physicians and in participating hospitals. Emergency care by nonplan physicians or hospitals is also covered when obtaining plan care is not reasonable because of distance and urgency.	Covered in full for around-the-clock emergency care by participating physicians and in participating hospitals. Emergency care by nonparticipating physicians or hospitals is also covered when obtaining plan care is not reasonable because of distance and urgency.
Ambulance service	Covered in full for local transportation after satisfying deductible	Covered in full	Covered in full
Maternity care:			
Hospital	Covered in full after deductible	Covered in full	Covered in full
Physician	Covered at 80% after deductible	Covered in full	Covered in full
Mental health care:			
Hospital	Covered as regular hospitalization, i.e., 365 day/lifetime limitation	Covered in full for 45 days per year	Covered in full for 30 days during 12-month period
Inpatient physician	Covered as regular inpatient physician care	Covered in full for 45 days per year	Covered in full for 30 days during 12-month period
Outpatient physician	Covered at 50% up to $20 per visit and $1,000 per year	Covered for 30 visits per year; first 3 visits covered in full, next 27 visits member pays $10 per visit	Covered for 20 visits per period; first 3 visits covered in full, next 7 visits member pays 25% of regular fee, next 10 visits member pays 50% of regular fee

	Plan A	Plan B	Plan C
Alcohol and drug addiction	Covered as other mental health services	No special limits, covered as other medical and mental health services	After detoxification treatment, covered as for mental health problems
Dental care:			
Hospital	Covered for hospital costs when confinement is necessary for dental care	Covered for hospital costs when confinement is necessary for dental costs	Covered for hospital costs when confinement is necessary for dental care
Dentist or dental surgeon	Covered for treatment of accidental injury to natural teeth	Covered for treatment of accidental injury to natural teeth and certain oral surgical procedures (e.g., impacted wisdom teeth)	Covered for treatment of diseases and injury to the jaw and removal of impacted wisdom teeth
Outpatient medication:			
Prescription drugs	Covered at 80% after deductible, if related to treatment of nonoccupational illness or injury	Not covered	Covered in full after $50 deductible per person per contract year
Injections	Covered at 80% after deductible, if related to treatment of nonoccupational illness or injury	Covered in full	Covered in full
Prescribed home health services	Covered at 80% after deductible	Covered in full	Covered in full
Allergy care	Covered at 80% after deductible	Covered in full	Covered in full
Eligibility	Spouse and unmarried dependent children to age 19 or age 23 if full-time students	Spouse and unmarried dependent children to age 19 or age 23 if full-time students	Spouse and unmarried dependent children to age 19 or age 23 if full-time students
Conversion	Conversion to individual coverage available	Conversion to nongroup coverage available	Conversion to individual enrollment available at same benefit level

STUDY QUESTIONS

1. How does a supplemental major medical contract broaden the benefits provided under the basic medical expense coverages?
2. Why are major medical contracts often written to supplement basic medical expense coverages rather than written as a single contract to provide comprehensive medical expense coverage for employees?
3. What types of exclusions are commonly found in major medical contracts?
4. What types of internal limitations are usually placed on the benefits provided under major medical contracts?
5. Nadine Swanson incurred $9,000 of covered medical expenses, $7,600 of which were paid under her Blue Cross and Blue Shield basic medical expense coverages. How much will Nadine collect under her supplemental major medical coverage if
   a. A $200 corridor deductible and 80 percent coinsurance are applicable?
   b. A $500 integrated deductible and 80 percent coinsurance are applicable?
6. Explain the carryover provision associated with a calendar-year deductible.
7. What is the significance of the accumulation period and the benefit period associated with a per-cause deductible?
8. Why do different coinsurance percentages sometimes apply to different categories of medical expenses?
9. Describe the methods used to place a limit on the amount of out-of-pocket medical expenses that must be borne by an individual under the coinsurance provision of a major medical contract.
10. What provisions are often included in major medical contracts to provide for a restoration of the lifetime maximum after it has been reduced by the payment of medical expenses?
11. To what extent are federally qualified HMOs allowed to require copayments for covered services?

12

Group Medical Expense Contract Provisions, Taxation and Cost Containment

Objectives

- Identify and explain the contract provisions common to both basic and major medical coverages.
- Explain the tax implications of employer-paid group medical expense premiums for the employer and the employees.
- Explain the tax implications of group medical expense benefits to employees.
- Explain the reasons for the increasing cost of health care and identify the measures used by employers to contain health care costs.

Many of the provisions found in both basic and major medical expense contracts are similar—if not identical—to those found in group term life insurance, discussed in Chapter 6. However, certain provisions are either unique to medical expense insurance contracts or differ substantially from those found in other types of group insurance. These pertain to eligibility, coordination of benefits, the effect of Medicare, termination and claims. In addition, some differences exist with respect to the taxation of benefits and contributions.

ELIGIBILITY

The eligibility requirements for medical expense insurance are essentially the same as those for group term life insurance: an employee must usually be in a covered classification, must satisfy any probationary period and must be full time. Coverage is rarely made available to part-time employees. In addition, medical expense contracts often contain an actively-at-work provision. This may be waived for larger employers for whom adverse selection tends to be less of a problem than for smaller groups, because any adverse selection for a large group will be reflected in future premiums through the experience-rating process.

Eligibility requirements may vary somewhat if an employer changes insurance companies. Even though it has been adopted by only a few states, most insurance companies follow the procedures established by the NAIC Model Regulation on Group Coverage Discontinuance and Replacement for medical expense coverage. This model regulation stipulates that coverage will be provided, but possibly limited, under a new plan to anyone who (1) was covered under the prior plan at the date it was discontinued and (2) is in an eligible classification of the new plan. Employees who are actively at work on the date coverage is transferred are automatically covered under the new plan and are exempt from any probationary periods. If the new plan contains a pre-existing-conditions provision, benefits applicable to an individual's pre-existing conditions are limited to the lesser of (1) the maximum benefits of the new plan (ignoring the pre-existing conditions) or (2) the maximum benefits of the prior plan.

Employees who are not actively at work on the date coverage is discontinued under the old plan (such as employees disabled by illness or injury or those suffering temporary interruptions of employment) must be included in the new plan. However, their benefits can be limited to the old plan's levels until they meet the actively-at-work requirement of the new plan. Two other points should be made concerning the transfer of coverage: First, the new plan will not pay benefits for expenses covered by the old plan under an extension-of-benefits provision (discussed later). Second, when applying any deductibles or waiting periods under the new plan, credit is usually given for the satisfaction, or partial satisfaction, of the same or similar provisions during the last three months of the old plan. For example, assume coverage is transferred in the middle of a calendar year and that the new plan contains the same $200-a-year calendar deductible as the old plan. If an employee had already satisfied the deductible under the old plan, no new deductible would be required for the remainder of the calendar year provided that (1) the expenses used to satisfy the deductible under the old plan would satisfy the deductible under the new plan and (2) the expenses were incurred during the last three months of the old plan. If only $140 of the $200 were incurred during the last three months, an additional $60 deductible would be required under the new plan for the remainder of the calendar year.

Dependent Eligibility

The same medical expense benefits that are provided for an eligible employee usually will also be available for that employee's dependents. Dependent coverage is rarely available unless the employee also has coverage. As long as any necessary payroll deductions have been authorized, dependent coverage is typically effective on the same date as the employee's coverage. If coverage under a contributory plan is not elected within 31 days after dependents are eligible, future coverage will be available only during an open enrollment period or when satisfactory evidence of insurability can be provided. However, if an employee was previously without dependents, and therefore had no dependent coverage, any dependents newly acquired by birth, marriage or adoption will be eligible for coverage as of the date they gain dependent status.

The term *dependents* is most commonly defined as an employee's spouse, who is not legally separated from the employee, and any unmarried children under the age of 19, including stepchildren and adopted children. However, coverage is usually provided for children to age 23 if they are full-time students. In addition, coverage may also continue—and is required to be continued in some states—for children who are incapable of earning their own livings because of physical or mental infirmities. Such children will be considered dependents as long as this condition exists, but periodic proof of the condition may be required by the insurance company. If an employee has dependent coverage, all newly acquired dependents are automatically covered.

Some persons who meet the definition of a dependent may be ineligible for coverage because they are in the armed forces or they are eligible for coverage under the same plan as employees themselves. This latter restriction, however, may not apply to a spouse unless the spouse is actually covered under the plan. Some plans also exclude coverage for any dependents residing outside the United States or Canada.

Most medical expense plans contain a nonconfinement provision for dependents, which is similar to the actively-at-work provision for employees. Under this provision, a dependent is not covered if he or she is confined for medical care or treatment in a hospital or at home at the time of eligibility. Coverage becomes effective when the dependent is released from such confinement.

When coverage is transferred, dependents are treated the same as employees, except that any actively-at-work provision is usually replaced by a nonconfinement provision.

COORDINATION OF BENEFITS

In recent years, the percentage of individuals having duplicate group medical expense coverage has increased substantially. Probably the most common situation is the one in which a husband and wife both work and have coverage under their respective employers' noncontributory plans. If the employer of either spouse also provides dependent coverage on a noncontributory basis, the other spouse will be covered under both plans. If dependent coverage is contributory, it will be necessary for a couple with children to elect such coverage under one of their plans. However, because a spouse is considered a dependent, he or she will also have duplicate coverage when the election is made. Duplicate coverage may also arise when:

- An employee has two jobs.
- Children are covered under both a parent's and a stepparent's plans.

- An employee elects coverage under a contributory plan even though he or she is covered as a dependent under another plan. This could result from ignorance or from an attempt to collect double the amount if a claim should occur. In many cases, this coverage is elected because it is broader, even though it still results in an element of duplicate coverage.

Duplicate coverage can also occur if an individual has coverage under a group plan that is not provided by an employer. A common example involves children whose parents have purchased accident coverage for them through their schools.

In the absence of any provisions to the contrary, group insurance plans are obligated to provide benefits in cases of duplicate coverage as if no other coverage exists. However, to prevent individuals from receiving benefits that exceed their actual expenses, most group insurance plans contain a *coordination-of-benefits (COB) provision*, under which priorities are established for the payment of benefits by each plan covering an individual.

Most COB provisions are based on the 1985 Model Group Coordination of Benefit Provisions promulgated by the NAIC. These provisions update earlier provisions, and all or portions have now been adopted by the majority of the states. All other states are expected to follow suit. As with all NAIC model legislation and regulations, some states have adopted the COB provisions with variations.

Although some flexibility is allowed, virtually all COB provisions apply when other coverage exists through the group insurance plans or group benefit arrangements (such as Blue Cross and Blue Shield HMOs or self-funded plans) of another employer. They may also apply to no-fault automobile insurance benefits and to coverage for students that is either sponsored or provided by educational institutions. However, these provisions virtually never apply (and cannot in most states) to any other coverages provided under contracts purchased on an individual basis outside of the employment relationship.

Determination of Primary Coverage

The usual COB provision stipulates that any other plan without the COB provision is primary, and that any plan with it is secondary. If more than one plan has a COB provision, the following priorities are established:

- Coverage as an employee is primary to coverage as a dependent.
- For dependent children of parents who are neither separated nor divorced, the plan covering the parent whose birthday falls earlier in the year is primary. Prior to the 1985 provisions, the policy of the father was primary to the policy of the mother. If the plan of one parent uses the birthday rule, and the plan of the other parent still uses the male/female rule, the latter rule is to be followed.
- For dependent children of parents who are separated or divorced, the following priorities apply:
    - The plan of the parent with custody is primary.
    - The plan of the spouse of the parent with custody (the stepparent) is secondary.

–The plan of the parent without custody pays last. However, if the specific terms of a court decree state that one of the parents is responsible for the child's health care expenses, the plan of that parent is primary as long as the insurance company or other entity obligated to provide the benefits has actual knowledge of the terms of the court decree. If benefits are paid under another plan before this knowledge is obtained, the "court decree rule" does not apply during the remainder of the plan or policy year.

- Coverage as an active employee (or as that person's dependent) is primary to coverage as a retired or laid-off employee (or as that person's dependent). However, this rule is ignored unless both plans contain the rule.
- If none of the previous rules establishes a priority, the plan covering the person for the longest period of time is primary.

Determination of Benefits Payable

The actual mechanics of the previously discussed COB provision are demonstrated in the following example, which assumes an individual has coverage under the plans of two employers:

- *Plan A* has basic benefits with a maximum of $150 per day for semiprivate hospital accommodations up to 31 days, $1,000 for hospital extras and $800 for surgery. It has no deductibles or coinsurance.
- *Plan B* has comprehensive major medical expense coverage with a $100-per-year calendar deductible, 80 percent coinsurance and a $250,000 maximum. Hospital benefits are limited to the cost of semiprivate accommodations.

Assume also that this individual incurs the following expenses:

Semiprivate room for 8 days at $250 per day	$2,000
Other hospital charges	1,200
Surgeon's fees	900
Total expenses	$4,100

If there were no COB provision in either plan, plan A would pay $3,000 ($1,200 for hospital room and board, $1,000 for hospital extras, and $800 for surgery), and plan B would pay $3,200 (assuming no portion of the deductible had been previously satisfied). This latter amount consists of 80 percent of covered expenses that exceed the $100 deductible. Consequently, the individual would collect benefits totaling $6,200 or $2,100 in excess of his or her actual expenses.

Before the COB provision is used, it must first be determined whether the provision applies to a given claim. It will apply only if the sum of the benefits under the plans involved (assuming there is no provision) exceeds an individual's "allowable expenses." Allowable expenses are defined as any necessary, reasonable and customary items of expense, all or a portion of which is covered under at least one of the plans that provides benefits to the individual for whom the claim is made.

When determining what the allowable expenses are, any deductibles, coinsurance and plan maximum are ignored.

In the previous example, the entire $4,100 is considered allowable expenses. Because the sum of the benefits otherwise payable under the two plans ($6,200) exceeds this amount, the COB provision applies. If the sum of the benefits did not exceed the allowable expenses, the COB provision would not apply, and each plan would pay its benefits as if it were the only existing plan.

When the COB provision applies, an individual receives benefits equal to 100 percent of his or her allowable expenses and no more. The primary plan pays its benefits as if no other coverage exists and the secondary plan (or plans) pays the remaining benefits. In this particular example, if plan A is primary, it will pay $3,000 and plan B will pay the remaining $1,100 of expenses. If plan B is primary, it will pay $3,200 and plan A will pay the remaining $900.

The Preservation of Deductibles and Coinsurance

The preservation of deductibles and coinsurance was acceptable under the original 1985 NAIC provisions. The major rationale for such a provision was that the traditional approach negated the cost-containment effects of deductibles and coinsurance since most persons would be indemnified for 100 percent of their expenses even if both plans contained these cost-saving features. However, most states did not adopt this portion of the provisions, and it was deleted in 1987 by the NAIC. However, a few states do allow the preservation of deductibles and coinsurance and permit one of two approaches to be used.

The first approach is similar to the previously described approach; however, it allows the secondary plan to pay the difference between 80 percent (or more if the plan so provides) of total allowable expenses actually incurred less whatever was paid by the primary plan. In the example, 80 percent of allowable expense is $3,280. If plan A is primary and pays its $3,000, plan B would only be required to pay $280 if it used the 80 percent figure.

The second approach for preserving deductibles and coinsurance does not use the concept of allowable expense. Rather, the secondary plan pays the difference, if any, between (1) what it would have paid if it had been primary and (2) the amount paid by the primary plan. This approach maintains the benefit provisions of the secondary plan—deductibles, coinsurance and any other policy limitations or exclusions. In the example, plan B would have paid $3,200 if it had been primary. If plan A is actually primary, it will pay $3,000 and plan B will pay an additional $200.

When it is permissible to preserve deductibles and coinsurance, most states require a plan to comply with certain rules that were contained in the deleted portion of the NAIC provisions:

- Covered persons must be given prior notice that they will not receive 100 percent of their expenses if duplicate coverage exists. This gives them an opportunity to discontinue the coverage under one of the plans if that is possible and within their best interest.
- The plan must allow a person who is otherwise eligible for coverage under the plan, but not enrolled in it, to enroll if his or her coverage under another

group plan terminates for any reason and cannot be replaced. The rationale for this provision is that the COB provision tends to encourage working families to drop duplicate coverage. This rule prevents a total loss of protection if coverage under the plan that was not dropped is later terminated.

- If a plan uses the second approach (the one without the concept of allowable expense), it cannot have a coinsurance factor of less than (1) 50 percent for mental or nervous disorders or alcohol and drug abuse treatments, (2) 50 percent for benefits if a covered person fails to obtain or follow cost containment provision, such as second surgical opinions or preadmission certification and (3) 75 percent for other covered expenses. The latter restriction, however, does not apply to dental care, vision care, hearing care, or prescription drugs.

THE RELATIONSHIP WITH MEDICARE

Since most employees and their dependents will be eligible for Medicare upon reaching age 65 (and possibly under other circumstances), a provision that will eliminate any possible duplication of coverage is necessary. The simplest solution would be to exclude any person eligible for Medicare from eligibility under the group contract. However, in most cases, this would conflict with the Age Discrimination in Employment Act, which prohibits discrimination in welfare benefit plans for active employees.

Medicare Secondary Rules

As mentioned in Chapter 5, employers with 20 or more employees must make coverage available under their medical expense plans to active employees age 65 or older and to active employees' spouses who are eligible for Medicare. Unless an employee elects otherwise, the employer's plan is primary and Medicare is secondary. Except in plans that require large employee contributions, it is doubtful that employees will elect Medicare to be primary since employers are prohibited from offering active employees or their spouses either a Medicare carve-out or a Medicare supplement.

Medicare is the secondary payer of benefits in two other situations. The first situation involves persons who are eligible for Medicare benefits to treat end-stage renal disease with dialysis or kidney transplants. Medicare provides these benefits to any insured workers (regardless of age) and to their spouses and dependent children, but the employer's plan is primary during the first 12 months of treatment only; after that time Medicare is primary and the employer's plan is secondary. It should be noted that the employer's plan could totally exclude dialysis and/or kidney transplants, in which case Medicare would pay. However, the employer is prevented by law from excluding these benefits for the first 12 months if they are covered thereafter. This rule for renal disease applies to medical expense plans of all employers, not just those with 20 or more employees.

Medicare is also the secondary payer of benefits to disabled employees (or the disabled dependents of employees) under age 65 who are eligible for Medicare and who are covered under the medical expense plan of large employers. It should be noted, however, that Medicare does not pay anything until a person has been eligible for social security disability income benefits for two years. This rule, which applies only to the plans of employers with 100 or more employees, will expire on January 1, 1992, unless it is extended. This rule applies only if an employer continues medical expense coverage for disabled persons; there is no requirement for such a continuation.

Medicare Carve-Outs and Supplements

An employer's plan may cover certain persons age 65 or older who are not covered by the provisions of the Age Discrimination in Employment Act. These include retirees and active employees of firms with fewer than 20 employees. There is nothing to prevent an employer from terminating coverage for these persons. However, many employers provide them with either a Medicare carve-out or Medicare supplement.

With a *Medicare carve-out,* plan benefits are reduced to the extent that benefits are payable under Medicare for the same expenses. (Medicare may also pay for some expenses not covered by the group plan.) For example, if an individual who incurs $1,000 of covered expenses is not eligible for Medicare, $720 in benefits would be paid under a medical expense plan that had a $100 deductible and an 80 percent coinsurance provision. However, if the same individual is eligible for Medicare, and if Medicare pays $650 for the same expenses, the employer's plan will only pay $70, for a total benefit of $720.

Some medical expense plans use a more liberal carve-out approach and reduce covered expenses (rather than benefits payable) by any amounts received under Medicare. In the previous example, the $650 paid by Medicare would be subtracted from the $1,000 of covered expenses, which would leave $350. After the deductible and coinsurance are applied to this amount, the employer's plan will pay $200. Therefore, the covered person will receive a total of $850 in benefits, or $130 more than a person not eligible for Medicare.

As an alternative to using a carve-out approach, some employers use a *Medicare supplement* that provides benefits for certain specific expenses which are not covered under Medicare. These include (1) the portion of expenses that is not paid by Medicare because of deductibles, coinsurance or copayments, and (2) certain expenses excluded by Medicare, such as prescription drugs. Such a supplement may or may not provide benefits similar to those available under a carve-out plan.

TERMINATION OF COVERAGE

In the absence of any provisions for continuation or conversion, group insurance coverage on an employee generally ceases on the earliest of the following:

- The date employment terminates. In some contracts, coverage ceases on the last day of the month in which employment terminates.

- The date the employee ceases to be eligible.
- The date the master contract terminates.
- The date the overall maximum benefit of major medical coverage is received.
- The end of the last period for which the employee has made any required contribution.

Coverage on any dependent usually ceases on the earliest of the following:

- The date on which he or she ceases to meet the definition of dependent.
- The date on which the coverage of the employee ceases for any reason except the employee's receipt of the overall maximum benefit.
- The date on which the overall maximum benefit of major medical coverage is received by the dependent.
- The end of the last period for which the employee has made any required contribution for dependent coverage.

However, coverage often continues past these dates because of federal legislation or employer practices.

Continuation of Coverage under COBRA

The Consolidated Omnibus Budget Reconciliation Act of 1985 (COBRA) requires that group health plans allow employees and certain beneficiaries to elect to have their current health insurance coverage extended at group rates for up to 36 months following a "qualifying event" that results in the loss of coverage. The term *group health plan* as used in the Act is broad enough to include medical expense plans, dental plans, vision-care plans and prescription drug plans, regardless of whether benefits are self-funded or provided through other entities, such as insurance companies or HMOs. COBRA applies even if the cost of a plan is paid solely by employees as long as the plan would not be available at the same cost to an employee if he or she were not employed. However, there is one exception to this rule: Mass-marketed plans under which the employer's only involvement is to process payroll deductions are not subject to COBRA.

The Act applies only to employers that had 20 or more employees on a typical business day during the preceding calendar year (church and government plans are exempt). Failure to comply with the Act will result in an excise tax of up to $100 per day for each person denied coverage. The tax can be levied on the employer as well as on the entity (such as an insurer or HMO) that provides or administers the benefits.

Under the Act, each of the following is a qualifying event if it results in the loss of coverage by an employee or the employee's spouse or dependent child:

- The death of the covered employee.
- The termination of the employee for any reason except for gross misconduct. This includes quitting, retiring or being fired for anything other than gross misconduct.
- A reduction of the employee's hours so that the employee or dependent is ineligible for coverage.

- The divorce or legal separation of the covered employee and his or her spouse.
- For spouses and children, the employee's eligibility for Medicare.
- A child's ceasing to be an eligible dependent under the plan.

The Act specifies that the beneficiary—any employee, spouse or dependent child who loses coverage because of any of these events—is entitled to elect continued coverage without providing evidence of insurability. The beneficiary must be allowed to continue identical coverage to that provided to employees and dependents to whom a qualifying event has not occurred. If a medical expense plan includes such items as dental care or vision care as an integral part of the plan, the beneficiary must also be allowed to continue coverage without these benefits, even though such an option is not available to active employees or their dependents.

Coverage for persons electing continuation can be changed when changes are made to the plan covering active employees and their dependents. The continued coverage must extend from the date of the qualifying event to the earliest of the following:

- 18 months for employees and dependents when the employee's employment has terminated or coverage has been terminated because of a reduction in hours. This period can be extended up to 29 months if the Social Security Administration determines that an employee met the social security definition of total disability at the time of the qualifying event.
- 36 months for other qualifying beneficiaries.
- The date the plan terminates for all employees.
- The date the coverage ceases because of a qualifying beneficiary's failure to make a timely payment of premium.
- The date a qualifying beneficiary becomes entitled to Medicare or becomes covered (as either an employee or dependent) under another group health plan provided the group health plan does not contain an exclusion or limitation with respect to any pre-existing condition. If the new plan does not cover a pre-existing condition, the COBRA coverage can be continued until the earlier of (1) the remainder of the 18- or 36-month period or (2) the time when the pre-existing-condition provision no longer applies.

If a second qualifying event occurs during the period of continued coverage (such as the divorce of a terminated employee), the maximum period of continuation is usually 36 months. One exception is if the second event is a former employee's eligibility for Medicare. In this case, other family members can continue COBRA's coverage for an additional 36 months. For example, an employee retires at age 64, creating a qualifying event entitling beneficiaries to 18 months of continued coverage. When the retiree becomes entitled to Medicare (at age 65), the dependents have a new qualifying event and can continue coverage for 36 more months.

At the termination of continued coverage, a qualified beneficiary must be offered the right to convert to an individual insurance policy if a conversion privilege is generally available to employees under the employer's plan.

Notification of the right to continue coverage must be made at two times by a plan's administrator. The first time is when a plan becomes subject to COBRA or when a person becomes covered under a plan subject to COBRA. Notification must be given to an employee as well as to his or her spouse. The second time is when a qualifying event occurs. In this case, the employer must notify the plan administrator, who then must notify all qualifying beneficiaries within 14 days. In general, the employer has 30 days to notify the plan administrator. However, an employer may not know of a qualifying event if it involves divorce, legal separation or a child's ceasing to be eligible for coverage. In these circumstances, the employee or family member must notify the employer within 60 days of the event or the right to elect COBRA coverage is lost. The time period for the employer to notify the plan administrator begins when the employer is informed of the qualifying event as long as this occurs within the 60-day period.

The continuation of coverage is not automatic; it must be elected by a qualifying beneficiary. The election period starts on the date of the qualifying event and may end not earlier than 60 days after actual notice of the event to the qualifying beneficiary by the plan administrator. Once coverage is elected, the beneficiary has 45 days to pay the premium for the period of coverage prior to the election.

Under COBRA, the cost of the continued coverage may be passed on to the qualifying beneficiary, but the cost cannot exceed 102 percent of the cost of the plan for the period of coverage for a similarly situated active employee to whom a qualifying event has not occurred. The extra 2 percent is supposed to cover the employer's extra administrative costs. The one exception to this rule occurs for months 19 through 29 if an employee is disabled when the premium can be as high as 150 percent. Qualifying beneficiaries must have the option of paying the premium in monthly installments. In addition, there must be a grace period of at least 30 days for each installment.

Continuation of Coverage in Addition to COBRA

Even before the passage of COBRA, it was becoming increasingly common for employers (particularly large employers) to continue group insurance coverage for certain employees—and possibly their dependents—beyond the usual termination dates. Obviously, when coverage is continued now, an employer must, at a minimum, comply with COBRA. However, an employer can be more liberal than COBRA, such as paying all or a portion of the cost, or providing continued coverage for additional categories of persons or for a longer period of time. It should also be noted that some states have continuation laws for insured medical expense coverage that might require coverage to be made available in situations not covered by COBRA. One example would be for employees who work for firms with fewer than 20 employees; another is coverage for periods longer than those required by COBRA.

Retired Employees

Even though not required to do so by the Age Discrimination in Employment Act, many employers continue coverage on retired employees. Although coverage can also be continued for retirees' dependents, it is often limited only to spouses. Retired employees under age 65 usually have the same coverage as do active employees. However, if included under the same plan, coverage for employees age 65 or older may be provided under a carve-out plan that includes Medicare or a Medicare supplement. The lifetime maximum for persons eligible for Medicare is often much lower, such as $5,000 or $10,000, than for active employees. In addition, this maximum is not usually subject to any provision that restores benefits which have been paid.

The subject of retiree benefits has become a major concern to employers since the Financial Accounting Standards Board (FASB) issued a set of rules in 1991 for the accounting for postretirement benefits other than pensions. Under the FASB Rule 106, to be phased in between 1993 and 1997, employers are required to do the following:

- Recognize the present value of future retiree medical expense benefits on the firm's balance sheet with other liabilities.
- Record the cost for postretirement medical benefits in the period when an employee performs services, which is comparable to pension cost accounting.
- Amortize the present value of the future cost of benefits accrued prior to the new rules.

These new rules are in contrast to the current practice of paying retiree medical benefits or premiums out of current revenue and recognizing these costs as expenses when paid. Although the rules are probably logical from a financial accounting standpoint, the effect on employers will be staggering. Estimates are that as many as half of the Fortune 500 companies will be required to report lower earnings, and some could even have their net worths wiped out completely.

The new FASB rules will result in two major changes by employers. First, some employers will lower and possibly eliminate retiree benefits. From a legal standpoint, this may be difficult to do for current retirees, but future retirees will bear the burden. Second, other employers will look for methods to prefund the benefits. However, there are no alternatives for prefunding that are as favorable as the alternatives for funding pension benefits. An employer can set money aside in a trust, but no current income tax deduction is allowed and the earnings are taxable. Another alternative is the use of a 501(c)(9) trust. As discussed in Chapter 14, there are limitations on the deductibility of contributions to a 501(c)(9) trust. In addition, a 501(c)(9) trust can be used to fund retiree benefits only if it is currently being used to fund benefits for active employees.

A third alternative is to prefund medical benefits within a pension plan. The IRS rules for qualified retirement plans permit the payment of benefits for medical expenses from a pension plan if certain requirements are satisfied:

- Medical benefits must be subordinate to retirement benefits. This rule is met if the cost of medical benefits provided does not exceed 25 percent of the employer's aggregate contribution to the pension plan. For many employers, this figure is too low to allow the entire future liability to be prefunded.

- A separate account must be established and maintained for the monies allocated to medical benefits. This can be an aggregate account for nonkey employees, but individual separate accounts must be maintained for key employees; medical benefits attributable to a key employee (and family members) can be made only from his or her account.
- The employer's contributions for medical benefits must be ascertainable and reasonable.

Although the rules for funding retiree medical benefits in a pension plan are restricted and administratively complex, they offer an employer the greatest opportunity to deduct the cost of prefunded benefits. It should also be noted that Congress is aware of the prefunding issue, and there are proposals to change the pension rules to allow a more liberalized approach to the prefunding of retiree medical benefits, including long-term care.

Surviving Dependents

Coverage can also be continued for the survivors of deceased active employees and/ or deceased retired employees. However, coverage for the survivors of active employees is not commonly continued beyond the period required by COBRA. In addition, coverage for the survivors of retired employees may be limited only to surviving spouses. In both instances, the continued coverage is usually identical to what was provided prior to the employee's death. It is also common for the employer to continue the same premium contribution level.

Laid-Off Employees

Medical expense coverage can be continued for laid-off workers, and large employers frequently provide such coverage for a limited period. Few employers provide coverage beyond the period required by COBRA, but some employers continue to make the same premium contribution, at least for a limited period of time.

Disabled Employees

As with group term life insurance, medical expense coverage can be continued for an employee (and dependents) when he or she has a temporary interruption of employment, including one arising from illness or injury. Many employers also cover employees who have long-term disabilities or who have retired because of a disability. In most cases, this continuation of coverage is contingent upon satisfaction of some definition of total, and possibly permanent, disability.

Extension of Benefits

When coverage is terminated rather than continued, most medical expense plans extend benefits for any covered employee or dependent who is totally disabled at the time of termination. However, the disability must have resulted from an illness or injury that occurred while the individual was covered under the group contract. Generally, the same level of benefits will be provided as before termination.

Although some contracts will only cover expenses associated with the same cause of disability, other contracts will cover any expenses that would have been paid under the terminated coverage, regardless of cause.

Under basic medical expense contracts, the extension of benefits generally ceases after three months, or when the individual is no longer totally and continuously disabled, whichever comes first. A similar provision is used in major medical contracts, but the time period is longer—generally 12 months or the end of the benefit period following the one in which termination took place.

Conversion

Except where termination results from the failure to pay any required premiums, medical expense contracts usually contain—and are often required to contain—a conversion provision, whereby most covered persons whose group coverage terminates are allowed to purchase individual medical expense coverage without evidence of insurability and without any limitation of benefits for pre-existing conditions. Covered persons commonly have 31 days from the date of termination of the group coverage to exercise this conversion privilege, and coverage is then effective retroactively to the date of termination.

This conversion privilege is typically given to any employee who has been insured for at least three months under the group contract or under any group contract it replaced, and it permits the employee to convert his or her own coverage as well as any dependent coverage. In addition, a spouse or child whose dependent coverage ceases for any other reason may also be eligible for conversion; for example, a spouse who divorces or separates, and children who reach age 19.

A person who is eligible for both the conversion privilege and the right to continue the group insurance coverage under COBRA has two choices at the time eligibility for coverage terminates. He or she can either elect to convert under the provisions of the policy or elect to continue the group coverage. If the latter choice is made, the COBRA rules specify that the person must again be eligible to convert to an individual policy within the usual conversion period (31 days) after the maximum continuation-of-coverage period ceases. Policy provisions may also make the conversion privilege available to persons whose coverage terminates prior to the end of the maximum continuation period.

The insurance company has the right to refuse the issue of a conversion policy to anyone (1) who is covered by Medicare or (2) whose benefits under the converted policy, together with similar benefits from other sources, would result in overinsurance according to the insurance company's standards. These similar benefits may be found in other group or individual coverages that the individual has or in coverages for which the individual is eligible under any group arrangement.

The use of the word *conversion* is often a misnomer. In actuality, a person whose coverage terminates is only given the right to purchase a contract on an individual basis at individual rates. Most Blue Cross and Blue Shield Plans offer a conversion policy that is similar or identical to the terminated group coverage. However, most insurance companies offer a conversion policy, or a choice of policies, with a lower level of benefits than existed under the group coverage. Traditionally, the conversion policy contained only basic hospital and surgical coverages even if major medical coverage was provided under the group contract. Now many insurance companies provide—and are required to provide in some states—a conversion policy that includes major medical benefits, but not necessarily with benefits as broad as the former group coverage.

CLAIMS

Medical expense contracts that provide benefits on a service basis generally do not require covered persons to file claim forms. Rather, the providers of services perform any necessary paperwork and are then reimbursed directly.

Medical expense contracts that provide benefits on an indemnity basis require that the insurance company or other provider be given a written proof of loss (that is, a claim form) concerning the occurrence, character and extent of the loss for which a claim is made. This form typically contains portions that must be completed and signed by the employee, a representative of the employer and the provider of medical services.

The period during which an employee must file a claim depends upon the insurance company and state requirements. An employee generally has at least 90 days, or as soon as is reasonably possible, after medical expenses are incurred to file. Some insurance companies require that they be notified within a shorter time, such as 20 days, about any illness or injury on which a claim may be based, even though they give a longer time period for the actual filing of the form itself.

Individuals have the right under medical expense plans to assign their benefits to the providers of medical services. Such an assignment, which authorizes the insurance company to make the benefit payment directly to the provider, may generally be made by completing the appropriate portion of the claim form. In addition, as in disability income insurance, the insurance company has the right to examine any person for whom a claim is filed at its own expense and with the physician of its own choice.

FEDERAL TAXATION

In many respects, the federal tax treatment of group medical expense premiums and benefits parallels that of other group coverages if they are provided through an insurance company, Blue Cross and Blue Shield or an HMO. Contributions by the employer for an employee's coverage are tax deductible to the employer under Code Section 162 as long as the overall compensation of the employee is reasonable. Under Code Section 106, employer contributions do not create any income tax liability for an employee. In addition, Code Section 105 provides that benefits are not taxable to an employee except when they exceed any medical expenses incurred.

One major difference between group medical expense coverage and other forms of group insurance is that a portion of an employee's contribution for coverage may be tax deductible as a medical expense if that individual itemizes his or her income tax deductions. Under the Internal Revenue Code, individuals are allowed to deduct certain expenses for medical care, including dental expenses, for which no reimbursement was received. This deduction is limited to expenses—including amounts paid for insurance—that exceed 7.5 percent of the person's adjusted gross income.

Under provisions of the Tax Reform Act of 1986, sole proprietors and partners can deduct 25 percent of the cost of any medical expense coverage provided to them or their families under a plan carried by their proprietorship or partnership. However, the deduction cannot exceed the taxpayer's earned income for the year. Under previous law, the proprietorship or partnership could deduct the cost of medical expense coverage for the proprietor or any partner, but the amounts deducted constituted fully taxable income to the proprietor or partner. The 25 percent deduction now allowable may be taken only if (1) the proprietorship's or partnership's plan meets the new nondiscrimination rules imposed by the Act and (2) the proprietor or partner is not eligible to participate in any subsidized medical expense plan of another employer of the proprietor or partner or of an employer of the proprietor's or partner's spouse. It should be noted that this deduction is not an itemized deduction, but rather a deduction in arriving at adjusted gross income. In addition, any amount deducted cannot be used to determine whether the 7.5 percent threshold for the regular medical expense deduction has been satisfied.

The tax situation may be different if an employer provides medical expense benefits through a self-funded plan, referred to in Code Section 105 as a self-insured medical reimbursement plan. Under this type of plan, employers either (1) pay the providers of medical care directly or (2) reimburse employees for their medical expenses. If a self-funded plan meets certain nondiscrimination requirements for highly compensated employees, the employer can deduct benefit payments as they are made, and the employee will have no taxable income. If a plan is discriminatory, the employer will still receive an income tax deduction. However, all or a portion of the benefits received by highly compensated employees, but not by other employees, will be treated as taxable income. A highly compensated employee of a company is (1) one of the five highest paid officers of the firm, (2) a shareholder who owns more than 10 percent of the firm's stock or (3) one of the highest paid 25 percent of all the firm's employees. There are no nondiscrimination rules if a plan is not self-funded and provides benefits through an insurance contract, a Blue Cross Plan or an HMO.

To be considered nondiscriminatory, a self-funded plan must meet certain requirements regarding eligibility and benefits. The plan must provide benefits (1) for 70 percent or more of all employees or (2) for 80 percent or more of all eligible employees if 70 percent or more of all employees are eligible. Certain employees can be excluded from the all-employees category without affecting the plan's nondiscriminatory status. These include:

- Employees who have not completed three years of service.
- Employees who have not attained age 25.
- Part-time employees. Anyone who works fewer than 25 hours per week is

automatically considered a part-time employee. Persons who work 25 or more hours, but fewer than 35 hours per week, may also be counted as part-time as long as other employees in similar work for the employer have substantially more hours.

- Seasonal employees. Anyone who works fewer than seven months of the year is automatically considered a seasonal employee. Persons who work between seven and nine months of the year may also be considered seasonal as long as other employees have substantially more months of employment.
- Employees who are covered by a collective bargaining agreement if accident and health benefits were a subject of collective bargaining.

Even if a plan fails to meet the percentage requirements regarding eligibility, it can still qualify as nondiscriminatory so long as the IRS is satisfied that the plan benefits a classification of employees in a manner that does not discriminate in favor of highly compensated employees. This determination is made on a case-by-case basis.

To satisfy the nondiscrimination requirements for benefits, the same type and amount of benefits must be provided for all employees covered under the plan, regardless of their compensation. In addition, the dependents of other employees cannot be treated less favorably than the dependents of highly compensated employees. However, because diagnostic procedures are not considered part of a self-funded plan for purposes of the nondiscrimination rule, a higher level of this type of benefit is permissible for highly compensated employees.

If a plan is discriminatory in either benefits or eligibility, highly compensated employees must include the amount of any excess reimbursement in their gross income for income tax purposes. If highly compensated employees receive any benefits that are not available to all employees covered under the plan, then these benefits are considered an excess reimbursement. For example, if a plan pays 80 percent of covered expenses for employees in general, but 100 percent for highly compensated employees, the extra 20 percent of benefits constitutes taxable income.

If a self-funded plan discriminates in the way it determines eligibility, then highly compensated employees will have excess reimbursements for any amounts they receive. The amount of this excess reimbursement is determined by a percentage that is calculated by dividing the total amount of benefits received by highly compensated employees, exclusive of any other excess reimbursements, by the total amount of benefits paid to all employees, exclusive of any other excess reimbursements. Using the previous example, assume a highly compensated employee receives $2,000 in benefits during a certain year. If other employees only receive 80 percent of this amount, or $1,600, then the highly compensated employee would have received an excess reimbursement of $400. If the plan also discriminates in the area of eligibility, the highly compensated employee will incur additional excess reimbursement. For example, ignoring any benefits already considered excess reimbursement, if 60 percent of the benefits were given to highly compensated employees, then 60 percent of the remaining $1,600 ($2,000 - $400) or $960 would be added to the $400, for a total excess reimbursement of $1,360.

If a plan provides benefits only for highly compensated employees, then all benefits received will be considered an excess reimbursement, as the percentage of total benefits received by the highly compensated group would be 100 percent.

COST CONTAINMENT

Since 1970, the average annual increases in the cost of medical care have been approximately twice the average annual increases in the consumer price index. No single factor accounts for these increases. Rather, it is a combination of reasons that include the following:

- Technological advances. In the last few years, many exciting technological advances have taken place. Numerous lives are now being saved by such techniques as CAT (computerized axial tomography) scans, fetal monitoring and organ transplants. As miraculous as many of these techniques are, they are also very expensive.
- Increasing malpractice suits. The providers of care are much more likely to be sued than in the past, and malpractice awards have outpaced the general rate of inflation. This has resulted in higher malpractice premiums, and these premiums are ultimately passed on to consumers. The increase in malpractice suits has also led to an increase in defensive medicine. More routine tests are likely to be performed more often.
- Increases in third-party payments. A growing portion of the country's health-care expenditures are now paid by private health insurers or the government. Patients and providers of health care often have no financial incentives to economize on the use of health-care service.
- Undercapacity of medical facilities. Currently, the United States has an over-abundance of hospital beds and a surplus of physicians is also beginning to develop. Empty hospital beds are expensive to maintain; an oversupply of physicians tends to drive up the average costs of medical procedures so that the average income of the physicians does not drop.
- Design of medical expense plans. Many medical expense plans now provide first-dollar coverage for many health care costs. There is often little incentive for patients to avoid the most expensive forms of treatment.
- AIDS. The continuing increase in the number of AIDS cases over the last ten years has resulted in increasing costs to employers. Costs in excess of $100,000 for an employee with AIDS are not unusual.

Increasing health care costs have become the concern of almost everyone—government, labor, employers and consumers. In the remainder of this chapter, many of the cost-containment measures used by employers will be discussed. Some of these measures have been discussed in the previous two chapters; others are discussed later in the textbook; still others will be briefly described here.

Cost containment can be broken into several components:

- Benefit plan design.
- Alternative providers.

- Alternative funding methods.
- Claims review.
- Health education and preventive care.
- Encouragement of external cost-control systems.
- Managed care.

No single cost-containment technique will usually produce great savings by itself, but a combination of these techniques may lead to significant cost reductions or a slowing of cost increases.

Benefit Plan Design

Numerous design features of a medical expense plan can control costs. These traditionally have been in the form of contractual provisions that shift costs to employees. Examples include:

- Deductibles.
- Coinsurance.
- Exclusions and limitations.
- Maximum benefits.

In recent years, design features have been aimed more at reducing costs than shifting them. And, in fact, benefit plans are often designed to provide a higher level of benefits if less costly alternatives are used. Examples of these cost-containment features include:

- Preadmission testing.
- Second surgical opinions.
- Coordination of benefits.
- The use of alternatives to the hospital—skilled nursing facilities, home health care, hospice care, birthing centers and ambulatory-care centers.

Alternative Providers

The use of HMOs and PPOs have both been popular as cost-containment methods. PPOs clearly accomplish this goal, but as mentioned earlier in the book, there is some controversy over the effectiveness of HMOs. HMOs and PPOs were discussed in Chapter 9.

Alternative Funding Methods

Employers are increasingly turning to funding methods that are alternatives to the traditional insurance company plan or Blue Cross and Blue Shield Plan. Chapter 14 is devoted to a discussion of these techniques.

Claims Review

There is no doubt that claims review can generate substantial cost savings. In general, this review is done by the provider of medical expense benefits, a third-party administrator or some independent outside organization (not the employer). At a minimum, claims should be reviewed for patient eligibility, eligibility of the services provided, duplicate policies and charges that are in excess of usual, customary and reasonable amounts. Many medical expense plans routinely audit hospital bills, particularly those that exceed some amount, such as $5,000 or $10,000. They check for errors in such items as length of stay, services performed and billed charges. Many insurance companies have found that each dollar spent on this type of review results in $2 or $3 of savings.

A newer trend in claims review is utilization review or case management. This may be done on either a prospective basis, a concurrent basis, a retrospective basis or a combination of the three. A prospective review involves analyzing a case to see what type of treatment is necessary. Hospital preadmission authorization, second surgical opinions and predetermination of dental benefits (see Chapter 13) fall into this category. However, when a patient is hospitalized, concurrent review can lead to shorter stays and the use of less expensive facilities. Concurrent review is normally carried out by a registered nurse and typically begins with precertification of a hospital stay for an initial specified length of time. The nurse then works with the patient's physician to monitor the length of stay and to determine whether other alternatives to hospitalization—such as hospice or home health care—can be used. Many providers of medical expense benefits will pay for these alternative forms of treatment even if they are not specifically covered under the medical expense plan—as long as their cost is lower than the cost of continued hospitalization.

A retrospective review involves an analysis of care after the fact to determine if it was appropriate. Such a review may lead to a denial of claims, but its purpose is often to monitor trends so that future actions can be taken in high-cost areas. For example, a retrospective review may lead to the establishment of a concurrent review program for a hospital with excessive lengths of stay.

Health Education and Preventive Care

There is little doubt that persons who lead healthy lifestyles will tend to have fewer medical bills, particularly at younger ages. It is also evident that healthier employees save an employer money by taking fewer sick days and having fewer disability claims. For these reasons, employers are increasingly establishing wellness programs and employee-assistance plans. Both of these programs are discussed in Chapter 16. With an increasing health awareness among the general population, the existence of these programs has a positive side effect—the improvement of employee morale.

Encouragement of External Cost Control Systems

While a certain degree of cost containment is within the control of employers, the proper control of costs is an ongoing process that requires participation by consumers (both employers and individuals), government and the providers of health care services. At the national level, the National Council on Health Planning and Development, an advisory body to the Secretary of Health and Human Services, identifies needs, monitors resources, establishes priorities, recommends courses of action and oversees laws pertaining to health care. The Council, which was created by the National Health Planning and Resources Development Act of 1974, oversees state and local activities that are carried out by state health planning and development agencies and local health system agencies. Many employers encourage and are actively involved with these agencies.

At the state and local level, many employers are active in coalitions whose purpose is to control costs and to improve the quality of health care. These groups—which may also involve unions, providers of health care, insurance companies and regulators—are often the catalyst for legislation, such as laws authorizing PPOs and establishing hospital budget review programs.

Managed Care

The current buzz word with respect to cost containment is *managed care*. In a general sense, the term can be defined to include any medical expense plan that attempts to contain costs by controlling the behavior of participants. However, in practice, the term is used by many persons to mean different things. At one extreme, traditional indemnity plans require second opinions and/or hospital precertification. At the other extreme, plans limit a participant's choice of medical providers, negotiate provider fees and use case management.

Managed-care plans have evolved over the last few years. Today, it is generally felt that a true managed-care plan should have five basic characteristics:

1. *Controlled access of providers.* It is difficult to control costs if participants have unrestricted access to physicians and hospitals. Managed-care plans attempt to encourage or force participants to use predetermined providers. Because a major portion of medical expenses results from referrals to specialists, managed-care plans tend to use primary care physicians as gatekeepers to determine the necessity and appropriateness of specialty care.
2. *Comprehensive case management.* Successful managed-care plans perform utilization review at all levels.
3. *Preventive care.* Managed-care plans encourage preventive care and the attainment of healthier lifestyles.
4. *Risk sharing.* Managed-care plans are most successful if providers share in the financial consequences of medical decisions. Newer managed-care plans have contractual guarantees to encourage cost-effective care. For example, a physician who minimizes diagnostic tests may receive a bonus. Ideally, such an arrangement will eliminate unnecessary tests, not discourage tests that should be performed.
5. *High-quality care.* A managed-care plan will not be well received and selected by participants if there is a perception of inferior or inconvenient medical care. In the past, too little attention was paid to this aspect of cost containment. Newer managed-care plans not only select providers more carefully but also monitor the quality of care on a continuing basis.

There seems to be a reasonable consensus among employers and benefit specialists that there is a negative correlation between benefit costs and the degree of managed care. That is, the greater the degree of managed care, the lower the cost. For example, studies generally rank benefit plans in the following order (from highest to lowest) with respect to annual benefit costs:

- Traditional plans without case management.
- Traditional plans with case management.
- PPOs.
- Open-ended HMOs.
- Independent practice association HMOs.
- Closed-panel HMOs.

It is interesting to note that the degree of care management increases as one goes down the list. In addition, there seems to be a high correlation between annual benefits costs and the rate of cost increases. For example, the cost of traditional benefit plans has recently been increasing at an annual rate in excess of 20 percent; closed-panel HMO costs have been increasing at an annual rate of about 10 percent.

STUDY QUESTIONS

1. Explain the effect of the NAIC Model Regulation on Group Coverage Discontinuance and Replacement when group insurance coverage is transferred.
2. What dependents are typically eligible for coverage under a major medical contract?
3. Holly incurred $5,000 of medical expenses that, except for deductibles and coinsurance, are fully covered under the medical expense plan provided by her employer. She is also covered as a dependent under her husband's plan. Holly's plan has a $100 deductible and an 80 percent coinsurance provision; her husband's plan has a $200 deductible and 90 percent coinsurance. How much will Holly collect from each plan if the usual coordination-of-benefits approach is used?
4. Under what circumstances is Medicare the secondary payer of medical expense benefits?
5. a. What employers are subject to the health insurance continuation provisions of COBRA?
   b. What are the penalties for noncompliance?
6. With respect to the health insurance continuation provisions of COBRA, answer each of the following:
   a. What is a qualifying event?
   b. Who are eligible qualifying beneficiaries?
   c. For what length of time must coverage be continued?
   d. When must a person be notified of his or her rights to continue health insurance coverage?
   e. What is the maximum charge that can be made for continuation of coverage?

7. Briefly describe how medical expense coverage provided to retired employees may differ from that provided to active employees.

8. a. Under what circumstances is an employee or dependent eligible to convert medical expense coverage that has terminated?

   b. What type of coverage can be obtained under the conversion provision?

9. How does the claims process differ with respect to medical expense contracts providing benefits on a service basis and medical expense contracts providing benefits on an indemnity basis?

10. What are some of the reasons for the significant increases in the cost of health care?

11. What are the major components of health care cost containment?

12. What are the ways in which utilization review can control health care costs?

13. What are the characteristics of an effective managed-care plan?

13

Group Dental Coverage and Other Group Insurance Benefits

Objectives

- Identify the sources of group dental insurance benefits and explain the provisions contained in dental insurance contracts.
- Describe the approaches used to provide group legal expense benefits.
- Explain the reasons why long-term care insurance is needed and describe the provisions found in group long-term care products.
- Explain the reasons for the slow growth of group property and liability insurance and describe the characteristics of the programs currently in existence.
- Describe the characteristics of mass-marketed individual insurance and explain its similarities and differences to group insurance.

Three traditional types of group insurance have been previously discussed—life insurance, disability income insurance, and medical expense insurance. This chapter will focus on four of the newer and/or less common types of group insurance coverage—dental insurance, long-term care insurance, legal expense insurance, and property and liability insurance. In addition, mass-marketed individual life and health insurance plans will be described. While these latter plans rely on individual insurance contracts, they are available only to a group of employees and have characteristics of both individual and group insurance.

GROUP DENTAL INSURANCE

Since the early 1970s, group dental insurance has been one of the fastest growing employee benefits. It has been estimated that between 1970 and 1990, the percentage of employees who had dental coverage grew from about 5 percent to over 60 percent. Many employee benefit consultants feel that most employees, except for those who work for small employers, will have dental coverage by the end of the century.

To a great extent, group dental insurance contracts have been patterned after group medical expense contracts, and they contain many similar, if not identical, provisions. Like group medical expense insurance, group dental insurance has many variations. Because of its newness as a major employee benefit, dental insurance contracts are even less standardized than medical expense contracts. Dental plans may be limited to specific types of expenses or they may be broad enough to cover virtually all dental expenses. In addition, coverage can be obtained from alternative types of providers, and benefits can be in the form of either services or cash payments. Dental benefits may also be self-funded.

Providers of Dental Coverage

Like medical expense coverage, employers have several sources from which they can purchase dental coverage for their employees. The three most common ones are insurance companies, dental service plans and Blue Cross and Blue Shield.

Insurance Companies

Approximately half the coverage for dental expenses is written on an indemnity basis by insurance companies. Coverage is usually offered independently of other group insurance coverages, but it may be incorporated into a major medical contract. However, if it is part of a major medical contract, the coverage is often referred to as an *integrated dental plan,* and the benefits are frequently subject to the same provisions and limitations as those benefits that are available under a separate dental plan.

Dental Service Plans

Most states have dental service plans, often called *Delta Plans,* that along with Blue Cross and Blue Shield, write approximately one-fourth of the dental coverage on a national basis. However, the extent of their use varies widely by state, and western states generally have larger and more successful plans than other parts of the country. The majority of these plans are nonprofit organizations that are sponsored by state dental associations. In addition, they are patterned after Blue Shield Plans, and dentists provide service benefits on a contractual basis. Also like Blue Shield, state Delta Plans are coordinated by a national board, Delta Dental Plans, Inc.

Blue Cross and Blue Shield

Many Blue Cross and Blue Shield Plans also provide dental coverage. In some cases, Blue Cross and Blue Shield have contractual arrangements with dentists that are similar to those of dental service plans; in other cases, benefits are paid on an indemnity basis, just as if an insurance company were involved. Finally, some Blue

Cross and Blue Shield Plans market dental coverage through Delta Plans in conjunction with their own medical expense plans.

Other Sources

A few HMOs offer dental benefits, but this is not very common. Any benefits that are provided—primarily check-ups, preventive services and routine fillings—are often limited to children.

Coverage may also be obtained from dental maintenance organization (DMO) plans, which operate like HMOs but only provide dental care. In addition, a few dental PPOs have started to operate. While the number of DMOs and dental PPOs is still small, they are growing at a rapid rate and may become major providers of dental care in the near future. Several factors would seem to make this growth logical. Dental expenses are more predictable than medical care expenses, and the preventive nature of much dental care provides a real potential to hold down future dental costs.

Employers are increasingly turning to self-funding of dental benefits. An employer may either self-administer the plan or use the services of a third-party administrator.

Contractual Provisions

Although group dental insurance contracts have been patterned after group medical expense contracts, some of their provisions are different, and others are unique to dental coverage. These provisions pertain to eligibility, benefits, exclusions, benefit limitations, predetermination of benefits and termination.

Eligibility

In noncontributory plans, most employers use the same eligibility requirements for dental coverage as they use for medical expense coverage. However, some employers have different probationary periods for the two coverages. Probationary periods are used because members of a group who previously had no dental insurance usually have a large number of untreated dental problems. In addition, many postponable dental care expenditures will be postponed by an employee who anticipates coverage under a dental plan in the future. Depending on the group's characteristics, the number of first-year claims for a new plan, or for new employees and their dependents under an existing dental plan, can be expected to run between 20 and 50 percent more than long-run annual claims. To counter this higher-than-average number of claims, some employers use a longer probationary period for dental benefits than for medical expense benefits. Other employers may have the same probationary period for both types of coverage but will impose waiting periods before certain types of dental expenses will be covered, such as 12 months for orthodontics.

Longer-than-usual probationary or waiting periods will initially minimize claims, but unless an organization has a high turnover rate, it may be false economy. Many of those persons who do not have coverage will merely postpone treatment until they do have coverage. This postponement may actually lead to increased claims, because existing dental conditions will become more severe and will require more expensive treatment. For this reason, some benefit consultants feel that probationary and waiting periods should be kept relatively short.

Another method of countering high first-year claims is to require evidence of insurability. For example, an insurance company might require any person who desires coverage from the dental plan to undergo a dental examination. If major dental problems are disclosed, the person must have them corrected before insurance coverage will become effective.

Since dental expenditures are postponable and somewhat predictable, the problem of adverse selection under contributory plans is more severe for dental insurance than for other types of group insurance. To counter this adverse selection, insurance companies impose more stringent eligibility and underwriting requirements on contributory dental plans than they do on other types of group insurance. In addition, most insurance companies insist upon a high percentage of participation, such as 80 or 85 percent, and a few will actually not write contributory coverage. Many insurance companies will also insist upon having other business besides dental coverage from the employer.

The problem of adverse selection is particularly severe when persons desire coverage after the date on which they were initially eligible to participate. These persons most likely want coverage because they or someone in their family needs dental treatment. Several provisions are contained in dental insurance contracts that try to minimize this problem. They include one or a combination of:

- Reducing benefits (usually by 50 percent) for a period of time (such as one year) following the late enrollment.
- Reducing the maximum benefit to a low amount, such as $100 or $200, for the year following the late enrollment.
- Excluding some benefits for a certain period, such as one or two years, following the late enrollment. This exclusion may apply to all dental expenses except those that result from an accident, or it may apply only to a limited array of benefits, such as orthodontics and prosthetics.

Benefits

Most dental insurance plans pay for almost all types of dental expenses, but a particular plan may provide more limited coverage. One characteristic of dental insurance that is seldom found in medical expense plans is the inclusion of benefits for both routine diagnostic procedures (including oral examinations and X-rays) and preventive dental treatment (including teeth cleaning and fluoride treatment). In fact, a few dental plans actually require periodic oral examinations as a condition of continuing eligibility. There is clear evidence that the cost of providing these benefits will be more than offset by avoiding expensive dental procedures that are required when a condition is not discovered early or when a preventive treatment has not been given.

In addition to benefits for diagnostic and preventive treatment, benefits for dental expenses may be provided for the following categories of dental treatment:

- Restoration, including fillings, crowns and other procedures used to restore the functional use of natural teeth.
- Oral surgery, including the extraction of teeth as well as other surgical treatment of diseases, injuries and defects of the jaw.
- Endodontics (treatment for diseases of the dental pulp within teeth, such as root canals).
- Periodontics (treatment of diseases of the surrounding and supporting tissues of the teeth).
- Prosthodontics (the replacement of missing teeth and structures by artificial devices, such as bridgework and dentures).
- Orthodontics (the prevention and correction of dental and oral anomalies through the use of correctional devices, such as braces and retainers).

Most dental plans will usually cover any expenses that arise from the first five categories listed above, and they may or may not include benefits for orthodontics. Whatever benefits are provided may be on a scheduled basis, on a nonscheduled basis or on some combination of the two.

Scheduled Plans. A scheduled dental plan is similar to a surgical expense plan in which benefits are paid up to the amount specified in the fee schedule. Here is an excerpt from one such dental schedule:

Dental Services	Maximum Benefit
Diagnostic:	
Initial oral examination	$ 15.00
Periodic oral examination	10.00
Preventive:	
Prophylaxis (14 years of age or older)	30.00
Prophylaxis (under 14 years of age)	20.00
Prosthodontics:	
Complete upper denture	400.00

Most scheduled dental plans provide benefits on a first-dollar basis and contain no deductibles or specified coinsurance percentage. However, benefit maximums are often lower than the usual-and-customary charges of dentists, thereby forcing employees to bear a portion of the costs of their dental services. For example, if a schedule is designed to provide maximum benefits that are equal to approximately 80 percent of the usual-and-customary charges, employees are in effect subject to an 80 percent coinsurance provision. In order to encourage diagnostic and preventive services, some dental schedules are designed so that the fees for these services are almost completely covered, while benefits for other dental services are paid at a lower level.

Unlike a surgical schedule, which only lists the more common surgical procedures, a dental schedule is essentially an all-inclusive list of the covered dental services. If a service is not on the list, most contracts will cover it, but only if the schedule contains what could be considered a suitable substitute. In addition, any benefits paid will be limited to the amount specified for the substitute service.

Although once common, scheduled dental plans are now used less frequently than either nonscheduled plans or combination plans.

Nonscheduled Plans. Nonscheduled dental plans, often called *comprehensive dental plans*, are the most common type of dental coverage. They resemble major medical expense contracts because dental expenses are paid on a reasonable-and-customary basis, subject to any exclusions, limitations or copayments contained in the contract. The use of the term *nonscheduled* is something of a misnomer, since many nonscheduled plans actually do contain a schedule of the covered dental services, but they do not list specific benefit amounts for individual services.

Nonscheduled dental plans usually contain both deductibles and coinsurance provisions. Although a single deductible and a single coinsurance percentage may apply to all dental services, the more common practice treats different classes of dental services in different ways. The typical nonscheduled dental plan breaks dental services into three broad categories:

1. Diagnostic and preventive services.
2. Basic services, such as fillings, oral surgery, periodontics and endodontics.
3. Major services, such as inlays, crowns, dentures and orthodontics.

Diagnostic and preventive services are typically covered in full and are not subject to a deductible or coinsurance. They are, however, subject to any other contract limitations. The other two categories, however, are generally each subject to an annual deductible, usually between $25 and $50 per person. In addition to the deductible, the cost of basic services may be reimbursed at a high percentage, such as 80 percent, while major services are reimbursed at a lower percentage, often 50 percent.

Combination Plans. Combination plans contain features of both scheduled and nonscheduled plans. The typical combination plan covers diagnostic and preventive services on a usual-and-customary basis, but uses a fee schedule for other dental services.

Exclusions

Exclusions are found in all dental plans, but their number and type vary. Some of the more common exclusions include charges for:

- Services that are purely cosmetic, unless necessitated by an accidental bodily injury while a person is covered under the plan. (Orthodontics, although often used for cosmetic reasons, can usually be justified as necessary to correct abnormal dental conditions.)
- Replacement of lost, missing or stolen dentures, or other prosthetic devices.
- Duplicate dentures or other prosthetic devices.
- Oral hygiene instruction or other training in preventive dental care.
- Services that do not have uniform professional endorsement.
- Occupational injuries to the extent that benefits are provided by workers' compensation laws or similar legislation.

- Services furnished by or on behalf of government agencies, unless there is a requirement to pay.
- Certain services that began prior to the date that coverage for an individual became effective; for example, a crown for which a tooth was prepared prior to coverage.

Limitations

Dental insurance plans also contain numerous limitations that are designed to control claim costs and to eliminate unnecessary dental care. In addition to deductibles and coinsurance, virtually all dental plans contain overall benefit maximums. Most plans contain a calendar-year maximum varying from $500 to $2,000, but no lifetime maximum. However, some plans have only a lifetime maximum such as $1,000 or $5,000, and a few plans contain both a calendar-year maximum and a large lifetime maximum. These maximums may apply to all dental expenses, or they may be limited to all expenses except those that arise from orthodontics and occasionally periodontics. In the latter case, benefits for orthodontics will be subject to a separate, lower lifetime maximum, typically between $500 and $2,000.

Most dental plans limit the frequency with which some benefits will be paid. Routine oral examinations and teeth cleaning are usually limited to once every six months and full mouth X-rays to once every 24 or 36 months. The replacement of dentures may also be limited to one time in some specific period, such as five years.

The typical dental plan also limits benefits to the least expensive type of accepted dental treatment for a given dental condition. For example, if either a gold or silver filling could be used, benefit payments will be limited to the cost of a silver filling, even if a gold filling is inserted.

Predetermination of Benefits

The majority of dental contracts provide for a pretreatment review of certain dental services by the insurance company. Although this procedure is not usually mandatory, it does allow both the dentist and the patient to know just how much will be paid under the plan before the treatment is performed. In addition, it enables the plan to have some control over the performance of unnecessary, or more-costly-than-necessary procedures, by giving the patients an opportunity to seek less costly care—possibly from another dentist—if they learn that benefits will be limited.

In general, the *predetermination-of-benefits provision*, which goes by several names, including precertification or prior authorization, applies only in non-emergency situations and when a dentist's charge for course of treatment exceeds a specified amount that varies from $100 to $300. The dentist, in effect, files a claim form, and X-rays if applicable, with the insurance company just as if the treatment had already been performed. The insurance company reviews the form and returns it to the dentist. The form specifies the services that will be covered and the amount of reimbursement. If and when the services are actually performed, payment is made to the dentist after the claim form has been returned with the appropriate signatures and the date of completion.

When the predetermination-of-benefits provision has not been followed, benefits will still be paid. However, neither the dentist nor the covered person will know in advance what services will be covered by the insurance company or how much the insurance company will pay for these services.

Termination

Coverage under dental insurance plans typically terminates for the same reasons as medical expense coverage; these were described in Chapter 12. Rarely is there any type of conversion privilege for dental benefits, even when the coverage is written as part of a major medical contract. However, dental coverage is subject to the continuation rules of COBRA.

Benefits for dental service received after termination may still be covered as long as (1) the charge for the service was incurred prior to the termination date and (2) treatment is completed within 60 or 90 days after termination. For example, the charge for a crown or bridgework is incurred once the preparation of the tooth or teeth has begun, even though the actual installation of the crown or bridgework (and the billing) does not take place until after coverage terminates. Similarly, charges for dentures are incurred on the date the impressions for the dentures are taken, and charges for root canal therapy are incurred on the date the root canal is opened.

GROUP LONG-TERM CARE INSURANCE

In the 1980s, insurance companies started to market long-term care insurance policies to individuals. Many of the earlier policies had limited benefits and expensive premiums. As the products have evolved, benefits have improved while premiums have remained stable or decreased. As with universal life insurance, success in the individual marketplace led to interest in group long-term care insurance as an employee benefit. The first group long-term plan was written in 1987, and a small but growing number of employers, mostly large ones, now make coverage available. The number of insurance companies writing coverage has also grown, but the number still remains relatively small and is primarily limited to the largest group insurance carriers.

At best, the growth of group long-term care insurance can be described as slow and cautious for several reasons.

1. The individual long-term care insurance market is still in an evolving state, due partially to the lack of adequate actuarial data to design and price coverage. The situation is not unlike the early days of disability income insurance.
2. The tax status of group long-term care coverage is uncertain. It appears that employer-provided benefits, unlike medical expense benefits, will result in taxation to employees. To the extent that employers want to spend additional benefit dollars, they want to spend them on benefits for which

employees receive favorable tax benefits. As a result, almost all group long-term care plans are financed solely by employee contributions.

3. There is uncertainty about whether long-term care can be included in a cafeteria plan on a tax-favored basis.

4. Finally, participation in group plans has been modest because older employees who feel they have a need for the coverage often find it too expensive. A surprise, however, with many of the early plans has been the higher-than-expected participation by employees in the 40-to-50 age bracket.

Before a description of the existing plans is undertaken, it is important to discuss the need for long-term care protection and the sources already available to meet this need.

The Need for Long-Term Care

The need for long-term care arises from the following factors:
- An aging population.
- Increasing costs.
- The inability of families to provide full care.
- The inadequacy of insurance protection.

An Aging Population

Long-term care has traditionally been thought of as a problem primarily for the older population. The population age 65 or over is the fastest-growing age group; today it represents about 11 percent of the population, a figure that is expected to increase to between 20 and 25 percent over the next 50 years. The segment of the population age 85 and over is growing at an even faster rate. While less than 10 percent of the over-65 group is over 85 today, this percentage is expected to double over the next two generations.

An aging society presents changing problems. Those who needed long-term care in the past were most likely to have suffered from strokes or other acute diseases. With today's longer life spans, a larger portion of the elderly will be incapacitated by chronic conditions such as Alzheimer's disease, arthritis, osteoporosis and lung and heart disease—conditions that often require continuing assistance with day-to-day needs. The likelihood that a nursing home will be needed increases dramatically with age. One percent of persons between the ages of 65 and 74 reside in nursing homes, and the percentage increases to 6 percent between the ages of 75 and 84. At ages 85 and over, the figure rises to approximately 25 percent.

It should be noted that the elderly are not the only group of persons who need long-term care. Many younger persons are unable to care for themselves because of handicaps resulting from birth defects, mental conditions, illnesses or accidents.

Increasing Costs

Today, nearly $50 billion is spent on nursing care. This cost is increasing faster than inflation because of the growing demand for nursing home beds and the shortage of skilled medical personnel. The cost of complete long-term care for an individual can also be astronomical, with annual nursing home costs of $30,000 not being unusual.

The Inability of Families to Provide Full Care

Traditionally, long-term care has been provided by family members, often at considerable personal sacrifice and great personal stress. However, it is becoming more difficult for families to provide long-term care for the following reasons:

- The geographic dispersion of family members.
- Increased participation in the paid work force by women and children.
- Fewer children in the family.
- More childless families.
- Higher divorce rates.
- The inability of family members to provide care because they themselves are growing old.

The Inadequacy of Insurance Protection

Private medical expense insurance policies (both group and individual) almost always have an exclusion for convalescent, custodial or rest care. Some policies, particularly group policies, do provide coverage for extended-care facilities and for home health care. In both cases, the purpose is to provide care in a manner that is cheaper than care in a hospital. However, coverage is provided only if a person also needs medical care; benefits are not provided if a person is merely "old" and needs someone to care for him or her.

Medicare is also inadequate because it does not cover custodial care unless this care is needed along with the medical or rehabilitative treatment provided in skilled nursing facilities or under home health-care benefits.

Sources of Long-Term Care

There are several sources other than insurance that are available for providing long-term care. However, there are drawbacks associated with each source.

One source is to rely on personal savings. Unless a person has substantial resources, however, this approach may force an individual and his or her dependents into poverty. It may also mean that the financial objective of leaving assets to heirs will not be met.

A second source is to rely on welfare. The Medicaid program in most states will provide benefits, which usually include nursing home care, to the "medically needy." However, a person is not eligible unless he or she is either poor or has exhausted most other assets (including those of a spouse). There is also often a social stigma associated with the acceptance of welfare.

Life-care facilities are growing in popularity as a source of meeting long-term care needs. With a life-care facility, residents pay an "entrance fee" that allows them to occupy a dwelling unit without actual ownership rights. The entrance fee is typically not refundable if the resident leaves the facility voluntarily or dies. (There may be some partial refund if a person leaves within a specified time period.) Residents pay a monthly fee that includes meals, some housecleaning services and varying degrees of health care. If a person needs long-term care, he or she must give up the independent living unit and move to the nursing home portion of the facility, but the monthly fee normally remains the same. The disadvantages of this option are that the costs of a life-care facility are beyond the reach of many persons, and a resident must be in reasonably good health and able to live independently at the time the facility is entered. Therefore, the decision to use a life-care facility must be made in advance of the need for long-term care. Once such care is needed or is imminent, this approach is no longer viable.

A few insurers have recently started to include long-term care benefits in some cash value life insurance policies. Essentially, an insured can begin to use the death benefit while still living. For example, if the insured is in a nursing home, he or she might receive a benefit equal to 1 or 2 percent of the face value of the policy. However, any benefits reduce the future death benefit payable to heirs.

Group Long-Term Care Policies

There are few standard group long-term care policies because most of the plans in existence have each been designed for a specific employer. However, virtually all group policies are consistent with the provisions contained in the NAIC Long-Term Care Insurance Model Act. The result is that group policies tend to be comparable to the broader policies that are sold in the individual marketplace.

Eligibility

The typical eligibility rules (that is, full time, actively at work and so on) apply to group long-term care policies. At a minimum, coverage can be purchased for an active employee and/or spouse. Some policies also provide coverage to retirees and to other family members such as children, parents, parents-in-law and possibly adult children. There is a maximum age for eligibility, but it may be as high as 80.

Cost

As previously mentioned, the cost of group long-term care coverage is almost always borne by the employee. Initial premiums are usually in five-year age brackets and increase significantly with age. For example, one plan has an annual premium of $200 for persons age 40–44 and $850 for persons age 60–65. Once coverage is elected, premiums remain level and do not increase when a person enters another age bracket. Coverage is guaranteed renewable, so premiums can be increased by class.

Under some plans, premiums are payable until a covered person either dies or starts to receive benefits. Under other plans, premiums are higher but cease at retirement age. Such a plan is analogous to a life insurance policy that is paid up at age 65.

Level of Care

There are four levels of care that can be provided by long-term care policies:

1. *Skilled nursing care,* which consists of daily nursing and rehabilitative care that can be performed only by, or under the supervision of, skilled medical personnel and must be based on a doctor's orders.
2. *Intermediate care,* which involves occasional nursing and rehabilitative care that must be based on a doctor's orders and can be performed only by, or under the supervision of, skilled medical personnel.
3. *Custodial care,* which is primarily to handle personal needs such as walking, bathing, dressing, eating or taking medicine and can usually be provided by someone without professional medical skills or training.
4. *Home health care,* which is received at home and includes part-time skilled nursing care, speech therapy, physical or occupational therapy, part-time services from home health aids and help from homemakers or chore-workers.

Most policies cover at least the first three levels of care. One problem with many individual group long-term care policies is that eligibility for one level of care is preconditioned on prior long-term care at a higher level. For example, custodial care in a nursing home can be received only if a person has already received skilled nursing care or intermediate care. There are no benefits if a person enters a nursing home and needs only custodial care. Group policies, on the other had, are much broader than individual policies because most of them pay for at least the first three levels of care and have no requirement that a prior higher level of long-term care has been received.

Most group policies do not require any hospitalization prior to qualification for long-term care benefits. Such a provision is desirable because many nursing home stays are not immediately preceded by a hospital stay. However, some group policies do require a prior hospital stay, usually of at least three days. The stay must also have ended within some time period, often 30 days, prior to entry into the nursing home.

Benefits

Benefits are usually limited to a specific dollar amount per day, with $50 to $100 being common. A few plans allow participants to select varying benefit levels (for example, $50, $75 or $100 per day) when coverage is initially elected. Benefits may vary by level of care, with the highest benefits being provided for skilled nursing care and the lowest level for home health care (if covered). For example, home health-care benefits are often paid at one-half the level of custodial care benefits. Some plans have protection against inflation, with benefits increasing periodically with some index like the consumer price index. However, inflation increases are often capped at some annual maximum, such as 3 percent.

While a few group long-term care plans provide benefits for an unlimited duration, most limit benefits to a period of time, ranging from three to six years, or to some equivalent dollar maximum. It should be noted that most persons who enter nursing homes either are discharged or die within two years. However, it is not unusual for stays to last six years or longer. As in the case of disability income insurance, benefits are often subject to a waiting period, which may vary from 10 to 150 days with 90 days being most common.

Pre-Existing Conditions

Almost all group long-term care policies have a pre-existing-conditions provision. Benefits typically are not paid during the first six months of plan participation for care needed for a condition that was treated within six months prior to participation.

Exclusions

Several exclusions are found in group long-term care policies:

- War.
- Institutional care received outside the United States.
- Treatment for drug or alcohol abuse.
- Intentionally self-inflicted injury.
- Attempted suicide.
- Confinement or care for which benefits are payable under workers' compensation or similar laws.
- Confinement or care for which the insured or the insured's estate is not required to pay.

In contrast to many individual policies, group contracts have not been written to exclude organic-based mental diseases, such as Alzheimer's.

Renewability and Portability

Group long-term care plans are guaranteed renewable. If a participant leaves, the group coverage can usually be continued on a direct-payment basis, under either the group contract or an individual contract.

GROUP LEGAL EXPENSE PLANS

Plans that cover the legal expenses of employees have been a common benefit in several European countries for many years. However, until the mid-1970s, the concept was not widely used in the United States. The plans that did exist were almost always established by unions and were financed from general union funds. Usually, the legal services were provided by attorneys who were employed by the unions, and the only legal services covered were those limited to job-related difficulties, such as suspensions or workers' compensation disputes.

The limited extent of legal expense plans was due to the existence of several obstacles, all of which have been substantially reduced or eliminated in recent years. Prior to 1971, all states had laws that made it illegal for insurance companies or other organizations to market group legal insurance plans under which contributions were paid in advance by the covered persons or by anyone else on their behalf. However, self-funded plans, whose benefits were paid from the general revenues of unions or employers as reimbursement for legal expenses, usually did not come under these limitations. In 1971, the U.S. Supreme Court declared that these state laws were unconstitutional, and the states have replaced them with laws that allow group legal benefits to be provided—subject to some restrictions—by a plan that is funded in advance.

The Supreme Court ruling actually did little to encourage the growth of legal expense plans, since federal tax laws did not give favorable treatment to legal expense benefits, and the Taft-Hartley Act did not allow legal expense benefits to be a subject of collective bargaining. However, in 1973, the Taft-Hartley Act was amended to make legal expense benefits a new subject of collective bargaining, and the Tax Reform Act of 1976 gave favorable tax treatment to certain legal expense plans by providing that neither the premiums paid by employers nor the benefits received under the plans constitute taxable income to employees. As a result of these changes, the number of legal expense plans has grown considerably, and several thousand employers now provide these benefits to their employees. However, as a result of collective bargaining, most of these employers offer group legal benefits only to union employees through negotiated trusteeships that provide the benefits on an uninsured basis. Although several insurance companies market group plans that include legal expense benefits, few plans of this type are currently in existence.

Requirements for Favorable Tax Treatment

Favorable tax treatment is given to group legal expense plans under Code Section 120 if they qualify as *prepaid legal services plans*. In order to obtain this qualification, a plan that provides benefits for legal expenses must meet the following requirements:

- The plan must be established under a separate written document that specifies the benefits that will be provided.
- The plan must be for the exclusive benefit of employees, their spouses or dependents.
- Contributions to the plan or benefits under the plan must not discriminate in favor of highly compensated employees.
- No more than 25 percent of the annual contributions to the plan may be made on behalf of the owners (or their spouses or dependents) of the organization that established the plan. An owner is defined as any person who, at any time during the year, owns more than 5 percent of the stock of the organization or who has more than a 5 percent interest in either the capital or profits of the organization.
- Amounts contributed under the plan must be paid to either (1) an insurance company in the form of a premium, (2) another organization or person that provides personal legal services or indemnification against the cost of legal services in exchange for a prepayment or the payment of a premium or (3) a

trust that is permitted by Code Section 501(c) to receive contributions for a legal services plan.

This last requirement is broadly written so that contributions can be made to negotiated trusteeships or to organizations that provide legal services on a prepaid basis. Self-funded plans of the employer are also permitted, so long as the appropriate trust is established and benefits are funded with contributions paid in advance. Self-funded plans with benefits paid from the current revenue of the employer cannot qualify, and any benefits paid to employees will result in taxable income.

Benefits from a prepaid legal services plan are tax-free. In addition, Section 120 provides that the first $70 of annual contributions to a plan on behalf of an employee do not result in taxable income. If, for example, an employer pays $100 per year for each employee to a trust or as an insurance premium, the $30 excess must be reported as income for the employee.

(Note: At the time of this writing, Section 120 was scheduled to expire on December 31, 1991. The section has been extended before and will most likely be extended again. If an extension does not occur, the amount of any insurance premiums or trust contributions will be included in an employee's income.)

Types of Plans

The types of group legal expense plans vary widely in the ways they provide legal services. When an employer or negotiated trusteeship establishes a group legal expense plan, benefits can be self-funded or purchased from another organization. In addition to insurance companies, these other organizations include prepaid plans that are sponsored by state bar associations, groups of attorneys or other profit or nonprofit organizations formed for this purpose.

Benefits can be provided on either a closed-panel or an open-panel basis, or on some combination of these two. By far, the most common are closed-panel plans, under which covered persons must obtain legal services from lawyers who are selected by the provider of benefits. These may be lawyers who are full-time employees of the plan, or lawyers who provide benefits for plan members, but who also have other clients. Under an open-panel plan, covered persons may be able to choose their own lawyer, or they may have to select one from a limited list of lawyers who have agreed to the terms and conditions of the plan, such as agreeing to charge no more than the plan's suggested fee schedule. When these two plan types are combined, the resulting plan will usually have its own lawyers provide routine legal services on a closed-panel basis, but will use an open-panel approach when a covered person has more serious legal problems.

Like medical or dental expense benefits, legal expense benefits can be provided either as services or as reimbursement for actual expenses. Virtually all closed-panel plans use a service approach and provide full benefits without requiring any copayments by the covered persons. Open-panel plans may also provide benefits on a service basis, primarily when eligible lawyers agree to the fee structure paid by the plan. When benefits are paid on the basis of actual charges incurred by a covered person, deductibles and coinsurance are sometimes used.

Benefit Schedules

Benefits under legal expense plans can be provided on either a scheduled basis or on a comprehensive basis. *Scheduled legal expense plans* list the specific types of legal expenses for which benefits will be paid. While considerable variations exist among plans, most cover at least:

- Consultation and advice on any legal matter.
- Preparation of legal documents, such as deeds, wills and powers-of-attorney.
- Adoption.
- Personal bankruptcy.
- Defense of civil suits.
- Juvenile delinquency proceedings.
- Domestic problems, such as separation, divorce or annulment.
- Criminal defense.

When benefits are provided on an indemnity basis, the maximum benefit for each covered legal service is usually limited to a flat amount or to a maximum hourly fee. In addition, there may be an overall maximum annual benefit, such as $1,000. Whether a plan provides benefits on a service or an indemnity basis, the plan may also limit the frequency with which benefits will be paid for each covered legal service. Under some plans the participating lawyers also agree to provide—at a discount—services that are not otherwise included in the plan.

Comprehensive legal expense plans are like major medical expense plans in that all legal expenses are covered except for those that are specifically excluded. Common exclusions include legal expenses that arise from:

- Business activities or transactions.
- Class action suits.
- Cases that have contingent fees.
- Actions against the legal expense plan.
- Actions against the employer.
- Actions against the union.
- Internal Revenue audits.

In addition, these plans generally exclude expenses that are not charged by a lawyer, such as court costs and fines. These plans usually provide benefits on a closed-panel basis, and have no overall benefit maximums or internal dollar limitations.

GROUP PROPERTY AND LIABILITY INSURANCE

In the mid-1960s, it was thought that property and liability insurance, especially automobile insurance, would be the next major employee benefit. However, by the late 1970s, most of the insurance companies that had entered this market were no longer willing to write property and liability coverage as an employee benefit. In fact, many began to dismiss this benefit as an idea whose time might never come.

The current status of property and liability insurance as an employee benefit is that it has generally been offered by only a few employers. Although this number is growing, it is doing so very slowly. Detailed statistics from the insurance industry are difficult to obtain, since most coverage is actually mass-marketed individual insurance and is not reported as a group benefit. However, various surveys and estimates indicate that approximately 10 percent of the employers that have more than 500 employees offer some form of property and liability coverage. For smaller employers, the percentage is significantly lower, and only a few plans exist for employers with under 50 employees. In the majority of cases, these plans are limited to automobile insurance, although some plans offer other coverages.

Reasons for Slow Growth

The slow growth of group property and liability plans can be traced to several factors, including unfavorable tax treatment, a low potential for cost savings, a lack of employer enthusiasm and regulatory restrictions.

Unfavorable Tax Treatment

The Internal Revenue Code specifically exempts employer contributions for certain employee benefits from being included in the taxable income of employees. This exemption does not apply to property and liability insurance. Although the employer is allowed an income tax deduction, an employee must report as taxable income any contributions made on his or her behalf for property and liability coverage. Note, however, that the portion of any premium that applies to medical or no-fault benefits is treated as health insurance and is not included in income.

In general, employers, unions and employees prefer that employer dollars be used to provide nontaxable benefits. Without employer contributions, it is often difficult to offer employees property and liability insurance at a substantial enough savings to encourage significant participation.

Lower Potential for Cost Savings

The potential for savings under group property and liability insurance plans is typically less than what exists under employee benefit plans that provide life, disability income or medical expense benefits. Under these latter plans, there is a substantial reduction in agents' commissions when compared to commissions received on individual coverage. Such savings do not occur in property and liability insurance, because commission scales for individual insurance are lower as a percentage of premium. The main reason for this lower scale is that a less intense marketing effort is required by agents, since consumers are more likely to seek out property and liability coverage on their own, rather than solicitation by agents. Therefore, a higher portion of commissions are for the services performed for the client, rather than for the agents' marketing efforts. Financial responsibility filings, automobile changes and certificates of insurance for mortgagees are examples of services that must still be performed for coverage that is provided on a group basis.

A second source of savings under most types of group insurance coverage results from the reduction or elimination of individual underwriting, which, together with other savings, more than offsets the cost of covering poor risks at group rates. However, this is not the case in property and liability insurance, particularly in automobile insurance. Not only are savings lower, but there are proportionately many more substandard drivers who must pay surcharged premiums in the individual property and liability insurance marketplace than there are persons with poor health in the individual life and health insurance marketplace. The absence of individual underwriting in property and liability insurance will usually mean that the average rate for the group members is higher than some persons would pay in the individual marketplace. Consequently, to avoid getting only the poor risks, group property and liability insurance plans generally use individual—but possibly liberalized—underwriting. As a result, poorer risks are charged a higher premium or, in some cases, are ineligible for coverage.

Under the most successful group property and liability plans, savings have averaged only between 5 and 15 percent when compared with the same insurance company's rates for individual coverage. However, property and liability rates vary widely among insurance companies, and the group rate may still be higher than many employees are paying for their individual coverage. Without a significant cost advantage, there is little incentive for an employee to switch to a group property and liability plan, except perhaps for the simplicity of paying premiums on a payroll-deduction basis. This is particularly true when the employee has an established relationship with his or her current property and liability insurance company or agent. Consequently, it may be difficult to enroll the minimum percentage (usually 30 or more) of employees required by the insurance company.

Lack of Employer Enthusiasm

In addition to the unfavorable tax treatment of employer contributions to the employee, many employers feel that group property and liability plans will place a strain on their relationship with employees. While the magnitude of the problem varies among employers that offer group property and liability plans, it is an undisputed fact that dissatisfaction with the plan and the employer occurs when employees (1) are ineligible for coverage because of underwriting considerations, (2) find the coverage more expensive than their current individual coverage or (3) have disputes over claims. In spite of this, however, many employers view property and liability insurance as a very desirable benefit because of its high visibility.

Regulatory Restrictions

Once common in almost all states, several states still have some type of regulation or statute that hinders the marketing of group property and liability insurance. These *fictitious group insurance statutes,* or similar regulations, prohibit the grouping of individual risks in order to give them favorable treatment in underwriting, coverage or rates, with the possible exception of rate reductions that are a result of savings in expenses. In effect, what is done for group life insurance, medical expense and disability coverages cannot be done for property and liability insurance. It should be noted that these laws apply only to true group insurance products; mass-marketed plans are not affected.

The laws of some states effectively prohibit true group insurance products because no specific statute is in effect that allows these products to be written. Late in 1986, the NAIC passed model legislation that, if adopted by a state, would permit and set standards for group personal property and liability insurance.

Many states also have regulations that prohibit any person who is not a licensed insurance agent from advising in the sale of property and liability insurance. This prevents the employer from performing any other functions besides those of a purely administrative nature, such as accepting applications or deducting premiums from payroll.

Federal regulatory restrictions are another reason for the lack of union interest since the Federal Labor Code prohibits a negotiated trusteeship from providing property and liability coverage. However, there is no prohibition against bargaining for this benefit and having it provided under a plan established by the employer.

Types of Plans

Traditional group property and liability insurance plans were not true group insurance, but were mass-marketed plans of individual insurance that are similar to the salary allotment plans described later in this chapter. Some companies still market group property and liability insurance in this form. Commonly referred to as quasi-group insurance, the cost of these plans is usually entirely borne by the participating employees. Besides handling the payroll deductions, the employer has little, if any, responsibility for the administration of the plan. Employees are solicited by representatives of the insurance company, usually by mail or phone. Some insurance companies may actually have agents located on or near the employer's premises, but the majority of insurance companies give group members toll-free numbers for contacting their representatives.

In general, these quasi-group plans are not experience rated but are offered at a slight discount because of the administrative savings associated with mass marketing. Premiums for employees vary because they are based on the same factors as individual property and liability insurance (such as age, driving record or value of the home), which also means that some employees may be ineligible for coverage. Most plans offer automobile insurance, and a few also offer other coverages, such as homeowner's insurance and umbrella liability insurance. Employees usually have the same choices regarding the amount and type of coverage as they would have in the individual marketplace, and the contracts offered are usually identical. However, sometimes modifications are made that attempt to decrease the cost of the mass-marketed coverage. These include larger deductibles and provisions in the automobile insurance policy that eliminate coverage for medical expenses to the extent that they are paid under the employer's medical expense plan.

A few companies now offer property and liability insurance on a true group basis, and use both a master contract and experience rating for the group. All employees are usually eligible. The coverages offered to the employees usually are the same as those offered under quasi-group plans, but the rating structure tends to be less refined, particularly for automobile insurance. Instead of having several dozen classifications that are based on factors such as age, sex and driving record, there may only be three or four classifications that are based on driving record. In virtually all cases when true group property and liability plans are made available, the insurance company will insist on employer contributions of between 25 and 50 percent of the cost of the coverage and on participation by a large percentage of employees, possibly as high as 75 percent.

The majority of group property and liability insurance plans fall somewhere between true mass-marketed plans and group insurance. Sometimes referred to as contributory franchise plans, they require employer contributions that are lower than under true group plans. This contribution may be either a percentage or a flat amount per employee. In addition, employers also perform numerous administrative functions associated with the plans. Underwriting tends to be liberal in that coverage will be written for most, if not all, employees, but poorer risks will be charged higher premiums. If state law permits, the rating structure, as with true group plans, tends to have a small number of classifications. The actual form of these plans varies from state to state. Coverage is usually written through master contracts with individual certificates of insurance, except in those states that require separate policies for each insured.

MASS-MARKETED INDIVIDUAL LIFE AND HEALTH INSURANCE

Some employers offer their employees individual insurance on a payroll-deduction basis.[1] Although this type of benefit has existed for many years, its character has changed in recent years.

Originally, such coverage was designed for employers who, because of their small number of employees, were ineligible for group insurance. Often referred to as wholesale life insurance or franchise health insurance, these plans were similar to group insurance in their plan design and the types of coverage they provided. In addition, amounts of insurance were predetermined and coverage under the plan ceased at termination of employment. However, these plans differed from group insurance in that individual policies and individual underwriting were used. In contrast to group insurance plans that insure a number of persons under one policy, these arrangements can best be described as *quasi-group* plans that insure a number of persons under individual policies. Since group insurance coverage is available for most small groups (usually through multiple-employer trusts), this type of mass-marketed individual insurance is not commonly written today.

While many variations exist, the majority of mass-marketed individual insurance plans currently made available to employees fall into two broad categories:

1. Salary allotment, or salary reduction, plans involving individual underwriting.
2. Money-purchase plans with simplified underwriting.

---

[1]Although this text refers only to mass-marketed individual insurance plans involving an employer-employee relationship, mass-marketed individual insurance is often used for other types of groups and is the common form of mail-order insurance.

Under either type of plan, the employer agrees to withhold premiums from participating employees' paychecks each pay period and submit them to the insurance company. Only in rare cases does the employer pay any portion of the premium. Arrangements are also made between the employer and the insurance company concerning how employees will be solicited. While the plan may be serviced by agents or company representatives, sales to individual employees are almost always done by regular agents of the insurance company. Each employee can determine the amount of coverage purchased, within limits, and coverage can be continued after termination of employment, normally at the same premium, as long as the employee continues paying the premium directly to the insurer. However, a less frequent mode of premium payment may be required. For example, instead of the previous payroll deduction each month, an annual premium of 12 times the monthly deduction may be required.

Salary Allotment Plans

Under salary allotment plans, employees have the option of purchasing some or all of the insurance products normally offered by the insurance company in the individual insurance market. Plans offered by life insurance companies are usually designed for executives or higher-paid employees. Policies with cash values are always available, but term insurance, long-term disability income insurance and other products may be offered. The premium per policy period normally is calculated by dividing the insurance company's regular annual rate-book premium by the number of payroll periods for which deductions will be made. For example, if the annual rate-book premium is $240, the monthly premium on a payroll-deduction basis would be $20. This is in contrast to the somewhat higher monthly premium that would be charged by most insurance companies if a policyholder paid the premium directly to the insurance company. In most cases, regular individual underwriting is used and regular commission scales are paid.

Some life insurance companies either will offer salary allotment plans at a discount from regular rate-book premiums or will use liberalized underwriting. To compensate for such practices, these insurers are generally more restrictive in making the plans available or employ cost-saving features such as lower commission scales.

Money-Purchase Plans

Money-purchase plans represent the fastest-growing form of mass-marketed individual insurance available to employees. Initially, these plans were marketed primarily to smaller employers with meager employee benefit plans, so that they could make life insurance coverage available to their employees with little cost to the employer other than the costs of publicizing the plan and administering the payroll deductions. However, a significant number of large firms now also offer such plans to their employees as a method of making additional insurance available.

To a large extent, money-purchase plans have been designed to meet the insurance needs of the lower paid employees who tend to purchase rather small amounts of insurance. Consequently, these plans are sometimes made available only to hourly paid employees. The main goal of most insurance companies in offering money-purchase plans is to market cash value life insurance, and hence this coverage is always offered. The term *money-purchase* comes from the fact that amounts of coverage are sold on the basis of what can be purchased with a given premium, such as $1, $2 or $5 per week. An employee must select one of the given premiums, with a maximum of $5 per week being common. Because the amount of coverage is governed by the employee's attained age, larger amounts of coverage are available to younger employees than to older employees. Furthermore, the cash-value policy used by an insurance company in its money-purchase plan may be a form normally sold in the individual market or may be one designed specifically for mass marketing. In some plans, this will be a whole life policy on which an employee can continue paying premiums after retirement or which can be converted to a paid-up policy with a lower face amount. In other plans, a limited-payment policy is used, enabling coverage to continue after retirement without reduction in amount and without the need to continue premium payments.

A rider that provides term life insurance coverage on an employee's children and possibly the employee's spouse is usually available. The coverage normally is a set amount, such as $1,000 per person, and results in either an additional premium, such as ten cents per month, or a reduction in the cash-value life insurance otherwise available at the premium selected by the employee. Term life insurance coverage for an employee is available under some plans, but its availability is often contingent upon the employee's purchase of cash value life insurance. Most plans also make cash-value life insurance available to an employee's children and spouse. Again, the amount of coverage is determined by what can be purchased with a given weekly premium. Some plans also offer deferred annuities by which an employee can supplement pension and social security benefits.

In most cases, coverage under money-purchase plans can be purchased at a cost lower than that for comparable benefits in the regular individual market. While there is individual underwriting, the underwriting standards of most insurers result in making at least 95 percent of all employees eligible for coverage. Many insurance companies use the same commission scales that are normally paid on individual insurance, but some companies use a reduced scale.

As in group insurance, insurance companies impose underwriting standards on money-purchase plans. These plans are not normally made available to employers who have high employee turnover or who are in industries characterized by a high turnover. In addition, employers in business for less than a minimum period of time are often ineligible. Employees typically must complete a waiting period of six months to one year before coverage may be purchased. Finally, most insurance companies will insist on a minimum number of participants, such as five, and/or a minimum percentage of participation. In addition, money-purchase plans may be available to employers with fewer than 25 employees only if there has been some type of prescreening to determine the suitability of the employer and the group of employees.

Variations for Universal Life Insurance

Universal life insurance is commonly sold in mass-marketed individual insurance plans and, for some insurance companies, it may be the only product marketed in this manner. Some insurers market it on a money-purchase basis as previously described.

Other insurers take a different approach with respect to the determination of the amount of insurance and the periodic premium. Rather than selecting the desired premium, employees choose the amount of pure death protection. Several options—such as $10,000, $25,000 and $50,000—may be chosen, and the available options may vary by salary level or position. A minimum periodic premium will then be specified for each option and a given employee's age. The premium will be sufficient to generate a cash value at retirement age, if the current interest assumptions of the insurer are met. Employees, however, can elect to pay higher premiums so that a larger cash value will develop. Some insurers set the initial premium at a multiple (such as two) of the pure insurance cost; others make it an amount that will generate a cash value equal to a percentage (such as 50 percent) of the original amount of insurance. After the policy has been in force for some time period, employees typically have similar flexibility with respect to premium levels as is available to persons purchasing group universal life insurance (discussed in Chapter 7). Except for this difference in premium determination, most mass-marketed universal life insurance products have the other characteristics of a money-purchase plan.

STUDY QUESTIONS

1. What types of limitations are often imposed upon benefits for a person enrolling in a dental insurance plan after his or her initial eligibility period has ended?
2. Why are dental insurance plans more likely than medical expense plans to include benefits for routine examinations and preventive medicine?
3. Describe the limitations often contained in dental expense plans to control claims costs and to eliminate unnecessary dental treatment.
4. a. What factors result in the need for long-term care insurance?
   b. What are the reasons for the cautious growth of group long-term care insurance?
5. What sources other than long-term care insurance coverage are available to meet the need for long-term care?
6. Describe the typical provisions found in group long-term care insurance policies for each of the following:
   a. Persons eligible.
   b. Current and future premiums.
   c. Levels of care covered.
   d. Level and duration of benefits.
   e. Treatment of pre-existing conditions.

  f. Exclusions.

  g. Renewability and portability.

 7. a. What makes a legal expense plan a "prepaid legal services plan" for purposes of Code Section 120?

  b. What are the tax benefits of a prepaid legal services plan?

 8. How do open-panel and closed-panel legal expense plans differ with respect to

  a. The ability to choose a lawyer?

  b. The form in which benefits are provided?

 9. Explain the reasons for the slow growth of group property and liability insurance.

10. Describe the types of plans that may be used to provide group property and liability insurance.

11. Under a mass-marketed individual insurance plan, how are premiums for employees paid

  a. While they are working for the employer?

  b. After they have left such employment?

12. Does the typical salary allotment plan provide coverage at a lower cost than is available if an individual pays premiums directly to an insurance company? Explain.

14

Alternative Funding Methods

Objectives

- Explain the reasons why employers may use alternative funding methods.
- Describe the characteristics and appropriateness of each of the following modifications of traditional group insurance arrangements:

  1. Premium-delay arrangements.
  2. Reserve-reduction arrangements.
  3. Minimum-premium plans.
  4. Cost-plus arrangements.
  5. Retrospective-rating arrangements.

- Describe the characteristics and appropriateness of each of the following methods of self-funding:

  1. Total self-funding.
  2. Self-funding with stop-loss coverage and/or ASO arrangements.
  3. Self-funding through a 501(c)(9) trust.

In recent years, employers have increasingly considered—and often adopted—benefit funding methods that are alternatives to the traditional fully insured group insurance contract. Under the traditional group insurance contract, the employer pays premiums in advance to the insurance company, which then has the financial responsibility for paying claims if and when they occur, and for assuming the administrative expenses associated with the contract. In addition, the insurance company bears the risk that claims will be larger than anticipated.

270

REASONS FOR ALTERNATIVE FUNDING

The increasing interest in alternatives to the traditional fully insured group arrangement has focused on two factors: cost savings and improved cash flow. To a large extent this interest has grown in response to the rising cost of medical care that has resulted in an increase in the cost of providing medical expense benefits. Even though alternative funding methods are most commonly used for providing medical expense benefits, many of the methods described here are also appropriate for other types of benefits.

Cost Savings

Savings may result to the extent that either claims or the insurance company's retention are reduced. Retention—which is discussed in more detail in Chapter 15—is that portion of the insurance company's premium over and above the incurred claims. This includes such items as commissions, premium taxes, risk charges and profit. Traditionally, alternative funding methods have not focused on reducing claims, since the same benefits will normally be provided and the same claims will be paid, regardless of which funding method is used. However, this focus has changed as state laws and regulations increasingly mandate the types and levels of benefits that must be contained in medical expense contracts. To the extent that these laws and regulations apply only to benefits that are included in insurance contracts, employers can avoid providing these mandated benefits by using alternative funding methods that do not involve insurance contracts.

Modifications of fully insured contracts are usually designed either to lower or eliminate premium taxes or to reduce the insurance company's risk and, consequently, the risk charge. Alternative funding methods that involve a degree of self-funding may be designed to also reduce other aspects of retention and to reduce claims by excluding mandated benefits.

Improved Cash Flow

Under a fully insured contract, an employer has the ability to improve cash flow because premiums are collected before the funds will actually be needed to pay claims. The employer will generally be credited with interest while these funds are held in reserves. Alternative funding arrangements that are intended to improve cash flow are designed either to postpone the payment of premiums to the insurance company or to keep the funds that would otherwise be held in reserves in the hands of the employer until they are needed by the insurance company. This is particularly advantageous to the employer when these funds can be invested at a higher rate of interest than that credited by the insurance company to reserves.

METHODS OF ALTERNATIVE FUNDING

Totally self-funded (or self-insured) employee benefit plans are the opposite of traditional fully insured group insurance plans. Under totally self-funded plans, the employer is responsible for paying claims, administering the plan, and bearing the risk that actual claims will exceed those expected. However, very few employee benefit plans that use alternative methods of funding have actually turned to total self-funding. Rather, the methods used typically fall somewhere between the two extremes.

The methods of alternative funding can be divided into two general categories: those that primarily modify traditional fully insured group insurance contracts, and those that have either partial or total self-funding. The first category includes:

- Premium-delay arrangements.
- Reserve-reduction arrangements.
- Minimum-premium plans.
- Cost-plus arrangements.
- Retrospective-rating arrangements.

These alternative funding methods are regarded as modifications of traditional fully insured plans because the insurance company has the ultimate responsibility for paying all benefits promised under the contract. Most insurance companies will only allow large employers to use these modifications, and although practices differ among insurance companies, generally a group insurance plan must generate between $150,000 and $250,000 in claims before these funding methods will be available to the employer.

The second category of alternative funding methods includes:

- Total self-funding from current revenue and self-administration.
- Self-funding with stop-loss coverage and/or administrative-services-only (ASO) arrangements.
- Funding through a 501(c)(9) trust.

In contrast to the first category of alternative funding methods, some of these alternatives can be used by small employers.

Premium-Delay Arrangements

Premium-delay arrangements allow the employer to defer payment of monthly premiums for some time beyond the usual 30-day grace period. In fact, these arrangements lengthen the grace period, most commonly by 60 or 90 days. The practical effect of premium-delay arrangements is that they enable the employer to have continuous use of that portion of the annual premium which is approximately equal to the claim reserve. For example, a 90-day premium delay allows the employer to use three months, or 25 percent, of the annual premium for other purposes. This amount roughly corresponds to what is usually in the claim reserve for medical expense coverage. Generally, the larger this reserve is on a percentage basis, the longer the premium payment can be delayed. The insurance company still has a statutory obligation to maintain the claim reserve and, therefore, it must use assets other than the employer's premiums for this purpose. In most cases, these assets come from the insurance company's surplus.

A premium-delay arrangement has a financial advantage to the extent that an employer can earn a higher return by investing the delayed premiums than by accruing interest on the claim reserve. In actual practice, interest is still credited to the reserve, but this credit is offset by either an interest charge on the delayed premiums or an increase in the insurance company's retention.

Upon termination of an insurance contract with a premium-delay arrangement, the employer is responsible for paying any deferred premiums. However, the insurance company is legally responsible for paying all claims incurred prior to termination, even if the employer fails to pay the deferred premiums. Consequently, most insurance companies are concerned about the employer's financial position and credit rating. For many insurance companies, the final decision of whether to enter into a premium-delay arrangement, or any other alternative funding arrangement that leaves funds in the hands of the employer, is made by the insurer's financial experts after a thorough analysis of the employer. In some cases, this may mean that the employer will be required to submit a letter of credit or some other form of security.

Reserve-Reduction Arrangements

A reserve-reduction arrangement is similar to the premium-delay arrangement. Under the usual reserve-reduction arrangement, the employer is allowed at any given time to retain an amount of the annual premium that is equal to the claim reserve. Generally, such an arrangement is allowed only after the contract's first year, when the pattern of claims and the appropriate amount of the reserve can be more accurately estimated. In succeeding years, if the contract is renewed, the amount retained will be adjusted according to changes in the size of the reserve. As with a premium-delay arrangement, the monies retained by the employer must be paid to the insurance company upon termination of the contract. Again, the advantage of this approach lies in the employer's ability to earn more on these funds than under the traditional insurance arrangement.

A few insurance companies offer another type of reserve-reduction arrangement for long-term disability income coverage. Under a so-called limited-liability arrangement, the employer purchases a one-year contract from the insurance company in which the insurer agrees to only pay claims for that year, even though the employer's plan provides benefits to employees for longer periods. Consequently, enough reserves are maintained by the insurance company to pay benefits only for the duration of the one-year contract. At renewal, the insurance company agrees to continue paying the existing claims as well as any new claims. In effect, the employer pays the insurance company each year for existing claims as the benefits are paid to employees, rather than when disabilities occur. A problem for employees under this type of arrangement is the lack of security for future benefits. For example, if the employer goes bankrupt and the insurance contract is not renewed, the insurance company has no responsibility to continue benefit payments. For this reason, several states do not allow this type of arrangement.

The limited-liability arrangement contrasts with the usual group contract in which the insurance company is responsible for paying disability income claims to a disabled employee for the length of the benefit period. On the average, each disability claim will result in the establishment of a reserve equal to approximately five times the employee's annual benefit.

Minimum-Premium Plans

Minimum-premium plans were primarily designed to reduce state premium taxes. However, many minimum-premium plans also improve the employer's cash flow.

Under the typical minimum-premium plan, the employer assumes the financial responsibility for paying claims up to a specified level, usually from 80 to 95 percent of estimated claims, with 90 percent most common. The specified level may be determined on either a monthly or an annual basis. The funds necessary to pay these claims are deposited into a bank account that belongs to the employer. However, the actual payment of claims is made from this account by the insurance company, which acts as an agent of the employer. When claims exceed the specified level, the balance is paid from the insurance company's own funds. No premium tax is levied by the states on the amounts deposited by the employer into such an account, as it would have been if these deposits had been paid directly to the insurance company. In effect, the insurance company, for premium-tax purposes, is only considered to be the administrator of these funds and not a provider of insurance. Unfortunately, the IRS also considers these funds to belong to the employer, and death benefits in excess of $5,000 represent taxable income to beneficiaries. Consequently, minimum-premium plans are used to insure disability and medical expense benefits rather than life insurance benefits.

Under a minimum-premium plan, the employer pays a substantially reduced premium, subject to premium taxation, to the insurance company for administering the entire plan and for bearing the cost of claims above the specified level. Because such a plan may be slightly more burdensome for an insurance company to administer than a traditional group arrangement, the retention charge may also be slightly higher. Under a minimum-premium arrangement, the insurance company is ultimately responsible for seeing that all claims are paid, and it must maintain the same reserves that would have been required if the plan had been funded under a traditional group insurance arrangement. Consequently, the premium will include a charge for the establishment of these reserves, unless some type of reserve-reduction arrangement has also been negotiated.

Some insurance regulatory officials view the minimum-premium plan primarily as a loophole used by employers to avoid paying premium taxes. In several states, there have been attempts to seek court rulings or legislation that would require premium taxes to be paid either on the funds deposited in the bank account or on claims paid from these funds. Most of these attempts have been unsuccessful, but recent court rulings in California require the employer to pay premium taxes on the funds deposited in the bank account. If similar attempts are successful in other states, the main advantage of minimum-premium plans will be lost.

Cost-Plus Arrangements

Cost-plus arrangements, often referred to by other names such as flexible funding, are frequently used by large employers to provide life insurance benefits.

Under such an arrangement, the employer's monthly premium is based on the claims paid by the insurance company during the preceding month, plus a specified retention charge that is uniform throughout the policy period. To the extent that an employer's loss experience is less than that assumed in a traditional premium arrangement, the employer's cash flow is improved. However, an employer with worse-than-expected experience, either during the early part of the policy period or during the entire policy period, could also have a more unfavorable cash flow than if a traditional insurance arrangement were used. To prevent this from occurring, many insurance companies place a maximum limit on the employer's monthly premium so that the aggregate monthly premiums paid at any time during the policy period do not exceed the aggregate monthly premiums that would have been paid if the cost-plus arrangement had not been used.

Retrospective-Rating Arrangements

Under retrospective-rating arrangements, the insurance company charges the employer an initial premium that is less than what would be justified by the expected claims for the year. In general, this reduction will be between 5 and 10 percent of the premium for a traditional group insurance arrangement. However, if claims plus the insurance company's retention exceed the initial premium, the employer will be called upon to pay an additional amount at the end of the policy year. Because an employer will usually have to pay this additional premium, one advantage of a retrospective-rating arrangement is the employer's ability to use these funds during the year.

This potential additional premium is subject to a maximum amount that is based on some percentage of expected claims. For example, assume a retrospective-rating arrangement bases the initial premiums on the fact that claims will be 93 percent of those actually expected for the year. If claims in fact are below this level, the employer will receive an experience refund. If they exceed 93 percent, the retrospective-rating arrangement will be triggered, and the employer will have to reimburse the insurance company for any additional claims paid, up to some percentage of those expected, such as 112 percent. Claims in excess of 112 percent are borne by the insurance company. Therefore, some of the risk associated with claim fluctuations is passed on to the employer. This will reduce both the insurance company's risk charge and any reserve for claim fluctuations. The amount of these reductions will depend upon the actual percentage specified in the contract; above this, the insurance company will be responsible for claims. This percentage and the one that triggers the retrospective-rating arrangement are subject to negotiations between the insurance company and the employer. In general, the lower the percentage that triggers the retrospective arrangement, the higher will be the percentage above which the insurance company is fully responsible for claims. In addition, the better cash-flow advantage the employer has, the greater will be the risk of claim fluctuations.

In all other respects, a retrospective-rating arrangement is identical to the traditional group insurance contract.

Total Self-Funding from Current Revenue and Self-Administration

The purest form of a self-funded benefit plan is one in which the employer pays benefits from current revenue rather than from a trust, administers all aspects of the plan, and assumes the risk that benefit payments will exceed those expected. In addition to eliminating state premium taxes and improving cash flow, the employer has the potential to reduce its operating expenses to the extent that the plan can be administered at a lower cost than the insurance company's retention (other than premium taxes). A decision to use this kind of self-funding plan is generally considered most desirable when all the following conditions are present:

- *Predictable claims*. Budgeting is an integral part of the operation of any organization, and it is necessary to budget for benefit payments that will have to be paid in the future. This can best be done when a specific type of benefit plan has a claim pattern that is either stable or shows a steady trend. This is most likely to occur in those types of benefit plans that have a relatively high frequency of low-severity claims. Although a self-funded plan may still be appropriate when the level of future benefit payments is difficult to predict, the plan will generally be designed to include stop-loss coverage, which will be discussed later in this chapter.
- *A noncontributory plan*. Several difficulties arise if a self-funded benefit plan is contributory. Some employees may resent paying their money to the employer for benefits that are contingent upon the firm's future financial ability to pay claims. If claims are denied, employees under a contributory plan are more likely to be bitter toward the employer than they would if the benefit plan were noncontributory. Finally, ERISA requires that a trust must be established to hold the employees' contributions until the funds are used by the plan. Both the establishment and maintenance of the trust will result in increased administrative costs to the employer.
- *A nonunion situation*. Self-funding of benefits for union employees may not be feasible if a firm is subject to collective bargaining. Self-funding by the employer clearly cannot be used if benefits are provided through a negotiated trusteeship. Even when collective bargaining results in benefits being provided through an individual employer plan, unions often insist that benefits be insured in order to guarantee that union members will actually receive them. An employer's decision about whether to use self-funding is most likely motivated by the potential to save money. When unions approve of self-funding, they frequently also insist that some of these savings be passed on to union members through additional or increased benefits.
- *The ability to handle claims effectively and efficiently*. One reason that many employers do not use totally self-funded and self-administered benefit plans is the difficulty in handling claims as efficiently and effectively as an insurance company or other benefit-plan administrator would handle them. Unless an employer is extremely large, only one person or a few persons will be needed to handle claims. Who in the organization can properly train and supervise these people? Can they be replaced if they should leave? Will

anyone have the expertise to properly handle the unusual or complex claims that might occur? Many employers want some insulation from their employees in the handling of claims. If employees are unhappy with claim payments under a self-administered plan, dissatisfaction and possibly legal actions will be directed toward the employer rather than toward the insurance company. The employer's inability to handle claims, or its lack of interest in wanting to handle them, does not completely rule out the use of self-funding. As will be discussed later, employers can have claims handled by another party through an administrative-services-only contract.

• *The ability to provide other administrative services.* In addition to claims, the employer must determine whether the other administrative services normally included in an insured arrangement can be provided in a cost-effective manner. These services are associated with plan design, actuarial calculations, statistical reports, communication with employees, compliance with government regulations and the preparation of government reports. Many of these costs are relatively fixed, regardless of the size of the employer, and unless the employer can spread them out over a large number of employees, self-administration will not be economically feasible. As with claims administration, an employer can purchase needed services from other sources.

The extent of total self-funding and self-administration differs significantly among the different types of group benefit plans. Plans that provide life insurance or accidental death and dismemberment benefits do not usually lend themselves to self-funding because of infrequent and large claims that are difficult to predict. Only very large employers can expect stable and predictable claims on an annual basis. In addition, federal income tax laws impede the use of self-funding for death benefits, since any payments to beneficiaries in excess of $5,000 are considered taxable income to the beneficiaries. Such a limitation does not exist if benefits are insured.

The most widespread use of self-funding and self-administration occurs in short-term disability income plans, particularly those in which the maximum duration of benefits is limited to six months or less. For employers of most any size, the number and average length of short-term absences from work are relatively predictable. In addition, the payment of claims is relatively simple, because benefits can be, and usually are, made through the usual payroll system of the employer.

Long-term disability income benefits are occasionally self-funded by large employers. Like death claims, long-term disability income claims are difficult to predict for small employers because of their infrequent occurrence and potentially large size. In addition, because small employers only receive a few claims of this type, it makes it economically unjustifiable to self-administer them.

The larger the employer is, the more likely its medical expense plan will be self-funded. The major problem with a self-funded medical expense plan is not the prediction of claims frequency, but rather the prediction of the average severity of claims. Although infrequent, claims of $100,000 to $250,000 or more do occasionally occur. Most small-and medium-sized employers are unwilling to assume the risk that they might have to pay such a large claim. Only employers with several thousand employees are large enough to anticipate that such claims will regularly occur and to have the resources that will be necessary to pay any unexpectedly large claims. This does not mean that smaller employers cannot self-fund medical benefits. To avoid the uncertainty of catastrophic claims, these employers often self-fund basic medical expense benefits and insure major medical expense benefits or self-fund their entire coverage but purchase stop-loss protection.

It is not unusual to use self-funding and self-administration in other types of benefit plans, such as those providing coverage for dental care, vision care, prescription drugs or legal expenses. Initially, it may be difficult to predict the extent to which these plans will be utilized. However, once these plans have "matured," the level of claims tends to be fairly stable. In addition, these plans are commonly subject to maximums so that the employer has little or no risk of catastrophic claims. Although larger employers may be able to economically administer these plans themselves, smaller employers commonly purchase administrative services.

Self-Funding with Stop-Loss Coverage and/or ASO Arrangements

Two of the problems associated with self-funding and self-administration are the risk of catastrophic claims and the inability of the employer to provide administrative services in a cost-effective manner. For each of these problems, however, solutions have evolved that still allow an employer to use elements of self-funding. These are stop-loss coverage and administrative-services-only (ASO) contracts. Although an ASO contract and stop-loss coverage can be provided separately, they are commonly written together.

Until recently, stop-loss coverage and ASO contracts were generally provided by insurance companies and were available only to employers with at least several hundred employees. However, these arrangements are increasingly becoming available to small employers. In many cases, the administrative services are now being purchased from third-party administrators who operate independently from insurance companies.

Stop-Loss Coverage

Aggregate stop-loss coverage is the most common form of protection for employers against an unexpectedly high level of claims. If total claims exceed some specified dollar limit, the insurance company assumes the financial responsibility for those claims that are over the limit, subject to the maximum reimbursement specified in the contract. The limit usually is applied on an annual basis and is expressed as some percentage of expected claims, typically between 120 and 140 percent. This arrangement can be thought of as a form of reinsurance and is treated as such by some regulatory officials. It is interesting to note that the employer is responsible for the paying of all claims to employees, including any payments that are received from the insurance company under the stop-loss coverage. In fact, since the insurance company has no responsibility to the employees, no reserve for incurred-but-unreported claims must be established.

Aggregate stop-loss coverage results in (1) an improved cash flow for the employer and (2) a minimization of premium taxes, because they must only be paid on the stop-loss coverage. However, these advantages will be partially, and perhaps totally, offset by the cost of the coverage. In addition, many insurance companies will insist that the employer purchase other insurance coverages or administrative services in order to obtain aggregate stop-loss coverage.

Stop-loss plans may also be written on a specific basis, similar to the way an insurance plan with a deductible is written. Most commonly used with medical expense plans, this arrangement is often referred to as a *big deductible plan* or as *shared funding*. The deductible amount, which varies from $500 to $25,000, is usually applied on an annual basis and pertains to each person insured under the contract. The deductible specified in the stop-loss coverage is the amount above which the stop-loss carrier will be responsible for claims, and it is different from the deductible that the employee must satisfy under the medical expense plan. Employees may have a small deductible to meet and the employer will then assume the financial responsibility for amounts between these two deductibles. For example, employees may be provided with a medical expense plan that has a $100 annual deductible and an 80 percent coinsurance provision. If stop-loss coverage with a $1,000 stop-loss deductible has also been purchased, an employee will have to assume the first $100 in annual medical expenses, the employer will then pay 80 percent of the next $900 in expenses, and the stop-loss insurer will pay 80 percent of any claims in excess of $1,000. The stop-loss insurer has no responsibility to pay the employer's share of claims under any circumstances, and most insurance companies will require that the employees be made aware of this fact.

In the past, specific stop-loss coverage was primarily written for large employers and had deductibles in the $5,000 to $10,000 range. More recently, this coverage has been written for small employers, usually with a $500 or $1,000 deductible. These plans have had particular appeal for small employers who have had better than average claims experience, but who are too small to qualify for experience rating and the accompanying potential premium savings.

ASO Contracts

Under an administrative-services-only contract, the employer purchases specific administrative services from an insurance company or from an independent third-party administrator. These services will usually include the administration of claims, but they may also include a broad array of other services. In effect, the employer has the option to purchase services for those administrative functions that can be handled more cost effectively by another party. Under ASO contracts, the administration of claims is performed in much the same way as it is under a minimum-premium plan; that is, the administrator has the authority to pay claims from a bank account that belongs to the employer. However, the administrator is not responsible for paying claims from its own assets if the employer's account is insufficient.

In addition to listing the services that will be provided, an ASO contract also stipulates the administrator's authority and responsibility, the length of the contract, the provisions for terminating and amending the contract, and the manner in which disputes between the employer and the administrator will be settled. The charges for the services provided under the contract may be stated in one or some combination of the following ways:

- A percentage of the amount of claims paid.
- A flat amount per processed claim.
- A flat charge per employee.
- A flat charge for the employer.

Payments for ASO contracts are regarded as fees for services performed; therefore, they are not subject to state premium taxes. However, two similarities to a traditional insurance arrangement may be present. If the administrator is an insurance company, it may agree to provide a conversion contract to employees whose coverage terminates. In addition, the administrator may agree to continue paying any unsettled claims after the contract's termination, but only with funds provided by the employer.

Funding Through a 501(c)(9) Trust

Section 501(c)(9) of the Internal Revenue Code provides for the establishment of *voluntary employees' beneficiary associations,* commonly called either *501(c)(9) trusts* or *VEBAs.* These are funding vehicles for employee benefits that are offered to members. The trusts have been allowed for many years, but until the passage of the 1969 Tax Reform Act, they were primarily used by negotiated trusteeships and association groups. Following that time, the liberalized tax treatment of the funds accumulated by these trusts resulted in their increased use by employers as a method of self-funding employee benefit plans. However, the Tax Reform Act of 1984 imposed more restrictive provisions on 501(c)(9) trusts, and their use has diminished somewhat, particularly by smaller employees who previously had overfunded their trusts primarily as a method of sheltering income from taxation.

Advantages

The use of a 501(c)(9) trust offers the employer some advantages over a benefit plan that is self-funded from current revenue. Contributions can be made to the trust and can be deducted for federal income tax purposes at that time, just as if the trust were an insurance company. Appreciation in the value of the trust assets or investment income earned on the trust assets is also free of taxation. The trust is best suited for an employer who wishes to establish either a fund for claims that have been incurred but not paid or a fund for possible claim fluctuations. If the employer does not use a 501(c)(9) trust in establishing these funds, contributions cannot be deducted until they are paid in the form of benefits to employees. In addition, earnings on the funds would be subject to taxation.

Although the Internal Revenue Code requires that certain fiduciary standards be maintained regarding the investment of the trust assets, the employer has some latitude and has the potential for earning a return on the trust assets that is higher than what is earned on the reserves held by insurance companies. A 501(c)(9) trust also lends itself to use by a contributory self-funded plan, since ERISA requires that under a self-funded benefit plan, a trust must be established to hold the contributions of employees until they are used to pay benefits.

There is also flexibility regarding contributions to the trust. Although the IRS will not permit tax deductions for overfunding a trust, there is no requirement that the trust must maintain enough assets to pay claims that have been incurred but not yet paid. Consequently, an employer can underfund the trust in bad times and make up for this underfunding in good times with larger than normal contributions. However, any underfunding must be shown as a contingent liability on the employer's balance sheet.

Disadvantages

The use of a 501(c)(9) trust is not without its drawbacks. The cost of establishing and maintaining the trust may be prohibitive, especially for small employers. In addition, the employer must be concerned about the administrative aspects of the plan and the fact that claims might deplete the trust's assets. However, as long as the trust is properly funded, ASO contracts and stop-loss coverage can be purchased.

Requirements for Establishment

In order to qualify under Section 501(c)(9), a trust must meet certain requirements, some of which may hinder its establishment. These requirements include:

- Membership in the trust must be objectively restricted to those persons who share a common employment-related bond. IRS regulations interpret this broadly to include active employees and their dependents, surviving dependents, and employees who are retired, laid-off or disabled. Except for plans maintained pursuant to collective-bargaining agreements, benefits must be provided under a classification of employees that the IRS does not find to be discriminatory in favor of highly compensated individuals. It is permissible for life insurance, disability, severance pay and supplemental unemployment compensation benefits to be based on a uniform percentage of compensation. In addition, the following persons may be excluded in determining whether the discrimination rule has been satisfied: (1) employees who have not completed three years of service, (2) employees under age 21, (3) seasonal or less than half-time employees and (4) employees covered by a collective bargaining agreement if the class of benefits was subject to good-faith bargaining.
- With two exceptions, membership in the trust must be voluntary on the part of employees. Members can be required to participate (1) as a result of collective bargaining, or (2) when participation is not detrimental to them. In general, participation is not regarded as detrimental if the employee is not required to make any contributions.
- The trust must only provide eligible benefits. The list of eligible coverages is broad enough so that a trust can provide benefits because of death, medical expenses, disability, legal expenses and unemployment. Retirement benefits, deferred compensation, state disability benefits and group property and liability insurance cannot be provided.

- The sole purpose of the trust must be to provide benefits to its members or their beneficiaries. Trust assets can be used to pay the administrative expenses of the trust, but they cannot revert to the employer. If the trust is terminated, any assets that remain after all existing liabilities have been satisfied must either be used to provide other benefits or be distributed to members of the trust.
- The trust must be controlled by (1) its membership, (2) independent trustees (such as a bank) or (3) trustees or other fiduciaries, at least some of whom are designated by, or on behalf of, the members. Most 501(c)(9) trusts are controlled by independent trustees selected by the employer.

Limitation on Contributions

The contributions to a 501(c)(9) trust (except collectively bargained plans for which Treasury regulations prescribe separate rules) are limited to the sum of (1) the qualified direct cost of the benefits provided for the taxable year, and (2) any permissible additions to a reserve (called a qualified asset account). The qualified direct cost of benefits is the amount that would have been deductible for the year if the employer had paid benefits from current revenue.

The permissible additions may be made only for disability, medical, supplemental unemployment, severance pay and life insurance benefits. In general, the amount of the permissible additions includes (1) any sums that are reasonably and actuarially necessary to pay claims that have been incurred but remain unpaid at the close of the tax year and (2) any administration costs with respect to these claims. If medical or life insurance benefits are provided to retirees, deductions are also allowed for funding these benefits on an actuarial level basis over the working lives of the covered employees. However, for retirees' medical benefits, current medical costs must be used rather than costs based on projected inflation. In addition, a separate account must be established with respect to postretirement benefits provided to key employees. Contributions to these accounts are treated as annual additions for purposes of applying the limitations that exist for contributions and benefits under qualified retirement plans.

The amount of certain benefits for which deductions will be allowed are limited. Life insurance benefits for retired employees cannot exceed amounts that are tax free under Section 79. Annual disability benefits cannot exceed the lesser of 75 percent of a disabled person's average compensation for the highest three years or $90,000. Supplemental unemployment compensation benefits and severance benefits cannot exceed 75 percent of average benefits paid plus administrative costs during any two of the immediately preceding seven years. In determining this limit, annual benefits in excess of $45,000 cannot be taken into account.

In general, it is required that the amount of any permissible additions be actuarially certified. However, deductible contributions can be made to reserves without such certification as long as certain safe-harbor limits with respect to the size of the reserve are not exceeded. The safe-harbor limits for supplemental unemployment compensation benefits and severance benefits are the same as the amounts previously mentioned. For short-term disability benefits, the limit is equal to 17.5 percent of benefit costs (other than insurance premiums for the current year), plus administrative costs for the prior year. For medical benefits, the percentage is 35. The Internal Revenue Code provides that the limits for life insurance benefits and long-term disability income benefits will be those prescribed by regulations. However, no regulations have been issued.

Employer deductions cannot exceed the limits as previously described. However, any excess contributions may be deducted in future years to the extent that contributions for those years are below the permissible limits.

There are several potential adverse tax consequences if a 501(c)(9) trust does not meet prescribed standards. If reserves are above permitted levels, additional contributions to the reserves are not deductible and earnings on the excess reserves are subject to tax as unrelated business income. (This effectively negates any possible advantage of using a 501(c)(9) trust to prefund postretirement medical benefits.) In addition, an excise tax is imposed on employers maintaining a trust that provides disqualified benefits. The tax is equal to 100 percent of the disqualified benefits. These benefits include (1) medical and life insurance benefits provided to key employees outside the separate accounts that must be established, (2) medical or life insurance benefits for retirees that are discriminatory and (3) any portion of the trust's assets that revert to the employer.

STUDY QUESTIONS

1. What are the reasons for increased employer interest in using alternative methods to fund employee benefit plans?
2. Why is an insurance company concerned with the financial position and credit rating of an employer to whom it issues a group insurance contract that contains a premium-delay arrangement?
3. a. Why are reserve-reduction arrangements usually not used during the first year of a group insurance contract?
   b. What is the responsibility of the employer under a reserve-reduction arrangement if an insurance contract is terminated?
4. a. Explain how minimum-premium plans minimize premium taxes.
   b. What is the responsibility of the insurance company under a minimum-premium plan for paying claims and maintaining reserves?
5. Explain the mechanics of retrospective rating.
6. Explain the conditions that are generally considered desirable before an employer should use total self-funding.
7. Why are life insurance benefits usually not self-funded?
8. What is the difference between aggregate stop-loss coverage and specific stop-loss coverage?
9. a. What are the tax advantages of a 501(c)(9) trust that are not present in benefit plans self-funded from current revenue?
   b. What conditions must be satisfied in order for a 501(c)(9) trust to meet IRS requirements?
   c. What are the limitations in amounts that may be contributed to a 501(c)(9) trust?

15

Group Insurance Rate Making

Objectives

- Describe the process by which manual premium rates are calculated.
- Explain how manual premium rates are used to determine group term life insurance premiums, both for large groups and for small groups.
- Identify the ways in which the manual rating process for other types of group insurance differs from the process for group term life insurance.
- Explain the rationale for experience rating.
- Describe the process of using experience rating to calculate dividends.
- Explain how experience rating for determining prospective premiums differs from experience rating for calculating dividends.

One of the least understood aspects of group insurance is the pricing process. In the simplest sense, group insurance pricing is no different from pricing in other industries. The insurance company must generate enough revenue to cover the costs of its claims and expenses and to contribute to the net worth of the company. However, this similarity is often overlooked because of the unique terminology that is associated with insurance pricing and because the price of a group insurance product is initially determined on the basis of expected, but uncertain, future events rather than on current tangible cost estimates. In addition, a group insurance plan may be subject to experience rating so that the final price to the consumer can only be determined after the coverage period has ended.

The purpose of this chapter is not to make readers experts in the actuarial intricacies of group insurance pricing, commonly referred to as *rate making*, but rather to provide an understanding of basic principles and concepts. Rate making consists of two distinct steps:

1. The determination of a unit price, referred to as a rate or premium rate, for each unit of benefit (such as each $1,000 of life insurance).
2. The determination of the total price, or premium, that will be paid by the policyholder for all of the coverage purchased.

The mechanics of rate making differ, depending upon whether a particular group is subject to manual rating or experience rating. When *manual rating* is used, the premium rate is determined independently of a particular group's claims; when *experience rating* is used, the past claims experience of a group is considered in determining future premiums for the group and/or in adjusting past premiums after a policy period has ended.

The major objective of rate making for all types of group insurance is to develop premium rates that are both adequate and equitable. Adequate rates must be sufficient to cover both incurred claims and expenses and to generate the desired profit or contribution to the insurance company's surplus. Obviously, the success and solvency of any group insurance operation is contingent upon the long-run adequacy of premium rates. Therefore, several states, concerned about the solvency of insurance companies, have laws and regulations regarding the adequacy of rates. The most significant of these is in New York. New York law prohibits any insurance company doing business in that state from issuing, in any state, a group health insurance contract for either medical expense or disability income that does not appear to be self-supporting on the basis of reasonable assumptions concerning expected claims and expenses. It also specifies the minimum group term life insurance rates that these companies may charge for any group which has not previously been insured for life insurance.

Equitable rates require each group to pay a premium which reflects the cost of providing coverage to that group. Again, practical considerations and state regulations act to encourage equity. The overpricing of group coverage for some segments of the market will result in lost business; the underpricing for other segments will attract unprofitable business. Most states also have laws and regulations that try to encourage equity by prohibiting unfair discrimination in insurance rates. The objective of equity has resulted in group insurance rates that may differ because of the age, sex and income distribution of a group's members and the size of a group, its geographic location, its occupational hazards and its claims experience. As will be discussed later, the factors that are considered vary with the type of group insurance coverage.

MANUAL RATING

In the manual rating process, premium rates are only established for broad classes of group insurance business. The insurance company does not consider the past claims experience of a particular group when determining that group's rates. However, claims experience is not entirely ignored since the aggregate claims experience for a business class is used to determine the premium rates for that class.

Manual rating is used with small groups for which no credible individual loss experience is available. This lack of credibility exists because the group's size is such that it is impossible to determine whether the other-than-average loss experience is due to random chance or is truly reflective of the group. Manual rating is also frequently used to determine the initial premiums for groups that are subject to experience rating, particularly when a group's past experience is unobtainable or when a group is being written for the first time. In addition, for all but the largest groups, experience rating uses a weighting of manual rates and the actual experience of a group to determine the final premium.

Rating Basis

Prior to the actual calculation of manual premium rates, it is necessary to develop a basis on which the rates will be determined. This involves a decision regarding (1) what benefit unit to use, (2) the extent to which rates will be refined by factors affecting claims and (3) the frequency with which premiums will be paid.

Benefit Unit

Subject to certain adjustments, the premium for a group is calculated by multiplying the premium rate by the number of benefit units provided. While variations occasionally exist, the following are the benefit units predominantly used for the most common types of group insurance:

Type of Group Insurance	Benefit Unit
Term life (including accidental death and dismemberment)	Each $1,000 of death benefit
Short-term disability income	Each $10 of weekly income
Long-term disability income	Each $100 of monthly income
Medical expense (including dental)	Each employee and each category of dependent

Factors Affecting Claims

As previously mentioned, equity requires that rates reflect those factors that result in different claims experience for different groups. Although there are variations among insurance companies, the following table represents the factors that are used by most insurance companies:

Type of Group Insurance	Age	Sex	Geographic Location
Term life	Yes	Yes	No
Short-term disability income	Yes	Yes	No
Long-term disability income	Yes	Yes	No
Medical expense	Yes	Yes	Yes
Dental	No	Yes	Yes

In addition, occupation is virtually always reflected in both group term insurance rates and accidental death and dismemberment rates. It may also be reflected in disability income, medical expense and dental insurance rates, but the number of groups for which it is of concern is relatively small. Consequently, some companies ignore it as a rating factor and may not write such coverages when certain occupations are involved.

At one time, the income level of group members was commonly used as a factor in establishing disability income, medical expense, and dental insurance rates. Currently, income level is still a factor in determining dental insurance premiums, but it is more likely only to be an underwriting consideration in disability income and medical expense insurance.

The size of a group will also affect rates since the proportion of the premium needed for expenses will decrease as the size of a group increases. All manual premium rates are based on an assumption that the size of a group falls within a certain range. If the size of a group varies from this range, an appropriate adjustment is made to the rate to reflect this differential.

A final factor considered in the calculation of rates is the length of time for which the rates will be used. This is a concern primarily for coverages that involve medical and dental claims, which over time will be expected to increase in severity because of inflation. In inflationary times, monthly rates that are guaranteed for three months may be lower than those guaranteed for one year.

Frequency of Premium Payment Period

Because group insurance premiums are usually paid monthly, this is the period for which rates are generally determined. When premiums can be paid less frequently, such as annually, they are usually slightly lower than the sum of the monthly premiums for the same period of coverage.

Calculation of Manual Rates

Manual rating involves the calculation of the *manual premium rates,* also called *tabular rates,* that are quoted in an insurance company's rate book. These manual rates are applied to a specific group insurance case in order to determine a *final premium rate,* or average premium rate, that will then be multiplied by the number of benefit units to obtain a premium for the group. There are three different manual rating methods. However, if identical assumptions are used, each method should result in approximately the same premium for any given group. The first method determines separate manual rates for groups that possess certain characteristics which an insurance company feels will affect claims experience. A second approach establishes a single standard manual rate that is adjusted in the premium-calculation process to compensate for any characteristics which deviate from those of the standard group. A third method merely combines the first two approaches and considers some factors in determining the manual rate and others in determining the final rate.

The first step in the calculation of manual premium rates is the determination of the *net premium rate,* which is the amount necessary to support the cost of expected claims. For any given classification, this is calculated by multiplying the probability (frequency) of a claim occurring by the expected amount (severity) of the claim. For example, if the probability that an employee, age 50, will die in the next month is .0005, then the net monthly premium for each $1,000 of coverage would be .0005 × $1,000 or $.50. Since premiums are collected before the claims will be paid, the insurance company will adjust this figure downward for anticipated interest earnings on these funds.

Insurance companies that write a large volume of any given type of group insurance will rely on their own experience in determining the frequency and severity of future claims. Insurance companies that do not have enough past data for reliable future projections can turn to many sources for useful statistics. Probably the major source is the Society of Actuaries, which regularly collects and publishes aggregate data on the group insurance business that is written by a number of large group insurance companies. Other sources of information include industry trade organizations and various agencies of the federal government.

The second and final step in the calculation of manual premium rates is the adjustment of the net premium rates for expenses, a risk charge and a contribution to surplus. Expenses include commissions, premium taxes, claims settlement costs and other costs associated with the acquisition and servicing of group insurance business. The risk charge represents a contribution to the insurance company's contingency reserve as a cushion against unanticipated and catastrophic amounts of claims. The contribution to surplus or net worth represents the profit margin of the insurance company. While mutual companies are legally nonprofit, they require a contribution to net worth that, as with stock insurance companies, is a source of financing for future growth.

From the standpoint of equity, the adjustment of the net premium rate is complex. Some factors such as premium taxes and commissions vary with the premium charge. However, the premium tax rate is not affected by the size of a group, whereas the commission rate decreases as the size of a group increases. To a large degree, the expenses of settling claims vary with the number, not the size, of claims. It costs just as much to pay a $10,000 claim under a group life insurance plan as it does to pay a $100,000 claim. Certain other costs also tend to be fixed regardless of the size of a group. For simplicity, some insurance companies adjust or load their net premium rates by a constant percentage. However, other insurance companies consider the different patterns of expenses by using a percentage plus a constant charge. For example, if the net premium rate is $.60, this might be increased by 20 percent plus $.10 to arrive at a manual premium rate of $.82 (that is, $.60 × 1.2 + $.10). Because neither approach adequately accounts for the difference in expenses as a result of the group's size, another adjustment, based on the size of the group, will be made in the calculation of the final premium rate.

Calculation of Premiums

Probably the best way to explain the actual calculation of group insurance premiums is to discuss some examples. The following analysis focuses primarily on group term life insurance, with some emphasis on how the structure of manual rates and the premium calculation process differ for certain other types of group insurance.

Group Term Life Insurance

The mechanics of calculating a final premium rate and the premium for a particular group will vary among insurance companies because of the differences in how manual premium rates are prepared and the process by which adjustments are made to these rates. The usual approach taken for all but the smallest groups parallels that used in the 1961 Standard Group Life Insurance Premium Rates. These rates, based on the 1960 Commissioners Standard Group Mortality Table, were jointly promulgated by the insurance commissioners of several states and were required to be used as minimum initial rates for new group insurance business, including groups that had previously been written by other insurance companies. The rationale for setting these minimum rates was to prevent insurance companies from adversely affecting existing policyholders by writing new business at a loss, with the hope of recovering that loss through rate increases in future years. In effect, an insurance company could not charge lower rates than these minimum rates during the first year it had a group insurance case on the books. However, the minimum rates did not apply upon renewal. Since New York applied these rates on an extraterritorial basis, any company licensed in New York had to use these rates in any state where it did business. Companies licensed in New York are still subject to the 1961 minimum rates on group insurance cases that have not been previously written; the rates no longer apply to transferred business. A few other states also have minimum rate laws, but their effect is primarily to apply the minimum rates to companies that do business in these states without New York licensing.

The following example is based on the 1961 minimum rates. It should be pointed out, however, that the manual premium rates of most insurance companies, except where the minimum rates apply, probably fall between 25 and 50 percent below these rates.

The 1961 minimum rates consist of a table of manual premium rates for males from ages 15 to 95, with female rates at 60 percent of the male rates. The following is an abbreviated version of these rates on a monthly basis per $1,000 of coverage at selected ages. As with most rate tables, the ages are those at a person's attained age, or nearest birthday.

Age at Nearest Birthday	Male Rate	Female Rate
20	$0.23	$0.14
25	0.25	0.15
30	0.27	0.16
35	0.32	0.19
40	0.45	0.27
45	0.68	0.41
50	1.06	0.64
55	1.65	0.99
60	2.51	1.51
65	3.78	2.27
70	5.81	3.49

These rates assume that the coverage contains both a waiver-of-premium provision on disabled lives and a conversion privilege. Consequently, they are higher than if neither of these additional benefits was included. When an employee converts coverage to an individual policy, a charge is assessed against the group insurance business of an insurance company to reflect the increased mortality that results from adverse selection on conversions. The amount of this assessment, commonly $50 to $75 per $1,000 of converted insurance, is transferred to the individual insurance department of the company to compensate it for having to write the converted business at too low a rate.

The premium-calculation process starts with the determination of an unadjusted cost, based on a census of the covered employees and the manual rates. For example, assume a firm has 230 employees. For the sake of simplicity, also assume that each of these employees is provided with $10,000 of life insurance and that the group has the following age distribution:

Age	Males	Females
25	20	30
30	0	30
35	10	30
40	30	10
45	30	10
50	20	10

The unadjusted cost is then calculated as follows:

Age	Sex	Employees	Coverage (in thousands)	Unadjusted Rate (per thousand)	Unadjusted Cost
25	M	20 ×	10 ×	$0.25 =	$ 50
35	M	10 ×	10 ×	0.32 =	32
40	M	30 ×	10 ×	0.45 =	135
45	M	30 ×	10 ×	0.68 =	204
50	M	20 ×	10 ×	1.06 =	212
25	F	30 ×	10 ×	0.15 =	45
30	F	30 ×	10 ×	0.16 =	48
35	F	30 ×	10 ×	0.19 =	57
40	F	10 ×	10 ×	0.27 =	27
45	F	10 ×	10 ×	0.41 =	41
50	F	10 ×	10 ×	0.64 =	64
Total Unadjusted Cost					$915

The unadjusted cost is then adjusted for expenses, a two-step process. First, an expense charge equal to the lesser of 20 cents per $1,000 of insurance provided or $8.00 is added to the unadjusted cost. In this example, the $8.00 is added because $.20 × 2,300 (based on providing $2.3 million of insurance) is $460. For all practical purposes, this charge can be treated as an $8 expense constant since virtually no groups exist that provide less than the $40,000 of coverage necessary for a lower charge.

The second step is to reduce the sum of the unadjusted cost and the expense charge calculated above by a percentage that is based on the volume of a group insurance case as determined by its monthly premium. The following reductions adopted in 1971 are used with the 1961 minimum rates:

Monthly Premium before Reduction	Percentage Expense Reduction
Under $200	0
200–224	1
225–249	2
250–299	3
—	—
—	—
700–799	12
800–899	13
900–999	14
1,000–1,199	15
—	—
—	—
45,000–59,999	33
60,000–79,999	34
80,000 and over	35

Thus, the initial monthly premium for the group in this example is:

Unadjusted cost	$915.00
+ lesser of $.20 per $1,000 and $8	8.00
Monthly premium before expense reduction	$923.00
– expense reduction (14%)	129.22
Adjusted monthly premium	$793.78

The initial monthly premium is also used to calculate the final monthly premium rate per $1,000 of protection for the group:

$$\text{Monthly premium rate per thousand} = \frac{\text{Adjusted monthly premium}}{\text{Total volume (in thousands)}}$$
$$= \frac{\$793.78}{2,300}$$
$$= \$0.345$$

This final monthly premium rate is usually rounded to either the nearest cent or one tenth of a cent and used throughout the first policy year; it is multiplied each month by the amount of insurance in force to calculate the monthly premium due. Adjustments to the final monthly premium rate as a result of changes in the makeup of employees by age or sex are not made until the beginning of the next policy year, when a new rate per $1,000 of coverage is determined as part of the renewal process. Thus, the initial rate is guaranteed for one year, assuming no change in the benefit structure of the plan.

It is possible to make one other adjustment to the 1961 minimum premium rates. Although the rates are designed so that most industries can be written at the manual rates, employers in industries that are considered hazardous can be charged a higher rate. This increased rate is in the form of a surcharge per $1,000 of coverage and is added to the sum of the unadjusted cost and the expense charge before the expense reduction percentage is applied. The industry ratings used with the 1961 rates are expressed as +1, +2, and so forth. For example, an industry with a +1 rating can be expected to have about one death claim per year per 1,000 employees in excess of those assumed in the manual rates. The charge for this excess mortality is eight cents per $1,000 of coverage per month for each unit of extra rating. In the previous example a +1 rating would have resulted in an increased charge of $184 (that is, 2,300 × $.08) before the expense reduction was made. Therefore, the adjusted monthly premium would have been calculated as follows:

Unadjusted cost	$915.00
+ lesser of $.20 per $1,000 and $8	8.00
+ industry surcharge	184.00
Total cost before expense reduction	$1,107.00
– expense reduction (15%)	166.05
Adjusted monthly premium	$940.95

Similarly, a +2 rating reflects the expectation of two extra death claims per year and would have resulted in an added premium of $.16 per $1,000 per month or $368.

Variations for Large Groups. The premium-calculation process discussed here is used by insurance companies for most groups above a certain size, commonly from ten or more to 50 or more lives. However, variations do exist. For example, some insurance companies do not incorporate a charge for a waiver of premium into their manual rates. An extra charge, that usually differs by industry, will instead be added for this coverage. In addition, a few companies use manual rates that vary by age but not sex. These unisex rate tables are based on assumptions about the ratio of males to females in the group. However, an adjustment will usually be made in the premium-calculation process if the actual ratio for the group differs from this assumption.

Insurance companies may or may not have a constant expense charge similar to the $8 previously described. Some companies incorporate a level of expenses into their manual rates so that there is no expense reduction for a certain size group. In the final premium-calculation process, an adjustment will be made, and larger groups will receive an expense reduction while smaller groups will receive an expense surcharge. Here is one such table of adjustments:

Monthly Premium before Adjustment	Percentage Adjustment
Under $200	+25
200–249	+22
250–299	+18
—	—
—	—
—	—
600–699	+2
700–799	+1
800–999	0
1,000–1,099	−1
1,100–1,200	−2
—	—
—	—
—	—
50,000–74,999	−14
75,000 and over	−15

Variations for Small Groups. The manual-rating process for small groups, including those written by METs, differs from that of large groups in several ways. In general, the manual rates are banded by age, typically in five-year intervals. Here is one such monthly rate table for each $1,000 of coverage:

Age at Nearest Birthday	Male Rate	Female Rate
Under 30	$ .25	$ .19
30–34	.30	.23
35–39	.35	.27
40–44	.50	.38
45–49	.80	.60
50–54	1.20	.90
55–59	1.70	1.25
60–64	2.50	1.90
65–69	3.70	2.75
70–74	5.50	4.00
75 and over	9.00	6.75

An unadjusted cost is developed based on a census of the employees by age and sex. Since the manual rates are loaded for most expenses, and since the groups written tend to be reasonably close in size, no adjustment for size is usually made. However, to compensate for the expenses of periodic billings, most insurance companies apply a flat fee to all groups, commonly between $10 and $20 per billing. Some companies do not levy this charge if the premium is paid annually. To reflect the administrative costs associated with record keeping, some insurance companies also levy a modest one-time expense charge when coverage is added for a new employee.

In contrast to large groups for which the initial monthly premium is used to determine a monthly premium rate that will apply for a specified period of time, the monthly premium rate for small groups will be recalculated each month based on the volume of insurance and on the changes in the makeup of employees by age and sex, just as if the group was being newly written. However, for purposes of this recalculation, most insurance companies do guarantee that both the manual rates that were used when the group was initially written and any future rates applicable to the group will remain applicable for some period of time. This time period may vary from 60 days to one year, but six months is most common.

Accidental Death and Dismemberment Insurance

Accidental death and dismemberment insurance is usually not written as a separate coverage, but rather is added by an endorsement to a group term insurance contract. A single manual rate typically applies to all employees regardless of age or sex, but it will vary depending on whether coverage is written (1) for nonoccupational accidents or (2) on a 24-hour basis for both nonoccupational and occupational accidents. The rate for nonoccupational coverage generally does not vary by industry and ranges from four to six cents per $1,000 of principal sum per month. However, the rate for coverage on a 24-hour basis does vary by industry and although it falls within this same range for low-risk industries, it may be several times higher for hazardous industries. Some companies calculate a separate charge for the accidental death and dismemberment coverage and add it to the charge for the group term life insurance. However, since most employers purchase accidental death and dismemberment coverage, many insurance companies incorporate the cost into the manual rates for group term life insurance. When this is done, the principal sum will be equal to the amount of life insurance protection that is purchased, and an additional charge will be levied only if a higher level of accidental death and dismemberment coverage is desired.

Dependent Life Insurance

Dependent life insurance is virtually always added as additional coverage to a group life insurance contract that provides life insurance protection for employees. Because dependent life insurance coverage usually is a modest fixed amount (such as $2,000 on the spouse and $1,000 on each child) that generates a relatively small additional premium, a very simplified rate structure tends to be used. However, several variations do exist: Some insurance companies have a single flat rate, independent of the type or number of dependents, for each employee who has dependent coverage. Other companies have two separate flat rates: one for the spouse's coverage; the other for the children's coverage. The rate for the children's coverage is a family rate regardless of the number of children, and it is based upon an average-sized family.

Flat rates are based on the assumption that the group has an average age mix of employees. If the group of employees is older than average, the flat rate for dependent coverage may be adjusted when applied to spouses to reflect the likelihood that the dependents are also above average in age when compared to the dependents of most other groups. A flat rate is commonly used when the cost of dependent coverage is paid entirely by the employees. The uniform charge is easy to communicate to employees, and it simplifies the payroll-deduction process for the employer.

Some insurance companies also use a rate for dependent coverage that varies with the employee's age, thereby assuming that older employees have older dependents. Basing the rate on the employee's age may seem illogical, but it is administratively simpler and less expensive than having to determine the ages of dependents. A single variable rate may apply to the total family coverage for the spouse and all children, or it may apply only to the spouse. In this latter case, a flat rate is generally used if coverage for children is also provided.

Short-Term Disability Income Insurance

In addition to varying by age and sex, manual rates for disability income insurance also differ by the maximum benefit period, the length of the waiting period and whether coverage is written on a 24-hour basis or only for nonoccupational disabilities.

Particularly for small groups, some insurance companies have only a single standard short-term disability income plan that they will sell, and therefore, they only need a single manual rate table. Other companies allow the employer some flexibility in designing the plan to be purchased and, rather than make adjustments to a single rate table, these companies will usually have several rate tables that vary by such factors as maximum benefit period (such as 13 or 26 weeks) and waiting period (such as seven days for all disabilities or seven days for illnesses and no waiting period for injuries). If any other variations are allowed, appropriate adjustments will be made.

An adjustment may be made for the nature of the industry represented by the group. Ignoring the occupational injuries and diseases that are covered under workers' compensation, a few occupations are still characterized by higher-than-average disability income claims. As an alternative to a rate adjustment, some insurance companies have underwriting standards that prohibit the writing of coverage for these groups.

Until the passage of the amendments to the Civil Rights Act pertaining to pregnancy, it was common for insurance companies to have one manual rate for plans that did not provide benefits for pregnancy-related disabilities and another for plans that did provide such benefits. Since most employers can no longer exclude pregnancy as a cause of disability, rates for coverage without this benefit are usually published only for the small business employers that still have an option regarding this benefit.

In contrast to group life insurance for which the rates for females are lower than the rates for males, disability income rates are higher for females. Ignoring pregnancy-related disabilities, the claims of females at younger ages still somewhat exceed those of males. However, because male and female claims are comparable at older ages, the rates for later years seldom vary. The following illustration of one insurance company's monthly rates per $10 of weekly benefit shows how this rate differential is even more pronounced at younger ages if maternity coverage is included:

Age	Male	Female
Under 30	$0.27	$0.91
30–34	0.42	0.91
35–39	0.48	0.91
40–44	0.63	0.91
45–49	0.71	1.03
50–54	1.12	1.12
55–59	1.26	1.26
60–64	1.62	1.62
65–69	2.27	2.27

In the past, it was common for short-term disability income rates to be expressed on the basis of each $10 of weekly benefit. This is probably still the norm, but many insurance companies are now expressing their rates in terms of a higher weekly benefit, such as $50 or $100.

Long-Term Disability Income Insurance

Like short-term disability income rates, the manual rates for long-term coverage vary by age, sex, the length of the benefit period and the length of the waiting period. In addition, the manual rates reflect the fact that benefits will be integrated with social security and certain other disability income benefits for which an employee might be eligible. To the extent that variations are allowed in the integration provision that was assumed in developing the manual rates, an adjustment will be made in the premium-calculation process. Also like short-term rates, an adjustment might be made for certain occupations.

Unlike short-term disability income rates that commonly are expressed on the basis of a weekly benefit, long-term rates typically are expressed on the basis of a monthly benefit, usually per $100. In contrast to the coverages previously discussed, long-term disability claims fluctuate with general economic conditions. Consequently, insurance companies review, and possibly revise, their manual rates and/or their underwriting standards as economic conditions change.

Medical Expense Insurance

In many ways, the manual rates for medical expense insurance, and also dental insurance, are similar to those for disability income insurance because variations exist by age, sex and the provisions of the plan, including the size of the deductible, the coinsurance percentage and the level of benefits. Most insurance companies have manual rates for the few standard plans that will be sold, and only large employers are given the flexibility to deviate from these plans. Any such deviation will then be reflected in adjustments to the manual rates. Adjustments may also be made to the manual rates if the employer is in an industry characterized by higher-than-average claims.

One other factor, geographic location, is a variable in the manual rates because of the significant differences in medical costs across the country. Depending on group size, an adjustment for location may be made in one of two ways: For large groups, the rating process usually starts with a manual rate that does not consider employee location. Each county (or other geographic subdivision) where coverage will be written is then assigned a factor that is based on the cost of health care in that location as compared with the average cost assumed in the manual rates. For example, if Seattle were 20 percent higher than average, it would have a factor of 1.2. If all of a firm's employees were there, the manual rates for that group would be multiplied by a location factor of 1.2 in the process of determining the group's premium. If employees were in several locations, a composite factor would be calculated as shown in the following example:

	Employees		Location Factor		Product
Seattle	100	×	1.2	=	120
Kansas City	70	×	1.0	=	70
Birmingham	30	×	0.7	=	21
	200				211

$$\text{Location factor} = \frac{\text{Total product}}{\text{Total employees}} = \frac{211}{200} = 1.055$$

Consequently, the manual rate for this group would be increased by 5.5 percent because of the location of the employees.

A slightly different approach is used for small groups. Because employees are usually in one location, most companies have manual rate tables for between ten and 15 rating territories and each county in which employees are located is assigned a specific territorial rating. The following territorial classifications are from the rating manual of one insurance company for counties in three states where it writes business:

California:	
Los Angeles	10
Alameda, Contra Costa, Marin, Orange, Riverside, San Bernardino, San Francisco, San Mateo, Santa Clara, Solano	9
Imperial, Kern, San Diego, San Luis Obispo, Santa Barbara, Ventura	8
All other counties	7

(continued)

Georgia:	
Clayton, Cobb, DeKalb, Fulton	6
Catoosa, Chatham, Gwinnett, Walker	4
All other counties	3
Maine:	
Entire state	2

An excerpt from the manual rate tables of the same company shows how the monthly cost for coverage under a plan written through one of their METs varies by geographic area:

Age	Class of Coverage	Area 2	Area 4	Area 7	Area 10
Under 30	Male	$ 56.00	$ 65.70	$ 82.30	$ 90.30
Under 30	Female	60.80	72.00	92.10	120.68
Under 30	Male and dependents	163.80	195.60	254.80	334.60
Under 30	Female and dependents	159.30	191.20	248.40	330.12
30–44	Male	83.90	97.60	122.80	157.20
30–44	Female	89.70	106.40	135.80	177.80
30–44	Male and dependents	219.80	261.70	337.30	445.80
30–44	Female and dependents	212.70	254.80	330.10	438.60

The previous example lists manual rates for dependent coverage that are applied regardless of the number of dependents, the relationship of the dependents to the employee or the ages of the dependents. For any size group, this is one of the three common methods for pricing dependent coverage. Under all three methods, the rate for dependent coverage is usually based on the employee's age rather than the dependents' ages. However, two methods do take the number of dependents and their relationship to the insured into consideration. One method uses a certain rate for dependent coverage if there is only one dependent and another rate if there are two or more dependents. In addition, the third method has three rates: one for coverage that is elected only for a spouse, another for coverage that is elected only for children and a third for coverage that is elected for both a spouse and children.

Because medical expense claims are continually increasing as a result of inflation, a trend factor must be applied to past claims experience when developing manual rates. This is a complex and often perplexing task for most insurance companies. As measured by the consumer price index, not only has the overall cost of medical care increased faster than the general cost of living, but the increases have been erratic from year to year and virtually impossible to predict with any degree of accuracy. In addition, because these increases vary significantly for each category of medical expenses, different trend factors must be applied to different categories of claims.

Group insurance rates at one time were guaranteed by insurance companies for at least 12 months and possibly for as long as two or three years. However, to protect themselves against unexpected increases in claims as a result of increases in the cost of medical care, many insurance companies now will only guarantee medical expense rates for at most six months. In fact, a number of METs have only three-month guarantees, or they contain provisions whereby rates can be increased at any time, provided notice of the rate increase is given 30 or 60 days in advance. Some companies allow an employer to select the length of rate guarantee, such as six months or one year. However, the longer the rate guarantee, the higher the rate.

Dental Insurance

In many ways, the rating of dental insurance is similar to the rating of medical expense insurance. However, there are some significant differences: Most insurance companies do not vary their rates by the ages of group members. Rather, an adjustment is usually made for the income levels of employees since higher paid persons are much more likely to obtain dental care. This adjustment is usually in the form of a percentage that is based on the extent to which the portion of employees with incomes higher than some figure (such as $20,000) exceeds the proportion of such employees that is assumed in the manual rates. An adjustment is also made for certain occupations (such as salespeople or teachers) that use dental services more frequently than average. Finally, the rates will usually be increased when a plan is new or expands benefits if the employees have been informed beforehand. Under these circumstances there is a tendency to postpone needed dental care until the plan is installed.

EXPERIENCE RATING

With experience rating, an insurance company considers a group's claims experience, either at the issue date or at the end of a policy period, when determining the premium rate for that group. When applied prospectively (that is, to future periods), experience rating is used to determine (1) upward or downward adjustments in renewal premiums for those groups whose claims experience has deviated from what was expected and (2) initial premiums for large groups that change insurance carriers.

In addition to determining the premium rate for the next policy period (usually 12 months), experience rating is also used to compute the refund for those groups that had better claims experience than anticipated. This refund is commonly referred to as a *dividend* by mutual insurance companies and a *retrospective rate credit* or premium refund by stock insurance companies. Since the majority of group insurance business is written by mutual companies, the term *dividend* will be used here. Under some experience-rating arrangements, the premium at the end of a policy period may also be retroactively adjusted upward if a group's claims experience has been worse than anticipated, and an additional premium will be charged. These arrangements are not very common and were discussed as an alternative funding method in Chapter 14.

Rationale for Experience Rating

One argument in favor of experience rating is that it achieves the ultimate degree of premium equity among policyholders. Even though manual rating also results in equity because it considers the obvious factors that affect claims, it is impossible to measure and make adjustments in the manual rates for such factors as lifestyle, working conditions and morale—all of which contribute to the level of claims experience. Experience rating is also the most cost-effective way to reflect the general health of a group in the premium that is charged.

Probably the major reason for using experience rating is the competition that exists in the group insurance marketplace. If an insurance company were to use identical rates for all groups regardless of their experience, employers with good experience would soon seek out insurance companies that offered lower rates, or they would turn to self-funding as a way to reduce costs. The insurance company that did not consider claims experience would therefore be left with only the poor risks. This is exactly the situation that led most Blue Cross and Blue Shield Plans to abandon community rating for group insurance cases above a certain size. Experience rating allows an insurance company to acquire and retain the better cases based on claims experience and to determine an appropriate premium for the groups that have worse than average claims experience.

Dividend Calculation

It is perhaps putting the cart before the horse to explain experience rating for dividend purposes, which occurs at the end of a policy period, before discussing the use of experience rating to determine premiums, which occurs at the beginning of that period. However, the process of calculating dividends tends to be somewhat more complex and is easier to discuss first. This discussion is followed by an explanation of how the experience-rating process is different for determining premiums on a prospective basis.

At first glance, the process of using experience rating to determine dividends appears complex. However, the actual mechanics are relatively simple and much of the confusion stems from the fact that the process is lengthy. In addition, both the format and the terminology vary somewhat among insurance companies. This discussion will focus on Table 15-1 and will explain the steps used to calculate the dividend for a group term life insurance contract. Although this illustration can be considered a typical example of a dividend calculation, variations could have been, and often are, used in several steps. Therefore, the more commonly used and significant variations will be described for group term life insurance as well as for other types of group insurance.

Premiums Paid

Step 1 shows the total amount of premiums that were actually paid by the policyholder during the experience-rating period, which usually is one year, before any adjustment has been made to reflect the actual experience of the group. In most instances, this will be the sum of 12 monthly premiums. The premiums paid may have been based on manual rates or on the past experience of the group.

TABLE 15-1
Illustrative Dividend Calculation

1. Premiums paid		$100,000
2. Incurred claims [a + (c - b) + d + e]		79,800
a. Paid death claims	$70,000	
b. Beginning reserve for death claims	14,000	
c. Ending reserve for death claims	15,000	
d. Charge for approved disability claims	7,500	
e. Conversion charges	1,300	
3. Stop-loss limit (120% of premium paid)		120,000
4. Incurred claims subject to experience rating (lesser of 2 and 3)		79,800
5. Expected claims		84,000
6. Credibility factor		0.8
7. Claims charge [(0.8 × 4) + (0.2 × 5)]		80,640
8. Retention charge (f + g + h + i + j - k)		9,800
f. Charge for stop-loss coverage	2,500	
g. Commissions	2,000	
h. Premium taxes	2,000	
i. Administration	1,500	
j. Contingency reserve (risk charge) and surplus contribution	3,000	
k. Interest on reserves	1,200	
9. Dividend earned [1 - (7 + 8)]		9,560
10. Deficit carried forward from prior periods		3,000
11. Deficit to be carried forward to future periods (9 - 10) if less than 0		—
or		
Dividend payable (9 - 10) if greater than 0		$ 6,560

Incurred Claims

Step 2 involves the determination of incurred claims, which are those claims attributable to the recently ended period of coverage that was subject to experience rating (the *experience period*). It may seem as if the incurred claims are those claims that were paid during the experience period. Unfortunately, it is not this simple. Some of the claims that were paid during the experience period may actually be attributable to prior periods and must be subtracted from the incurred claims. In addition, other claims that are attributable to the experience period may not have been reported or may be in the course of settlement. However, the value must be estimated. Therefore, an appropriate determination of incurred claims is:

Incurred claims = Claims paid during the experience period
           - Claims paid during the experience period, but incurred during prior periods
           + Estimate of claims incurred during the experience period, but to be paid in future periods

In actual practice, incurred claims usually are expressed as:

> Incurred claims = Paid claims
> + Ending claim reserve
> – Beginning claim reserve
> *or*
> Incurred claims = Paid claims
> + Change in claim reserve

This *claim reserve*, which is often referred to as the open-and-unreported claim reserve, represents an estimate by the insurance company for (1) claims that have been approved but not yet paid, (2) claims that are in the course of settlement and (3) claims that have been incurred but not yet reported. In addition, when disability income coverage or medical expense coverage is experience rated, an additional amount must be added to this estimate for any claims that have been incurred, reported and approved but are not yet payable. Essentially, these claims arise from disabilities or current medical claims that will continue beyond the experience period.

Based upon past experience, most insurance companies can fairly accurately estimate the percentage of claims that will be paid after the close of the experience period for a given type of coverage. While this estimate reflects company-wide experience and may not reflect the experience of a particular policyholder, it is usually applied to each group insurance contract rather than determining the claim reserve on a contract-by-contract basis. In general, the claim reserve is based either on a percentage of the annual premium before experience rating or on a percentage of claims paid. The first approach is most common for small groups and the latter approach tends to be used for large groups. This percentage varies considerably by type of coverage, with the claim reserve for group term life insurance usually ranging between 10 to 15 percent of the annual premium—and up to 25 percent if a waiver of premium for disability is included; the claim reserve for medical expense coverage often ranges from 20 to 65 percent, depending upon what benefits are involved.

Two other factors enter into the incurred claims amount for group term life insurance: disability claims and conversion charges. In addition to death claims, there may be disability claims if a group insurance contract contains a waiver-of-premium provision or other type of disability provision. Once a waiver-of-premium claim has been approved, a charge is made for future death claims since no future premiums will be received for the disabled employee. This charge is based on the probability that the disabled employee will die prior to recovery or termination of coverage, for example, at age 65. On the average, the charge will be about $750 for each $1,000 of coverage. If the insurance contract continues, an additional $250 per $1,000 of coverage will be charged if a death claim is paid. If the employee recovers or coverage terminates prior to death, the $750 charge will be credited back to the policyholder.

As mentioned earlier in this chapter, a conversion charge is levied against the group insurance department of an insurance company to reflect the increased mortality on converted coverage. In the experience-rating procedure, this is transferred to the group policyholder as a charge per $1,000 of coverage converted, commonly $50 to $75.

Stop-Loss Limit

The stop-loss limit is specified in Step 3. This is the maximum amount of claims that will be charged to the group in Step 4 of the experience-rating calculation. Its purpose is to minimize the effect of any chance fluctuations that might occur from year to year, including catastrophic losses within the group, such as an accident that kills several employees. These chance fluctuations tend to become relatively smaller as the size of a group increases, and a stop-loss limit may not be used for very large groups.

The stop-loss limit is usually expressed as a percentage of the premiums paid, and the actual percentage is subject to negotiation between the policyholder and the insurance company. In this illustration, 120 percent is used. Therefore, the amount of incurred claims that will enter into the experience-rating calculation is limited to a maximum of $120,000. Since this exceeds the actual amount of incurred claims, the latter amount is used in Step 4.

Obviously, a charge must be made somewhere for incorporating a stop-loss provision into an experience-rated contract since the insurance company is obligated to pay any excess amount over the stop-loss limit. The charge in this illustration is shown in Step 8. In practice, this charge will be the same for all similar-sized groups that use the same stop-loss percentage. Because the charge is a percentage of premiums paid, it becomes smaller as either the size of the group or the stop-loss percentage increases. In effect, this charge for stop-loss coverage can be viewed as a manual rate charge for losses in excess of some limit, with only those losses below the limit subject to experience rating.

Expected Claims

The amount of expected claims in Step 5 represents that portion of the premiums paid that the insurance company had anticipated would be necessary to pay claims during the experience period. This may have been derived either from average experience as in manual rating or from the past experience of the particular group.

Credibility

The credibility factor, which can vary from zero to one (Step 6), is a statistical measure of the reliability of the group's past experience. In other words, it is a measure of the probability that the group's actual experience is a true reflection of the group and is not the result of chance occurrences. The credibility factor varies with the size of the group and the type of coverage. In general, the larger the group is, the greater the reliability of estimates will be because of the law of large numbers. In addition, actual experience tends to deviate less from the estimates of expected claims (on a relative basis) as the frequency of claims rises. Therefore, a greater degree of credibility can be attributed to a group's medical expense claims than to its life insurance claims.

In actual practice, credibility factors are usually based on the size of a group as determined by the number of lives who are insured. However, some insurance companies base their credibility factors on the annual premium of a group. The factors vary somewhat among insurance companies, but the following excerpt from the rate manual of one insurance company is a typical example of the first approach:

Size of Group (lives)	Life Insurance and Long-Term Disability Income Insurance	Medical Expense Insurance and Short-Term Disability Income Insurance
100	0.0	0.2
200	0.2	0.5
400	0.4	0.8
600	0.7	1.0
800	0.9	1.0
1,000 or more	1.0	1.0

Adjustments may be made in these factors to reflect any characteristics of either the group or the insurance contract that are not the norm. For example, an older group of employees might be assigned a higher credibility factor than a younger group whose claims are more likely to be due to random fluctuations. In addition, the level of any stop-loss limit may have an effect. As the stop-loss charge is increased, meaning the stop-loss limit is lowered, the credibility that can be assigned to the remaining claims below the stop-loss limit also increases.

Similarly, the size of the credibility factor may be influenced by the amount of the risk charge that is levied on the group for the establishment of a contingency reserve. If an insurance company has an adequate contingency reserve for a group insurance contract, it is more likely to allow the use of a higher credibility factor than can be justified from a statistical standpoint. This practice will result in reduced claims charges for years in which the employer has good experience, and an increased claims charge for years in which it has bad experience. Although it is desired by employers that have a history of better-than-average claims experience, a higher-than-justified credibility factor will lead to a larger-than-usual deficit for a group whose experience is bad. It will also increase the probability that the employer will terminate the contract before the deficit is eliminated. A larger contingency reserve can balance the financial consequences of this possibility.

Claims Charge

Once the credibility factor is determined, the process of calculating what claims will be charged against the group in the experience period is relatively simple and can be expressed by the following formula:

> Claims charge = (z)(Incurred claims subject to experience rating)
> + (1 − z)(Expected claims),
> where z is the credibility factor.

In effect, the claims charge is a weighted average of (1) the incurred claims that are subject to experience rating and (2) the expected claims, with the incurred claims being assigned a weight equal to the credibility factor and the expected claims being assigned a weight equal to one minus the credibility factor. In Step 7 of Table 15-1, the claims charge is calculated as follows:

$$
\begin{aligned}
\text{Claims charge} &= 0.8(\$79{,}800) + (1 - 0.8)(\$84{,}000) \\
&= 0.8(\$79{,}800) + 0.2(\$84{,}000) \\
&= \$63{,}840 + \$16{,}800 \\
&= \$80{,}640
\end{aligned}
$$

Note that if a credibility factor of 1.0 is used, the claims charge will be equal to the incurred claims that are subject to experience rating and the expected claims will not be taken into consideration.

Large Amounts of Coverage

In many group term life insurance contracts, there is considerable disparity in the amounts of coverage, and top executives often have much greater coverage than the lowest paid employees. Claims that arise from the deaths of employees who have large amounts of coverage can have a significant impact on a group's experience for the years in which they occur. Consequently, several methods have been used to exclude these claims, or at least a portion of these claims, from the process of determining the claims charge in experience rating. One of these methods is the stop-loss limit that was previously mentioned. However, its primary purpose is to limit the claims charge because of a higher than anticipated frequency of claims, rather than because of a few high-severity claims. Some of the other methods used to handle these large claims include:

- *Excess-amounts pooling.* Under this approach, the amount of insurance that is subject to experience rating on any one person is limited. Amounts in excess of the limit are not experience rated, but are subject to manual rates that are based upon the ages of the individuals involved. This results in a pooling or an insurance charge being added to either the claims charge or the retention charge depending upon the practice of the insurance company. These excess amounts may also be subject to evidence of insurability.
- *A lower credibility factor.* Under this method, the credibility factor normally used for a certain-size group is reduced if there is a significant difference between the smallest and largest amounts of coverage. This results in more weight being placed on the group's expected claims than on its incurred claims.

- *An extra contingency reserve.* Under this approach, the excess of claims above a certain limit is ignored in the experience-rating process for dividend purposes, but is charged against a contingency reserve that has been established (with an appropriate annual charge) for this purpose.

Retention

The retention (Step 8) in a group insurance contract is usually defined as the excess of premiums paid over claims payments and dividends. It consists of charges for the stop-loss coverage, expenses (commissions, premium taxes and administrative expenses), a risk charge and a contribution to the insurance company's surplus. As in this illustration, the risk charge and contribution to surplus are often lumped together and treated as a single item. The sum of these retention charges is reduced by the interest that is credited to certain reserves which the insurance company holds in order to pay future claims attributable to this contract. These include the claim reserve and any contingency reserves. However, some insurance companies do not subtract this interest when determining retention but rather treat it as an additional premium paid.

For large groups, each item in the retention is calculated separately, based on the group's experience. For small groups, a formula is usually applied that is based on insurance company averages. This formula varies by the size of a group and the type of coverage involved, and most often it is either a percentage of the claims charge or a flat charge plus a percentage of the claims charge.

Dividend Earned

The dividend earned (Step 9) is computed by adding the retention to the claims charge and then subtracting this amount from the premiums paid. This is the dividend amount attributable to the group insurance contract for a particular experience period.

Prior Deficits

Under most experience-rated group insurance plans, any deficits from past periods must be made up before any future dividends will be paid. Whenever the sum of the claims charge and the retention charge for any experience period exceeds the premiums paid and results in a negative dividend earned, there is a deficit. In Table 15-1 (Step 10), a $3,000 deficit from prior periods exists. Interestingly, the insurance company will have no opportunity to recover this deficit if the insurance contract is not renewed. However, because there is always a chance of nonrenewal, this is one of the reasons a risk charge is levied.

As additional protection against the nonrenewal of insurance contracts that have a deficit, some insurance companies require that part of any dividend earned be placed in a *claims fluctuation reserve* when experience is favorable. Monies are drawn from the reserve to indemnify the insurance company for those years in which there is a deficit. Because this lessens the possibility that the insurance company will lose money on a group insurance contract, it is usually accompanied by a lower risk charge.

Dividend Payable

The final step in the dividend-calculation process (Step 11) is to establish whether a dividend is payable. This is determined by subtracting any deficit that has been carried forward (or placed in a claims fluctuation reserve) from the dividend earned for the experience period. If this figure is positive, it is the amount of the dividend; if the figure is negative, it is the amount of the cumulative deficit that is to be carried forward.

In Table 15-1, only one type of coverage is experience rated. However, when an employer has more than one type of coverage that is experience rated with the same insurance company, a single dividend is usually determined for the combined package. This typically involves the determination of a separate claims charge for each coverage and a single retention charge for the entire package. Because "losses" for one type of coverage will often be offset by "gains" for other types of coverage, the relative fluctuation in the overall experience will tend to be less than the fluctuations in the experience of some or all of the individual coverages. Therefore, the overall premium can often be reduced (or the dividend increased) because the insurance company will levy a lower risk charge and/or require a lower contingency reserve.

Renewal Rating

Experience rating also is often used to develop future premiums for group insurance contracts based on the past experience of the group. For the most part, the procedure is similar to that for determining dividends, and in fact, the two procedures usually are done at the same time. However, there are some differences: In most cases, the experience-rating period will be three to five years instead of one year, and thus cumulative premiums and charges for this period will be used. In addition, a more conservative (lower) credibility factor will normally be applied. For example, an insurance company that uses a credibility factor of 0.8 for dividend purposes for a particular contract might use a factor of 0.6 for renewal-rating purposes. Furthermore, since a premium is being developed for the future, it is also necessary to adjust past claims and the retention, not only to reflect current cost levels, but also to include expected trends for the next year. Adjustments must also be made to account for any changes in the coverage. Once a renewal premium is calculated that is expected to be sufficient to cover claims and retention, an additional amount is added for future dividends. This, in effect, becomes a safety margin for the insurance company should both claims and retention be higher than anticipated; otherwise it is returned as an experience dividend to the policyholder.

Experience rating may also be used to develop the initial premiums for any transferred business. This will require the insurance company to obtain past data from the policyholder regarding its experience with the previous carrier. A policyholder may be reluctant to provide this information because poor experience, and the resulting rate increase, is often the reason for changing insurance companies. However, the existence of the poor claims experience is exactly the information needed by the insurance company. In fact, some insurance companies actually refuse to write transferred coverage, particularly for large groups, unless verifiable prior claims experience is provided.

If possible, the past data are used to determine what the premiums and charges would have been if the new contract had been written by the new carrier in previous years. If this can be accomplished, the procedure is a simplified application of the principles previously described. If it cannot be accomplished, manual rating may be used for small groups, but judgment may play a large role in determining the premiums for large groups.

STUDY QUESTIONS

1. The major objective of rate making is to develop rates that are adequate and equitable. What is meant by adequate and equitable?
2. In addition to determining the benefit unit, what decisions must be made in developing a basis on which manual premium rates can be established?
3. The Powell Company has 200 employees covered for $30,000 each under a group term life insurance contract. The sex and age distribution of the employees is as follows:

Sex	Age	Number of Employees
M	30	40
M	40	20
M	50	20
F	30	60
F	40	60

   Determine the initial monthly premium and the monthly premium rate for this group on the basis of the New York minimum premium rates described in this chapter.
4. What characteristics of a group are usually considered in determining disability income rates that are not likely to be considered in determining term life insurance rates?
5. How do insurance companies protect themselves against increases in medical expense claims costs due to inflation?
6. a. What is the rationale for the use of experience rating?
   b. Identify the situations in which experience rating may be used.
7. Given the following information for a group insurance contract, calculate its claims charge:

Premiums paid	$250,000
Claims paid	$190,000
Beginning claim reserve	$ 25,000
Ending claim reserve	$ 35,000

Stop-loss limit	120% of premiums paid
Expected claims	$160,000
Credibility factor	0.7

8. Explain how claims for large amounts of coverage might be treated in the experience-rating process.
9. Explain why paid claims differ from incurred claims.
10. What is the purpose of a stop-loss limit?
11. How does the credibility factor for a group vary by the size of the group and the type of insurance coverage?
12. Why might the full amount of a dividend earned not be paid to a group insurance policyholder?
13. How does experience rating for determining renewal rates differ from experience rating for calculating dividends?

PART
FOUR

Other Nonretirement Benefits and Cafeteria Plans

16

Other Nonretirement Benefits

Objectives

- Explain why employers often provide fringe benefits.
- Identify the types of payments that employers may make to employees for time not worked and explain the tax consequences of each benefit.
- Describe the types of extra cash payments that employers may provide to employees and explain the tax consequences of each.
- Describe the types of services employers often provide to employees and explain the tax consequences of each.

In the first chapter of this book, employee benefits were divided into five categories:

1. Legally required social insurance payments.
2. Payments for private insurance and retirement plans.
3. Payments for time not worked.
4. Extra payments to employees.
5. Services to employees.

Variations exist among employers, but typically about one-third of the sum spent on employee benefits is devoted to payments for legally required social insurance programs. Another one-third spent on employee benefits is devoted to payments for retirement plans and group insurance. Often overlooked is the significance of the remaining types of benefits that may be provided to employees, which—as a group—account for the final one-third of the employee benefit dollars spent by employers. Since the list is extensive, not every possible benefit will be described. Rather, the discussion will be devoted to the following list of more commonly provided "fringe" benefits:

- Vacations.
- Holidays.
- Personal time off with pay.
- Personal time off without pay.
- Supplemental unemployment benefit plans.
- Educational assistance.
- Moving-expense reimbursement.
- Suggestion awards.
- Service awards.
- Productivity and safety achievement awards.
- Holiday bonuses and gifts.
- No-additional-cost services.
- Employee discounts.
- Free parking.
- Transportation.
- Company cars.
- Subsidized eating facilities.
- Dependent-care assistance.
- Wellness programs.
- Employee-assistance programs.
- Financial-planning programs for executives.
- Preretirement-counseling programs.

These benefits are conveniently classified as payments for time not worked, extra cash payments and services. Some of these benefits, such as holidays and vacations, are provided by most employers; other benefits, such as financial planning, are provided by relatively few employers. Some employers provide many such benefits; others provide few. The reasons one employer may provide a certain array of benefits are many: to satisfy the specific needs of its employees, for competitive reasons or because of traditions within its area or industry. Collective bargaining, the personal whims of the employer and state laws may also play a role.

In general, fringe benefit design tends to favor nontaxable benefits because of the additional amount effectively contributed toward such benefits by the U.S. Treasury, thereby resulting in lower compensation costs for the employer. The federal income tax treatment of group insurance, qualified plans, nonqualified deferred compensation and certain types of executive benefits have long been the subject of the statutory rules described throughout this book. Many other areas remained uncertain until the Tax Reform Act of 1984 added Code Section 132, substantially clarifying the tax treatment of fringe benefits by making certain benefits specifically nontaxable and others taxable.

MEANING OF HIGHLY COMPENSATED EMPLOYEE

Several of the benefits discussed in this chapter are subject to nondiscrimination rules. Specifically, these benefits are educational assistance, service awards, safety achievement and productivity awards, no-additional-cost services, employee discounts, dependent-care assistance and employee-assistance programs. In each case, there are rules designed to prevent or discourage the benefit plan from discriminating in favor of highly compensated employees.

The consequences of a discriminatory plan vary. In some cases, no employees can receive benefits on a tax-favored basis; in other cases, this penalty applies to highly compensated employees only.

As used in this chapter, a highly compensated employee is one who meets the definition in Code Section 414(q). This definition is also used for the nondiscrimination rules that apply to qualified retirement plans. A highly compensated employee is an employee who at any time during the current year or the preceding year was one of the following:

- A 5-percent owner of the firm.
- An employee who earned more than $90,803 in annual compensation in 1991 from the employer.
- An employee who earned more than $60,535 in annual compensation in 1991 from the employer and was in the top 20 percent of the firm's employees in terms of compensation.
- An officer of the firm who earned more than $54,481.50 in 1991. In firms with fewer than 500 employees, no more than the greater of three employees or 10 percent of all employees are treated as officers. In firms with 500 or more employees, no more than 50 employees are treated as officers.

All of the above dollar figures are subject to annual indexing.

It is interesting to note that this definition of a highly compensated employee is not the same as the one used with the nondiscrimination rules for self-insured medical reimbursement plans (Chapter 12) or the one used for cafeteria plans (Chapter 17).

PAYMENTS FOR TIME NOT WORKED

Vacations

Paid vacation plans vary widely. Since paid vacations are an important employee incentive, most employers take considerable interest in the details of the vacation plan and design it to closely fit their own objectives and company or industry traditions, with some influence from competitive forces. There has been a long-term trend toward increasing the amount of paid vacation time in all industries in the United States; however, the current interest in increasing productivity may result in a slowing of this trend.

Typical design features of paid vacation plans include a specified waiting period for new employees before the full amount of paid vacation is earned, and some increase in the amount of vacation time for a specified number of years of service. Some employers allow employees to carry over unused vacation days from year to year, usually within limits, while others require vacation days to be used during the current year or be forfeited. There are very few governmental regulatory constraints on the design of vacation plans. However, paid vacations are an issue that must be the subject of good-faith bargaining for a group of employees forming a collective bargaining unit under applicable federal or state labor law.

The tax treatment of vacation pay is straightforward. In general, employees are individuals using the cash method of accounting, so they pay taxes on vacation pay in the year the payments are received. If the employer uses the accrual method of accounting, as most businesses do, the employer obtains a tax deduction under Code Section 463 for accrued vacation pay reasonably expected to be paid during the current and succeeding taxable year.

Vacation pay plans are almost always funded on a pay-as-you-go method. However, some employers pay money into a trust fund that is used to make vacation payments—a case usually the result of collective bargaining agreements.

Holidays

Almost all employers pay employees for some holidays on which the business is closed, such as Christmas Day or New Year's Day. However, the calendar is full of holidays, and not all businesses elect to close their doors on all of them, or to pay employees for all days on which the business is closed. This decision is not entirely an employee benefits decision, because marketing factors in the particular business also play a part. Also, in some states, certain businesses, such as banks, are required to close on certain legal holidays.

Personal Time Off with Pay

Personal situations that require an employee to be away from work often arise. Consequently, many employers allow employees to take time off with pay for certain reasons, the more common of which include the following:

- *Reserve/National Guard duty.* Laws sometimes require that employees be given time off for reserve or National Guard duty, but there is no stipulation that pay continue during this period. However, the majority of employers compensate their employees for the difference between their regular pay and any compensation received for the reserve or National Guard duty.
- *Voting time.* Many states require that employees be given time off to vote, but most of these laws do not require the employee to be compensated for this time. However, the time period is short, usually no more than two hours, and most employers who grant such time off continue regular pay. Since polls are typically open 12 hours or more, it is questionable whether this benefit is necessary in the absence of state law.
- *Jury duty.* Most employers grant (and may be required to grant) time off for jury duty. Since employees are usually compensated for jury duty, some employers pay only the difference between this amount and an employee's regular pay. However, the amount paid for jury duty is small and often just barely covers an employee's extra expenses. Therefore, many employers continue regular compensation with no deduction.

- *A death in the family.* Employers often allow up to five days off with pay because of the death of a family member. At a minimum, this usually includes the death of a parent, child, spouse or other relative residing in the household. Some employers allow a shorter period of time, such as a day or a half day, to attend funerals of other relatives and sometimes even persons other than relatives.
- *Sabbatical leaves.* Sabbatical leaves are well established as employee benefits at educational institutions. Typically, faculty members are permitted an extended leave of a semester or a year after a specified period of service, such as seven years. During the sabbatical leave, the faculty member receives full or partial pay while performing no services for the employer. However, the faculty member is often required to complete a research project or some similar activity as a condition of the sabbatical. Noneducational employers, particularly those having employees with professional degrees, sometimes provide similar benefits to professional employees in order to afford them an opportunity to engage in research or study that is not directly job related.

Some less common reasons that employers may allow time off with pay include an employee's marriage and serving as a witness in a court proceeding. Since other personal reasons for needing time off may occasionally arise, employers may grant two or three days of personal leave that can be taken at an employee's discretion.

Personal Time Off without Pay

In addition to granting time off with pay, employers may allow employees to take time off without pay. Reasons for such leave may include active military duty, extended vacations, honeymoons, education and maternity leave after maternity disability has ended. Usually such time off is subject to the approval of the employer.

Recent years have seen the introduction in Congress of several bills that would mandate employers to allow employees, both male and female, to take unpaid leaves of absence because of the birth or adoption of a child or serious illness of a child, spouse or parent. Most of the bills would require at least 10 weeks of unpaid leave but would apply only to employers with some minimum number of employees, ranging from 20 to 50.

Supplemental Unemployment Benefit Plans

A supplemental unemployment benefit (SUB) plan is designed to supplement state unemployment insurance benefits for workers who are unemployed. These plans are most common among larger employers in industries where cyclical unemployment prevails, such as the steel and automobile industries. Most such plans are negotiated as part of collective bargaining agreements.

SUB plans are attractive to employees in cyclical industries as a way of maintaining income levels through periods of layoff, and this is obviously why workers negotiate for them. However, employers can find some benefit in these plans as well, because they help to increase management's flexibility when layoffs are required because of economic conditions or technological change.

SUB plans negotiated as part of collective bargaining agreements almost always require employers to contribute to a SUB fund in an amount based on the compensation of currently active employees. The employer receives a current deduction for contributions to the fund, and the fund itself may be exempt from federal income taxes under Code Section 501(c)(17). Benefit payments to employees are fully taxable. The fund is typically maintained by trustees chosen by the labor union that is the collective bargaining agent, and often a common fund is maintained for several employers.

The two principal methods of designing the plan are the pooled fund method and the individual account method. Under the pooled fund method, which is the most common, employer contributions are determined on the basis of hours worked and paid into a pooled SUB fund. Benefits are paid to workers out of this fund as they become due. Under the individual account method, the funding is similar but the plan establishes a separate account for each eligible employee, somewhat similar to an account in a qualified defined-contribution plan. The employee is given certain rights to draw on the account during periods of layoff, with the employee often having a right to the entire account balance in the event of permanent unemployment. Some plans of this type involve contributions by employees as well as the employer.

EXTRA CASH PAYMENTS

Educational Assistance

For several years, the Internal Revenue Code has provided favorable tax treatment to employees who receive benefits from their employers for educational assistance. At this writing, Code Section 127 allows employees to receive annually the first $5,250 of these benefits on a tax-free basis, but this Code section is scheduled to expire on December 31, 1991. (This date has been extended several times before and will probably be extended again, or the Code section may be made permanent.) In order for benefits to be tax free, the employer's plan cannot discriminate in favor of officers, shareholders, highly compensated employees or their dependents. In addition, no more than 5 percent of the benefits may be paid out to shareholders or owners (or their dependents) who are more-than-5-percent owners of the firm.

Eligible benefits include tuition, fees and books. The costs of supplies and equipment are also included as long as they are not retained after completion of the course. Meals, lodging and transportation associated with educational expenses cannot be received tax free.

There are also some limitations on the types of education that may be received. As a general rule, benefits cannot be paid for graduate-level courses leading to a law, business, medical or other advanced, academic or professional degree. Courses involving sports, games or hobbies are also ineligible for favorable tax treatment. Although an employer's plan *could* pay for any of these types of courses, an employee would be taxed on the value of the employer's contribution to their cost.

One change made by the 1989 Budget Act allows benefits to be paid in excess of $5,250 and for graduate courses to the extent that an employee would have been eligible to take an income tax deduction if the employee had paid for them.

If Congress fails to extend the favorable tax treatment of a broadly defined educational assistance program, employees will still be allowed to deduct any educational expenses that are incurred (1) to maintain or improve a skill required in employment or (2) to meet the express requirements of the employer as a condition for retaining employment. To the extent that these benefits are paid for by the employer, they will be treated as taxable compensation. However, the corresponding deduction effectively makes them a tax-free benefit. Other types of educational expenses, such as costs incurred to qualify the employee for a new trade or business, are not deductible.

Moving-Expense Reimbursements

Most large employers encourage geographical mobility by their work force and like to be able to recruit workers from a large geographical area. Therefore, a plan for reimbursing employees for moving expenses can significantly serve the employer's interests, by offering an inducement to employees to move in accordance with the employer's needs.

Under Code Section 217, an employee is allowed an itemized deduction for moving expenses (without any "floor" limitation like that applicable to itemized medical deductions) if the moving expenses were incurred in connection with the commencement of work at a new principal place of work. Moving expenses for this purpose include only expenses for:

- Moving household goods and personal effects.
- Traveling, including meals and lodging, from the old residence to the new.
- Travel, meals and lodging for house-hunting purposes.
- Meals and lodging in temporary quarters during any 30 consecutive days after obtaining the new job.
- Selling the old residence, purchasing the new residence or corresponding lease expenses for renters.

There is no dollar limit on the deduction for the first two items. However, the house-hunting and temporary living items together are deductible only up to $1,500; sale, purchase or lease expenses are deductible only up to $3,000, reduced by any deductible house hunting and temporary living expenses.

If the employee itemizes deductions, any employer reimbursement of these expenses to the employee involves a compensating tax deduction by the employee, so that the moving expense reimbursement is a form of compensation income that is tax free. If the employer reimbursement exceeds the amount deductible, the additional amount is taxable income to the employee. If the reimbursement does not fully cover the moving expense, the employee can deduct the additional unreimbursed moving expense within the limits of Section 217.

However, if the employee does not itemize deductions, moving expenses are not deductible and any employer reimbursement is taxable income that is not offset by any deduction. Thus, employer reimbursements to employees who do not itemize are a significantly less valuable benefit than corresponding payments to employees who do itemize. Some employers may consider making additional payments to nonitemizers to equalize moving expense benefits.

Suggestion Awards

Some employers, particularly those in manufacturing industries, give awards to employees who make suggestions that, if implemented, will improve the operating efficiency of the firm. The awards are often a percentage of the firm's estimated savings over some specified future period of time but may be subject to a maximum dollar amount. If a suggestion plan is properly administered, the benefits of the plan may far exceed its costs while at the same time increasing the motivation and involvement of employees.

Suggestion awards are included in an employee's gross income for tax purposes.

Service Awards

Many employers provide awards to employees for length of service. These awards are often nominal for short periods of service (five or ten years) and may consist of such items as key chains, flowers or pens. Awards typically increase in value for longer periods of service, and employees may actually be given some choice in the award received.

If the value of a service award is *de minimis*, it is not included in an employee's income. To be *de minimis*, the value of the benefit must be so minimal that accounting for the cost of the benefit would be unreasonable or administratively impractical. Service awards of higher value may also be excludible from an employee's income if they are considered *qualified plan awards*. However, the total amount excludible from an employee's income for qualified plan awards (which also include awards for safety) cannot exceed $1,600 per year. Qualified plan awards must be provided under a permanent written program that does not discriminate in favor of officers, shareholders or highly compensated employees. In addition, the average annual cost of all awards under the plan cannot exceed $400.

Productivity and Safety Achievement Awards

Some employers provide awards for productivity and safety achievement. Productivity awards are fully treated as compensation. While awards for safety achievement that are given to professional, administrative, managerial or clerical employees are fully taxable, such awards are treated as qualified plan awards for other employees and are included in the $1,600 figure mentioned previously under service awards.

Holiday Bonuses and Gifts

Many employers give gifts or bonuses to employees, particularly around Christmas. Since the value of such gifts is typically small, some employees tend to resent gifts of money. Therefore, gifts such as liquor or a ham are often given.

As with service awards, a holiday gift does not result in taxation for an employer as long as the market value of the gift is small.

EMPLOYER-PROVIDED SERVICES

Employer-provided services are an important benefit, particularly for businesses where valuable services can be provided as an employee benefit without significant additional costs to the employer—for example, free travel for the employees of airlines. The fringe benefit provisions of Code Section 132 have a significant impact on this type of benefit planning, as will be discussed.

No-Additional-Cost Services

No-additional-cost services are those that are sold to the public in the ordinary course of the employer's business and can be provided by the employer to employees without incurring any substantial additional costs. The transportation, communications, lodging and entertainment businesses are the most likely businesses able to provide employee benefits in this category. As long as the following rules are satisfied, the cost of these services is not includable in an employee's gross income for tax purposes:

- The services cannot be provided on a basis that discriminates in favor of highly compensated employees.
- The employer must not incur any significant additional cost or lost revenue in providing the service. For example, giving a standby ticket to an airline employee if there were unsold seats on a flight would satisfy this requirement, but giving an airline ticket to an employee when potential paying customers were denied seats would not.
- The services must be those that are provided in the employer's line of business in which the employee actually works. Therefore, if a business owns both an airline and a chain of hotels, an employee of the hotels can be given a room as a tax-free benefit but not an airline ticket. However, unrelated employers in the same line of business, such as airlines, may enter into reciprocal arrangements under which employees of any party to the arrangement may obtain services from the other parties.

Employee Discounts

Discounts on merchandise sold by the employer are an important employee benefit, especially in retail industries. Sometimes, there is an additional business reason for such benefits; for example, a retailer may wish to have its salespeople wearing clothing or cosmetics from the store as a way of demonstrating these products to customers.

These discounts are not includable in the taxable income of employees if the discounts are available on a nondiscriminatory basis, in the same sense as discussed in the preceding section. The exclusion does not apply to discounts on employee purchases of investment property, such as securities or real estate, that could typically be resold by the employee as a way of obtaining additional cash compensation.

The goods or services available for tax-free discounting must be those that are offered for sale by the employer to nonemployee customers in the ordinary course of the employer's line of business in which the employee works. This line of business limitation is similar to that applicable to the services described in the preceding section.

Free Parking

Free parking for employees during working hours is often not even thought of as an employee benefit if the business premises are in suburban locations where parking is customarily provided. However, where parking is scarce, free parking near the business premises may be considered as a form of employee benefit.

Free parking for employees is not considered taxable income to employees, even if the parking is available on a basis favoring officers, owners or highly compensated employees.

Transportation

Some employers provide benefits to employees for transportation to and from work. This benefit may be in the form of reimbursement for commuting expenses, but such reimbursement generally creates additional taxable income for employees. However, tokens, vouchers and reimbursements to cover the cost of commuting by public transportation are considered a *de minimis* benefit under Code Section 132 as long as the subsidy does not exceed $15 per month.

As a method of conserving energy, many employers were encouraged in the early 1980s to provide vanpools for employees. While few new plans have been established recently, a number of such plans still exist. Essentially, the employer purchases vans, and one employee is designated as the driver. The driver then picks up several other employees and takes them to and from work. The cost to employees is usually modest and often covers only the cost of maintaining the van. Even though the employer may bear all the cost of purchasing the van, savings do arise from having to provide fewer parking places. Also, traffic congestion at the work site is reduced.

The cost of any employer subsidy for a vanpool is passed on to riders as additional compensation.

Company Cars

Employers often provide employees with company cars (or other types of vehicles). In addition to using a vehicle for business proposes, an employee may also be allowed to use the car for commuting to and from work and for other personal uses. However, an employee who drives a company car for personal use must include the value of this use in his or her taxable income.

The method for valuing the use of a car is determined by the employer. There are three alternatives available. The first alternative is for the employer to report the entire value of the car as taxable income. This value is the amount an unrelated third party would charge for the use of the vehicle in an arms-length transaction. The IRS has prepared a schedule of amounts based on a vehicle's fair market value that should be used for this purpose unless an employer can clearly justify the use of a lower value. If the employer uses this alternative, the employee can claim an income tax deduction for any business use of the vehicle. However, this deduction is subject to the 2 percent floor requirement for miscellaneous deductions.

A second alternative is to report a value that is based solely on the employee's use of the vehicle. Under IRS regulations, a mileage rate of 24 cents per mile of personal use must be used for the first 15,000 miles, after which a rate of 11 cents per mile is used. This alternative is available only if car's fair market value is less than $12,800 and one of the following criteria is satisfied:

- The car is used more than 50 percent for business.
- The car is used each day in an employer-sponsored commuting pool.
- The car is driven at least 10,000 miles per year and is used primarily by employees.

The final alternative is available if the employer has a written policy that the employee must commute in the vehicle and cannot use the vehicle for other than minimal personal use. In this case, the value of the car's use is $1.50 times the number of one-way commutes or $3.00 times the number of round-trip commutes.

Subsidized Eating Facilities

Employers often provide fully or partially subsidized eating facilities for employees. While lunch is the most commonly served meal, breakfast and dinner may also be provided. Such facilities provide a place for employees to discuss common issues and may minimize the chance that employees will take prolonged lunch periods at off-site restaurants. The popularity of these facilities will tend to vary with the price of meals, the convenience of alternative places to eat and the quality of the food served.

The value of meals served to employees may or may not result in taxable income. If the meals are provided without charge, they are tax free as long as they are provided on the business premises and are furnished for the convenience of the employer. In general, meals are considered to be furnished for the employer's convenience if there are inadequate facilities in the area for employees to obtain meals within a reasonable period of time.

The situation is different when a charge is made for meals. If the employees have the option of purchasing the meals, employees who do purchase them will have taxable income to the extent of any subsidy in excess of the employer's cost. However, if a periodic deduction of meals is made from an employee's paycheck regardless of whether the employee eats the meals, the amount of this deduction will be excludible from income only if the meals are furnished for the convenience of the employer.

Dependent-Care Assistance

As the number of families headed by two wage earners or by a single parent has increased, so has the need for child-care facilities. As a result, child-care assistance has become a popular benefit offered by a growing number of employers, particularly those in the service industries. Some firms also provide benefits for the care of other dependents, such as parents. The assistance may be in the form of employer-provided day-care centers or payments to employees.

Under Code Section 129, dependent care is a tax-free benefit to employees up to statutory limits as long as certain requirements are met. The amount of benefits that can be received tax free is limited to $5,000 for single parents and married persons who file jointly and to $2,500 for married persons who file separately. The benefits must be for care to a qualifying individual—a child under age 13 for whom the employee is allowed a dependency deduction on his or her income tax return and a taxpayer's spouse or other dependent who is mentally or physically incapable of caring for himself or herself. Although benefits must generally be for dependent care only, educational expenses at the kindergarten or preschool level can also be paid.

Dependent-care benefits are subject to a series of rules. If the rules are not met, highly compensated employees are taxed on the amount of benefits received. However, the benefits for other employees still retain their tax-free status. The rules are as follows:

- Eligibility, contributions and benefits under the plan cannot discriminate in favor of highly compensated employees or their dependents.
- No more than 25 percent of the benefits may be provided to the class composed of persons who own more than a 5 percent interest in the firm.
- Reasonable notification of the availability of benefits and the terms of the plan must be provided to eligible employees.
- By January 31 of the following year, each employee must receive an annual statement that indicates the amounts paid or expenses incurred by the employer to provide benefits.
- The average benefit provided to nonhighly compensated employees must be at least 55 percent of the average benefit provided to highly compensated employees.

In meeting the 55 percent benefit test, an employer can exclude employees earning under $25,000 if benefits are provided through a salary reduction agreement. For both the 55 percent benefit test and the nondiscrimination rule for eligibility, an employer can exclude employees who (1) are under age 21, (2) have not completed one year of service or (3) are covered under a collective bargaining unit that has bargained over dependent-care benefits.

Even if an employer does not provide assistance for dependent care, other tax-saving options may be available to employees. Under the Code, a tax credit is available so that employees can deduct a portion of unreimbursed expenses. In addition, the employer may have the opportunity to make before-tax contributions to a cafeteria plan that includes dependent care as an option.

Wellness Programs

Traditionally, benefit programs have been designed to provide benefits (1) to employees for their medical expenses and disabilities or (2) to their dependents if the employee should die prematurely. In the last few years, there has been an increasing trend among employers, particularly large corporations, to initiate programs that are designed to promote the well-being of employees and, possibly, their dependents. Some of these programs have been aimed at the discovery and treatment of medical conditions before they become severe and result in large medical expenses, disabilities or death. Other programs have focused on changing the lifestyles of employees in order to eliminate the possible causes of future medical problems. Recent studies have shown that the cost of establishing and maintaining many of these programs are more than offset by the lower amounts paid for medical expense, disability and death benefits. In addition, if long-term disabilities and premature deaths can be eliminated, the expenses associated with training new employees can be minimized. Many firms also feel these programs increase productivity by improving the employees' sense of well-being, their work attitudes and their family relationships.

Medical-Screening Programs

The use of a medical-screening program to discover existing medical conditions is not new, but it has often covered the costs, frequently up to a specific dollar limit, of routine physical examinations only for selected groups of management employees. Although this benefit may be highly valued by these employees, and its use as an executive benefit has been increasing somewhat, there are doubts—even among the medical profession—as to its cost effectiveness, particularly when it is provided on an annual basis. Certain medical conditions will undoubtedly be discovered during a complete physical, but most of them could also be diagnosed by less frequent and less costly forms of medical examinations.

Although the number of employers that provide preemployment physicals for new employees has grown, there has been an even greater increase in the number of employers that sponsor periodic medical-screening programs. These screenings detect specific medical problems, such as hypertension (high blood pressure), high cholesterol levels, breast cancer and colon-rectal cancer. Generally, they are conducted at the employment site during the regular working hours of the employees. Sometimes, a screening will be conducted by a physician, but it is usually performed by other lower paid medical professionals. In addition, screenings can sometimes be obtained at little or no cost through such organizations as the American Red Cross, the American Heart Association or the American Cancer Society.

Lifestyle Management Programs

Lifestyle management programs are primarily designed to encourage employees, and occasionally their dependents, to modify their behavior so that they will lead healthier lives. Most of these programs strive to discover and eliminate those conditions that increase the likelihood of cardiovascular problems—the source of a significant percentage of medical expenses and premature deaths. Some of these conditions, such as obesity or smoking, are obvious, but medical screening can also detect less obvious conditions like hypertension, high cholesterol levels and the degree of an employee's physical fitness. The types of programs often instituted to promote cardiovascular health include:

- Fitness programs. These may consist of formal exercise programs or of exercise facilities, such as swimming pools, exercise rooms or jogging tracks. Some employee benefit consultants question whether facilities for competitive sports, such as racquet ball courts, can be cost justified because their availability is limited, and they are often a source of injuries.
- Weight-reduction programs.
- Nutrition programs. These are often established in conjunction with weight-reduction programs, but they can also teach methods of cholesterol reduction even if there is no weight problem.
- Smoking-cessation programs.
- Stress-management programs.

These programs may be available to any employee who expresses an interest in them, or they may be limited only to those employees who have been evaluated and found to be in a high-risk category for cardiovascular disease. This evaluation may consist of questionnaires regarding health history, blood pressure readings, blood chemistry analyses and fitness tests. Generally, these evaluations and meetings to describe the programs and their value are conducted during regular working hours. However, the programs themselves are usually conducted during nonworking hours, such as at lunchtime.

Many wellness programs are designed to include employees, their spouses and sometimes other family members. In many instances, it will not be possible to change an employee's lifestyle unless the lifestyle of his or her entire family also changes. For example, it is not very probable that an employee will stop smoking if his or her spouse also smokes and is making no attempt to stop. Similarly, a weight-reduction or nutrition program will most likely be more effective if all family members alter their eating habits.

Programs designed to eliminate alcohol or drug abuse are another example of lifestyle management. Participation may be voluntary or it can be mandatory for employees who are known to have alcohol or drug problems and who want to keep their jobs. When these programs have been successful, many employers have found a decrease in employee absenteeism.

Some employers have also instituted programs that seek to minimize back problems—the reason for a large percentage of employee absenteeism and disability claims. These programs are generally intended for those employees who have a history of back trouble; they consist of exercises as well as education in how to modify or avoid activities that can aggravate existing back conditions.

More recently, many employers have become concerned with the spread of AIDS and its effect on the cost of benefit plans. As a result, they have instituted educational programs aimed at encouraging employees to avoid those activities that may result in the transmission of AIDS.

Like prescreening programs, the employer may either conduct these activities on the premises or use the resources of other organizations. For example, overweight employees might be sent to Weight Watchers, employees with alcohol problems might be encouraged to attend Alcoholics Anonymous and employees with back problems might be enrolled in programs at a local YMCA or YWCA.

Federal Income Taxation

Most employer expenditures for wellness programs can probably be justified as deductible ordinary and necessary business expenses. It is more difficult to summarize the tax treatment to the employee. Some types of benefits could possibly be excluded from taxation as health or accident benefits. Certain athletic facilities for employees are tax free under Code Section 132(h)(5); other aspects of wellness programs may also be tax free under Code Section 132(e) if they have relatively little monetary value. It is possible, however, that some of these benefits could constitute taxable income.

Employee-Assistance Programs

As the trend toward fostering wellness in the workplace continues, an increasing number of employers are establishing employee-assistance programs. These programs are designed to help employees with certain problems that result in poor job performance, such as the following:

- Alcohol abuse.
- Drug abuse.
- Marital problems.
- Legal problems.
- Financial problems.

Numerous studies have shown that proper treatment of these problems is very cost effective and leads to reduced sick days, hospital costs, disability and absenteeism. It is also argued that employee morale and productivity are increased as a result of the concern shown for employees' personal problems.

An employee-assistance plan uses job performance as the basis for employer concern. Essentially, an employee is told that his or her work is substandard and asked if a problem exists that he or she would like to discuss with someone. If the employee says yes, referral is made to a counselor. No attempt is made by the employee's supervisor to diagnose the specific problem.

The counselor may be a company employee; most often, however, an employer establishes the plan through a hospital or through a professional organization that specializes in such programs. Information provided to the counselor by the employee is kept confidential. Many problems can be solved by discussion between the counselor and the employee, and most plans have 24-hour counseling available, through either a telephone hotline or on-duty personnel. If the counselor cannot solve an employee's problem, it is the counselor's responsibility to make a preliminary determination as to the type of professional help the employee should receive. In many cases, this treatment can be provided under existing medical expense or legal expense plans. The cost of other types of treatment is usually paid totally or in part by the employer. As long as the treatment is for the purpose of alleviating medical conditions, including mental illness, an employee has no taxable income. If the treatment is for a nonmedical condition, the employee will have taxable income as the result of employer payments.

Financial-Planning Programs for Executives

Employers are increasingly providing financial planning as a benefit to employees. Traditionally, this benefit was limited to a small number of top executives. However, many firms are now expanding their programs to also include members of middle management. In addition, financial-planning education and advice are now offered to many employees as part of a broader preretirement-counseling program. Any program in overall financial planning must take into consideration the benefits available under group insurance plans, under social insurance programs and through the individual efforts of employees.

Financial planning is composed of many separate, but interrelated, segments, including:

- Compensation planning. This includes the explanation of employee benefits and an analysis of any available compensation options.
- Preparation of tax returns.
- Estate planning. This includes the preparation of wills and planning to both minimize estate taxes and maintain proper estate liquidity.
- Investment planning. This includes both investment advice and investment management.
- Insurance planning. This includes information on how to meet life insurance, medical expense, disability and property and liability needs.

A financial-planning program may be designed to provide either selected services from the list above or a comprehensive array of services. Comprehensive financial planning can be thought of as a series of interrelated and continuing activities that begin with the collection and analysis of personal and financial information, including the risk attitudes of an employee. This information is used (1) to establish the priorities and time horizons for attaining personal objectives and (2) to develop the financial plan that will meet these objectives. Once the plan is formulated, the next critical step is the actual implementation of the plan. A proper financial-planning program should also include a process for measuring the performance of any plan so that, if unacceptable, either the plan can be changed or the objectives of the employee revised.

Financial-planning services may be (1) provided by an organization's own employees; (2) purchased from outside specialists, such as lawyers, accountants, insurance agents or stockbrokers; or (3) purchased from firms that do comprehensive financial planning. Significant differences exist among financial-planning firms; some operate solely on a fee basis and give only advice and counseling. If this is the case, it is then the employee's responsibility to have his or her own attorney, insurance agent or other financial professional implement any decisions. These financial-planning firms will often work closely with these other professionals in handling the employee's affairs.

Other financial-planning firms operate on a product-oriented basis and sell products (usually insurance or investments) in addition to other financial-planning services. These firms receive commissions from the products they sell in addition to any fees paid by the employer. However, the fees of such firms may be lower to reflect the commissions. The insurance or investment advice of these firms may be slanted in favor of the products they sell. Therefore, employers must make sure that this advice will be unbiased and will be presented in a professional manner.

Taxation

Fees paid for financial planning are deductible by the employer as long as the total compensation paid to an employee is reasonable. The amount of any fees paid to a financial-planning firm or other professional on behalf of individual employees becomes taxable income to the employee. However, an employee may be allowed an offsetting income tax deduction for certain services relating to tax matters and investment advice.

Preretirement-Counseling Programs

Organizations, aware of the pitfalls that can await unprepared retired employees, have increasingly begun to offer preretirement counseling. It has been estimated that this benefit is offered by approximately 75 percent of companies with 20,000 or more employees. For companies with under 1,000 employees, the figure is closer to 15 or 20 percent. Most of these firms have made this benefit available to all employees over a specific age (such as 50 or 55), but some organizations allow employees of any age to participate. Preretirement-counseling programs differ from financial-counseling programs in that there is very little individual counseling. Rather, employees meet in groups to listen to media presentations and speakers, and they are given the opportunity to ask questions and discuss their concerns. This counseling typically may take place during nonworking hours, but there is an increasing trend to have it provided during work hours, often in a concentrated one or two-day period. Most organizations encourage spouses to participate. Although one program is often developed for all employees, some organizations vary their programs for different classifications of employees, such as management employees and blue-collar workers.

When these programs are successful, the fears that many employees have about retirement can be alleviated. They will learn that with proper planning, retirement cannot only be financially possible, but it can also be a meaningful period in their lives.

Financial Planning

Some preretirement-counseling programs devote at least half their time to the financial aspects of retirement. Because proper financial planning for retirement must begin many years prior to actual retirement, the amount of time that will be devoted to this subject will be greatest in those programs that encourage employees to begin participation at younger ages.

Some financial-planning meetings help employees identify and determine what their financial needs will be after retirement, and what resources will be available to meet these needs from the organization's benefit plans and from social security. If retirement needs will not be met by these sources, employees are informed about how individual effort can supplement retirement income through savings or investments. They are also told about the specific advantages and risks associated with each method of savings or investment. Unlike financial-planning programs for executives, preretirement financial counseling is conducted on a group basis and is unlikely to provide investment advice on an individual basis or through an investment management service.

Other Aspects of Preretirement Counseling

Preretirement counseling focuses on other aspects of retirement besides financial need. Some of the following questions must also be faced by most retired workers and are often addressed by preretirement-counseling programs:

- Living arrangements. What are the pros and cons of selling a house and moving into an apartment or condominium? Is relocation in a sun-belt state away from family members and friends advisable?
- Health. Can changes in lifestyle lead to healthier retirement years?
- Free time. How can the time that was previously devoted to work be used? What opportunities are available for volunteer work or part-time employment? What leisure activities or community activities can be adopted that will continue into retirement? Studies have shown that alcoholism, divorce and suicide tend to increase among the retired. Most of this increase has been attributed to the lack of activities to fill free time and to the problems encountered by husbands and wives who are constantly together for the first time in their lives.

Sources of Preretirement Counseling

An organization may establish and maintain its own program of preretirement counseling. However, many organizations, such as benefit counseling firms, the National Council on the Aging and the American Association of Retired Persons, have developed packaged programs that are sold to other organizations. These programs typically consist of media presentations and information regarding the types of speakers that should be used in counseling sessions. Generally, these packaged programs are flexible enough to be used with almost any type of employee group.

Taxation

The costs of preretirement-counseling programs are deductible business expenses to employers. As long as no specific services are provided to employees on an individual basis, the employees do not have taxable income to report as a result of participating in these programs.

STUDY QUESTIONS

1. What design features are usually found in paid vacation plans?
2. What factors other than employee benefit decisions determine the holidays on which a business is closed?
3. Under what circumstances might an employer allow employees to have time off with pay?
4. a. Describe the two principal methods for designing supplemental unemployment benefit plans.
   b. What is the tax treatment of employer contributions to such funds?
   c. How are benefit payments taxed to employees?
5. With respect to an educational-assistance plan that meets the requirements of Code Section 127, explain
   a. The amount of benefits that may be received tax free.
   b. The types of benefits that may be received.
   c. The nondiscrimination rules that apply.
6. Under what circumstances may each of the following employer-provided services be received tax free by employees?
   a. Moving expenses.
   b. No-additional-cost services.
   c. Employee discounts.
   d. Free parking.
   e. Transportation reimbursement.
   f. Subsidized eating facilities.
   g. Dependent-care assistance.
7. What are the advantages that may offset the cost of wellness programs?
8. Why are many wellness programs designed to include family members of employees?
9. a. What is the purpose of employee-assistance plans?
   b. How do employee-assistance plans operate?
10. Explain how financial-planning programs for executives differ from the financial planning that is available under preretirement-counseling programs.
11. In addition to financial planning, what are the other aspects of preretirement-counseling programs?

17

Cafeteria Plans

Objectives

- Explain the rationale for the use of cafeteria plans.
- Describe the general nature of cafeteria plans and identify the various types of cafeteria plans.
- Explain the barriers that must be overcome before a cafeteria plan can be implemented.
- Explain the issues that must be resolved to properly design a cafeteria plan.

For several years, some organizations have had benefit plans that give a limited number of key executives some choice in the selection of types and levels of employee benefits that will be provided with employer contributions. Although many organizations have benefit programs in which optional or supplemental benefits may be elected by all (or many) employees, the cost of these benefits must normally be borne by the employees on an aftertax, payroll-deduction basis. With the possible exception of an HMO option, employees have no choice about how employer dollars will be spent.

In the past few years, however, many organizations have established benefit programs in which all (or almost all) the employees can design their own benefit packages by purchasing benefits with a prespecified amount of employer dollars from a number of available options. Generally, these *cafeteria plans* (often referred to as flexible benefit plans or cafeteria compensation plans) also allow additional benefits to be purchased on a payroll-deduction basis. Today, it is estimated that at least 25 percent of employers with more than 1,000 employees have a full-fledged cafeteria plan. Even more of these employers and many smaller employers offer flexible spending accounts.

THE RATIONALE FOR CAFETERIA PLANS

The growth in employee benefits has caused two problems. First, some employers feel that many employees do not recognize and appreciate the magnitude of their employee benefits because as benefits increase, employee appreciation often seems to decrease. Advocates of cafeteria plans argue that by giving employees a stated dollar amount with which they must select their own benefits (from a list of options), employees will become more aware of the actual cost of these benefits and will be more likely to appreciate the benefits they choose.

A second problem is that the inflexible benefit structure of conventional employee benefit plans does not adequately meet the various benefit needs of all employees, often leading to employee dissatisfaction. For example, single employees often resent the medical coverage that married employees receive for their families, since single employees receive no benefit of corresponding value. Similarly, employees who have no dependents often see little value in life insurance and would prefer other benefits. Those who favor the concept of cafeteria plans feel that such dissatisfaction can be minimized if employees have the option to select their own benefits. Advocates of cafeteria plans hope that this increased employee satisfaction will result in a better employee-retention record and in greater ability to attract new employees.

Some employers see the cafeteria approach to benefit planning as an opportunity to control the escalating benefit costs associated with inflation and with the new requirements of recently enacted federal and state legislation. Since a cafeteria plan is essentially a defined-contribution plan rather than a defined-benefit plan, it provides a number of opportunities for controlling increases in costs. For example, it may encourage employees to choose medical expense options that have larger deductibles so they can more efficiently use the fixed number of dollars allotted to them under the plan. A cafeteria plan may also enable the employer to pass on to employees any increased benefit costs that result from having to comply with legislation that mandates additional benefits. In addition, since increases in employer contributions for optional benefits are not directly related to increases in benefit costs, the employer can grant percentage increases in the amounts available for benefits that are less than the actual overall increase in employee benefit costs.

It should be noted that early cafeteria plans were designed primarily to meet the varying needs of employees. In contrast, newer plans are much more likely to be instituted as a cost-saving technique.

THE NATURE OF CAFETERIA PLANS

In its purest sense, a cafeteria plan can be defined as any employee benefit plan that allows an employee to have some choice in designing his or her own benefit package by selecting different types or levels of benefits that are funded with employer dollars. At this extreme, a benefit plan that allows an employee to select an HMO as an option to an insured medical expense plan can be classified as a cafeteria plan. However, the more common use of the term *cafeteria plan* denotes something much broader—a plan in which choices can be made among several different types of benefits, including cash.

Prior to the addition of Code Section 125 by the Revenue Act of 1978, the use of cafeteria plans had potentially adverse tax consequences for an employee. If an employee had a choice among benefits that were normally nontaxable (such as medical expense insurance or disability income insurance) and benefits that were normally taxable (such as life insurance in excess of $50,000 or cash), then the doctrine of constructive receipt would result in an employee's being taxed as if he or she had elected the maximum taxable benefits that could have been obtained under the plan. Therefore, if an employee could elect cash in lieu of being covered under the employer's medical expense plan, an employee who elected to remain in the medical expense plan would have taxable income merely because cash could have been elected. Obviously, this tax environment was not conducive to the use of cafeteria plans unless the only benefits contained in them were normally of a non-taxable nature.

Permissible Benefits

Currently, Code Section 125 defines a cafeteria plan as a written plan under which all participants are employees and under which all participants may choose between two or more benefits consisting of *qualified benefits* and cash. Qualified benefits essentially include any welfare benefits excluded from taxation under the Internal Revenue Code except scholarships and fellowships, transportation benefits, educational assistance, no-additional-cost services and employee discounts. Thus medical expense benefits, disability benefits, accidental death and dismemberment benefits, vacations, coverage under a qualified legal expense plan and dependent-care assistance (such as day care centers) can be included in a cafeteria plan. The Code also allows group term life insurance to be included even in amounts exceeding $50,000. In general, a cafeteria plan cannot include benefits that defer compensation except for a qualified Section 401(k) or similar plan.

The prohibition of benefits that defer compensation has an important impact on vacation benefits. If an employee elects vacation benefits for the plan year of a cafeteria plan, the vacation days cannot be carried over into the following plan year because this would be a deferral of compensation. (Note: Regular vacation days are considered to have been taken before the additional days elected under the cafeteria plan.) However, an employee can elect to exchange these days for cash as long as the election is made and the cash is actually received prior to the end of the plan year. If this is not done, the days are forfeited and their value is lost.

Because of recent IRS regulations, the term *cash* is actually broader than it would otherwise appear. In addition to the actual receipt of dollars, a benefit is treated as cash as long as (1) it is not a benefit specifically prohibited by Section 125 (one that defers compensation or is among the list of previously mentioned exceptions, such as scholarships and educational assistance) and (2) it is provided on a taxable basis. This latter provision means that either (1) the cost of the benefit is paid by the employee with aftertax dollars on a payroll-deduction basis or (2) employer dollars are used to obtain the benefit, but the employer reports the cost of the benefit as taxable income for the employee. This recent change, for example, would allow the inclusion of group automobile insurance in a cafeteria plan. It also allows long-term disability coverage to be provided on an aftertax basis, so that disability income benefits can be received tax free.

As long as a benefit plan offering choice meets the definition of a cafeteria plan, the issue of constructive receipt does not apply. Employees will have taxable income only to the extent that normally taxable benefits are elected. These include group term life insurance in excess of $50,000 and cash. An employer can have a benefit plan that offers choice but does not meet the statutory definition of a cafeteria plan. In such a case, the issue of constructive receipt will come into play if the plan contains any benefits that normally result in taxable income.

Benefit Election

Section 125 requires that benefit elections under a cafeteria plan be made prior to the beginning of a plan year. These elections cannot be changed during the plan year except under certain specified circumstances if the plan allows such changes. While there is no requirement that these changes be included in a plan, some or all of them are included in most plans.

Changes in benefit elections are permissible under the following circumstances:

- *Changes in family status.* IRS regulations do not specifically define what is meant by changes in family status. However, the regulations include examples of the following:
  1. An employee's marriage or divorce.
  2. The death of an employee's spouse or a dependent.
  3. The birth or adoption of a child.
  4. The commencement or termination of employment by the employee's spouse.
  5. A change from part-time to full-time employment status or vice versa by the employee or the employee's spouse.
  6. An unpaid leave of absence taken by either the employee or the employee's spouse.
  7. A significant change in an employee's or spouse's health coverage that is attributable to the spouse's employment.
- *Separation from service.* An employee who separates from service during a period of coverage may revoke existing benefit elections and terminate the receipt of benefits. However, the plan must prohibit the employee from making new benefit elections for the remainder of the plan year if he or she returns to service for the employer. It should be noted that an employee must be allowed to continue health insurance coverage under COBRA upon separation from service.
- *Cessation of required contributions.* A cafeteria plan can terminate coverage if an employee fails to make the required premium payments for the benefits elected. The employee is then prohibited from making new elections for the remainder of the plan year.

- *Plan cost changes.* A cafeteria plan can allow for an automatic adjustment of employee contributions if the cost of a health plan is increased or decreased by an insurance company or other independent third-party provider of benefits. Such an adjustment is not allowed because of changes in self-insured health plans. Regulations also allow the revocation of previous elections and the selection of another health plan with *similar* coverage if costs are increased *significantly.* IRS regulations do not define either of the italicized terms.
- *Plan coverage changes.* An employee may also change to a *similar* health plan if a third-party provider of health benefits *significantly* curtails or ceases to provide health coverage during a plan year. This provision is particularly helpful in situations involving the insolvency of a provider of health benefits.

TYPES OF PLANS

Core-Plus Plans

Probably the most common type of cafeteria plan is one that offers a basic core of benefits to all employees, plus a second layer of optional benefits that permits an employee to choose which benefits he or she will add to the basic benefits. These optional benefits can be "purchased" with dollars, or credits, that are given to the employee as part of the benefit package. If these credits are inadequate to purchase the desired benefits, an employee can make additional purchases with aftertax contributions or with before-tax reductions under a flexible spending account.

Perhaps the best way to demonstrate how cafeteria plans operate is to include a brief description of some existing plans.

> EXAMPLE 1: This is the core-plus plan of an educational organization with 3,000 employees. While this type of plan is common, it should be noted that the list of optional benefits is more extensive than what is found in most cafeteria plans.
>
> All employees receive a minimum level of benefits, called *basic benefits.* These include
>
> - Term life insurance equal to 1½ times salary.
> - Travel accident insurance (when on the employer's business).
> - Medical expense insurance for the employee and dependents.
> - Disability income insurance.
>
> Employees are also given *flexible credits,* equal to between 3 and 6 percent of salary (depending on length of service, with the maximum reached after ten years), which can be used to purchase additional or "optional" benefits. There is new election of benefits each year, and no carryover of any unused credits is allowed. The optional benefits include:

- Additional life insurance equal to one times salary.
- Accidental death insurance when the basic travel accident insurance does not apply.
- Term life insurance on dependents.
- Dental insurance for the employee and dependents.
- An annual physical examination for the employee.
- Up to two weeks additional vacation time.
- Cash.

If an employee does not have enough flexible credits to purchase the desired optional benefits, additional amounts may be contributed on a payroll-deduction basis for all but more vacation time. In addition, a salary reduction may be elected for contributions to a flexible spending account that provides dependent-care-assistance benefits.

A variation of the core-plus approach is to have the plan be an "average" plan for which the employee makes no contribution. If certain benefits are reduced, the employee may then receive credits that can be used either to increase other benefits or, if the plan allows, to increase cash compensation. Additional benefits can also be typically obtained through employee payroll deductions.

EXAMPLE 2: This plan covers 15,000 nonunion employees in one division of a major industrial conglomerate.

Employees may elect to reduce certain benefits and receive credits that can be used to purchase additional benefits, can be taken in cash, or can be contributed to the company's 401(k) plan. Additional benefits may be purchased on a payroll-deduction basis.

The plan applies to four types of benefits:

1. Medical expense insurance.
2. Employee life insurance.
3. Accidental death and dismemberment insurance.
4. Dependent life insurance.

Several medical expense insurance options are available. The standard coverage, for which there is neither a charge nor a credit, provides basic hospitalization coverage for 120 days, surgical coverage based on a predetermined schedule and major medical coverage for 80 percent of expenses after a yearly deductible ($100 for an individual and $200 for a family) has been met. Lifetime benefits are limited to a maximum of $100,000. Employees may elect a more comprehensive option that offers 365 days of hospital coverage, a higher surgical schedule and major medical coverage with a larger maximum and more favorable coinsurance and deductible provisions. This option results in an additional charge to the employee. On the other hand, employees may elect a less comprehensive option that results in a credit. In addition, several HMO options are available, all of which provide credits.

There are several employee life insurance options that range from ½ to five times salary. The standard coverage for which there is no credit or charge is 1½ times salary.

Although several supplemental accidental death and dismemberment options and a single dependent life insurance option are available, they result in a charge to the employee. In effect, there is no basic benefit in these areas.

Modular Plans

Another type of cafeteria plan is one in which an employee has a choice among several predesigned benefit packages. Typically, at least one of the packages can be selected without any employee cost. If an employee selects a more expensive package, the employee will be required to contribute to the cost of the package. Some employers may also include a bare-bones benefit package, which results in cash being paid to employees who select it.

Under some cafeteria plans using this approach (often referred to as a modular approach), the predesigned packages may have significant differences. A comparison of two packages may show one to be better than others in certain cases but inferior in other cases. Other employers using this approach have virtually identical packages, with the major difference being in the option selected for the medical expense coverage. For example, the plan of one large bank offers three traditional insured plans, two HMOs and a PPO.

> **EXAMPLE 3:** This is a large financial institution whose cafeteria plan covers almost 20,000 employees.
>
> There are seven predesigned benefit packages that can be chosen, with each package designed for a specific segment of the employee population. Each package contains one of three medical expense plans and varying amounts of group term life insurance. The packages contain differing combinations of dental insurance, vision coverage and dependent care benefits. All packages contain the same level of disability income coverage.
>
> A "cost" is associated with each package. Some packages cost an employee nothing, other packages require an employee contribution and at least one option has a negative cost—an employee who selects it gets additional cash compensation. The cost of each package can vary for two reasons. First, an employee can elect whether to have medical expense coverage for dependents. Second, HMO and PPO choices are available in many of the employee locations.

Flexible Spending Accounts

Section 125 also allows employees to purchase certain benefits on a before-tax basis through the use of a flexible spending account (FSA). FSAs, which technically are cafeteria plans, can be used by themselves or incorporated into a more comprehensive cafeteria plan. They are most commonly used alone by small employers who are unwilling to establish a broader plan, primarily for cost reasons. The cafeteria plans of most large employers contain an FSA as an integral part of the plan.

An FSA allows an employee to fund certain benefits on a before-tax basis by electing to take a salary reduction, which can then be used to fund the cost of any qualified benefits included in the plan. However, they are most commonly used for health insurance premiums, medical expenses not covered by the employer's plan and dependent-care expenses.

The amount of any salary reduction is, in effect, credited to an employee's reimbursement account. Benefits are paid from this account when an employee properly files for such reimbursement. Reimbursements are typically made on a monthly or quarterly basis. The amount of the salary reduction must be made on a benefit-by-benefit basis prior to the beginning of the plan year. Once made, changes are allowed only under the specified circumstances previously mentioned for benefit elections.

If the monies in the FSA are not used during the plan year, they are forfeited and belong to the employer. Although some employers keep the forfeited money and use it to offset the cost of administering the FSA program, almost anything can be done with the money, except for giving it back to the persons who have forfeited it. Some employers give the money to charity; others credit it on a pro rata basis to the amounts of all participants in the FSA program for the following year or use it to reduce future benefit costs (such as contributions to a medical expense plan) for all employees.

An election to participate in an FSA program not only reduces salary for federal income tax purposes, but also lowers the wages on which social security taxes are levied. Therefore, those employees who are below the wage-base limit after the reduction will pay less in social security taxes. Their future income benefits under social security will also be smaller. However, the reduction in benefits will be small in most cases unless the salary reduction is large. It should be noted that the employer's share of social security tax payments will also decrease. In some cases, the employer's savings may actually be large enough to fully offset the cost of administering the FSA program.

One issue faced by employers over the years has been whether to limit benefit payments to the amount of an account balance or to allow an employee at any time during the year to receive benefits equal to his or her annual salary reduction. For example, an employee might contribute $100 per month to an FSA to provide benefits for the cost of unreimbursed medical expenses. During the first month of the plan, the employee would have made only $100 of the $1,200 annual contribution. If the employee incurred $300 of unreimbursed medical expenses during the month, should he or she be allowed to withdraw $100 or the full $300? The objection to allowing a $300 withdrawal is that the employer would lose $200 if the employee terminated employment before making any further contributions. Consequently, most plans limit aggregate benefits to the total contributions made until the time benefits are received.

However, a new IRS regulation has changed the rules. FSAs that provide health benefits (medical and dental expenses) must now allow an amount equal to the full annual contribution to be taken as benefits anytime during the year. Therefore, the employee in the previous example would be entitled to a benefit payment of $300 after the first month. This regulation, however, does not apply to other types of benefits, and employers still have a choice of reimbursement policies.

EXAMPLE 4: This is a cafeteria plan that consists solely of an FSA. Employees are allowed to elect salary reductions for each of the following:

- *Qualifying medical care expenses.* These are monthly premiums for the employer's contributory medical expense plan and any medical expenses normally deductible on Schedule A of an employee's federal income tax return (without regard to any gross income limitations). These deductible expenses must not have been reimbursed by insurance.
- *Eligible dependent-care expenses.* These are expenses for the types of benefits that could be provided in a qualified dependent-care-assistance program as described in Chapter 16. The maximum annual salary reduction for this category of benefits is limited to $5,000 to prevent the plan from being discriminatory because too large a portion of the benefits would be provided to key employees.

Employees can request reimbursements at the end of each month and must file an appropriate form accompanied by documentation (bills and receipts) to support their request. For administrative purposes, reimbursement requests must be for at least $50 except in the last quarter of the year.

The maximum reimbursement at any time for dependent-care expenses is the accumulated amount in an employee's account. Unused amounts in reimbursement accounts at the end of the year are donated to the United Way.

OBSTACLES TO CAFETERIA PLANS

Certain obstacles must be overcome before a cafeteria plan can be successfully implemented. Recent changes in federal tax laws and proper plan design would seem sufficient to overcome many of these obstacles. However, it must be realized that any organization that adopts a cafeteria plan other than a simple FSA will face a complex, costly and time-consuming project.

The Legislative Environment

Undoubtedly, the largest obstacle to cafeteria plans for several years was the unsettled federal income tax picture. This picture was finally clarified in 1984 by the passage of the Tax Reform Act and the IRS issuance of regulations governing cafeteria plans. Since then, the number of cafeteria plans has grown significantly, particularly among large firms. However, almost every year either a federal tax bill alters Section 125 in some way or new IRS regulations are issued. The benefits that can be included in a cafeteria plan are changed, the nondiscrimination rules are altered or the rules for FSAs are "clarified." This continuing uncertainty has caused many employers to take a wait-and-see attitude toward cafeteria plans.

Meeting Nondiscrimination Rules

Section 125 imposes complex nondiscrimination tests on cafeteria plans, causing many employees to view the establishment of a cafeteria plan unfavorably. If these tests are not met, adverse tax consequences for key employees and/or highly compensated employees may actually result in higher taxable income for these employees than if no cafeteria plan existed. From a practical standpoint, the test will usually be met if an employer has a full-fledged cafeteria plan that applies to all employees. However, care must be exercised in designing a plan that either covers only a segment of the employees or has only a small percentage of employees participating. The latter situation often occurs with FSAs.

As is often the case, the nondiscrimination tests are not applicable if a plan is maintained under provisions of a collective bargaining agreement.

The Concentration Test

Under the concentration test, no more than 25 percent of the tax-favored benefits provided under the plan can be provided to *key employees* (as defined in Chapter 6 for the Section 79 nondiscrimination rules). This test is a particular problem if an employer has a large percentage of key employees and if key employees, being higher paid, contribute large amounts to an FSA.

If a plan fails the concentration test, key employees must include in gross income the maximum taxable benefits that could have been elected under the plan. In effect, these employees are subject to the doctrine of constructive receipt.

The Eligibility Test

Cafeteria plans are subject to a two-part eligibility test, both parts of which must be satisfied. The first part stipulates that no employee be required to complete more than three years of employment as a condition for participation and that the employment requirement for each employee be the same. In addition, any employee who satisfies the employment requirement and is otherwise entitled to participate must do so no later than the first day of the plan year following completion of the employment requirement unless the employee has separated from service in the interim.

The second part requires that eligibility for participation must not be discriminatory in favor of highly compensated employees, who are defined as any of the following:

- Officers.
- Shareholders who own more than 5 percent of the voting power or value of all classes of the firm's stock.
- Employees who are highly compensated based on all facts and circumstances.
- Spouses or dependents of any of the above.

The eligibility test uses the table below, which is contained in IRS regulations and can best be explained with an example.

Nonhighly Compensated Employee Concentration Percentage	Safe Harbor Percentage	Unsafe Harbor Percentage
0–60	50	40
61	49.25	39.25
62	48.50	38.50
63	47.75	37.75
64	47	37
65	46.25	36.25
66	45.50	35.50
67	44.75	34.75
68	44	34
69	43.25	33.25
70	42.50	32.50
71	41.75	31.75
72	41	31
73	40.25	30.25
74	39.50	29.50
75	38.75	28.75
76	38	28
77	37.25	27.25
78	36.50	26.50
79	35.75	25.75
80	35	25
81	34.25	24.25
82	33.50	23.50
83	32.75	22.75
84	32	22
85	31.25	21.25
86	30.50	20.50
87	29.75	20
88	29	20
89	28.25	20
90	27.50	20
91	26.75	20
92	26	20
93	25.25	20
94	24.50	20
95	23.75	20
96	23	20
97	22.25	20
98	21.50	20
99	20.75	20

An employer has 1,000 employees, 800 nonhighly compensated and 200 highly compensated. The percentage of nonhighly compensated employees is 80 percent (800/1,000), for which the table shows a safe harbor percentage of 35. This means that if the percentage of nonhighly compensated employees eligible for the plan is equal to at least 35 percent of the percentage of highly compensated employees eligible, the plan satisfies the eligibility test. Assume that 160 people, or 80 percent of the highly compensated employees, are eligible. Then at least 28 percent, or 224, of the nonhighly compensated employees must be eligible (calculations: .80 × .35 = .28 and .28 × 800 = 224).

The table also shows an unsafe harbor percentage of 25 percent. Using this figure instead of 35 percent yields 160 employees. If fewer than this number of nonhighly compensated employees are eligible, the eligibility test is failed.

If the number of eligible nonhighly compensated employees falls between the numbers determined by the two percentages (from 160 to 223 employees in this example), IRS regulations impose a facts-and-circumstances test to determine whether the eligibility test is passed or failed. According to the regulations, the following factors will be considered:

- The underlying business reason for the eligibility classification.
- The percentage of employees eligible.
- The percentage of eligible employees in each salary range.
- The extent to which the eligibility classification is close to satisfying the safe harbor rule.

However, the regulations also state that none of these factors alone is determinative; other facts and circumstances may be relevant.

If a plan fails the eligibility test, highly compensated employees must include in gross income the maximum taxable benefits that could have been elected under the plan.

Nondiscriminatory Contributions and Benefits

Cafeteria plans cannot discriminate in favor of highly compensated participants with respect to contributions or benefits. Section 125 states that a cafeteria plan is not discriminatory if the plan's nontaxable benefits and total benefits (or the employer contributions allocable to each) do not discriminate in favor of highly compensated employees. In addition, a cafeteria plan providing health benefits is not discriminatory if contributions under the plan for each participant include an amount equal to one of the following:

- 100 percent of the health benefit cost for the majority of similarly situated (family or single coverage) highly compensated employees.
- At least 75 percent of the health benefit cost for the similarly situated participant with the best health benefit coverage.

Contributions exceeding either of these amounts are nondiscriminatory if they bear a uniform relationship to an employee's compensation.

The Obligation of the Employer

Under the most liberal cafeteria plan, each employee has an unrestricted choice of the benefits provided by his or her employer. Some critics of this concept argue that both the motivational and security aspects of a cafeteria plan may be damaged by unwise employee selection because many employees may not have the expertise to select the proper benefits. In addition, there is concern about the organization's moral and perhaps legal obligation to prevent employees from financial injury through faulty decisions. These concerns have been incorporated into the design of most plans presently in existence. Employees are given both certain basic benefits that provide a minimum level of security and a series of optional benefits on top of the basic ones.

Negative Attitudes

Some negative attitudes toward cafeteria plans have been expressed by employees, insurers and unions. No cafeteria plan can be truly successful without the support of the employees involved. In order to win the employees' initial support and to overcome any potential negative attitudes, companies that contemplate the development of such programs must spend a considerable amount of time and resources in making sure that employees are adequately informed about the reasons, advantages and disadvantages and future implications of the proposed program. For best results, the opinions of employees should be solicited and weighed; employees should be involved in various aspects of the decision-making process.

Some insurers have been reluctant to participate in cafeteria plans. A few seem unwilling to try anything new; others are concerned about the problem of adverse selection as a result of employee choice. However, as explained below, the problem of adverse selection can be minimized.

The attitude of unions has also generally been negative. Union management often feels that bargaining for a cafeteria plan is contrary to the practice of bargaining for the best benefit program for all employees. There is also a concern that a cafeteria plan will be used primarily as a cost-containment technique to pass on the cost of future benefit increases to union members. Consequently, the programs in existence often apply only to nonunion employees.

Adverse Selection

When employees are allowed a choice in selecting benefits, the problem of adverse selection arises. This means that those employees who are likely to have claims will tend to pick the benefits that will minimize their out-of-pocket costs. For example, an employee who previously selected a medical expense option with a high deductible might switch to a plan with a lower deductible if medical expenses are ongoing. An employee who previously rejected dental insurance or legal expense benefits is likely to elect these benefits if dental care or legal advise is anticipated in the near future.

It should be noted that adverse selection is a problem whether a plan is insured or self-funded. The problem even exists outside of cafeteria plans if choice is allowed. However, the degree of choice within a cafeteria plan tends to make the potential costs more severe unless actions are taken to combat the problem.

Several techniques are used to control adverse selection in cafeteria plans. Benefit limitations and restrictions on coverage can be included if a person wishes to add or change coverage at a date later than initial eligibility. This technique has been common in contributory benefit plans for many years. Another technique is to price the options accordingly. If an option is likely to encourage adverse selection, the cost to the employee for that option should be higher than what would have been charged if the option had been the only one available. Such pricing has been difficult in the past, but it is becoming easier and more accurate as more experience with cafeteria plans develops. The control of adverse selection is also one reason for the use of predesigned package plans. If, for example, the medical expense plan in one option is likely to encourage adverse selection, the option may not include other benefits for which adverse selection is also a concern (such as dental or legal expense benefits). To further counter increased costs from the medical expense plan, the option may also offer minimal coverage for other types of benefits.

Cost

It is an accepted fact that an organization that adopts a cafeteria plan will incur initial development and administrative costs that are over and above those of a more traditional benefit program. One benefit consultant estimated that an organization with 10,000 employees could expect initial development costs of approximately $500,000. About half this amount represents the value of the employee hours that would be spent in preparing the program for implementation. Another sizable portion would be paid for the reprogramming of the organization's computer system to include necessary information and to accept the employees' benefit elections. Although this figure appears substantial, it represents a cost of $50 per employee—a small fraction of the annual cost of each employee's benefits.

Until recently, the cost of a cafeteria plan was beyond the means of all but large employers. However, package plans developed by many insurers now make this approach financially available to employers with only a few hundred employees.

Continuing costs will depend on such factors as the benefits included in the plan, the number of options available with each benefit, the frequency with which employees may change benefit elections and the number of employees covered by the plan. Firms with cafeteria plans have incurred increased costs because of the need for additional employees to administer the program and additional computer time to process employee choices. However, the costs have been regarded as small in relation to the total cost of providing employee benefits. In addition, as cafeteria plans have grown in popularity, many vendors have developed software packages that can be used to provide administrative functions more cost effectively.

ISSUES IN PLAN DESIGN

Before committing itself to the establishment of a cafeteria plan, an employer must be sure a valid reason exists for converting the company's traditional benefit program to a cafeteria plan. For example, if there is strong employee dissatisfaction with the current benefit program, the solution may lie in clearly identifying the sources of dissatisfaction and making appropriate adjustments in the existing benefit program, rather than making a shift to a cafeteria plan. However, if employee dissatisfaction arises from their widely differing benefit needs, conversion to a cafeteria plan may be quite appropriate. Beyond having a clearly defined purpose for converting from a traditional benefit program to a cafeteria plan and being willing to bear the additional administrative costs associated with a cafeteria plan, the employer must face a number of considerations in designing the plan.

The Type and Amount of Benefits to Include

Probably the most fundamental decision that must be made in designing a cafeteria plan is determining what benefits should be included. An employer who wants the plan to be viewed as meeting the differing needs of employees must receive employee inputs concerning the types of benefits perceived as being most desirable. An open dialogue with employees will undoubtedly lead to suggestions that every possible employee benefit be made available. The enthusiasm of many employees for a cafeteria plan will then be dampened when the employer rejects some—and possibly many—of these suggestions for cost, administrative or psychological reasons. Consequently, it is important that certain ground rules be established regarding the benefits that are acceptable to the employer.

The employer must decide whether the plan should be limited to the types of benefits provided through traditional group insurance arrangements or be expanded to include other welfare benefits, retirement benefits and possibly cash. At a minimum, it is important to ensure that an overall employee benefit program provide employees with protection against all major areas of personal risks. This suggests a benefit program with at least *some* provision for life insurance, disability income protection, medical expense protection and retirement benefits, but it is not necessary that *all* these benefits be included in a cafeteria plan. For example, most employers have a retirement plan separate from their cafeteria plan because of Section 125 requirements. Other employers make a 401(k) plan one of the available cafeteria options.

In some respects, a cafeteria plan may be an ideal vehicle for providing less traditional types of benefits. Two examples are extra vacation time and child care. Some plans allow an employee to use flexible credits to purchase additional days of vacation. When available, this option has proven a popular benefit, particularly among single employees. A problem may arise, however, if the work of vacationing employees must be assumed by nonvacationing employees in addition to their own regularly assigned work. Those not electing extra vacation time may resent doing the work of someone else who is away longer than the normal vacation period.

In recent years, there has been increasing pressure on employers to provide care for employees' children, which represents an additional cost if added to a traditional existing benefit program. Employees who include child care benefits in a cafeteria plan can pay for the cost of such benefits, possibly with dollars from an

FSA. However, lower-paid employees may be better off financially be paying for child care with out-of-pocket dollars and electing the income tax credit available for dependent-care expenses.

Cost is an important consideration in a cafeteria plan. The greater the number of benefits, particularly optional benefits, the greater the administrative costs. A wide array of options may also be confusing to many employees and require extra personnel to counsel employees or to answer their questions.

Level of Employer Contributions

An employer has considerable latitude in determining the amount of dollars that will be available to employees to purchase benefits under a cafeteria plan. These dollars may be a function of one or more of the following factors: salary, age, family status and length of service.

The major difficulty arises in situations in which the installation of a cafeteria plan is not accompanied by an overall increase in the amount of the employer's contributions to the employee benefit plan. It is generally felt that each employee should be provided with enough dollars so that he or she can purchase optional benefits, that, together with basic benefits, are at least equivalent to the benefits provided by the older plan.

Including an FSA Option

An FSA option under a cafeteria plan enables employees to lower their taxes and, therefore, increase their spendable income. Ignoring any administrative costs, there is probably no reason not to offer this option to employees for benefits such as dependent care. However, salary deductions for medical expenses pose a dilemma. While such deductions save taxes for an employee, they may also result in his or her obtaining nearly 100 percent reimbursement for medical expenses, which may negate many of the cost-containment features in the employer's medical expense plan.

Change of Benefits

Because employees' needs change over time, a provision regarding their ability to change their benefit options must be incorporated into a cafeteria plan. Since the changing of options results in administrative costs and possibly adverse selection, employees should probably not be permitted to change their benefit selections more often than once a year.

Two situations may complicate the issue of the frequency with which benefits may be changed. First, the charges to employees for optional benefits must be adjusted periodically to reflect experience under the plan. If the charges for benefits rise between dates on which employees may change benefit selections, the employer must either absorb these charges or pass them on to the employees, probably through increased payroll deductions. Consequently, most cafeteria plans allow benefit changes on annual dates that are the same as the dates when charges for benefits are recalculated as well as the date on which any insurance contracts providing benefits under the plan are renewed.

The second situation arises when the amount of the employer's contribution is based on compensation. If an employee receives a pay increase between selection periods, should he or she be granted more dollars to purchase additional benefits at that time?

Under most cafeteria plans, the dollars available to all employees are calculated only once a year, usually before the date by which any annual benefit changes must be made. Any changes in the employee's status during the year will have no effect on the employer's contribution until the following year on the date on which a recalculation is made.

STUDY QUESTIONS

1. Explain the advantages claimed for cafeteria plans.
2. a. What types of welfare benefits can be provided under a cafeteria plan?
   b. What types of retirement benefits can be provided?
   c. What is meant by a cash benefit?
3. A benefit plan may offer employees a choice among benefits but not satisfy the statutory definition of a cafeteria plan. What are the implications of such a situation?
4. a. When must benefit elections be made under a cafeteria plan?
   b. To what extent can a cafeteria plan permit changes in benefit elections?
5. What is the difference between a core-plus cafeteria plan and a modular plan?
6. a. What is the advantage of funding employee benefits through an FSA?
   b. What types of benefits can be funded by an FSA salary reduction?
   c. What happens to balances in an FSA if they are not used for expenses incurred during the election period?
7. Other than meeting nondiscrimination rules and adverse selection, what are the obstacles to establishing cafeteria plans?
8. What types of nondiscrimination rules apply to cafeteria plans?
9. What techniques can be used to control adverse selection in a cafeteria plan?
10. Briefly discuss the issues that must be addressed in designing a cafeteria plan.

PART
FIVE

Retirement Plans

18

Introduction to Qualified Plans

Objectives

- Describe the fundamental management objectives in designing and implementing pension plans.
- Identify major policy issues motivating government regulation of qualified retirement plans.
- Explain the general requirements that must be met by qualified pension plans with respect to
  1. Eligibility and plan coverage.
  2. Nondiscrimination in benefits and contributions.
  3. Funding requirements.
  4. Vesting.
  5. Limitations on benefits and contributions.
  6. Payout restrictions.
  7. Top-heavy rules.
- Identify the tax advantages of qualified pension plans.
- List the broad types of qualified plans and their primary characteristics.
- Briefly explain the government's regulatory structure for qualified plans.

Retirement plans are among the most common employee benefits offered by employers. Nearly half of all benefit spending by employers goes to retirement benefits, and employees rate retirement benefits as the second most important employee benefit, after health insurance.[1] Moreover, retirement plans are probably the most complicated benefit—in terms of design, administration, and taxation—commonly provided by employers. The purpose of this chapter is to explain the reasons for

---

[1]Employee Benefit Research Institute, Issue Brief Number 111, Washington, D.C. (2/91).

this importance and complexity, and to provide an introduction to pension plan design and government regulation of pension plans.

MANAGEMENT OBJECTIVES IN PENSION PLAN DESIGN

Generally, a primary management objective in designing and maintaining a pension program is to maximize those factors by which the plan improves employee productivity. In other words, to maximize the extent to which the costs of the plan represent investment rather than pure expense. A pension plan improves productivity by attracting and keeping a better work force and providing incentives for good work performance. Although the quantitative evidence for the productivity relationship for specific pension plan features is relatively scanty at this time, there has been much qualitative experience in this area.

Benefit managers and pension planners must begin with an overall idea of what employer objectives can be promoted by a pension plan. While not every potential objective can be met with a single plan—in fact, some are conflicting—it's useful to begin this chapter by noting broadly what pension plans can do. Here are the basic objectives:

1. *Help Employees with Retirement Saving.* This is the most fundamental reason for pension plans and it shouldn't be overlooked. Most employees, even highly compensated employees, find personal savings difficult. It is difficult not merely for psychological reasons, but also because our tax system and economy are oriented toward consumption rather than savings.

   For example, the federal income tax system imposes tax on income from savings (even if it is not used for consumption) with only three major exceptions: (1) deferral of tax on capital gains until realized; (2) benefits for investment in a personal residence; and (3) deferral of tax and other benefits for qualified retirement plans and IRAs. In other words, a qualified retirement plan is one of only three ways our government encourages savings through the tax system—but it is available only if an employer adopts the plan. (IRA benefits are very limited.)

2. *Tax Deferral for Owners and Highly Compensated Employees.* While many employees in all compensation categories can benefit from pension plans, owners and other key employees have more money available for saving, have higher compensation, have longer service with the employer and often are older than regular employees; thus they can benefit more from pension plans. When designing a plan for a business owner, a typical objective is to maximize the benefits for the owner (or, in some cases, to minimize the discrimination *against* the highly compensated employee that is built into some of the qualified pension plan rules.)

3. *Help Recruit, Retain and Retire Employees.* These "three Rs" of compensation policy are important in designing pension plans. The plan can help recruit employees by matching or bettering pension benefit packages offered by competing employers; it can help retain employees by tying maxi-

mum pension benefits to long service; and it can help retire employees by allowing them to retire with dignity—without a drastic drop in living standard—when their productivity has begun to decline and the organization needs new members.

4. *Encourage Productivity Directly.* Certain types of plan design can act as employee incentives; this is particularly true of plans whose contributions are profit-based or those providing employee accounts invested in stock of the employer.

5. *Discourage Collective Bargaining.* An attractive pension package—as good as or better than labor union-sponsored plans in the area—can help to keep employees from organizing into a collective bargaining unit. Collective bargaining often poses major business problems for some employers.

THE GOVERNMENT'S ROLE—PENSION POLICY ISSUES

Management objectives are one major factor in pension design; the other is the government regulatory structure. This section discusses the development of the government's role in this area.

A relatively complete discussion of plan types and terminology will appear later in this chapter, but one very important concept must be understood at the outset. Most employees covered under an employer-sponsored retirement plan are covered under what is known as a *qualified* retirement plan. A qualified plan is one that receives certain valuable federal tax benefits, but its design, funding and administration must meet an extraordinarily complex set of federal statutory and regulatory requirements. Most federal regulation in this area specifically preempts state and local regulation. The tax benefits from such plans to both employer and employee are generally (though not always) adequate to justify the inconvenience of this severe regulatory regimen. A *nonqualified* plan is any other retirement or deferred compensation plan. Nonqualified plans are subject to much simpler federal regulation, along with less favorable tax treatment. Nonqualified plans are used primarily for executive compensation arrangements that replace or supplement qualified plan coverage for a selected group of highly compensated executives. These are discussed in Chapter 28.

The government's role in the retirement income area has been dictated primarily by historical factors. Beginning in the late 19th century, the economy of the United States changed fairly rapidly from predominantly agricultural to predominantly industrial and service oriented. Coinciding with this change—and probably in response to it—the large, supportive extended family of the agricultural economy was largely replaced by smaller, more fragmented family units. The shift away from agriculture has reduced the amount of economically useful work available to older people, and family structural changes have reduced the amount of family support for the aged.

Because of these economic and social trends, people generally must make specific plans for their retirement. This is a difficult matter for most individual employees to do alone and, consequently, employer-sponsored pension plans have become increasingly important.

In the 20th century, federal government involvement in retirement plans for the aged has also greatly expanded. The federal government's involvement is twofold. For most people, the most obvious federal government program in this area is the social security system adopted in the 1930s to provide direct benefit payments to the aged. But even before the social security system was adopted, the federal government became involved in a more traditional way by measures designed to encourage the private pension system.

Governments tend to be reluctant to adopt direct payment arrangements for dependent individuals, particularly in the United States—a reflection of the generally conservative social values of the American public. Historically, governments have tended to look first at private organizations to act in this area. This is one reason why charitable institutions, such as orphanages and hospitals, have for centuries been granted various forms of tax exemption.

In the tradition of encouraging private initiatives, in the 1920s, the federal government began encouraging private, employer-sponsored retirement plans by providing two kinds of tax benefits. First, pension funds were made tax exempt under the Revenue Acts of 1921 and 1926. Then, in the Revenue Act of 1928, employer contributions to plan funds were made currently deductible by the employer, even though benefits were not paid to employees until later years. These basic provisions still apply and form the basis for today's vast federal regulatory scheme for qualified plans.

The embryonic private pension system of the 1920s declined significantly during the depression of the 1930s. This was one reason for the adoption of the social security system. However, since the 1940s, private pension plans have revived to an enormous degree. Assets in private pension plans now amount to almost three trillion dollars,[2] which constitutes a very substantial portion of the nation's entire capital.

Because of the large sums involved, any tax benefits provided to qualified plans cost the government a great deal in lost tax revenues; the government estimate is well over $50 billion annually.[3] This large "tax expenditure" is often given as a primary justification for the exhaustive scheme of government regulation that now applies to qualified pension plans. Fundamentally, the argument is that the large tax expenditure is designed to help prevent individuals from becoming dependent on the government in retirement. Consequently, the government attempts to make sure that plan benefits go where they are most needed so that this tax expenditure is cost effective. Much pension regulation is aimed at discouraging plans that primarily benefit highly-compensated employees who have other sources of retirement income. Other rules are intended to assure that the large sums set aside

---

[2]Employee Benefit Research Institute, *EBRI Databook on Employee Benefits,* Washington, D.C. (figures as of end of 1989).

[3]Office of Management and Budget, *Special Analyses: Budget of the United States Government, Fiscal Year 1992.* The estimated total annual tax loss for all employee benefit provisions was $134 billion.

for plan benefits are managed in the exclusive interest of plan participants and beneficiaries.

In practice, the government frequently adopts new or modified statutes and regulations relating to pensions without clear or articulated long-range policy objectives. The absence of a coherent federal retirement policy is currently a critical federal policy issue. Current issues in pension regulation include the following.

Tax Revenue Loss

At times, revenue-raising needs outweigh retirement policy issues in Congress. The tax benefits for qualified plans cause a substantial apparent decrease in tax revenues. The criticism is also frequently made that too much of the tax benefit goes to high-income individuals who don't need government help. Whatever the merits of this argument, it is indisputable that "fine tuning" the rules to reduce tax benefits for certain plan participants can increase tax revenues in the short run, without the political pain of visibly "raising taxes." The need to raise revenue has motivated many recent changes in the qualified plan law, and it probably will be a factor in future legislation. Changes of this type are often enormously complex as a result of the need to carefully target the group whose benefits are to be reduced, typically the owner-employees of closely-held businesses. Revenue-motivated changes are often criticized as resulting in bad retirement policy.

Discrimination in Favor of Highly Compensated Employees

Although a major thrust of virtually all qualified plan legislation since the 1940s has been to discourage employers from discriminating in their plans in favor of highly compensated employees, a considerable amount of such discrimination is still possible, as discussed throughout this text. Because of this, much qualified plan legislation has been designed to reduce the "tax shelter" aspects of qualified plans, particularly those for smaller businesses where owner-employees receive substantial benefits. Many of the most complex and awkward provisions of the law, such as the top-heavy rules discussed in Chapter 25, were designed in this vein.

Seemingly, it would be easy to eliminate the discrimination problem by simple, appropriate benefit or contribution limits. However, there is a countervailing policy consideration. Small businesses, collectively, employ a large and increasing segment of the work force. Owners of these businesses may not be interested in maintaining a qualified plan for their employees unless the plan provides substantial, and possibly disproportionate, benefits for the owners themselves. This policy issue, therefore, involves tension between tax-benefit equity and efficiency on the one hand, and the need to encourage small business retirement plans on the other. No simple resolution of this is likely in the near future, and complex legislative compromises on this issue will probably continue to emerge from Congress.

Encouraging Private Saving

Surprisingly, in view of the trillions invested in pension plans, relatively little policy emphasis has been given to the role of the qualified plan rules in encouraging private savings. One problem is that policy makers do not agree on the appropriate level for private savings, nor whether government policy should encourage savings, rather than allowing the free market to set the level. Another factor is that economists are divided about the efficacy of the qualified plan provisions in encouraging savings. Some economists argue that these plans merely displace private saving that would take place in any event. Nevertheless, the savings issue is an ongoing factor in the policy debate.

Interest-Group Pressures

As the foregoing discussion indicates, retirement policy poses difficult problems even if viewed from a neutral intellectual viewpoint. The actual political climate, of course, is not neutral The qualified plan business is large and involves many firms and individuals. Most of these organizations eagerly and frequently convey their views to Congress in great technical detail. This complicates the resolution of issues and makes change more difficult.

Mandatory Retirement Plan Coverage

A presidential commission, formed in the late 1970s to study pension policy, recommended the establishment of a Minimum Universal Pension System (MUPS) for all workers, to be funded by employers at an initial rate of at least 3 percent of payroll.[4] The MUPS benefit would be completely portable from job to job. In general, the MUPS approach is not popular with employers and benefit plan designers who prefer the flexibility of current rules and, at the present time, Congress is not considering it seriously.

Age and Sex Discrimination

Age and sex discrimination have not been addressed by Congress specifically as retirement plan issues. However, recent federal legislative and regulatory activity related to employment discrimination in general has affected retirement plans, as discussed later in this text.

QUALIFIED PLAN CHARACTERISTICS

The term *qualified plan* is not amenable to a simple definition; in a sense, it requires all of Part Five of this text to provide an adequate definition. Nevertheless, it is helpful to take a brief overall look at the most significant requirements before getting into the details. These requirements are discussed in appropriate detail in subsequent chapters.

---

[4]*Coming of Age: Toward a National Retirement Income Policy,* President's Commission on Pension Policy, 1981.

Eligibility and Plan Coverage

The plan can have almost any kind of initial eligibility provision, except for specific restrictions based on age or service. Generally, no minimum age over 21 can be required, nor can more than one year of service be required for eligibility. In addition, the plan *in operation* must generally cover at least 70 percent of all nonhighly compensated employees. These rules have many complex exceptions and limitations, as discussed in Chapter 19.

Nondiscrimination in Benefits and Contributions

Generally speaking, a qualified plan may not discriminate, either in plan benefits or employer contributions to the plan, in favor of highly compensated employees. The law includes a detailed definition of *highly compensated* for this purpose. However, the plan contribution or benefit can be based on the employee's compensation or years of service, which often will provide a higher benefit for certain highly compensated employees. In addition, the qualified plan can be integrated with social security so that a greater contribution or benefit is available for higher paid employees whose compensation is greater than an amount based on the social security taxable wage base. Because of the possibilities for abuse in these areas, the rules for social security integration, discussed in Chapter 20, are complex.

Funding Requirements

Generally, a qualified plan must be funded in advance of the employee's retirement. This can be done either through contributions to an irrevocable trust fund for the employee's benefit or under an insurance contract. There are strict limits on the extent to which the employer can exercise control over the plan fund. The fund must be under the control of a *fiduciary*—the legal designation for a person who holds funds of another—and must be managed solely for the benefit of plan participants and beneficiaries.

Vesting Requirements

Under the vesting rules, an employee must be given a nonforfeitable or *vested* benefit at the normal retirement date specified in the plan and, in case of termination of employment prior to retirement, after a specified period of service. For example, one common vesting provision grants a fully vested benefit after the employee has attained five years of service, with no vesting until then. If the plan has this vesting provision, an employee who leaves after, say, four years of service with the employer will receive no plan benefit even though the employer has put money into the plan on his behalf over the four-year period. However, an employee who leaves after five or more years of service will receive the entire plan benefit earned up until that time.

The vesting rules are discussed more fully in Chapter 21. These rules are designed to make it more difficult for employers to deny benefits to employees by selectively discharging or turning over employees.

Limitations on Benefits and Contributions

In order to limit the use of a qualified plan as a tax shelter for highly compensated employees, Section 415 of the Internal Revenue Code contains a limitation on the plan benefit or employer contributions, depending on the type of plan. Under these limitations, a plan cannot generally provide an annual pension of more than $90,000 (as indexed for inflation) or annual employer and employee contributions of more than $30,000. The limitations are discussed further in Chapter 25. Practically speaking, these limits are high enough so that only highly compensated participants are likely to encounter them.

Benefits for highly compensated employees are further limited by a requirement that only the first $200,000 (as indexed) of a participant's compensation can be taken into account in a plan's contribution or benefit formula.

Payout Restrictions

In order to insure that qualified plan benefits are used for their intended purposes, there are various restrictions on benefit payouts. Certain plans (pension plans in particular) do not allow withdrawals of funds before termination of employment. In addition, there is a 10 percent penalty on withdrawal of funds from any qualified plan before early retirement, age 59½, death or disability, with certain exceptions. Funds cannot be kept in the plan indefinitely; generally, the payout must begin by April first of the year after the participant's attainment of age 70½, in specified minimum annual amounts. Loans from the plan to participants are restricted.

Top-Heavy Rules

To reduce the possibility of excessive discrimination in favor of business owners covered under a qualified plan, special rules are provided for *top-heavy plans*. Basically, a top-heavy plan is one that provides more than 60 percent of its aggregate accumulated benefits or account balances to key employees. A plan that is top-heavy must meet a special rapid vesting requirement and provide minimum benefits for nonkey employees.

 TAX BENEFITS OF QUALIFIED PLANS

The most important tax advantage of a qualified plan is best understood by comparison with the rules applicable to a nonqualified deferred compensation plan. In a nonqualified plan, the timing of the employer's income tax deduction for compensation of employees depends on when the compensation is included in the employee's income. If the employer puts no money aside in advance to fund the plan, there is no deduction to the employer until the retirement income is paid to the employee, at which time the employee also reports the compensation as taxable income. If the employer puts money aside into an irrevocable trust fund, insurance contract or similar fund for the benefit of the employee, the employer can get an immediate tax deduction, but then the employee is taxed immediately; there is no tax deferral for the employee.

These rules do *not* apply to a qualified plan. In a qualified plan, the employer obtains a tax deduction for contributions to the plan fund (within specified limits) for the year the contribution is made. Employees pay taxes on benefits when they are received. The combination of an immediate employer tax deduction plus tax deferral for the employee can be obtained only with a qualified plan.

Besides this basic advantage, there are other tax benefits for qualified plans. Four advantages are usually identified:

1. The employer gets an immediate deduction, within certain limits, for amounts paid into the plan fund to finance future retirement benefits for employees.
2. The employee is not taxed at the time the employer makes contributions for that employee to the plan fund.
3. The employee is taxed only when plan benefits are received. If the full benefit is received in a single year, it may be eligible for special favorable "lump sum" income taxation.
4. Earnings on money put aside by the employer to fund the plan are not subject to federal income tax while in the plan fund; thus the earnings accumulate tax free.

CLASSIFICATION OF QUALIFIED PLANS

There are two broad classifications of qualified plans. Plans are either pension plans or profit-sharing plans; they are also classified either as defined-benefit or defined-contribution plans. These broad classifications are useful in identifying plans which meet broad overall goals of the employer. Once detailed employer objectives have been determined, a specific qualified plan program can be developed for the employer using one or more of the types of plans from a menu of specific plan types. The specific plan types contain a lot of flexibility in design to meet employer needs, and one or more different plans or plan types can be designed covering the same or overlapping groups of employees to provide the exact type of benefits that the employer desires.

Pension and Profit-Sharing Plans

One way of broadly classifying qualified plans is to distinguish between pension plans and profit-sharing plans. A *pension plan* is a plan designed primarily to provide income at retirement. Thus, benefits are generally not available from a pension plan until the employee reaches a specified age, referred to as the *normal retirement age*. Some plans also provide an optional benefit at an earlier age (the *early retirement age*). The design of a pension plan benefit formula must be such that an employee's retirement benefit is reasonably predictable in advance. Because the object of a pension plan is to provide retirement security, the employer must keep the fund at an adequate level. Pension plans are subject to the *minimum funding* rules of the Code, and these generally require the employer to make regular deposits to avoid a penalty.

By contrast, a *profit-sharing plan* is designed to allow a relatively short-term deferral of income; it is a somewhat more speculative benefit to the employee because the employer's contribution can be based on profits. Furthermore, a profit-sharing plan can provide for a totally discretionary employer contribution, so that even if the employer has profits in a given year, the employer need not make a contribution for that year. The minimum funding rules do not apply. However, there must be substantial and recurring contributions or the plan will be deemed to be terminated.

In a profit-sharing plan, it is difficult to determine the employee's benefit in advance, and the plan is considered more an incentive to employees than a predictable source of retirement income. Because it is not exclusively designed for retirement income, employees may be permitted to withdraw funds from the plan before retirement. The plan may allow amounts to be withdrawn as early as two years after the employer has contributed them to the plan. However, as with any qualified plan, preretirement withdrawals may be subject to a 10 percent penalty. Finally, the deductible annual employer contribution is limited to 15 percent of payroll, an amount less than would usually be deductible under a pension plan.

Defined-Benefit and Defined-Contribution Plans

Qualified plans are also divided into defined-benefit and defined-contribution plans. A *defined-contribution plan* has an *individual account* for each employee; defined-contribution plans are, therefore, sometimes referred to as individual-account plans. The plan document describes the amount the employer will contribute to the plan, but it does not promise any particular benefit. When the plan participant retires or otherwise becomes eligible for benefits under the plan, the benefit will be the total amount in the participant's account, including past investment earnings on the amounts put into the account. The participant can look only to his or her own account to recover benefits; the participant is not entitled to amounts in any other account. Thus, the participant bears the risk of bad plan investments.

In a *defined-benefit plan*, the plan document specifies the amount of benefit promised to the employee at normal retirement age. The plan itself does not specify the amount the employer must contribute annually to the plan. The plan's actuary will determine the annual contribution required so that the plan fund will be sufficient to pay the promised benefit as each participant retires. If the fund is inadequate, the employer is responsible for making additional contributions. There are no individual participant accounts, and each participant has a claim on the entire fund for the defined benefit. Because of the actuarial aspects, defined-benefit plans tend to be more complicated and expensive to administer than defined-contribution plans.

Specific Types of Qualified Plans

As Figure 18-1 indicates, within the broad categories (pension, profit-sharing, defined-benefit, defined-contribution), there are specific types of plans available to meet various retirement-planning objectives.

FIGURE 18-1

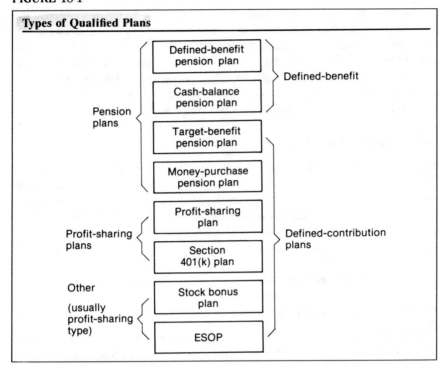

Defined-Benefit Pension Plan

All defined-benefit plans are pension plans; they are designed primarily to provide income at retirement. A defined-benefit plan specifies the benefit in terms of a formula, of which there are many different types. Such formulas may state the benefit in terms of a percentage of earnings measured over a specific period of time, and might also be based on years of service. For example, a defined-benefit plan might promise a monthly retirement benefit equal to 50 percent of the employee's average monthly earnings over the five years prior to retirement. Or instead of a flat 50 percent, the plan might provide something like 1.5 percent for each of the employee's years of service, with the resulting percentage applied to the employee's earnings averaged over a stated period. Employer contributions to the plan are determined actuarially. Thus, for a given benefit, a defined-benefit plan will tend to result in a larger employer contribution on behalf of employees who enter the plan at older ages, since there is less time to fund the benefit for them.

Cash-Balance Pension Plan

In a cash-balance plan (also called a guaranteed account plan and various other titles), each participant has an "account" which increases annually as a result of two types of credits: a compensation credit based on the participant's compensation and an interest credit equal to a guaranteed rate of interest. As a result of the guarantee, the participant does not bear the investment risk. Unlike defined-benefit formulas, the plan deposits are not based on age, and younger employees receive the same benefit accrual as those hired at older ages. The plan is funded by the employer on an actuarial basis; the plan fund's actual rate of investment return may be more or less than the guaranteed rate and employer deposits are adjusted accordingly. Technically, because of the guaranteed minimum benefit, the plan is treated as a defined-benefit plan. From the participant's viewpoint, however, the plan appears very similar to a money-purchase plan, described below.

Target-Benefit Pension Plan

A target plan uses a benefit formula (the "target") like that of a defined-benefit plan. However, a target plan is a defined-contribution plan and, therefore, the benefit consists solely of the amount in each employee's individual account at retirement. Initial contributions to a target plan are determined actuarially, but the employer does not guarantee that the benefit will meet the target level, so the initial contribution level is not adjusted to reflect actuarial experience. Like a defined-benefit plan, a target-benefit plan provides a relatively higher contribution on behalf of employees entering the plan at older ages.

Money-Purchase Pension Plan

A money-purchase pension plan is a defined-contribution plan that is in some ways the simplest form of qualified plan. The plan simply specifies a level of contribution to each participant's individual account. For example, the plan might specify that the employer will contribute each year to each participant's account an amount equal to 10 percent of that participant's compensation for the year. The participant's retirement benefit is equal to the amount in the account at retirement. Thus, the account reflects not only the initial contribution level, but also any subsequent favorable or unfavorable investment results obtained by the plan fund. The term *money purchase* arose because in many such plans, the amount in the participant's account at retirement is not distributed in a lump sum but rather is used to purchase a single or joint life annuity for the participant.

Profit-Sharing Plan

As described earlier, the significant features of a profit-sharing plan are that employer contributions are, within limits, discretionary on the part of the employer and that employee withdrawals before retirement may be permitted. Profit-sharing plans that are designed to allow employee contributions are sometimes referred to as *savings* or thrift plans.

Section 401(k) Plan

A Section 401(k) plan, also called a *cash or deferred plan,* is a plan allowing employees to choose (within limits) to receive compensation either as current cash or as a contribution to a qualified profit-sharing plan. The amount contributed to the plan is not currently taxable to the employee. Such plans have become popular because of their flexibility and tax advantages. However, such plans must include restrictions that may be burdensome to the employer or the employees. The most significant restrictions are a requirement of immediate vesting for amounts contributed under the employee election, and restrictions on distribution of these amounts to employees prior to age 59T.

Stock Bonus Plan

The stock bonus plan resembles a profit-sharing plan except that employer contributions are in the form of employer stock rather than cash and the plan fund consists primarily of employer stock.

The fiduciary requirements of the pension law forbid an employer from investing more than 10 percent of a pension plan fund in stock of the employer company. This prevents the employer from utilizing pension plan funds primarily for financing the business rather than providing retirement security for employees. However, the 10-percent restriction does not apply to profit-sharing or stock bonus plans.

Stock bonus plans are intended specifically to give employees an ownership interest in the company at relatively low cost to the company. Stock bonus plans are often used by closely held companies to help create a market for stock of the employer.

ESOP

Employee stock ownership plans (ESOPs) are similar to stock bonus plans in that most or all of the plan fund consists of employer stock; employee accounts are stated in shares of employer stock. However, ESOPs are designed to offer a further benefit: the employer can use an ESOP as a mechanism for financing the business through borrowing or "leveraging." Various tax incentives exist to encourage this.

PLANS FOR SPECIAL TYPES OF ORGANIZATIONS

Plans Covering Partners and Proprietors

Under federal tax law, partners and proprietors (sole owners) are not considered employees of their unincorporated business, even if they perform substantial services for the business. By comparison, shareholders of a corporate business who are employed by the business are considered employees for retirement planning and other employee benefit purposes. For many years, there were restrictions on the benefits available from a qualified plan to partners or proprietors. Special plans called *Keogh* or *HR#10* plans were used if partners or proprietors were covered. Since 1983, most of these restrictions no longer apply, and qualified plans can cover partners and proprietors on virtually the same terms as regular employees of the business.

S Corporations

An S corporation is a corporation that has made an election to be treated substantially like a partnership for federal income tax purposes. Certain shareholder-employees of S corporations were once subject to qualified plan restrictions similar to those for partners and proprietors; however, after 1983, most of these restrictions do not apply. Thus, as with partners and proprietors, S corporation shareholder-employees are now treated basically like regular employees for qualified plan purposes. However, S corporations generally cannot adopt stock bonus plans or ESOPs. Also, an S corporation employee who owns more than 2 percent of the corporation's stock is treated as a partner for *other* employee benefit purposes, such as group life and health plans.

Multiple Employer, Collectively Bargained and Multiemployer Plans

In this text, if not stated otherwise, it is assumed that any qualified plans referred to are maintained by a single employer or by a group of related employers. It is possible, however, for more than one employer or related group to participate in a single qualified plan. If such a plan is established under a collective bargaining agreement (as is usually the case), it is referred to as a *collectively bargained plan*. With a collectively bargained plan, the plan is usually designed and maintained by a labor union, and employers who recognize the union as a bargaining agent for their employees agree to contribute to the plan on a basis specified in the collective bargaining agreement. If the plan is not the result of a collective bargaining agreement, it is referred to as a *multiple employer plan*. Such plans might, for example, be maintained by trade associations of employers in a certain line of business. There are special rules for applying the participation and other requirements to these plans.

There are also provisions for a special type of collectively bargained plan known as a *multiemployer plan* (Code Section 414(f)). A multiemployer plan is a plan to which more than one employer is required to contribute and which is maintained under a collective bargaining agreement covering more than one employer; the Department of Labor can also impose other requirements by regulation. Presumably, most large collectively bargained plans will qualify as multiemployer plans. Because of the nature of the multiemployer plan, the funding requirements are somewhat more favorable than for other plans. However, the employer may incur a special liability on withdrawing from the plan.

GOVERNMENT REGULATION OF QUALIFIED PLANS

It was noted earlier in this chapter that a qualified retirement plan receives special federal tax benefits in return for being designed in accordance with rules imposed by the federal government. This section of the chapter will discuss how the federal government imposes these rules. The federal rules are the most important because federal law generally preempts state and local laws in the qualified plan area.

Benefit planners need a basic understanding of the federal regulatory scheme. Planners must often interpret the significance of various official rules and interact with governmental organizations. These governmental rules and organizations must be understood in order to be effective in plan design and management.

Government regulation is expressed through the following, in the order of their importance: (1) statutory law; (2) the law as expressed in court cases; (3) regulations of government agencies; and (4) rulings and other information issued by government agencies.

Statutory Law

Theoretically, the highest level of regulatory law is the U.S. Constitution, since all regulation must meet constitutional requirements, such as due process of law and equal protection for persons under the law. However, relatively few issues of federal regulation are actually resolved under constitutional law. For practical purposes, the "law" as expressed by statutes passed by the U.S. Congress is the highest level of authority and is the basis of all regulation; court cases, rulings and regulations are simply interpretations of statutes passed by Congress. If the statute was detailed enough to cover every possible case, there theoretically wouldn't be any need for anything else. But despite the best efforts of Congressional drafting staffs, the statutes can't cover every situation.

Benefit planners should become as familiar as possible with statutory law since it is the basis for all other rules, regulations and court cases. One of the main causes for confusion among nonexperts is a lack of understanding of the relative status of sources of information. That is, while a rule found in the Internal Revenue Code is fundamental, a statement in an IRS ruling or instructions to IRS forms may be merely a matter of interpretation that is relatively easy to "plan around."

In the benefits area, the sources of statutory law are:

- *Internal Revenue Code (the Code).* The tax laws governing the deductibility and taxation of pension and employee benefit programs are fundamental. These are found primarily in Sections 401–425, with important provisions also in Sections 72, 83, and other sections.
- *ERISA (Employee Retirement Income Security Act of 1974) as amended and other labor law provisions.* Labor law provisions such as ERISA govern the nontax aspects of federal regulation. These involve plan participation requirements, notice to participants, reporting to the federal government and a variety of rules designed to safeguard any funds that are set aside to pay benefits in the future. There is some overlap between ERISA and the Code in the area of plan participation, vesting and prohibited transactions.
- *Pension Benefit Guaranty Corporation (PBGC).* The PBGC is a government corporation set up under ERISA in 1974 to provide termination insurance for participants in qualified defined-benefit plans up to certain limits. In carrying out this responsibility, the PBGC regulates plan terminations and imposes certain reporting requirements on covered plans that are in financial difficulty or in a state of contraction.

- *Securities laws.* The federal securities laws are designed to protect investors. Benefit plans may involve an element of investing the employee's money. While qualified plans are generally exempt from the full impact of the securities laws, if the plan holds employer stock, a federal registration statement may be required and certain securities regulations may apply.
- *Civil Rights laws.* Benefit plans are part of an employer's compensation policies; these plans are subject to the Civil Rights Act of 1964 which prohibits employment discrimination on the basis of race, religion, sex or national origin.
- *Age Discrimination.* The Age Discrimination Act of 1978, as amended, has specific provisions aimed at benefit plans, as discussed throughout this book.
- *State legislation.* ERISA contains a broad "preemption" provision under which any state law in conflict with ERISA is preempted—has no effect. If ERISA does not deal with a particular issue, however, there may be room for state legislation. For example, there is considerable state legislation and regulation governing the types of group-term life insurance contracts that can be offered as part of an employer plan. There are also certain areas where states continue to assert authority even though ERISA also has an impact; such as in the area of creditors' rights to pension fund assets.

Court Cases

The courts enter the picture when a taxpayer decides to appeal a tax assessment made by the IRS. The courts don't act on their own to resolve tax or other legal issues. Consequently, the law as expressed in court cases is a crazy-quilt affair that offers some answers but often raises more questions than it answers. However, after statutes, court cases are the most authoritative source of law. Courts can and do overturn regulations and rulings of the IRS and other regulatory agencies.

A taxpayer wishing to contest a tax assessment has three choices: (1) the Federal District Court in the taxpayer's district; (2) the United States Tax Court; or (3) the United States Claims Court. Tax law can be found in the decisions of any of these three courts.

All three courts are equally authoritative. Most tax cases, however, are resolved by the U.S. Tax Court, because it offers a powerful advantage: The taxpayer can bring the case before the Tax Court without paying the disputed tax. All the other courts require payment of the tax followed by a suit for refund.

Decisions of these three courts can be appealed to the Federal Court of Appeals for the applicable federal "judicial circuit"—the U.S. is divided into 11 judicial circuits. The circuit courts sometimes differ on certain points of tax law; as a result, tax and benefit planning may depend on what judicial circuit the taxpayer is located in. Where these differences exist, one or more taxpayers will eventually appeal a decision by the Court of Appeals to the United States Supreme Court to resolve differences of interpretation among various judicial circuits, but this process takes many years and the Supreme Court may ultimately choose not to hear the case. Congress also sometimes amends the Code or other statute to resolve these interpretive differences.

Regulations

Regulations are interpretations of statutory law that are published by a government agency; in the benefits area, the most significant regulations are published by the Treasury Department (the parent of the IRS), the Labor Department and the PBGC.

Regulations are structured as abstract rules, like the statutory law itself. They are not related to a particular factual situation, although they often contain useful examples that illustrate the application of the rules. Currently, Treasury regulations are often issued in question-and-answer form.

The numbering system for regulations is supposed to make them more accessible by including an internal reference to the underlying statutory provision. For example, Treasury Regulation Section 1.401(k)–2 is a regulation relating to Section 401(k) of the Internal Revenue Code. Labor Regulation Section 2550.408b–3 relates to Section 408b of ERISA.

Issuance of regulations follows a prescribed procedure involving an initial issuance of *proposed regulations,* followed by hearings and public comment, then *final regulations.* The process often takes years. Where taxpayers have an urgent need to know answers, the agency may issue *temporary regulations* instead of proposed regulations. Technically, temporary regulations are binding while proposed regulations are not. However, if a taxpayer takes a position contrary to a proposed regulation, the taxpayer is taking the risk that the regulation will ultimately be finalized and be enforced against him.

Rulings and Other Information

IRS Rulings

IRS rulings are responses by the IRS to requests by taxpayers to interpret the law in light of their particular fact situations. A *General Counsel Memorandum (GCM)* is similar to a ruling except that the request for clarification and guidance is initiated from an IRS agent in the field during a taxpayer audit, rather than directly from the taxpayer.

There are two types of IRS rulings—*Revenue Rulings,* which are published by the IRS as general guidance to all taxpayers, and *Private Letter Rulings (PLRs),* which are addressed only to the specific taxpayers who requested the rulings. The IRS publishes its Revenue Rulings in IRS Bulletins (collected in Cumulative Bulletins [CB] each year). Revenue rulings are binding on IRS personnel on the issues covered in them, but often IRS agents will try to make a distinction between a taxpayer's factual situation and a similar one covered in a ruling if the ruling appears to favor the taxpayer.

PLRs are not published by the IRS, but are available to the public with taxpayer identification deleted. These "anonymous" PLRs are published for tax professionals by various private publishers. They are not binding interpretations of tax law except for the taxpayer who requested the ruling, and even then they apply only to the exact situation described in the ruling request and do not apply to even a slightly different fact pattern involving the same taxpayer. Nevertheless, PLRs are very important in research since they are often the only source of information about the IRS position on various issues.

Other Rulings

The Department of Labor and the PBGC issue some rulings in areas of employee benefit regulation under their jurisdiction. DOL rulings include the *Prohibited Transaction Exemption (PTEs)* which rule on types of transactions that can avoid the prohibited transaction penalties—for example, sale of life insurance contracts to qualified plans.

Other Information

Because of frequent changes in the tax law, the IRS has been unable to promulgate regulations and rulings on a timely basis, and has increasingly used less formal approaches to inform taxpayers of its position. These include various types of published *Notices* and even speeches by IRS personnel. Finally, many important IRS positions are found only in *IRS Publications* (pamphlets available free to taxpayers) and *instructions* for filling out IRS forms. The IRS also maintains telephone question-answering services, but the value of these for information on complicated issues is minimal.

STUDY QUESTIONS

1. List four major management objectives for a pension plan and explain how the plan helps achieve these objectives.
2. What are the underlying social and historical reasons for the federal government's involvement in regulating private pension plans?
3. List some of the general features required for qualified retirement plans.
4. Identify the tax benefits available to the employer and the employees from a qualified plan.
5. Explain the difference between a pension plan and a profit-sharing plan.
6. Compare defined-benefit plans with defined-contribution plans with respect to
   a. Administrative costs.
   b. Individual account balances for participants.
   c. Risk of bad plan investments.
   d. Need for an actuary.
7. Identify the types of defined-contribution plans and their primary features.
8. Discuss the coverage available to partners and sole proprietors under qualified plans.
9. How are shareholder-employees treated under an S corporation for purposes of qualified plans?
10. Distinguish between multiple-employer plans, collectively bargained plans and multiemployer plans.
11. Explain the role of the courts in interpreting the tax laws pertaining to qualified plans.
12. What are the respective regulatory roles of Treasury Regulations, IRS Revenue Rulings and IRS private letter rulings?

19

Pension Plan Design: Eligibility, Contributions and Retirement Age

Objectives

- Explain the eligibility and participation requirements that must be met by qualified retirement plans with respect to
  1. Age and service requirements.
  2. Maximum age limits.
  3. Years of service.
  4. Breaks in service.
  5. Overall coverage tests.
- Explain the coverage rules when an employer has
  1. A group of employees in a collective bargaining unit.
  2. Separate lines of business.
  3. Affiliated or comonly controlled related employers.
- Explain why most pension plans are noncontributory.
- Discuss the importance of normal, early and late retirement ages in a qualified plan.

A basic problem in discussing qualified plans is the great variety of possible plan types. Many of the qualified plan rules apply to all types of qualified plans. In any complete discussion, there is a possibility that the same rules will be repeated again and again in different contexts. To minimize this problem, this chapter and the next three chapters will contain a relatively complete discussion of pension plans and the rules that apply to them. This is appropriate because pension plans are the most complex and significant of qualified plans, involving the majority of employees covered under qualified plans and well over half of the funds held by qualified plans. Because the qualified plan rules will be discussed thoroughly in these four chapters, only a brief review of these rules is necessary in Chapter 23, which discusses profit sharing and similar plans.

Qualified plan design is particularly complicated because there is constant interaction between the employer's objectives and the limits imposed by the qualified plan rules of the Internal Revenue Code and other provisions of the law. In this text, the approach will be to discuss both aspects of plan design together—plan design topics will be discussed from the standpoint of employer objectives and how these objectives can be accomplished within the limitations imposed by the qualified plan rules.

STRUCTURE AND DESIGN OF A PENSION PLAN

A qualified pension plan is a labyrinth of concepts and terminology. One way to thread the labyrinth is to follow an employee covered under a typical plan. This may help to illustrate the process of qualified pension plan design discussed here.

> **EXAMPLE:** Suppose Clutch Company has a qualified defined-benefit plan. When employee Tom Bill is hired, he does not automatically become a participant because he must first meet the plan's eligibility requirements, basically consisting of a definition of the covered group and a waiting period. When Tom enters the plan and becomes a plan *participant*, Clutch Company must begin to put money into a fund designed to accept, invest, accumulate and pay out money belonging to the plan. Also, when Tom enters, he begins to *accrue benefits* under the plan. In the Clutch Plan, as in many plans, the amount of benefit accrued each year is determined by estimating the benefit Tom will receive at retirement and allocating that amount in a specified manner over each of Tom's anticipated years of employment prior to his expected retirement date.
>
> Since the Clutch Plan does not allow loans to participants or provide incidental insurance coverage (although it could do these things), Tom will receive no benefit from the plan until he terminates employment with Clutch. If he terminates before retirement and before he has served Clutch long enough to be *vested*, he will receive nothing even though he has accrued a benefit under the plan. If he terminates after vesting, he will receive all or a portion of his benefit accrued to that date. This benefit will begin immediately if he has reached the plan's specified early retirement age or normal retirement age. These ages are 62 and 65 in the Clutch Plan, a typical choice of ages that is within the limits of the qualified plan law. If Tom has not reached either of these ages, the Clutch Plan will not pay benefits until he reaches age 65. If the benefit is very small, Tom will be paid his benefit immediately in a

cash lump sum. Except for this, the plan gives Tom a choice of various forms of benefit at retirement; all of these are of equal value to the plan—a life annuity, an annuity for the joint lives of Tom and his wife, and several others.

This little scenario illustrates the major planning decisions. These are, as discussed in this and the next several chapters:

- What group of employees should be covered under the plan? (Chapter 19)
- Should there be a waiting period for plan entry by new employees? (Chapter 19)
- Should the plan be funded solely by the employer or should employees contribute? (Chapter 19)
- What is the plan's normal retirement age and how are earlier and later retirement treated? (Chapter 19)
- What is the plan benefit at retirement? (Chapter 20)
- How fast do benefits accrue to employees? (Chapter 21)
- What do employees receive upon termination of employment before retirement (what is the vesting schedule)? (Chapter 21)
- What provisions should the plan have for employees who terminate employment because of death or disability? (Chapter 21)
- Who should hold the plan funds and on what terms? (Chapter 22)
- What will the plan cost the employer each year? (Chapter 22)
- In what form are benefits paid? (Chapter 23)

ELIGIBILITY AND PARTICIPATION

The employer must decide what group is to be covered by the qualified plan. In a closely held business, the employer will often want to provide a large portion of the plan's benefits to controlling and key employees and minimize benefits for rank and file employees. In larger plans, employers will often want to provide a different qualified plan (or no plan) for different groups of employees for various reasons; for example, the existence of collective bargaining units with separate plans, a desire for different benefit structures for hourly and salaried employees or differences in benefit policy for employees at different geographical locations.

In reviewing the many limitations imposed on the plan designer by the qualified plan rules, note that the overriding purpose for most of these rules is to prevent discrimination by the employer in favor of highly compensated employees. A secondary purpose, related to the first, is to provide and maintain some security of benefits for participants, particularly participants who are not highly compensated. Most of the qualified plan rules can be explained by these rationales; most questions about the meaning of particular rules and how they apply in a particular situation can be resolved by referring to these basic purposes of the law.

The Code imposes two types of limitations on the employer's freedom to designate the group of employees to be covered under the plan. The first limitation applies to the plan as it exists on paper—the eligibility provisions written into the plan. The second type of limitation applies to the plan in operation and provides minimum coverage requirements in the form of three alternative coverage tests. Both limitations are contained in Code Section 410 and its accompanying regulations and rulings.

First of all, as to plan coverage in the document itself, the designer has a good deal of freedom. The plan may cover only employees at a certain geographical location, employees in a certain work unit, salaried employees only, hourly employees only or almost any other variation. However, when eligibility is restricted on the basis of age or service with the employer, there are specific limits.

AGE AND SERVICE REQUIREMENTS

Although not all plans have age or service conditions for entry, many employers prefer such conditions because they help to avoid the cost of carrying an employee on the records as a plan participant when the employee quits after a short period of service. Generally, a plan cannot require more than one year of service before eligibility, and an employee who has attained the age of 21 must be permitted to participate in the plan if the employee has met the other participation requirements of the plan. Both age and service requirements can be imposed. For example, for an employee hired at age 19, the plan can require that employee to wait until age 21 to participate in the plan. However, an employee hired at age 27 cannot be required to wait more than one year before participating in the plan.

As an alternative to the one-year waiting period, a plan may provide for a waiting period of up to two years if the plan provides immediate 100 percent vesting upon entry. (In most other cases, graduated vesting is allowed—see the discussion in Chapter 21.) The two-year provision is often used by employers with very few employees and a high turnover rate—for example, a self-employed physician with one or two clerical or technical employees who have high mobility in their labor market. With a two-year provision, few of the employees may ever be covered.

One problem with these age and service requirements is that it is often desirable for a plan to have *entry dates*—that is, specific dates during the year in which plan participation is deemed to begin—in order to simplify recordkeeping. The regulations provide that no employee may be required to wait for participation more than six months after the plan's age and service requirements are met.[1] Thus, a plan having entry dates must adjust its eligibility provisions accordingly.

> **EXAMPLE:** The Blarp, Inc. pension plan wishes to have a one-year, age 21 entry requirement and to use an entry date or dates. Any of the following options will meet the requirement in the regulations:
>
> - Two entry dates in the year, six months apart, with participants entering on the next entry date after they satisfy the one-year, age 21 condition.

---

[1]Regulations Section 1.410(a)–4(b)(1).

- One entry date, but a minimum entry age of no more than 20½ and a maximum waiting period of six months.
- One entry date, with participants entering the plan on the date nearest (before or after) the date on which the one-year, age 21 requirement is satisfied.

All qualified plans are subject to the age 21 requirement, except for a plan maintained exclusively by a tax-exempt educational institution as defined in Code Section 170(b)(1)(a)(ii). To avoid coverage of temporary employees such as graduate teaching assistants, such a plan may provide a minimum age of 26, but the plan must have 100 percent vesting after one year of service.

Maximum Age Limits and Coverage of Older Employees

Coverage of employees who enter a defined-benefit or target plan when they are close to the plan's retirement age can present a funding problem, since there are relatively few years available to fund the benefit. If the participant enters the plan within a few years of retirement, the employer contribution may be burdensome. For example, using a given set of actuarial assumptions, the annual cost to fund the same benefit of $1,000 per month at age 65 varies with age at entry as follows:

Age at Plan Entry	Annual Cost
30	$ 537
50	3,410
55	6,391
60	15,783
62	28,521
64	92,592

The age discrimination law prohibits exclusion of employees who enter at later ages. However, as discussed later under "Retirement Age," a plan can define normal retirement age as the fifth anniversary of plan entry for a participant entering within five years of normal retirement age. This provides at least five years for funding. Alternatively, the time for funding the benefit can be extended simply by having the plan delay the beginning of benefit payments beyond retirement age, but payments cannot be delayed beyond the 10th anniversary of plan participation, and benefit payments must begin no later than April 1 of the year after attainment of age 70½; see Chapter 23.

Definition of Year of Service

The term *year of service* is used in different ways in the qualified plan rules. It is used to define the age and service rules for eligibility that were just discussed, and is also used in connection with the vesting and benefit accrual rules discussed in Chapter 21. Since it plays such an important part in these rules, it has a specific definition under the law.

Generally, a year of service is a 12-month period during which the employee has at least 1,000 hours of service.[2] For purposes of determining eligibility, the *initial* 12-month period must be measured beginning with the date the employee begins work for the employer. For other purposes, the 12-month accounting period used by the plan (the *plan year*) can generally be used. For example, suppose the plan uses the calendar year as the plan year. If an employee began work on June 1, 1992, the initial 12-month period for determining whether the 1,000-hour requirement had been met would be June 1, 1992 through May 31, 1993. If the employee did not perform 1,000 hours of service during that period, the plan could begin the next measuring period on January 1, 1993, with subsequent years being determined similarly on the basis of the plan year.

The employer may determine hours of service using payroll records or any other type of records that accurately reflect the hours worked. Alternatively, the regulations allow a plan to use "equivalency" methods for computing hours of service. These equivalencies allow employees to be credited with hours worked based on completion of some other unit of service such as a shift, week or month of service, without actual counting of hours worked.

Breaks in Service

A larger employer may reduce the cost of a plan somewhat by including a *break-in-service provision* in the plan's eligibility requirements. Under such a provision, an employee whose continuous service for the same employer is interrupted loses credit (upon returning to work) for service prior to the break and must again meet the plan's waiting period for eligibility. For a smaller employer, breaks in service followed by reemployment are relatively rare and such a provision may have no substantial cost impact other than possibly to complicate plan administration.

The rules under which a plan may interrupt service credits for breaks in service are somewhat complicated. The rules are set out in Code Section 410(a)(5) and regulations thereunder, as well as Labor Regulations Section 2530.200b. A one-year break in service for this purpose is defined as a 12-month period during which the participant has 500 or fewer hours of service. Service prior to a break cannot be disregarded until there is a one-year break in service. If the employee then returns to work, prebreak service may be disregarded (and the participant regarded as a new employee for participation purposes) within the following three limitations:

1. Service prior to the one-year break in service does not have to be counted unless the returned employee completes a year of service. Participation is then effective as of the first day of the plan year in which eligibility was reestablished.
2. If the plan has a two-year/100 percent vesting eligibility provision, prebreak service need not be counted if the employee did not complete two years of service before the break.
3. If the participant had no vested benefits at the time of the break, prebreak service need not be counted if the number of consecutive one-year breaks in

---

[2]See Code Sections 410(a)(3) (eligibility) and 411(a)(5) (vesting), and regulations thereunder.

service equals or exceeds the greater of five or the participant's years of service before the break. For example, suppose that participant Arlen works for Maple Corporation for eight months, quits, and then returns seven years later. For purposes of determining eligibility in the Maple Corporation Plan, Arlen's eight months of prebreak service do not have to be counted.

Other Eligibility Criteria Related to Age and Service

Since the age and service limitations must be met by the plan document as drafted, the IRS will scrutinize the plan to ascertain whether there are eligibility criteria that indirectly base eligibility on age and service. For example, the employer may wish to exclude part-time employees. The IRS views an exclusion of part-timers as a service-based eligibility provision. If the plan has a one-year service requirement for entry, it will exclude all employees who never work 1,000 hours or more in any year. However, the plan cannot exclude part-timers who work 1,000 hours or more in a year, but less than a full year, because such a requirement would be seen as a service requirement that violated the one-year, 1,000 hour rule. However, even if some part-timers must be included, the plan is allowed to have a benefit formula that provides smaller benefits for them because of their lesser compensation, or because part-time service is given less credit for benefit purposes than full-time service.

The IRS will also look at how a plan is actually operated to make sure that the age and service limitations are not violated. For example, suppose an employer has a plan for Division B of the business, and employment in Division B requires five years of service in Division A. Division B has a qualified plan and Division A does not. This service requirement, although outside the plan itself, could be seen as an attempt to circumvent the service limitation for the plan maintained by Division B.

OVERALL COVERAGE TESTS

H.C. – 70% } *Covered*
No H.C. [49%]
↘ *rest may be covered by S.S.*

In addition to the specific rules relating to age and service eligibility provisions, the second major limitation on the employer's freedom to exclude employees from a qualified plan is a set of two alternative statutory tests (Code Section 410) to be applied to the plan in actual operation to determine if coverage is discriminatory. A qualified plan must satisfy one of two coverage tests:

1. The *ratio percentage test:* The plan must cover a percentage of nonhighly compensated employee that is at least 70 percent of the percentage of highly compensated employees covered.
2. The *average benefit test:* The plan must benefit a nondiscriminatory classification of employees, and the average benefit, as a percentage of compensation, for all nonhighly compensated employees of the employer, must be at least 70 percent of that for highly compensated employees.

In addition, no plan can be qualified unless it covers, on each day of the plan year, the lesser of (1) 50 employees of the employer or (2) 40 percent or more of all employees of the employer (Code Section 401(a)(26)).

Employees Excluded

In applying these tests, certain employees are not taken into account:

- Employees who have not satisfied the plan's minimum age and service requirements, if any.
- Employees included in a collective bargaining unit, if there is evidence that retirement benefits were the subject of good-faith bargaining under a collective bargaining agreement.
- Employees excluded under a collective bargaining agreement between air pilots and employers under Title II of the Railway Labor Act.
- Employees who are nonresident aliens and who receive no earned income from sources within the United States.

The coverage tests apply not only at the plan's inception, but on an ongoing basis. Generally, all of the nondiscrimination requirements must be met by a plan on at least one day of each quarter of the plan's taxable year (Code Section 401(a)(6)). Although the IRS does not perpetually monitor a plan's compliance with the percentage coverage requirements, these requirements give the IRS an ongoing weapon to challenge a plan that may have become discriminatory.

Highly Compensated

For purposes of the coverage tests just described (and for many other employee benefit purposes as well), Code Section 414(q) provides a specific definition of a *highly compensated employee*. A highly compensated employee is any employee who during the year or the preceding year meets any of the following tests:

- Was at any time an owner of a more than 5 percent interest in the employer, or
- Received compensation from the employer in excess of $75,000 (this nominal $75,000 amount is indexed annually for inflation; in 1991 the amount was $90,803), or
- Received compensation from the employer in excess of $50,000 (as indexed; in 1991: $60,535), and was in the highest paid 20 percent of the employer's employees for the year, or
- Was at any time an officer and received compensation greater than 50 percent of the indexed Section 415 defined-benefit dollar limit (1991 limit: $108,963; 50 percent of this was $54,481.50). If the employer has fewer than 500 employees, no more than the greater of (a) three employees or (b) 10 percent of all employees, are treated as officers. If the employer has 500 or more employees, no more than 50 employees can be treated as officers.

Features of the Average Benefit Test

In some respects, the average benefit test is the least stringent of the two coverage tests, and many types of plan design will be able to qualify only under this test. For example, a common plan design provides separate plans for salaried and hourly employees. In many cases, neither plan individually—the salaried plan in particular—can meet the ratio percentage test and thus meets the average benefit test.

The average benefit test is two-pronged. First, the plan must cover a *nondiscriminatory classification* of employees. Because of this aspect of the test, the IRS has a degree of discretion in the determination of whether a classification is nondiscriminatory. However, the IRS has issued detailed regulations as guidance in interpreting whether there is a nondiscriminatory classification.

The second requirement of the average benefit test is that the *average benefit*, as a percentage of compensation for nonhighly compensated employees, must be at least 70 percent of that for highly compensated employees. In making this determination, all employees, whether covered or not under the plan in question, are counted and benefits from all qualified plans are taken into account.

Examples of Plan Coverage Meeting Various Tests

- Acme Trucking Company has ten employees, three of whom are highly compensated. A qualified plan covers the three highly compensated employees and five of the seven nonhighly compensated employees. This plan meets the ratio percentage test, since it covers at least 70 percent of nonhighly compensated employees.
- Barpt Products, Inc. has 20 employees, five of whom are highly compensated. If a qualified plan covers four of the highly compensated employees (80 percent), then the plan meets the ratio percentage test if it covers at least 56 percent of nonhighly compensated employees—70 percent of 80 percent—or, in this case, nine nonhighly compensated employees.
- Flim Company, Inc. has 500 employees, 100 of whom are salaried. Flim has a plan for salaried employees that covers 50 employees. Flim has received a determination from the IRS that the 50 salaried employees covered do not form a discriminatory classification, presumably because some low-paid salaried employees are covered as well as highly paid employees. The Flim Company Plan will qualify, so long as benefits are provided for nonhighly compensated employees as a group that are at least 70 percent of those for highly compensated employees as a group. Thus, some kind of retirement plan coverage for the hourly employees would be necessary.

Plans for Separate Lines of Business

If an employer has separate lines of business, the participation tests can be applied separately to employees in each line of business (Code Section 414(r)). A separate line of business must be operated for bona fide business reasons and must have at least 50 employees. If highly compensated employees constitute more than a specified percentage of the employees in the separate line of business, special guidelines apply or IRS approval may be required to use the separate line of business provision.

The separate line of business provision may allow a larger employer, or a controlled group of employers, to design separate plans—with separate coverage provisions—for its various operations. This increases the flexibility available in plan design to some extent.

SERVICE FOR PREDECESSORS AND OTHER EMPLOYERS

A plan of one employer generally does not need to give an employee credit for service with another employer. There are some situations, however, in which this is required. Under collectively bargained, multiemployer or multiple employer plans, service with more than one employer may have to be taken into consideration. Also, if the employer has chosen to take over or maintain the plan of a predecessor employer, service for the predecessor must be given credit. The IRS has not yet made clear what is meant by "predecessor employer," leaving some doubt as to the rules in this area. A common situation is the incorporation of a partnership and the continuation of the qualified plan of that partnership by the new corporation. The IRS once took the position that corporate employees who were partners in the prior partnership may not be given credit for prior service as partners. However, the IRS currently will probably permit this so long as regular employees receive full credit for service under the partnership.

Finally, service credit must be given for service with all employers under common control. The definition of *common control*, an important concept in the qualified plan area, is discussed in general terms below.

COMMONLY CONTROLLED EMPLOYERS

Often an employer organization (incorporated or unincorporated) is owned or controlled in common with other such organizations. The qualified plan designer must often coordinate plan coverage for the first employer with plan coverage for employees of other members of the commonly controlled group of employers.

The Code has several provisions relating to this issue; their basic objective is to prevent a business owner from getting around the coverage and nondiscrimination requirements for qualified plans by artificially segregating employees to be benefited from the plan into one organization with the remainder being employed by subsidiaries or organizations with lesser plan benefits or no plan at all. While this is still technically possible, the controlled group rules restrict this practice considerably.

Controlled Group Rules in General

Because the forms of business ownership can be tangled and complex, the common control rules for qualified plans are appropriately complicated. There are four sets of these rules.

1. Under Code Section 414(b), all employees of all corporations in a *controlled group* of corporations are treated as employed by a single employer for purposes of Sections 401, 408(k), 410, 411, 415 and 416. The major impact

of this comes from the participation rules of Section 410, which require the participation and coverage tests to be applied to the entire controlled group rather than to any single corporation in the group. Code Section 414(c) provides similar rules for commonly controlled partnerships and proprietorships.

2. Code Section 414(m) provides that employees of an *affiliated service group* are treated as employed by a single employer. This requirement similarly has its major impact in determining participation in a qualified plan; however, it applies to other employee benefit requirements as well.

3. A *leased employee* is treated as an employee of the lessor corporation under certain circumstances, under Code Section 414(n).

4. If a qualified plan covers a partner or proprietor who owns more than 50 percent of another business, then the plan or comparable plan must provide for employees of the controlled business (Code Section 401(d)).

Some examples will give a general idea of the impact of these provisions on plan design; a detailed discussion is beyond the scope of this book. Note that the common thread of these examples is that the related organization's employees must be *taken into account* in applying the participation rules. This does not mean that these employees must necessarily be covered.

- Alpha Corporation owns 80 percent of the stock of Beta Corporation. Alpha and Beta are members of a parent subsidiary controlled group of corporations. In applying the participation and coverage rules of Code Section 410, Alpha and Beta must be considered as a single employer.
- Bert and Harry own stock as follows:

Owner	Corporation A	Corporation B
Bert	60%	60%
Harry	30	30
	90%	90%

Corporations A and B are a brother-sister controlled group. Thus, A and B must be considered as a single employer for purposes of Code Section 410 and most other qualified plan rules.

- Medical Services, Inc. provides administrative and laboratory services for Dr. Sam and Dr. Joe, each of whom is an incorporated sole practitioner. Dr. Sam and Dr. Joe each own 50 percent of Medical Services, Inc. If either Dr. Sam or Dr. Joe adopts a qualified plan, employees of Medical Services, Inc. will have to be taken into account in determining if plan coverage is nondiscriminatory.
- Calculators Incorporated, an actuarial firm, contracts with Temporary Services, Inc., an employee-leasing firm, to lease employees on a substantially full-time basis. The leased employees will have to be taken into account in determining nondiscrimination in any qualified plan of Calculators, unless

Temporary maintains a minimum (10 percent nonintegrated) money-purchase pension plan for the leased employees.

- Stan and Fran are partners in a construction business. Fran is also a 60 percent partner in a road-paving business with 50 employees. If the Stan and Fran partnership adopts a qualified plan covering Stan and Fran, then the plan must either cover the 50 employees of the road-paving business or the road-paving business must provide a plan with coverage comparable to that provided for Stan and Fran.

WHO WILL PAY FOR THE PLAN?

Most qualified pension plans are funded entirely by the employer. Pension plans requiring contributions by employees, referred to as *contributory* plans, were once popular but are currently of diminishing importance. There are two reasons for this. First, employee contributions to a qualified plan other than "salary reductions" (see below) are *aftertax* contributions—the employee receives no tax deduction or exclusion for the contribution. Also, employee contributions involve administrative complications that have been aggravated by recent tax law changes, particularly Code Section 401(m), discussed in Chapter 23.

Many employers believe that retirement plan benefits are appreciated more by employees if the employees themselves contribute (or feel that they are contributing) toward their cost. In most cases, of course, most of an employee's income comes in the form of compensation from the employer, so there is some degree of illusion in this approach. Some employers may also believe that a contributory approach lowers plan costs, but this is not actually true. To the extent that a contributory approach results in the loss of tax benefits (in effect, a contribution to the plan by the U.S. Treasury), a contributory plan actually costs the employer more for the same level of benefits. A better justification for contributory plans is that they give the employee some degree of choice in allocating his or her compensation between cash and deferred benefits.

Currently, the most favorable contributory plan design is to use *salary reductions* in a plan that is permitted to use salary reductions—a Section 401(k) plan, a Section 403(b) plan, a Section 457 plan, or a simplified employee pension (SEP) plan (discussed in later chapters). Qualified pension plans cannot use salary reductions, except for some older plans that were "grandfathered" (permitted to use older law) when current law was enacted. Salary reductions are subject to FICA and FUTA (social security and federal unemployment) taxes but not to federal income tax. Thus, the tax benefits of qualified plans are not completely lost to the employee if the salary reduction approach is used.

RETIREMENT AGE

A plan's *normal retirement age* is the age at which a participant can retire and receive the full specified retirement benefit. A defined-benefit plan must specify a normal retirement age in order to fully define the benefit. Defined-contribution plans do not need a normal retirement age for this purpose, but they may have a normal retirement age in order to specify an age at which participants can retire and begin to receive benefits or, as discussed below, an age beyond which no further employer contributions will be made.

Under Code Section 411(a)(8), a plan's normal retirement age can be no greater than the latest of:

- Age 65.
- The fifth anniversary of plan entry if a participant entered within five years of normal retirement age.

Thus, for example, a plan having a normal retirement age of 65 could provide normal retirement at age 67 for a participant entering at age 62.

Although most plans use 65 as the normal retirement age, the plan may specify an earlier normal retirement age. The use of an earlier normal retirement age in a defined-benefit plan requires that funding be accelerated—larger amounts must be contributed to the plan each year to fund each employee's benefit because the benefit will become payable at an earlier date. For plans in which tax sheltering is a primary consideration, such as plans oriented toward key employees in a closely held business, the use of the earliest possible normal retirement age can provide significant additional tax benefits by increasing the deductible plan contributions each year. However, if the normal retirement age is less than the social security retirement age, the Section 415 limitations are reduced, as discussed in Chapter 25. This tends to provide some limit on the use of unrealistically low normal retirement ages.

The IRS considers a plan's retirement age to be an actuarial assumption. Therefore, the requirement of "reasonableness" for actuarial assumptions, as discussed in Chapter 22, also puts some limit on the use of unrealistically low normal retirement ages.

Early Retirement

A qualified plan may designate an *early retirement age* at which an employee may retire and receive an immediate benefit. The early retirement benefit is usually reduced below that payable at normal retirement. The plan may have some service requirement for early retirement, such as ten years of service, or it may permit early retirement simply upon attainment of the early retirement age.

Under most defined-benefit plans, the monthly early retirement benefit is reduced below the monthly normal retirement benefit payable at age 65 because of two factors. First, the early retirement benefit will usually be limited to the participant's accrued benefit, and the participant will often have not accrued the full benefit at early retirement. Second, most plans require an actuarial reduction. The actuarial reduction is a mathematical adjustment based on (1) longer life expectancy at early retirement, (2) loss of investment earnings to the plan fund due to payments beginning earlier and (3) loss of the possibility that the participant might die before payments begin—mortality.

Most plans do not require employer consent for early retirement. If employer consent is required, the IRS limits the early retirement benefit to the vested accrued benefit that would be payable if the employee terminated employment unilaterally, in order to avoid the possibility that the employer will favor highly compensated employees in granting early retirement benefits.

For defined-contribution plans, early retirement is usually treated the same as a termination of employment, and the benefit payable at early retirement is simply the amount of the participant's account balance as of that date. Thus, many defined-contribution plans do not specify an early retirement age.

Some employers offer a "subsidized" early retirement benefit—one that is reduced by less than the full amount dictated by the three factors discussed above—as an incentive for retirement. The subsidized benefit is often offered during a limited "window" period, during which the employee must either choose the benefit or lose the opportunity to receive it forever (or at least until the employer decides to offer another window benefit). There are specific legal protections under the Age Discrimination Act for employees in this situation.

Late Retirement

A qualified plan design should also cover the possibility of late retirement— retirement after the normal retirement age. Under the age discrimination rules discussed below, the plan must continue benefit accruals for employees who continue working after the normal retirement age unless the plan's benefit formula stops benefit accruals after a specified number of years and the employee has enough years of service to cease accruals for that reason. Benefit formulas must be designed carefully to insure appropriate treatment of older employees. In smaller businesses, older participants are often owners or key employees who will want the plan to provide substantial benefits. On the other hand, many larger employers want to encourage earlier retirement and will want to provide only the minimum late retirement benefit required under the law.] *College Prof < 70 yrs old)*

Age Discrimination

The Federal Age Discrimination Act, as amended in 1978, 1986 and 1989, has an impact on qualified plans. The Age Discrimination Act applies to workers and managers of any business that engages in interstate transactions (a very broad category) and employs at least 20 persons during the year. Certain hazardous occupations are excluded as well as executive employees who would be entitled, upon retirement, to an annual pension of $44,000 or more over and above social security benefits.

The main provision of the Age Discrimination Act that affects qualified plans is that which prohibits involuntary retirement at any age. A qualified plan must not in any way require mandatory retirement.

In addition, the 1986 legislation added specific provisions (Code Sections 411(b)(1)(H) and 411(b)(2)) dealing with benefits for older workers. In general, older workers must be treated the same as younger workers with regard to plan contributions (for a defined-contribution plan) and benefit accruals (for a defined-benefit plan). However, for a defined-benefit plan, the benefit formula can provide that benefits are fully accrued not at a specified age but after a specified number of years of service, such as 25. This will cut off further benefit accrual for many older employees, but it is permitted. If a plan provides for normal retirement at 65 with actuarial increases for later retirement, the actuarial increases are credited toward any requirement of benefit accrual that applies. For example, if a plan provides a benefit of $1,000 per month beginning at age 65 or an actuarially adjusted $1,100 per month beginning at age 66, the extra $100 is counted as an additional benefit accrual.

STUDY QUESTIONS

1. Describe the coverage of employees who enter into a defined-benefit or a target plan when they are close to the plan's normal retirement age.
2. For purposes of a qualified plan, explain what requirements an employee must satisfy to earn credit for a year of service.
3. Jane Chaney worked two years for BIGGO, and acquired two years of service under BIGGO's defined-benefit plan. The BIGGO Company has a vesting schedule that grants a fully vested benefit after the employee has attained five years of service with no vesting until then. Jane left after two years, but returned to work after a four-year absence. Will Jane's break in service cause her to lose her pre-break service? Explain.
4. Which of the following employees of the Kelvin Company are considered highly compensated employees for nondiscrimination purposes?

	Salary
Kathy Kelvin (100 percent stock owner/president)	$400,000
Lou Jane (vice president/treasurer)	$180,000
Manny Martin	$ 47,000
Nancy Norris	$ 40,000
Oprah Oliver	$ 22,000
Peter Peaquin	$ 20,000

5. a. The Alpha Company has 20 employees, six of whom are highly compensated. The Alpha Plan covers the six highly compensated employees and 11 of the 14 employees who are not highly compensated. Does the Alpha Plan pass the ratio percentage test?
   b. The Beta Company has ten employees, two of who are highly compensated. The Beta Plan covers the two highly compensated employees and covers seven of the eight employees who are not highly compensated. Does the Beta Plan pass the ratio percentage test?
6. For qualified plan purposes, what is the significance of treating more than one business as a controlled group of corporations?
7. The president of The New England Cannery (250 employees) is undecided about whether her company's qualified pension plan should provide for employee contributions.

   a. Explain the advantages and disadvantages of including mandatory employee contributions in the plan.

   b. What type of plan eliminates the problem of lost tax benefits arising from employee contributions?

8. a. Why do defined-benefit plans use a normal retirement age requirement?

   b. What is the latest normal retirement age that a qualified plan may use?

   c. What are the advantages and disadvantages of using a pre-65 normal retirement age in a closely held business?

9. Why are early retirement benefits typically reduced below the monthly normal retirement benefit payable at age 65?

20

Pension Benefit Formulas

Objectives

- Describe the types of retirement benefit formulas that can be included in defined-contribution pension plans and in defined-benefit plans.
- Explain the planning reasons for integrating a qualified plan formula with social security benefits.
- Describe offset and integration level formulas and explain the integration rules applying to such formulas.

A pension plan's benefit formula is obviously the central issue in plan design. Great variety is possible, within the restrictions to be discussed here. Some simple rules should be set forth at the outset. First, the plan formula cannot, on its face, discriminate in favor of highly compensated employees. Also, civil rights laws prevent discrimination with respect to race, religion or national origin. Age discrimination issues were discussed in Chapter 19.

The discussion of benefit formulas in this chapter is organized as follows:

- Defined-contribution formulas.
- Defined-benefit formulas.
- Inflation and pension planning.
- Integration of plan formulas with social security.

DEFINED-CONTRIBUTION FORMULAS

A defined-contribution plan is much simpler than a defined-benefit plan. In a defined-contribution plan, the plan specifies the amount that the employer will contribute to the plan. There are two basic types of contribution formulas for defined-contribution pension plans—the *money-purchase* formula and the *target-benefit* formula. For a money-purchase formula, the annual employer contribution is usually a stated percentage of each employee's compensation—for example, 6 percent of compensation. The target-benefit formula uses an actuarial approach, providing larger contribution percentages for older plan entrants.

The great advantage of a defined-contribution plan, particularly a money-purchase plan, is simplicity. The benefit formula is readily understandable by employees and employer, actuarial services are not required and plan installation and drafting are simpler. Also, the PBGC insurance and reporting requirements (Chapter 26) do not apply to defined-contribution plans.

In terms of the number of plans, defined-contribution plans—including profit sharing and pension plans—constitute about 70 percent of all qualified plans. However, if a comparison is made on the basis of employees covered under qualified plans, the result is the opposite—about 60 percent of such employees are in defined-benefit plans. This indicates, not surprisingly, that defined-benefit plans tend to cover larger groups. However, defined-benefit plans are often used for smaller groups as well.

Money-Purchase Formulas

In a money-purchase plan, as in all defined-contribution plans, there is an individual account for each employee. The amount of the benefit at retirement is equal to the employee's account balance at the retirement date or at a valuation date near the time of the retirement date. The plan may provide for payment of the benefit in a lump sum; a variety of payment options, including annuity benefits, may also be made available. The accounts of all employees are usually commingled for investment purposes; each account is kept separate administratively, so that the account increases and decreases in accordance with the investment performance of the fund. Thus, the benefit available at retirement cannot be predicted exactly. Investment risk lies with the employee. If the employee's account is less than anticipated, the employer is not required to make additional contributions.

As Table 20-1 shows, money-purchase plans tend to provide a better benefit for employees who enter the plan at younger ages, because a longer period of time is available to accumulate plan contributions and compound these contributions with investment earnings. If the employer has employees with a wide range of ages at the inception of the plan, this feature of a money-purchase plan makes it impossible to provide older employees with retirement income that is comparable, as a percentage of their preretirement income—the *replacement ratio*—to that of the younger employees. As discussed later, comparable replacement ratios for older and younger employees can be better achieved with a target plan or defined-benefit plan.

Target Plans

From a planning point of view, the target plan is a hybrid of the defined-contribution and defined-benefit approaches. Under a target plan, the employer

TABLE 20-1
Defined-Contribution Plan Accumulations

Age at Plan Entry	Account Balance at Retirement
25	$213,609
30	147,913
40	67,676
50	26,888
55	14,783
60	6,153

Assumptions: Annual employer contributions: $1,000 per employee; retirement age: 65; average investment return: 7%.

chooses a target level of retirement benefit using a benefit-formula approach similar to that used in designing a defined-benefit plan.

For example, the target level might be some percentage of each participant's final-average compensation. An actuarial calculation is made at the plan's inception of the level annual contribution amount (for each participant) that would be required to fully fund this benefit at the participant's normal retirement date. These level amounts are then actually contributed by the employer to the plan each year. Unlike a defined-benefit plan, however, there is no change in the level contribution amount if actual investment return or mortality varies from the assumptions used in determining the initial contribution level, unless the plan is actually amended. Therefore, at retirement, the amount actually available may be more or less than anticipated. The plan has individual accounts for each participant and unlike a defined-benefit plan, each employee's benefit is limited to the amount actually in his or her individual account.

The best way to understand how a target plan works is to examine Table 20-2. This example uses a somewhat unrealistic employee census for illustrative purposes only—the employees vary in age but the same annual compensation of $30,000 is assumed for each. The target benefit is 50 percent of the final-average compensation and for purposes of funding the plan initially, the current compensation is used. This is the usual approach even though it might theoretically be possible to use an assumption of salary increases (salary scale). However, this ordinarily would not be feasible because the projected compensation levels, particularly for younger employees, would tend to reach very high levels. In this illustrative plan, the 50 percent target benefit would provide a pension of $15,000 annually for each employee.

The column of the table headed "Annual Contribution" represents the annual level employer contribution required to fund this pension beginning at age 65, using an actuarial computation. Actuarial methods and assumptions are discussed in Chapter 22. For reference, the assumptions here are a 5 percent interest rate and an annuity purchase rate at age 65 of $1,400 for $10 per month. At that annuity purchase rate, it would be necessary to have $175,000 in the fund for each participant at age 65 to provide a pension of $15,000 annually. The annual contribution is the level-funding amount that will provide a fund equal to $175,000 for each employee as that employee reaches age 65. The calculation does not use a

TABLE 20-2* Target Plan (nonintegrated)							
Employee's Age	50% "Target" Compensation Pay Benefit	Annual Contribution	5½% "Target" Maturity Value‡	4% Average Return Maturity Value	8% Average Return Maturity Value	10% Average Return Maturity Value
20	$30,000	$15,000	$ 901	$175,000	$113,398	$376,067	$712,506
30	30,000	15,000	1,655	175,000	126,739	307,998	493,400
40	30,000	15,000	3,243	175,000	140,451	256,030	350,833
45	30,000	15,000	4,757	175,000	147,327	235,117	299,703
50	30,000	15,000	7,402	175,000	154,146	217,056	273,502
55	30,000	15,000	12,883†	175,000	160,866	201,554	255,854
60	30,000	15,000	29,721†	175,000	167,418	188,312	199,594

*This table is adopted from an illustration used in The American College's Advanced Pension Planning program.

†Since a target plan is subject to the defined-contribution maximum annual additions limitation of 25% or $30,000, the contribution for these two employees would have to be limited to $7,500 ($30,000 × 25%).

‡Based on a 5½% interest rate and an annuity purchase rate of $1,400 for $10 per month.

mortality assumption. This will be appropriate for a small employee group and a plan that provides a death benefit equal only to the participant's account balance.

Note first of all that the annual contribution on behalf of the employees of varying ages is radically different. The contribution for older employees is much greater, relatively speaking, because less time is available to fund the benefit. In this respect, a target plan is similar to a defined-benefit plan. In some cases, this may allow the plan to discriminate significantly in favor of employees who are older when the plan is initiated—typically the owners of the company or other members of the prohibited group. The extent to which such discrimination is possible is somewhat limited, however, as will be discussed below.

The second point to note is that a target plan is a defined-contribution plan for purposes of the Section 415 limits (see Chapter 25). Thus, the annual addition to each participant's account cannot exceed the lesser of 25 percent of compensation or the applicable dollar figure for the year in which the annual addition is made ($30,000, as indexed for inflation). In this example, it means that the contribution determined by the actuary for employees age 55 and 60 is too much. For those employees, only $7,500 (25 percent of $30,000) can be contributed because of the annual-additions limit. Thus, because the annual-additions limit applies to a target plan, it restricts to some degree the amount of discrimination in favor of older employees that is possible in a target plan as compared with a defined-benefit plan. If the plan in this example were a defined-benefit plan, the corporation could contribute the actuarially determined amount for the two employees age 55 and 60 ($12,883 and $29,721, respectively) because the annual-additions limit would not apply, and the benefit of 50 percent of final average compensation would be well within the Section 415 limit for defined-benefit plans.

A third important feature of the target plan illustrated here is that even though the actuarially determined contribution level is designed to provide the same pension benefit for all participants (50 percent of compensation or $15,000), if the actual rates of return vary from the actuarial assumptions, the benefits will differ. A lower rate of return will produce a lower benefit for everyone (refer to the column headed "4% Average Return Maturity Value"); older employees will do better at retirement than younger employees. Conversely, a return higher than the assumed rate will provide everyone with a better pension than expected; the higher rate will tend to favor younger employees (refer to the column headed "8% or 10%' Average Return Maturity Value").

This feature of the target plan provides a possibility for manipulating the initial interest assumption to discriminate in favor of older or younger employees, depending on which group the planner desires to favor. Because of this, the IRS imposes a restriction on assumed investment rates in Revenue Ruling 76-464; the assumed rate must be between 5 and 6 percent to avoid special IRS scrutiny. If a different assumed rate is used, the employer will have to prove that the plan does not discriminate in favor of the prohibited group.

The contributions to a target plan may be invested in a variety of ways. Generally, the approach is to invest in a separate equity portfolio to obtain the benefits of equity growth and provide a hedge against inflation. At retirement, the existing account may be used to provide a benefit in whatever form is appropriate. A lump sum or an annuity are the usual forms of benefit.

It is possible to integrate a target plan with social security. The rules for this are complex and will not be given in detail here.

DEFINED-BENEFIT FORMULAS

The basic difference between a defined-benefit plan and a defined-contribution plan is that in a defined-benefit plan, the plan formula specifies the benefit that will be paid to the employee. There are no individual accounts for employees and, consequently, the employee does not bear the risk of bad investment results. Payment of the promised benefit is an obligation of the employer and the employer is required to fund the plan in advance so that sufficient funds will be available. Within certain limits, benefits in a defined-benefit plan are insured by the federal government through the Pension Benefit Guaranty Corporation (PBGC).

Defined-benefit plans are the most complex of all qualified plans. The benefit formulas themselves tend to be complex because of the variety of employer objectives sought. The actuarial funding approach requires additional administrative costs for the plan. Hence, the law dealing with defined-benefit plans is appropriately complex.

General Characteristics of Defined-Benefit Formulas

Defined-benefit formulas have two basic characteristics that determine their use in pension plan design. First, the amount of an employee's benefit is not necessarily directly related to total compensation from the employer during the period the employee is covered under the plan. This means that the employer can design the plan with reference to a desired retirement income level for an employee, even if the employee had relatively low compensation in certain years or participated in the plan for a relatively short time.

The second basic characteristic is that defined-benefit formulas can favor those employees who enter the plan at later ages. This is because the benefit for such employees is a stated amount—often the same amount payable to employees who entered the plan at earlier ages—even though the employer's annual cost for funding the benefit is greater for employees entering the plan at later ages. As an example, consider three employees having the same compensation of $50,000 annually and a plan providing a benefit of 50 percent of this compensation at age 65. If these employees entered the plan at ages 30, 40 and 50, the employer's level annual cost to provide the same retirement benefit for each is illustrated in Table 20-3.

These basic characteristics relate to the two principal types of employer objectives that can be met with a defined-benefit plan. One objective is to provide a reasonable income replacement ratio for all covered employees. The flexibility of defined-benefit formulas permits this. The other type of objective is philosophically quite different—the objective of providing the maximum tax shelter under the plan for key employees. In a closely held business where this objective is often dominant, key employees are typically older at the plan's inception. Thus, the second basic defined-benefit plan characteristic illustrated in Table 20-3 is significant, as is the flexibility of defined-benefit formula design.

Replacement Ratio Approach

In adopting an income replacement ratio approach to benefit formula design, the starting point is to examine the census of the employees to be covered and determine an appropriate level of retirement income. For all but the lowest paid employees, a retiree's standard of living can usually be maintained with less than 100 percent of preretirement income. Some reasons for this are that there are no work-related expenses after retirement, that the need to save after retirement is reduced and that living expenses of older persons tend to be less than those of working persons. Certain expenses of older persons that tend to go up, such as medical care, are often covered under Medicare or other health insurance. Replacement ratios for lower income employees should be higher because an individual closer to the subsistence level tends to spend most of his or her income for basic

---

TABLE 20-3
Entry Age and DB Contribution

Age at Entry	Employer Contribution Each Year to Retirement
30	$ 1,971
40	4,309
50	10,847

Assumptions: 7 percent investment return, no mortality, unisex annuity purchase rate $1,400 per $10 monthly at age 65.

items such as food and shelter, and these expenses at a basic level are not likely to decline after retirement. Qualified plans that use this approach typically aim at providing about 50 to 75 percent of preretirement gross (before-tax) income from the plan plus social security retirement benefits.

An appropriate benefit formula is designed to provide the desired replacement ratio, using the design rules discussed in the rest of this chapter. The annual cost of the plan is then determined. If this exceeds the employer's cost objectives, the plan must be redesigned until the cost comes within the appropriate range. It is also possible to vary the annual cost by varying the actuarial methods and assumptions used, as discussed in Chapter 22.

Types of Formulas

Many different benefit formulas have been developed to meet various plan design objectives. A large degree of variation is possible, within the limits of the rules for integration with social security, discussed later, the benefit accrual rules discussed in Chapter 21 and the general nondiscrimination requirements for qualified plans. The possible benefit formulas can be divided into specific types. The IRS distinguishes two types of benefit formulas, the flat-benefit formula and the unit-benefit formula.

Flat-Benefit Formula

This type of formula does not take an employee's service into account. Such a benefit formula might be either a *flat-amount* formula, such as a formula providing a benefit of $100 per month at retirement for each employee, or a *flat-percentage* formula—for example, a benefit of 40 percent of compensation at retirement.

The flat-amount approach is usually suitable only for a group of employees having almost the same compensation levels, because most pension planners would want to take differing compensation levels into account in determining the retirement income level. However, the flat-amount formula has the advantage of simplicity. The flat-percentage approach takes differing compensation into account and is frequently used. The plan's definition of compensation, as discussed below, is an important element of this formula.

All flat-benefit formulas raise the problem of fairness among employees with differing amounts of service with the employer. Many employers would prefer not to give the same benefit to short- and long-service employees, even though they have the same compensation levels. This objection can often be resolved by having a minimum period of service required in order to receive the full stated dollar amount or percentage, with reductions for lesser amounts of service. A more definite solution is to use a unit-benefit formula, discussed next.

Unit-Benefit Formula

A unit-benefit formula is based on the employee's service. Some unit-benefit formulas take only service into account, with no compensation factor—for example, a benefit of $10 per month for each year of service. As with the flat-benefit formula, such a formula is usually only suitable for a group having a fairly narrow range of compensation. Such formulas are sometimes used in collectively bargained plans, for example. A unit-benefit formula may also take account of compensation—for example, a formula providing a benefit of 1 percent of compensation for each year of service (or to state it another way, 1 percent of compensation times the employee's years of service). *Career avg. - % of service*

Find avg. -

Past Service

When a unit-benefit plan is installed for an existing—rather than new—employee group, the employer must decide whether to give service credit only for prospective or future service or to give some credit for existing employees' prior service for the employer. In small, closely held businesses, the owners and key employees often have considerable past service compared with other employees; it is particularly common to have past-service provisions in such plans. Past-service credit can be provided in many ways, so long as there is no discrimination in favor of highly compensated employees. Past service can be treated the same as future service, or the formula can provide lesser credit for past service.

The ability to utilize past service is one of the major advantages of a defined-benefit plan over a defined-contribution plan. For example, suppose a plan is adopted by an employer with two employees, one age 30 with five years of prior service and the other age 50 with 25 years of prior service. If a defined-contribution plan is adopted, the younger employee will have at age 65 a plan account representing 35 years of employer contributions, while the older employee will have only 15 years of contributions at retirement. However, a unit-benefit plan providing an annual benefit of 1 percent of compensation for each year of past and future service would allow each employee to retire at age 65 with an annual benefit of 40 percent of compensation.

The Cash-Balance Formula

The cash-balance formula—sometimes referred to as a guaranteed-account formula, as well as by other names—is a type of hybrid between defined-benefit and defined-contribution approaches that is in a sense the opposite of the other hybrid, the target formula. In the target formula, employer contributions are based on age at entry, but ultimate benefits are not guaranteed. With a cash-balance formula, employer contributions are based on compensation, not on age at entry; the ultimate benefit (account balance) is subject to a guaranteed rate of return.

In a cash-balance plan, "accounts" for each participant are set up. Unlike the accounts in a defined-contribution plan, there is no investment risk—the accounts are merely a computational formality. The accounts are credited at least annually with two types of credits—a pay credit and an interest credit.

The pay credit is generally a percentage of compensation. The pay credit formula may be integrated with social security; for example, the plan might provide a pay credit each year of 2 percent of each participant's total earnings plus

3 percent of the participant's earnings above an integration level related to the social security taxable wage base. A cash-balance formula must meet the rules for integrating a defined-benefit plan (see below). The actuary typically will do this by showing that the "worst case"—the most discriminated-against participant—will receive at least as much as under the defined-benefit integration rules.

The interest credit is an amount representing earnings on the participant's account balance. To meet the definitely determinable rule applicable to pension formulas, the interest credit must be an amount that is defined in the plan and not subject to the employer's discretion. For example, the interest credit each year might be defined as the lesser of the change in the Consumer Price Index (CPI) for the preceding year or the one-year rate for Treasury securities. However, the employer can have the option of crediting actual plan earnings, if these are higher.

Because there are no true individual accounts—participants have a guaranteed minimum benefit that can be legally satisfied out of the entire plan fund—the plan does not meet the definition of a defined-contribution plan and is thus technically a defined-benefit plan. Consequently, the plan is subject to a more complex legal environment; it is subject to PBGC reporting and termination requirements and the requirement of actuarial certification.

The employer's cost for the plan is determined actuarially because of the guarantee features. Costs can be controlled to some extent by choosing appropriate factors for the interest credits. However, if interest credits do not keep pace with actual plan earnings, participants are likely to be dissatisfied with the plan.

Despite the plan's technical status as a defined-benefit plan, a cash-balance plan looks very much like a money-purchase plan and serves some of the same objectives. Typically, the cash-balance plan will be attractive to younger employees, for the reasons already discussed. Thus, it is attractive to employers wishing to retain younger employees or allocate pension costs in a way that does not discriminate against younger employees. At the same time, the guarantee features help to meet some of the retirement security objectives of the traditional defined-benefit plan.

Definition of Compensation

For formulas that are based on compensation, the definition of compensation provides some flexibility in planning. Definitions of compensation can be classified into two categories: *career average* and *final average*. With a career-average formula, the employee's compensation over the entire working period is averaged. Another way of putting this is that the benefit earned in a given year of service is based on the compensation for that year. Any defined-contribution formula is effectively a career-average formula, but defined-benefit plans can also use the career-average approach. In a final-average formula, the compensation used is averaged over a specified period of years, usually chosen to produce a relatively high benefit. For example, the compensation used in the benefit formula could be defined as compensation over the employee's five final years of service. To guard against the possibility of a salary decrease in the final years of service due to partial disability or other cause, many plans define compensation as the compensation over a specified consecutive period during which the average compensation is the highest.

In defining compensation for plan purposes, a decision must be made whether to use total compensation (salary or wages plus bonuses, overtime and so forth) or some lesser amount such as base salary only. Flexibility is permitted here, but if anything other than total compensation is used, the method chosen must not produce discrimination. For example, excluding overtime pay in the benefit formula might be discriminatory if lower paid workers typically receive substantial overtime pay while prohibited group employees do not.

Sex Discrimination

Sex discrimination as it relates to qualified plans, annuities and life insurance is a subject that is not yet completely resolved, but some clear rules for qualified plan design have emerged. The issue arises from the statistical fact that women, as a group, live longer than men. This means that if actuaries make separate calculations for men and women, the same periodic annuity costs more for women than for men of the same age. Or, for a given annuity premium, the periodic annuity amount is lower for women than for men.

The Civil Rights Act of 1964, like its predecessor, the Equal Pay Act of 1963, provides that it is an unlawful employment practice for an employer

> to discriminate against any individual with respect to his compensation, terms, conditions or privileges of employment, because of such individual's race, color, religion, sex or national origin [Section 2000e-2(a), Civil Rights Act of 1964].

It is clear that qualified plan benefits are part of an employee's compensation; it was not originally clear, however, what constituted sex discrimination in a qualified plan.

- Must the plan provide the same periodic *benefit* for both men and women employees?
- Must the plan provide only the same employer *contribution* to the plan?

Early federal administrative guidelines under the Equal Pay Act of 1963 indicated that an employer satisfied the nondiscrimination requirement if it provided *either* equal periodic benefits or equal contributions. However, in 1972, the Equal Employment Opportunities Commission (EEOC) issued a revised sex discrimination guideline under the Civil Rights Act of 1964: To avoid sex discrimination in retirement plans, the employer must provide equal periodic benefits to men and women employees in all circumstances. Employers originally resisted this guideline, but recent court cases clearly point in this direction. The first significant case went to the United States Supreme Court, *Los Angeles Department of Water and Power v. Manhart*, 435 US 702 (1978). That case involved a contributory pension plan of a municipality. The Supreme Court held that the plan could not require women to pay higher contributions than men in order to receive equal periodic benefits upon retirement. Subsequently, the Supreme Court held in *Arizona Governing Committee v. Norris*, 103 S.Ct. 3492 (1983), that a municipal retirement plan could not provide sex-based annuity choices at retirement. No employer contributions were involved—only employee contributions.

Neither the Manhart and Norris cases nor any other case has yet clearly settled the question whether the Civil Rights Act requires equal periodic benefits for men and women in an employer-provided retirement plan under all circumstances. Each case depends on specialized facts. However, the trend favors an equal-benefit approach and virtually all planners assume this to be the law.

Most qualified plans already avoid obvious sex discrimination problems. Most defined-benefit plans provide the same normal retirement benefit for men and women employees; most defined-contribution plans provide the same employer contribution for men and women employees. Discrimination problems arise when a qualified plan (either defined-benefit or defined-contribution) offers participants a choice of benefits including a retirement annuity. Most plan designers advise using only "unisex" annuities (those providing the same annuity rate for both men and women) for this purpose. Similarly, if a qualified plan offers life insurance as an incidental benefit (see Chapter 21), the life insurance cost to the employee must be determined on a unisex basis. However, in determining the annual deposit to a defined-benefit plan, the sex of covered employees may be taken into account, since it affects only the employer's costs and not the ultimate benefit that the employee will receive.

The sex discrimination issue is complicated by the fact that the Civil Rights Act does not govern the pricing of insurance products; private insurance companies, therefore, currently are allowed to use sex as a factor in determining life insurance and annuity rates. The argument has been made that when a qualified plan uses a group pension contract for funding, sex-based annuity options should be allowed under the group contract. However, it is the employer, not the insurance company, that provides the pension as part of an employee's compensation. In view of this and the trend of the court cases, insurance companies no longer offer sex-based annuities as part of a group pension contract.

Even if employers remove any conceivable sex discrimination from qualified plan documents, if the plan is designed so that participants can withdraw their benefits at retirement, effective sex discrimination will still be possible so long as sex-based annuities are available from insurance companies. In that situation, men can withdraw their benefits and purchase an annuity from an insurance company providing greater periodic payments than women would be able to purchase for the same amount (or payments greater than those available under the plan if the plan provides a unisex annuity). Because of this and other related problems, Congress may reconsider the question whether insurance companies should be allowed to determine annuity and life insurance premiums on the basis of sex.

There is no doubt that sex is a relevant actuarial classification, as is any ascertainable factor affecting life expectancy, which could conceivably include such things as race, religion or national origin. Insurance companies do not commonly use race or other potentially offensive actuarial factors, regardless of their relevance as predictors of life expectancy. However, they are strongly attached to the use of sex classifications and have vigorously opposed restrictions proposed in Congress.

Both sides of the controversy view the issue as one of fairness. Advocates of sex classification argue that unisex annuity rates are unfair to men, who should be allowed to purchase annuities reflecting their group's life expectancy. Opponents argue that it is unfair to attribute to an individual the characteristics of a group to which that individual belongs, regardless of whether the individual actually possesses those characteristics. Ultimately, Congress may have to determine the appropriate social policy in connection with insurance company practices.

INFLATION AND PENSION PLANNING

Inflation has been a persistent feature of the U.S. economy since World War II. Although the rate of inflation has gone up and down during that period, many economists believe that some degree of inflation is a permanent structural feature of our economy. A qualified plan, particularly a defined-benefit pension plan, is a theoretically long-range program; benefit levels are often determined for a 25-year-old employee that will not be paid until 40 years later. Thus, inflation is a serious problem in the design of pension plans.

Although no really satisfactory solution to the problem of inflation in private pension plans has yet been devised, there are some planning approaches that can help with this problem. A distinction can be made between approaches that are applied in the preretirement period while the employee is still at work, and in the postretirement period, when the employee is least able to protect against inflation.

Preretirement Inflation

Some types of benefit design are inherently better able to cope with preretirement inflation than others. If the plan benefit depends upon employee compensation, the final-average definition of compensation usually does a better job in protecting the employee against inflation than the career-average definition because the final-average definition bases benefits on the employee's highest compensation level. Much of the increase in an employee's compensation level over a working career merely reflects inflation. Other reasons for compensation increases are increases in general employee productivity and increases in the individual employee's merit, and both are also appropriately reflected in the retirement benefit. If the plan does not use a final-average formula, the employer should consider periodically reviewing the plan's benefit level in light of inflation and amending the plan to increase benefits as appropriate. It is also possible to include an automatic mechanism in the plan under which future benefit levels for current employees are increased in accordance with some kind of formula based on the inflation rate; however, this is rarely done.

Defined-contribution plans provide some inflation protection not available under defined-benefit plans because the benefit in the defined-contribution plan depends upon the value of the investments in each participant's account. In the long run, a reasonably diversified investment portfolio tends to increase in value to keep pace with inflation. This is not necessarily true for short periods; in the 1970s, for example, common stocks often declined even as inflation reached new heights. However, most economists believe that the long-range linkage between asset values and inflation will continue, so defined-contribution plans can be useful in dealing with inflation. Naturally, for this to occur the investment portfolio has to be chosen to emphasize the types of assets—common stocks, for example—that typically show inflation-related growth.

A defined-contribution plan, however, has a disadvantage similar to that of a career-average benefit formula; contributions to the participant's account in the early years are based on then-current compensation, which typically is at a low level compared with later years. This disadvantage tends to mitigate the advantage of possible investment-related growth.

Postretirement Inflation

In the postretirement period, one approach to inflation protection in defined-benefit plans is *indexation* of retirement benefits. With an indexed formula, the plan provides that the benefit is to be increased after retirement in accordance with some formula contained in the plan. The design problem here is the choice of a formula that is affordable by the employer and that accurately reflects the impact of inflation on retirees.

One approach is to use the CPI, a price index provided by the government. The CPI is a measure of the relative rise from month to month of a "market basket" of consumer products purchased by a hypothetical average consumer. There is some debate as to whether the CPI accurately reflects the impact of inflation on retired persons, since it may emphasize rising prices of items not normally purchased by retirees or conversely, may understate the impact of rising prices for items particularly important to retirees. At one time, for example, the CPI had a large component reflecting the cost of new housing, which typically is not a significant item in retirees' budgets.

The government also provides various types of wage indexes indicating the increase in wages in specific portions of the work force. Theoretically, it is possible to index retirement benefits in accordance with a wage index. Based on past experience, this would produce a larger increase in retirement benefits than a price index, because wage indexes reflect increases in productivity that have historically outdistanced inflationary price increases. However, in short-term periods, wage indexes can fall behind cost indexes such as the CPI. A theoretical advantage of wage indexing is that retirees will obtain the same protection against inflation as people currently in the work force (but no better). Whatever the merits of this argument, however, wage indexes are rarely used.

A third approach to indexation is to use a formula for increasing benefits that is included in the plan itself and is not dependent on external price or wage indexes. Such a formula makes it easier for the employer to anticipate the cost of the benefit increases. The risk of possibly running ahead of the CPI can be minimized by providing that the formula increase will not exceed an amount determined by reference to the CPI or other chosen economic indexes.

Indexed pension benefits are obviously attractive to participants, but currently they are not extensively used in the private pension system. This is because even a small annual or periodic percentage increase in pension benefits can result in a very large increase in the ultimate cost of the benefit. Private employers, therefore, often avoid indexation because of the possibility of incurring an uncontrollable future liability. However, indexation is quite common in pension programs of federal, state and local government units. Elected officials often grant indexed pensions to government employees with the implicit expectation that taxpayers in the future (after current officials' terms have expired) will accept tax increases to fund the increased pension costs.

In the private sector, probably the most common mechanism for dealing with postretirement inflation is to increase pension benefits through ad hoc "supplemental payments" to retirees. At one time, there was some concern that a program of supplemental payments might be deemed a separate pension plan involving various federal regulatory complexities. However, in order to encourage employers to make such supplemental payments, the Labor Department has issued relatively permissive regulations concerning these payments. Under these regulations (Labor Regulations Section 2510.3–2(g)), a supplemental payment plan will not be treated as a separate pension plan but rather as a welfare plan, which is subject to much simpler regulatory requirements, if the amount paid is limited by a formula that effectively restricts it to the cost-of-living increases that have occurred since the retirees' pension payments commenced. The supplemental payments can be made out of the employer's general assets or a separate trust fund can be established for them. In addition, there are special provisions (Code Section 415(k)(2)) allowing employees to contribute additional amounts to a defined-benefit plan to provide cost-of-living adjustments to benefits.

INTEGRATION OF QUALIFIED PLANS WITH SOCIAL SECURITY

Integration of a plan with social security further complicates the design of the benefit formula. More than half of all private qualified plans are integrated with social security, and the percentage is even higher among defined-benefit plans considered separately. The reason for this is the obvious overlap between private retirement benefits and the social security benefit. Although this is a complication, it also provides advantages in private plan design.

Purpose and Effect of Social Security Integration

The existence of social security benefits is relevant to a number of objectives in designing a qualified plan.

- The objective of providing an appropriate income replacement ratio must take into account the fact that the employee will receive social security benefits as well as benefits from the plan. If plan benefits alone are considered for this purpose, the actual replacement ratio will often be very different from what was intended.
- The objective of plan efficiency can be met only if retirement benefits from social security are considered in designing the plan. Otherwise, private plan

benefits for some employees may duplicate benefits they already receive from social security.

- For a small business owner who is interested in maximizing the tax sheltering benefits from the qualified plan, an integrated plan provides a method by which the plan itself can, to a considerable extent, discriminate in favor of higher paid employees. Therefore, the objective of maximizing the tax sheltering benefits of the qualified plan may lead to a consideration of integrating the plan with social security.
- Finally, with regard to the employer's cost objectives, an integrated plan may provide a satisfactory level of retirement benefits to all employees at the lowest possible employer cost.

The integration rules are based on the way the OASDI social security benefit is calculated. For simplicity, this benefit will be referred to in this chapter as OASDI.

OASDI uses a unit-benefit type of formula based on the employee's past years of work experience and the employee's compensation income in each of those years. More credit is given for the "first dollars" of compensation than for larger amounts; for compensation in a given year that exceeds the taxable wage base for that year, there is no benefit credit. The OASDI calculation was covered in detail in Chapter 3.

The integration rules are designed to allow a private qualified plan to provide a benefit that is a "mirror image" of OASDI so that the two sources of retirement income together form a retirement program that is nondiscriminatory. Because of the nature of the OASDI calculation, social security alone provides a higher percentage of income replacement for lower paid employees than for higher paid employees. Thus, the private plan may correspondingly provide a proportionately greater benefit for the *higher* paid. Figures 20-1 and 20-2 illustrate this qualitatively. In all cases, note how OASDI integration allows the private plan—considered alone—to discriminate substantially in favor of the highly compensated, both in terms of benefit amounts and percentages of compensation.

An employer has much less freedom in integrating a qualified plan with OASDI than in integrating other types of benefit plans such as disability income plans. Because of the potential for discrimination, Code Section 401(a)(5) and 401(l) and associated regulations and IRS rulings impose detailed limitations on integrating qualified plans.

Under the principles of Code Section 401(l), there are two basic approaches by which a qualified plan can be integrated with OASDI—the *offset* approach and the *integration-level* approach (sometimes called the "excess" approach). Under the offset approach, a specified fraction of the benefit is subtracted from the benefit otherwise payable under the plan. The offset approach can be used only with a defined-benefit plan. Under the integration-level approach, the plan specifies a level of compensation called the integration level. Benefits or contributions below this integration level are provided at a lower rate than benefits or contributions for compensation above the integration level. An integration-level approach can be used with both defined-benefit and defined-contribution plans. The rules will be discussed in detail next, beginning with the integration of defined-benefit plans.

FIGURE 20-1

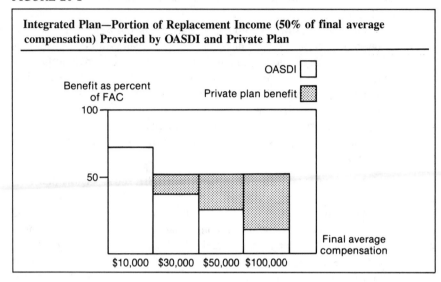

Integrated Plan—Portion of Replacement Income (50% of final average compensation) Provided by OASDI and Private Plan

FIGURE 20-2

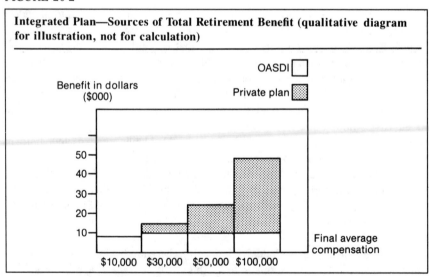

Integrated Plan—Sources of Total Retirement Benefit (qualitative diagram for illustration, not for calculation)

INTEGRATION OF DEFINED-BENEFIT PLANS

Offset Approach

As indicated above, a defined-benefit plan can be integrated with OASDI using either the offset approach or the integration-level approach. Since the offset approach is simpler, it will be discussed first.

With the offset method, the private plan benefit is initially structured to provide the replacement ratio desired, without taking OASDI into account. Then the benefit formula is modified to subtract a specified amount to reflect the employee's OASDI benefit. For example, an offset formula might read as follows:

Upon retirement, the participant shall be entitled to a monthly retirement benefit equal to 60 percent of the participant's final average monthly compensation, less ½ percent of the participant's monthly final average compensation for each year of service.

An offset approach cannot result in a complete elimination of the private plan benefit. The plan benefit may not be reduced by more than the *maximum offset allowance*, which is:

- For any year of service, 4 percent of the participant's final average compensation.
- For total benefits, ¾ percent of the participant's final average compensation multiplied by the participant's years of service with the employer, not in excess of 35.

Furthermore, in no event can the maximum offset allowance be more than 50 percent of the plan benefit that would have accrued without the offset.

The ¾ percent fraction is reduced if the participant's final average compensation exceeds an amount referred to as covered compensation (see Table 20-4 and the explanation below). The IRS is scheduled to publish annually a table with the appropriate offset factors for brackets of final average compensation that exceed covered compensation.

An offset plan must base benefits on average annual compensation for at least a three-year period, or the total number of the participant's years of service, if less. The ¾ percent factor in the maximum excess allowance is actuarially reduced for early retirement benefits. For this purpose, an early retirement benefit is any unreduced benefit other than disability benefits beginning before the social security retirement age. The ¾ percent factor is to be reduced by one-fifteenth for each of the first five years that the benefit's commencement date precedes social security retirement age, and by an additional one-thirtieth for each of the next five years that the benefit commencement date precedes the social security retirement age, with actuarial reductions for additional years (more than ten) of commencement prior to the social security retirement date.

OASDI is currently subject to indexing to reflect increases in the cost of living. However, the benefit paid by a private integrated plan cannot be reduced to reflect postretirement increases in OASDI, even if an offset formula is used. In other words, the amount of benefit payable to a participant from the plan itself generally will be fixed when the participant retires, regardless of changes in OASDI paid thereafter to the participant.

As will be evident after reviewing the rules for social security integration using the integration-level approach, the principal advantage of an offset formula is its simplicity, both in designing the plan and in communicating the plan effectively to employees.

Integration-Level Approach

Under the integration-level approach in a defined-benefit plan, a specified level of compensation, called the integration level, is defined by the plan. The plan then

TABLE 20-4
Official 1989 IRS Tables of Covered Compensation

Calendar Year of Birth	Year of Social Security Retirement Age	1989 Covered Compensation	
		Table II	Table I
1907	1972	$ 4,488	$ 4,200
1908	1973	4,704	4,800
1909	1974	5,004	4,800
1910	1975	5,316	5,400
1911	1976	5,664	5,400
1912	1977	6,060	6,000
1913	1978	6,480	6,600
1914	1979	7,044	7,200
1915	1980	7,692	7,800
1916	1981	8,460	8,400
1917	1982	9,300	9,600
1918	1983	10,236	10,200
1919	1984	11,232	11,400
1920	1985	12,276	12,000
1921	1986	13,368	13,200
1922	1987	14,520	14,400
1923	1988	15,708	15,600
1924	1989	16,968	16,800
1925	1990	18,228	18,000
1926	1991	19,476	19,200
1927	1992	20,724	21,000
1928	1993	21,972	22,200
1929	1994	23,208	23,400
1930	1995	24,444	24,600
1931	1996	25,680	25,800
1932	1997	26,916	27,000
1933	1998	28,152	28,200
1934	1999	29,388	29,400
1935	2000	30,612	30,600
1936	2001	31,800	31,800
1937	2002	32,988	33,000
1938	2004	35,280	35,400
1939	2005	36,432	36,600
1940	2006	37,572	37,800
1941	2007	38,688	38,400
1942	2008	39,756	39,600
1943	2009	40,752	40,800
1944	2010	41,712	42,000
1945	2011	42,648	42,600
1946	2012	43,548	43,800
1947	2013	44,412	44,400
1948	2014	45,132	45,000
1949	2015	45,768	45,600
1950	2016	46,284	46,200
1951	2017	46,740	46,800
1952	2018	47,088	46,800
1953	2019	47,376	47,400
1954	2020	47,616	48,000
1955	2022	47,904	48,000
1956 or later	2023 or later	48,000	48,000

provides the participant a higher rate of benefits for compensation above the integration level than for compensation below the integration level. This clearly is a mirror image to the OASDI benefit structure, which provides a *lower* (zero) rate of benefits above a specified compensation level (the taxable wage base) than it does for compensation below the taxable wage base.

An example of a formula using an integration-level approach is:

> Upon retirement, a participant will be entitled to an annual retirement benefit equal to 30 percent of the participant's final average annual compensation up to $7,000, plus 56 percent of the participant's final average annual compensation in excess of $7,000.

Another way of drafting the same formula is:

> Upon retirement, a participant will be entitled to an annual retirement benefit equal to 30 percent of the participant's full final average annual compensation, plus 26 percent of the participant's final average compensation in excess of $7,000.

The integration level in both plans is $7,000.

Under the Code, two percentages are defined. The *excess benefit percentage* is the benefit as a percentage of compensation above the integration level. The *base benefit percentage* is the percentage of compensation provided for compensation up to and including the integration level. The difference between these two percentages cannot exceed the *maximum excess allowance*. The maximum excess allowance is ¾ percent for any year of service, or in total, ¾ percent multiplied by the participant's years of service up to 35.

For example, if the plan provides a benefit of 1 percent of compensation below the integration level for each year of service, then it can provide no more than 1.75 percent of compensation above the integration level for each year of service. Or, for a participant with 35 years of service, if the plan provides a benefit of 30 percent of final average compensation below the integration level, it cannot provide more than 56.25 percent of compensation above the integration level. (The spread of 26.25 percent is three-fourths of one percentage point multiplied by 35 years of service.)

Furthermore, the maximum excess allowance can be no greater than the base percentage. Thus, if a plan provides 10 percent of final average compensation below the integration level, it can provide no more than 20 percent of compensation above the integration level.

The maximum permitted integration level is the appropriate amount from the IRS table of *covered compensation* (Table 20-4). This table essentially gives the average of the taxable wage base over the 35-year period prior to an employee's retirement, as explained further below. Covered compensation can be taken from either Table I or Table II in Table 20-4. Since this amount varies with each participant's age, some planners may prefer to use a uniform dollar amount as the integration level for all participants in order to make the plan simpler and easier to communicate to participants. It should be permissible to use any uniform dollar amount that does not exceed the covered compensation from Table I or II for the oldest possible prospective employee of the employer.

The Covered Compensation Table

In specifying the maximum integration levels and the maximum percentages that may be used in integration-level plans, IRS actuaries have made a computation based on the value of OASDI benefits. Since the integrated private plan is designed to be a mirror image of the OASDI benefit, the maximum integration level in private plans should correspond generally to the maximum compensation taken into account in determining the OASDI benefit. For this purpose, the IRS has promulgated the *covered compensation* table. Covered compensation represents an averaging of the taxable wage base that has been in effect over each employee's working career. The covered compensation figure will, therefore, vary depending upon the year in which the employee reaches age 65 and becomes eligible for full OASDI retirement benefits. The 1989 IRS table of covered compensation is given in Table 20-4. Table II gives the exact covered compensation level. The IRS has also provided Table I, containing the covered compensation level rounded to the nearest multiple of $600 (i.e., $50 per month). The IRS does not always update its covered compensation table as rapidly as the taxable wage base changes, and when this is the case, it is permissible to use a covered compensation table computed by a private actuary in lieu of the official IRS table.

The relevance of the table of covered compensation is that, as described above, it specifies the maximum integration level permitted for most types of defined-benefit plans.

INTEGRATION OF DEFINED-CONTRIBUTION PLANS

Since the benefits in a defined-contribution plan are based on the participant's account balance, the integration rules for defined-contribution plans apply to the amounts allocated to participants' accounts rather than to the benefits. Only an integration-level approach (not an offset) can be used.

The integration level for a defined-contribution plan is generally the taxable wage base for the year. While other integration levels may be used, under IRS regulations, this generally reduces the excess contribution percentage allowable. Table 20-5 gives the taxable wage base for recent years. The integration rules for defined-contribution plans are further stated in terms of two defined quantities: The *base contribution percentage* is the plan's contribution level for compensation below the integration level, while the *excess contribution percentage* is the contribution level for compensation above the integration level. The difference between the excess contribution percentage and the base contribution percentage cannot be more than the lesser of

- The base contribution percentage, or
- The greater of (a) 5.7 percent or (b) the old-age social security tax rate.

Under this rule, a plan having a zero base contribution percentage would also have to have a zero excess contribution percentage; therefore, it is not possible to have a plan that provides no contribution at all for participants at compensation levels below the integration level.

TABLE 20-5 Social Security Taxable Wage Base	
Year	Taxable Wage Base (Annual)
1972	$ 9,600
1973	10,800
1974	13,200
1975	14,100
1976	15,300
1977	16,500
1978	17,700
1979	22,900
1980	25,900
1981	29,700
1982	32,400
1983	35,700
1984	37,800
1985	39,600
1986	42,000
1987	43,800
1988	45,000
1989	48,000
1990	51,300
1991	53,400

Some examples of the application of the rules are as follows:

- A plan providing a 4 percent base contribution percentage could provide no more than 8 percent excess contribution percentage.
- A plan providing a 6 percent base contribution percentage could provide no more than an 11.7 percent excess contribution percentage, assuming the old-age social security tax rate is less than 5.7 percent.

Multiple Plans

If the employer has more than one plan covering the same employee, both plans cannot be fully integrated. The degree of integration must be cut back in one or both. The most common approach is to fully integrate one plan (typically a defined-benefit plan) and not to integrate the other (typically a defined-contribution plan).

SUMMARY OF INTEGRATION RULES

Qualified plan benefit or contribution formulas can be integrated with OASDI to reflect the value of the employer's OASDI contribution for the employee. This reduces plan costs by avoiding duplication of benefits provided by OASDI. It also tends to provide relatively higher plan benefits for highly compensated employees.

Defined-Benefit Plans

A *defined-benefit* plan can be integrated using either the offset or the integration level method.

The maximum offset allowance is ¾ percent of final average compensation for any year of service, or a total of ¾ percent multiplied by years of service up to 35; total offset can't exceed 50 percent of benefit otherwise payable.

The maximum integration level is covered compensation. Maximum excess allowance is ¾ percent for any year of service, or, in total, ¾ percent multiplied by years of service up to 35.

Defined-Contribution Plans

A *defined-contribution* plan may use only the integration level approach. The maximum integration level is the taxable wage base for the year. The difference between the base contribution percentage and the excess contribution percentage can't exceed the lesser of the base contribution percentage or the non-Medicare OASDI tax rate.

STUDY QUESTIONS

1. a. How are employer contributions usually determined under a money-purchase plan?
   b. What determines the amount of an employee's retirement benefit under a money-purchase plan?
2. Explain why a target plan is considered a hybrid of the defined-contribution and defined-benefit approaches.
3. Why are defined-benefit plans the most complex of all qualified plans?
4. Explain how you can design a defined-benefit formula to favor employees who enter a plan at a later age.
5. Describe the replacement ratio approach to benefit formula design.
6. a. What is a flat-benefit formula?
   b. Explain how a flat-benefit formula may create a problem of fairness among employees.
   c. How can this problem be resolved?
7. A firm has two long-time, devoted employees. A retirement plan is about to be adopted and the employer desires to provide these two older employees with an adequate retirement benefit at retirement.
   a. What type of plan should the employer adopt?
   b. What special provision should be included in the plan to achieve the employer's objective?
8. Distinguish between a career-average formula and a final-average formula in a defined-benefit plan.
9. Explain how sex discrimination is still possible even if the employer removes any conceivable sex discrimination from the plan documents of a qualified plan.

10. What kinds of qualified plans are inherently better able to cope with preretirement inflation?
11. What is the purpose of the rules for integrating qualified plans with social security?
12. Briefly describe the integration rules for
    a. Offset plans.
    b. Integration-level plans.
    c. Defined-contribution plans.

21

Pension Plan Design: Additional Benefits

Objectives

- Describe the purpose for the accrued-benefit rules.
- Explain the vesting requirements for qualified plans.
- Describe the preretirement and postretirement survivorship benefits that must be provided by qualified plans.
- Explain the extent to which incidental death benefits and disability benefits may be included in qualified plans.

Qualified plans can—and in some cases must—provide benefits other than retirement benefits. Benefits can be paid also as a result of termination of employment other than retirement, and specific provisions can be made for terminations resulting from death or disability. These are discussed in this chapter.

THE ACCRUED BENEFIT

Under the vesting rules discussed in this chapter, many employees will be entitled to a benefit from their qualified plan if they terminate employment before retirement. Therefore, the plan must provide a means of determining the amount of benefit payable to employees with a given termination date. In order to do this, the qualified plan benefit is treated as having been earned over the employee's entire period of employment. The amount of benefit earned as of a given date is referred to as the *accrued benefit* at that date. The concept of the accrued benefit is also important in certain actuarial methods for determining annual plan costs, as discussed in Chapter 22.

Every qualified plan must include a means for determining the participant's accrued benefit. Furthermore, to prevent discrimination, Code Section 411(b) and extensive IRS regulations under Code Section 401(a)(4) require benefits to accrue at minimum specified rates. The purpose of the Section 411(b) benefit accrual rules is to prevent the plan from having an excessive amount of what is known as *backloading*. An extreme example of a backloaded plan would be one that had a normal retirement age of 65 with a provision that no employee who terminated employment prior to age 63 would receive any benefit under this plan. In effect, all of the benefits under this plan would accrue during the two years between ages 63 and 65. This much backloading is not permitted under current rules. Obviously, the purpose of the accrual rules is to prevent employers from favoring highly compensated employees who are the ones most likely to continue employment to later ages. Incidentally, the benefit accrual rules do not prevent *frontloading*—rapid benefit accrual during a participant's earlier years of employment. However, few employers would have any reason for designing a frontloaded plan.

Benefit Accrual Rules

In a defined-contribution plan, a participant's accrued benefit is simply equal to the balance in that participant's account under the plan. The account balance includes employer and employee contributions, forfeitures from accounts of other employees and investment earnings on the account, less any distributions from the account. If a defined-contribution plan has a nondiscriminatory contribution formula, there normally is no problem of backloading. Consequently, there are no specific rates of accrual required for defined-contribution plans.

For defined-benefit plans, however, benefits must accrue at a rate specified in Code Section 411(b). The plan's accrual rate must be at least as fast as one of three alternative minimum rules:

1. *3 Percent Rule.* Under this rule, the benefit accrued by a participant during each year of participation must be at least 3 percent of the maximum benefit that a hypothetical participant can accrue by entering at the plan's earliest entry age and participating until normal retirement.
2. *133⅓ Percent Rule.* Under this rule, the rate of benefits accrued in any given plan year cannot be more than 133⅓ percent of the rate of benefit accrual during any prior year.
3. *Fractional Rule.* Under this rule, the benefit the employee has accrued at the date of termination must be proportionate to the normal retirement benefit. The following requirement must be satisfied:

$$\frac{\text{Benefit on}}{\text{termination}} = \frac{\text{Normal retirement benefit if}}{\text{participant continued to normal}} \times \frac{\text{Years of actual participation}}{\frac{\text{Years of participation if}}{\text{terminated at normal retirement}}}$$

EXAMPLE: Suppose that an employee has participated in the plan for 20 years and terminates at age 55. The plan's normal retirement age is 65. If the employee had continued working to age 65, the plan would have provided an annuity of $12,000 per year beginning at age 65. The fractional rule would require a termination benefit of at least two-thirds of this, or $8,000 annually beginning at age 65. If the plan does not provide at least this amount, it must meet one of the other two benefit accrual rules or it will be disqualified.

The tendency is for most plans to provide a termination benefit based on the fractional rule, since it is simpler to design and explain to participants.

Fully-insured plans—plans that are funded exclusively by the purchase of insurance contracts providing level annual premium payments to retirement and providing benefits guaranteed by an insurance company—are not specifically subject to the preceding three accrual rules, if the accrued benefit meets the following tests:

- The accrued benefit is not less than the cash surrender value of the participant's insurance contracts at any time.
- The insurance premiums are paid up, the insurance contracts are not subject to a security interest and there are no policy loans outstanding.

The assumption is that if all these conditions are satisfied, plans funded with insurance contracts will automatically meet or exceed the benefit accrual test. Note that this exception applies only to fully insured plans, not to all plans that use an insurance contract or contracts for funding. The use of insurance contracts in plan funding is discussed in Chapter 22.

VESTING

A qualified plan must provide a minimum nonforfeitable or vested benefit for participants who attain certain service requirements. Once vested, the participant cannot forfeit this minimum vested benefit. For example, the plan cannot contain a clause that requires an employee to forfeit part or all of the vested benefit required by the Code if the employee commits an act of misconduct, such as embezzlement or going to work for a competitor. The strictness of the vesting rules was designed to provide additional benefit security and to protect employees against arbitrary acts of the employer.

Vesting at Normal Retirement Age and Termination of Employment

The plan must provide a fully vested benefit at the normal retirement age. The plan must also provide that benefits are vested under a specified "vesting schedule" during the participant's employment, so that if the participant terminates employment prior to retirement age, he or she is entitled to a vested benefit with some stated minimum amount of service.

If the plan provides for employee contributions, the participant's accrued benefit is divided between the part attributable to employee contributions and the part attributable to employer contributions. The part attributable to employee contributions must at all times be 100 percent vested. The part attributable to employer contributions must be vested in accordance with a vesting schedule set out in the plan.

There is some flexibility in designing a vesting schedule in order to meet various employer objectives. However, the vesting schedule must be at least as favorable as one of two alternative minimum standards, five-year vesting or three- to seven-year vesting.

Five-Year Vesting

The vesting schedule satisfies this minimum requirement if an employee with at least five years of service is 100 percent vested in the employer-provided portion of the accrued benefit. This rule is satisfied even if there is no vesting at all before five years of service. This rule is sometimes referred to as "cliff" vesting.

Three- to Seven-Year Vesting

A vesting schedule satisfies this minimum standard if the vesting is at least as fast as under the following table:

Years of Service	Vested Percentage
3	20
4	40
5	60
6	80
7 or more	100

In applying the vesting rules, all of a participant's years of service for the employer must be taken into account, even years prior to plan participation, except that years of service prior to age 18 may be excluded. The plan's vesting schedule may also ignore service prior to a break in continuous service with the employer; however, there are elaborate restrictions on how this may be done (Code Section 411(a)(6)).

Probably the most common vesting provision in defined-benefit plans is the five-year provision, because of its simplicity and because it is generally the most favorable to the employer. Defined-contribution plans are often designed with a more generous (to the employee) vesting schedule using the three- to seven-year schedule or one that is even faster.

Top-Heavy Vesting

To complete this discussion, it should be mentioned that plans that are top-heavy as defined in the code are required to provide faster vesting than under most of the schedules previously mentioned. The top-heavy minimum vesting schedule is:

Years of Service	Vested Percentage
2	20
3	40
4	60
5	80
6 or more	100

A 100 percent vesting provision with two years eligibility also meets the top-heavy minimum vesting requirement. Top-heavy plans are discussed in detail in Chapter 25. As discussed below, the top-heavy requirements have a significant impact in designing a vesting schedule for plans of smaller employers.

Choosing a Vesting Schedule

Choosing an appropriate vesting schedule is an important plan design decision. When a pension plan participant terminates employment, invested funds contributed to the plan for that participant (*forfeitures*) are generally used to reduce future employer costs for the pension plan. Strict vesting, therefore, can reduce a pension plan's cost to the employer. In a defined-contribution plan, forfeitures also can be reallocated to remaining participants' accounts. Thus, there should be a reason for adopting more than a strict minimum vesting schedule. Some reasons for using liberal vesting include the need to provide employee incentive and involvement in situations where a five-year vesting schedule might appear too remote and therefore of no value to employees. Also, a simplified liberal vesting schedule may reduce administrative costs.

Vesting on Plan Termination

The final vesting rule relates to a plan that has terminated. The IRS will regard a plan as having terminated either if it is formally terminated or if the employer permanently ceases to make contributions to the plan (see Chapter 26). When a plan is terminated, all benefits must be fully vested to the extent funded. Therefore, when a defined-contribution plan terminates, all participants are immediately 100 percent vested in their account balances. When a defined-benefit plan terminates, participants are 100 percent vested in their accrued benefits; however, if the plan funds are insufficient, they are vested only to the extent that the plan is funded. Many terminated qualified defined-benefit plans are insured by the Pension Benefit Guaranty Corporation (PBGC). The provisions that come into operation on plan termination under the PBGC rules will be discussed in Chapter 26.

Benefits at Termination of Employment

The vesting provisions of a plan determine the amount of benefit that a participant is entitled to receive upon terminating employment prior to retirement.

In a defined-contribution plan, the termination benefit is the vested portion of the participant's account balance. In defined-contribution plans, particularly profit-sharing plans, the account balance usually is distributed to the participant in full at termination of employment. It is technically possible to defer the distribution to the participant's normal retirement date, but this is rarely done in defined-contribution plans because it causes additional expense to the plan with little or no corresponding benefit to the employer or the plan. However, the plan may give the participant the option to leave the funds on deposit in the plan for withdrawal at a later date, in order to allow the participant to take advantage of the tax-deferred investment medium afforded by the plan, with a possible loss of favorable income tax treatment on the later plan distribution (Chapter 24) and the use of tax-free rollovers (Chapter 27).

For a defined-benefit plan, the benefit on termination of employment is more complicated. The benefit will be the vested accrued benefit as of the date of termination, determined under the vesting and the accrual rules already described. Using the same example as in the discussion of the fractional accrued-benefit rule, suppose that an employee terminates employment at age 55 after 20 years of service and the plan's normal retirement age is 65. If the participant is fully vested and the accrued benefit is $8,000 as discussed in the earlier example, an annuity of $8,000 per year will be payable beginning at age 65.

To make sure that terminated participants actually receive deferred vested benefits at retirement, which may be many years after termination, the employer must report all deferred vested benefits of terminated participants to the Social Security Administration, which then can inform retirees of their rights to benefits from plans of former employers. This reporting is done on the Form 5500 series (Chapter 26).

In some cases, the deferred vested benefit may be such a small amount that keeping track of it until the participant's retirement is merely a nuisance for both employer and employee. The employer can *cashout* a distribution, that is, pay cash to the employee in lieu of the deferred vested benefit, without the employee's consent, so long as the entire benefit is distributed and the employer portion of the benefit so distributed does not exceed $3,500. The involuntary cashout must be within one year of termination of participation in the plan; the plan must have a provision permitting the employee to repay the cashout to the plan if the employee was not fully vested at the time of termination, in case the employee should resume participation in the plan. A cashout of a benefit that exceeds the $3,500 limit can be made, but only with the consent of the employee.

DEATH AND DISABILITY BENEFITS

Qualified plans are intended primarily to provide retirement benefits—or in the case of profit sharing and similar plans, deferred-compensation benefits. However, the regulations indicate that a plan may provide for the payment of incidental death benefits through insurance or otherwise, and also that the plan may provide for the payment of a pension due to disability. Moreover, a qualified plan must in certain circumstances provide a survivorship pension to the participant's spouse.

Currently under Code Section 401(a)(11), two types of survivorship benefits are required: the *qualified joint and survivor annuity* and the *qualified preretirement survivor annuity.* All pension plans must provide these, but profit-sharing plans need not provide them if the participant's vested account balance is payable as a death benefit to the spouse. ESOPs and stock bonus plans generally do not have to provide spousal survivorship benefits.

Qualified Joint and Survivor Annuity

The qualified joint and survivor annuity is a postretirement death benefit for the spouse. Plans subject to this requirement must provide, as an automatic form of benefit, an annuity for the life of the participant with a survivor annuity for the life of the participant's spouse. The survivor annuity must be not less than 50 percent of nor greater than the annuity payable during the joint lives of participant and spouse. The spouse annuity must be continued even if the spouse remarries. The joint and survivor annuity must be at least the actuarial equivalent of the plan's normal form of benefit or any optional form of benefit offered under the plan. Optional benefit forms are discussed further in Chapter 24.

The qualified joint and survivor form must be offered automatically to a married participant at retirement. The participant may elect to receive another form of benefit if the plan so provides; however, the spouse must consent in writing to the election and the consent form must be notarized or witnessed by a plan representative. An election to waive the joint and survivor form must be made during a 90-day period ending on the annuity starting date. A waiver of the joint and survivor annuity can be revoked—the participant can change the election during the 90-day period. The plan administrator must provide the participant with a notice of the election period and an explanation of the consequences of the election within a reasonable period before the annuity starting date.

Preretirement Survivor Annuity

Code Section 401(a)(11) mandates a preretirement death benefit for the spouse of a vested plan participant. The survivor annuity payable if the participant dies before retirement is the amount that would have been paid under a qualified joint and survivor annuity, computed as if the participant had either (1) retired on the day before his or her death or (2) separated from service on the date of death and survived to the plan's earliest retirement age, then retired with an immediate joint and survivor annuity. For a defined-contribution plan, a qualified preretirement survivor annuity is an annuity for the life of the surviving spouse actuarially equivalent to at least 50 percent of the participant's vested account balance as of the date of death.

As with the qualified joint and survivor annuity, a participant can elect to receive an alternative form of preretirement survivorship benefit, including a benefit that does not provide for the spouse. However, written consent by the spouse is required for such an election. The right to make such an election must be communicated to all participants with a vested benefit who have attained age 32, and the participant can elect to waive the preretirement survivor annuity at any time after age 35.

Subsidizing Survivor Annuities

A plan can provide that when a participant receives either the qualified joint and survivor annuity or the preretirement survivor annuity, the annuity payment is reduced from the amount that would be paid under a straight-life annuity; the reduction reflects the extra cost to the plan for the survivorship feature. For example, the normal form of benefit might be a straight-life annuity of $1,000 per month, but the joint and survivor annuity might pay only $800 per month while both spouses survived, then $400 per month to the survivor. However, a plan is permitted to subsidize all or part of the cost of the survivorship feature. If the survivorship feature is fully subsidized, the plan does not have to allow the participant to elect an alternative form of benefit.

Incidental Death Benefits

A qualified plan may provide a death benefit over and above the survivorship benefits required by law. In a defined-contribution plan, probably the most common form of death benefit is a provision that the participant's vested account balance will be paid to the participant's designated beneficiary in the event of the participant's death before retirement or termination of service. Defined-benefit plans, unless they use insurance as discussed later, usually do not provide an additional death benefit; in such cases, the survivors receive no death benefit except for whatever survivor annuity the plan provides.

In order to provide any substantial preretirement death benefit, it is usually necessary for the plan to purchase life insurance. This provides the plan with significant funds at a participant's death; it is particularly important in the early years of a participant's employment, when the participant's accrued benefit is still relatively small. An insured preretirement death benefit can be provided in either a defined-benefit or defined-contribution plan. Contributions to the plan by the employer may be used to pay life insurance premiums, so long as the amount qualifies under the tests for incidental benefits.

In general, the IRS considers that nonretirement benefits such as life, medical or disability insurance in a qualified plan will be incidental, and therefore permissible, so long as the cost of providing these benefits is less than 25 percent of the cost of providing all the benefits under the plan. In applying this approach to life insurance benefits, the 25 percent rule is applied to the portion of any life insurance premium that is used to provide current life insurance protection. Any portion of the premium used to increase the cash value of the policy is considered a contribution to the plan fund available to pay retirement benefits and is not considered in the 25 percent limitation.

The IRS has ruled, using its general 25 percent test, that if a qualified plan provides death benefits using ordinary life insurance (life insurance with a cash value), the death benefit will be considered incidental if either (1) less than 50 percent of the total cumulative employer contribution credited to each participant's account has been used to purchase ordinary life insurance; or (2) the face amount of the policies does not exceed 100 times the anticipated monthly normal retirement benefit, or the accumulated reserve under the life insurance policy, whichever is greater. In practice, defined-benefit plans using ordinary life insurance are usually designed to take advantage of the 100-times rule, while defined-contribution plans, including profit-sharing plans, that use ordinary life contracts generally make use of the 50 percent test.

If term insurance contracts are used to provide the death benefit, the 25 percent test will be applied to the entire premium, and the aggregate premiums paid for insurance on each participant should be less than 25 percent of aggregate additions to the employee's account. Term insurance is sometimes used to fund death benefits in defined-contribution plans but rarely in defined-benefit plans.

The discussion so far is somewhat simplified, because insurance can be used in qualified plans in many ways, and the IRS has issued many rulings, both revenue rulings and letter rulings, applying the basic 25 percent test to a variety of different fact situations. Thus, there is considerable room for creative design of life insurance-funded death benefits within qualified plans.

If life insurance is provided for a participant through a qualified plan (i.e., by using employer contributions to the plan to pay premiums for the insurance), part or all of the cost of the insurance is currently taxable to the participant. Life insurance provided by the plan is not considered part of a Section 79 group term plan, and consequently the $50,000 exclusion under Section 79 does not apply.

If cash value life insurance is used, and if all of the death proceeds are payable to the participant's estate or beneficiary, the term cost or cost of the "pure amount at risk" is taxable income to the employee. The term cost is the difference between the face amount of insurance and the cash surrender value of the policy at the end of the policy year. In other words, the cost of the policy's cash value is not currently taxable to the employee because the cash value is considered part of the plan fund to be used to provide the retirement benefit. The term cost is calculated using either a table of rates (Table 21-1) provided by the Internal Revenue Service known as the PS 58 table or the insurance company's rates for individual one year term policies, if these are lower and if the insurance company actually offers such policies.

If the plan uses term insurance rather than cash-value insurance to provide an insured death benefit, the cost of the entire face amount of insurance is taxable to the employee. Similarly, if the plan provides medical or disability insurance for participants, the entire cost of the insurance is taxable to the employee, unless the insurance can be excluded under Code Section 106 as part of the employer's medical or disability plan.

Planning Considerations

It is relatively uncommon for a qualified plan to provide medical, disability or term life insurance to participants, because the tax treatment provides no advantage to the employee in so doing. It is more common, however, to use cash-value life insurance as funding for the plan, because the cost to the employee using the PS 58 table or the insurance company's term rates may prove to be a relatively favorable way to provide life insurance. The use of life insurance for funding qualified plans will be discussed further in Chapter 22.

TABLE 21-1
PS 58 Rates, One-Year Term Premiums for $1,000 of
Life Insurance Protection*

Age	Premium	Age	Premium	Age	Premium
15	$1.27	37	$ 3.63	59	$ 19.08
16	1.38	38	3.87	60	20.73
17	1.48	39	4.14	61	22.53
18	1.52	40	4.42	62	24.50
19	1.56	41	4.73	63	26.63
20	1.61	42	5.07	64	28.98
21	1.67	43	5.44	65	31.51
22	1.73	44	5.85	66	34.28
23	1.79	45	6.30	67	37.31
24	1.86	46	6.78	68	40.59
25	1.93	47	7.32	69	44.17
26	2.02	48	7.89	70	48.06
27	2.11	49	8.53	71	52.29
28	2.20	50	9.22	72	56.89
29	2.31	51	9.97	73	61.89
30	2.43	52	10.79	74	67.33
31	2.57	53	11.69	75	73.23
32	2.70	54	12.67	76	79.63
33	2.86	55	13.74	77	86.57
34	3.02	56	14.91	78	94.09
35	3.21	57	16.18	79	102.23
36	3.41	58	17.56	80	111.04
				81	120.57

*These rates are used in computing the cost of pure life insurance protection that is taxable to the employee under qualified pension and profit-sharing plans.

The rate at insured's attained age is applied to the excess of the amount payable at death over the cash value of the policy at the end of the year.

The decision whether to include life insurance in a qualified plan relates to the employee benefit design objective of efficiency. The employer must first decide whether and to what extent it will provide death benefits to employees. Death benefits can be provided for employees under group term plans and other plans as well as providing them as an incidental benefit in qualified plans. The death benefit should be designed to produce the lowest employer and employee cost for the benefit level desired. A death benefit should be included in the qualified plan only to the extent it is consistent with this objective.

Disability Benefits from Qualified Plans

A qualified plan may provide as an incidental benefit a pension payable upon disability. The plan must provide a specific definition of disability. Usually some minimum service or age requirements are imposed to appropriately restrict the class of participants entitled to the disability pension. The disability benefit may be the participant's accrued benefit actuarially reduced because of a commencement date earlier than normal retirement, or the plan may provide some subsidy of the disability benefit in order to be sure that it is adequate for the participant's needs.

It is becoming increasingly common for companies to cover disability through separate benefit programs, often insured. These were discussed in Chapter 8. Such programs tend to be fairer and more efficient than providing disability coverage as an incidental benefit under a qualified plan. In all events, the planner should be sure that there is no duplication of disability coverage between the qualified plan and a separate short-term or long-term disability plan of the employer.

Qualified plans that do not provide immediate disability coverage prior to normal retirement age should, however, include some provision for the treatment of the employee's retirement benefit if the employee becomes disabled. Separate long-term disability programs usually cease paying benefits when the participant reaches age 65 or other normal retirement age. After this age, the company's retirement plan must provide whatever income the participant will receive from the employer. Therefore, from an employee's standpoint, the plan should be designed so that the retirement benefit will be adequate when long-term disability benefits cease. For example, the plan might provide that a participant who is disabled as defined in the plan will continue to receive service credit for purposes of vesting or benefit accrual or both. The definition of disability in the plan should be coordinated with the definition in the employer's long-term disability plan. The plan also should indicate what definition of compensation will be used to determine retirement benefits if the participant becomes disabled before retirement.

STUDY QUESTIONS

1. For defined-benefit plans, benefits must accrue at an accrual rate that must be at least as rapid as one of the three alternative minimum rules. What are these rules?
2. What is the effect on the use of the three accrual rules of the plan is funded exclusively by insurance contracts?
3. Explain whether the following vesting schedules comply with the vesting rules.

a.

Years of Service	Percentage Vested
0–9	0%
10	100%

b.

Years of Service	Percentage Vested
1	50%
2	60%
3	70%
4	80%
5	90%
6	100%

c.

Years of Service	Percentage Vested
0–4	0%
5	50%
6	100%

4. Explain whether the following vesting schedule meets the vesting schedule rules for top-heavy plans.

Years of Service	Percentage Vested
0–1	0%
2	20%
3	40%
4	60%
5	80%
6 or more	100%

5. a. Under what conditions would you recommend that an employer choose a restrictive vesting schedule for the plan?
   b. Under what conditions would you recommend that an employer choose a liberal vesting schedule for the plan?
6. a. What is a qualified joint and survivor annuity?
   b. What rules affect the amount of the joint and survivor annuity?
   c. What requirements apply to a joint and survivor annuity that must be offered to married parties as part of a qualified plan?
7. a. What is a preretirement survivor annuity?
   b. How is the amount of a preretirement survivor annuity determined?
8. Explain the rules that determine whether a death benefit that is funded with life insurance is considered incidental in a qualified plan.
9. Explain how the taxable income to an employee is determined when employer-provided life insurance is included in a qualified plan.
10. Why might you recommend that an employer include life insurance in a qualified plan?

22

Pension Plan Funding

Objectives

- Describe the general features of each of the following pension funding instruments and explain when each might best be used:
  1. Trusts.
  2. Individual life insurance and annuity contracts.
  3. Group permanent contracts.
  4. Group deposit administration contracts.
  5. Immediate-participation guarantee contracts.
- Explain how separate accounts and the new money technique can overcome the disadvantages associated with the commingling of pension funds.
- Identify the circumstances under which a plan sponsor should use a guaranteed investment contract and an investment-guarantee contract.
- Distinguish between accrued-benefit actuarial cost methods and projected-benefit methods for determining pension costs.
- Explain the concept of a supplemental liability and how the use of a supplemental liability increases flexibility in pension funding.
- Describe the actuarial cost methods that are specifically permitted by ERISA.
- Explain the minimum funding standards of the Internal Revenue Code and the operation of the funding standard account.
- Explain the rules for deductibility of employer contributions to qualified pension plans.

The assets of a qualified plan must be held either by a trustee or by an insurance company. It is also possible to hold plan funds in a bank custodial account that is not technically a trust, but under Code Section 401(f), such an account is treated

420

the same as a trust for all practical purposes. The trustee or insurance company is referred to as the plan's *funding agency.*

Plan assets are held by a funding agency under a legal document called a *funding instrument*—either a *trust agreement* or *insurance contract,* depending on the funding agency. There are many legal requirements applicable to a funding instrument; these are discussed in this chapter and in Chapter 26. Within these requirements, however, there is opportunity for flexibility in plan design, funding procedures and investment policy. The employer's choices in these areas are an important part of qualified plan design.

TRUSTS

The trust is the leading funding agency for qualified plans, both in terms of the number of employees covered and aggregate plan assets. A trust used for qualified plan funding is based on the same general principles of trust law as trusts used for other purposes, such as estate planning and administering the affairs of minors or incompetent persons. A trust is an arrangement involving three parties—the grantor of the trust, the trustee and the beneficiaries. In qualified plan funding, the grantor is the employer and the beneficiaries are the employees. The trustee is a party holding funds contributed by the employer for the benefit of employees.

Legally speaking, a trustee is a fiduciary. A fiduciary is a person or organization that holds money on behalf of someone else (here the plan participants and beneficiaries) and that must administer that money solely in the interest of those other persons. The trustee's compensation is a fee for services rendered; the trustee is prohibited from personally profiting as a result of investing the trust funds.

The duties of a qualified plan trustee, like those of any other trustee, are set out in a formal trust agreement. Usually, the duties of a plan trustee are to accept employer contributions, invest those contributions and accumulate the earnings and pay benefits to plan participants and beneficiaries out of the plan fund. The trustee performs these acts only at the direction of the plan administrator and not at the trustee's own discretion. However, in some cases, a trustee is given direct responsibility for choosing plan investments or choosing an investment adviser. The trustee must account periodically to the plan administrator or the employer for all investments, receipts and disbursements. The trustee does not guarantee the payment of benefits or the adequacy of the trust fund to pay benefits. That remains the obligation of the employer.

A trustee may be an individual or group of individuals or a corporation such as a bank or trust company. Often employers name individual trustees, such as the company president or a major shareholder, to obtain an extra measure of control over plan assets. This is permissible under the law; however, when acting as trustee, such an individual is legally obligated to act solely in the interests of the plan participants and beneficiaries and not in the interests of the employer or shareholders.

Although a qualified plan trust is created and exists under the laws of the state in which it is established, the most significant provisions of trust law affecting qualified plan trusts have been codified in federal statutes that supersede state law whenever they apply. The area of trust investments and related issues is treated in more detail in Chapter 26.

INSURANCE CONTRACTS

Allocated and Unallocated Funding in Insurance Contracts

Insurance companies offer a variety of contracts either designed specifically for qualified plan funding or adaptable to it. In theory, an employer could negotiate a contract with the insurance company with provisions specifically tailored to the employer's needs. In practice, however, insurance contracts tend to fall into specific types, with some but not complete flexibility in their terms. This is partly a result of the fact that an insurance contract—particularly a life insurance contract—cannot be the subject of unfettered negotiation between insurer and contractholder. Often, the terms of the contract require state regulatory approval and, consequently, the insurer is not interested in varying them for each individual contractholder. Also, historical practices and needs in the insurance industry have determined the form of many of the contracts.

Insurance contracts used in funding qualified plans can be divided into *allocated* and *unallocated* types. When funding is allocated under an insurance contract, this means that the insurer has assumed the employer's obligation to pay specific benefits to specific participants. The employer is still primarily responsible, but under the terms of the insurance contract, participants and the employer can look to the insurance company for payment of specific amounts. With unallocated funding, the insurance company acts as a holder of the funds, much like a bank trustee. With unallocated funding, the insurance company is, of course, obligated to deal prudently with the funds, but it makes no guarantee that the funds will be adequate to pay any specific benefits under the plan. An insurance contract used in a qualified plan can be either purely allocated or purely unallocated, or can offer a mixture of both.

Insurance contracts can be classified—and will be discussed—in this order:

Allocated Contracts

- Individual life insurance or annuity contracts.
  1. Fully insured plans.
  2. Combination plans.
- Group permanent contracts.
- Group deferred annuity contracts.

Unallocated Contracts

- Deposit administration contracts.
- Immediate participation guarantee contracts.

INSURANCE CONTRACTS USING ALLOCATED FUNDING

Individual Life Insurance and Annuity Contracts

For qualified plans of employers with few employees, particularly defined-benefit plans, one of the most common funding methods traditionally has been the use of individual life insurance or annuity contracts. These contracts are typically level-premium contracts. Once a benefit level for a given employee has been determined, the benefit is funded using a single insurance or annuity contract with equal annual premiums paid by the employer until the employee's retirement. It is relatively simple to see how annuity contracts can be used in this manner; however, the use of life insurance contracts requires some explanation.

The somewhat complex spectrum of life insurance products can be divided into two types of contracts—those providing only term insurance and those with a cash value. Term insurance contracts are not suitable as funding instruments for qualified plans, although they can be used by the plan to provide incidental insurance. Cash value contracts, on the other hand, can be used in a qualified plan to provide both retirement benefits and death benefits. This is because these contracts are designed to accumulate a reserve that, if the insured lives long enough, grows to a size sufficient to pay the entire face amount of the contract's death benefit. The purpose for the accumulation of this reserve is to allow the policy to be offered to the insured with the assurance of a level premium for a long period of time—the excess cost in early years is used to provide insurance in later years. Term insurance, by comparison, increases in cost each year as the insured grows older; there is no reserve for any period longer than one year. The reserve feature of cash value contracts means that such a contract is an investment medium that can be used in funding a qualified plan.

The most familiar cash value insurance contract, usually referred to as the whole life contract, provides increasing cash values up to a quite advanced age, such as 90 or more. Prior to that time, the scheduled cash value is usually less than the face amount of the death benefit, although many policies provide dividends that accelerate the cash value increase considerably. A whole life policy cannot be used to provide the sole funding for the retirement benefit in a qualified plan with a normal retirement age of 65, because the cash value at age 65 is usually insufficient. Under the incidental test for death benefits described in the preceding chapter, the death benefit in a qualified plan cannot be more than 100 times the expected monthly pension. For example, if the plan provides a monthly pension of $100 per month, no more than $10,000 of whole life insurance can be provided, and the cash value of a $10,000 policy at age 65 is usually insufficient to provide a pension of $100 per month. If whole life policies are used to fund a qualified plan, the plan fund must be supplemented with a side fund or conversion fund, as discussed under "Combination Plans" below. In order to fund a qualified plan benefit with life insurance alone, policies with rapidly increasing cash values must be used; one such policy commonly used is referred to as a *retirement income* policy. The difference in cash value buildup between a retirement income policy and a whole life policy is represented in Figure 22-1.

FIGURE 22-1

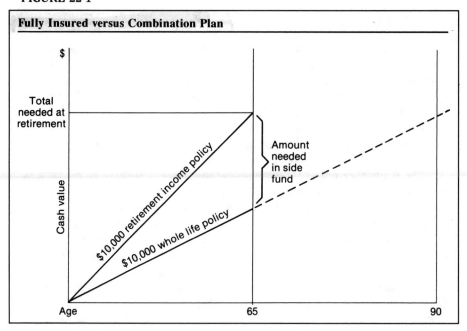

Fully Insured versus Combination Plan

Use of Retirement Income Policies

The individual retirement income policies used in qualified plans are usually similar to such policies offered to the general public for use outside of qualified plans. The plan design options for a plan funded with such policies are somewhat limited because of the characteristics of the policies themselves. The plans are usually defined-benefit plans providing a life income at retirement in a specified amount, usually expressed in units of $10 per month. When the plan is initially installed, benefit levels are projected for each employee, and a policy is purchased for each employee sufficient to provide these projected benefits. If an employee's projected benefit increases—for example, if the benefit formula is based on compensation and the employee's compensation increases—then a second, additional policy must be purchased for the employee to provide the benefits in excess of the original amount. Thus, the employee's eventual benefit at retirement may be provided under more than one policy.

Since retirement income contracts are basically life insurance policies, the plan provides a preretirement death benefit usually determined under the 100 to 1 formula. Death benefits may be made subject to medical examinations or insurance may be made available on a guaranteed issue basis (i.e., without medical examinations), usually subject to a minimum number of participants, such as five. If medical examinations are required and a participant is uninsurable, the retirement benefit is unaffected, but the death benefit may be reduced or eliminated.

The plan's vesting provisions must, of course, meet the vesting rules described in the preceding chapter. In order to accomplish this, at termination of employment, the policies may be distributed to the participant in return for a payment by the participant to the plan of the amount of any nonvested cash values in the policy. Alternatively, the plan may retain the policy and use it to provide a deferred vested benefit at the participant's retirement age.

Use of Retirement Annuity Contracts

Retirement annuity contracts are individual contracts used in funding qualified plans in a manner similar to retirement income contracts. However, as the name implies, these are not life insurance contracts; therefore, the plan usually provides no death benefit other than a return of the annuity premiums or the annuity's cash value, whichever is greater. Thus, the death benefit under a retirement annuity contract is relatively small in a participant's earlier years in the plan.

The employer is the contractholder under both types of fully-insured individual contract plans, although sometimes a trustee is designated as contractholder for administrative convenience. The employer's sole responsibility for funding the plan is to make the premium payments when due. All benefits are guaranteed by the insurance company and if the employer has paid all premiums, it has no further responsibility so long as the insurance company remains solvent.

Under these contracts, the insurance company provides certain credits to the employer to offset premium costs. Because the plan must meet the "exclusive benefit" rule applicable to all qualified plans, these credits cannot be paid to the employer in cash. Credits include policy dividends, credits for withdrawal of a participant who is not fully vested and credits for participants who continue working beyond the normal retirement date.

Combination Plans

A combination plan is a plan that funds a participant's benefit with a whole life policy or policies (i.e., policies whose cash value buildup is relatively slow), plus an additional unallocated trust fund called a *side fund* or *conversion fund* to provide the additional amount needed at retirement to fund the retirement benefit. This type of funding is frequently used for defined-benefit plans of small employers, because it combines the advantages of an insured death benefit with some of the flexibility of an unallocated trust fund.

The whole life policies used in combination plans are generally the same as those offered by insurance companies to individuals for purposes other than retirement plans. Almost any type of cash value policy can be used, including some of the newer forms, such as universal life policies, that provide substantial investment return compared with older types of cash value policies. As with fully insured plans, the employer is the policyholder although, again, a trustee can be used to hold the policies; this trustee can be the same as the trustee of the side fund.

As with fully insured plans, the plan design is to some extent based on the features of the policy used. However, additional flexibility is provided because of the side fund. A whole life policy is purchased for each participant when initial projected benefit levels are established; additional policies are provided for each participant if that participant's projected benefit increases because of increases in compensation or changes in the plan. The employer is responsible for paying premiums on policies, with the insurance company guaranteeing the death benefit and the cash value of the policies. However, the employer is responsible for insuring the adequacy of the side fund. The employer may use its own consulting actuary for purposes of determining funding levels for the side fund, although the insurance company can provide these services if the employer wishes. The employer also determines how the side fund will be invested, although, again, the insurance company can hold these funds under a deposit administration type of contract to be discussed later.

Table 22-1 illustrates the typical features of a combination plan. Note that the amount of life insurance (face amount of each policy) is determined using the 100 to 1 test. The total cost to the employer is the sum of the annual premiums plus the deposit to the side fund. At each participant's retirement, the policy cash value and the balance in the side fund will be combined to provide the retirement benefit. Typically, the plan will provide that an annuity will be purchased from the insurance company at this time at guaranteed rates. If the amount in the side fund is more than is necessary to provide the benefit specified in the plan, the excess remains in the plan, thus allowing the employer to reduce future contributions to the side fund. On the other hand, if the side fund is insufficient at retirement to provide the plan benefit, the employer must make up the difference.

In the event of death before retirement, the combination plan typically provides a death benefit to the participant's beneficiary equal to the policy's full face amount. This is particularly beneficial in the case of a participant who dies early before the cash value or the side fund have built up to significant amounts. If the participant terminates employment with a vested benefit, the plan provides a deferred vested benefit using a portion of the cash value of insurance contracts on the participant's life plus a portion of the side fund.

Combination funding can also be used for defined-contribution plans, such as money-purchase pension plans or profit-sharing plans. Since the 100 to 1 test for incidental insurance benefits is difficult to apply in such situations, the amount of insurance is usually designed to meet the other "incidental" test—aggregate insurance premiums less than 50 percent of total contributions. In a defined-contribution plan, individual accounts in the side fund must be maintained for each participant. The retirement benefit is usually a lump sum equal to the cash value of the policy or

TABLE 22-1
Illustration of Defined-Benefit Combination Plan

	Employee	
	A	B
Age at entry	48	30
Projected monthly retirement benefit	$ 2,250	$ 1,250
Face amount of insurance	225,000	125,000
Gross annual premium	6,399	1,647
Annual side fund deposit	10,174	1,405
Policy cash value at retirement	81,225	65,250
Side fund at retirement (5 percent assumed return)	276,075	133,250

policies plus the amount in the participant's individual side fund account. Alternatively, this amount could be distributed as an equivalent annuity. If the participant dies before retirement, the death benefit in such a plan usually is the face amount of the life insurance plus the participant's individual side fund account, although the plan may limit the death benefit to the insurance amount alone.

Group Permanent Contract

In order to facilitate the use of cash-value life insurance contracts in qualified plans of larger employers, insurance companies can write these contracts on a group basis. Such contracts are referred to as *group permanent* contracts. The group permanent contract is used to provide a funding structure similar to that of corresponding individual contracts, with similar plan design considerations and costs. The major difference is group underwriting. Sometimes, a minimum number of employees is required, usually 10 to 25. With group underwriting, life insurance is written without evidence of insurability up to a limit specified in the plan.

A group permanent (whole life) contract can be designed to provide relatively slow buildup of cash values and, therefore, a lower cost to the employer, so that it can be used together with a side fund in much the same manner as a combination plan utilizing individual policies.

Group Deferred Annuity Contract

The group deferred annuity contract is, historically, an important form of allocated funding for pension plans. Under this contract, there is no life insurance. Employer contributions are used to purchase single premium deferred annuities for employees based on the amount of annuity accrued by the participant each year.

As an illustration, suppose that in a given year, an employee earns (accrues) a pension increment of $10 per month beginning at age 65. The premium for this amount of deferred annuity is determined and similar determinations are made for other covered employees. The total annuity premium charged to the employer this year is the sum of all such premiums for all employee credits earned during the year. Next year, the premium is the cost of all deferred annuities earned by employees during that year. Thus, unlike the types of contracts discussed so far, the group deferred annuity contract does not generate a level premium but, other things being equal, tends to produce an increasing premium because the cost of a given amount of deferred annuity increases with increasing age. For an entire employee group, however, the annual premium will not necessarily show an increasing trend because of retirements, deaths and terminations of employment.

Since the entire premium under a group deferred annuity contract is determined by the insurance company, the employer has little control over the amount and timing of pension costs. There are typically withdrawal credits, deferred retirement credits and dividends or premium rate adjustments, but these also are largely beyond the control of the employer. Because of the lack of employer flexibility in funding, as well as the availability of better investment results using other contracts, group deferred annuity contracts are rarely used today.

INSURANCE CONTRACTS USING UNALLOCATED FUNDING

The basic characteristic of unallocated funding instruments in a qualified plan is that employer contributions to the plan are not initially allocated to provide specific benefits. In an insurance contract with unallocated funding, the insurance company thus does not assume the risk of paying specific benefits. Instead, the contributions are held in an undivided fund, similar to a trust fund, until annuities are purchased at an employee's retirement or until benefits are actually paid to employees. Where long-term investment results are more favorable than the investment assumptions used by insurance companies for allocated contracts, the unallocated type of contract provides an advantage to the employer because the employer contribution level can be made lower initially and the employer can retain use of the money saved. Thus, unallocated contracts have been developed by insurance companies primarily to compete with other funding agencies, such as bank trust departments.

Group Deposit Administration Contract

In the conventional type of group deposit administration (DA) contract, employer contributions to fund benefits for employees who have not yet retired are held in an unallocated account, referred to as the *active life fund, annuity purchase fund, deposit administration fund, purchase payment fund* or something similar. As each participant reaches retirement age, an amount is taken from the active life fund sufficient to purchase an annuity for that participant in the amount provided by the plan. The annuity purchase rate is determined by the insurance company under the terms of the DA contract. Typically, a DA contract provides a limited guarantee of annuity purchase rates. For example, the contract may guarantee annuity purchase rates for contributions paid during the first five years of the contract, with a year-to-year guarantee thereafter. More liberal guarantees are sometimes made available by insurers to remain competitive.

Under a DA contract, the rate of contributions to the fund is determined by the employer, using a reasonable actuarial method of the employer's choosing, subject to the minimum funding standards and other rules discussed later in this chapter. The employer is entirely responsible for the adequacy of the active life fund and must make contributions accordingly. The insurance company does not determine the premium or funding level. Also, the lack of allocated funding allows the same flexibility in designing the plan's benefit structure as is available under a trust fund plan. Benefit and funding flexibility are the main reasons for the attractiveness of unallocated funding instruments to employers.

In addition to design flexibility, insurance companies can provide investment features under DA contracts that make these contracts attractive. Most DA contracts provide a minimum investment rate guarantee. As with annuity purchase rate guarantees, the investment rate guarantee will typically apply to contributions paid during the first five years of the contract, with a year-to-year guarantee thereafter; more liberal guarantees may be made available from time to time to increase the attractiveness of these contracts.

Immediate Participation Guarantee Contract

The conventional DA contract just described retains one difference from a fully unallocated fund—the purchase of annuities as participants reach retirement. In determining annuity purchase rates, the insurer includes a factor for expenses, and also a factor for a "contingency reserve," to cover the possibility of adverse actuarial experience. This amount must be conservatively determined by the insurance company, because if the annuity purchase rate turns out to be excessive, the company can return part of the excess through dividends on the contract; if the purchase rate is insufficient, the insurance company cannot require the contractholder to make additional payments.

Many employers, particularly those with many employees, would prefer to assume all of the risks of making postretirement benefit payments in order to avoid the withdrawal of funds to purchase annuities, thereby maintaining control of the funds for a longer period of time. The immediate participation guarantee (IPG) contract was developed to provide for this market.

In most respects, the IPG contract is similar to the conventional DA contract. The principal difference is in the method of providing annuities to participants reaching retirement. Under an IPG contract, there is a single fund into which all plan contributions by the employer are deposited. Under some IPG contracts, the fund is charged directly with benefit payments as they are made. Under other contracts, the IPG fund is charged as each employee reaches retirement with a single annuity premium; however, this is done in such a way as to provide the effect of a trust fund; for example, through annual cancellation and reissuance of annuities.

Although some insurers offer no guarantees under IPG contracts, principal and minimum investment return guarantees are sometimes made available. As with conventional DA contracts, separate accounts funding can be made available under an IPG contract.

SEPARATE ACCOUNTS FUNDING AND NEW MONEY

The investment of qualified plan funds under an insurance contract can involve certain disadvantages relating to the commingling of the employer's pension funds with those of other employers or with other funds of the insurance company. Separate accounts funding and the new money technique are methods by which two of these disadvantages can be mitigated.

Separate Accounts

Separate accounts funding was developed to avoid commingling pension assets with all of the general assets of the insurance company, since an insurance company's general assets have traditionally been invested in long-term, low-return investment vehicles, sometimes subject to legal restrictions on investments. With separate accounts funding, the insurance company makes available one or more special accounts, separate from its general asset accounts, solely for investment of pension money. Such separate accounts may have a specified investment philosophy; for example, one type of account might be invested in common stocks, another in bonds, another in real estate mortgages, another in money market instruments and so forth. The qualified plan sponsor is then given the option to invest various portions of the plan fund in one or more of the separate accounts. The funds so designated are commingled with similar funds of other qualified plans, as in a common or collective trust fund. If an individual plan fund is large enough, an insurer may also offer the employer an individual separate account only for that employer with whatever mix of assets the employer designates.

New Money

Because many of the insurance contracts available for qualified plan funding involve the mingling of an employer's pension contributions with money invested in previous years, the investment return credited on a given year's contributions is not necessarily equal to the return that could have been earned if the amounts contributed had been newly invested that year. This can present a problem under contracts giving employers discretion as to how much to contribute to the fund during a given year, as is generally true under DA and IPG contracts. Where the composite return provided under the insurance contract is greater than that available for new investments, the employer will tend to maximize contributions, while contributions will be minimized when new outside investments can obtain a higher rate of return than under the contract. To alleviate such problems, insurers have developed methods to credit each block of qualified plan contributions with the rate of return at which the funds were actually invested. There are a number of ways of accomplishing this; such techniques are referred to as *new money, investment year* or *investment generation* methods.

New money methods must not only credit plan contributions for a given year with the current investment rate for that year, but must also take account of the fact that contributions from past years are constantly being reinvested at current rates. Thus, a plan contribution made in Year 1 is credited with the new money rate for Year 1. For Year 2, the Year 1 contribution is credited not with the Year 2 rate, but with a composite of the Year 1 rate and the Year 2 rate, to reflect the fact that a portion (but only a portion) of the Year 1 money will be reinvested in Year 2.

Two broad methods of accounting for these changes are the *declining-index* method and the *fixed-index* method. Under the declining-index method, the amount of money associated with a particular year gradually declines as the amount originally invested in that year is reinvested in later years. Thus, under the declining-index method, the amount invested in Year 1 in the previous example would decline in Year 2 to reflect the fact that part of it was reinvested in Year 2. Under the fixed-index method, the amount associated with the initial investment year remains the same, and the rate of return credited to that amount is adjusted to reflect reinvestments without changing the original principal amount. The two methods generally produce the same results.

ACTUARIAL METHODS AND ASSUMPTIONS

The final or ultimate cost of a qualified plan cannot be determined until the last benefit dollar has been paid to the last surviving plan participant. However, the ultimate cost is not of immediate concern to the employer. Rather, the employer wants to know what the annual cost burden of the plan will be, particularly over the first several years of the plan. For a defined-contribution plan, this is not difficult to determine; the plan document itself specifies the amount of annual contribution that is required, usually in terms of some parameter of business operations, such as payroll or profits. Thus, it is not difficult to get an idea of the kind of burden the business will be assuming if it adopts this kind of plan. For a defined-benefit plan, however, actuarial methods and assumptions determine the annual cost, since the plan itself specifies only the benefits that will be paid.

In the past, employers had a great deal of flexibility in funding defined-benefit plans. In fact, prior to ERISA, it was not necessary even to fund such plans in advance; benefit payments could be made as they came due. Another method sometimes used was terminal funding—funding the benefit in full at the participant's retirement, usually through purchase of an annuity from an insurance company. Under current law, however, all qualified defined-benefit plans subject to the funding provisions of ERISA must provide advance funding over the working lives of the participants using an actuarial cost method and assumptions. The ERISA funding requirements apply basically to all qualified defined-benefit plans of private employers. Certain government and church plans are exempted from coverage, as well as certain types of plans having no employer contributions. Also, fully insured plans are treated under special rules described later in this chapter in the discussion of minimum funding standards.

An *actuarial cost method* is a method of determining an annual employer contribution for a given set of plan benefits and group of employees. The method produces a schedule of annual contributions aimed at providing a plan fund sufficient to make all benefit payments when they come due without any further contributions by the employer. *Actuarial assumptions* refer to assumptions about future investment return and the character of the employee group that are made in order to determine the annual contribution.

Great variety and complexity are possible in actuarial methods and assumptions. Because of this, many people who are otherwise experts in the benefits area tend to regard actuarial methods as a technical subject that should be left solely to actuaries. However, the choice of actuarial methods and assumptions is such an important factor in determining the timing of plan costs—and, therefore, the tax benefits from the plan—that anyone involved in the benefits area should have a basic knowledge of actuarial concepts.

Because of the complexity of the subject and the specialized terminology involved, it is difficult to treat actuarial methods in a brief and concise way. As with so many considerations in the design of qualified plans, there are two interrelated aspects to the issue. First are the basic concepts used by pension actuaries; then there are the limits imposed by the Internal Revenue Code and ERISA on the types of methods and assumptions permitted for a qualified plan.

Accrued-Benefit and Projected-Benefit Approaches for Determining the Plan's Normal Cost

We will begin with a discussion of the basic concepts and terminology. The actuary's starting point is a determination of the amount that will be required at retirement to fully fund each active employee's benefit. For example, suppose that Clutch Company is planning to adopt a defined-benefit plan. The annual retirement benefit will be 50 percent of each employee's salary at retirement, with the benefits payable as a straight-life annuity. Clutch's employee census and projected benefits look like this:

Employee	Age	Current Salary	Projected Annual Retirement Benefit
A	60	$100,000	$50,000
B	50	60,000	30,000
C	45	40,000	20,000
D	30	25,000	12,500

For simplicity, it is assumed in this example that salary at retirement is equal to current salary, even though it is permissible for funding purposes to make certain assumptions about salary changes, as discussed later. At any rate, the actuary's task is to determine an annual deposit to the plan fund that will insure that as each employee retires there is enough money in the fund to fully fund the retirement benefit.

Initially, this discussion will focus on methods for determining annual deposits over each employee's working career prior to retirement, designed to fully fund that employee's benefit. The total of such amounts for all employees is the plan's annual *normal cost*. In some actuarial methods, the total cost is divided into two elements. Under this approach, only part of the cost is funded by deposits calculated over employees' working careers (the normal cost). The remainder of the plan's cost, or the *supplemental liability*, which is usually an amount attributable to past service, is funded through deposits over a fixed period of years without reference to participants' retirement dates. This type of funding can provide flexibility in the annual contribution level, as will be discussed.

The Internal Revenue Code does not specifically prescribe what actuarial methods must be used, only that a method must be "reasonable" (Section 412(c)(3)). However, the regulations state that in order to be reasonable, the actuarial method must determine the normal cost in one of two ways:

1. The normal cost must be an "amount equal to the present value of benefits accruing under the method for a particular plan year."
2. The normal cost must be expressed as "a level dollar amount or a level percentage of pay."

Actuarial cost methods used for qualified plans determine the normal cost using one of these two approaches: the first is referred to as the *accrued-benefit* approach and the second is the *projected-benefit* approach.

Accrued-Benefit Approach

Under this method of determining the normal cost, the normal cost for a particular year is the amount needed to currently fund all the benefits earned for service with the employer that year. The first step in the method, therefore, is to determine the amount of retirement benefit accrued by each employee during the current year. This depends on the plan formula; some formulas may specify the amount accrued for each year of service while for others, the total amount will have to be determined and then spread over the years of service remaining to retirement, usually on a pro rata basis, although the plan can specify otherwise within the limits of the benefit accrual rules. Pro rata accrual will be used for the plan of the Clutch Company described above. Thus, if normal retirement age is 65, the annual benefit accrual under the Clutch Plan would be:

Employee	Projected Annual Retirement Benefit	+ Years to Retirement	= Annual Benefit Accrual
A	$50,000	5	$10,000
B	30,000	15	2,000
C	20,000	20	1,000
D	12,500	35	357

The next step is to compute the amount that must be contributed this year to fund each of these benefits currently—that is, the present value of the annual accrual. For simplicity, we will assume that all employees survive and continue in service with the employer until age 65. (Mortality and turnover assumptions are permitted, however, as discussed later.) The only factor in the present-value calculation then is an assumption as to the rate of investment return. The actuary must determine the rate of investment return to be assumed. The Code does not put specific limits on the range of permissible rates, but the rate must be reasonable, as with other actuarial assumptions. For reference, Table 22-2 is a present-value factor table for a 6 percent investment return assumption. Either a table or a formula may be used.

The final factor needed is the annuity purchase rate. This is the lump sum needed at retirement to provide a straight-life annuity of $1 per year. The annuity

TABLE 22-2 Present-Value Factors	
Years to Retirement	Present Value at 6 Percent
5	.7473
15	.4173
20	.3118
25	.2330
35	.1301
40	.0972

purchase rate is based on the plan's retirement age, the life expectancy of the retiree and the assumed investment return in the postretirement period. For illustration, an annuity purchase rate of $9.50 will be used for the Clutch Plan. As an example, an accrued benefit of $10,000 per year at that rate would require an accumulation of $95,000 at age 65. Our calculation under the accrued-benefit method then is:

Employee	Annual Accrual	×	Annuity Rate	×	Present Value Factor	=	Present Value
A	$10,000		$9.50		.7473		$70,993
B	2,000		9.50		.4173		7,929
C	1,000		9.50		.3318		2,962
D	357		9.50		.1301		441
Total							$83,325

This calculation shows, for example, that $70,993 must be deposited now to provide a benefit of $10,000 per year for Employee A at age 65 (five years from now), $70,993 being the present value of the $95,000 required to purchase the $10,000 annuity at age 65. The normal cost for the current year is the sum of the present values of the annual accruals for all employees, or $83,325.

It should be noted from the present-value table that the present-value factor increases as the participant gets closer to retirement. The accrued-benefit method, therefore, produces a steadily increasing normal cost for a given group of active employees. However, as employees leave the group by retiring or terminating employment, their benefit no longer enters the calculation. Correspondingly, new employees entering the plan will add to the normal cost. Thus, when the accrued-benefit method is used in actual situations, the employer's annual normal cost may increase, decrease or level off.

Projected-Benefit Methods

The projected-benefit methods determine the normal cost by developing a level annual cost for each employee's benefit instead of the steadily rising costs resulting under the accrued-benefit method. A simple illustration of this can be provided using the data and assumptions for the Clutch Plan discussed previously.

(1) Employee	(2) Projected Annual Benefit	×	(3) Annuity Rate	=	(4) Accumulation Required at Age 65	(5) Years to Retirement	(6) Level Annual Deposit (6%) Required to Attain (4)
A	$50,000		$9.50		$475,000	5	$79,494
B	30,000		9.50		285,000	15	11,551
C	20,000		9.50		190,000	20	4,872
D	12,500		9.50		118,750	35	1,005
Total							$96,922

The calculation of the normal cost under the projected-benefit approach begins with the entire projected benefit at retirement, then a calculation (column six) of the level deposits necessary each year to provide an ultimate accumulation at retirement age sufficient to provide the projected benefit at an assumed annuity rate. (Column six can be calculated from the information in columns four and five, plus an interest assumption—6 percent was used here—using a pocket calculator having an installment savings program, a computer with the same program or actuarial tables.) The normal cost for the Clutch Plan is the total of the amounts in column six, or $96,922. The addition of mortality, turnover or other actuarial assumptions would complicate the calculation, but the principles are the same. Note that the normal cost provided initially under this method is higher than the normal cost using the accrued-benefit method. This is what one would expect because of the level funding approach in the projected-benefit approach.

Several actuarial cost methods use the projected-benefit approach. These can be divided into *individual* and *aggregate* methods. With individual methods, the plan's normal cost is determined as the sum of separate annual costs determined for each employee. This is the approach used in the example just completed. With aggregate methods, the normal cost is determined by reference to the total benefits and salaries of all employees covered under the plan rather than on an individual basis. Basically, this is done by determining the normal cost as a percentage of payroll of all employees covered by the plan. The normal cost percentage is defined as:

$$\frac{\text{Present value of projected benefits} - \text{Plan assets}}{\text{Present value of future salaries}}$$

For a new plan, of course, the value of plan assets will initially be zero.

An advantage of an aggregate method is that, as the above formula indicates, the value of plan assets is taken into account in determining each year's normal cost percentage; thus, the method automatically makes adjustments for investment results or other fund experience, such as mortality or turnover, that deviate from the actuarial assumptions. With individual methods, such adjustments are made after an actuarial valuation and are amortized separately over a period of years, as will be discussed.

Amortization of Past Service Cost (Supplemental Liability)

Flexibility in funding is gained by splitting the funding into two elements—the normal cost and a *supplemental liability*. As previously discussed, the supplemental liability is usually related to an initial liability for funding past service benefits. While the normal cost of a plan is designed to be funded over the period prior to each employee's retirement, the entire supplemental liability may be funded or *amortized* over a fixed period of years, even if this period extends beyond the retirement dates of some plan participants. Under ERISA, the amortization period for new single-employer plans cannot exceed 30 years. A full tax deduction for the supplemental liability amortization, however, can be obtained for an amortization over as little as ten years, as discussed under "Deductibility of Pension Plan Contributions."

An actuarial cost method that includes a supplemental liability provides some flexibility in the amount the employer must contribute each year. Once a plan's actuarial methods and assumptions have been determined, the amount of the normal cost has been correspondingly determined. It may be difficult for an employer to change actuarial methods and assumptions to adjust the normal cost to a more financially comfortable level in the future. However, the portion of the plan funding attributable to amortizing the supplemental liability can be varied by the employer from year to year so long as the amount is at least enough to meet the 30-year amortization requirement.

Actuarial Assumptions

The importance of actuarial assumptions has been mentioned previously. The following are some commonly used actuarial assumptions with some indication of when and how they are used.

Interest or Investment Return

This is the actuarial assumption that is most basic and must always be used. It reflects the time value of money—the fact that $1 deposited currently will grow over the years to some amount greater than $1. Actuaries typically use conservative rates of return for defined-benefit plans because of the plan's long range nature and the necessity for security. The lower the rate used, the greater the annual deposit required.

Mortality

A mortality assumption reflects the possibility that some participants in the employee census may die before reaching retirement age and the amounts contributed to the plan on their behalf will be available to fund benefits of other participants, assuming the plan does not pay these amounts out fully as a death benefit. A mortality assumption accordingly reduces the current contribution to the plan. A mortality assumption may not be appropriate for a small group—say less than ten employees. It is hard to predict mortality in such a small group; often all the members of the group will live to retirement, thus producing underfunding if a mortality assumption has been used.

Turnover

A turnover assumption reflects the possibility that some employees will terminate employment without a fully vested retirement benefit. Again, a turnover assumption tends to reduce current costs for the plan. But, as with mortality, a turnover assumption may not be appropriate for a small group of employees where turnover is difficult to predict.

Salary Scale

If plan benefits depend on future salaries, it is unrealistic to make a benefit projection based on current salaries. Therefore, the plan may include an assumption that salaries will increase at a specified rate over time. It is impractical to assume an increase based on a high inflation rate, because this would produce enormous projected benefits for younger employees. Therefore, a salary scale typically uses a relatively conservative long-term rate based on annual increases of a few percentage points.

Choosing Actuarial Assumptions

The regulations under Code Section 412 permit assumptions of the four types indicated above, so long as they use "reasonable" factors. Each assumption must be reasonable under IRS guidelines.

Certain types of assumptions that might be considered actuarially appropriate are specifically prohibited by the regulations. The regulations do not allow a funding method to anticipate changes in plan benefits that become effective in a future plan year, except for collectively bargained plans. Also, a funding method may not anticipate the future entry of new employees into the plan, except for current employees who have not yet satisfied the plan's participation requirements.

Penalty for Overstatement of Pension Liabilities

If the IRS assesses additional taxes because an employer's pension plan used unreasonable actuarial assumptions, under Code Section 6662, it can also impose a penalty on the additional tax liability ranging from 10 to 30 percent, based on the extent of the actuarial overstatement.

Some Specific Permissible Actuarial Cost Methods

The choice of actuarial cost method is limited only by the code requirement that the method be reasonable and a few corresponding requirements in the regulations. Thus, a wide variety of actuarial cost methods is available through variations on the concepts discussed earlier.

- Accrued-benefit or projected-benefit approach for determining normal cost.
- Individual or aggregate methods, if the projected-benefit approach is used.
- Whether to use a supplemental liability.

Six specific methods are briefly discussed here because they are specifically mentioned in ERISA Section 3(31) as acceptable methods. Because of this legislative endorsement, many plans use one of these methods.

Accrued-Benefit Method

The accrued-benefit method, sometimes called the unit-credit method, is a method under which future service costs are funded using a normal cost determined by an accrued-benefit method; past service liability is treated separately. This is essentially the method discussed earlier in some detail in the first example for the Clutch Plan.

Individual Level-Premiums Method

This is a method without separate funding for past service benefits, so that the entire cost of the plan is funded through the normal cost. In this method, the normal cost is determined on a projected benefit or level cost basis for each participant separately, with the total normal cost for the plan being the sum of the level cost computed for each participant. The second example for the Clutch Plan illustrates this method.

Entry-Age Normal Method

This is another method under which past service liability is funded separately from the normal cost. The normal cost of the plan each year is the sum of the level costs for each participant. However, the level cost for each participant is determined as if the participant had entered the plan at the age when that participant's benefits began to accrue—the entry age. If entry ages occur before the plan is instituted— that is, if the plan provides past service benefits—then the normal cost will not by itself fully fund the plan. The amount of the past service liability is the present value of the total normal costs, which were never actually paid, occurring between each employee's entry age and the establishment of the plan. This past service liability is then amortized under the applicable rules.

Aggregate Method

This method and the next two methods are aggregate cost methods since they determine normal cost with reference to total benefits and salaries of all plan participants, rather than making determinations on an individual basis. The "plain" aggregate method does not separately fund past service cost, so there is no initial past service liability. The normal cost percentage is determined from the formula:

$$\frac{\text{Present value of projected benefits – Plan assets}}{\text{Present value of future salaries}}$$

Attained-Age Normal Method

This is a variation of the plain aggregate method designed to create an initial past service liability to increase funding flexibility. Under the attained-age normal method, the amount of the initial past service liability is determined using the accrued-benefit method. The normal cost percentage is then determined under the following formula:

$$\frac{\begin{array}{c}\text{Present value of projected}\\\text{benefits}\end{array} - \left(\text{Plan assets} + \begin{array}{c}\text{Unfunded initial past service}\\\text{liability under the accrued-benefit}\\\text{method}\end{array}\right)}{\text{Present value of future salaries}}$$

Frozen Initial Liability Method

This is a further variation on the aggregate method, and it also determines an initial past service liability to increase funding flexibility. The frozen initial liability method uses a projected-benefit method, such as the entry-age normal method, to determine the initial past service liability. As with the attained-age normal method, the remaining benefits are funded through future normal cost determined under the aggregate method. Accordingly, the normal cost percentage formula is:

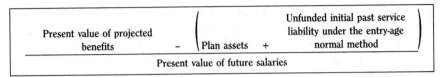

$$\frac{\text{Present value of projected benefits} \quad - \quad \left(\text{Plan assets} \quad + \quad \begin{array}{c} \text{Unfunded initial past service} \\ \text{liability under the entry-age} \\ \text{normal method} \end{array}\right)}{\text{Present value of future salaries}}$$

The best way to understand how these actuarial cost methods operate is to work through examples of the various types for a given plan and employee group. A good example is found in "How to Select Acceptable Actuarial Methods for Defined-Benefit Pension Plans," by Kirk F. Maldonado in *The Journal of Taxation,* July 1982.

A comparison of the annual cost for a given plan under the six methods shows how important the choice of method is and how much flexibility is available. In the Maldonado article, the cost for a given plan for each of the six ERISA methods was determined. The plan provides an annual retirement benefit of 40 percent of the employee's salary for his or her final year, and the benefits are to be paid monthly in the form of a straight-life annuity. For simplicity, possible deferred vested benefits for terminating employees were not taken into account. The employee census data are:

Age	Age When Hired (entry age)	Years of Past Service	Current Salary
60	40	20	$10,000
50	45	5	50,000
30	30	0	25,000
25	25	0	10,000

For the first year, the cost comparison from the article is:

Comparison of First-Year Funding Cost		
Funding Method	Minimum Contribution	Maximum Deduction
Individual methods:		
Accrued-benefit	$34,742	$50,162
Individual level-premiums	81,938	81,938
Entry-age normal	34,546	51,831
Aggregate methods:		
Aggregate	52,318	52,318
Attained-age normal	36,594	52,014
Frozen initial liability	34,668	51,953

The column headed "minimum contribution" indicates the normal cost plus a 30-year amortization of the supplemental liability, if any, for each method. The column headed "maximum deduction" indicates the normal cost plus a ten-year amortization of the supplemental liability. The employer's actual first-year contribution, for a given funding method, could be either amount or any amount in between, as the employer determines.

Choosing an Actuarial Cost Method

The initial choice of an actuarial cost method may be affected by the employer's concerns as to how plan costs will be spread over future years. The accrued-benefit method will often produce a lower initial cost than other methods and might be chosen if the employer wishes to minimize costs at the plan's inception with the expectation of increased funding in later years. Sometimes, this deferral of funding can be a problem. For example, in the 1950s, plans of large manufacturing companies often used the accrued-benefit method since they expected continuing expansion of their work force and thus increasing contributions. However, with the decline in manufacturing in the 1970s, many such plans became underfunded.

Some employers might prefer to *maximize* initial contributions. This is often the case when a plan benefits mostly key employees and the employer wishes to maximize tax sheltering effects. In that case, a level cost method such as the individual level-premiums method may produce the highest annual cost. A very high initial annual cost can sometimes be provided using the individual level-premiums method with past service liability amortized over a ten-year period. However, if highly paid participants are within ten years of retirement, the individual level-premiums method *without* a supplemental liability will generally provide a higher annual tax deductible contribution.

Sometimes, employers wish to match pension costs as closely as possible to payroll costs. In that situation, the aggregate method is typically used since it expresses normal cost as a percentage of participants' compensation and thus rises automatically with payroll costs. The aggregate method is typically used with larger employee groups for this reason, although it produces the same results with a smaller group of employees as well.

Methods that spread costs over too many years can produce problems of underfunding. For example, using a supplemental liability for past-service benefits and spreading these benefits over a 30-year period can result in underfunding if participants with large projected benefits are close to retirement.

If a plan's initial funding method proves unacceptable in practice, the plan administrator can change the method. Code Section 412(c)(5) requires IRS approval for a change in funding method; however, under Revenue Procedure 85-29, such changes will be automatically approved in most routine situations. Changes in actuarial assumptions generally do not require IRS approval.

Ongoing Actuarial Valuations

The discussion so far has focused on actuarial methods for determining plan costs for the initial year. In subsequent years, the plan experience is likely to deviate somewhat from the assumptions made in determining first-year cost. If the deviations are significant enough, one response may be to change the actuarial methods or assumptions. There are, however, other ways to deal with variations from the initial assumptions.

The assets of all qualified plans are valued periodically by the actuary. Under ERISA, the valuation must be made at least once every three years. If the plan assets are found to be insufficient, there is an actuarial deficiency (or *experience loss*) which is made up with increased contributions that are usually deposited (*amortized*) over a period of years. Similarly, if there is an actuarial surplus (or *experience gain*), contributions are decreased over future years. The minimum funding standards, discussed below, determine how rapidly these experience gains and losses must be amortized.

The valuation of the plan's assets may be made on the basis of any reasonable valuation method, as long as the method takes into account the fair market value of the assets—rather than using cost or some other purely formal method of valuation. The regulations under Section 412 specify rules that must be used in valuation. For example, debt instruments may be valued by amortizing the difference between initial cost and maturity value over the life of the bond, since it may not be possible to determine current fair market value by market quotations. Also, since valuations are relatively infrequent, the plan can use any reasonable and consistent procedure for averaging actual market value over a period of years or smoothing out the fluctuations in the market value of assets.

MINIMUM FUNDING STANDARDS

The minimum funding standards of Code Section 412 and corresponding ERISA provisions provide the legal structure for enforcing the advance funding requirement that applies to qualified pension plans. A plan to which the minimum funding standard applies must maintain a *funding standard account.* The funding standard account is annually charged with the plan's normal cost and certain other costs and credited with certain items that benefit the plan. At the end of the year, if the charges exceed the credits, there may be an *accumulated funding deficiency.* In that case, there is a penalty tax and other enforcement provisions. The penalty tax consists of an initial tax of 5 percent of the deficiency, with an additional 100 percent tax if the deficiency is not corrected after notification by the IRS.

Obviously, the employer's objective is to *balance* the funding standard account for each year. If the employer is unable to make sufficient contributions to do this, the employer can request a waiver from the IRS of the minimum funding standard for the plan year or request an extended amortization period for certain plan liabilities.

The employer is not required to contribute annually any more to the plan than an amount referred to as the *full funding limitation* even if the funding standard account would then be left with a deficit for the plan year. This important limitation is defined as the difference between the accrued actuarial liability of the plan computed under the plan's funding method (or if this is not possible, under the entry-age normal method) less the value of the plan assets. Finally, certain plans are allowed to establish an *alternative minimum funding standard account* and can then avoid a funding deficiency by avoiding a deficit in either the funding standard account or the alternative minimum funding standard account, whichever is lesser. The alternative minimum funding standard account is somewhat simpler than the funding standard account and it is usually possible to avoid a deficit with a lower employer contribution.

Exemptions from the Minimum Funding Standard

The minimum funding standard rules basically apply to all qualified pension plans. However, governmental plans, church plans that have not elected to be treated as qualified plans and various types of plans having no employer contributions are exempted in Code Section 412.

More significantly, the minimum funding standards do not apply to profit-sharing or stock bonus plans. Technically, the standards apply to defined-contribution pension plans as well as defined-benefit pension plans. However, for defined-contribution pension plans (money-purchase and target plans), the minimum funding standard will be met so long as the employer contributes the amount required under the plan's contribution formula each year.

Fully insured plans—those funded exclusively by the purchase of individual insurance or annuity contracts—are specifically exempted from the minimum funding standards so long as the following requirements are met:

- The contracts provide for the payment of premiums in equal annual amounts over a period no longer than the preretirement period of employment.
- The plan benefits are equal to those guaranteed by the insurance carrier under the contracts.
- The premiums on the contracts have been paid when due or, if there has been a lapse, the policy has been reinstated.
- No rights under the insurance contract have been subject to a security interest at any time during the plan year.
- No policy loans are outstanding at any time during the plan year.

Plans that are fully insured under group contracts are also exempt from the minimum funding standard so long as the contracts meet conditions similar to those previously listed. These would ordinarily have to be group contracts providing fully allocated funding.

DEDUCTIBILITY OF PENSION PLAN CONTRIBUTIONS

Excessive contributions to a pension plan fund, if they are allowed to be deducted, will accelerate the employer's tax deduction and thereby increase the tax benefit of the qualified plan beyond what is considered appropriate. To prevent this, there are specific limits on the amount of pension plan contributions that an employer can deduct in a given plan year.

Unlike the deduction limit for profit-sharing plans, which is 15 percent of payroll (see Chapter 23), the deduction limit for pension plans is based on actuarial considerations. For a given plan year, an employer can deduct contributions to a pension plan up to a limit determined by the largest of three amounts (Code Section 404(a)(1)):

1. The amount necessary to satisfy the minimum funding standard for the year.
2. The amount necessary to fund benefits based on past and current service on a level funding basis over the years remaining to retirement for each employee. However, if the remaining unfunded cost for any three individuals is more than 50 percent of the total of the unfunded costs, funding for those three individuals must be distributed over a period of at least five taxable years.
3. An amount equal to the normal cost of the plan plus, if there is a supplemental liability, an amount necessary to amortize the supplemental liability in equal annual payments over a ten-year period.

In determining the applicable limitation, the funding methods and the actuarial assumptions used must be the same as those used for purposes of the minimum funding standards. Furthermore, the tax deduction for a given plan year cannot exceed the full funding limitation that was discussed earlier. Thus, there is little incentive for the employer to contribute beyond the full funding limitation.

Although these limits are expressed in actuarial language, the implications are relatively easy to understand. First of all, if the plan is funded on the basis of individual insurance contracts, the second limit will generally be the one applicable to the plan, since most such contracts have premiums determined on the basis of level funding for the years remaining until retirement for each employee. On the other hand, plans funded with group contracts and trust funds using a variety of actuarial methods and assumptions will generally be governed by the third alternative limit.

Note that this limit specifies the *maximum* deductible amount. The amount required to be contributed under the minimum funding standard as applied to the plan may be somewhat less than this limit. Therefore, in a given plan year, the employer's actual contribution and deduction may be less than the maximum limit that applies. This is one of the reasons why a defined-benefit plan with a group pension contract or trust fund can be relatively flexible for the employer. Between the minimum limit required by the minimum funding standards and the maximum deductible limit discussed earlier, there may be a relatively comfortable range of contributions that can be adjusted according to the employer's specific financial situation.

The rules previously stated technically apply to both defined-benefit and defined-contribution pension plans. However, for defined-contribution plans, the minimum funding standards are satisfied whenever the employer makes the annual contributions specified by the plan document. In other words, the limit on the amount deductible under a defined-contribution pension plan is simply the amount specified in the plan document. For example, the plan document in a money-purchase plan might require that each year the employer must contribute an amount equal to 6 percent of each employee's compensation to that employee's account. The total of such contributions would then be both the amount required by the minimum funding standard and the maximum amount deductible.

If an employer has a combination of defined-benefit and defined-contribution plans covering the same employee or employees, a percentage deduction limit applies. The deduction for a given year cannot exceed the greater of 25 percent of the common payroll (compensation of employees covered under both plans) or the amount required to meet the minimum funding standard for the defined-benefit plan alone. As discussed in Chapter 25, this provision has its greatest impact on highly compensated employees.

Penalty for Nondeductible Contributions

Generally, there is no advantage in contributing more to a plan than is deductible, because not only is the deduction for the excess unavailable but under Code Section 4972, a 10 percent penalty is imposed on the nondeductible portion of the contribution. However, if nondeductible contributions are made, they can be carried over and deducted in future years. The deduction limit for future years, however, applies to the combination of carried-over and current contributions.

Timing of Deductions

The rules for timing of contributions and deductions for qualified plans are relatively favorable. Contributions will be deemed to be made by the employer for a given taxable year of the employer, and will be deductible for that year, if they are made by the time prescribed for filing the employer's tax return for that year, including extensions. For example, a corporation using a calendar year could contribute to the plan for 1991 as late as September 15, 1992 (the basic tax filing date of March 15, plus the maximum six-month extension). The rules for timing of contributions and deductions are the same for both cash and accrual-method taxpayers; there is no advantage for this purpose in using the accrual method.

STUDY QUESTIONS

1. a. What is a trust?
   b. What is the role of a trustee?
2. Explain why a retirement income policy can be the sole funding vehicle for a qualified pension plan, but an ordinary life insurance policy cannot normally be so used.
3. a. Describe a combination plan.
   b. What are the typical features of a combination plan?
4. How does a group permanent contract differ from individual policies used to fund qualified plans?
5. a. What are the basic characteristics of unallocated funding instruments in a qualified plan?
   b. What is the advantage in using them?
6. What makes an IPG contract different from the conventional DA contract?

7. Why is it important for anyone involved with employee benefits to understand actuarial cost methods and actuarial assumptions?

8. a. Explain how an accrued-benefit approach is used to determine the normal cost for a qualified plan.

   b. How does the projected-benefit approach for determining the normal cost of a qualified plan differ from the accrued-benefit approach?

9. a. Under what circumstances is supplemental liability incurred?

   b. Over what period of time may supplemental liability be amortized?

10. Which actuarial cost method should be chosen in each of the following situations?

   a. The Metro Company, a growing corporation, wishes to minimize costs at the plan's inception with the expectation of increased funding in later years.

   b. Infant Care, Inc., a small, closely held pediatric care group with highly paid participants who are within ten years of retirement, wishes to maximize initial contributions in order to maximize tax shelter.

   c. Middleco, a mid-sized manufacturing firm, wishes to match pension costs as closely as possible to payroll costs.

23

Profit-Sharing and Other Nonretirement Qualified Plans

Objectives

- Describe the characteristics of profit-sharing plans with respect to
    1. Eligibility.
    2. Vesting.
    3. Contribution provisions.
    4. Allocations to employee accounts.
    5. Forfeitures.
    6. Integration with social security.
    7. Deductibility of employer contributions.
    8. Section 415 limits.
    9. Investment earnings and account balances.
    10. Incidental benefits.
- Describe the characteristics of a savings plan.
- Describe the characteristics of a 401(k) plan.
- Explain the actual deferral percentage test.
- Describe the characteristics of stock plans.

"NONRETIREMENT" QUALIFIED PLANS

Qualified plans are a particularly useful employee benefit because they can be designed for purposes other than simply retirement income. This chapter will discuss qualified plans that are designed primarily as incentive-type employee benefits, with an element of retirement savings that may, in some cases, only be incidental. These plans are:

- Qualified profit-sharing plans.
- Savings or thrift plans.
- Cash or deferred (Section 401(k)) plans.
- Employer stock plans (stock bonus plans and ESOPs).

All of the plans discussed in this chapter are defined-contribution plans because they inherently have individual accounts for each employee.

Planners should also be aware that there are other benefit arrangements similar to these nonretirement qualified plans (simplified employee pensions [SEPs], Section 403(b) tax-deferred annuity plans and Section 457 plans). These alternative arrangements are covered in Chapters 27 and 28, because they are *not* qualified plans and have quite different rules and limitations. However, in planning for certain types of employers, these alternative plans should be considered as supplements to or alternatives to qualified plans. SEPs can be used by virtually any employer, while Section 403(b) plans and Section 457 plans are available only to certain tax-exempt and governmental employers, as discussed later.

QUALIFIED PROFIT-SHARING PLANS

The basic profit-sharing plan is a defined-contribution plan in which employer contributions are typically based in some manner on the employer's profits, although there is no actual requirement for the employer to have profits in order to contribute to the plan. Even a nonprofit organization may have a "profit-sharing" plan. The general characteristics are as follows:

- The employer contribution may be specified as a percentage of annual profits each year or, for even more flexibility, the plan may provide that the employer determines the amount to be contributed on an annual basis, with the option of contributing nothing even in years in which there are profits or conversely, making contributions in unprofitable years.
- The plan must have a nondiscriminatory formula for allocating the employer contribution to the accounts of employees.
- Since the plan is a defined-contribution plan, the benefit from it consists of the amount in each employee's account, usually distributed as a lump sum at retirement or termination of employment.
- The plan may permit employee withdrawals or loans during employment.
- Eligibility and vesting are usually liberal because of the incentive nature of the plan.
- Forfeitures from employees who terminate employment are usually reallocated to the accounts of remaining participants, thus making the plan particularly attractive to long-service employees.
- The main price for the advantages of the design is that the employer's annual deduction for contributions to the plan is limited to 15 percent of the payroll of employees covered under the plan.

Eligibility and Vesting

Profit-sharing plans are typically designed with relatively liberal eligibility and vesting provisions as compared with pension plans. This is because the employer generally wishes the incentive objective of the plans to operate for short-term as well as long-term employees, and also because the simplicity of administering a profit-sharing plan makes it less necessary to exclude short-term employees to reduce plan administrative costs. Thus, many profit-sharing plans permit employees to enter the plan immediately upon becoming employed, or after a short waiting period—for example, until the next date on which the plan assets are valued. A great variety of vesting provisions are used and they are typically tailored to the employer's specific needs.

As a qualified plan, a profit-sharing plan is subject to the restrictions on eligibility and vesting provisions discussed in detail in earlier chapters. In summary, a minimum age requirement greater than 21 is not permitted, nor can a waiting period for entry be longer than one year, or up to 1½ years if entry is based on plan entry dates. Under the age discrimination law, no maximum age for entry can be prescribed (and contributions must continue for as long as the employee continues to work). The coverage tests discussed in Chapter 19 apply to a profit-sharing plan as they do to all qualified plans.

The vesting requirements discussed in Chapter 21 are also applicable to profit-sharing plans. A profit-sharing plan is more likely to discriminate in favor of highly compensated employees as a result of high employee turnover and the use of forfeitures, as discussed below. Therefore, the IRS may require the more stringent three- to seven-year vesting schedule in new profit-sharing plans. Most profit-sharing plans use a vesting schedule that is at least as generous as this schedule. Even more stringent vesting is required if the plan is top-heavy (Chapter 25).

Employer Contribution Provision

There is great flexibility in designing an employer contribution provision for a profit-sharing plan. The contribution provision can be either *discretionary* or of the *formula* type.

With the discretionary provision, the company's board of directors determines each year what amount will be contributed. It is not necessary for the company actually to have current or accumulated profits. Many employers will wish to contribute the maximum deductible amount each year, but a lesser amount can be contributed.

Although employers are permitted to omit contributions under a discretionary provision, the IRS requires that contributions be "substantial and recurring." If too many years go by without contributions, the IRS is likely to find that the plan has been terminated, with the consequences discussed in Chapter 26 (basically, 100 percent vesting for all plan participants and distribution under a specified payment schedule). No specific guidelines are given by the IRS as to how many years of omitted contributions are permitted, so the decision to skip a profit-sharing contribution must always be made with some caution.

With a formula contribution provision, a specified amount must be contributed to the plan whenever there are profits. Typically, the amount is expressed as a percentage of profits determined under generally accepted accounting principles. There are no specific IRS restrictions on the type of formula so flexibility is possible. For example, the plan might provide for a contribution of 7 percent of all current profits in excess of $50,000, possibly with a limitation to the amount deductible for the year. There is also considerable freedom in defining the term *profit* in the plan. For example, profit before taxes or after taxes can be used, with before-tax profits being the most common. Profit as defined in the plan can also include capital gains and losses, or accumulated profits from prior years. Even an employer that is organized under state law as a "nonprofit" corporation can have a profit-sharing plan funded from a suitably defined surplus account.

The advantage of the formula approach is that it is more attractive to employees than the discretionary approach and more definitely serves the incentive purpose of the plan. However, if a formula approach is adopted, the employer must remember that the formula amount must always be contributed to the plan; the formula constitutes a continuing legal and financial obligation for the business. It is possible to draft formulas that take into account possible adverse financial contingencies. Without such provisions, the formula may have to be amended in the future in the event of financial difficulty.

Allocations to Employee Accounts

The plan's contribution provision determines the total amount contributed to the plan for all employees. The plan must also have a formula under which appropriate portions of this total contribution are allocated to the individual accounts of employees. Here there is less flexibility because the allocation provision must meet nondiscrimination requirements. The law provides that contributions must be allocated under a definite formula that does not discriminate in favor of highly compensated employees. Any formula that meets these requirements can be acceptable, but most formulas allocate to participants on the basis of their compensation as compared to the compensation of all participants. That is, after the total employer contribution is determined, the amount allocatable to a given participant is:

$$\text{Total employer contribution} \quad \times \quad \frac{\text{Participant's compensation}}{\text{Compensation of all participants}}$$

If compensation is used in the allocation formula, the plan must define compensation in a way that does not discriminate. Compensation might include only base pay, or might be total compensation including bonuses or overtime. Only the first $200,000 (as indexed for inflation) of each employee's compensation can be taken into account in the plan formula.

Service is another factor often used in the formula for allocating employer contributions. However, since highly compensated employees are likely to have long service, the IRS will probably require a showing that any service-based formula will not produce discrimination.

Age-Based Allocation Formula

Under IRS regulations adopted recently, it is possible for a profit sharing plan's allocation formula to take the participant's *age at plan entry* into account. That is, the plan can provide a greater allocation percentage of compensation to a participant who entered the plan at, say age 55, than to a participant who entered at age 25. The purpose of this allocation method is to provide the late entrant with a more adequate benefit at retirement, given the fact that the late entrant has fewer years to accumulate plan contributions. The advantages of this approach are similar to those for the target pension plan discussed in Chapter 20. The age-based profit-sharing plan has the additional advantage that the employer is not "locked-in" to an annual contribution obligation, which may make this approach attractive to smaller or less stable businesses.

Forfeitures

A forfeiture is an unvested amount remaining in a participant's account when the participant terminates employment without being fully vested under the plan's vesting schedule. Thus, forfeitures can occur in any defined-contribution plan that does not have 100 percent immediate vesting. Forfeitures can be reallocated to accounts of other participants or used to reduce future employer contributions. In a profit-sharing plan, forfeitures are usually reallocated to participants in order to provide an additional incentive for continuing service.

Forfeitures must be allocated in a nondiscriminatory manner. In most plans, forfeiture allocations are made in the same manner as allocations of employer contributions—on the basis of compensation or a combination of compensation and service. The IRS usually will not accept a forfeiture allocation provision based on account balances of remaining participants because such a provision may provide substantial discrimination.

Analysis of profit-sharing plans of smaller employers that have existed for a number of years generally shows that by far the largest account balances are those for highly compensated participants. This is because the combination of higher compensation, longer service (and therefore more years in the plan) and low turnover among the highly compensated group eventually produces a great disparity in account balances. This phenomenon is, in fact, one of the reasons why closely held businesses adopt profit-sharing plans. As such, it is not deemed to be discriminatory. However, if the plan contains any features designed to multiply this inherent discrimination (such as forfeiture allocation based on account balances) the IRS generally will not approve it.

Integration with Social Security

The allocation formula of a profit-sharing plan may be integrated with social security in order to avoid duplication of benefits and reduce plan costs to the employer. Under those rules, as discussed earlier, the integration level is generally equal to the taxable wage base for the year, although other levels are used in some cases. The difference between the plan's excess contribution percentage (contribution percentage for compensation above the integration level) and its base contribution percentage (contribution percentage for compensation up to the integration level) cannot be more than the lesser of

- The base contribution percentage, or
- The greater of (a) 5.7 percent or (b) the old-age social security tax rate.

The integrated plan gives credit to the employer for contributions made to social security as if they had been made to the plan, thus overall providing a nondiscriminatory allocation formula.

As an example of integrated formulas, if the plan uses an integration level of $53,400, it could provide a base allocation percentage of 10 percent of compensation below $53,400, plus an allocation of 5.7 percent of compensation above $53,400, assuming the old-age social security tax rate is less than 5.7 percent. Or, if the plan provided 4 percent of compensation below the integration level, it could provide no more than 4 percent of compensation above the integration level.

Plan allocations counted toward the 5.7 percent limitation must include not only employer contributions for the year but also any forfeitures allocated to the participant's account. For example, suppose that for the year 1991 a plan has two participants with compensation as shown below. For 1991, the employer contributes $5,000 to the plan and a forfeiture of $8,000 is available for allocation to participants' accounts. The plan's integration level is $53,400. Under the plan's allocation formula, each participant's account is to receive the maximum permitted percent of plan contributions plus forfeitures for compensation above $53,400 (up to 5.7 percent). The remaining amount of the plan contributions plus forfeitures are allocated in proportion to total compensation. Plan allocations would then be as follows:

Employee	1991 Compensation	Compensation above $53,400	5.7% of Excess	Allocation of Remainder	Total Allocation
A	$63,400	$10,000	$570	$10,051	$10,621
B	15,000	0	0	2,379	2,379
Payroll	$78,400				$13,000

The amount in the fifth column is arrived at by subtracting the excess allocation (total of column four) from the $13,000 of contributions plus forfeitures; this remaining amount of $12,430 is multiplied by a fraction, the numerator which is the participant's total compensation and the denominator of which is the total payroll. This allocation meets the integration rules since the amount allocated to compensation below $53,400 is more than 5.7 percent.

Deduction of Employer Contributions

Under Code Section 404(a)(3), the maximum amount that an employer can deduct for contributions to a profit-sharing plan is 15 percent of the compensation paid or accrued during the taxable year to all employees who participate in the profit-sharing plan. This is an employer deduction limit based on compensation of all covered employees; it is not a rule stating that allocations to individual participants' accounts are limited to 15 percent of their compensation. The limitation on annual additions to individual accounts, the Section 415 limit, is discussed below.

An employer can contribute to a profit-sharing or a stock bonus plan in excess of the 15 percent limit, but the excess is not deductible and is subject to a 10 percent penalty under Section 4972. The excess amount can be carried over to a future year and deducted then, but deductions in the future year for current contributions plus carryovers are still subject to the 15 percent of payroll limit.

Combined Profit-Sharing and Other Plans

If an employer has both a defined-benefit plan and a profit-sharing or other defined-contribution plan covering a common group of employees, the total contribution for both plans cannot exceed 25 percent of compensation of the common group of employees. However, if a greater contribution is necessary to satisfy the minimum funding standard for the defined-benefit plan, the employer will always be able to make and deduct this contribution.

Section 415 Limits

The Section 415 limits (discussed in more detail in Chapter 25) that apply to profit-sharing plans are those applicable to all defined-contribution plans. The annual addition to any participant's account cannot exceed the lesser of 25 percent of the participant's compensation or $30,000 (as indexed for inflation). For a profit-sharing plan, the annual addition usually includes the participant's share of any forfeitures as well as employer and employee contributions. This means that when forfeitures are allocated to a participant's account, the amount of employer contributions that can be allocated may be reduced. The Section 415 limits usually affect only highly compensated employees covered under the plan.

Investment Earnings and Account Balances

As a defined-contribution plan, a profit-sharing plan must provide separate accounts for each participant. However, unless the plan contains a provision permitting participants to direct investments (discussed below), the plan trustee or other funding agents will generally pool all participants' accounts for investment purposes. The plan must then provide a mechanism for allocating investment gains or losses to each participant. Most methods for doing this effectively allocate such gains and losses in proportion to the participant's account balance.

IRS revenue rulings require accounts of all participants to be valued in a uniform and consistent manner at least once each year, unless all plan assets are immediately invested in individual annuity or retirement contracts meeting certain requirements. The plan usually will specify a *valuation date* or dates on which valuation occurs. Investment earnings, gains and losses are allocated to participants' accounts as of this date.

Participant-Directed Investments

Under ERISA Section 401(c), any "individual account" plan (such as a profit-sharing, stock bonus or money-purchase pension plan) can include a provision allowing the participant to direct the trustee or other funding agent as to the investment of the participant's account.

If the plan administrator provides a reasonably wide range of investment choices—so that the participant's choice has real meaning—then the trustee and other plan fiduciaries are not subject to fiduciary responsibility for the investment decision.[1] A plan can technically allow unlimited choice of investments, but this increases the plan's administrative burdens. Often, a family of mutual funds is offered as investment options to increase the administrative feasibility of participant direction. At least one "cash equivalent" option, such as a money market fund, must be included.

Investment direction gives the participant a considerable degree of control over the funds in his or her account. It is frequently used in profit-sharing plans, particularly those for closely held businesses where the controlling employees have by far the largest accounts. On the other hand, to the extent that participant direction of investments removes the security provided by the fiduciary rules, such a provision is at odds with a plan objective of providing retirement security, and would not be appropriate if this were a major objective of the plan for a particular employee group.

To prevent certain abuses associated with participant-directed investments, the Code provides that an investment by a participant-directed qualified plan account in a *collectible* will be treated as if the amount invested were distributed to the participant as taxable income to the participant. A collectible is defined in Code Section 408(m) as a work of art, rug or antique, metal or gem, stamp or coin (excluding certain federal and state-issued coins), alcoholic beverage or any other tangible personal property designated as a collectible by the IRS.

Withdrawals During Employment and Loan Provisions

The incentive (rather than retirement security) focus of profit-sharing plans tends to dictate that participants be given the opportunity to control or benefit from their accounts even before retirement or termination of employment. There are various ways to do this. One such provision is a participant-directed account as discussed above. Another is a special feature permitted in profit-sharing plans, but not in pension plans—a provision for account withdrawals from the plan during employment.

The regulations require that employer contributions under a profit-sharing plan must be accumulated for at least two years before they can be withdrawn by participants.[2] However, in some revenue rulings, the IRS has permitted a plan provision allowing employees with at least 60 months of participation to withdraw employer contributions including those made within the previous two years. Also,

---

[1]Labor Regulation Section 2550.404c–1.

[2]Revenue Ruling 73–55, 1973–2 CB 130; Rev. Rul. 71–295, 1971–1 CB 184; Rev. Rul. 80–155, 1980–1 CB 84.

revenue rulings have permitted a plan provision for withdrawal in the case of "hardship" including contributions made within the previous two years. Hardship must be sufficiently defined in the plan and the definitions must be consistently applied.[3] All these limitations apply only to amounts attributable to employer contributions to the plan. If the plan permits employee contributions, the employee contributions can be withdrawn at any time without restriction.

In considering the design of withdrawal provisions, it is important to keep in mind that the taxation and early-withdrawal penalty rules act as disincentives for participants to withdraw plan funds. These rules (discussed in Chapter 24) indirectly reduce the advantages of using a qualified plan as a medium for preretirement savings.

Many plan designers prefer to have a prohibition or at least restrictions on withdrawals from the employer-contributed portion of the account. This is because favorable investment results sometimes depend on having a pool of investment money that is relatively large and not subject to the additional liquidity requirements imposed by the possibility of participant withdrawals. Some typical restrictions found in profit-sharing plans include a requirement that the participant demonstrate a need for the money coming within a list of authorized needs either set out in the plan or promulgated by the plan administrator and applied consistently. Such needs might include educational expenses for children, home purchase or remodeling, sickness or disability and so forth. Another method of restricting plan withdrawals is to provide a penalty on a participant who withdraws amounts from the plan (in addition to the 10 percent federal penalty tax which also applies). A plan penalty might include suspension of participation for a period of time, such as six months after the withdrawal. The plan penalty cannot, however, deprive a participant of any previously vested benefit.

Loan provisions are appropriate for profit-sharing plans. Again, however, a generous loan provision in a plan may have the effect of reducing the amount of funds available for other plan investments.

Incidental Benefits

The regulations permit profit-sharing plans to provide as an incidental benefit life, accident or health insurance for the participant and the participant's family. Incidental life insurance is the only one that is commonly provided. If employer contributions are used to provide insurance, the incidental benefit limitations described in Chapter 21 must be met.

If the plan provides incidental whole life insurance, the usual test is that aggregate premiums for each participant must be less than 50 percent of the aggregate of employer contributions allocated to the participant's account. If the plan purchases term insurance or accident and health insurance, the aggregate premiums must be less than 25 percent of the employer contributions allocated to the participant's account. The current IRS position is that universal life premiums also must meet the 25 percent limit. Note that these tests apply to the *aggregate*—that is, the total contributions made for all years at any given time. If either of these limits is

---

[3]Rev. Rul. 68–24, 1968–1 CB 150.

exceeded, the plan could be disqualified. However, insurance premiums paid with employer-contributed funds that have accumulated for at least two years are not subject to these limitations.

If the employee dies before normal retirement age, the plan can provide that the face amount of the policies plus the balance credited to the participant's account in the profit-sharing plan can be distributed to the survivors without the life insurance violating the incidental benefit requirement. This can be done even though the amount of life insurance might be more than 100 times the account balance expressed as an expected monthly pension.

If life insurance is provided by the plan, the term insurance cost is currently taxable to the employee under the PS 58 table (see Chapter 21) or the insurer's term insurance rates, as discussed in Chapter 6. Accident and health insurance provided by an employer under the plan might not be taxable because of the exclusion provided for employer-provided health insurance. However, there is usually no particular benefit in providing accident and health insurance under a profit-sharing plan. It is usually provided in a separate plan not connected with the profit-sharing plan.

SAVINGS PLANS

Almost any qualified plan can have a provision for employee contributions to supplement the plan fund or benefit. A plan that is designed particularly to exploit the possibility of employee contributions is often referred to as a *savings plan* or *thrift plan*. The term *savings plan* will be used here to describe a plan featuring employee *aftertax* contributions. Salary-reduction (401(k)) plans will be discussed in the next section.

Design of Savings Plans

A savings plan is a defined-contribution plan so that employees can have separate accounts. Usually, qualified savings plans are designed as profit-sharing plans (rather than money-purchase pension plans) because only a profit-sharing plan permits account withdrawals during employment, and this is an important feature of the plan if the plan is to be described to employees as a savings medium. Thus, a savings plan can generally be described as a contributory profit-sharing plan.

The typical savings plan features employee contributions matched by the employer. Plan participation is voluntary; employees elect to contribute a chosen percentage of their compensation up to a maximum percentage specified in the plan. The employer then makes a matching contribution to the plan. The matching may be dollar for dollar, or the employer may put in some multiple or submultiple of the employee contribution rate. For example, typically a plan might permit an employee to contribute annually any whole percentage of compensation from 1 to 6 percent. The plan might then provide that the employer contributes at the rate of half the chosen employee percentage; thus, if the employee elects to contribute 4 percent of compensation, the employer would contribute an additional 2 percent.

If the plan's maximum contribution level is too high, there is a possibility of discrimination because only higher paid employees would be in a position to contribute to the plan, and only they would receive full employer matching contributions. To prevent this type of discrimination, there is a specific numerical test applicable to after-tax employee contributions. Under this test (Code Section 401(m)), a plan is not deemed discriminatory for a plan year if, for highly compensated employees, the total of employee contributions (both matched and voluntary) plus employer matching contributions does not exceed certain numerical limits similar to those applicable to Section 401(k) plans, discussed later. Administration of the Section 401(m) limits can be complex and costly.

Apart from the features relating to employee contributions, savings plans generally follow the rules for profit-sharing plans described earlier. In designing a savings plan, emphasis is usually put on features relating to the objective of providing a savings medium for employees. Thus, a savings plan usually has generous provisions for vesting, employee withdrawal of funds, plan loans and investment flexibility.

Advantages and Disadvantages of Savings Plans

Savings plans have been very popular in the past and continue to be so, despite the advent of other types of plans, such as Section 401(k) plans, that provide greater tax leverage. Some older savings plans have been converted to add a 401(k) feature while retaining the provision for additional aftertax contributions by employers. Like all qualified plans, a savings plan provides a tax-deferred savings medium, since earnings in the plan fund are not taxable until the employee's account is distributed.

A savings plan usually does not maximize the potential tax deduction available for plan contributions, because it involves aftertax contributions by the employee— contributions that are not deducted or excluded for federal income or social security tax purposes. A greater degree of tax deductibility can be provided with other types of plans, such as regular profit-sharing plans or Section 401(k) plans. However, some of these plans may require a greater employer outlay for the plan itself (although not necessarily for the overall compensation package). These other plans may also entail greater restrictions on the funds which may make them a less attractive savings medium from the employee's standpoint.

SECTION 401(k) PLANS (CASH OR DEFERRED PLANS)

A qualified cash or deferred profit-sharing plan, usually referred to as a 401(k) plan since the special rules for these plans are found in Code Section 401(k), is a qualified profit-sharing or stock bonus plan that incorporates an option for participants to put money into the plan or receive it as taxable cash compensation. In other words, a 401(k) plan differs from a regular profit-sharing plan in that employees can participate in deciding how much of their compensation is deferred. Amounts contributed to the plan are not federal income taxable to participants until they are withdrawn; this is a significant advantage over contributions to a savings plan, which are taxable to the employee before contribution to the plan. However, 401(k) amounts for which the employee can elect to receive either cash or a plan contribution—*elective deferrals*—are subject to an annual limit of $7,000, indexed for inflation.

A 401(k) plan can be an independent plan, or the 401(k) feature can be included with a regular profit-sharing, savings or stock bonus plan of the employer. The plan can be designed in a number of ways to combine both employer and employee contributions, or the entire plan can be funded through salary reductions by employees.

Section 401(k) plans can be adopted only by private employers who pay taxes; they are not available to tax-exempt or governmental employers. Tax-exempt and governmental employers may instead adopt Section 403(b) or Section 457 plans, described in Chapters 27 and 28, to provide results somewhat similar to 401(k) plans.

Advantages and Disadvantages

Section 401(k) plans are currently very attractive to employees. First, they have the basic attraction of all qualified plans: They provide a tax-deferred savings medium. But 401(k) plans have an additional advantage by giving employees an opportunity to choose the amount of deferral according to their individual need for savings. From the employee's viewpoint, a 401(k) plan appears much like an individual IRA, but with additional advantages: The 401(k) plan has higher contribution limits than an IRA, it permits five-year averaging on qualifying lump-sum withdrawals, and the withdrawal provisions during employment are slightly less restrictive.

From the employer's viewpoint, 401(k) plans are favorable because the entire plan can be funded through salary reductions by employees. Thus, the plan provides no direct additional compensation costs to the employer. Because of the popularity of the plan with employees, partly due to good publicity for these plans in the media, the employer can obtain employee goodwill with this type of plan at a relatively low cost. There are also some actual dollar savings in using the 401(k) type of design, since salary reductions by employees may reduce employer expense for workers' compensation and unemployment compensation insurance by reducing the payroll subject to those taxes.

The 401(k) type of design has some disadvantages, but in reviewing these it is important always to ask: Disadvantages to whom and disadvantages compared with what? First of all, the $7,000 (indexed) annual limit on elective deferrals is lower than that for other types of qualified plan contributions. However, as a practical matter, this limit primarily affects highly compensated employees only. Another disadvantage is that a 401(k) plan is a qualified plan and as such is much more complicated than simply leaving savings up to individual employees, either through individual IRAs or otherwise. Also, the 401(k) plan is a qualified profit-sharing plan, not a pension plan, so the employer's deduction is limited to 15 percent of the covered payroll. That is, the total of the employer contribution and nontaxable employee salary reductions cannot exceed 15 percent of covered payroll. Generally speaking, integration of a 401(k) formula with social security is not possible; but the

401(k) nondiscrimination rules nevertheless permit significant discrimination in favor of higher paid employees. Section 401(k) plans are more difficult to administer than regular qualified plans, because of the additional rules (discussed later) that must be satisfied. Deferral amounts must be 100 percent vested; thus, there is no opportunity for the employer to save on plan costs by making use of employee forfeitures on Section 401(k) deferral amounts. Finally, distributions to employees prior to termination of employment are more restrictive than for a regular qualified plan. However, these restrictions are more liberal than those for an IRA.

Salary-Reduction 401(k) Plan

The regulations permit a 401(k) plan to be funded entirely through employee elections to reduce salary by a specified amount and contribute the reduced amount to the plan. The major appeal of this approach is that the plan can be funded based on existing salary scales without any specific additional costs to the employer. Also, the plan can be described to employees as being somewhat like an IRA.

For purposes of the 15 percent deduction limit and the annual-additions limit of Section 415(c), salary reductions are treated as employer contributions to the plan.

> **EXAMPLE:** Suppose an employer has two employees, and for a given year their gross salaries and salary-reduction contributions to a 401(k) plan are as follows:

	Gross Salary	Salary Reduction Elected	Salary after Reduction
Pat	$21,000	$1,000	$20,000
Mike	31,000	1,000	30,000
			$50,000

> Neither participant exceeds the $7,000 limit on elective deferrals. The deduction limit for plan contributions in this case is 15 percent of the payroll of reduced salaries—here, 15 percent of $50,000 or $7,500, which is well in excess of the $2,000 actually contributed to the plan. The annual-additions limit for each participant is 25 percent of the reduced salary, or $30,000 if less. For example, for Pat, the annual-additions limit is 25 percent of $20,000 or $5,000. Note that for both Pat and Mike the annual-additions limit is lower than the $7,000 elective deferral limit, indicating how little impact the $7,000 limit has on lower income employees.

Salary reductions must be elected by employees before compensation is earned; that is, before they render the services for which compensation is paid. If elections are made after compensation has been earned, the doctrine of constructive receipt would prevent the employee from excluding the salary reduction from taxable income. The regulations indicate that salary reductions must be made before the beginning of the calendar year for which the reduction is effective.

Employer Matching Plan

Under this approach, participating employees can elect salary reductions, with the employer making a matching contribution to the plan. The employer share can be dollar-for-dollar, or some specified fraction of the employee's contribution. Matching can be limited to a specified percentage of each employee's compensation. For example, a plan might provide that an employee can elect salary reductions up to 6 percent of compensation, with the employer contributing an additional 1 percent of compensation for each 2 percent of employee salary reduction.

A significant advantage to this approach is that employer matching encourages plan participation by lower paid employees. This helps to meet the qualification tests for 401(k) plans—the actual deferral percentage tests—discussed later.

Coverage Requirements

Since a 401(k) plan is a qualified profit-sharing plan, it must meet all the eligibility and coverage requirements discussed earlier. However, substantial additional participation by lower paid employees may indirectly be required in order to meet the actual deferral percentage requirements applicable under Section 401(k) as discussed below.

Vesting of Employee Accounts

Vesting requirements in a 401(k) plan may depend upon the source or identity of the plan contributions.

- Nontaxable employee salary reductions or elective deferrals made under a Section 401(k) cash or deferral option must be immediately 100 percent vested.
- Any aftertax employee contributions must be 100 percent immediately vested, as in regular qualified plans such as savings or thrift plans.
- All employer contributions to the plan must meet the usual vesting rules for qualified plans, discussed in Chapter 21. That is, the plan must have a vesting schedule that at least meets one of the ERISA minimum vesting standards (five-year vesting or three- to seven-year vesting).

$7,000 Limit on Elective Deferrals

Code Section 402(g) imposes a $7,000 annual limit on elective deferrals for each plan participant. The limit is imposed on the total of elective deferrals under all 401(k) plans, Section 403(b) tax-deferred annuity plans and salary-reduction simplified employee pensions (SEPs) covering the participant. (In the case of a 403(b) plan, a higher limit of $9,500 applies; see Chapter 27.) Any excess over the $7,000 limit is treated as taxable income to the participant. The $7,000 limit is adjusted for cost-of-living changes in the same manner as the Section 415 dollar limit on annual benefits under defined-benefit plans.

Actual Deferral Percentage Tests

It has long been recognized that since higher paid employees have more discretionary income and, in particular, more income to save, any qualified plan that allows employees to choose deferral or cash will be used disproportionately by higher paid employees. The concept of cash or deferral plans has existed for a long time, but until Congress enacted Section 401(k) in 1978, they were not permitted by statute because of this potential discrimination problem. The most important provision of Section 401(k) is a series of tests designed to prevent disproportionate use of these plans by higher paid employees. These are the actual deferral percentage (ADP) tests.

These tests are in the nature of an additional nondiscrimination rule that must be met by 401(k) plans in addition to the usual rules for qualified plans. A qualified 401(k) plan must meet one of the following two tests in actual operation:

1. The ADP for eligible highly compensated employees must not be more than the ADP of all other eligible employees multiplied by 1.25 (i.e., it must not exceed this percentage by more than 25 percent); or
2. The ADP for eligible highly compensated employees must not exceed the lesser of (a) 200 percent of the ADP of all eligible nonhighly compensated employees or (b) the ADP for all eligible nonhighly compensated employees plus 2 percentage points.

The ADP for a given year is

$$\frac{\text{Employer contribution to plan for employee (or salary reduction)}}{\text{Employee's compensation}}$$

This amount is computed for each employee and averaged for each of the two groups (highly compensated, nonhighly compensated).

A few examples will illustrate the operation of the ADP tests better than any extended explanation.

> **EXAMPLE 1:** 10 percent of compensation bonus which the employee can take as cash or as a contribution (deferral) to the 401(k) plan; only employee A is highly compensated.

Employee	Compensation	Cash	Deferral	ADP
A	$30,000	$1,350	$1,650	5.5%
B	15,000	750	750	5
C	10,000	600	400	4

Test 1 is satisfied; ADP for highly compensated (A only) is 5.5%; ADP for nonhighly compensated is 4.5% (average of 4% and 5%) 1.25 times 4.5% is 5.625%.

EXAMPLE 2: 6 percent of compensation bonus; D, E and F are highly compensated.

Employee	Compensation	Cash	Deferral	ADP
D	$100,000	$ 0	$6,000	6%
E	80,000	0	4,800	6
F	60,000	0	3,600	6
G	40,000	800	1,600	4
H	30,000	600	1,200	4
I	20,000	400	800	4

Plan fails test 1 (1.25 × 4% is less than 6%) but passes test 2 (ADP for highly compensated is no more than two percentage points greater and less than two times 4%).

Designing a Plan to Meet the ADP Tests

Obviously, it is critical to design the 401(k) plan so that the ADP tests are met; otherwise the plan will fail to qualify and all tax benefits will be lost. Fortunately, it is not as difficult as plan designers once believed and disqualifications are rare. Some of the methods used to ensure compliance are as follows:

- *Mandatory deferral.* For example, an employer contributes 5 percent of compensation for all employees that must be deferred and allows an additional 2 percent under a cash or deferral option. This plan will always meet the second ADP test.
- *Limiting deferral by the higher paid.* This approach involves administrative problems. The higher paid group must be identified and deferral must be monitored, with a mechanism to stop deferrals at an appropriate point during the year if necessary. One approach is making monthly contributions from salary reductions of the highly paid to a nonqualified investment annuity and transfering at the end of the year the maximum amount possible to a 401(k) plan, with the remainder at the participant's option paid in cash or retained in the investment annuity vehicle.
- *Redesignating 401(k) amounts.* Under this approach, a non-401(k) plan is maintained; the employer redesignates amounts contributed to the regular plan as 401(k) amounts to the maximum extent after the year is finished and the plan administrator knows how much can be contributed. The redesignated amounts, of course, will be subject to all of the 401(k) restrictions, such as 100 percent vesting and the distribution restrictions. This approach, in most cases, has been found by many planners to be too administratively difficult.
- *Counting on the popularity of the 401(k).* In actual practice, many companies find that participation by lower paid employees is substantial. It is not unusual for 75 percent of all employees of an organization to participate in the plan. This may eliminate the problem without any special mechanisms coming into effect.

Because of the ADP tests, not every employer is suitable for a 401(k) plan. Since substantial participation by lower paid employees is necessary, pay levels must be reasonably high in the organization, at least high enough so that some amount of retirement saving is possible by most of the employees.

Distribution Restrictions

Account balances attributable to amounts subject to the cash or deferral election—the 401(k) amounts—are subject to special distribution restrictions. These amounts may not be distributed earlier than upon retirement, death, disability, separation from service, hardship, age 59½ or termination of the plan. Also, as with any qualified plan distribution, the 10 percent early withdrawal penalty applies.

The income taxation of distributions from 401(k) plans, including both 401(k) and non-401(k) amounts in the plan, follows the usual rules for qualified plan distributions. The qualified plan rules relating to loans and plan distributions are discussed in detail in Chapter 24.

Social Security and Employment Taxes

Section 401(k) plans are an exception to the general rule that contributions by an employer to a qualified plan are free of federal employment taxes (social security [FICA] and unemployment tax [FUTA]). The popularity of 401(k) plans when first introduced caused such a noticeable reduction in federal employment tax revenues that Congress made special rules for 401(k) plans. Under current law, 401(k) amounts, subject to an employee election to defer instead of receiving cash, are subject to FICA and FUTA, whether these are contributed through salary reduction or employer bonuses. FICA and FUTA do not apply to non-401(k) amounts—contributions made by the employer to the plan that are not subject to deferral.

In general, state unemployment compensation and workers' compensation payments are not required for either employer contributions or salary reductions in a 401(k) plan.

USING EMPLOYER STOCK IN QUALIFIED PLANS

For a number of years, the Internal Revenue Code has included special provisions for qualified plans that invest primarily in employer securities. Congress wants to encourage these plans on the premise that it is desirable to give employees some ownership interest in the company for which they work. The most important special benefit is the leveraging technique for ESOPs, described below, that allows the employer to use the ESOP as a means of financing corporate growth. There are also provisions that encourage the use of a stock plan to help create a market for employer stock.

There are two types of qualified plans that invest primarily in employer securities, the traditional *stock bonus plan* and the *employee stock ownership plan* (ESOP). In addition, a regular profit-sharing plan may invest in employer stock without limit, and profit-sharing plans are sometimes used, formally or informally, for this purpose. Qualified pension plans may not invest more than 10 percent of their assets in employer stock, so pension plans are not very useful as employer stock plans.

Advantages of Investing in Employer Stock

There are certain employer and employee advantages to any plan that invests in employer stock, including a regular profit-sharing plan, a stock bonus plan or an ESOP.

- A market can be created for employer stock. This has many planning implications and is discussed in detail below.
- The employer can obtain a deduction for noncash (that is, employer stock) contributions to the plan.
- Employees receive an ownership interest in the company, which may act as a performance incentive.
- As described below, unrealized appreciation of stock is not taxed to the employee at the time of distribution.

These advantages are available only to a regular or C corporation. An S corporation cannot adopt a stock plan because the plan is not a permissible shareholder in an S corporation. Also, of course, an unincorporated business (proprietorship or partnership) can't have a stock plan because it has no stock.

Stock Bonus Plan

The stock bonus plan is the older of the two types of qualified plans that invest primarily in employer securities. Under the regulations, a stock bonus plan is a qualified defined-contribution plan similar to a profit-sharing plan, except that the employer's contributions are not necessarily dependent on profits; benefits are distributable in the stock of the employer company.

Typically, the plan contribution formula is based on employee compensation. Employer contributions to the plan may be made in cash or directly in the form of employer securities, newly issued or otherwise. Shares of stock are allocated to participants' accounts under a formula that must meet the same nondiscrimination requirements as the allocation formula in a profit-sharing plan. Some stock bonus plans also provide for aftertax employee contributions or salary reductions. (A salary reduction stock plan is sometimes referred to as a KSOP.)

The value of each participant's account in a stock bonus plan is stated in terms of a certain number of shares of employer stock. The value of the account varies with the value of the underlying employer stock. Dividends on the shares can be used to increase participants' accounts, or cash dividends can be paid through the plan directly to participants as currently taxable income, in which case the employer gets a tax deduction.

Plan Distributions

Distributions from both stock bonus plans and ESOPs are generally subject to the same restrictions applicable to distributions from any qualified plan. Thus, distributions prior to age 59½, death, disability or retirement are subject to a 10 percent penalty, with some exceptions. However, for a stock bonus plan or ESOP, there is no requirement of providing a joint and survivor annuity or other spousal death benefit.

Since an employee retains the investment risk in the employer company until the stock is distributed, a deferred distribution to a terminated employee would not be appropriate, so payouts from stock bonus plans or ESOPs have a special earlier beginning date than that for other qualified plans. Distributions from a stock bonus plan or ESOP must occur no later than one year after the end of the fifth plan year after the employee's separation from service, or no later than one year after retirement, disability or death.

In general, the plan must distribute benefits in the form of employer stock. However, the participant can be given the option of receiving cash of equal value, subject to a right to receive employer stock. If the participant receives stock that is not traded on an established market, the participant has a right to require that the employer repurchase the securities under a fair valuation formula. This is referred to as the "put" requirement. If an employee exercises the put option on distribution—that is, sells the securities back to the plan—the participant must be paid over no more than five years, and during that time the plan must provide adequate security for the payment.

Voting Rights

If the employer company is closely held, plan participants must be given the right to vote with respect to stock held for them in the plan on corporate issues requiring more than a majority of the outstanding common shares. If the employer stock is publicly traded, participants must be permitted to vote on all issues.

Taxation of Employees

In addition to the usual tax advantages for qualified plans, the basic employee tax benefit provided by the Code for a plan holding employer stock is the deferral of taxation of unrealized appreciation. When the plan makes a lump-sum distribution including employer stock, the unrealized appreciation of the stock—that is, the difference between the value of the stock when contributed to or purchased by the trust and its value when distributed to the employee—is not taxable to the employee at the time of the distribution to the extent that it (1) represents nondeductible employee contributions, or (2) represents employer contributions, and the participant's entire account is distributed within one taxable year as a result of death, the attainment of age 59½ or the employee's separation from the service of the employer.

This means that the taxable amount of a lump-sum distribution from a stock bonus plan does not include unrealized appreciation of employer securities if the recipient is entitled to the special tax treatment for lump-sum distributions in general. The unrealized appreciation is taxable only when the employee or other recipient sells the securities at a later date. The unrealized appreciation amount is taxable as a capital gain when the stock is sold.

Deductibility of Contributions

As indicated above, the employer can deduct a contribution to a stock bonus plan in the form of employer securities as well as cash. Deductions for contributions can be taken even if there are no current or accumulated profits. The deduction limit is the same as that for a profit-sharing plan—15 percent of covered payroll.

Employee Stock Ownership Plan (ESOP)

The ESOP, first introduced in 1974, is basically a stock bonus plan with an important additional feature: If certain requirements are met, the plan can be used by the employer company as a means of raising funds on a tax-favored basis. The funds can be used for any corporate purposes, which can include acquiring the assets or stock of another company.

In effect, an ESOP allows an employer to indirectly borrow money from a bank and repay the loan with fully deductible repayment amounts. The repayment amounts are deductible in full because they are structured as contributions to an ESOP; normally, only the interest portion of a loan repayment would be tax deductible.

This bit of tax magic (see Figure 23-1) is accomplished by first having the plan trustee borrow money from a bank or other lender. The borrowed money is then used to purchase a block of employer stock from the employer. Shares of this stock also will subsequently be allocated to participants' accounts in the ESOP as plan contributions are made. The employer makes periodic plan contributions to the ESOP and obtains a tax deduction for them. These plan contributions are designed to be enough to enable the plan trustee to gradually repay the loan to the bank. The net result is that the employer immediately receives the full proceeds of the bank loan and in effect pays off the loan through tax-deductible contributions to the plan on behalf of plan participants.

Since the ESOP normally has no financial status independent of the employer, the employer usually must guarantee the loan to the bank. If the plan gives collateral for the loan, the collateral may consist only of qualifying employer securities.

These transactions are made attractive to lenders by a provision (Code Section 133) that allows the lender to exclude 50 percent of the interest income from a loan

FIGURE 23-1

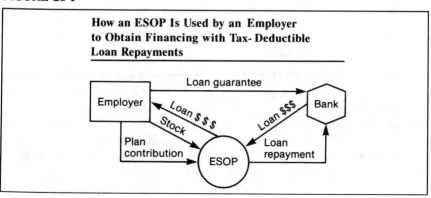

How an ESOP Is Used by an Employer to Obtain Financing with Tax-Deductible Loan Repayments

to an ESOP for acquiring employer securities. To qualify for this exclusion, the lender must be a bank, an insurance company, a corporation actively engaged in the business of lending money to ESOPs or a regulated investment company. Also, the ESOP must own more than 50 percent of the outstanding stock of the employer corporation.

Contribution Formulas and Accounts

An ESOP's contribution allocation formula may not be integrated with social security, since plan allocations must be based on total compensation. In other respects, contribution formulas and participants' accounts are handled in the same manner as for the stock bonus plan described earlier.

Deductibility of Contributions

The rules for contribution deductibility for an ESOP are somewhat different from those for a stock bonus plan or profit-sharing plan. If employer contributions to the ESOP are applied to the repayment of a loan, amounts applied by the plan to repay the loan principal are deductible by the employer up to a limit of 25 percent of compensation of employees covered under the plan. Amounts used to repay interest are deductible without any percentage limit.

Plan Distributions

The distribution rules, voting rights and taxation considerations regarding ESOP distributions are the same as those discussed earlier in connection with stock bonus plans.

Diversification Requirement

To reduce investment risks, participants in ESOPs who have reached age 55 with ten years of service are entitled to an annual election requiring the employer to diversify investment in the participant's account. The plan must offer at least three investment options, other than employer stock, to the participant for diversification purposes.

Creating a Market for Closely Held Stock

In small companies, it is often important for shareholders to find a market for their stock for financial and estate planning purposes. Many types of plans have been designed to enable the use of company funds for purchasing stock, such as stock redemption and corporate-owned life insurance plans. An ESOP or stock bonus plan can also be helpful for this purpose. The shareholder can sell stock to the plan during lifetime or at death, generally with favorable tax results. These techniques involve various complexities and must be designed with some care.

STUDY QUESTIONS

1. a. What is a profit-sharing plan?
   b. Explain how the eligibility and vesting requirements of profit-sharing plans differ from the eligibility and vesting requirements of pension plans.
2. a. Describe the two types of contribution formulas that can be used for a profit-sharing plan.
   b. Why is a formula approach more attractive to employees?
3. a. Explain the importance of the allocation formula in a profit-sharing plan.
   b. What is the usual allocation formula?
4. Explain how the allocation formula of a profit-sharing plan may be integrated with social security.
5. a. What is the maximum amount that an employer can deduct for contributions to a profit-sharing plan?
   b. What is the maximum annual addition to any participant's account in a profit-sharing plan?
6. Explain the ramifications of participant-directed investments.
7. a. To what extent are preretirement withdrawals allowed from profit-sharing plans?
   b. Describe the restrictions on withdrawals of employer contributions from profit-sharing plans.
8. a. What incidental benefits are allowed in profit-sharing plans?
   b. What limitations are placed on incidental life insurance benefits?
9. a. What are the typical features of savings (thrift) plans?
   b. What are the advantages and disadvantages of savings plans?
10. Describe a qualified Section 401(k) plan. Include the following points in your description.
    a. What are the advantages and disadvantages of a 401(k) plan?
    b. What are the vesting requirements in a 401(k) plan?
    c. What is the limit on elective deferrals under a 401(k) plan?
11. Fixemup, P.C. is a professional corporation for a group of four doctors, two nurses, and one receptionist. The census data for the current year is as follows:

	Salary/Percentage of Stock Ownership	401(k) Contributions
Dr. Able	$90,000/50%	8%
Dr. Baker	85,000/30%	8%
Dr. Resident	44,000/20%	8%
Dr. Intern	35,000/0%	8%
Nurse Marmer	25,000/0%	5%
Nurse Devries	25,000/0%	5%
Receptionist Smith	15,000/0%	0%

Does the Fixemup, P.C. 401(k) plan meet the ADP test? Explain.
12. a. Describe the characteristics of a stock bonus plan.
    b. How do ESOPs differ from stock bonus plans?

24

Qualified Plan Distributions and Loans

Objectives

- Review the management issues in designing plan distribution provisions.
- Describe the normal and optional forms of benefit payments that are available for distributions from qualified plans and explain the restrictions imposed on distributions.
- Describe the federal taxation of distributions from a qualified plan that occur
  1. Over more than one taxable year.
  2. In one taxable year.
  3. At death.
- Explain the rules applying to loans from qualified plans.

MANAGEMENT ISSUES IN DESIGN OF DISTRIBUTION PROVISIONS

Employee interests are best served by maximum flexibility in plan distribution provisions. However, plan designers may find it necessary to reduce this flexibility somewhat in order to meet the employer's management objectives.

First of all, flexibility increases administrative complexity and costs. In addition, flexibility can potentially cause cash-flow and liquidity problems to the plan fund. Finally, flexibility can create extremely complex federal income tax problems, due to the inordinately complex rules in this area. The rules are merely summarized in this chapter, but the reader will undoubtedly note that even this summary is startlingly complicated. The complexity is probably due more to congressional inattention to this issue rather than to any clear policy rationale. Simplification is on the congressional agenda.

The complex distribution rules are management's problem as well as the participant's, since employees often ask employers about the tax treatment of a plan distribution. An employer's wrong answer likely will subject the employer to liability to reimburse the employee for any excess tax payments that result. And management cannot simply "stonewall" on this issue by refusing to advise employees on tax treatment of distributions, since employee resentment as well as legal liability may result that can negate the value of the plan as an employee incentive.

The planner's objective in designing plan distribution provisions is to provide employees with the maximum amount of distribution flexibility that is consistent with management's needs as outlined above. In a small business with limited personnel management resources, this may dictate only very limited distribution flexibility. For example, some smaller plans provide for distributions only in the form of a lump sum at retirement or termination of employment.

Normal Form of Benefit

A qualified plan must specify not only the amount of the benefit but the form of the benefit. In a defined-benefit plan, the *normal form of benefit* is the basic "defined benefit," the form that quantifies the benefit due and provides a standard for calculating equivalent alternative benefits. At one time, the normal form was the form a participant received if he or she did not choose an alternative form, but this is not necessarily true because of joint and survivor provisions.

The normal form in a defined-benefit plan is usually either a straight-life annuity or a life annuity with period certain. A straight-life annuity simply provides periodic (usually monthly) payments for the participant's life. A life annuity with period certain provides periodic payments for the participant's life, but additionally provides that if the participant dies before the end of a specified period of years, payments will be continued until the end of that period to the participant's designated beneficiary. Specified periods of 10, 15 and 20 years are commonly used.

In comparing defined-benefit plans, it must be remembered that straight-life and life annuities with periods certain are not equivalent; a plan providing an annuity of $100 per month for life with period certain as the normal form of benefit provides a significantly larger benefit than a plan providing $100 per month as a straight-life annuity. Period-certain annuities as the normal form of benefit are most commonly found in plans using insurance contracts for funding.

As discussed in Chapter 20, a pension plan must provide a qualified joint and survivor annuity for the participant and spouse automatically to a married participant (unless the participant elects otherwise). To avoid discrimination against single participants, most plans provide that the qualified joint and survivor annuity is "actuarially equivalent" to the normal form. For example, if the normal retirement benefit would be $1,000 per month as a straight-life annuity, the qualified joint and survivor annuity might be something like $800 per month to the participant for life, then $400 per month to the spouse for life. However, the plan can partially or fully subsidize the joint and survivor annuity; for example, it might provide a straight-life annuity of $1,000 per month or a $1,000/$500 joint and survivor annuity. This might be desirable to the employer even though it would discriminate against unmarried participants.

Defined-contribution pension plans can provide an annuity as the normal benefit form. This is particularly common if an insurance contract is used for funding. The amount of the annuity depends on the participant's account balance at retirement, with annuity purchase rates specified in the insurance contract, if any. Optional forms of benefit, particularly a lump sum, are usually provided in defined-contribution plans.

Optional Alternative Forms of Benefit

Participants generally benefit from having a choice of benefit forms as an alternative to the normal form. Participants can then choose a benefit that is structured in accordance with their individual financial needs, family situations and retirement activities. In defined-benefit plans, the most common alternative forms (assuming a straight-life annuity as the normal form) are, in addition to the qualified joint and survivor annuity that must be offered, (1) joint and survivor annuities for the participant and spouse or other beneficiary with varying survivorship annuity percentages such as 50 percent, 75 percent and 100 percent, and (2) annuities for the participant and beneficiary with varying periods certain such as 5, 10, 15 or 20 years. The plan also can allow payouts over a fixed period of years without a life contingency. All these options are subject to the limitations described below.

In order to avoid undesirable or prohibited discrimination among employees in different situations, the plan should provide that any optional benefit is actuarially equivalent to the normal form of benefit. Under Code Section 401(a)(25), the actuarial assumptions used for this purpose must be specified in the plan, either by stating the actuarial interest and other factors or by specifying an equivalency table for the various benefits, in order to avoid employer discretion in favor of highly compensated employees.

Lump-Sum Option

A lump-sum distribution can provide planning flexibility for participants. Lump-sum distribution provisions are most common in defined-contribution plans; in fact, in a profit-sharing plan, the lump sum is often the only distribution option. However, even a defined-benefit plan can offer a lump-sum option.

A lump sum may be beneficial for participants because of the special five-year averaging tax treatment discussed below. However, the same or greater tax savings can often be obtained by a distribution spread over a period of years, so tax savings as such usually are not a dominant factor in choosing a lump-sum distribution.

Higher income participants often would like a lump sum because they have other sources for retirement income and wish to invest their plan funds in riskier, high-return investment vehicles. A defined-contribution plan can be designed to accommodate this need to some extent within the plan, however, by providing participant investment direction. Also, investment results within the plan are enhanced by the tax deferral on plan income and may provide an effective rate of return that the participant cannot match outside of the plan. However, funds cannot be left in the plan indefinitely; distributions must generally begin at age 70½.

In some defined-benefit plans, particularly insured plans, the assumptions used for funding are too conservative. For example, a plan may have accumulated $140,000 to fund a benefit of $12,000 per year to a retiree. In many cases, however, it might be possible for a retiree to individually invest $140,000 and receive a better return than $12,000 per year for life. Thus, the retiree might rather have a $140,000 lump sum from the plan fund than the plan's annuity benefit. In some cases, this situation results from bad plan design, while in others it is done deliberately to increase the benefit for key employees.

Distribution Restrictions

Plan distributions can be designed to provide considerable flexibility, but they must be designed within a rather complex network of rules that have been accumulating in the law over many years. These rules are aimed at protecting the financial interests of participants and, more significantly, they are designed to limit the use of qualified plans merely as a tax-sheltered investment medium for key employees. The significant rules are as follows:

- Distinctions between the types of distributions permitted in pension plans as opposed to profit-sharing plans.
- Rules preventing employers from unjustly delaying benefit payments.
- Minimum distribution requirements.
- Early distribution penalties.
- Incidental benefit requirements.
- Nonalienation rules.

Pension versus Profit-Sharing Plans

The IRS generally will not allow a pension plan to pay benefits prior to retirement, early retirement, death or disability, although some limited cash-out provisions may be allowed in the event of termination of employment prior to these events, as previously discussed. With a profit-sharing plan, there is much more flexibility, and the plan may allow in-service distributions, as discussed in Chapter 23. However, the 10 percent penalty described below may deter employees from making certain withdrawals.

Delaying Benefit Payments

Under Code Section 401(a)(14), all qualified plans must provide for payment not later than the 60th day after the latest of the following three dates:

1. The earlier of age 65 or the plan's normal retirement date.
2. The tenth anniversary of the participant's entry into the plan.
3. The participant's termination of service with the employer.

The plan may allow the participant to elect a payout that begins at a date later than this maximum limit. However, the extent to which a participant can stretch out payments is limited by the rules discussed in the next section.

Minimum Distribution Rules

Congress does not like qualified plans to be used as tax shelters for funds that are not actually needed by participants for retirement income. Therefore, Code Section 401(a)(9) requires plan distributions to begin no later than April 1 of the calendar year following the year in which the employee attains age 70½, even if the participant continues working for the employer.

Furthermore, the distribution must be either in a lump sum or a periodic distribution over a specified period. Basically, the distribution must be paid in substantially equal annual amounts over the life of the employee or the joint lives of the employee and a designated beneficiary. Alternatively, the distribution may be made over a stated period that does not exceed the life expectancy of the employee or the life expectancy of the employee and a designated beneficiary. This permits period-certain annuity payouts, so long as the period certain does not exceed the life expectancy limits. A periodic distribution based on an ongoing recalculation of life expectancy is permitted, which tends to stretch out payments somewhat since life expectancy is extended by continuing survival. However, life expectancy can be recalculated no more often than annually. Cost-of-living increases in pension payments to retirees are permitted so long as they are not designed to circumvent the minimum distribution rules.

The minimum distribution rules also have provisions applicable to distributions made to a beneficiary if the employee dies before the entire plan interest is distributed. If distributions to the employee have already begun, the remaining portion of the employee's interest must be distributed at least as rapidly as under the method in effect prior to death. For example, if the employee elected a 20-year period-certain annuity and the employee died after ten years, the remaining interest could be distributed in equal annual installments over a term not exceeding ten years. The beneficiary could, however, elect to accelerate these payments.

If the employee dies before distributions have begun, the plan's death benefit must be distributed within five years after the employee's death, with an exception. The five-year restriction is not applicable if (1) any portion of the plan benefit is payable to a designated beneficiary, (2) the beneficiary's interest will be distributed over the life of the beneficiary or over a period not extending beyond the life expectancy of the beneficiary and (3) distributions begin no later than one year after the employee's death. If the designated beneficiary is the surviving spouse, the beginning of the distribution can be delayed to the date on which the employee would have attained age 70½.

Early Distribution Penalty

Code Section 72(t) provides a tax penalty for early distributions from qualified plans. This penalty provision was added by Congress in order to encourage plan participants to use qualified plans primarily for retirement and not merely for deferral of compensation. The 10 percent penalty tax applies to distributions from a broad range of tax-advantaged retirement plans, including regular qualified plans, Section 403 tax-deferred annuity plans, individual retirement arrangements and SEPs. The penalty applies to all distributions *except* distributions:

- Made on or after attainment of age 59½.
- Made to a beneficiary or employee's estate on or after the employee's death.
- Attributable to disability.
- That are part of a series of substantially equal periodic payments made at least annually over the life or life expectancy of the employee, or the joint lives or life expectancies of the employee and beneficiary (separation from service is required, except for IRAs).
- Made after a separation from service after age 55 (not applicable to IRAs).
- Related to certain tax credit ESOP dividend payments.
- To the extent of medical expenses deductible for the year under Code Section 213, whether or not actually deducted (not applicable to IRAs).

Under this penalty provision, a plan may be permitted to make a distribution to an employee without disqualifying the plan, but the distribution may nevertheless be subject to penalty. For example, many hardship distributions from 401(k) plans or 403(b) tax-deferred annuity plans will be subject to the penalty tax.

Despite the penalty, withdrawals from qualified plans may still be important to participants in many situations—to obtain emergency funds, for example. Therefore, plan designers may wish to provide withdrawals in plans, where permitted, despite the existence of the 10 percent penalty.

Incidental Benefit Requirements

Some types of optional benefit forms provide substantial payments to persons other than the participant after the participant's death—for example, a 20-year-certain annuity with payments continued to a beneficiary. Since these are death benefits, they must be incidental.

Code Section 401(a)(9)(G) and corresponding regulations provide rules for determining whether survivorship benefits are incidental. For example, if a participant has a 10-year life expectancy at retirement, he or she could not elect a 25-year-certain annuity, since this would result in too much of the expected benefit to be paid as a death benefit. This incidental rule does not apply to a survivor annuity for spouses; thus, for example, a plan could provide a joint and 50 percent survivor annuity for a 65-year-old retiree and his 25-year-old spouse, even though actuarially, the participant's present interest in the benefit would be less than half of the total.

Nonalienation Rules

A qualified plan must provide that plan benefits may not be assigned or alienated (Code Section 401(a)(13)). This means, for example, that a plan participant can't pledge future anticipated qualified plan payments as security for a bank loan. For divorce, child support and similar domestic disputes, there are special provisions discussed later in this chapter.

Examples

The distribution restrictions described in the preceding pages appear so complex as to defy summary. Probably the best way to see how these restrictions work is to look at some examples. Consider the following proposed plan distribution options, offered to a married male participant in a qualified defined-benefit plan retiring at age 65. Assume that the participant and his spouse have waived any required joint and survivor annuity. The following options will be analyzed to see if they are permissible under the distribution restrictions:

- A joint and 100 percent survivor annuity for the lives of the participant and his daughter age 35.
- A 25-year period-certain annuity for the lives of the participant and his spouse.
- Equal periodic distributions over five years beginning when the participant reaches age 75.
- Equal monthly payments over a fixed period equal to the participant's life expectancy, but if the participant survives, the payout period is extended (the monthly payments are actuarially reduced) annually to reflect the increased life expectancy.

The first potential distribution would meet the first restrictions of Section 401(a)(9), since it extends over the lives of a participant and named beneficiary, but it does not meet the incidental benefit tests under the regulations. According to tables in the regulations, no more than a 60 percent survivor annuity could be payable to the daughter.

The second distribution—the 25-year period-certain annuity for the lives of the participant and spouse would meet Section 401(a)(9) so long as the joint life expectancy of the participant and spouse is at least 25 years. As for the incidental test, the regulations provide that a survivor annuity for a spouse will generally qualify regardless of the difference in ages.

The third option, a distribution beginning at age 75, is not permitted because distributions must begin not later than April 1 following the calendar year in which the employee reaches age 70½.

Finally, a fixed-period payout over the participant's life expectancy, with annual recalculations of life expectancy, is permitted. This can be an advantageous way of receiving the benefit, since payments can continue to a relatively advanced age, reducing the danger that retirement income will stop while the participant is still living.

FEDERAL TAXATION OF DISTRIBUTIONS

A qualified plan participant is taxed advantageously on a distribution that qualifies as a *lump-sum distribution*, the definition of which is discussed below. Other types of plan distributions are taxed in accordance with the rules for taxing annuity payments found in Code Section 72. The tax treatment of both types of payments will be discussed here. This section deals with *federal* income and estate taxation. Some states apply similar tax treatment, but there is considerable variation. Federal taxes are usually the dominant factor in the overall tax burden on plan distributions.

The initial step in determining the taxation of a qualified plan distribution is determining the *taxable amount* of the distribution. For a distribution upon retirement, disability or termination of employment, the taxable amount consists of the total amount of the distribution less the following amounts, sometimes referred to as the employee's *cost basis* in the plan:

- The total nondeductible contributions made by the employee (in the case of a contributory plan).
- The total cost of life insurance reported as taxable income by the participant, assuming that the plan distribution is received under the same contract that provided the life insurance protection.
- Any employer contributions previously taxed to the employee (for example, where a nonqualified plan later became qualified).
- Certain employer contributions attributable to foreign services performed before 1963.
- Amounts paid by the employee in repayment of loans that were treated as distributions.
- In the case of a stock bonus plan or other stock plan, the net unrealized appreciation, as discussed in Chapter 23.

The first two items in the list are the ones most frequently encountered. If the employee is self-employed or was self-employed in the past, the items excludible from the taxable amount are slightly different from the above list. The most important difference is that for a self-employed person who is an owner/employee (a more than 10-percent owner of an unincorporated business), the insurance costs (the second item above) are not part of the cost basis.

The simplest way to describe the taxation of qualified plan distributions is to distinguish between those benefits that are paid out fully in a single taxable year of the participant and those that are spread out over more than one taxable year. The latter are discussed first.

Payment over More than One Taxable Year

If the plan distribution is made over more than one taxable year of the employee, the usual annuity rules apply to taxation of the distribution. The distribution will be taxable to the participant or beneficiary in the year received, except to the extent that there is a cost basis to be recovered. The cost basis is recovered by calculating an *exclusion ratio* and applying it to each payment to determine the nontaxable amount. The exclusion ratio is defined as

$$\frac{\text{Investment in the contract}}{\text{Expected return}}$$

"Investment in the contract" in this context is the amount of the cost basis; the expected return is determined by multiplying the total annual payment by the participant's life expectancy according to tables in the regulations—see Table 24-1.

EXAMPLE: Employee Green is entitled to a pension at retirement of $200 per month. Green's cost basis in the plan is $8,000. Green retires at age 65. The exclusion ratio will be

$$\frac{\$8,000}{\$48,000}$$

TABLE 24-1
Life Expectancies, from Reg. Sec. 1.72-9 (unisex tables)

Age	Multiple	Age	Multiple	Age	Multiple
5	76.6	42	40.6	79	10.0
6	75.6	43	39.6	80	9.5
7	74.7	44	38.7	81	8.9
8	73.7	45	37.7	82	8.4
9	72.7	46	36.8	83	7.9
10	71.7	47	35.9	84	7.4
11	70.7	48	34.9	85	6.9
12	69.7	49	34.0	86	6.5
13	68.8	50	33.1	87	6.1
14	67.8	51	32.2	88	5.7
15	66.8	52	31.3	89	5.3
16	65.8	53	30.4	90	5.0
17	64.8	54	29.5	91	4.7
18	63.9	55	28.6	92	4.4
19	62.9	56	27.7	93	4.1
20	61.9	57	26.8	94	3.9
21	60.9	58	25.9	95	3.7
22	59.9	59	25.0	96	3.4
23	59.0	60	24.2	97	3.2
24	58.0	61	23.3	98	3.0
25	57.0	62	22.5	99	2.8
26	56.0	63	21.6	100	2.7
27	55.1	64	20.8	101	2.5
28	54.1	65	20.0	102	2.3
29	53.1	66	19.2	103	2.1
30	52.2	67	18.4	104	1.9
31	51.2	68	17.6	105	1.8
32	50.2	69	16.8	106	1.6
33	49.3	70	16.0	107	1.4
34	48.3	71	15.3	108	1.3
35	47.3	72	14.6	109	1.1
36	46.4	73	13.9	110	1.0
37	45.4	74	13.2	111	.9
38	44.4	75	12.5	112	.8
39	43.5	76	11.9	113	.7
40	42.5	77	11.2	114	.6
41	41.5	78	10.6	115	.5

The numerator is equal to Green's cost basis while the denominator is Green's annual pension of $2,400 multiplied by his life expectancy of 20 years as determined from the tables in the regulations. Thus, one-sixth of each payment that Green receives will be nontaxable, while the remainder will be taxable as ordinary income.

Under the annuity rules, once an exclusion ratio has been determined, it continues to apply only until the cost basis is fully recovered (as would be the case if the participant lived longer than the life expectancy described in the regulations). Payments thereafter are fully taxable. If the participant dies before the cost basis has been fully recovered, there is an income tax deduction allowable to the participant's estate representing the unrecovered basis.

The same cost recovery rules apply, with some modifications, if the annuity has a period-certain feature, or is some form of joint and survivor annuity. With a period-certain feature, the cost basis in determining the exclusion ratio is reduced in accordance with factors in the regulations. For a joint and survivor annuity, the expected return is adjusted to take the joint life expectancy into account.

Survivorship and period-certain annuities can be paid out in many forms, and the tax consequences of all of these cannot be discussed here; however, the same principles apply in all cases.

There is an alternative simplified "safe harbor" method for computing the amount of each periodic payment excluded from tax (IRS Notice 88-118). The safe harbor applies only to payments from a qualified plan or Section 403(b) tax deferred annuity plan which are to be paid for the life of the employee or the joint lives of the employee and beneficiary. Under the safe harbor method, the employee's investment in the contract is divided by the number of expected monthly payments set out in the IRS table below. The number of payments is based on the employee's age at the annuity starting date and the same table is used for both single life and joint and survivor annuity payments. The resulting dollar amount is excluded from each payment until the cost basis is fully recovered.

Age	Number of Payments
55 and under	300
55–60	260
61–65	240
66–70	170
71 and over	120

Payment in One Taxable Year

If the qualified plan distribution is paid to the participant in a single taxable year, the taxable amount (the amount in excess of the participant's cost basis as described above) potentially is all taxable to the participant as ordinary income in the year received. Since this can increase the participant's effective tax rate by pushing up the marginal tax bracket in that year, a special one-time relief provision applies if the distribution qualifies as a *lump-sum distribution* and is received after age 59½. A lump-sum distribution must meet all of the following requirements:

- It is made in one taxable year of the recipient.
- It represents the entire amount of the employee's benefit in the plan.
- It is payable on account of the participant's death, attainment of age 59½, separation from service (non-self-employed person only) or disability (self-employed person only).
- It is from a qualified plan.
- Except for death benefits, the employee must have participated in the plan for at least five years prior to the distribution.

In determining whether the entire amount of the employee's benefit has been distributed, all pension plans maintained by the employer are treated as a single plan, all profit-sharing plans are treated as one plan, and all stock bonus plans are treated as one plan.

If the distribution qualifies as a lump-sum distribution, the taxable amount of the distribution (the amount remaining after the cost basis is subtracted) is eligible for special tax treatment.

The special tax treatment for qualifying lump-sum distributions has changed over the years. Before 1974, the applicable provision allowed the taxable amount of the lump-sum distribution to be treated as long-term capital gain for tax purposes. After 1973, the taxable amount became eligible for a special provision referred to as *ten-year averaging*, subject to rules somewhat more liberal than the current *five-year averaging* provision that replaced ten-year averaging in 1987. Ten-year averaging is "grandfathered" for participants who attained age 50 before 1986; that is, such participants may elect to use it rather than the current five-year averages.

The current five-year averaging treatment is a special tax calculation. It can be elected only if the distribution is received on or after the plan participant has attained age 59½, and can be elected only once. First, a minimum distribution allowance of the lesser of $10,000 or one-half of the total taxable amount is subtracted from the taxable amount. The minimum distribution allowance, however, must be reduced by 20 percent of the total taxable amount in excess of $20,000; therefore, if the taxable amount is $70,000 or more, there is no minimum distribution allowance. The remaining taxable amount after the minimum distribution allowance is divided by five and a separate tax is determined on this portion; the tax so determined is then multiplied by five. In making this calculation, the tax is determined apart from the employee's other taxable income, without the usual deductions or exclusions, and the single taxpayer rate is used. The computation is described on the IRS form for reporting lump-sum distributions (currently Form 4972) and it is unnecessary to go into the computational details here.

A taxpayer who participated in the plan prior to 1974 has an option to forego capital gain treatment on the pre-1974 portion of the taxable amount and use the five-year averaging method for the entire taxable amount. Normally, such a taxpayer will elect whichever option provides the lowest amount of tax.

Taxation of Death Benefits from Qualified Plans

The income tax treatment described above also applies in general to plan death benefits paid to beneficiaries of participants. That is, if the death benefit is paid as periodic payments, the annuity rules described above generally apply; if the death benefit qualifies as a lump-sum distribution, the special favorable tax treatment is available to the beneficiary. However, some additional income tax benefits under Code Section 101 are also available to the beneficiary.

One such benefit is an income tax exclusion of up to $5,000 for a death benefit paid by an employer by reason of the death of the employee. If the benefit qualifies as a lump-sum distribution, the full exclusion is available without qualification. However, if the benefit is in the form of periodic payments, the $5,000 exclusion is only available to the extent the employee's benefit was nonvested prior to death.

Another income tax exclusion applies if the death benefit is payable under a life insurance contract held by the plan. The amount excluded from income tax is the pure insurance amount paid—the difference between the policy's face amount and its cash value.

> **EXAMPLE:** Employee Haines dies before retirement and his beneficiary receives a lump-sum death benefit from the plan consisting of $100,000 of the proceeds of a cash-value life insurance contract, the cash value of which was $50,000. The plan was noncontributory and Haines reported a total of $8,000 of insurance costs on his income tax returns during his lifetime as a result of the plan's insurance coverage. The taxable amount of this distribution to the beneficiary is the total distribution of $100,000 less the following:
>
> - The pure insurance amount ($100,000 minus the cash value of $50,000),
> - The $5,000 employee death benefit exclusion, and
> - Haines's cost basis—in this case, only the $8,000 of insurance cost reported during his lifetime.
>
> The taxable amount is therefore $37,000. This amount is taxable income to the beneficiary, subject to the special five-year averaging and capital gain provisions described above, if they are applicable.

Excess Distribution Tax

There is a penalty tax of 15 percent, in addition to the regular income tax, on the taxable amount of a distribution that exceeds $112,500 annually (as adjusted in certain cases). Since this affects primarily highly compensated plan participants, it is discussed in detail in Chapter 25.

Federal Estate Tax

The federal estate tax on qualified plan death benefits affects only highly compensated participants (those with a gross estate of at least $600,000) and is discussed further in Chapter 25. There is also an *excess accumulation* tax of 15 percent imposed on estates that is the counterpart of the excess distribution tax.

QUALIFIED DOMESTIC RELATIONS ORDERS

The prohibition against nonalienation of benefits does not apply to an assignment of a benefit under a *qualified domestic relations order* (QDRO). Under Code Section 414(p), a QDRO is a decree, order or property settlement under state law relating to child support, alimony or marital property rights that assigns a participant's plan benefits to a spouse, former spouse, child or other dependent of the participant. Currently, therefore, a participant's plan benefits generally become the subject of negotiation in domestic disputes. The pension law itself does not indicate how such benefits are to be divided; this is still a matter of state domestic relations law. The QDRO provision simply provides a means by which state court orders in domestic relations issues can be enforced against plan trustees.

To protect plan administrators and trustees from conflicting claims, a QDRO cannot assign a benefit that the plan does not provide. Also, a QDRO cannot assign a benefit that is already assigned under a previous order. If, under the plan, a participant has no right to an immediate cash payment from the plan, a QDRO cannot require the trustees to make such a cash payment. If a cash settlement is desired, the parties will generally agree to allow one participant to keep the entire plan benefit and pay compensating cash to the other.

LOANS FROM QUALIFIED PLANS

The law permits loans, within limits, to participants in regular qualified plans and Section 403(b) tax-deferred annuity plans. However, a participant cannot borrow from a plan unless the plan document specifically permits loans, and as discussed below, loan provisions may not be appropriate for all plans. Loans from IRAs and SEPs are effectively prohibited; they are treated as taxable distributions and may be subject to penalties for premature distribution. Also, loans from a qualified plan to an owner/employee (a proprietor or more than 10 percent partner in an unincorporated business) or to an employee of an S corporation who is a more than 5 percent shareholder in the corporation are prohibited transactions subject to the prohibited transaction penalties.

Limits on Loan Amount

Under Code Section 72(p), loans will be recognized as loans (rather than taxable current distributions) only to the extent that the loan, together with all other outstanding loans, does not exceed the lesser of

- $50,000 reduced by the highest outstanding loan balance during the preceding one-year period, or

- One-half of the present value of the vested accrued benefit of the employee under the plan.

A loan up to $10,000 may be made even if this is more than one-half of the present value of the employee's vested accrued benefit. Some examples:

Vested Accrued Benefit	Maximum Aggregate Loans
$120,000	$50,000
40,000	20,000
15,000	10,000

Terms of Loans

In order to obtain loan treatment, the loan must be repayable by its terms within five years. The rule noted above for reducing the $50,000 limit by the loan balance in the preceding year was designed to prevent avoidance of the five-year limit by simply repaying then immediately reborrowing the same amount every five years. The five-year requirement does not apply to any loan used to acquire a principal residence of the participant.

Transactions with an effect similar to that of loans (for example, the pledging of an interest in a qualified plan or a loan made against an insurance contract purchased by a qualified plan) are also covered by the loan limitations and rules.

If the plan permits loans, they must be made available on a nondiscriminatory basis. Also, the loans must be adequately secured and bear a reasonable rate of interest. Usually, the security for a plan loan is simply the participant's vested accrued plan benefit. Interest on the loan is generally consumer interest that is not deductible as an itemized deduction unless secured by a home mortgage. However, if the loan is to a key employee as defined in the top-heavy rules or is secured by 401(k) or 403(b) elective deferrals, interest is not deductible in any event.

Any loan that does not meet these requirements will be treated as a current distribution and may be currently taxable to the employee when received.

Should the Plan Permit Loans?

Whether the plan should permit loans depends on the employer's objectives for the plan. Plan loan provisions are often desired by the controlling employees of closely held businesses because a plan loan provides the advantage of tax sheltering the plan funds without losing control of the cash. However, the same considerations may make plan loans desirable for regular employees as well. A disadvantage of plan loans is that if they are too extensively utilized, they deplete the plan funds available for investment. More fundamentally, however, plan loan provisions are inconsistent with a primary plan objective of providing retirement security. Thus, they are less common in pension plans than in profit-sharing plans. Plan loan provisions are particularly uncommon in defined-benefit plans because such plans have no individual participant accounts; it is complicated to convert a participant's vested accrued benefit to a cash equivalent at a given time to determine the amount of loan that can be allowed. Plan loans also add significant administrative costs to the plan.

STUDY QUESTIONS

1. a. What is meant by the "normal form of benefit" in a defined-benefit plan?
   b. What optional forms of benefit are commonly made available to participants?
2. What is the distinction between types of preretirement distributions allowable in a pension plan and types allowable in a profit-sharing plan?
3. a. What is the latest date on which a qualified plan may allow retirement benefits to commence?
   b. What is the latest age at which a participant of a qualified plan must begin to receive benefits?
4. Explain the minimum distribution rules applicable to a beneficiary if
   a. The employee dies before the entire plan interest is distributed.
   b. The employee dies before distributions have begun.
5. Which of the following plan distributions is not subject to the 10 percent Section 72(t) penalty?
   a. A lump-sum distribution to a participant age 55.
   b. A death benefit payable to a beneficiary upon the death of an employee age 52.
   c. A lump-sum benefit payable to a disabled employee age 57.
   d. A life annuity payable beginning immediately upon separation from service to an employee age 45.
   e. A distribution of $30,000 to employee Slick who plans to use the money to build a swimming pool prescribed by his doctor for arthritis treatments.
   f. A distribution from a 401(k) plan to an employee age 52 who qualifies under the plan's "extreme hardship" distribution provision.
6. Joe Smith retired at age 65 with a pension of $400 per month. His life expectancy is 20 years. To what extent is his pension benefit taxable if Smith's cost basis is $16,400?
7. a. What requirements must a lump-sum distribution meet in order to qualify for special tax treatment?
   b. What is the special tax treatment that is available?
8. Explain how death benefits from a qualified plan are taxed.
9. The ABC Company (an S corporation) has a qualified money-purchase plan that allows employees to take loans up to the maximum legal limit. What is the maximum loan that can be taken by the following employees?

Employee	Vested Account Balance	Percentage of Corporate Ownership
a. Don Taich	$ 17,000	0%
b. Peter Demunney	$160,000	0
c. Dana N. Runn	$200,000	50

10. What are the advantages and disadvantages of designing a plan that includes a loan provision?

25

Plan Restrictions Aimed at Highly Compensated Employees

Objectives

- Describe the limitations on compensation, benefits and contributions that apply to qualified plans.
- Explain the purpose of the top-heavy rules and describe their effect on smaller employers.
- Describe the status of the self-employed person with respect to coverage under a qualified plan.
- Discuss the federal estate tax treatment of qualified plan benefits.
- Discuss the excess distribution and excess accumulation penalties.

Congress and the IRS have long been convinced that the tax advantages of qualified plans can be abused by plans that confer most of their benefits on highly paid key employees, typically employees who are stockholders or partners in a closely held business. Such plans are arguably inconsistent with the social policy behind the qualified plan provisions. Therefore, the law contains a variety of provisions particularly aimed at this type of abuse. The provisions discussed in this chapter will have little actual effect on plans typically designed for larger employers. However, these rules technically apply to *all* plans, and thus they must be considered at least in drafting every plan.

There is a large community of pension planners who specialize in designing plans to avoid the provisions discussed in this chapter, so from time to time Congress and the IRS add new rules to close various "loopholes" that plan designers have found. Thus, the provisions discussed here have become the most complex in the entire pension law.

CEILING ON COMPENSATION

The most fundamental limit of this type is the rule (Code Section 401(a)(17)) that only the first $200,000 of each employee's compensation (as indexed for inflation; in 1991: $222,220) can be taken into account in a qualified plan's contribution or benefit formula. For example, if an employee earns $300,000 in 1991 and is covered under a money-purchase pension plan with a 10 percent of compensation contribution formula, the contribution for that employee in 1991 is limited to $22,222 (10 percent of $222,200, rather than 10 percent of $300,000).

For family businesses, the impact of this limit is heightened by the aggregation rule. Under the aggregation rule, any compensation paid to an employee who is a member of the family of a 5-percent owner or of one of the ten highly compensated employees paid the greatest compensation during the year, will be treated as paid to the 5-percent owner or highly compensated employee. For this purpose, family members include the spouse of an employee and the employee's lineal descendants who have not attained age 19 by the close of the year. For example, suppose a husband and wife own and operate a business that pays each one of them $150,000 in 1991. They have a pension plan that provides a contribution of 20 percent of compensation annually. Without the aggregation rule, the plan would provide a $30,000 contribution for each spouse ($60,000 total), but with aggregation, the total contribution is limited to 20 percent of $222,220, or $44,444.

LIMITATIONS ON INDIVIDUAL BENEFITS OR ANNUAL ADDITIONS (SECTION 415 LIMITS)

Section 415 of the Internal Revenue Code contains limitations on the amount of benefit or annual account additions that any participant can receive under a qualified plan. These limitations are intended to prevent the qualified plan from being used as an individual tax-sheltering device beyond any reasonable need for retirement savings. They have their greatest impact on small businesses where one or more of the business owners are plan participants. However, the limitations also can have an impact on larger plans that cover high-salaried executives. There are two types of Section 415 limits—one for defined-benefit plans and one for defined-contribution plans.

Defined-Benefit Plans

For defined-benefit plans, the applicable limitation restricts the amount of *benefit* that any individual can receive. Basically, the plan cannot permit a benefit at age 65 (or the social security retirement age, if later) that exceeds the lesser of 100 percent of the participant's compensation averaged over the three years of highest compensation, or $90,000 annually. A pension of up to $10,000 annually can be paid even if it exceeds the 100 percent limit, but this $10,000 floor applies only if the participant has never been covered by a defined-*contribution* plan.

The benefit limit of Section 415 applies to employer-provided benefits only. If the plan provides for employee contributions (which is relatively rare in defined-benefit plans), these employee contributions can be used to increase benefits above the Section 415 limit.

The limits as stated above apply to a benefit in the form of either a straight-life annuity or a qualified joint-and-survivor annuity. However, the limits must be actuarially adjusted if the normal retirement benefit is something else—for example, a ten-year period-certain annuity. No adjustment is made for preretirement death or disability benefits. Also, there is an increase in the limit in the event of late retirement.

The $90,000 limit is now adjusted for inflation under a formula based on social security benefit amounts in effect. In 1991, for example, the limit had reached $108,963.

The $90,000 limit is actuarially adjusted for retirement ages earlier or later than the social security retirement age. This prevents acceleration of funding (and tax deductions) simply by choosing a normal retirement age earlier than 65. The limit is also actuarially increased for retirement later than the social security retirement age. Table 25-1 illustrates the adjustments to the basic $90,000 limit for a participant born before 1938 whose social security retirement age is 65.

As indicated above, the Section 415 benefit limitation must be part of every qualified plan document. The plan language must, therefore, prohibit the accrual of any benefit in excess of the limit. For any given employee, however, except an employee who is contemplating retirement in the current plan year, it is impossible to know what the applicable dollar limitation under Section 415 will be in the year of retirement. Nevertheless, the IRS does not allow benefits to be accrued in excess of the Section 415 limits based on current compensation and the current dollar limit, even for a participant far from retirement.

Defined-Contribution Plans

For a defined-contribution plan, the Section 415 limitation is a restriction not on the benefit, but on the *annual addition* to each participant's account. The annual

---

TABLE 25-1
Retirement Age and Maximum Benefit

Retirement Age	Maximum Dollar Benefit
55	42,400
60	61,419
62	72,000
65	90,000
70	155,843

Assumptions: 1971 Group Annuity (Male) Table with interest at 5 percent, life annuity. Revenue Ruling 80–253 indicates what assumptions will be considered reasonable for this purpose. For the actuarial increase after age 65, under Code Section 415(b)(2)(E)(ii), the interest rate assumption cannot be greater than the lesser of 5 percent or the plan's actuarial interest rate assumption.

addition cannot exceed the lesser of 25 percent of the participant's annual compensation or $30,000. Like the dollar limit for defined-benefit plans, the $30,000 limit was frozen through 1987, after which it will be adjusted until the adjusted defined-benefit limit reaches $120,000; thereafter, the defined-contribution limit will be set at one-fourth the defined-benefit limit.

The annual addition to each participant's account includes three elements:

1. Employer contributions including employee salary reductions.
2. Reallocated forfeitures from other participants' accounts.
3. Nondeductible (aftertax) employee contributions.

The following example shows how the annual-additions limit will affect a participant's account in a hypothetical plan. In the example, a forfeiture amount is available that is allocated to the employee's account in proportion to compensation.

Employee Compensation	Maximum Annual Addition	Forfeiture Allocated	Maximum Employer Contribution
$ 20,000	$ 5,000	$ 2,000	$ 3,000
50,000	12,500	5,000	7,500
100,000	25,000	10,000	15,000
200,000	30,000	20,000	10,000

It is important to note that both of the Section 415 limitations apply to individual participants, not to the plan as a whole. Also, it should be noted that the annual-additions limit is not a limit on the amount that the employer can deduct for income tax purposes. The deduction limits are a separate set of rules from the Section 415 limits and the two items should not be confused. However, no deduction can ever be taken for an employer contribution that causes an employee's benefit or account to exceed the Section 415 limit.

Combined Limit

Often, it is good retirement planning to have both a defined-contribution and a defined-benefit plan covering the same employee, since the different advantages of the two approaches can thereby be combined. If each of the Section 415 limitations were applied separately in this case, the amount of tax benefit to the participant would be far above that available through one type of plan only. Therefore, Section 415 contains special limitations that apply to a participant who is covered under a defined-benefit plan and a defined-contribution plan of the same employer. The purpose of this limitation is to scale back the benefit so that the overall intention of Section 415 is carried out. Even with the combined limit, however, it is still possible for an individual participant to obtain somewhat more tax benefit through a combination of the two plans than would be available through only one type of plan.

The combined rule can be summarized as follows. Two fractions are determined—the *defined-benefit fraction* and the *defined-contribution fraction*. Each fraction more or less represents the benefit or contribution level the participant actually receives in each plan as compared with the maximum amount available in each plan separately. Then, the rule further provides that where an individual is a participant in both a defined-benefit plan and a defined-contribution plan maintained by the same employer, the *sum of the defined-benefit fraction and the defined-contribution fraction for any year may not exceed one;* that is,

$$\text{D.B. fraction} + \text{D.C. fraction} = 1$$

The detailed definitions of the fractions will not be covered here.

Combined Deduction Limit

A combined deduction limit (Code Section 404(a)(7)) has the effect of restricting the benefits of many combination plans even though they meet the combined rule discussed above. If an employer maintains a defined-contribution and a defined-benefit plan covering the same employer or employees, the employer's annual tax deduction for the plans cannot exceed 25 percent of the compensation of the employees covered under both plans. The 25 percent deduction limit can be exceeded only to meet the minimum funding requirements for the defined-benefit plan. For older plan entrants, the defined-benefit funding level will often exceed 25 percent of compensation, thus (depending on the overall nature of the employee group) potentially eliminating the possibility of adding a defined-contribution plan. For example, if there is only one participant, or only one highly paid participant and a few others (such as the typical plan for a doctor or dentist) this will be the case.

> EXAMPLE: Dr. X, age 55, adopts a plan providing a pension of $75,000 a year (50 percent of compensation) at retirement age 65. Annual cost is $44,428 (8 percent interest assumption) which is 30 percent of Dr. X's compensation. Thus, if Dr. X is the only employee, there is no room for a defined-contribution plan.

TOP-HEAVY PLANS

The *top-heavy* rules are another addition to the arsenal of weapons Congress has provided against the use of qualified plans by small businesses primarily as tax shelters for owners and highly compensated employees. The rules (Code Section 416) provide additional requirements that must be met by all qualified plans that meet the definition of top-heavy. To summarize, the top-heavy requirements

- Put a ceiling on the amount of a participant's compensation that may be taken into account in plan contribution or benefit formula.
- Provide faster vesting of benefits for plan participants who are not key employees.

- Provide minimum unintegrated benefit or contribution levels for plan participants who are not key employees.
- Reduce the aggregate Section 415 limit on contributions and benefits for key employees in certain situations.
- Restrict distributions to key employees.

The top-heavy restrictions must be written into the plan document itself, even a plan for a large employer that is unlikely ever to be top-heavy. The plan document must provide that if the plan meets the definition of top-heavy on a given determination date, all of the top-heavy restrictions automatically become part of the plan. So long as the plan is not top-heavy, the top-heavy restrictions need not necessarily apply, although, of course, the planner is free to add these restrictions to the plan even if it is not top-heavy.

Definition of Top-Heavy

A defined-benefit plan is a top-heavy plan for a given plan year if (as of the determination date—see below) the present value of the accumulated accrued benefits for participants who are key employees is more than 60 percent of the present value of all accumulated accrued benefits in the plan. A defined-contribution plan is considered top-heavy if, as of the determination date, the sum of the account balances of participants who are key employees exceeds 60 percent of the aggregate value of the accounts of all employees. Benefits and account balances attributable to both employer and employee contributions are to be taken into account, except for accumulated voluntary deductible employee contributions or rollovers from other plans. The present value of a participant's accrued benefit or the value of the participant's account balance is to be increased by any aggregate distributions made with respect to the participant during the five-year period ending on the determination date. Plans of related groups can be lumped together and if the contributions or benefits of the overall group are top-heavy, each plan in the group will be considered top-heavy.

Determination Date

The determination date for any given plan year is the last day of the preceding plan year. For the first year of the new plan, the determination date is the last day of the first plan year. The IRS also has the authority to apply the top-heavy provisions on the basis of years other than plan years.

Definition of Key Employee

A key employee is any participant in the plan, including a self-employed person, who at any time in the four preceding years was an officer earning more than 50 percent of the Section 415 defined-benefit dollar limit, an employee owning one of the ten largest interests in the employer (under attribution-of-ownership rules), a more-than-5-percent owner or a more-than-1-percent owner earning more than $150,000. Since the term *officer* is not clearly defined, there is a limit on the number of employees that can be treated as officers. No more than 50 employees can be treated as officers in general, while for small employers the limit on the number of officers is the greater of three individuals or 10 percent of the employees (presumably the highest paid). For example, suppose a small company has 25 employees. In determining who are key employees, the IRS cannot designate more than three of these employees (the greater of three individuals or 10 percent of the employees) as officers.

In determining ownership in the business for purposes of identifying key employees, the top-heavy provisions have rules for attributing stock ownership from related persons, and there are special rules for aggregating commonly controlled groups of employers and affiliated service groups.

An illustration of what constitutes a top-heavy plan might be helpful in defining the concept of top-heavy.

> **EXAMPLE:** Suppose that a corporation with ten employees has a defined-contribution money-purchase pension plan. The employees include Wolfe (president and sole shareholder), Hare (vice-president) and Flynn (foreman). All of the other employees are clerical or production workers paid by the hour. The IRS would most likely identify the three named employees as the plan's key employees. As of the end of the 1991 plan year, aggregate account balances of all participants in the plan total $200,000. The account balances for Wolfe, Hare and Flynn total $100,000. On these facts, the plan is not top-heavy for the plan year 1992, since the aggregate account balances for the three key employees total less than 60 percent of the total account balances as of the determination date, the end of 1991. However, suppose that in 1990 Wolfe received a distribution of $100,000 from the plan. In this case, the account balances as of the end of 1991 would have to be increased by the amount of this distribution, so they would total $300,000. The account balances for the key employees would then be $200,000, because the $100,000 distribution to Wolfe would have to be included for this purpose. Now the plan would be deemed to be top-heavy for the plan year 1992, since the account balances for key employees would be more than 60 percent of the total.

Although the example above involved a plan of a small employer that fell on the line between being top-heavy and avoiding that status, planners find that virtually all plans of employers with fewer than about ten employees will be top-heavy at all times. Key employees in such businesses usually have not only higher salaries but also much longer service than regular employees, so their account balances or accrued benefits are much higher as a percentage of the total. Therefore, the top-heavy rules become an additional set of qualification requirements that must be met by all small plans.

Additional Vesting Requirements for Top-Heavy Plans

If a plan meets the definition of top-heavy, the plan provisions must meet one of two special vesting schedules applicable during years in which the plan is top-heavy. One alternative is 100 percent after two years of service. The other alternative is six-year graded vesting, as follows:

Years of Service	Vesting Percentage
2	20
3	40
4	60
5	80
6 or more	100

Minimum Benefit Requirements

A qualified plan must provide minimum benefits or contributions for top-heavy years. For defined-benefit plans, the benefit for each nonkey employee must be at least a minimum percentage of average compensation. The applicable minimum percentage of compensation for a given employee is two multiplied by the number of the employee's years of service, with a maximum percentage of 20 percent (i.e., ten years of service or more). The average compensation used for this test will generally be based on the highest five years of compensation.

For a defined-contribution plan, employer contributions during a year of top-heaviness must be not less than 3 percent of each nonkey employee's compensation.

A top-heavy plan can consider only nonintegrated benefits in meeting the vesting and minimum benefit requirements. That is, these requirements must be met based on benefits from the plan itself. Benefits received by the participant from social security cannot be taken into account.

Modification of Section 415 Combined Fraction

If a plan is top-heavy, the defined-benefit or defined-contribution fraction is modified to make it more restrictive. The result of this is to increase the fraction for highly paid employees (those affected by the dollar limit) and, therefore, limit the total benefits for an employee covered by both a defined-benefit and defined-contribution company plan. The biggest impact is on very small organizations, such as a self-employed professional.

The modification of the fractions does not apply to a regular top-heavy plan if the plan provides minimum benefits or contributions at least 1 percent higher than the basic minimum—that is, if the plan provides a 4 percent (rather than 3 percent) defined-contribution or a 3 percent per year (rather than 2 percent) defined-benefit. However, if the plan is *super top-heavy* (more than 90 percent of accrued benefits or account balances for key employees), the modified fractions apply regardless of the amount of minimum benefits or contributions.

Effect of Top-Heavy Rules on Integration

If a qualified plan is top-heavy in a given year, one of the restrictions that will apply is that there must be a minimum benefit or contribution level for nonkey employees. In such cases, therefore, a pure "excess" type of integrated formula with zero benefits below the integration level cannot be used for nonkey employees. Since 1989, excess-type integrated formulas are no longer possible in most cases, top-heavy or not (see Chapter 20).

QUALIFIED PLANS FOR OWNERS OF UNINCORPORATED BUSINESSES

The owner of an unincorporated business often works full time or performs substantial services for the business as its proprietor or one of its partners. However, under the law such a person is not technically an employee of the business, but is referred to instead as a *self-employed person*. For many years, partners and proprietors were not eligible to be covered under qualified plans adopted by their unincorporated businesses. Beginning in 1962, qualified plan coverage was allowed, but only under very restricted conditions. In particular, there was a relatively low limit on the amount that could be contributed to the plan (or on the benefit provided by the plan) for partners and proprietors. The special plans designed under these restrictions were known as *Keogh* or *HR-10* plans. These restrictions were enough to induce many unincorporated businesses to incorporate, simply in order that the partner or proprietor could become a legally recognized *employee* of the business and be eligible for full qualified plan coverage. However, for plan years beginning after 1983, most of these previous restrictions were eliminated and partners and proprietors were able to participate fully in qualified plans adopted by their unincorporated businesses. There are, however, a few differences in the treatment of unincorporated businesses, most of them related to basic differences in the form of business.

Earned Income

An unincorporated business is not treated for federal income tax purposes as a taxable entity but rather as a conduit for passing the business's taxable income or loss through to the partners or proprietor. By comparison, a corporation is a tax-paying entity, and income can be passed through to owners only in the form of salaries representing reasonable compensation for services rendered, or as dividends. Because of this difference, plan benefits or contributions for partners and proprietors are based on a defined amount referred to as *earned income* which is intended to be comparable to the *compensation* that employees receive.

Earned income is the partner's or proprietor's share of the net earnings of the business after taking all appropriate business deductions, and without including nontaxable income. However, earned income includes only earnings with respect to the trade or business in which the personal services of the partner or proprietor are a material income-producing factor. For example, the net profits of an investment-type business could not be treated like compensation in order to provide a benefit under a qualified plan for a partner who provided no personal services to the business.

The fact that earned income is determined after all business deductions creates a computational complication. Business deductions include the plan contribution itself, as well as one-half the social security self-employment tax which is based on net income [Code Section 164(f)]). An illustration will show this without getting into the details of the algebra:

> **EXAMPLE:** Dot Matrix is a self-employed computer consultant with no regular employees. She earned $100,000 of net income in 1990, not counting her Keogh plan contribution and the deduction for self-employment tax. Her deduction for self-employment tax is $3,924.45. The Keogh plan is a money-purchase plan calling for an annual contribution of 25 percent of earned income. How much can Dot contribute? The answer is $19,215.11. This amount is 25 percent of Dot's earned income. Her earned income is equal to

Initial net income		$100,000.00
less self-employment tax deduction	$ 3,924.45	
Keogh contribution	19,215.11	
Earned income		$76,860.44

Insurance

Another group of special rules applies to a qualified plan providing insurance for a partner or proprietor. No deduction can be taken by the business for plan contributions that are allocatable to the purchase of incidental life, health or accident insurance for the partner or proprietor. If cash-value life insurance is used, the deduction is denied for the portion of the premium allocatable to pure insurance protection, but the remainder of the premium is deductible as a plan contribution. The amounts not deducted are taxable income to the business owners, since all taxable income of a partnership or proprietorship flows through to the individual owners. Therefore, there are no PS 58 costs to include in the owner's income if insurance has been purchased, because the full cost of the insurance has already been included in the owner's income. However, unlike regular employees, the owners do not obtain a cost basis for the cost of the insurance to apply to any distribution from the qualified plan.

Aggregation Rule for Unincorporated Businesses

As discussed in Chapter 19, the Code has various provisions under which all businesses (both incorporated and unincorporated) under common control are treated as a single employer for qualified plan purposes. There is an additional common-control rule that affects primarily unincorporated businesses. Under this rule (Sections 401(d)(1)–(2)), if a qualified plan covers a partner or proprietor who controls another business (control here means more than 50 percent ownership), then the plan must either cover the employees of the controlled business or a comparable plan must be provided for employees of the controlled business.

EARLY TERMINATION RULE FOR 25 HIGHEST PAID EMPLOYEES

Potentially, a qualified defined-benefit plan can be used as a one-time tax shelter for key employees if it is designed with the expectation that most of the key employees will retire within a few years, taking most of the plan assets out for their retirement, thus terminating the plan. For many years, the Regulations (Section 1.401–4(c)) have contained a provision designed to limit this abuse by requiring defined-benefit plans to limit benefits for the 25 highest paid employees if they are paid out within ten years of the plan's establishment or the plan terminates within ten years.

In such cases, benefits to the 25 highest paid employees are limited by limiting the total employer contributions used to fund such benefits. The employer contributions for each such employee cannot exceed the greater of $20,000 or 20 percent of the first $50,000 of employee compensation multiplied by the number of years the plan was in effect prior to the benefit payment or plan termination. Often, this will produce a lower limit on benefits than the Section 415 benefit limit.

FEDERAL ESTATE TAX TREATMENT OF QUALIFIED PLAN BENEFITS

The federal estate tax is a tax separate from the income tax that is imposed on the value of a decedent's property at the time of death. The estate tax is payable out of the decedent's estate and, therefore, reduces the amount available to the beneficiaries. Only a small percentage of decedents—less than 5 percent—have enough wealth to be concerned about the estate tax because of a high initial minimum tax credit applicable to the estate tax. No estate tax return need be filed for a decedent whose gross estate is less than approximately $600,000. Also, there is an unlimited marital deduction for federal estate tax purposes—that is, there is no federal estate tax imposed on property transferred at death to a spouse, regardless of the amount.

As a general rule, a lump-sum death benefit, or the present value of an annuity payable to a beneficiary from a qualified plan, is includable in the estate of a deceased participant for federal estate tax purposes. For some high-income participants, avoiding federal estate taxes on the plan benefit (and also the excess accumulation tax described below) will be important. Their estates may be large enough to attract some federal estate tax. The marital deduction may not be significant, since they may not wish to pay the plan benefit to a spouse—they may be widowed or divorced, or may wish to provide for another beneficiary. Also, even if the benefit is payable to a spouse, a spouse is often about the same age as the decedent, and thus within relatively few years most of the property transferred to the spouse is potentially subject to federal estate tax again at the spouse's death. As a result, it is often useful to design a qualified plan death benefit that can be excluded from the participant's estate.

The general rule of the federal estate tax is that all items of property are includable unless a specific code provision excludes them. Thus, qualified plan death benefits are generally includable because there is no specific exclusion. However, the estate tax law does have a specific provision dealing with life insurance, Section 2042. Under Section 2042, life insurance proceeds are includable in a decedent's estate only if the decedent has "incidents of ownership" in the insurance policies. Incidents of ownership are various rights under the policy, particularly the right to designate the beneficiary. It therefore seems possible to exclude a qualified plan death benefit if the benefit is provided through a life insurance policy in which the decedent has no incidents of ownership. Noninsured death benefits, however, presumably would not be excludable in any event.

There are no definite rules as to how to avoid incidents of ownership in a life insurance policy held in a qualified plan for a participant. However, design techniques currently being used for this purpose include the use of a separate trust or subtrust under the plan for holding the policies and a provision for irrevocable beneficiary designations.

EXCESS DISTRIBUTION AND EXCESS ACCUMULATION PENALTIES

In order to further limit the tax benefits from qualified plans for highly compensated participants, Congress has added penalties for plan distributions in excess of certain specified amounts (Code Section 4980A). These penalties apply even if plan contributions or benefits are within the Section 415 limits discussed earlier.

Excess Distribution Penalty

In addition to any regular income tax payable, there is a tax of 15 percent on any excess distribution made in any year from a qualified plan or plans to an individual participant. Distributions from all IRAs, Section 403(b) tax-deferred annuities and qualified plans of all employers covering the participant are aggregated. A 15 percent tax is imposed on the participant to the extent that the aggregate distributions exceed a specified limit. The distribution limit is $150,000 for individuals participating in plans before 1989 (or in some cases, the participant's accrued benefit as of August 1, 1986). The limit is now indexed so that it is always equal to at least 125 percent of the Section 415 defined-benefit dollar limit. At some point, it will catch up with the $150,000 limit for pre-1989 participants; after that, the $150,000 limit will no longer apply.

The excess distribution tax does not apply to the following distributions:

- Death benefits paid to a beneficiary (but there may be an excess accumulation tax, as discussed below).
- A distribution to an alternate payee under a QDRO, if includable in income of the alternate payee. However, the alternate payee must then pay the 15 percent penalty.
- A distribution of the employee's own after-tax contributions.
- A distribution that is not included in income because it is rolled over (see Chapter 27).

For a lump-sum distribution, the limitation is five times the $112,500 limit, or $562,500, subject to indexing as described earlier. If a lump-sum payment exceeds $562,500 (or the indexed limit), then in addition to the regular tax payable, there is a 15 percent penalty on the amount above $562,500.

The amount of any 15 percent penalty is reduced by any 10 percent early distribution tax imposed on the same distribution.

Excess Accumulation Penalty

If an individual participating in a qualified plan dies with an *excess accumulation*, there is an additional tax, over and above any federal estate tax that applies. The additional tax is equal to 15 percent of the excess accumulation. An excess accumulation is defined as the excess of the value of the qualified plan retirement accumulation over the present value of an annuity paying $112,500 (or the applicable indexed limit) annually over the individual's life expectancy, determined at the date of death.

The additional 15 percent excess accumulation tax is not eligible for the unified credit under the estate and gift tax law, and cannot be reduced by the marital deduction or the charitable deduction, even if the qualified plan accumulation is actually given to a spouse or a charity. Thus, this tax adds an additional complication to estate planning for high-income individuals participating in qualified plans.

STUDY QUESTIONS

1. a. Why are so many provisions of the qualified plan law aimed primarily at the closely held business?
   b. How do Congress and the IRS often react to aggressive design by pension planners?
2. What is the purpose of the Section 415 limitations on qualified plan benefits and contributions?
3. a. What is the basic Section 415 limitation on benefits from a defined-benefit plan?
   b. Under what circumstances might this basic limit be adjusted?
4. a. What is the basic Section 415 limitation on annual additions to a defined-contribution plan?
   b. What elements are included in annual additions?
5. a. Describe the reasons for the combined limit under Section 415 when an employee is a participant in a defined-benefit and a defined-contribution plan with the same employer.
   b. Briefly describe the rule that applies to benefits and contributions when such dual participation exists.
6. Assume a corporation has 15 employees and that three employees, Tom, Ed and Jim, individually earn more than $60,000 annually. They are the only officers of the corporation. The remaining employees are hourly paid and clerical workers. Assume that the aggregate account balances of all participants in

the firm's defined-contribution plan are equal to $200,000, and for Tom, Ed and Jim the total is $100,000.
   a. Who are the plan's key employees? Explain.
   b. Is the plan top-heavy? Explain.
 7. Explain how each of the following is affected if a qualified plan is top-heavy:
   a. Vesting.
   b. Minimum benefits.
   c. Section 415 limits.
 8. Explain how the rules applying to qualified plans of unincorporated businesses differ from those applying to the qualified plans of corporations.
 9. Explain the early termination rule for the 25 highest-paid employees of a qualified plan.
10. What is the federal estate tax treatment of qualified plan benefits?
11. Describe the excess distribution and excess accumulation penalties.

26

Plan Installation and Administration; Investments; Plan Termination

Objectives

- Describe the basic steps that must be taken to install a qualified plan and explain the significance of an advance-determination letter.
- Explain the reporting and disclosure requirements that apply to qualified plans.
- Describe the impact of the ERISA fiduciary requirements and other investment restrictions on qualified plans.
- Explain the procedures for terminating a qualified plan and describe the general coverage of plan termination insurance provided by the Pension Benefit Guaranty Corporation (PBGC).

PLAN INSTALLATION

Installing a qualified plan can be fairly complex, particularly if the plan is complicated and the employer wishes to maximize the tax benefits by having the plan effective at the earliest possible date. The best way to discuss the installation process is to use as a framework for reference the checklist for the installation of a hypothetical qualified plan provided in Table 26-1. This checklist should be used for general discussion only; IRS guidelines for plan installation are frequently revised, and procedures may even vary from one Internal Revenue district to another.

497

TABLE 26-1

Checklist for Installation of Quicklime Construction Company, Inc. (calendar-year taxpayer) Employees' Profit-Sharing Plan (*effective January 1, 1991*)

BEFORE DECEMBER 31, 1991

1. Board must pass resolution adopting the plan. It is sufficient for the board to adopt either a preliminary draft of the plan or a simple resolution listing the major provisions of the plan.
2. Trust instrument must be executed. (Under state law, a nominal contribution to the trust corpus may also be necessary in order to establish the existence of the trust.) If there is a separate group pension contract, the contract need not be in final form before December 31, 1991, but application must have been accepted by insurer and partial payment made.
3. Plan should be communicated to employees. (There is no specific statutory deadline for this, but communication before the end of the year is recommended.) Communication can be oral (e.g., at employee meetings) or written. Alternatively, the Summary Plan Description (SPD) can be used for his purpose.

BEFORE EMPLOYER'S TAX-FILING DATE (March 15, 1992; extension to September 15, 1992, is possible)

1. Execute plan in final form. (Plan may be adopted subject to right to rescind if determination letter is not obtained.)
2. Make 1991 contribution to trust. (Plan may allow contribution to be returned if plan does not qualify.)

WITHIN 120 DAYS AFTER PLAN IS ADOPTED BY BOARD OF DIRECTORS (e.g., if resolution adopted December 31, 1991, by April 30, 1992)

1. Furnish SPD to participants. (See "Reporting and Disclosure" in this chapter.)
2. File SPD with Department of Labor.

BEFORE FILING APPLICATION FOR DETERMINATION WITH IRS

Provide notice to interested parties (i.e., employees) by mail 10 to 24 days before filing or posting 7 to 20 days before filing.

FILE APPLICATION FOR DETERMINATION WITH IRS

Time

No statutory deadline. However, should be filed before employer's tax-filing date (March 15, 1992, plus extensions). Filing of letter will extend the retroactive amendment date to give time to amend plan to meet IRS objections, if any.

What to file

Form 5300/5301

Form 5302, employee census (data concerning 25 highest-paid employees)

Other schedules as required under Form 5300/5301 instructions

Plan—executed

Trust Agreement—executed (or Insurance Contract)

Other items (e.g., Power of Attorney)—depending on circumstances

ON OR BEFORE JULY 31, 1992 (AND EACH JULY 31 THEREAFTER)

File Annual Report (Form 5500 Series) with IRS (see "Reporting and Disclosure")

ON OR BEFORE SEPTEMBER 30, 1992 (AND EACH SEPTEMBER 30 THEREAFTER)

Furnish Summary of Annual Report to participants.

Adoption of the Plan

In order to be effective during a particular year, the plan must be adopted by the employer during that year. For a corporation, the corporate board should pass a resolution adopting the plan before the end of its year in order for the plan to become effective during that year. It is not proper to back date documents for this purpose—the board must actually act legally before the end of the year. It may not be necessary to draft the final form of the plan at this time, however; the board usually can adopt a resolution merely outlining the basic provisions of the plan. If the plan uses a trust, the trust must be established before the end of the year in which the plan is to be effective. This means that a trust agreement must be executed between the employer and the trustee, and at least a nominal principal contribution may be necessary to establish the existence of the trust. If the plan uses an insurance contract as a funding instrument, the insurer must have accepted the terms of the agreement before the end of the year, although the contract may not be put into final form until sometime later. The plan and insurance contract should be finalized prior to the time the employer makes its first plan contribution other than a nominal contribution required to establish the trust or insurance contract; this usually means the employer's tax filing date, because as discussed in Chapter 22, the plan contribution for a given year can be deferred to the tax filing date for that year.

Plan Year

It is possible to establish a plan with a plan year that is different from the employer's taxable year. In that case, one plan year will end and another will begin in the same taxable year of the employer. The employer can then take a deduction that taxable year for a contribution on behalf of either plan year or for partial contributions for both taxable years; however, the employer must follow a consistent procedure so there is no undue tax benefit. For simplicity, unless otherwise indicated in this chapter, it will be assumed that the plan year is the same as the employer's taxable year.

Advance Determination Letters

A central feature of the plan installation process is usually an application to the IRS District Director for a determination letter stating that the plan as designed is a qualified plan eligible for the accompanying tax benefits. It is not necessary for the plan to have such a letter in order to be qualified; any plan that complies with the applicable Code provisions is a qualified plan. However, if there is no advance determination by the IRS, the IRS will not examine the plan until the time comes for an audit of the employer's tax returns. If the IRS finds at that time that the plan is not qualified, the possible tax consequences can be disastrous: the loss of the employer's tax deductions for plan contributions, the taxation of all plan contributions to participants and the loss of the trust's tax exempt status. To avoid this, most employers consider it desirable to have the IRS review the plan in advance and issue a determination letter. There are some other advantages to the determination letter procedure. The process of IRS review will often reveal drafting problems that might otherwise have gone unnoticed. During the review procedure, the IRS usually suggests any changes in the plan that are necessary to make it qualify.

There is a retroactive amendment procedure that allows the employer to make amendments to the plan effective for a prior year if the amendments are necessary to make the plan qualify. In general, retroactive plan amendments may be made up to the employer's tax filing date for the year in question, plus extensions. For example, if a corporate employer uses a calendar year, the tax filing date for the year 1991 is March 15, 1992, with possible extensions to September 15, 1992. Thus, an employer could install a qualified plan effective January 1, 1991, and could amend the plan retroactively to January 1, 1991, as late as September 15, 1992. The filing of a determination letter prior to this deadline extends the retroactive amendment procedure while the determination letter request is pending—this is another advantage of requesting an IRS determination letter.

Generally, the employer wishes to make the plan effective as early as possible to obtain the maximum tax deduction at the outset. This can present a problem if, upon filing the application for determination, the IRS finds the plan not qualified and retroactive amendments are unavailable or the employer does not wish to make the amendments the IRS suggests. The employer's prior contributions to the plan then might not be retrievable since the trust generally must be an irrevocable trust. To avoid this problem, the plan can be drafted making the plan's existence and the employer's contribution contingent on obtaining a determination letter.

The IRS provides various forms for purposes of making an application for determination. Some of these are described in the checklist (Table 26-1).

One final point should be made concerning IRS determination letters. Determination letters indicate that the IRS has approved the plan on the basis of the plan documents and the facts submitted to it. They are no guarantee that the plan qualifies and will continue to qualify if these facts are not accurate or if the facts change at a subsequent date. Therefore, the continuing qualification of the plan must always be a concern of the employer and its employee benefit advisers.

Master, Prototype and Pattern Plans

A qualified plan must be evidenced by a formal written document. Because of the many complex provisions that must be included, it is not unusual for such documents to run to 50 pages or more. If all of the plan language is custom designed, the drafting expense alone can be considerable.

Various methods have been devised to simplify plan drafting for smaller employers. One of the most common is the use of master and prototype plans offered by financial institutions and other types of plan advisers. A *prototype plan* is a standardized plan form, such as a prototype profit-sharing plan or a prototype money-purchase pension plan, usually offering some choice of provisions in the important features. For example, the plan might allow the employer to specify the contribution rate or choose the vesting schedule. A master plan is similar to a prototype plan, but the term *master plan* usually refers to a plan form designed by a financial organization and adopted only by employers that wish to use that financial organization for plan funding. The IRS also allows law firms to use *pattern* plans; these are plans using language that has been examined and approved by the IRS, thus allowing speedier IRS approval of plans to the extent they use the pattern language. Also, most qualified plan consultants use standardized plan language of one kind or another to a considerable extent to reduce drafting costs, even if they do not provide formal master, prototype or pattern plans.

PLAN ADMINISTRATION

Plan administration encompasses a host of clerical and managerial functions related to a plan, including record-keeping, receipt and disbursement of funds, claim administration and investments. The discussion of plan administration in this chapter will focus on specific obligations imposed by ERISA and the Internal Revenue Code affecting plan administration.

Many of the administrative requirements of the law involve penalties for noncompliance, so it is important to impose these duties on specific individuals or groups of individuals to limit the scope of this liability to a known group. Otherwise, persons involved with the plan might find themselves held responsible for actions over which they may think they have no control. This problem is greatest in the area of investment decisions; therefore, it is important to be as specific as possible in the plan and trust agreement as to who has responsibility for making investment decisions and how these persons are chosen.

Employee Benefit Plans Other than Qualified Plans

As discussed in Chapter 5, many of the requirements of ERISA apply to a broad range of employee benefit plans as well as to qualified plans. In general, all of the rules discussed in this section through the heading "Unrelated Business Income" apply to all employee benefit plans, with the exceptions noted in the next paragraph. The rules are discussed in detail here because they typically have a much greater impact on qualified plans than on other plans, particularly the fiduciary rules.

The following employee benefit plans (retirement and other) are exempt from the fiduciary and reporting and disclosure requirements of ERISA:

- Governmental plans.
- Church plans (unless they elect to be covered).
- Plans maintained solely to comply with workers' compensation, unemployment compensation or disability insurance laws.

In addition, through regulations issued by the Secretary of Labor, certain types of plans have been declared not to be employee welfare benefit plans and are thus exempt from the regulations of ERISA. Among these are:

- Compensation for work performed under other than normal circumstances, including overtime pay and shift, holiday or weekend premiums.

- Compensation for absences from work due to sickness, vacation, holidays, military duty, jury duty or sabbatical leave and training programs to the extent such compensation is paid out of the general assets of the employer.
- Group insurance programs under which (1) no contributions are made by the employer; (2) participation is completely voluntary for employees; (3) the sole function served by the employer, without endorsing the program, is to collect premiums through payroll deduction and remit the amount collected to the insurer; and (4) no consideration is paid to the employer in excess of reasonable compensation for administrative services actually performed. (Most of the mass-marketed plans described in Chapter 13 fall into this category.)

Plan Administrator

Any employee benefit plan subject to ERISA is required to name in the plan document a plan administrator. If none is named, the employer is assumed to be plan administrator. Some employers prefer to designate a plan committee to be the plan administrator. This committee is usually made up of a group of management and sometimes rank and file employees responsible for administering the plan. If this is done, the plan should spell out how committee members are to be named, so that there can be no doubt who has the responsibility of plan administrator. Many employers prefer to simply designate the employer as plan administrator, with administration duties delegated to specific employees, usually in the personnel department, in the same manner as other management functions are carried out. Where the plan is funded through an insurance contract, some administrative duties may be carried out by the insurance company for a fee; this is particularly likely for smaller employers where the amount of administrative work involved does not justify the employment of a qualified plan specialist. Often, plan administrators also rely on outside benefit consultants for assistance with various administrative duties.

Claims Procedure

One of the plan administrator's duties is to evaluate employee claims for benefits and to direct the trustee or other fund holder to make payments as appropriate. If the plan is properly drafted, there should be little ambiguity about whether a particular participant or beneficiary is entitled to a plan benefit. However, due to the complexity of many plan provisions, disputes sometimes arise.

Every plan must include a written procedure under which a claimant can appeal the denial of a plan benefit to the plan administrator. There are specific time limits, 60 to 120 days generally, within which the plan administrator must make a decision on the appeal. The purpose for the claims procedure requirement is to require plans to develop internal procedures for evaluating claims so that participants will not always be compelled to bring a lawsuit against the plan if a claim is denied. If a claim dispute cannot be satisfactorily resolved internally, however, claimants have the right to sue and many will do so.

Tax Withholding

Distributions from a qualified retirement plan are subject to federal income tax withholding in a manner similar to payments of wages or other compensation. However, a recipient can elect not to have tax withholding on the qualified plan distribution, without providing any reason. (This, of course, will not relieve the recipient of any obligation to pay whatever income taxes are due.) The payer of the plan distribution must notify the recipient of the right not to have taxes withheld.

The withholding requirement applies to both lump-sum distributions and periodic payments. The liability for withholding is imposed on the payer of the distribution, but the plan administrator will be held liable unless the plan administrator directs the payer to withhold the tax and provides the payer with the information necessary to make the withholding. If the payer is a different person from the plan administrator, a trustee for example, it is important that there is a clear understanding between the parties about the responsibilities for withholding.

Reporting and Disclosure

The reporting and disclosure provisions, enacted as part of ERISA in 1974, impose a variety of duties on employee benefit plans to report or disclose various plan information to the government and plan participants. The purpose of the reporting and disclosure provisions is to indirectly discourage various plan abuses on the theory that wrongdoers will be deterred by knowing that their wrongdoing may be exposed to public view. This approach to federal regulation is based on the success of the securities laws of the 1930s and is common in other areas of federal regulation. The statutory format in ERISA for reporting and disclosure is extremely complex and confusing, and many modifications of the original statutory procedure have since been made by regulation, although the underlying statutes remain the same.

The reporting and disclosure requirements currently consist of this series of reports, some annual and some not, that must be provided to the participant or filed with the government or both:

- *Summary Plan Description (SPD).* The SPD is a document intended to describe the plan to its participants in plain language. It must be furnished to participants whether they ask for it or not and must also be filed with the Department of Labor, in both cases within 120 days after the plan is established or 90 days after a new participant enters the plan. There is no government form for the SPD; it can be designed according to the employer's specifications. However, the contents of the SPD are specified in minute detail by Department of Labor regulations. These regulations require, among other things, clear identification of the plan sponsor and funding entities, the plan's eligibility requirements, any possibilities of losses or forfeiture of benefits, procedures for making claims for benefits under the plan and a prescribed statement of the participant's rights under the law.

  There is also a plain language requirement, and this can be extremely important in practice. If a participant or beneficiary claims a benefit and is disappointed to find that the benefit was not provided under the plan, it is quite likely that the disappointed claimant will find a lawyer who will look closely at the SPD for any ambiguities that might provide grounds for a lawsuit. Such lawsuits sometimes prove successful.

- *Annual Report (Form 5500 Series).* This form is the centerpiece of the reporting requirements. The form is filed only with the IRS, but is made available to both the IRS and the Department of Labor. The form includes detailed financial information about the plan, including a signed report by an independent, qualified public accountant, along with any separate financial statements forming the basis of the independent accountant's report. If a qualified plan is subject to the minimum funding requirements, a signed report by the plan's enrolled actuary must be included, along with a certified actuarial valuation.

  Plans covering fewer than 100 participants are subject to simpler reporting requirements designed to reduce the cost of compliance for these plans. These plans file a simplified Form 5500 C/R. There is also a Form 5500-EZ for plans with only one participant—typically a self-employed person. Other plans must file the full Form 5500 each year. To get a better idea of the scope of the reporting requirements, it is useful to obtain from the IRS copies of these forms and accompanying instructions and review them.

  Form 5500 also includes schedule SSA, a schedule identifying participants who have separated from service during the year with deferred vested benefits under the plan. It is provided by the IRS to the Social Security Administration so that at retirement any former participant may be notified of a deferred vested benefit from the plan.

- *Summary of Annual Report (SAR).* The plan administrator must provide participants and beneficiaries with an SAR within nine months after the end of the plan year. There is a prescribed format for the SAR, consisting of selected financial information derived from the Form 5500 series annual report plus a prescribed notice that additional information may be obtained from the plan administrator.

- *Report on Termination, Merger or Other Changes (Forms 5310 and 5310A).* The plan administrator of a plan covered under the PBGC plan termination insurance discussed later in this chapter must notify the PBGC in advance of the termination. The Code and ERISA also contain a number of other reporting requirements in the event of a plan termination, merger, split up, transfer of assets and various other similar events. These are generally reported on Form 5310.

- *Individual Benefit Statement.* On written request, the plan administrator must furnish an individual participant or beneficiary with a prescribed statement of his or her vested and unvested current plan benefits. This need not be furnished more than once a year. Some plan administrators provide these individual statements annually, even without a request from participants or beneficiaries.

The reporting requirements are enforced by various types of penalties, including criminal penalties for willful violations or false statements.

In addition to the specific forms that must be filed or distributed, the reporting and disclosure requirements include a variety of sunshine provisions that give government agencies and participants rights to inspect and copy various documents and records relevant to the plan and its operation. Also, in order to obtain an advance determination letter or other IRS ruling, the plan documents must usually be submitted to the IRS.

INVESTMENT ISSUES

Investment issues are among the most complex and significant issues relating to employee benefit plans, involving the fiduciary relationship of plan sponsors to participants and beneficiaries, as well as larger issues of public policy. In this section, some basic rules and some of the more frequently occurring investment issues are discussed.

Fiduciary Requirements of ERISA and the Internal Revenue Code

A relationship in which one person holds and administers money belonging to another is legally described as a *fiduciary* relationship. A funded employee benefit plan, therefore, involves fiduciary relationships—plan assets are held by a trustee or insurance company, under the direction of the employer, on behalf of plan participants and beneficiaries. The rules governing fiduciary relationships are generally a subject of state law; however, in the case of qualified plans and other employee benefit plans, federal law (primarily ERISA) has superimposed specific federal fiduciary requirements that supersede state law where applicable. The federal requirements are usually stricter than the superseded state law requirements. While these rules are applicable to most employee benefit plans, they have their greatest impact on qualified pension and profit-sharing plans because welfare-benefit plans are typically insured or unfunded, although the use of funded welfare-benefit plans is increasing.

The fiduciary requirements were not intended as a helpful guide for employers and trustees in administering qualified plans. They do not spell out the specific responsibilities of each person involved in designing and maintaining the plan. Rather, the rules are intended to spread a net of liability over various persons involved with the plan, aimed at maximizing the protection of participants and beneficiaries. Thus, there are not always simple rules explaining how employers, trustees and other persons should act with regard to qualified plans; rather, they must be aware of their fiduciary responsibilities and do their best to comply with them or avoid them.

The definition of fiduciary is broad enough to include the employer, the plan administrator and the trustee. It also includes a wide variety of other possible targets. However, the government has stated that an attorney, accountant, actuary or consultant who renders legal, accounting, actuarial or consulting services to the plan will not be considered a fiduciary solely as a result of performing those services. Also, labor regulations exclude broker/dealers, banks and reporting dealers from being treated as fiduciaries simply as a result of receiving and executing buy-sell instructions from the plan. Furthermore, a person giving investment advice will be considered a fiduciary only with respect to the assets covered by that investment advice.

Every plan must specify a *named fiduciary* in the plan document. The purpose of this requirement is not to limit liability to named persons, but rather to provide participants and the government with an easy target in case they decide to take legal action against the plan. Of course, other unnamed fiduciaries can also be included in the legal action.

The duties of fiduciaries specified in the law are primarily of an investment nature. According to ERISA Section 404, a fiduciary must:

- Discharge duties with respect to a plan solely in the interest of the participants and the beneficiaries.
- Act for the exclusive purpose of providing benefits to participants and their beneficiaries and defraying the reasonable expenses of administering the plan.
- Act with the care, skill, prudence and diligence under the prevailing circumstances that a prudent man acting in a like capacity and familiar with such matters would use in the conduct of an enterprise of a like character and with like aims.
- Diversify the investments of the plan to minimize the risk of large losses, unless under the circumstances it is clearly prudent not to do so.
- Follow the provisions of the documents and instruments governing the plan, unless inconsistent with ERISA provisions.

In interpreting the prudent-man requirement, labor regulations indicate that the fiduciary must, in making an investment, determine that the particular investment is reasonably designed as part of the plan's portfolio to further the purposes of the plan. The fiduciary must consider (1) the composition of the portfolio with regard to diversification, (2) the liquidity and current return of the portfolio relative to the anticipated cash flow requirements of the plan and (3) the projected return of the portfolio relative to the funding objectives of the plan.

A major exception to the diversification requirement applies to holdings of employer securities and employer real property. An eligible individual account plan (a profit-sharing, stock-bonus or employee stock ownership plan that specifically permits the holding of employer real property or qualifying employer securities) may hold such property in any amount, and may even hold such property as the exclusive assets of the plan. Other plans can hold such property only up to the extent of 10 percent of the fair market value of the plan assets. The purpose of this exception is, of course, to encourage the adoption of employer stock plans of the type discussed in Chapter 23. A qualifying employer security means employer stock or marketable debt obligations meeting the various requirements of ERISA Section 407. Employer real property is real property owned by the plan and leased to the employer, again under limitations set out in ERISA Section 407.

Fiduciaries can delegate fiduciary responsibilities and, therefore, avoid direct responsibility for performing the duty delegated. For example, the employer can delegate duties relating to the handling and investment of plan assets to a trustee, and investment management duties can be delegated to an appointed investment manager. The plan must provide a definite procedure for delegating these duties. The delegation of a fiduciary duty does not remove all fiduciary responsibility. A fiduciary will be liable for a breach of fiduciary responsibility of any other fiduciary under certain circumstances.

The broad scope of the fiduciary liabilities indicates that, in addition to careful delegation of fiduciary duties to well-chosen trustees and advisors, the employer should take care that its liability insurance coverage adequately covers any liabilities that might arise out of the fiduciary responsibility provisions. ERISA specifically prohibits a plan from excusing or exculpating any person from fiduciary liability, but individuals and employers are permitted to have appropriate insurance and employers can indemnify plan fiduciaries.

Prohibited Transactions

In addition to the general fiduciary requirements already described, both Code Section 4975 and ERISA Section 406 include a specific list of "don'ts" for employee benefit plans, including qualified plans. Under these rules, a *party-in-interest* is forbidden from any of the following, with a number of exceptions described later:

- Sale or exchange, or leasing, of any property between the plan and a party-in-interest;
- Lending of money or other extension of credit between the plan and a party-in-interest;
- Furnishing of goods, services or facilities between the plan and a party-in-interest;
- Transfer to, or use by or for the benefit of, a party-in-interest, of any assets of the plan; or
- Acquisition, on behalf of the plan, of any employer security or employer real property in excess of the limits described previously in this chapter.

A party-in-interest—the Code uses instead the term *disqualified person*—is defined very broadly, again in order to bring the largest possible number of persons into the net to provide the maximum protection for plan participants. A party-in-interest includes:

- Any fiduciary, counsel or employee of the plan.
- A person providing services to the plan.
- An employer, if any of its employees are covered by the plan.
- An employee organization, any of whose members are covered by the plan.
- An owner, direct or indirect, of a 50 percent or more interest in an employer or employee organization.
- Various individuals and organizations related to those on this list, under specific rules given in Code Section 4975 and ERISA Section 406.

Because of the breadth of the prohibited transaction rules, certain specific exclusions are provided in the law, and the IRS and Labor Department are also given the authority to waive the prohibited transaction rules in certain circumstances.

First, the specific statutory exemptions: Loans to participants or beneficiaries are permitted under the rules discussed in Chapter 24. A loan to an ESOP by a party-in-interest is also permitted under certain circumstances in order to permit the ESOP to function as described in Chapter 23. Similar provisions permit such a plan to acquire employer securities or real property without violating the prohibited transaction rules. Also, the plan is allowed to pay a reasonable fee for legal, accounting or other services performed by a party-in-interest. There are provisions permitting various financial services to the plan by a bank or insurance company that is a party-in-interest. Other provisions exempt normal benefit distributions from any possible conflict with the prohibited transaction rules.

In addition to the specific statutory exemptions, the Department of Labor has broad authority to grant an exemption to the prohibited transaction rules for a transaction or a class of transactions, after finding that the exemption is administratively feasible, in the interest of the plan and its participants and beneficiaries, and protective of their rights. There are specific administrative procedures for obtaining such exemptions. Pursuant to this authority, the Labor Department has granted, among others, a class exemption permitting the sale of life insurance policies by participants to the plan or by the plan to participants. Another exemption, PTE84–14, permits a wide variety of transactions by qualified plan asset managers (QPAMs), such as banks and insurance companies. Individual exemptions have been granted for a variety of transactions, usually involving a sale to the plan by a party-in-interest of property that represents a particularly favorable investment opportunity for the plan.

Penalties

A violation of the prohibited transaction rules can result in a two-step penalty under the Internal Revenue Code, with the initial penalty equal to 5 percent of the amount involved, and an additional 100 percent penalty if the transaction is not corrected within a certain period of time. A violation of the prohibited transaction rules can also result in penalties for breach of fiduciary liability.

Unrelated Business Income

The trust fund under a qualified plan and trust funds used in some other self-insured employee benefit plans, such as Section 501(c)(9) trusts, are given a broad exemption from federal income tax similar to that granted to a variety of other institutions and organizations, such as churches, schools and charities. However, such tax-exempt organizations are subject to federal income tax on *unrelated business taxable income* according to Code Sections 511–514. Unrelated business taxable income is income of a tax-exempt organization from a trade or business that is not related to the function that is the basis for the tax exemption. For example, if a charitable organization operates a full-time shoe store in a shopping center, the shoe store income would be taxable to the charity. However, the charity's tax exemption for its other income probably would not be jeopardized unless the effect of operating the shoe store was to shift the focus of the organization totally away from its exempt function.

The basic function of an employee benefit plan trust is to receive, invest and distribute plan funds to participants and beneficiaries. Thus, passive investment income of the plan trust is usually not unrelated business income unless the investment is debt-financed, as described in the next paragraph. Problems sometimes arise in distinguishing passive investments from activities that might be considered a trade or business. The law specifically exempts dividends, interest, annuities and royalties, as well as rents from real property and from personal property leased with real property. However, the wide variety of possible leasing arrangements indicates that each rental arrangement must be looked at on the basis of its own facts and circumstances. For example, a number of revenue rulings have held that investments in manufacturing or railroad equipment for leasing constituted an unrelated trade or business, even though these leasing arrangements are usually looked upon by investors as strictly investment activities. Another revenue ruling, however, allows a qualified plan trust to hold shares in a real estate investment trust without incurring unrelated business taxable income. In short, the possible impact of unrelated business taxable income is an additional factor that must be taken into account by the investment advisers of a benefit plan trust.

Code Section 514 specifies that income from *debt-financed property* is to be treated by a tax-exempt organization as unrelated business taxable income. However, there is an exception in Section 514(c)(9) for qualified plans holding certain real estate investments that typically are highly leveraged or debt-financed. Therefore, such investments may still be advantageous to a qualified plan, particularly if they provide long-term growth or other benefits.

Investment Policy

The policy baseline for the investment of qualified plan funds is set by the rules previously discussed—the exclusive-benefit rule, the prudent-expert rule, the diversification requirement, liquidity requirements, the plan document itself and the additional limitations imposed by the prohibited transaction and unrelated business income provisions. Within these constraints, however, a broad range of investment strategies is possible.

Growth-Oriented Strategies

Trustees governed by fiduciary rules aimed primarily at the preservation of principal generally do not follow aggressive, growth-oriented investment strategies, and pension trustees are no exception. However, qualified plan design offers a number of opportunities for incorporating growth-oriented investment strategies without running into fiduciary problems.

Defined-contribution plans can provide that part or all of each participant's account be put in a participant-directed account, with the participant then choosing the investment strategy and relieving the trustee of liability for that choice. Also, defined-contribution plan funds can be invested in pooled accounts of a bank or insurance company that offer participants choices of investment strategies—an equity fund, a fixed-income fund and so on.

For defined-benefit plans, there is no provision for participant direction of investment; however, as discussed in Chapter 22, defined-benefit plan funds can be invested in insurance company funds utilizing separate account funding, with a choice by the employer of investment strategies such as equity or fixed income. It is also possible to structure the trust agreement to allow the employer to recommend investments, and the employer can pursue a growth-oriented strategy. In such a case, of course, the employer is still responsible for the adequacy of the pension fund and is subject to full fiduciary liability for its investment recommendations. Finally, there is the possibility of designing a plan to invest primarily in employer securities, which can be viewed as a type of growth-oriented investment strategy.

Risk

Most of the ERISA investment rules can be seen as prescriptions for avoiding risk, particularly the risk of large losses; for example, the requirement for diversification of investments. Within the ERISA limits, however, the qualified plan investment manager, like any investor, must balance risk and return.

Social Effects

According to the Employee Benefit Research Institute,[1] at the end of 1989, private pension funds (trusted and insured) in the United States totaled about $1.8 trillion, with government-employee funds comprising an additional $950 billion. This is a sizable portion of the nation's capital. If there is any pattern to the investment strategies of qualified plan investment managers, such a pattern is likely to have an effect on the economy and on society. Because so much pension money is held and invested by large institutions such as banks and insurance companies, current pension investment policies largely reflect the views of these organizations. In general, such organizations will tend to invest in conventional ways that support the status quo. The question is often raised whether there is a role in pension investing for active attempts to support a particular social result not dictated merely by market conditions.

Existing legislation and other laws relating to qualified plan investments focus primarily on fiduciary aspects of the relationship between plan managers and participants; it does not address issues of social policy. That is, it encourages investment managers to invest so as to prevent direct losses to participants and beneficiaries, but it does not deal with possible indirect losses that may accrue to participants and beneficiaries as a result of trends in overall pension investment policy that may be contrary to the social and economic interests of plan participants.

Social Investing

In recent years, objections to prevailing pension investment policies have been raised, particularly on behalf of unionized employees in large manufacturing industries. Although these objections are not always clearly stated, four types of argu-

---
[1]*EBRI Databook on Employee Benefits.*

ments can be distinguished. First, it is stated that the usual pension investment policies contribute to the disinvestment in basic manufacturing industries that is now occurring, particularly in certain geographical areas such as the Midwest. This results in the loss of jobs for persons covered under the pension plans, with the attendant economic and social costs, and also in disinvestment in housing and other facilities in communities where plan participants live. Second, it is stated that pension investors can undercut the union movement by investing in nonunionized corporations. Third, pension investment policies allegedly can affect the welfare of workers adversely by investing in corporations that violate health, safety or nondiscrimination principles. Finally, some object to investing in certain corporations on moral or political grounds (not directly related to the interests of plan participants), such as environmental pollution, involvement in South Africa or weapons production. Although advocates of social investment for union pension funds sometimes make common cause with religious and academic groups who advocate social investment policies for church or university endowment funds, it is clear that on this issue the interests of unionized employees are quite distinct.

A decision by a pension investment manager to pursue a social investment strategy that attempts to avoid one or more of these objections raises a number of issues. The first relates to fiduciary responsibility. Does a social investment strategy result in a lower return on the fund? There are some studies indicating that an investment portfolio of "good guy" investments has a lower return. However, such studies usually choose the "good" investments using a broad range of criteria, so they do not indicate the effects of narrower targeting such as simply excluding nonunion employers. The "efficient markets" theory proposed by some economists would suggest that in the long run an investment strategy based on social investing should have no effect on investment return, so long as investments are sufficiently diversified and the market includes other investors who do not use the same social criteria.

Some social investment advocates suggest that even if the return is lower, the indirect social and economic benefits to plan participants are a compensating factor. However, under current fiduciary law, both state and federal, this argument probably could not protect an investment manager in the event of a lawsuit by a plan participant injured directly by a low return on the fund. Suggestions have been made in Congress to amend federal legislation to permit social investment of various types, but no such provision has yet been enacted. The Department of Labor is reportedly studying the issue, but no regulations or rulings in this area have been issued.

A second problem is, assuming a social investment strategy has been chosen, how does the investment manager evaluate possible investments to determine their compliance with the chosen social criteria? It is currently difficult to identify corporations that meet even such simple criteria as compliance with health and safety legislation. There are various social investment indices available, but these are generally inadequate as guidance in any specific program of social investing. Because of these difficulties, social investing usually involves additional administrative costs.

The pension investment community has generally reacted with some hostility to social investing, with most pension advisers taking the view that any considerations other than the traditional ones of risk and return have no part in pension investment decisions, and that it would be a violation of fiduciary responsibility to use other criteria.

PLAN TERMINATION

In order to be qualified, the regulations require that a plan be "permanent." By this is meant only that the employer must not have an *initial* intention of operating the plan for a few years to obtain tax benefits and then terminating it. Thus, despite the permanence requirement, qualified plans can be terminated and often are.

A plan can be terminated unilaterally by the employer, unless a collective bargaining agreement or other employment contract prohibits it. If an employer does not formally terminate a plan, but merely discontinues contributions to it, the IRS may find that the plan has been terminated, with the same consequences as if a formal termination had been made by the employer. It is also possible to have a *partial termination* of a plan, which usually means that the plan is terminated for an identifiable group of employees, such as employees at a given geographical location, while it is continued for other employees.

When Should a Plan Be Terminated?

If a qualified plan ceases to be an effective method of compensating employees, or becomes too expensive for the employer, it should be terminated. However, under the rules discussed in this chapter, a proposed termination may have such undesirable consequences that the employer will decide to continue the plan, possibly in amended form. As discussed below, the substitution of a different plan or plans may avoid some of the undesirable consequences of simply terminating the old plan.

Asset-Reversion Terminations

Defined-benefit plans are sometimes terminated not because they are too costly or ineffective, but because the employer wants to take out some of the plan's assets. If the plan is fully funded, excess plan assets will revert to the employer, if the plan so provides. The assets that revert are taxable income to the employer.

For some time, commentators have expressed concern that the applicable law in this area favors stripping of assets from qualified plans, with a possible detriment to the retirement security of employees. Congress initially responded to this concern by imposing a 10 percent tax on asset reversions, in addition to the income tax payable on the reversion amount. This tax was criticized as merely penalizing employers slightly without any direct benefit to employees. Consequently, the law was changed; the penalty is now set at 50 percent of the reversion amount unless (1) the employer adopts a replacement plan; (2) the employer provides pro rata increases in the benefits of participants in the terminated plan totaling at least 20 percent of the reversion, or (3) the employer is in bankruptcy. If any of these three conditions is met, the excise tax is 20 percent rather than 50 percent (Code Section 4980).

Consequences of Termination

If an employer terminates a plan within a few years after its inception, the employer must usually show that the termination resulted from *business necessity* or the IRS will infer that the permanence requirement for qualification never existed. The plan will thus be treated as a nonqualified deferred compensation arrangement, resulting in a loss of tax benefits for both employer and employees. If the plan is terminated after many years of operation, the IRS will not raise a presumption of impermanence so long as the plan is properly funded and termination does not result in prohibited discrimination.

Plan termination results in immediate 100 percent vesting for some or all employees. With a defined-benefit plan, 100 percent vesting means that the accrued benefits of affected participants become 100 percent vested at the time of termination, to the extent the plan is funded. Most defined-benefit plans are insured by the PBGC, and the further complications involved are discussed below. At termination, with a defined-contribution plan, participants become 100 percent vested in their account balances derived from employer contributions, regardless of where they stand otherwise on the vesting schedule. This precludes the possibility of any future forfeitures (and therefore, in a profit-sharing plan, any future reallocation of forfeitures). Obviously, the purpose of the vesting remedy is to limit the possibility of any discrimination resulting from termination of the plan.

THE PENSION BENEFIT GUARANTY CORPORATION AND ITS PLAN INSURANCE (PBGC)

If an employer encounters financial difficulty and is forced to terminate or curtail a qualified defined-benefit plan, the ultimate payment of plan benefits is often jeopardized. If the plan uses an insurance company contract as the funding medium, the employee's benefit is usually to some extent guaranteed by the insurance company. However, the use of trust funds predominates in defined-benefit plans, and these funds usually involve no insurance company guarantees. Actuarial funding methods assume that plans will be in existence indefinitely. As a result, the plan fund in many cases is, at a given moment, inadequate to fund all of the benefits accrued under the plan if the plan terminates at that moment.

Recognizing this problem, Congress established a scheme of mandatory plan insurance for certain defined-benefit plans as part of ERISA (Title 4) in 1974. The insurance is administered by a quasi-governmental corporation called the Pension Benefit Guaranty Corporation (PBGC). Defined-contribution plans do not involve the same benefit security problems as defined-benefit plans because the participant's accrued benefit is always equal to the participant's account balance. Therefore, the PBGC plan insurance scheme does not apply to defined-contribution ("individual account") plans.

Plans Covered

PBGC coverage can be summarized by stating that, in general, all qualified defined-benefit plans are covered, while individual account (defined-contribution) plans are not covered. With respect to defined-benefit plans, the usual exclusions applicable to ERISA provisions apply; there is no PBGC coverage for federal, state and local government plans; church plans (unless the plan elects coverage); plans with no employer contributions; plans for highly compensated individuals or substantial owners; plans frozen prior to ERISA; and various other exclusions.

Benefits Insured

The PBGC does not insure or guarantee all benefits provided under a qualified defined-benefit plan covered by PBGC insurance. A distinction is made between *basic* and *nonbasic* benefits. The PBGC is required under the terms of its federal charter to insure basic benefits. PBGC is allowed to extend coverage to nonbasic benefits, but it has not yet done so.

There are numerous conditions and limitations on what qualifies as a guaranteed basic benefit, set out in Part 2613 of the PBGC regulations. The most significant limitations are as follows:

- The benefit must be nonforfeitable or vested. This refers to vesting that existed under the terms of the plan immediately prior to plan termination, not to benefits that became vested solely on account of plan termination.
- The benefit must be a "pension benefit"—a benefit payable as an annuity to a retiring or terminating participant or surviving beneficiary, providing a substantially level retirement income to the recipient. Consequently, the PBGC generally does not insure a lump-sum benefit.
- There is a dollar limitation on the amount of monthly payment the PBGC will guarantee. Regardless of the plan provisions, the insured monthly benefit is limited to one-twelfth of the participant's average annual gross income from the employer during the highest paid five consecutive calendar years or lesser number of years of active participation. Furthermore, in no event will the insured benefit exceed a dollar limit, originally $750 monthly in 1974, which is subject to an indexation procedure. For plans terminated in 1991, the limit was $2,250 monthly. The dollar limitation applies to a benefit in the form of a straight-life annuity beginning at age 65 and payable monthly. The limit is adjusted actuarially for other forms of benefits.
- The participant must be "entitled" to the benefit as of the date of plan termination. Generally, this means that the recipient must have satisfied the conditions of the plan necessary to establish the right to receive the benefit (other than mere application for it or satisfying a waiting period) prior to the plan termination date. Also, the benefit must be payable to or for the benefit of a natural person (not, for example, a corporation).

PBGC Funding and Premiums

The PBGC has established several funds to provide benefit guarantees. It has the power to borrow up to $100 million from the U.S. Treasury if necessary. However, the PBGC is expected to be self-supporting and is therefore required to charge insurance premiums for its guarantees. For single employer plans, the annual premium for 1991 is $16 per participant. An additional annual premium of up to $34 per participant may be required, depending on the amount of the plan's unfunded vested benefits. Congress has the authority through a joint resolution procedure to review and change PBGC rates from time to time, based on various factors set out in the law. Payment of the premiums is mandatory, and is enforced by various penalties.

Plan Termination Procedures

Reportable Events

The PBGC becomes involved with a plan that is terminating or encountering various difficulties in somewhat complex ways. First of all, the plan administrator is obligated to report to the PBGC certain events that could potentially cause financial difficulty. There is a long list of these *reportable events*; some significant ones include:

- An IRS or Department of Labor disqualification of the plan.
- A plan amendment decreasing retirement benefits.
- A decrease in the number of active participants to less than 80 percent of the number at the beginning of the plan year or 75 percent of the number at the beginning of the previous plan year.
- A determination by the IRS that there has been a termination or partial termination of the plan.
- A failure to meet the minimum funding standards.
- An inability by the plan to pay benefits when due.
- Certain large distributions to a substantial owner.
- A plan merger, consolidation or transfer of its assets.
- The occurrence of another event indicative of a need to terminate the plan— the regulations refer to such items as insolvency of the employer or a related employer and certain breakups of commonly controlled groups of employers.

If the consequences of these reportable events are significant enough, the plan can be *involuntarily terminated* by the PBGC. Also, of course, a *voluntary termination* can be carried out by the plan administrator under one of the two procedures described below. In any event, the actual termination of a plan covered by PBGC guarantees is carried out under detailed procedures set out in the law.

Allocation of Plan Assets on Termination

The PBGC termination procedures revolve around the rules for allocation of the assets of a terminated defined-benefit plan under ERISA Section 4044. On termination, such plan assets must be allocated in descending order to the following categories:

- Benefits attributable to voluntary employee contributions.
- Benefits attributable to mandatory employee contributions.

- Annuity benefits attributable to employer contributions that were, or could have been, in "pay status" as of three years prior to termination. A benefit in "pay status" means a benefit being paid to a retired (nonactive) employee. The high priority reflects the fact that such employees are least able to protect themselves against a failure of the plan fund.
- All other PBGC guaranteed benefits.
- All other vested benefits.
- All other plan benefits.

Any amount remaining after these categories may revert to the employer, if the plan so provides.

Voluntary Plan Termination

ERISA Section 4041(a) provides for two types of voluntary termination procedures, the *standard termination* and the *distress termination*. A plan is eligible for the standard termination only if assets at the termination date are sufficient to provide for all *benefit commitments* as of the termination date. A benefit commitment to a participant or beneficiary means all benefits guaranteed by the PBGC as described earlier, but determined without certain limitations, such as the maximum dollar limit or the restriction on benefits in effect for less than 60 months before plan termination. Certain early retirement supplements and plant closing benefits also come within the definition of benefit commitments. If benefit commitments are not met, a voluntary termination must follow the distress termination procedures.

With a standard termination, the plan administrator must provide 60 days advance notice of intent to terminate to participants, beneficiaries and other affected parties.

The plan administrator must begin distributing plan assets at the end of the 60-day determination period if the PBGC has not issued a notice of noncompliance and if the plan assets are sufficient to meet benefit commitments. The assets are distributed in accordance with the priorities of ERISA Section 4044 described above. Assets must be distributed either through the purchase of annuities from an insurance company to provide plan benefits or in some other manner providing adequate benefit security.

A distress termination is available only if one of three distress criteria is met:

1. Each contributing sponsor of the plan or substantial member of a controlled group sponsoring the plan must be in a liquidation proceeding under federal bankruptcy law or similar state law; or
2. The sponsor must be involved in a reorganization in bankruptcy or an insolvency proceeding; or
3. The plan administrator demonstrates to the PBGC that unless the termination occurs, the sponsor will not be able to pay its debts and will be unable to continue in business, or the cost of providing benefits under the pension plan has become unreasonably burdensome (for example, because of a declining work force).

Upon a distress termination, the plan administrator must submit to the PBGC information similar to that required under a standard termination, plus information related to the distress criteria. If the PBGC determines that there are sufficient plan assets to fulfill benefit commitments, the plan administrator may begin to distribute the assets in accordance with ERISA Section 4044. If the PBGC determines that the plan is sufficient only to provide guaranteed benefits, the plan administrator may distribute plan assets and terminate the plan, but the PBGC will establish a separate trust under ERISA Section 4049 for the terminating plan to pay non-guaranteed benefits. If the PBGC determines that plan assets are not sufficient even for guaranteed benefits, the PBGC will proceed to terminate the plan in accordance with the procedures for involuntary terminations, and also must establish a separate Section 4049 trust for any benefit commitments under the plan that are not guaranteed.

A Section 4049 trust, as indicated above, is established by the PBGC whenever additional benefit commitments are unfunded under a terminating plan. As long as the employer remains in business, it continues to be obligated to fund these benefit commitments, and the trust is used to receive payments from the employer and to distribute benefits to plan participants and beneficiaries accordingly. The trust continues as long as is necessary to pay all benefit commitments.

Contingent Liability of Employer

In the event of a plan termination covered by PBGC insurance, the employer must reimburse the PBGC for the PBGC's liability for guaranteed benefits in excess of the plan's assets. However, the employer liability to reimburse in full is limited to 30 percent of the "net worth" of the employer. Above the 30 percent limit, the employer need reimburse only 75 percent of the liability. Net worth is determined as of a date chosen by the PBGC which is not more than 120 days prior to the date of termination. This remedy has proven to be of somewhat limited value, particularly in the case of large bankrupt employers where the PBGC's liability is the greatest, since a bankrupt company has no net worth.

Multiemployer Plans

The previous discussion of termination procedures applies primarily to single employer plans or plans of controlled groups of employers. The termination problems are somewhat different where contributions to the plan are made by a number of unrelated employers—that is, a multiemployer plan such as a plan adopted under industry-wide collective bargaining agreements. For such plans, there are different asset allocation provisions and somewhat different provisions for involuntary termination by the PBGC.

The most significant difference from single employer plans involves the *withdrawal liability* of an employer that completely or partially withdraws from a multiemployer plan. A sale of the employer's assets in an arms-length transaction will not be treated as a withdrawal as long as the purchaser of the business continues the plan, the purchaser provides an acceptable surety bond or escrow deposit for five years after the sale and the seller of the business remains secondarily liable for five years. If an employer withdraws from the plan, the employer's withdrawal liability is an amount based on the withdrawing employer's share of unfunded vested benefits under the plan. The withdrawing employer must pay all or a substantial portion of the withdrawal liability to the plan on a periodic basis over a number of years. The law provides for the PBGC to establish a supplemental fund to reimburse multiemployer plans for any uncollectible employer withdrawal liabilities.

STUDY QUESTIONS

1. What are the steps necessary for an employer to adopt a qualified plan for a given year?
2. a. Why is it desirable to obtain an advance determination letter for a qualified plan?
   b. What recourse might be available to an employer if the IRS finds a plan is not qualified?
3. What types of employee benefit plans are exempt from the fiduciary, reporting and disclosure requirements of ERISA?
4. a. What is the purpose of the reporting and disclosure provisions of ERISA?
   b. Briefly describe the reports ERISA requires qualified plans to provide to participants or to the federal government.
5. What objectives were the fiduciary requirements of ERISA enacted to accomplish?
6. What are the investment responsibilities of a fiduciary under ERISA?
7. Explain why each of the following is, or is not, a prohibited transaction.
   a. The sale of real estate owned by the ABC Plan to the wife of the treasurer of the ABC Company.
   b. Loaning money from the plan to an officer of the corporation. The plan contains a loan provision that permits loans on a nondiscriminatory basis.
   c. The acquisition of 25 percent of employer stock by a defined-benefit plan.
   d. The acquisition of real estate from the plan for less than its market value by the plan's trustee.
8. What is unrelated business taxable income and what is the effect of having it?
9. The Faulty Corporation installed a pension plan five years ago and because of declining profits, the firm is considering terminating the plan to help prevent insolvency.
   a. What will be the IRS's likely reaction to this termination? Explain.
   b. What alternatives are available to the corporation other than terminating the plan?
10. What qualified plan benefits are insured by the Pension Benefit Guaranty Corporation?

27

Individual Retirement Plans, Simplified Employee Pensions and Section 403(b) Plans

Objectives

- Describe individual retirement plans with respect to
  1. Eligibility.
  2. Deduction limit.
  3. Spousal IRAs.
  4. Nondeductible IRAs.
  5. Timing of contributions.
  6. Distributions.
  7. Funding.
- Explain the rollover rules.
- Describe simplified employee pensions (SEPs) with regard to
  1. Eligibility and coverage.
  2. Contributions and deductions.
  3. Salary reduction SEPs (SARSEPs).
- Describe the types of employers and employees who may benefit through Section 403(b) plans and describe such plans with respect to
  1. Coverage and participation tests.
  2. The annual exclusion allowance.
  3. Salary reduction plans.
  4. Catch-up alternatives.
  5. Investments.
  6. Distributions and loans.
  7. Taxation.

Certain tax-favored arrangements that are not technically qualified plans can offer employees the same tax deferral advantages as the qualified plans discussed in previous chapters. These nonqualified but tax-favored arrangements are individual retirement accounts, simplified employee pensions and Section 403(b) tax-deferred annuity plans. Where these plans are available, they can be a useful supplement or alternative to a qualified plan adopted by an employer.

INDIVIDUAL RETIREMENT PLANS

Complete retirement planning, at least from the employee's viewpoint, requires consideration of individual retirement accounts or annuities (IRAs), which allow individuals to adopt a plan that provides tax deferral benefits somewhat similar to those available from an employer plan. The role of IRAs is a limited one, however. Individuals who are participants in qualified plans and whose income exceeds specified limits are limited or excluded altogether from eligibility for IRA deductions. And no employee can contribute more than $2,000 annually to an IRA (or $2,250 including a spousal IRA).

IRAs can be used by employers as part of their employee plan design, either through simply sponsoring an IRA plan or adopting an arrangement known as a *simplified employee pension* (SEP), under which employer contributions or employee salary reductions are made systematically to employees' IRAs. SEPs permit a contribution level similar to that for a qualified plan and are viewed as an alternative to a qualified plan.

Eligibility for IRAs

In order to be eligible for an IRA, an employee or self-employed person must have compensation or earned income.[1] Compensation or earned income means income received from services actually performed by the individual. This includes compensation from self-employment as well as from an employer. The definition has been extended to also include taxable alimony received by a divorced spouse. It does not include investment income, any amount received as a pension or annuity or any amount received as deferred compensation.

Deduction Limit

The annual IRA deduction limit for an individual is the lesser of $2,000 or the individual's earned income.

Deductible IRA contributions are restricted to:

- Individuals who are not active participants in an employer-maintained retirement plan for any part of the retirement plan year ending with or within the individual's taxable year.

---

[1]Most of the IRA rules are found in Code Sections 219 and 408 and related regulations; these references will not be repeated in this chapter.

• Any other individual, as long as the individual (or married couple if a joint return is filed) has adjusted gross income below a specified limit. If the adjusted gross income exceeds this limit, the $2,000 IRA limit is reduced under a formula that eventually permits no deduction.

The *active participant* restriction applies if the individual (or if a joint return is filed, either the individual or spouse) is an active participant in

• A regular qualified plan.
• A Section 403(b) tax-deferred annuity plan.
• A simplified employee pension (SEP).
• A federal, state or local government plan, not including a Section 457 non-qualified deferred-compensation plan.

Active plan participants can make deductible IRA contributions only if their income falls within certain income limits, as shown below:

IRA Deduction/Compensation Limits *(taxpayer or spouse active plan participant)*			
	Full IRA Deduction	Reduced IRA Deduction	No IRA Deduction
Individual	$25,000 or less	$25,000–$35,000	$35,000 or over
Married couple, joint return	$40,000 or less	$40,000–$50,000	$50,000 or over
Married, filing separately	not available	$0–$10,000	$10,000 or over

The reduction in the IRA deduction for those affected is computed by multiplying the IRA limit ($2,000 or 100 percent of compensation) by a fraction equal to

$$\frac{\text{Taxpayer's adjusted gross income} - \text{full deduction limit}}{\$10,000}$$

There is a $200 floor under this equation—if the result comes out to less than $200, the taxpayer can contribute and deduct $200.

> **EXAMPLE:** A married couple, one of whom is an active participant in a regular qualified plan, files a joint return and has an adjusted gross income of $43,000.

$$\frac{\$\,3,000}{\$10,000} \times \$2,000 = \$600$$

$$\$2,000 - \$600 = \$1,400 \text{ IRA deduction limit}$$

> **EXAMPLE:** A single person, an active participant in a qualified plan, has an adjusted gross income of $34,500.

$$\frac{\$\,9,500}{\$10,000} \times \$2,000 = \$1,900$$

$$\$2,000 - \$1,900 = \$100$$

However, the individual may contribute $200, the floor amount.

Spousal IRAs

If an individual has a spouse who has no compensation or earned income, the working individual may also set up an IRA for the spouse. In that case, the total contribution to both IRAs is the lesser of $2,250 or 100 percent of compensation or earned income. If the working spouse is an active participant in an employer retirement plan, the $2,250 is reduced in the same manner as described above, and is thus phased out for joint adjusted gross incomes of $50,000 or more.

A spouse with earned income can elect to be treated as having no earned income in order to use the spousal IRA provision; this is useful if the earned income is small (e.g., $250 or less). If both spouses have compensation or earned income, however, it generally is beneficial for each to set up his or her own IRA, within the available deduction restrictions.

Nondeductible IRAs

Individuals not permitted to make deductible IRA contributions may, nevertheless, make such contributions on a nondeductible basis, up to the usual $2,000/100 percent/$2,250 limit. Nondeductible contributions (but not income on those contributions) are tax free when ultimately distributed to the individual. If nondeductible contributions to an IRA are made, any amounts withdrawn are treated as partly tax free and partly taxable under rules similar to the exclusion ratio calculation for annuities under Code Section 72.

The law allows individuals to designate deductible contributions as nondeductible contributions in order to be able to receive distributions tax free. This might be a useful technique in a year in which taxable income has been reduced to zero through other deductions or losses.

Other Restrictions

Since the IRA is designed primarily for retirement savings, no IRA deduction is allowed to an individual for the taxable year in which the individual attains age 70½ or any later year.

Contributions to an IRA must be made in cash; contributions of property such as an insurance policy are not permitted.

Excess Contributions

A contribution in excess of the deductible limits described above is an *excess contribution* subject to an annual nondeductible 6 percent excise tax (Code Section 4973). The excise tax continues to be applied each year until the contribution is withdrawn from the IRA. Many complex rules apply to excess contributions; their complexity seems out of proportion to the actual issue involved.

Timing of Contributions

An IRA for any given year may be established up to the time for filing the tax return for the given year, not including extensions. Deductible contributions for a given year may be made within the same time limit. This "last minute" feature of IRAs helps to explain a lot of their popularity. For example, suppose Frank Filer works out a draft of his 1991 tax return on April 1, 1992, and discovers that he owes the government $600. His local savings bank is running an advertising campaign touting its IRAs and offering to lend money to contribute to an IRA. Frank does some quick figuring and discovers that if he borrows $2,000 from the bank and contributes it to an IRA, it will wipe out his tax liability and he will be entitled to a $160 tax refund, enough to make the first monthly payment on the loan. This may be a more attractive deal to Frank than borrowing $600 to pay taxes.

Limitations on IRA Distributions

In order to limit any benefits for nonretirement distributions from IRAs, there is a penalty under Code Section 72(t) for certain early IRA distributions similar to the early distribution penalty applicable to qualified plans. The IRA early distribution penalty is 10% of the taxable amount of any distribution except for:

- Distributions made on or after attainment of age 59½.
- Distributions made to a beneficiary or employee's estate on or after the employee's death.
- Distributions attributable to disability.
- Distributions that are part of a series of substantially equal periodic payments made at least annually over the life or life expectancy of the participant, or the joint lives or life expectancies of the participant and beneficiary.

Loans from IRAs are treated as distributions and, therefore, are not available for practical purposes. This is another aspect of IRAs that makes them less flexible than regular qualified plans, which allow loans.

There is an *upper limit* on the length of time amounts may be maintained in an IRA. Distributions from an IRA must begin no later than April 1 of the year following the year in which the individual attains age 70½. The distribution may be in the form of a lump sum or periodic payments. The minimum annual distribution is a periodic payment determined on the basis of a period not extending beyond the life expectancy of the individual or the joint life expectancy of the individual and a designated beneficiary. If an individual or beneficiary dies before the entire interest is distributed, the remaining amount must, within five years after the death, be distributed or applied to the purchase of an immediate life annuity for the beneficiary for a term not exceeding the life expectancy of the beneficiary. In general, these rules are the same as the rules under Section 401(a)(9) for distributions from qualified plans, discussed in Chapter 24.

If the assets of the IRA are not distributed at least as rapidly as described above, there is an excise tax of 50 percent of the *excess accumulation* (Code Section 4974). The excess accumulation is the amount by which the minimum amount required to be distributed during a given year (under the above rules) exceeds the amount actually distributed during the year. The IRS is allowed to waive the 50 percent penalty in order to avoid penalizing reasonable errors.

Taxation of Distributions

The amount distributed from an IRA is taxable as ordinary income in the year of receipt. Lump-sum distributions are taxable when received and do not qualify for the special capital-gain or averaging provisions applicable to lump-sum distributions from qualified plans. An IRA annuity is taxed under the Section 72 annuity rules—payments based on deductible contributions and all investment earnings are ordinary income and are taxable in full as received. Nondeductible IRA contributions, if any, are recovered tax free through an exclusion ratio applied to each payment.

The value of an annuity or lump sum received by any beneficiary of a participant in an IRA is included in the deceased participant's gross estate for federal estate tax purposes. However, if the beneficiary is a spouse, there is no estate tax because of the unlimited marital deduction under the estate tax. Even for a non-spouse beneficiary, there may be no estate tax if the estate is relatively small—less than about $600,000.

Funding of IRAs

The code provides for two types of IRAs: individual retirement accounts and individual retirement annuities.

Individual Retirement Accounts

An individual retirement account must be a plan established under a written trust created or organized in the United States for the exclusive benefit of the individual creating the IRA. A written custodial agreement can also be used. The written instrument must include the following provisions:

- The contributions must be in cash and not exceed $2,000 on behalf of any individual.
- The trustee must be a bank or "other person" approved by the IRS.
- No part of the trust fund will be invested in life insurance contracts. Annuities, however, can be purchased.
- An individual's account is nonforfeitable.
- The assets of the trust will not be commingled with other property except in a common trust fund or common investment fund.
- The individual's account must be distributed in accordance with certain distribution requirements, such as the age 70½ provision and the minimum distribution requirement.

Many banks and other savings institutions are actively marketing trusteed IRAs. Brokerage houses and mutual funds also market trusteed IRAs. These technically use a bank as trustee but the bank's role is purely formal and the investor views the broker or fund as the sponsor of the IRA.

A bank or institution acting as trustee or custodian may prepare its own prototype trust agreement and submit the agreement to the IRS for approval on Form 5306. Alternatively, the IRS has issued prototype trust and custodial agreements (Forms 5305 and 5305A) which, if used, are automatically qualified. An individual who deposits funds in an IRA that uses an approved form of trust agreement does not have to submit the IRA to the IRS for approval.

Individual Retirement Annuities

An individual may fund an IRA by purchasing an *individual retirement annuity.* An individual retirement annuity is a contract that is issued by an insurance company and that meets requirements parallel to those listed above for individual retirement accounts. The premium for the annuity may not be fixed, so the only insurance product that can be used is a flexible premium annuity. Both fixed-dollar and variable annuities can be used.

Insurance companies that wish to market individual retirement annuities may apply for IRS approval of their own prototype contracts. As with trusteed plans, an individual who purchases an approved prototype individual retirement annuity contract does not apply separately for IRS approval of the individual IRA plan.

Retirement Bonds

To facilitate the use of IRAs, the federal government issued a special series of bonds designed specifically for funding IRAs. These bonds contain a number of restrictions similar in purpose to those described earlier for individual retirement accounts and annuities. The bonds made no significant impact on the IRA market and sales were suspended in 1982.

Rollovers

In order to increase the amount of investment flexibility available to participants in IRAs and qualified plans, the Code contains a number of provisions relating to the use of IRAs as vehicles for investment *rollovers.* Three types of tax-favored rollovers are possible.

Rollover from One IRA to Another

There is no current taxation if an individual withdraws an amount out of an IRA trust fund, IRA annuity or retirement bond plan and invests part or all of it in another IRA plan. In order to receive this treatment, the amount to be rolled over must be paid into another IRA plan not later than the sixtieth day after the withdrawal. If such a rollover is made, no additional tax-free rollover of this type is permitted for a period of one year thereafter.

A direct transfer of an account from one IRA trustee to another (with the participant never receiving the money) is not treated as a rollover for purposes of these rules. Thus, a direct transfer can be used as a way of avoiding the one-year rule.

Rollover of Distribution from Qualified Plan or Annuity

An IRA may be used as a vehicle for receiving the proceeds of a distribution from a qualified plan or a Section 403(b) plan, thereby avoiding immediate taxation on the distribution. The distribution from the qualified plan or Section 403(b) plan must be at least 50 percent of the employee's account balance in the plan to be eligible for rollover. All or any portion of the amount received can be rolled over. The 100 percent/$2,000 limit does not apply to a rollover contribution. The rollover contribution must be made on or before the sixtieth day after receipt of the distribution. An existing IRA can be used, or a new one may be set up.

The part of the distribution that is rolled over into the IRA will not be currently taxable to the recipient. The usual rules for taxation of IRA distributions will apply when this amount is subsequently withdrawn. Any part of the distribution from the qualified plan or Section 403(b) plan that is not rolled over into the IRA will be taxable at the time of receipt under the usual rules for taxation of distributions, except that the capital-gain and averaging provisions may not be used.

In deciding whether or not to roll over all or part of the proceeds of a distribution from a qualified plan to an IRA, the alternatives must be considered. A lump-sum distribution from a qualified plan may qualify for the special capital-gain and averaging provisions of the Code. Thus, even though a distribution that is not rolled over is taxable immediately, it is taxable under advantageous provisions, if it qualifies as a lump-sum distribution. A distribution that is rolled over will not be taxed immediately; taxation will be deferred to the time when it is withdrawn from the IRA. However, this subsequent distribution, like any IRA distribution, is not eligible for the capital-gain or averaging provisions; rather, the taxable amount is taxed as ordinary income. Furthermore, the $5,000 income tax exclusion for employee death benefits is not available for a distribution from an IRA.

Despite the possible loss of averaging, however, the mere deferral of taxes resulting from a rollover may be advantageous. Furthermore, taxes on investment earnings of the IRA are also deferred until the rollover amount is distributed. Although it is somewhat complex, the tax consequences of the two alternatives can be calculated (under appropriate assumptions) and compared; some financial planners provide such advice to their clients. Computer software for this purpose is now widely available.

Some tax planners have devised methods of obtaining tax deferral and rollover results in general without using an IRA with all its restrictions. For example, if the plan administrator is willing to cooperate, the plan distribution can be made in the form of a nontransferable deferred annuity instead of cash. This will not result in tax to the recipient until annuity proceeds are withdrawn, just as with an IRA. In most of these situations, if there is deferral of the distribution, the averaging and capital-gain treatment is lost, just as with an IRA rollover. Also, careful planning is necessary to obtain the proper tax result.

IRA as Conduit for Transfer from One Plan to Another

Finally, an IRA may be used as a conduit to carry out a tax-free transfer of cash or property from one corporate qualified plan to another. Basically, if the amount received from the qualified plan is transferred within 60 days to an IRA, the transfer is tax free as described earlier. In addition, if the IRA plan contains no assets other than those attributable to the distribution from the qualified plan, then the amount in the IRA may subsequently be transferred tax free to another qualified plan if the transfer is made within 60 days after the property is received. Similar provisions allow an IRA to be used as a conduit between two Section 403(b) annuity plans.

An alternative procedure known as a *trustee-to-trustee transfer* may be a better way to accomplish the same result as a conduit IRA. This procedure has been approved by the IRS and is often used by smaller employers to close out a superseded plan. For example, suppose Dr. Messer has practiced medicine as a sole practitioner for a number of years and has a qualified ("Keogh") plan. In 1987, he agrees to form a professional corporation with Dr. Couteau. The new company will have a qualified plan. Dr. Messer's account in the old plan may be transferred directly from the trustee of the Messer plan to the trustee of the Messer/Couteau plan without adverse tax consequences. It is important to observe the formalities carefully in a procedure like this, or the IRS might claim that a taxable distribution took place.

Employer-Sponsored IRAs

Although the IRA is viewed primarily as a device for facilitating individual retirement savings, an employer may sponsor an IRA for some or all employees. A labor union may also sponsor an IRA plan for its members. There is no requirement that employer-sponsored IRAs be available to all employees or be nondiscriminatory in coverage.

The contributions to the employer-sponsored IRA may be made as additional compensation or as a salary reduction. Any amount contributed by the employer to the IRA is taxable to the employee as additional compensation income. The employee is then eligible for the IRA tax deduction up to the 100 percent/$2,000 limitation. Since the amounts contributed are additional compensation, they are subject to FICA and FUTA taxes, therefore adding to employer costs. No federal income tax withholding is required if the employer believes that the employee will be entitled to the offsetting IRA tax deduction.

SIMPLIFIED EMPLOYEE PENSIONS

The simplified employee pension (SEP) is an expanded version of the employer-sponsored IRA, designed by Congress to make it easy and attractive for employers to adopt a retirement plan which, although not a qualified plan as such, has similar features. A SEP is designed much like an employer-sponsored IRA, but the deduction limits are much higher—instead of a $2,000 annual deduction limit, the limit on deductible contributions for each employee is the lesser of $30,000 or 15 percent of the employee's compensation. The price for this expanded deduction limit is that the employer loses discretion as to who must be covered; there is a coverage requirement that in some ways is more stringent than that for regular qualified plans.

Eligibility and Coverage

If the employer has a SEP plan, it must cover all employees who are at least 21 years of age and who have worked for the employer during three out of the preceding five calendar years. Part-time employment counts in determining this; there is no 1,000-hour definition of a year of service. However, contributions need not be made on behalf of employees whose compensation for the calendar year was less than $300 (as indexed for inflation). The plan can exclude employees who are members of collective bargaining units if retirement benefits have been the subject of good-faith bargaining, and it can also exclude nonresident aliens. Employer contributions to a SEP can be made for employees over age 70½; these employees are not eligible for regular IRAs, as discussed earlier.

Contributions and Deductions

An employer need not contribute any particular amount to a SEP in a given year or even make any contribution at all. In this respect, a SEP is more flexible than any type of qualified plan, even a profit-sharing plan, which requires substantial and recurring employer contributions. However, any employer contribution that is made must be allocated to employees under a definite written formula. The formula may not discriminate in favor of highly compensated employees. In general, the formula must provide allocations as a uniform percentage of total compensation of each employee, taking only the first $200,000 (as indexed for inflation) of compensation into account. The SEP allocation formula can be integrated with social security under the usual integration rules for qualified defined-contribution plans.

Each individual in a SEP maintains an IRA and employer contributions to the SEP are channeled to each employee's IRA. For tax purposes, the employer contributions are treated as if they are paid to the employee in cash and included in income and then contributed to the IRA. The Code provides a deduction to both the employer and to the employee for these amounts.

If the employer maintaining a SEP also has a regular qualified plan, contributions to the SEP may reduce the amount that can be deducted for contributions to the regular plan.

Salary Reduction SEPs

A salary reduction SEP, sometimes referred to as a SARSEP, can be used as an alternative to a 401(k) plan for smaller employers (but not by state or local government employers). If the employer has 25 employees or less during the preceding year, salary-reduction SEPs are permitted. Employees may elect to receive cash or have amounts contributed to the SEP. The $7,000 (indexed) limit for 401(k) plans also applies in this case to the total of the salary-reduction SEP and 401(k) salary reductions, if any.

In order to utilize the salary-reduction SEP alternative, not less than 50 percent of the employees must elect to make contributions to the SEP. Also an average deferral percentage rule similar to the 401(k) rules must be satisfied. The annual deferral percentage for each highly compensated employee who participates must be no more than 1.25 times the average deferral percentage for the year of non-highly compensated employees. For example, if nonhighly compensated employees elect salary reductions of 6 percent of compensation, no highly compensated employee can elect more than a 7.5 percent salary reduction.

Other Requirements

Except for the contribution, allocation and deduction provisions, the IRAs maintained as part of a SEP are the same as other IRAs and the rules discussed in the previous section apply to them as well. For example, the rules for taxation of distributions from SEP–IRAs are the same as those for other IRAs. As with regular IRAs, loans to participants from SEP–IRAs are not permitted.

Labor and IRS regulations contain certain reporting and disclosure provisions for SEPs. These are simplified if the employer uses the IRS prototype SEP contained on Form 5305–SEP. This form was designed to simplify the adoption of SEPs by employers; however, it uses a nonintegrated formula.

When Should an Employer Use a SEP?

The term *simplified* in the name of these plans is somewhat misleading; a SEP is not really much simpler than a regular qualified profit-sharing plan, especially where a qualified master or prototype plan is used. However, installation costs are minimal where the government Form 5305–SEP is used; administration costs are low since the annual report form (5500 series) need not be filed. Thus, SEPs are attractive for cases where administrative costs must be absolutely minimized, such as a one-person plan. In other specific situations, the special coverage rules for SEPs may be more attractive than the regular coverage rules. From an employee viewpoint, the complete portability of the SEP benefit is attractive.

SECTION 403(b) TAX-DEFERRED ANNUITY PLANS

Some years ago, Congress was concerned by the possibility that employees of tax-exempt organizations might not have adequate qualified plan coverage. Tax-exempt employers may have relatively little money available for employee benefits and the tax deductibility of a qualified plan does not act as an incentive since the tax-exempt employer pays no federal income taxes. As a result, Congress enacted Code Section 403(b) which, within limits, allows employees of certain tax-exempt organizations to have money set aside for them by salary reductions or direct employer contributions in a tax-deferred plan somewhat similar to a qualified plan.

Section 403(b) plans are an important consideration in designing the benefit program for any tax-exempt employer. However, today many tax-exempt employers have regular qualified plans for their employees, with the Section 403(b) plan being made available as a supplemental retirement or savings program. In particular, tax-exempt and governmental employers are not permitted to adopt a Section 401(k) plan, so a 403(b) plan is clearly an alternative to a 401(k) plan in such cases.

Section 403(b) plans are sometimes referred to as tax-deferred annuity (TDA) plans or tax-sheltered annuities, but because these terms also can refer to annuities not covered under Section 403(b), the term *Section 403(b) plans* will be used here to avoid confusion.

Eligible Employers

Employees of two types of organizations are eligible for Section 403(b) plans. These employer organizations are:

1. A tax-exempt employer described in Code Section 501(c)(3)—an employer "organized and operated exclusively for religious, charitable, scientific, testing for public safety, literary or educational purposes, or to foster national or international amateur sport competition . . . or for the prevention of cruelty to children or animals." Section 501(c)(3) also requires that the organization benefit the public rather than a private shareholder or individual and that the organization refrain from political campaigning or propaganda to influence legislation.

2. An educational organization with a regular faculty and curriculum and a resident student body that is operated by a state or municipal agency—in other words, a public school or college.

Thus, Section 403(b) plans are available to a wide range of familiar nonprofit institutions such as churches, private and public schools and colleges, hospitals and charitable organizations.

To participate in a Section 403(b) plan of an eligible employer, the participant must be a full- or part-time employee. This is significant because tax-exempt organizations often have ties with persons who are independent contractors rather than employees. For example, many physicians on a hospital staff are not technically employees, but rather independent contractors. A person is an employee when the employer exercises control or has the right to control the person's activities as to what is done and when, where and how it is done. The question of employee status also affects federal income tax withholding, employment taxes (social security and federal unemployment) and participation in other fringe benefit plans of the employer. If the employer wishes to cover a person under a Section 403(b) plan, it must at least treat that person consistently as an employee for all these purposes.

To be eligible for a Section 403(b) plan, a public school employee must perform services related directly to the educational mission. The employee can be a clerical or custodial employee, as well as a teacher or principal; a political officeholder is eligible only if the person has educational training or experience.

Coverage and Participation Tests

Section 403(b) plans, to which the employer makes contributions, are subject to the minimum coverage requirements of Section 410(b). These are the same coverage tests applicable to qualified plans—the percentage ratio test and the average benefit test. Under prior law, no coverage tests were applicable to Section 403(b) plans, and employers could cover even a single highly compensated employee.

A Section 403(b) plan is covered under the age and service provisions of ERISA Section 202, which are the same as the analogous age and service code provisions for qualified plans. Thus, if a Section 403(b) plan uses age or service eligibility, these can be no greater than age 21 and one year of service. However, age and service requirements are rarely used in Section 403(b) plans.

The Annual Exclusion Allowance

An employer may contribute annually to a participant's account in a Section 403(b) plan up to that participant's *exclusion allowance* for the year. As in a qualified defined-contribution plan, contributions may not discriminate in favor of highly compensated employees. A contribution equal to a uniform percentage of annual compensation up to $200,000 would be nondiscriminatory, for example. All amounts contributed to the plan must be immediately 100 percent vested.

The formula for the annual exclusion allowance for an employee is:

- 20 percent of the participant's *includable compensation* (taxable compensation) from the employer multiplied by
- The employee's total years of service for the employer, minus
- Amounts contributed to the plan in prior years that were excluded from the employee's income.

The third item—the amount subtracted from the 20 percent times years of service amount—must include contributions by the employer to regular qualified plans on behalf of the employee. If the qualified plan is a defined-benefit plan, the amount deemed to be contributed for the employee is to be determined under recognized actuarial principles or under a formula provided in the regulations.

The determination of the exclusion allowance for higher income employees is complicated by the fact that although a Section 403(b) plan is not a qualified plan, the Section 415 limitation for defined-contribution plans applies. Thus, the annual addition to any participant's account cannot exceed the lesser of 25 percent of compensation or $30,000, even if the exclusion allowance would produce a higher figure.

> Doctor Staph is an employee of the Tibia Hospital and has annual compensation of $200,000 this year. She has four prior years of service for Tibia Hospital, during which the hospital has contributed $5,000 to her account in a Section 403(b) plan. No amounts have been contributed to any qualified plan on her behalf. The maximum amount that can be contributed to the Section 403(b) plan this year is 20 percent of her includable compensation of $200,000 times her five years of service, or a total of $200,000, less contributions for prior years of $5,000, or $195,000. Since this exceeds the applicable Section 415 limit of $30,000, $30,000 is the most that can be contributed to the Section 403(b) plan for Doctor Staph this year.
>
> If the participant has more than one employer, all Section 403(b) plans of all employers must be combined for purposes of

the Section 415 limit. However, if the employee participates in a regular qualified plan or plans as well as the Section 403(b) plan, it usually is not necessary to combine the qualified plans and the 403(b) plan for purposes of the Section 415 limit (Section 415(g) and Regulations Section 1.415–8).

Salary Reduction Plans

The preceding discussion of the exclusion allowance assumed a noncontributory plan in which the employer made a contribution to the Section 403(b) plan over and above the employee's regular compensation. Most Section 403(b) plans are *not* designed this way. Instead, such plans are usually *salary-reduction* plans. Under a salary-reduction plan, the employee is given the option to elect to contribute part of his or her regular salary to the 403(b) plan instead of receiving it in cash. There is a nondiscrimination requirement: if the plan permits salary reductions of more than $200 by any participant, then all employees in the organization must be given the same option, except for those covered under a Section 457 plan or Section 401(k) plan, or part-time student employees.

There is a $9,500 limit on annual salary reductions for each participant. This limit applies to the total (for each employee) of Section 403(b) salary reductions, salary-reduction SEPs and 401(k) salary reductions under plans of all the employee's employers. The $9,500 is indexed for cost-of-living increases in connection with the $7,000 401(k) limit: once the 401(k) limit reaches $9,500 through indexing, the two limits will become the same and will be indexed together. The $9,500 limit does not apply to direct employer matching contributions to the participant's account; thus, the total can be more than $9,500, as long as the 20 percent exclusion allowance is not exceeded.

The amount contributed to the plan will not be subject to income taxes if the salary-reduction election is made properly. For these amounts to avoid taxation, the employee must make the election in advance of the period in which the compensation is to be earned and the salary-reduction agreement between the employer and employee must be legally binding. If an employee makes such an agreement after the right to receive the compensation has been earned, the election will not be effective for tax purposes because of the tax doctrine of constructive receipt.

Although the amounts contributed to the plan under a properly designed salary reduction agreement are not currently subject to income tax to the participant, they are subject to social security and federal unemployment (FICA and FUTA) taxes.

In order to apply the exclusion allowance formula given above to a salary reduction plan, the amount of *includable compensation*—compensation included in taxable income—must be used instead of total salary.

If an employee's stated salary is $30,000, and the employee elects to receive $25,000 in cash and have $5,000 contributed to a Section 403(b) plan, the amount of includable or taxable compensation is $25,000; therefore, the exclusion allowance is 20 percent of $25,000 times the employee's years of service, less prior years' plan contributions. In other words, other things being equal, for an employee in the first year of service an employer can contribute up to 20 percent of the full stated salary, but if the employee elects to reduce salary and contribute the reduction to a Section 403(b) plan, then the maximum salary reduction is 16⅔ percent of the full stated salary or 20 percent of the stated salary after reduction.

Catch-Up Alternatives

The Section 415 limit (25 percent/$30,000) may not be exceeded in any year, while the regular exclusion allowance is increased by prior service. This works a hardship on long-service employees who have had relatively low Section 403(b) contributions in prior years. Under the regular exclusion allowance, their prior service would otherwise permit large contributions to catch up for past years. For employees of educational institutions, hospitals and home-health service agencies—but not other employers—the Code contains catch-up alternatives to the regular Section 415 limitation that are aimed at long-service employees. Under the catch-up alternatives, the 25 percent of compensation limit under Section 415 is not always applied, thus permitting Section 403(b) contributions in excess of 25 percent of the current year's compensation. However, in no event can the $30,000 limitation be exceeded even under the catch-up alternatives.

There is also a catch-up provision to raise the $9,500 salary reduction limit for employees having at least 15 years of service with the employer. The catch-up limit (Code Section 402(g)) allows additional salary reductions above the $9,500 limit (as indexed) equal to the lesser of:

- $3,000.
- $15,000 less prior catch-up contributions.
- The excess of ($5,000 × prior number of years of service) over prior salary reductions.

Types of Investments for 403(b) Plans

Section 403(b) plan funds must be invested in either

- Annuity contracts purchased by the employer from an insurance company, or
- Mutual fund shares held in custodial accounts (referred to as 403(b)(7) accounts).

Many different types of annuities may be used for Section 403(b) plans. Thus, the annuities can be individual or group contracts, level or flexible premium annuities and fixed dollar or variable annuities. Face-amount certificates providing a fixed maturity value and a schedule of redemptions are also permitted. In addition, the annuity contract may provide incidental amounts of life insurance for the employee; however, the value of such insurance is taxable to the employee each year under the PS 58 table. The annuity contracts can provide the employee a choice of broad types of investment strategy—for example, a choice between investment in a fixed-income fund and an equity-type fund. However, if the contract gives the employee specific powers to direct the investments of the fund, the IRS will regard the employee as in control of the account for tax purposes and the employee will be currently taxed on the fund's investment income.

Annuity contracts used in Section 403(b) plans must be nontransferable. This means that they cannot be sold or assigned as collateral to any person other than the insurance company issuing the contract. However, the employee is permitted to designate a beneficiary for death benefits or survivorship annuities. Since similar restrictions apply to annuities transferred to participants from qualified plans, most insurance companies use the same standard provisions for both types of annuity contracts.

Distributions and Loans from Section 403(b) Plans

Distributions from Section 403(b) plans are subject to much the same rules applicable to qualified plans; in particular, those rules applicable to 401(k) plans.

Withdrawals are not permitted from 403(b)(7) custodial accounts (mutual funds) or from any salary-reduction 403(b) account except for withdrawals after age 59½, or upon death, disability, separation from service or financial hardship. These withdrawal restrictions technically do not apply to annuity-type 403(b) accounts funded by direct employer contributions rather than salary reductions. However, this "loophole" is of limited usefulness because all early withdrawals are subject to the 10 percent early distribution penalty of Code Section 72(t). As discussed in Chapter 24, this penalty applies to most distributions prior to age 59½ from qualified plans, IRAs and Section 403(b) plans. The penalty applies even to distributions that are permitted; for example, many hardship distributions from Section 403(b) plans will be subject to the penalty.

Other qualified plan distribution rules also apply to Section 403(b) plans. Distributions must begin by April 1 of the calendar year following the attainment of age 70½. The minimum annual distribution thereafter is a level amount spread over the participant's life expectancy or over the joint life expectancies of the participant and beneficiary, as discussed in Chapter 24. Failure to make a minimum annual distribution results in a 50 percent penalty under Code Section 4974.

Loans

Section 403(b) plans with either annuity or mutual-fund accounts may permit loans on the same basis as regular qualified plans. Plan loans are discussed in Chapter 24. Because of the restrictions on Section 403(b) distributions, plan loan provisions are particularly important to employees and should be considered in any Section 403(b) plan.

Taxation of Section 403(b) Plans

A Section 403(b) plan provides the same general tax advantages as a qualified plan. Thus, plan contributions within the limits of the exclusion allowance are not currently taxable to the employee. Investment earnings on plan funds are also not currently taxable.

However, the taxation of distributions from Section 403(b) plans is somewhat less favorable than for qualified plans. The full amount of any distribution from a Section 403(b) plan, whether during employment or at termination of service, is fully taxable as ordinary income to the participant, except for any cost basis the participant has in the distribution. A cost basis could result if the employee paid tax previously on any amount contributed to the plan, or reported PS 58 costs if the plan provides incidental life insurance. There are no averaging or capital-gain provisions for the taxable amount of a distribution from a Section 403(b) plan. The bad tax effect of having all of the income taxable in a single year can be alleviated only by having a periodic form of payout from the plan. A periodic distribution from a Section 403(b) plan is taxed under the annuity rules the same as an annuity from a qualified plan.

Death benefits are also subject to somewhat less favorable income tax treatment than death benefits from qualified plans. The averaging and capital-gain provisions are not available to the beneficiary. Also, the $5,000 employee death benefit exclusion of Code Section 101(b) is available only for a lump-sum distribution from a Section 403(b) plan, and only if the employer was one of a limited subclass. This subclass is defined in a rather complex way, but most private religious, educational and charitable organizations are included; however, it has been held that a state university is included but not a public elementary or high school system.

Section 403(b) death benefits are included in the gross estate of the deceased participant for federal estate tax purposes. However, if they are paid to a spouse, they escape estate taxation under the unlimited marital deduction. In other cases, there may be no estate tax because the tax applies only to relatively large estates (those over about $600,000).

Section 403(b) plan amounts are included in determining the excess distribution and excess accumulation taxes (Code Section 4981) discussed in Chapter 25. These taxes can be significant for highly compensated employees. In some cases, the potential effect of these taxes may make it advisable for highly compensated employees to discontinue participation in Section 403(b) or other plans.

Regulatory and Administrative Aspects

A Section 403(b) plan is considered a pension plan, rather than a welfare-benefit plan, for purposes of the reporting and disclosure provisions. The reporting and disclosure requirements applicable are similar to those applicable to qualified plans, as discussed in Chapter 26. However, as with qualified plans, Section 403(b) plans of governmental units and churches that have not elected to come under ERISA are exempt from these requirements, unless mutual funds rather than annuity contracts are used for funding. If a Section 403(b) plan is purely of the salary reduction type and does not include any direct employer contributions, the reporting and disclosure and other regulatory requirements are greatly reduced.

STUDY QUESTIONS

1. Who is eligible to make deductible IRA contributions?
2. George and Mary Barke (marrieds filing jointly) have an adjusted gross income of $44,317. What is the amount of the deductible IRA contribution that they can make if they do not contribute toward a spousal IRA?
3. How are IRA distributions taxed?
4. What are the financial planning advantages associated with IRA rollovers?
5. What are the major similarities and differences between an SEP and a qualified profit-sharing plan?
6. Explain how SEPs can use salary reductions.
7. What types of organizations may adopt a 403(b) plan for employees?
8. Ed Greave's salary in his first year of employment with a nonprofit, charitable organization is $50,000. He elects a salary reduction under a Section 403(b) plan. What is the maximum salary reduction possible for Ed Greaves?
9. Describe the major differences between a salary-reduction type Section 403(b) plan and a qualified Section 401(k) plan.

28

Executive Benefits and Nonqualified Deferred-Compensation Plans

Objectives

- Review the types and objectives of benefits often provided to select groups of executives.
- Explain why supplemental nonqualified deferred-compensation plans are often provided for executives.
- Explain the distinction between funded and unfunded nonqualified deferred-compensation plans.
- Describe the types of benefits available and the employer's tax treatment with respect to nonqualified deferred-compensation plans.
- Describe a Section 457 plan.
- Describe the distinction between nonqualified deferred-compensation plans that are funded with restricted property, stock options or incentive stock options.
- Describe the uses of life insurance in deferred-compensation plans.

The employee benefit plans discussed so far in this text usually are designed for relatively broad groups of employees. Some of the more tax-favored plans, such as qualified retirement plans, actually include specific nondiscriminatory coverage provisions. However, employers often wish to provide special or additional employee benefits to key employees.

In designing plans for executives and key employees, the first step is to identify the employer and employee objectives that the plan is to meet. Then, the plan must be designed to prevent—as far as possible—any undesirable tax or other legal consequences. Employer objectives for executive benefit plans usually include the attraction of appropriate key employees and the retention of such employees once they are hired. In particular, the employer may wish to prevent the employee from going to work for a competing organization. Key employees themselves are usually concerned about their high marginal income tax brackets and their need for savings and estate planning. They therefore favor benefit plans that provide them with tax-favored current compensation or a tax-favored savings medium. There are many types of plans that can be designed to meet employer or employee objectives of this type. In smaller organizations, key employees are often the owners of the business, so there is no difference between employer and employee objectives.

Some common types of executive benefit plans will be listed here at the beginning of the chapter. In the rest of the chapter, some of these benefits will be discussed in more detail, particularly those involving design features that must be coordinated with tax and other laws.

EXECUTIVE BENEFIT CHECKLIST

1. *Nonqualified Deferred-Compensation or Supplemental Retirement Plans.* A nonqualified deferred-compensation plan provides additional retirement or deferred-compensation benefits to key employees in addition to, or in place of, the amounts received under the employer's qualified plan, if any. There is a great deal of flexibility in the design of such plans, and many approaches have been used. (See later discussion.)

2. *Restricted Stock or Other Property.* Restricted property plans provide compensation to executives in the form of property, usually stock of the employer company, that is restricted in such a way as to help retain the services of the executives or provide an incentive for good executive performance. (See later discussion.)

3. *Stock Options.* Stock option plans are used for purposes similar to restricted stock plans; however, with an option plan, the employee is given an option to buy the stock at a stated price rather than an outright grant of the stock subject to restrictions. (See later discussion.)

4. *Life Insurance.* Life insurance is a valuable benefit for key employees. As discussed later, it can be provided in a variety of ways.

5. *Severance Pay.* Most employers have some form of severance pay policy for employees, often at a minimal level for rank-and-file employees. Executives, however, often negotiate favorable severance pay provisions as part of their compensation package. One particular type of contract regarded by Congress as abusive is the "golden parachute" contract, under which a company agrees to pay an executive large amounts of severance pay if the company changes ownership. Under Code Section 280G, tax deductions for golden parachute payments can be denied to the employer if the amount is excessive—generally, if it is at least three times the executive's average annual salary.

6. *Cash Bonus and Incentive Plans.* Executive compensation plans often include plans for cash bonuses paid currently or deferred for a relatively short period of time that are tied to company or executive performance. Most of these programs are based in some manner on growth in company earnings during the executive's tenure in office. Often the bonus or incentive award depends on the attainment of specified target earnings objectives. There are many design considerations for such plans, including eligibility for the plan, the amount of the award and the benefit formula, and the period of time over which executive performance will be assessed. All these design features must be tailored to the employer's specific situation. There are no special tax complications for these plans; generally, the compensation is taxable to the executive when received, and deductible to the employer at the same time.

7. *Additional Medical Expense Benefits.* Additional health insurance is an attractive executive benefit, particularly where the company's basic plan has gaps in coverage.

8. *Disability Income Plans.* As with health insurance, the company may wish to provide a disability income (salary continuation) plan for executive employees to cover any gaps in or to supplement the company's broad-based disability income plan. If the additional coverage is provided through insurance owned by the company, the premium is fully deductible to the employer, but benefits are taxable to the employee when paid, subject to a disability income tax credit which disappears for higher income employees. If instead of relying on a company-provided plan, the executive purchases his or her own disability income insurance, the premium payments by the employee are nondeductible, but disability income payments are nontaxable. Because of this, many companies may prefer simply to provide extra compensation income to executives with the understanding that the executive will have the option of obtaining personally owned disability income insurance coverage.

9. *Loans to Executives.* A plan providing loans from company funds to executives on favorable terms may be attractive to executives. If the executives are owners of the company, such a program also provides a means of withdrawing corporate funds on a favorable basis, that is, without being taxed on the receipt of a dividend. While interest-free and bargain loans were once used for this purpose, Code Section 7872 now prescribes a minimum interest rate for such loans, which is basically the interest rate applicable during the same period for federal marketable securities of similar term. If the employee loan has a lower interest rate, the bargain element is taxed as if the employee had received that amount as cash compensation. The purpose of this Code provision is to treat as nearly as possible a bargain-rate loan as if it is a market-rate loan, in order to discourage bargain-rate loans.

Any employee loan should be a bona fide loan, and should be evidenced by a formal written note with a fixed maturity date or a repayment schedule. The employee could be required to provide security for the loan, such as a home mortgage. Loan plans can be relatively unrestricted or can restrict executive loans to specific purposes, such as the purchase of a home or children's educational expenses.

Interest on the loan will generally be consumer interest that is nondeductible to the employee unless secured by a home mortgage. Interest could also be deductible as investment interest if the loan proceeds are used for investments.

10. *Other Fringe Benefits.* An infinite variety of perquisites and fringe benefits for executives is possible; for example, executive dining rooms, favorable expense account provisions, financial counseling and estate planning for executives, additional moving expense reimbursements, payment of professional association dues and trips to professional seminars. The usefulness of these benefits depends entirely on individual facts and circumstances.

The decision whether to provide any of these benefits is often affected by their federal income tax treatment because executives tend to be in high marginal income tax brackets and prefer to receive extra compensation in tax-free form.

NONQUALIFIED DEFERRED-COMPENSATION PLANS

For qualified plans, Code Section 415, as discussed in Chapter 25, imposes limits on the benefits or contributions that can be provided to any one individual. Annual additions to a qualified defined-contribution plan are limited to the lesser of 25 percent of the employee's compensation or $30,000. Correspondingly, for a defined-benefit plan, the maximum projected annual benefit is the lesser of 100 percent of the employee's compensation or $90,000. For very highly paid executives, it may be desirable to provide additional retirement income in excess of these limits. Also, in some cases, an employer does not have a qualified plan because the employer does not want to provide the kind of broad retirement plan coverage required by the nondiscriminatory coverage requirements. Thus, a common form of executive benefit is the provision of retirement income or deferred compensation outside of a qualified plan. Plans that do this are generally referred to as nonqualified deferred-compensation plans. Many names have been coined by consulting firms and insurance companies to describe specific plans of this type—for example, supplemental retirement plans, top-hat plans and the like. The design of nonqualified deferred-compensation plans is open-ended and almost any combination of features can be provided in one way or another.

Objectives for the Plan

The design of a nonqualified deferred-compensation plan will reflect the objectives of the person establishing it. A broad distinction can usually be made between plans designed to meet employer objectives and those designed primarily to meet employee objectives. The employer's objectives in instituting the plan are usually to provide an inducement for hiring key employees and then to provide additional inducements to the key employees to continue working for the employer—especially so that employees do not leave and go to work for a competitor. Employee objectives are usually to obtain an additional form of compensation at retirement or termination of employment, with tax on the additional amounts deferred, if possible, until the money is actually received.

Employer-Instituted Plan

Eligibility in an employer-instituted plan is usually confined to key executives or technical employees who are difficult to recruit and keep. The plan does not have to specify a class of employees to be covered; it can simply be adopted for specific individuals as the need arises. However, the need for fairness among a similarly situated group of executives often dictates that the plan cover a specified class of employees rather than individuals.

A plan instituted for employer objectives usually has some kind of forfeiture provision in order to discourage key employees from leaving. The plan may require the employee to forfeit all rights under the nonqualified deferred-compensation plan in the event of termination of employment prior to normal retirement age without the employer's consent. The employer might wish to soften this forfeiture provision somewhat by including graduated vesting similar to that required under a qualified plan. However, as long as the plan avoids the applicability of the ERISA vesting provisions discussed later, no particular vesting schedule is required and complete forfeiture can be provided for any reason. The plan might include additional forfeiture provisions, such as a forfeiture of any unpaid benefits, if the employee enters into competition with the employer or goes to work for a competitor. The courts have held that such covenants not to compete can be enforced by the employer, so long as the scope of the prohibited competition is reasonable in terms of the geographical area over which it applies and the period of time during which it is in effect.

Nonqualified deferred-compensation plans often require that the employee remain available for consulting services to the employer after retirement, with possible forfeiture of benefits if the employee does not comply. Actually, consulting services provisions can be beneficial to the employee, as they often provide a means for the employee to receive additional amounts from the employer after retirement in return for relatively nominal consulting services.

Employee-Option Nonqualified Deferred Compensation

Different objectives for a nonqualified deferred-compensation plan come from the employee's side. Employees with enough income to have substantial savings programs often seek tax-favored methods of saving. Additional amounts of tax-favored savings can be provided beyond the limits of a qualified plan through a salary-reduction arrangement, with the amount of the salary reduction paid to the employee after retirement instead of currently. This provides tax savings because income tax on the salary reduction is paid in the future instead of currently, a valuable benefit because of the time value of money. It is also possible that the employee may be in a lower marginal tax bracket after retirement.

The initial problem in designing a plan for this objective is to insure that the employee is not taxed currently on the salary reduction that goes into the plan. The salary-reduction arrangement must avoid the constructive receipt doctrine, under which income is taxable to a taxpayer if it is credited to the taxpayer's account, set apart or otherwise made available, even though it is not actually received. To avoid this doctrine, the amount set aside must be subject to substantial limitations. This can generally be accomplished if the salary-reduction agreement is made prior to the time the income is earned by the employee and if the employee's receipt of it is deferred for a period of time, such as to termination of employment or retirement, which constitutes a substantial limitation.

Plans designed to meet employee objectives generally will have generous provisions and, in particular, there will be few forfeiture provisions—usually 100 percent immediate vesting—unless the plan is formally funded.

Funded and Unfunded Plans

A nonqualified deferred-compensation plan can be either funded by the employer or unfunded. With a funded plan, the employer sets aside money or property to the employee's account in an irrevocable trust or through some other means that restricts access by the employer and the employer's creditors to the fund. With an unfunded plan, either there is no fund at all, or the fund that is set up is accessible to the employer and its creditors at all times, so that it provides no particular security to the employee other than the knowledge that the fund exists.

It might appear desirable from the employee's point of view to have a funded plan. However, there are significant disadvantages: The amounts put into a funded plan generally are taxable to the employee at the time the employee's rights to the fund become nonforfeitable, or substantially vested, a concept to be discussed under "Compensation with Restricted Property." This may occur well in advance of the time these funds are actually received by the employee, thus producing a tax disadvantage. Also, funded plans are subject to the ERISA vesting and fiduciary requirements, as discussed later, and this is usually undesirable from the employer's point of view.

As a result of these disadvantages, nonqualified deferred-compensation plans generally are unfunded. The employee relies only on the employer's unsecured contractual obligation to pay the deferred compensation. Since such plans provide no real security to the employee, their value as an inducement may be minimal if the company is risky; employees will then probably opt for greater benefits in current cash or property rather than deferred compensation.

Informal Funding

To provide some assurance, the employer can informally fund the plan by setting money aside in some kind of separate account, with this arrangement known to the employee but with no formal legal rights on the part of the employee and with the amount in the fund therefore available to the employer's creditors. Life insurance policies on the employee's life (owned by and payable to the employer) are often used to provide this kind of informal funding. Life insurance is particularly useful for this purpose if the deferred-compensation plan provides a death benefit to the employee's designated beneficiary, since if the employee dies after only a few years of employment, the life insurance will make sufficient funds available immediately to pay the death benefit. Sometimes a trust is set up by the employer to finance the plan. If the trust assets are available to the employer's creditors, the arrangement is deemed unfunded by the IRS. This type of arrangement is sometimes referred to as a *rabbi trust,* since an early IRS ruling on this issue involved a rabbi.

Form of Benefits

Most nonqualified deferred-compensation plans provide for benefit payments in installments beginning at retirement or termination of employment. The five-year averaging provision available for qualified plan lump-sum benefits does not apply to nonqualified plans; benefits are taxable as ordinary income when received at the taxpayer's regular tax rates, assuming that the taxpayer has not already paid taxes on the amounts in prior years.

Nonqualified deferred-compensation plans often provide a death benefit, usually in the form of a benefit to a designated beneficiary in the amount the employee would have received if he or she had lived. If the plan uses life insurance as an informal funding medium, it usually also provides a flat-amount death benefit—usually related to the face amount of the life insurance policies—that is payable regardless of how much deferred compensation has accrued to the date of death. Death benefits are taxable as ordinary income to the beneficiary, except for the possible availability of the $5,000 employee death benefit exclusion under Code Section 101(b). For this to apply, the employee must not have vested rights to the benefit immediately before the employee's death.

Employer's Tax Treatment

In a nonqualified deferred-compensation plan, the employer does not receive a tax deduction for deferred compensation until the year in which the employee must include the compensation in taxable income. This is the case even if the employer has put money aside through formal or informal funding of the plan in an earlier year. For an unfunded plan, the year of inclusion for the employee is the year in which the compensation is actually or constructively received. If the plan is formally funded, the employee includes the compensation in income in the year in which it becomes substantially vested.

Impact of ERISA and Other Regulatory Provisions

In order to retain design flexibility and keep administrative costs down, most deferred compensation plans are designed to avoid the fiduciary, vesting and reporting and disclosure requirements of ERISA to the maximum extent possible. Generally, if the plan is unfunded and is maintained by an employer primarily for the purpose of providing deferred compensation for a select group of management or highly compensated employees, the plan will be exempt from all provisions of ERISA except for a simple reporting requirement notifying the Department of Labor of the existence of the plan and some basic facts about it. However, if the plan does not come within this exemption, most of the provisions of ERISA become applicable and the plan must comply with almost all of the ERISA provisions that apply to a qualified plan. The nonqualified plan could discriminate in participation, benefits or contributions, but for all other purposes—vesting, fiduciary and reporting and disclosure—the plan would have to be designed like a qualified plan without the tax benefits for qualified plans. Consequently, most nonqualified deferred-compensation plans are designed to be unfunded and are limited to management or highly compensated employees.

SECTION 457 DEFERRED-COMPENSATION PLANS FOR GOVERNMENTAL EMPLOYEES

In a nonqualified deferred-compensation plan, an employee may defer tax on compensation income, but with a twofold cost. First, there is a loss of benefit security because there can be no irrevocable trust fund for the employee, and second, the employer's tax deduction is also deferred.

Neither of these two factors imposes much disadvantage to state and local government employers or employees, because there is little risk of the employer's becoming insolvent and because the employer is nontaxable and derives no benefit from tax deductions. For private tax-exempt employers, the second disadvantage also does not apply, although the first could be significant. To avoid potentially unlimited use of nonqualified deferred compensation by state and local government employees and employees of private tax-exempt employers, Section 457 therefore imposes restrictions on such plans.

Limit on Amount

The amount deferred annually by an employee under these plans cannot exceed the lesser of $7,500 or one-third of the employee's taxable compensation, reduced by any salary reductions under a Section 403(b) plan or SEP. The $7,500 limit is *not* indexed for inflation. However, the ceiling can be increased, in each of the last three years before normal retirement age, to the lesser of $15,000 or the regular ceiling plus the total amount of potential deferral that was not used in prior years. If an individual has more than one employer, the total deferred for all employers must not exceed these limits.

Other Rules

- Elections to defer compensation under Section 457 are made monthly, under an agreement entered into before the beginning of the month.
- The plan cannot be funded—all deferred compensation and income therefrom remains the property of the employer.
- Plan distributions cannot be made before separation from service or "unforeseeable emergency." Also, plan distributions must meet the rules of Section 401(a)(9)

regarding beginning date (April 1 after age 70½). A special incidental death benefit provision applies—the participant must expect to receive at least two-thirds of the total payout where there is a survivor annuity.

- There are no specific coverage requirements—the plan can be offered to all employees, or any group of employees, even a single employee. However, for a tax-exempt organization (but not for a governmental organization) the participation, fiduciary and other ERISA rules may apply.

- If the state or local government employer or tax-exempt employer has a nonqualified deferred-compensation plan that does not comply with Section 457—for example, one that exceeds the limits—then it is treated for tax purposes as a funded plan, whether or not it is actually funded. This means that the deferred amount is includable in the participant's income when there is no substantial risk of forfeiture. This does, however, provide some opportunity for governments and tax-exempts to design plans for top executives above the $7,500 limit by including forfeiture provisions.

COMPENSATION WITH RESTRICTED PROPERTY

An employee's compensation can be paid in either cash or noncash property. It is common for an executive's compensation to include payment in property, usually employer stock or securities, that is subject to some form of restriction at the time it is paid. The restriction on the property is usually designed to serve an employer goal, such as retaining a valued employee, and the restriction also can be designed to postpone taxability of the compensation to the employee and correspondingly postpone the employer's tax deduction.

Restricted stock or other restricted property is not an attractive benefit to an executive if the executive must pay income tax on the property when it is received, even though it is subject to restrictions. Therefore, most restricted property plans are designed around Code Section 83 that allows deferral of taxation to the employee if the restrictions meet certain requirements. Basically, the rules provide that an employee is not subject to tax on the value of restricted property until the year in which the property becomes *substantially vested*. Property is not considered substantially vested if it is subject to a *substantial risk of forfeiture* and not transferable by the employee free of the risk of forfeiture. As with most types of nonqualified compensation plans, the employer does not get a tax deduction until the year in which the property becomes substantially vested and includable in the employee's income.

The question whether there is a substantial risk of forfeiture depends on the facts and circumstances of each case. However, a substantial risk of forfeiture usually exists when the employee must return the property if a specified period of service for the employer is not completed—for example, five years of service. A forfeiture that results only from an unlikely event, such as the commission of a crime by the executive, probably would not constitute a substantial risk of forfeiture. Forfeitures as a result of failing to meet certain sales targets or going to work for a competitor could constitute substantial risks, depending on the facts and circumstances. If the employee is an owner of the company, the IRS is likely to be skeptical of any forfeiture provision in the plan, no matter how rigid it may appear on paper.

The nontransferability provision—the second half of the test—can be complied with in the case of the company stock by inscribing a statement on the share certificate to the effect that the shares are part of a restricted property plan. Thus, any prospective transferee is aware that the employee is not free to sell the shares to an outsider without restriction.

> Suppose that executive Rita Bill is permitted to buy 500 shares of company stock at $10 per share in 1989, while the current market value is $100 per share. Rita must resell the shares to the company for $10 per share if she terminates employment with the company at any time during the next five years. The share certificates are also stamped with an appropriate statement to meet the nontransferability requirement. Rita pays no taxes on this arrangement until the restriction expires in 1994. If the unrestricted shares in 1994 have a market value of $200 per share, Rita has additional taxable compensation income for 1994 of $100,000, the market value of the shares, less $5,000, the amount Rita paid, or a net additional compensation income of $95,000. The company gets a tax deduction of $95,000 in 1994, but gets no deduction for 1989. Also, the allowance of the tax deduction to the company is, like all tax deductions for compensation paid, subject to the requirement that the total compensation package for the employee constitutes reasonable compensation for services rendered.

Many variations are possible in the design of restricted stock plans. The plan, for example, may provide that dividends on the restricted stock are payable to the executive during the restriction period; if so, these dividends are taxable currently to the executive as compensation income. The plan also might provide graduated vesting over a period of years, rather than full vesting at the end of a specified period like five years; this would mean that the executive would be taxed each year on the value of the property that became substantially vested that year.

In some plans, there are no forfeiture provisions; instead the stock is subject to other restrictions. For example, the employee may have a fully vested interest in the stock but may not be permitted to resell the stock without first offering it back to the company at a specified price. In that case, the value of stock to the executive would not be its market value, but would be a reduced value reflecting the restriction. Under the Internal Revenue Code, a restriction will be taken into account in valuing the property for tax purposes only if it is a *nonlapse restriction*—a restriction which by its terms will never lapse. The restriction in the example with a requirement of resale to the company at a fixed price would qualify as a nonlapse restriction. Other types of restrictions must be assessed on their own facts and circumstances, and the IRS tends to take a very limited view of what constitutes a nonlapse restriction.

Once an executive has become substantially vested in the restricted property and paid any tax on the compensation element involved, gain on a subsequent sale of the property is usually taxed as capital gain just as in the case of the sale of such property acquired by other means.

STOCK OPTION PLANS FOR EXECUTIVES (NONSTATUTORY)

A stock option is an offer to sell stock at a specified price at some time in the future or over a limited period of time with a specific termination date. Stock options have long been used for executive compensation to accomplish some of the same purposes as compensation with restricted stock. Over the years, Congress has designed special tax incentives to make certain types of stock option plans attractive. The type of tax-favored plan currently in effect is known as an incentive stock option (ISO) plan which will be discussed separately. In this section, stock options in general—sometimes referred to as *nonstatutory* or *nonqualified stock options*—will be discussed first.

Options to buy stock in the employer company are typically granted to executives as additional compensation at a favorable price, with the hope that the value of the stock will rise and make the option price a considerable bargain for the executive. If the stock price declines, the executive simply declines to exercise the option to buy the stock. This gives the executive a benefit whose potential value is tied to the fate of the company, but with no downside risk. This valuable incentive to the executive appears to cost the company very little, although this is somewhat misleading as discussed below.

Stock options other than ISOs can be designed in any manner the employer and employee desire. Typically, a stock option runs for a period such as ten years, and is granted at a price equal to the fair market value of the stock on the date that it is granted.

> Bill Kate is given an option in Year 1 to purchase up to 1,000 shares of stock at $50 per share, which is the current market price, with the option to be exercised over the next ten years. The plan may provide a waiting period before the option may be exercised, or may provide that the option can be exercised only in successive installments—i.e., only 20 percent of the option can be exercised during the first two years, 40 percent over the first four years, and so on. The option has no value to Bill at the date of the grant because the option price was the same as the market price. Therefore, as of Year 1, there was no taxable income to Bill. Under the general tax rules in this situation, Bill will not be taxed until shares are actually purchased.
>
> Suppose Bill purchases 400 shares in Year 4 for a total of $20,000. If the fair market value of the shares in Year 4 has risen to $40,000, the executive has $20,000 of ordinary income in Year 4. The company will get a tax deduction of $20,000 in Year 4, the

same as the amount of Bill's compensation income, again assuming that Bill's compensation meets the reasonable compensation test for deductible compensation. However, the company gets no further deduction if Bill resells the stock and realizes a capital gain.

Options with an immediate value to the executive are sometimes used in executive compensation.

Suppose that the option had been granted at $40 per share, a bargain over the prevailing market price of $50 at the time of the grant. If the option has a determinable value and the option could be traded on an established market, the value of the option is taxable as ordinary income to Bill at the time of the grant, with a corresponding deduction to the employer. If tax is payable at the grant of the option, there is no further taxable compensation income when the option is exercised later. This can be an advantageous approach if the stock is expected to appreciate substantially in value, because the taxable compensation income at the time of the grant is relatively small, while the remainder of the gain on the overall deal will be taxed as capital gain only when the stock is sold.

Suppose that Bill is granted an option for 500 shares of company stock at $40 per share in Year 1, the current market price being $50 per share. Bill has $5,000 of ordinary compensation income in Year 1, the year of the grant. In Year 4, Bill exercises the option and buys 400 shares for $16,000. There is no ordinary income tax to Bill at the time of the exercise in Year 4.

The stock option appears to be an almost ideal method of compensating executives, providing a valuable incentive-based compensation arrangement at practically no cost to the company. However, the company's cost is comparable to the cost of cash compensation. While it costs the company almost nothing to grant options and print stock certificates to provide shares when the options are exercised, the executive will exercise the option only when the stock has a substantial market value. If this is the case, the company could itself have sold the stock used in the option arrangement on the open market and received the full proceeds. However, the grant of an option does not result in a charge to the company's income statement, so this form of compensation can be attractive from an accounting point of view.

The tax rules applicable to nonstatutory stock options do not provide any particular tax advantage to the employer company in using stock option plans. Therefore, in designing a stock option plan the company must look for benefits to itself just as in the case of any other kind of executive compensation. Typically, stock option plans would be used where the executive has a strong desire to obtain an interest in the business, or where the executive has a direct impact on the company's profits and, therefore, its stock value.

INCENTIVE STOCK OPTIONS

The incentive stock option (ISO) is the current form of stock option plan eligible for special tax benefits, which are provided by Code Section 422. Under an ISO plan, the usual tax rules previously discussed do not apply. Instead, for stock purchased under an ISO plan, there is no taxation to the employee until the stock is sold. Employees do not realize any taxable income when they receive the option, even if the option has an ascertainable fair market value and, furthermore, there is no taxable income when the option is exercised. However, the difference between the option price and the fair market value at the time of exercise is a tax preference item that may be subject to the alternative minimum tax. Since there is no regular taxable income to the employee at either the grant or the exercise of the option, the corporation gets no deduction at any time.

Options under an ISO plan must generally be granted to employees within ten years of the plan's adoption or approval by the shareholders, and an option must be exercised by the employee within ten years after it is granted. The option price must equal or exceed the stock's fair market value at the time the option is granted. Any good faith attempt to value stock will be acceptable if there is no readily established market.

ISO plans increase the tax benefit of stock options as a form of compensation by providing increased tax deferral and, therefore, represent an attractive executive benefit. However, they are most likely to be used in large corporations. If an option holder has stock with more than 10 percent of the total combined voting power of the employer corporation, taking certain stock attribution rules into account, there are additional restrictions on ISO plans that may make them unattractive for closely held corporations. In such cases, the option price must be at least 110 percent of the stock's fair market value at the time it is granted and the option must be exercised within five years after it is granted rather than ten. Also, an employee receives the maximum tax benefit from an ISO plan only when the stock is sold, and there may be no ready market for a stock of a closely held corporation. Furthermore, it may be undesirable to pass ownership of stock in a closely held corporation to outsiders. However, the plan may permit the employee to exercise an option and pay for the shares of stock with other stock of the employer.

The aggregate fair market value of stock for which an employee can be granted an option under an ISO plan during a single calendar year cannot exceed $100,000. There are carryover provisions if the employee does not use the full limit in any year.

LIFE INSURANCE FOR EXECUTIVES

Life insurance can be an important executive benefit. Life insurance is important to high income employees as a means of providing income security to their families during the early part of their careers. In later years, it can provide or augment the executive's estate to be left to family and other heirs, or it can help provide liquidity to the estate to meet estate taxes and other expenses. A number of methods with favorable tax consequences have been devised to provide life insurance to executives. Generally, the aim is to provide insurance in a way that minimizes the current year-to-year income tax cost of the plan to the employee, and also keeps the life insurance out of the employee's estate for federal estate tax purposes. Some of the methods used include:

- *Split-Dollar Plans.* In a split-dollar plan, cash-value life insurance is used, with the death benefit divided or split between the employer and the employee's designated beneficiary. The premium can be paid entirely by the employer, or premium costs can be shared between employer and employee. The employer does not receive a tax deduction for its share of the premium payments. However, the plan is designed so that the employer is reimbursed for its premium payments by its share of the death benefit, which is received by the employer tax-free. Thus, the employer's cost for a split-dollar plan is the loss of the use of its share of the premium payments during the time in which the plan is in effect.

  In Revenue Ruling 64–328 the IRS has held that the employee pays tax only on the term insurance cost of the portion of the death benefit payable to the employee's beneficiary, using the PS 58 table (Table 21-1 in Chapter 21) or the insurance company's term rates for valuation. From this is subtracted any amount paid by the employee toward the premium.

  Many variations on the basic split-dollar approach are possible. For example, the tax advantages can be increased by using a plan that features borrowing against the cash value of the insurance policy, with corresponding interest deductions. Also, to avoid federal estate taxes, the plan is often designed so that the employee has no incidents of ownership in the policy. This can be done, for example, by having the policy applied for by a beneficiary such as a spouse or a family trust, with a split-dollar arrangement between the employer company and the policyholder. Although this arrangement may eliminate the federal estate tax in the employee's estate, it is still considered by the IRS to result in compensation income to the employee.

- *Death Benefit Only (DBO) Plans.* A DBO plan is a form of deferred-compensation plan in which the benefits are paid only to a designated beneficiary upon the death of the employee. The purpose of this arrangement is to avoid federal estate taxes on the death benefit.

  Under the federal estate tax law, a death benefit from a deferred-compensation plan is included in the employee's estate if the employee had a nonforfeitable right to receive benefits while living, even if the employee never actually received such benefits while alive. Thus, the DBO benefit is designed to be paid only at death. If there is a DBO plan, the employer's fringe benefit arrangements for the employee must also be designed carefully to make sure the DBO plan will accomplish its intended purpose. The IRS will lump other deferred-compensation plans—not including qualified plans—together with the DBO plan to determine if the company provides a lifetime benefit to the employee.

In order to provide a substantial death benefit even during the early years of the plan, DBO plans are usually funded informally with life insurance. That is, the employer owns insurance on the life of the employee, with the employer itself as beneficiary. At the death of the employee, the policy provides funds enabling the employer to pay the death benefit to the employee's beneficiary.

For income tax purposes, a DBO plan is treated the same as any other deferred-compensation plan—death benefits are taxable in full to the beneficiary as ordinary income when received, except for the $5,000 employee death benefit exclusion of Code Section 101(b).

- *Group Term Life Insurance Plan.* Under Section 79, a group term life insurance plan can have a special class for executives and provide them with amounts of group term insurance relatively greater than the amounts provided for other employees. However, if the plan provides amounts of insurance that are higher multiples of compensation for key employees, it probably will be deemed discriminatory and, therefore, the tax exclusion for the value of the first $50,000 of insurance will be lost by key employees. Section 79 plans can also provide permanent insurance to a specified executive class of employees. Such arrangements are often referred to as *top-hat* or *superimposed plans*. Unless these plans are carefully designed, however, the entire premium for the permanent insurance will be taxable to the employee.

STUDY QUESTIONS

1. Briefly describe the present rules for interest-free and bargain loans made by a company to its executives.
2. What management objectives can be accomplished by using a nonqualified deferred-compensation plan for a selected group of executives?
3. What features does an executive typically want in his or her nonqualified deferred-compensation plan?
4. a. What is the usual form of benefit payments from a nonqualified deferred-compensation plan?
   b. How are these payments taxed?
5. When does the employer receive a tax deduction for nonqualified deferred-compensation payments made under an unfunded plan?
6. Why are nonqualified plans generally unfunded in the tax sense?
7. How can a nonqualified plan be informally funded (while remaining unfunded in the tax sense) in order to provide covered executives with some degree of benefit security?
8. What are the special rules applicable to state and local government employers installing nonqualified deferred-compensation plans for employees?
9. Jim Franco purchased 100 shares of company stock at $5 per share. At the time of purchase, the market price for the shares was $50 per share. Jim must resell the shares back to the company for $5 per share if he terminates

employment within three years of the purchase. The stock is nontransferable.
   a. Is there a tax impact on Jim when the shares are purchased? Explain.
   b. Will there be a tax impact on Jim if the stock is worth $100 per share when the restriction expires in three years? Explain.
   c. When will the company be allowed a tax deduction for the additional compensation to Jim?
   d. What amount will be deductible by the corporation?
10. In what ways does an incentive stock option differ from a nonstatutory stock option?
11. Describe a split-dollar plan by explaining the roles played by the employer and employee in order to achieve the intended benefits from the arrangement.
12. Explain DBO plans with respect to
   a. The primary purpose of the arrangement.
   b. How the plan is funded.
   c. The income tax impact to the beneficiary.

Additional Readings

PERIODICALS

Benefits Quarterly. Brookfield, Wis.: International Foundation of Employee Benefits Plans. (quarterly)

Best's Review (Life and Health Edition). Oldwick, N.J.: A. M. Best Company, Inc. (monthly)

BNA Pension Reporter. Washington, D.C.: Bureau of National Affairs. (weekly)

Business Insurance. Chicago: Crain Communications, Inc. (weekly)

Employee Benefit Plan Review. Chicago: Charles D. Spencer & Assocs. (monthly)

IF Employee Benefits Journal. Brookfield, Wis.: International Foundation of Employee Benefits Plans. (quarterly)

Journal of the American Society of CLU and ChFC. Bryn Mawr, Pa.: American Society of CLU and ChFC. (bimonthly)

Journal of Pension Planning and Compliance. Greenvale, N.Y.: Panel Publishers. (quarterly)

Life Insurance Fact Book. Washington, D.C.: American Council of Life Insurance. (annual)

National Underwriter (Property Casualty/Employee Benefits Edition). Chicago: National Underwriter Co. (weekly)

Pension Facts. Washington, D.C.: American Council of Life Insurance. (annual)

Pension Handbook. Larchmont, N.Y.: Maxwell MacMillan. (annual)

Pension World. Atlanta: Communication Channels, Inc. (monthly)

Pensions & Investments. Chicago: Crain Communications, Inc. (biweekly)

Personnel Administration. Alexandria, Va.: American Society for Personnel Administrators. (monthly)

Personnel Journal. Costa Mesa, Calif.: A. C. Craft, Inc. (monthly)

Social Security Bulletin. Washington, D.C.: U.S. Dept. of Health and Human Services. (monthly)

Social Security Manual. Cincinnati: The National Underwriter Company. (annual)

Source Book of Health Insurance Data. Washington, D.C.: Health Insurance Association of America. (annual)

Tax Facts on Life Insurance. Cincinnati: The National Underwriter Company. (annual)

LOOSE-LEAF SERVICES

EBPR Research Reports. Chicago: Charles D. Spencer & Assocs.

Pension and Profit-Sharing Service. Englewood Cliffs, N.J.: Prentice-Hall.

Pension Plan Forms. Jacksonville, Fla.: Corbel & Company.

Pension Plan Guide. Chicago: Commerce Clearing House.

BOOKS

Allen, Everett T., Jr.; Melone, Joseph J.; Rosenbloom, Jerry S.; and Van Derhei, Jack L. *Pension Planning.* 6th ed. Homewood, Ill.: Richard D. Irwin, 1988.

Beam, Burton T., Jr. *Group Benefits: Basic Concepts and Alternatives.* 4th ed. Bryn Mawr, Pa.: The American College, 1991.

Canan, Michael J. *Qualified Retirement and Other Employee Benefit Plans.* St. Paul: West Publishing Co., 1991.

Canan, Michael J. and Mitchell, William D. *Employee Fringe and Welfare Benefit Plans.* St. Paul: West Publishing Co., 1990.

Dunkle, David S. *Guide to Pension and Profit Sharing Plans.* Colorado Springs, Co.: Shepard's/McGraw-Hill, Inc., 1990.

Employee Benefit Research Institute. *Fundamentals of Employee Benefit Programs.* 4th ed. Washington, D.C.: Employee Benefit Research Institute, 1990.

Fielding, Jonathan E. *Corporate Health Management.* Reading, Mass.: Addison-Wesley Publishing, 1984.

Gee, Judith B. *Pensions in Perspective.* 3rd ed. Cincinnati: The National Underwriter Co., 1990.

Gifford, Dale L. and Seltz, Christine A. *Fundamentals of Flexible Compensation.* New York: John Wiley & Sons, 1988.

Harker, Carlton. *Self-Funding of Welfare Benefits.* Brookfield, Wis.: International Foundation of Employee Benefit Plans, 1989.

Health Insurance Association of America. *A Course in Group Life and Health Insurance.* Washington, D.C.: Health Insurance Association of America, 1990.

———. *A Course in Group Life and Health Insurance (Advanced Subject Areas)*. Washington, D.C.: Health Insurance Association of America, 1988.

International Foundation of Employee Benefit Plans. *Corporate Benefits: Retirement Plan Design and Other Perspectives*. Brookfield, Wis.: International Foundation of Welfare Benefit Plans, 1990.

———. *Health Care Cost Containment*. Brookfield, Wis.: International Foundation of Employee Benefit Plans, 1987.

Johnson, Richard E. *Flexible Benefits—A How-To-Guide*. 3rd ed. Brookfield, Wis.: International Foundation of Employee Benefit Plans, 1990.

Kordus, Claude L., ed. *Employee Benefits Today: Concepts and Methods*. Brookfield, Wis.: International Foundation of Employee Benefit Plans, 1989.

Leimberg, Stephan R. and McFadden, John J. *Tools and Techniques of Employee Benefit and Retirement Planning*. 2nd ed. Cincinnati: The National Underwriter Co., 1990.

Mamorsky, Jeffrey D. *Employee Benefits Handbook*. Boston: Warren, Gorham & Lamont, 1987. (with annual supplements)

McFadden, John J. *Retirement Plans for Employees*. Homewood, Ill.: Richard D. Irwin, 1988.

McGill, Dan M. *Fundamentals of Private Pensions*. 6th ed. Homewood, Ill.: Richard D. Irwin, 1989.

Myers, Robert J. *Social Security*. 3rd ed. Homewood, Ill.: Richard D. Irwin, 1985.

Osgood, Russell K. *The Law of Pensions and Profit-Sharing*. Boston: Little, Brown, 1984.

Rejda, George M. *Social Insurance and Economic Security*. 3rd ed. Englewood Cliffs, N.J.: Prentice-Hall, 1988.

Rosenbloom, Jerry S., ed. *The Handbook of Employee Benefits*. 2nd ed. Homewood, Ill.: Dow Jones-Irwin, 1988.

Rosenbloom, Jerry S. and Hallman, G. Victor. *Employee Benefit Planning*. 3rd ed. Englewood Cliffs, N.J.: Prentice-Hall, 1990.

Index